BATTERY FLASHES
OF
W.W. II

*A thumb-nail sketch of Canadian artillery
batteries during the 1939-1945 conflict*

by

D.W. Falconer

Canadian Cataloguing in Publication Data

Falconer, D.W. (David W.), 1921-
  Battery flashes of W.W. II

  Bibliography: p.
  Includes index.
  ISBN 0-9691865-0-9

  1. Canada. Canadian Army. Artillery —
History — World War, 1939-1945.   I. Title.
UF26.F34 1984   358'.1'0971   C84-091438-5

Printed and bound in Canada

Thanks to the British Columbia Heritage Trust, a grant will be forwarded to
The 5th British Columbia Regiment, Royal Canadian Artillery Museum and
Archives Society upon completion of this book.

Cover photo courtesy of
the Royal Canadian Artillery Museum, Shilo, Manitoba

FOREWORD

On September 21, 1959, the Artillery Memorial was unveiled in Ottawa by the Governor-General of Canada, His Excellency, Major-General Georges P. Vanier, who in concluding his tribute, stated: "... in their memory and to their glory the cry of hope which has arisen on so many occasions from infantry and other arms — 'The Guns, thank God, the Guns!'"

D.W. (Wilf) Falconer, who served the Guns from Dieppe to The Dollart has, through his dedication and untiring efforts, produced a reference work ensuring the units and details of their histories will always be remembered. The degree of accuracy and attention to detail contained in this work are second to none.

It is my pleasure to recommend this book as a reference source to all students of military history and to all collectors of memorabilia of the Royal Regiment of Canadian Artillery.

To Wilf Falconer, I take great pride, as one old Gunner to another, in saying —"Good Shooting!, Stand Easy!"

J.P. Beer, MBE, CD,
Colonel, R.C.A. (Ret'd)

CONTENTS

BATTERY FLASHES OF W.W. II

PREFACE

Battery Flashes of W.W. II is a thumb-nail sketch of Royal Canadian Artillery batteries mobilized for service during the 1939 to 1945 conflict. In many cases the battery had no militia affiliate and mobilized for service during the emergency, then with cessation of hostilities disappeared from sight.

Unlike infantry regiments completely recruited in a city, town or county, the component batteries of an artillery regiment often originated in several provinces and were brought together under a regimental headquarters, ofttimes from yet another sector.

As you thumb through the pages with a brief account of each battery, it is hoped that its history will "flash" before your eyes, along with the "flash" of a fired gun.

The pages on shoulder "flashes" are included to revive memories and to help the reader visualize the "Red Patch Devils" going ashore in Sicily, the royal blue "flash" of 2nd Div of Dieppe, the French grey of 3rd Div "Water Rats" storming ashore on D-Day in Normandy, the Pegasus "flash" of 1st Canadian Parachute Battalion floating from the sky in the early hours of the 6th of June, the 4th Div green in the breakout from Caen and the "Mighty Maroon Machine" clawing its way up the Italian boot.

The diamond "flashes" of First Canadian Army, 1st Canadian Corps, 2nd Canadian Corps, 1st Canadian Army Tank Brigade, redesignated 1st Canadian Armoured Brigade (Dieppe, Sicily, Italy and NW Europe), 2nd Canadian Armoured Brigade (D-Day). The grey Atlantic Command and green Pacific Command diamonds, the diagonal "flashes" of 6th, 7th and 8th Divisions of home defence, 6th Division Canadian Army Pacific Force, the Hong Kong battle "flash", 1st Special Service Force arrow and the polar bear of Iceland duty are included.

General Orders authorizing the mobilization of the CASF in 1939 required very few changes considering the course of the war was unknown, and provides an interesting study. A number of changes were made on "paper" causing little or no disruption.

Corps Headquarters was authorized under General Order 135/39, 1st September 1939, along with 1st and 2nd Divisions but the headquarters was not required until December 1940 when 2nd Div joined 1st Division overseas and the Canadian Corps was formed.

3rd and 4th Divisions mobilized in 1940, 5th Canadian Armoured Division mobilized early 1941 and during the year proceeded overseas as did 3rd Division and 1st Canadian Army Tank Brigade.

4th Division was converted to an Armoured Division in 1942 and proceeded overseas before the end of the year. 6th, 7th and 8th Divisions mobilized for home defence in 1942 and fear of attack on the west coast saw 6th Division and the greater part of 8th Division assembled in British Columbia under Pacific Command and with the coastal defences at Prince Rupert, Yorke Island, Vancouver, and Victoria-Esquimalt, formed the first line of defence.

13th Brigade Group of 6th Division participated in the US-Canadian attack on Kiska Island in the Aleutian Chain, August 1943, and upon finding the Japanese had vacated the island remained on garrison duty until the end of the year.

On the east coast, Headquarters Atlantic Command encompassed 7th Division Headquarters at Debert, Nova Scotia, coast and anti-aircraft units in Newfoundland, Nova Scotia and New Brunswick. Coast defences outside Atlantic Command included a coast battery at Lauzon and an anti-aircraft regiment at Arvida, P.Q.

The fear of attack lessened with the Aleutian Islands free of the enemy and the run-down of units on home defence was begun. 7th and 8th Divisions received authorization to disband in October 1943.

Overseas, Headquarters First Canadian Army was authorized in April 1942, and Headquarters 2nd Canadian Corps was formed in January 1943. The existing Canadian Corps became 1st Canadian Corps and General A.G.L. McNaughton readied his First Canadian Army for the invasion of the Continent. 1st Canadian Infantry Division and 1st Canadian Army Tank Brigade departed for the invasion of Sicily, 10th July 1943 and were followed to the Mediterranean by Headquarters 1st Canadian Corps and 1st Canadian AGRA toward the end of the year. The decision was made to retain army headquarters and replace the departed formations with British or other Allied units.

It was early in 1944, that 1st Canadian Corps became operational in Italy with 1st Canadian Infantry Division, 5th Canadian Armoured Division and 1st Canadian AGRA under command. 1st Canadian Armoured Brigade remained with 13 British Corps. 1st Canadian Corps battled its way up the Liri Valley toward Rome which was captured by US troops, 4th June 1944.

The fighting in Italy was soon to be overshadowed, for on the 6th of June 1944 the greatest armada of all time crossed the English Channel to launch the invasion of Normandy. The assault force consisted of one Canadian division, two British divisions and two US divisions. 3rd Canadian Infantry Division supported by 2nd Canadian Armoured Brigade, 19th Army Field Regiment

RCA, 1st Canadian Parachute Battalion, the Royal Canadian Navy and the Royal Canadian Air Force, was Canada's contribution.

Headquarters First Canadian Army became operational 23rd July with 1 British Corps under command (replacing 1st Canadian Corps), and on the 31st of July 1944 all Canadian units in Normandy came under command including Headquarters 2nd Canadian Corps, 2nd and 3rd Canadian Infantry Divisions, 4th Canadian Armoured Division, 2nd Canadian Armoured Brigade and 2nd Canadian AGRA.

Following vicious fighting the breakout from Caen was effected, the Falaise Gap closed and the River Seine crossed. First Canadian Army moved to the left to clear the coastal area with 2nd Div entering Dieppe where it paused for a service of remembrance and a divisional parade through the city.

First Canadian Army entered Belgium and began the battle of the Scheldt in Belgium and Holland, to free the port of Antwerp to shipping. The army then moved to the Nijmegen salient in Holland and was entrusted with the attack into the Rhineland and the advance to the River Rhine.

The First Canadian Army attack was launched 8th February 1945 by 30 British Corps with 2nd and 3rd Canadian Divisions under command for the initial attack, returning to 2nd Canadian Corps for a two corps advance.

The Siegfried Line was breached, the Reichswald and Hochwald forests cleared and the River Rhine crossed. Upon crossing the Rhine the three Canadian Divisions advanced northward side by side to clear NE Holland from the river to the North Sea.

During this interval 1st Canadian Corps arrived from Italy and became operational under First Canadian Army in the Arnhem Sector. First Canadian Army now had both 1st Canadian Corps and 2nd Canadian Corps under command and was predominently Canadian, fulfilling the dream of its founders.

1st Canadian Corps busied itself clearing the western Netherlands liberating the starving people and 2nd Canadian Corps continued its drive to the North Sea in NE Holland and a section of Germany. The advance was interrupted when the "Cease Fire" was received 5th May, and discontinued with the designation of the 8th of May 1945 "VE" Day.

With the cessation of hostilities the Canadian units operated equipment dumps and staging camps for the troops marching back to Germany. An occupation force was formed of a reconstituted 3rd Canadian Infantry Division and the rundown of Canadian units was begun. The Canadian Army Pacific Force was being formed when "VJ" Day intervened and the force disbanded. The occupation force remained in Germany almost a year before returning to Canada.

All units of the Pre-war Permanent force returned to the Postwar Permanent Force with the exception of 3rd Medium Battery RCA which during the war had served as a component of 1st Medium Regiment RCA.

4th AA Battery RCA, PF served as 4th LAA Battery, 2nd LAA Regiment RCA, 1st Div and 4th LAA Battery, 11th LAA Regiment RCA, Army Troops, disbanded in March 1944 and was the only Pre-war PF unit not to go beyond England. The battery surfaced again in the Postwar PF.

The trust shown in the retention of Headquarters First Canadian Army the latter part of 1943 when split in two with the departure of 1st Canadian Corps to the Mediterranean had been repaid bountifully, for First Canadian Army with its multi-national components played a leading role in the ultimate defeat of the enemy.

May 1985 heralds the fortieth anniversary of the liberation of Holland and the cessation of hostilities in NW Europe. The war in the Pacific came to a conclusion in September 1945 bringing World War II to an end. The eyes of the world will be focused on the anniversary celebrations and seems an appropriate occasion to publish "Battery Flashes of W.W. II", a compilation of Canada's contribution.

D.W.F.

ACKNOWLEDGEMENTS

The completion of a project the size of "Battery Flashes of W.W. II" would not have been possible without the assistance cheerfully given by historians, archival and library staff, veterans, family and friends. It is indeed an exhilarating experience to meet people with a similar interest and all most eager to share their knowledge and experiences.

Included in this category were Mr. P.A.C. Chaplin, Mr. Winston MacIntosh and the staff at the Directorate of History, Ottawa; Captain R.J. Banks, Master Gunner (CWO) W.M. Lunan, Curator of the RCA Museum and Sergeant R.W. Andrews, Canadian Forces Base Shilo, Shilo, Manitoba; 5th (B.C.). Regiment Unit Historian Colonel A.E. Sherwin, CD, RCA, former Commanding Officer, former Commander Military District No. 11 and former President Royal Canadian Artillery Association; Major P.A. Sherwin, CD, Commanding Officer 5th (B.C.) Field Battery RCA; and Mr. Robert L. Clapp, Curator of 5th (B.C.) Regiment RCA Museum and Archives, Bay Street Armoury, Victoria, B.C.

Phylis Bowman of Prince Rupert, British Columbia, author of a number of books including "We Skirted The War!", kindly provided a photo of her CWAC uniform with Pacific Command flash and Mars trained soldier badge prominently displayed on the right sleeve. Roy's Photography Ltd., Victoria, highlighted the flashes in the photo.

Mr. Jack Rippengale, Master Gunner, Captain RCA retired, former Area Superintendent National Historic Parks and Sites Vancouver Island, readily spoke of Fort Rodd Hill and the contribution of the Permanent Force 5th Heavy Battery RCA to the forts at Victoria-Esquimalt, Vancouver, Yorke Island and Prince Rupert, British Columbia.

Lt.-Colonel F.D.H. Nelson, CD (Retired), Archivist, CFB Esquimalt Museum, generously donated the 2nd Canadian Corps artillery flash he wore while serving overseas with 112th Battery, 6th Light Anti-Aircraft Regiment RCA for inclusion in the colour section.

Major R.V. Stevenson, CD, Regimental Historian, 15th Field Artillery Regiment RCA, Vancouver, kindly checked the 15th (Vancouver) Coast Regiment RCA script. Mr. Stu Maitland of 15th Field Artillery Regiment Museum confirmed the wearing of 2nd Canadian Corps artillery flash while with 2nd Survey Regiment RCA and Mr. J.G. McDaniels of Pembroke, Ontario wrote

xii   ACKNOWLEDGEMENTS

to say he wore the 2nd Canadian Corps artillery flash as a member of 6th LAA Regiment RCA.

Major E.J.D. Edmonds, Vancouver, provided information on 1st AA Regiment, 16th Light Anti-Aircraft Battery and 42nd Composite Anti-Aircraft Battery (Type 1H and 1L) RCA.

Mr. George A. Warren, Victoria, provided information on 4th AA S/L Battery RCA, a shoulder flash and a photo of its personnel. Mr. Jim McCague aided with the 22nd AA Battery story.

Mr. Max Uhl, Victoria, B.C., former Sergeant with 84th Field Battery RCA which had mobilized at Moosomin, Saskatchewan, as a component of 24th Field Regiment RCA, related his experiences of August 1943 when as part of the combined Canadian-US Force, his battery and regiment landed on the Island of Kiska, in the Aleutians.

Mr. Bill Irwin's 79th Armoured Division flash is displayed in the colour section, along with Mr. Larry Stilling's Exercise "Eskimo" flash and the Army Troops Artillery flash contributed by Mrs. D.M. Judson, Thunder Bay, Ontario.

Three ships were missing from the record of ships carrying the batteries overseas during the war and the list was completed thanks to Mr. F.A. Stanway, Montreal (5th LAA Battery), Mr. D.J. MacDougall, Harriston, Ontario (100th LAA Battery) and Dr. F.G. Holbertson, Calgary, Alberta (39th Field Battery), upon the receipt of letters informing me that 5th LAA Battery sailed overseas February 1941 on board the SS Dempo (Netherlands), the Oronsay transported 100th LAA Battery overseas in November 1941, and 21st Field Regiment RCA sailed overseas on the Queen Mary in August 1943 (39th, 59th and 64th (Yorkton) Field Batteries RCA).

In response to an inquiry on artillery by Lieutenant Colonel Wyn van der Schee of The King's Own Calgary Regiment (RCAC), the latent interest was roused resulting in this compilation. Mr. Robert L. Clapp, former Interpretive Officer at Fort Rodd Hill, strongly advocated publishing the manuscript, and Mr. Jack Falconer of Winnipeg supplied the legwork.

Colonel J.P. Beer, MBE, CD, R.C.A. Retired, kindly consented to aid with the Foreword, and, thanks to the above mentioned enthusiasts, along with all who contributed in some way and whose names are not listed, the book became a reality.

Victoria, B.C.
January 1985   D.W. Falconer.

SECTION I

ANTI-AIRCRAFT ARTILLERY

Section I includes anti-aircraft sections, troops and batteries mobilized under Headquarters Victoria and Esquimalt Fortress at the West Coast and under Headquarters Halifax Fortress on the East Coast. The sections, troops and batteries became components of anti-aircraft regiments formed to give anti-aircraft protection to military installations, ports, airfields and other vulnerable locations.

Anti-aircraft regiments of Coast Defence comprised both (H) heavy batteries equipped with 3.7 inch anti-aircraft guns, and (L) light batteries equipped with Bofors 40mm light anti-aircraft guns. (M) medium batteries manned 3 inch anti-aircraft guns.

The number preceding the H or L denoted the number of 4-gun components. 55th and 62nd Anti-Aircraft Troops (Type LS), denoting six Bofors 40mm light anti-aircraft guns was an exception to the rule.

Each anti-aircraft regiment had under command a static anti-aircraft gun operation room which was the control centre for the anti-aircraft defences.

Overseas, a Canadian Anti-Aircraft Operations Room served as a mobile anti-aircraft operations room for First Canadian Army and with 2nd Canadian Heavy Anti-Aircraft Regiment came under command 107th British Anti-Aircraft Brigade which had replaced the disbanded 1st Canadian Anti-Aircraft Brigade in First Canadian Army.

No. 1, 2 and 3 Anti-Aircraft Machine Gun Troops mobilized in October 1941.

16th Anti-Aircraft Machine Gun Battery (CD) RCA mobilized in March 1941 for service in Newfoundland and served until the 15th of November 1942. No. 1 and 2 Anti-Aircraft Machine Gun Troops disbanded in 1943. No. 3 Anti-Aircraft Machine Gun Troop became 12th Anti-Aircraft Troop in December 1941 and was enlarged to a battery in April 1942, serving until January 1945.

Four anti-aircraft searchlight batteries mobilized in October 1941 for service at Halifax, Gander, Arvida, and Victoria, then in June 1942, 5th Special Mobile Anti-Aircraft Searchlight Troop was formed. However, only 1st Anti-Aircraft Searchlight Battery and 5th Special Mobile Anti-Aircraft Searchlight Troop, in Atlantic Command, remained operational until cessation of hostilities as 2nd, 3rd and 4th Anti-Aircraft Searchlight Batteries had been phased out during 1943.

An anti-aircraft unit staging camp mobilized in April 1942 and was redesignated Artillery Anti-Aircraft Reinforcement Camp before the year's end.

1 Canadian Training Brigade Group was formed at Debert, Nova Scotia, to upgrade the general standard of overseas-bound reinforcements. No. 1 Light Anti-Aircraft Training Battery RCA, redesignated a troop in December 1944, served as a component.

All four Batteries of 3rd Light Anti-Aircraft Regiment RCA accompanied 2nd Canadian Infantry Division on the Dieppe Raid, 19th August 1942.

1st Light Anti-Aircraft Regiment RCA of 1st Canadian Corps became the Lanark and Renfrew Scottish and served as an Infantry Battalion with 5th Canadian Armoured Division in Italy during 1944.

46th Light Anti-Aircraft Battery RCA of 6th Division, Home Defence, served at Kiska, in the Aleutians, the latter part of 1943, and during January and February 1945 participated in Exercise "Eskimo" in Northern Saskatchewan.

Light anti-aircraft batteries also mobilized for service with the Canadian Army Occupational Force in Germany and served under Headquarters 3rd Canadian Infantry Division CAOF, June 1945 to May 1946

*　　*　　*

1st Anti-Aircraft Battery RCA, Halifax, N.S. — Serial 344

1st Halifax Regiment CGA was to comprise a headquarters, four companies, and one anti-aircraft section, under Provisional Peace Establishment — A regiment of Garrison Artillery, Non-Permanent Active Militia, authorized strength of a regiment — Canadian Garrison Artillery, in General Order 142/1921, 15th May 1921.

The Section was enlarged to a battery in 1936, and during the precautionary period in 1939, 1st Anti-Aircraft Battery RCA is listed with NPAM Units called out on service in Military District No. 6, under General Order 124/39 (Effective 26th August 1939), to assist in protecting the port and vulnerable points in the Halifax area.

The mobilization order for the Canadian Active Service Force (CASF) in Military District No. 6 included Serial 344, 1st Anti-Aircraft Battery RCA, CASF (Details), authorized under General Order 135/39 1st September 1939.

The CASF "Details" were absorbed into the battery and Serial 344, 1st Anti-Aircraft Battery RCA was placed on active service under General Order 44/41 (Effective 1st January 1941). The Battery continued to serve under Headquarters Halifax Fortress, Atlantic Command.

1st Anti-Aircraft Battery RCA, Serial 344, was redesignated 1st Anti-Aircraft Battery (Type "H"), RCA, Serial 344, under General Order 297/41 (Effective 1st October 1941).

1st Anti-Aircraft Battery Type H, RCA, Serial 344, was redesignated 1st Anti-Aircraft Battery Type 2H, RCA, Serial 344, under General Order 257/42 (Effective 15th May 1942).

Headquarters 21st Anti-Aircraft Regiment RCA, Serial 527, was authorized under General Order 256/42 (Effective 1st June 1942), to encompass the anti-aircraft units under Headquarters Halifax Fortress. 1st Anti-Aircraft Battery became a component of 21st Anti-Aircraft Regiment RCA, and served at Morris Lake, Russell Lake, and Dartmouth.

1st Anti-Aircraft Battery Type 2H, RCA was posted to Goose Bay, Labrador in June 1943, and returned to Halifax in July 1944.

1st Anti-Aircraft Battery Type 2H, RCA, Serial 344, received authorization to disband, along with Headquarters 21st Anti-Aircraft Regiment RCA, and Headquarters Atlantic Command, under General Order 305/45 (Effective 31st July 1945).

*   *   *

No. 1 AA GOR (Class B) RCA, Halifax, N.S. — Serial 1341

No. 1 Anti-Aircraft Gun Operation Room (Class B), Royal Canadian Artillery, Serial 1341, mobilized under General Order 332/42 (Effective 1st July 1942).

No. 1 Anti-Aircraft Gun Operation Room served with 21st Anti-Aircraft Regiment RCA under Headquarters Halifax Fortress, in Atlantic Command.

No. 1 Anti-Aircraft Gun Operation Room (Class B) Royal Canadian Artillery, Serial 1341, received authorization to disband under General Order 305/45 (Effective 31st July 1945).

*   *   *

No. 1 AA Machine Gun Troop RCA, N.S., P.Q. and B.C. — Serial 428

No. 1 Anti-Aircraft Machine Gun Troop RCA, Serial 428, mobilized under General Order 87/41 (Effective 25th March 1941), in Military District No. 6. —(Nova Scotia).

No. 1 Anti-Aircraft Machine Gun Troop RCA with its four Colt Browning. .5 inch machine guns proceeded to Patricia Bay, (Pat Bay) in British Columbia, January 1942, following service at Arvida, P.Q.

2nd Anti-Aircraft Battery RCA, Victoria-Esquimalt, Part II Orders early 1942, include No. 1 Anti-Aircraft Machine Gun Troop Strength Returns and Postings.

No. 1 Anti-Aircraft Machine Gun Troop became a component of 27th Anti-Aircraft Regiment RCA in June 1942, under Headquarters Victoria and Esquimalt Fortress. Sections of the troop also served at Esquimalt Dry Dock, on Vancouver Island, and at Sea Island on the mainland.

No. 1 Anti-Aircraft Machine Gun Troop RCA, Serial 428, received authorization to disband under General Order 367/43 (Effective 15th June 1943). — "its personnel posted to 13th AA Battery." — 13th Anti-Aircraft Battery RCA, CA, War Diary.

*   *   *

1st AA S/L Battery RCA, Halifax, N.S. — Serial 878 — 21st AA Regt.

1st Anti-Aircraft Searchlight Battery RCA, Serial 878, mobilized under General Order 296/41 (Effective 1st October 1941) for service in the Halifax area.

Headquarters 21st Anti-Aircraft Regiment RCA, Serial 527, was authorized to mobilize under General Order 256/42 (Effective 1st June 1942), to encompass all anti-aircraft units under Headquarters Halifax Fortress, Atlantic Command.

1st Anti-Aircraft Searchlight Battery RCA served with 21st Anti-Aircraft Regiment RCA under Headquarters Halifax Fortress in Atlantic Command, until Headquarters 21st Anti-Aircraft Regiment RCA, and Headquarters Atlantic Command were authorized to disband under General Order 305/45 (Effective 31st July 1945).

1st Anti-Aircraft Searchlight Battery RCA, Serial 878, continued to serve under Headquarters Halifax Fortress until authorized to disband under General Order 18/46 (Effective 30th September 1945).

Headquarters Halifax Fortress, Serial 2916, received authorization to disband under General Order 85/46 (Effective 29th November 1945).

* * *

Anti-Aircraft Unit Staging Camp — Serial 887 — Debert, N.S.

Anti-Aircraft Unit Staging Camp, Serial 887, mobilized under General Order 234/42 (Effective 1st April 1942).

The Staging Camp was formed at Debert Camp, Nova Scotia, to ease the forming of anti-aircraft units during this mass mobilization period. Cadres trained at A23 Coast Defence and Anti-Aircraft Artillery Training Centre, Halifax, proceeded to the Anti-Aircraft Unit Staging Camp and provided the base for each new battery or troop. The camp was capable of handling several H or L batteries at one time.

Anti-Aircraft Unit Staging Camp, Serial 887, was redesignated Artillery Anti-Aircraft Reinforcement Camp, under General Order 411/42 (Effective 15th September 1942).

Serial 887, Artillery Anti-Aircraft Reinforcement Camp received authorization to disband under General Order 18/46 (Effective 30th October 1945).

* * *

1st HAA Battery RCA, Montreal — Serial 69C — Army Troops

1st Heavy Anti-Aircraft Battery, RCA, Serial 69C, mobilized as 1st Medium Battery RCA, CASF, Serial 73, under General Order 135/39, 1st September 1939, with Headquarters of 2nd Medium Brigade RCA, CASF, Corps Troops mobilizing with 1st Division.

Headquarters of 2nd Medium Brigade RCA, CASF, was redesignated Headquarters of 2nd Medium Regiment RCA, CASF, and the Batteries paired in a two-battery Regiment.

1st Medium Battery, RCA, CASF, Serial 73, combined with 57th Medium Battery (Howitzer) RCA, CASF, Serial 71, to become 1st/57th Medium Battery RCA, CASF, Serial 71, under General Order 123/40 (Effective 1st June 1940).

1st Battery regained individual identity as 1st Medium Battery RCA and was allotted Serial Number 459, then redesignated 1st Heavy Anti-Aircraft Battery RCA, Serial 459, under General Order 149/41 (Effective 24th May 1941).

Headquarters 2nd Medium Regiment RCA, Serial 69, was redesignated Headquarters, 2nd Heavy Anti-Aircraft Regiment (Mobile) RCA, Serial 69, under General Order 149/41 (Effective 24th May 1941), and 1st Battery remained with the regiment in its new role.

1st Heavy Anti-Aircraft Battery, 2nd Heavy Anti-Aircraft Regiment RCA departed for overseas 19th September 1941 on board the Pasteur and disembarked at Gourock, Scotland, on the 26th September 1941.

1st Heavy Anti-Aircraft Battery RCA was allotted Serial Number 69C under General Order 54/42 (Effective 22nd December 1941).

The Battery and Regiment joined 1st Canadian Anti-Aircraft Brigade in the air defence of Great Britain (ADGB) and served with the brigade until its disbandment, listed in General Order 357/44 (Effective 1st March 1944).

1st Heavy Anti-Aircraft Battery RCA landed in Normandy 6th August 1944 with 107th British Anti-Aircraft Brigade which had replaced 1st Canadian Anti-Aircraft Brigade in First Canadian Army.

1st Heavy Anti-Aircraft Battery, 2nd Heavy Anti-Aircraft Regiment RCA, with 107th Anti-Aircraft Brigade Royal Artillery, joined the action under command of First Canadian Army on the Caen sector, the night of 8th/9th August 1944.

As a component of First Canadian Army the battery and regiment served in France, Belgium, Holland, and Germany.

1st Heavy Anti-Aircraft Battery RCA served until cessation of hostilities and received authorization to disband under General Order 401/45 (Effective 7th September 1945).

*   *   *

1st LAA Battery RCA, Ottawa — Serial 991E — 2nd Canadian Corps

1st Light Anti-Aircraft Battery RCA, Serial 991E, mobilized as a component of 6th Light Anti-Aircraft Regiment RCA, authorized under General Order 240/41 (Effective 5th September 1941), to serve with 4th Division.

Battery headquarters was established in the Regal Building, Ottawa, with barracks located at Lansdowne Park. The Battery remained in Ottawa until moving to join the regiment at Petawawa in February 1942.

Headquarters 4th Division, Serial 900, however, was redesignated Headquarters 4th (Armoured) Division, Serial 900, under General Order 132/42 (Effective 26th January 1942). 6th Light Anti-Aircraft Regiment RCA was replaced by 8th Light Anti-Aircraft Regiment RCA in the new Formation.

6th Light Anti-Aircraft Regiment reorganized to a three battery regiment and 101st Light Anti-Aircraft Battery RCA moved to 8th Light Anti-Aircraft Regiment RCA. 6th Light Anti-Aircraft Regiment RCA which now comprised 1st, 30th and 112th Light Anti-Aircraft Batteries, congregated at Petawawa in February 1942.

In March 1942 a composite troop, designated "G" Troop, 112th Battery, which included 21 members of 1st Light Anti-Aircraft Battery RCA was posted to Prince Rupert, British Columbia, to man two Bofors 40mm Light Anti-Aircraft guns in the Prince Rupert defences.

In April, 30 more other ranks proceeded to Prince Rupert, and on the 5th June the remainder of 112th Light Anti-Aircraft Battery departed for Prince Rupert and duty on Annette Island, Alaska.

30th Light Anti-Aircraft Battery also moved to the West Coast in June 1942 to man sites under Headquarters Victoria-Esquimalt Fortress on Vancouver Island, and on Yorke Island, under Headquarters Vancouver Defences. 1st Light Anti-Aircraft Battery and regimental headquarters remained at Petawawa where the Battery took part in manouvres, special demonstrations and Light Anti-Aircraft training.

6th Light Anti-Aircraft Regiment assembled at Petawawa in September prior to going overseas and moved to Halifax in October to board the Queen Elizabeth. 1st Light Anti-Aircraft Battery RCA with the regiment departed for overseas 30th October 1942 and disembarked at Gourock, Scotland, on the 5th of November 1942.

The first home for the Battery was at Colchester, Essex, where 1st Canadian Anti-Aircraft Brigade took the regiment under its wing, and mid-February 1943, 6th Light Anti-Aircraft Regiment RCA came under command of 2nd Canadian Corps for all purposes.

Visits to firing camps, training schemes, a trip to the Battle Training School in Wales and duty on the South coast of England kept the regiment occupied during 1943 as it readied itself for the invasion of the continent.

1st Light Anti-Aircraft Battery, 6th Light Anti-Aircraft Regiment RCA landed in Normandy on the 9th and 10th of July 1944 and moved to the Cairon area 15th July to protect the AGRA guns. A and B Troops were credited with downing two enemy aircraft from this location 16th July.

1st Battery and regimental headquarters crossed the Orne River 21st July. The regiment and 2nd Canadian Corps were under command of Second British Army at this time.

2nd Canadian Corps, the regiment and 1st Light Anti-Aircraft Battery moved under command of First Canadian Army 31st July 1944 and took part in the vicious fighting in the breakout from Caen and closing of the Falaise Gap. The regiment continued the struggle in Belgium, Holland, and Germany, culminating with the unconditional surrender of the enemy.

The 8th of May 1945 was designated "VE" Day and 1st Light Anti-Aircraft Battery RCA, Serial 991E, received authorization to disband under General Order 321/45 (Effective 24th June 1945), in NW Europe. Personnel proceeded to the Canadian Army Pacific Force (CAPF), the Canadian Army Occupational Force (CAOF), or were posted to divisional units from the military district of their enlistment for the return to Canada.

*   *   *

No. 1 LAA Training Troop RCA, Debert, N.S. — Serial 1480

No. 1 Light Anti-Aircraft Training Troop RCA, Serial 1480, mobilized as No. 1 Light Anti-Aircraft Training Battery RCA, under General Order 419/44 (Effective 1st October 1943) — (Serial Number not listed).

The Battery was formed as a component of 1st Canadian Training Brigade Group at Debert to upgrade the general standard of the reinforcements before they proceeded overseas.

Light Anti-Aircraft training was carried out to the battery level, beginning with detachment training in Phase I, troop training in Phase II and Phase III, to battery training in Phase IV.

No. 1 Light Anti-Aircraft Training Battery RCA, Serial 1480, was redesignated No. 1 Light Anti-Aircraft Training Troop RCA, Serial 1480, under General Order 560/44 (Effective 15th December 1944).

No. 1 Light Anti-Aircraft Training Troop RCA (no Serial Number), was authorized to disband under General Order 18/46 (Effective 15th April 1945).

*   *   *

S 1 Coast and Anti-Aircraft Artillery School, Serial 489, is included in the *Coast Artillery Section, Section III.*

*   *   *

2nd Anti-Aircraft Battery RCA, Victoria, B.C. — Serial 392

5th (British Columbia) Regiment CGA was to comprise headquarters, two companies, and one anti-aircraft section, under Provisional Peace Establishment — A regiment of garrison artillery, Non-Permanent Active Militia, authorized strength of a regiment — Canadian Garrison Artillery, in General Order 142/21, 15th May 1921.

The Section was enlarged to a battery in 1936, and during the precautionary period in 1939, 2nd Anti-Aircraft Battery RCA is listed with NPAM Units called out on Service in Military District No. 11, under General Order 124/39 (Effective 26th August 1939).

2nd Anti-Aircraft Battery Part II Order No. 1 issued 26th August 1939, notes that — "3 Officers (amended to 4 officers in General Order No. 4), and 30 ORs of the battery marched to Fort Macaulay and taken on strength 26th August 1939. Attached were 15 members of the permanent force and a member of 13th Field Ambulance. 1 Officer and 15 ORs from 17th Searchlight Battery were attached for rations and stores on 26th August 1939". The battery and attached permanent force personnel assumed the duty of manning the 12 pounder and 6" Battery at the Fort.

"Details" of 2nd Anti-Aircraft Battery RCA, CASF, Serial 392, were authorized as components of the Canadian Active Service Force under General Order 135/39, 1st September 1939. The serving members of the battery became "Details" in the CASF.

At Fort Macaulay the battery administered to a large number of local, and transient personnel. In September 1939, 1 Officer and 30 Other Ranks of 11th Fortress Signals were attached for rations, 2 Officers, 10 ORs of 60th Heavy Battery, and 5 ORs of the 17th Searchlight Co. stationed at the Breakwater Battery were attached for rations until messing facilities became available at the Breakwater. A number of NCOs from 55th, 56th, and 60th Batteries, and 17th Searchlight Battery RCA were attached for rations while attending a school of instruction.

The pattern continued into 1940 with Officers and ORs attached for rations while attending courses of instruction. Members of "Z" Force Special Coast Defence Unit RCA, CASF, were attached for rations during July (Part II Order No. 172, 11th July 1940). During 1940 the Battery also contributed to the overseas-bound 16th Light Anti-Aircraft Battery RCA, 3rd Light Anti-Aircraft Regiment RCA, of 2nd Division.

Macaulay Fort transferred from 2nd Anti-Aircraft Battery RCA, CASF, to 60th Heavy Battery RCA, CASF, 15th September 1940.

The designation "Details" was discontinued and members absorbed into the

Battery, upon Serial 392, 2nd Anti-Aircraft Battery RCA being placed on active service under General Order 44/41 (Effective 1st January 1941).

Battery headquarters moved from Fort Macaulay to Triangle Mountain 6th May 1941, returning to Fort Macaulay 19th June 1941. The next location was Fort Mary Hill, 8th July to 15th December 1941.

While at Fort Mary Hill, Serial 392, 2nd Anti-Aircraft Battery RCA was redesignated Serial 392, 2nd Anti-Aircraft Battery (Type "H") RCA under General Order 297/41 (Effective 1st October 1941). Battery strength which had declined since the latter part of 1940, rebounded toward the end of October 1941 when 121 Home Defence members were taken on strength.

Next stop for battery headquarters was Fort Rodd Hill from 15th of December 1941 to 1st July 1942, then on to RCA Camp Area, 3rd July 1942. It was from this location that the last Battery Part II Order (No. 113) was issued.

Early in 1942, Anti-Aircraft Regiment Headquarters were authorized to encompass the large number of batteries being formed at Halifax for the East Coast, and at Macaulay Plains, Esquimalt, British Columbia for duty at the West Coast. Headquarters 28th Anti-Aircraft Regiment RCA was given responsibility for the Vancouver Defences, Headquarters 27th Anti-Aircraft Regiment RCA, with 2nd Anti-Aircraft Battery (Type "H") RCA as a component was to serve under Headquarters Victoria and Esquimalt Fortress on Vancouver Island. Headquarters 29th Anti-Aircraft Regiment RCA, at Prince Rupert and Headquarters 30th Anti-Aircraft Regiment RCA, at Port Alberni, British Columbia, were formed in March 1943,

Excerpts from unit records confirm the areas protected by 2nd Anti-Aircraft Battery — 13th AA Battery War Diary — "27th Apr (1942) 2 guns taken over from 2 AA Bty at Esq. drydock". — 10th AA Battery War Diary — "Took over 3 Bofors Guns at Pat Bay from 2nd AA Bty, 1st May 42".

2nd Anti-Aircraft Battery is listed as a component of 27th Anti-Aircraft Regiment, Victoria & Esquimalt in Operational Units — Artillery — Cdn Army North American Zone, 24 April 1943 — D. Hist., Ottawa.

Fort Record Book, Fort Black Rock, November 1943, extract — "Immediately behind Macaulay Fort towards Work Point Barracks the 2nd AA Battery has sited four 3.7" Heavy AA guns".

Duntze Head Fort Record Book, 19th December 1944, extract — "2nd AA Bty have sited four 3.7" HAA guns adjacent to Fort Macaulay".

2nd Battery is also listed as having been on duty at VH 3 — Tillicum Road site, in Pacific Command — AA Radars — Time in Operating Condition. January

1944 — July 1945, Headquarters Victoria — Esquimalt Fortress, 27th AA Regiment.

In the Site Fighting Book, VH 2 — Colwood, B.C. — detachments manning this site, date of taking over, 2nd AA Battery assumed responsibility on the 19th February 1945. The site was under the control of 27th Anti-Aircraft Regiment RCA, Esquimalt Fortress.

2nd Anti-Aircraft Battery (Type "H") RCA, Serial 392, remained operational until receiving authorization to disband under General Order 18/46 (Effective 31st October 1945). Headquarters 27th Anti-Aircraft Regiment RCA, and Headquarters Esquimalt Fortress also disbanded at that time.

* * *

No. 2 AA GOR (Class B) RCA - Serial 1342 — Victoria-Esquimalt

No. 2 Anti-Aircraft Gun Operation Room (Class B) RCA, Serial 1342, mobilized under General Order 332/42 (Effective 1st July 1942), and served as a component of 27th Anti-Aircraft Regiment RCA under Headquarters Victoria-Esquimalt Fortress, and its later designation, Headquarters Esquimalt Fortress.

No. 2 Anti-Aircraft Gun Operation Room (Class B) RCA, Serial 1342, received authorization to disband under General Order 18/46 (Effective 31st October 1945).

* * *

No. 2 AA Machine Gun Troop RCA, Halifax, N.S. — Serial 429

No. 2 Anti-Aircraft Machine Gun Troop RCA, Serial 429, mobilized under General Order 87/41 (Effective 25th March 1941), for service in the Halifax defences.

Headquarters 21st Anti-Aircraft Regiment RCA, Serial 527, was authorized to mobilize under General Order 256/42 (Effective 1st June 1942), to encompass all anti-aircraft units serving under Headquarters Halifax Fortress, in Atlantic Command, and No. 2 Anti-Aircraft Machine Gun Troop became a component.

No. 2 Anti-Aircraft Machine Gun Troop RCA, Serial 429, served with 21st Anti-Aircraft Regiment RCA until receiving authorization to disband under General Order 367/43 (Effective 15th June 1943).

* * *

2nd AA Searchlight Battery RCA - Serial 879 — "W" Force

2nd Anti-Aircraft Searchlight Battery RCA, Serial 879, mobilized under General Order 296/41 (Effective 1st October 1941) and served with the original

26th Anti-Aircraft Regiment RCA in the Gander Lake Area, Newfoundland, "W" Force, Atlantic Command.

2nd Anti-Aircraft Searchlight Battery RCA, Serial 879, received authorization to disband under General Order 301/43 (Effective 1st May 1943).

*   *   *

2nd (Yorkton) LAA Battery RCA, Yorkton, Sask. — Serial 141B — 1 Div

1st (Yorkton) Light Anti-Aircraft Battery RCA, CASF, Serial 131, mobilized with Headquarters 2nd *Anti-Aircraft* Regiment RCA, CASF, Serial 127, under General Order 135/39, 1st September 1939.

Headquarters 2nd Anti-Aircraft Regiment RCA, CASF, Serial 127 was not required at this time and disbanded under General Order 438/43 (Effective 1st September 1939), and its batteries moved to other formations.

Headquarters 2nd Light Anti-Aircraft Regiment RCA, CASF, Serial 141, mobilized under General Order 184/40 (Effective 24th May 1940), to become 1st Division's Light Anti-Aircraft Regiment.

1st (Yorkton) Light Anti-Aircraft Battery departed for overseas 27th August 1940 on board the Oronsay, and disembarked on the 5th September 1940 at Greenock, Scotland.

1st (Yorkton) Light Anti-Aircraft Battery RCA, Serial 131, was redesignated 2nd (Yorkton) Light Anti-Aircraft Battery RCA, Serial 131, under General Order 86/41 (Effective 18th March 1941), and was allotted Serial Number 141B, under General Order 54/42 (Effective 22nd December 1941).

The Battery trained with the division and manned Air Defence of Great Britain (ADGB) sites until June 1943, then accompanied 1st Canadian Infantry Division to the Mediterranean for the assault on the island of Sicily, with 30 British Corps, British Eighth Army.

The Regiment sailed 25th June 1943, and 2nd (Yorkton) Light Anti-Aircraft Battery aligned with 3rd Canadian Infantry Brigade, the reserve Brigade, landed 11th July 1943.

With the fall of Sicily, the Battery crossed to the Italian mainland with the assaulting 3rd Canadian Infantry Brigade under 13 British Corps, 3rd September 1943.

1st Canadian Infantry Division moved to 1st Canadian Corps early in the new year, upon the Corps becoming operational and served as a component in Italy until March 1945, then moved with the corps to NW Europe.

The battery sailed to Marseilles from Naples, 15th March 1945, then joined the action 7th April 1945 with First Canadian Army in Holland, and served until cessation of hostilities.

2nd (Yorkton) Light Anti-Aircraft Battery RCA received authorization to disband under General Order 401/45 (Effective 7th September 1945).

*   *   *

3rd AA Battery RCA, Quebec and Levis, P.Q. — Serial 320

6th Quebec and Levis Regiment CGA was to comprise, headquarters, three companies, and one anti-aircraft section, under Provisional Peace Establishment — A regiment of garrison artillery, Non-Permanent Active Militia, authorized strength of a regiment — Canadian Garrison Artillery, in General Order 142/21, 15th May 1921.

The Section was enlarged to a battery in 1936, and during the precautionary period in 1939, 3rd Anti-Aircraft Battery RCA is listed with NPAM Units called out on Service in Military District No. 5, under General Order 124/39 (Effective 26th August 1939).

"Details" of 3rd Anti-Aircraft Battery RCA, CASF, Serial 320, became a component of the Canadian Active Service Force in Military District No. 5, authorized under General Order 135/39, 1st September 1939.

3rd Anti-Aircraft Battery RCA, Serial 320, was placed on Active Service under General Order 44/41 (Effective 1st January 1941), and the CASF "Details" were absorbed into the Battery, and 3rd Anti-Aircraft Battery continued to serve independently in the Quebec Defences.

General Order 200/43, lists Serial 320, 3rd Anti-Aircraft Battery RCA, CASF (Details), being disbanded (Effective 16th October 1942).

The Unit War Diary lists the Battery disbanding for the forming of 60th (H) Anti-Aircraft Battery and 61st Anti-Aircraft Troop.

*   *   *

No. 3 AA GOR (Class B) RCA, Arvida, P.Q. — Serial 1343

No. 3 Anti-Aircraft Gun Operation Room (Class B) RCA, Serial 1343, mobilized under General Order 437/42 (Effective 3rd August 1942), and moved to Arvida, P.Q. as a component of 24th Anti-Aircraft Regiment RCA, for service in the Arvida defences.

In July 1943 all operational anti-aircraft units in Military District No. 5 came under command of Headquarters 24th Anti-Aircraft Regiment RCA for administration and training supervision.

The operational control of the three additional units, two in the Quebec area and one in the Gaspe Defences was to remain unchanged. This organization remained in effect until early November 1943 when four of the units became components of 26th Anti-Aircraft Regiment RCA, French speaking.

No. 3 Anti-Aircraft Gun Operation (Class B) RCA, Serial 1343, continued to control the fire of 24th Anti-Aircraft Regiment's guns in the Arvida defences until authorized to disband under General Order 208/45 (Effective 15th January 1945).

*   *   *

No. 3 AA Machine Gun Troop RCA (12th AA Bty, Arvida) — Serial 883

No. 3 Anti-Aircraft Machine Gun Troop RCA, Serial 883, mobilized under General Order 306/41 (Effective 10th October 1941).

No. 3 Anti-Aircraft Machine Gun Troop RCA, Serial 883, was redesignated 12th Anti-Aircraft Troop (Type L) RCA, Serial 883, under General Order 26/42 (Effective 12th December 1941).

12th Anti-Aircraft Troop Type L, RCA, Serial 883, was redesignated 12th Anti-Aircraft Battery Type 4L RCA, Serial 883, under General Order 182/42 (Effective 13th April 1942).

Headquarters 24th Anti-Aircraft Regiment RCA, Serial 533, was authorized under General Order 256/42 (Effective 1st June 1942), to encompass anti-aircraft units in the Arvida Defences, Arvida, P.Q., and 12th Anti-Aircraft Battery became a component.

12th Anti-Aircraft Battery Type "4L", RCA, Serial 883, was redesignated 12th Anti-Aircraft Battery Type "3L" RCA, Serial 883, under General Order 366/43 (Effective 15th June 1943), and the battery continued to serve in the Arvida defences.

12th Anti-Aircraft Battery Type "3L" RCA, Serial 883, was redesignated 12th Anti-Aircraft Battery (Type 2L) RCA, Serial 883, under General Order 493/43 (Effective 15th October 1943).

12th Anti-Aircraft Battery Type 2L RCA, Serial 883, remained at Arvida until authorized to disband along with Headquarters 24th Anti-Aircraft Regiment RCA, Serial 533, under General Order 208/45 (Effective 15th January 1945).

*   *   *

3rd Anti-Aircraft S/L Battery RCA, Arvida, P.Q. — Serial 880

3rd Anti-Aircraft Searchlight Battery RCA, Serial 880, mobilized under General Order 296/41 (Effective 1st October 1941), and upon the forming of 24th Anti-Aircraft Regiment RCA, 1st June 1942, 3rd Anti-Aircraft Searchlight Battery RCA became a component.

3rd Anti-Aircraft Searchlight Battery RCA, Serial 880, continued to serve with 24th Anti-Aircraft Regiment RCA, in the Arvida, P.Q. Defences, until authorized to disband under General Order 301/43 (Effective 1st May 1943).

*   *   *

4th AA Battery RCA, Halifax, Nova Scotia — Serial 890

4th Anti-Aircraft Battery (Type L) RCA, Serial 890, mobilized under General Order 25/42 (Effective 12th December 1941), for duty in the Halifax defences.

4th Anti-Aircraft Battery Type L, RCA, Serial 890, was redesignated 4th Anti-Aircraft Battery Type 4L, RCA, Serial 890, under General Order 182/42 (Effective 13th April 1942).

Headquarters 21st Anti-Aircraft Regiment RCA was authorized to mobilize under General Order 256/42 (Effective 1st June 1942) to encompass the anti-aircraft units serving under Headquarters Halifax Fortress, in Military District No. 6, and 4th Anti-Aircraft Battery became a component of 21st Anti-Aircraft Regiment.

4th Anti-Aircraft Battery Type "4L", RCA, Serial 890, was redesignated 4th Anti-Aircraft Battery Type "3L", RCA, Serial 890, under General Order 366/43 (Effective 15th June 1943).

Battery headquarters of 4th Anti-Aircraft Battery Type "3L", RCA, was located at Imperoyal, with 1 troop at Imperoyal, 1 troop at Dartmouth Airport, and 1 troop at the Seaplane Base, Dartmouth.

4th Anti-Aircraft Battery Type 3L, RCA, Serial 890 served with 21st Anti-Aircraft Regiment RCA, under Headquarters Halifax Fortress, Atlantic Command, until receiving authorization to disband, along with Headquarters 21st Anti-Aircraft Regiment RCA, and Headquarters Atlantic Command, under General Order 305/45 (Effective 31st July 1945).

Headquarters Halifax Fortress, Serial 2916, disbanded under General Order 85/46 (Effective 29th November 1945).

*   *   *

No. 4 AA GOR (Class B) RCA — Serial 1344 — Gander, "W" Force

No. 4 Anti-Aircraft Gun Operation Room (Class B) RCA, Serial 1344, mobilized under General Order 437/42 (Effective 3rd August 1942), and joined the original 26th Anti-Aircraft Regiment RCA at Gander, Newfoundland, "W" Force.

Upon the conversion of 26th Anti-Aircraft Regiment RCA to French speaking, No. 4 Anti-Aircraft Gun Operation Room (Class B) RCA, Serial 1344, was converted to French speaking and served with the new 26th Anti-Aircraft Regiment in the Newfoundland Defences.

No. 4 Anti-Aircraft Gun Operation Room (Class B) RCA, Serial 1344, received authorization to disband under General Order 305/45 (effective 31st July 1945).

Headquarters 26th Anti-Aircraft Regiment RCA, Serial 537, disbanded under General Order 379/45 (Effective 15th August 1945).

"W" Force Brigade Headquarters, Serial 1140, was authorized to disband under General Order 227/46 (Effective 30th July 1946).

*   *   *

4th Anti-Aircraft S/L Battery RCA, Victoria, B.C. — Serial 881

4th Anti-Aircraft Searchlight Battery RCA, Serial 881, mobilized under General Order 296/41 (Effective 1st October 1941), and served at Victoria, British Columbia, under Headquarters Victoria-Esquimalt Fortress.

4th Anti-Aircraft Searchlight Battery RCA manned two 18 inch searchlights atop the Bay Street Armoury, and later manned the same two searchlights on the ground in the vehicle compound adjacent to the Bay Street Armoury, from October 1941 to May 1943.

4th Anti-Aircraft Searchlight Battey RCA, Serial 881, as a group departed for Long Beach, on the west coast of Vancouver Island, to join 23rd Anti-Aircraft Battery RCA of 27th Anti-Aircraft Regiment RCA, and 4th Anti-Aircraft Searchlight Battery RCA, Serial 881, received authorization to disband under General Order 301/43 (Effective 1st May 1943).

*   *   *

4th LAA Battery RCA, Kingston — Serial 141C — (PF) — 1 Div — Army Tps

4th Anti-Aircraft Battery RCA, a Permanent Force battery, was formed in 1935 and with the threat of war the battery proceeded to the East Coast from Kingston, 26th August 1939, to provide protection to the port.

4th Anti-Aircraft Battery RCA was authorized as a component of the Canadian Active Service Force (CASF) and mobilized as 4th Anti-Aircraft Battery

RCA, CASF, Serial 128, with Headquarters 2nd Anti-Aircraft Regiment RCA, CASF, Serial 127, under General Order 135/39, 1st September 1939.

Serial 127, Headquarters 2nd Anti-Aircraft Regiment RCA, CASF, found itself without a role at this early date and was authorized to disband under General Order 438/43 (Effective 1st September 1939), its component Batteries moved to other units or disbanded.

4th *Anti-Aircraft* Battery RCA, CASF, Serial 128, was redesignated 4th *Light Anti-Aircraft* Battery RCA, CASF, Serial 128, authorized under General Order 184/40 (Effective 24th May 1940), and moved to *2nd Light Anti-Aircraft* Regiment RCA, CASF, Serial 141, mobilized to serve as 1st Division Light Anti-Aircraft Regiment in the CASF.

4th Light Anti-Aircraft Battery RCA, CASF, departed for overseas 16th December 1940 on board Troopship E-92, the Pasteur, and disembarked at Greenock, Scotland, 26th December 1940.

4th Light Anti-Aircraft Battery proceeded to Aldershot for organization and came under command 2nd Light Anti-Aircraft Regiment RCA effective 4th January 1941, then moved to Colchester, Essex, 6th February 1941, where the regiment assembled for training and duty.

On the 12th April 1941 the battery moved to the Dartford, Kent area and took over manning of Air Defence of Great Britain (ADGB) Sites.

In an alignment of Serial Numbers with 2nd Light Anti-Aircraft Regiment RCA, Serial 141, 4th Light Anti-Aircraft Battery RCA Serial Number was changed to 141C, under General Order 54/42 (Effective 22nd December 1941).

4th Light Anti-Aircraft Battery moved to Worthing in the 1st Division area, 11th February 1942 and received an official welcome by the GOC, 11th March 1942.

In corps schemes, 4th Light Anti-Aircraft Battery was aligned with 2nd Canadian Infantry Brigade, 1st Division, a duty later assumed by 54th Light Anti-Aircraft Battery RCA.

Shortly after the second anniversary of the forming of 2nd Light Anti-Aircraft Regiment RCA in Colchester reorganization to a three battery regiment was effected. 4th Light Anti-Aircraft Battery RCA departed 2nd Light Anti-Aircraft Regiment RCA and 1st Division to become a component of 11th Light Anti-Aircraft Regiment RCA which was in the process of being formed to serve as Army Troops, First Canadian Army.

Headquarters 11th Light Anti-Aircraft Regiment RCA, Serial 1170A was authorized under General Order 242/43 (Effective 6th March 1943).

In the role of army troops, 4th Light Anti-Aircraft Battery and 11th Light Anti-Aircraft Regiment RCA served with 1st Canadian Anti-Aircraft Brigade, First Canadian Army, in the defence of England.

To help ease the Canadian manpower shortage British units replaced a number of Canadian units in First Canadian Army. Headquarters 1st Canadian Anti-Aircraft Brigade RCA, Serial 842, Headquarters 11th Light Anti-Aircraft Regiment RCA, Serial 1170A, 62nd Light Anti-Aircraft Battery RCA, Serial 449C, 53rd Light Anti-Aircraft Battery RCA, Serial 142E, and 4th Light Anti-Aircraft Battery RCA, Serial 141C, along with 7th Light Anti-Aircraft Regiment RCA, Headquarters 7th Light Anti-Aircraft Regiment RCA and its three batteries were authorized to disband in England, under General Order 357/44 (Effective 1st March 1944).

* * *

5th Anti-Aircraft Battery RCA - Serial 891 — "W" Force

5th Anti-Aircraft Battery, (Type L) RCA, Serial 891, mobilized under General Order 25/42 (Effective 12th December 1941).

5th Anti-Aircraft Battery Type L, RCA, Serial 891, was redesignated 5th Anti-Aircraft Battery Type 2L, RCA, Serial 891, under General Order 235/42 (Effective 1st May 1942).

5th Anti-Aircraft Battery Type "2L", RCA, Serial 891, was redesignated 5th Anti-Aircraft Battery Type "4L", RCA, Serial 891, under General Order 366/43 (Effective 15th June 1943).

5th Anti-Aircraft Battery, Type "4L", RCA, Serial 891, was redesignated 105th Anti-Aircraft Battery (Type 4L) RCA, Serial 891, under General Order 412/43 (Effective 1st September 1943).

The battery under both designations served with the original 26th Anti-Aircraft Regiment RCA, in the Gander, Newfoundland, Defences, "W" Force, in Atlantic Command.

Upon the conversion of 26th Anti-Aircraft Regiment RCA to French speaking, 105th Anti-Aircraft Battery (Type 4L) RCA, Serial 891, disbanded under General Order 432/44 (Effective 31st December 1943).

* * *

No. 5 AA GOR (Class B) RCA — Serial 1345 — "W" Force

No. 5 Anti-Aircraft Gun Operation Room, (Class B), RCA, Serial 1345, mobilized under General Order 437/42 (Effective 3rd August 1942), and served with 25th Anti-Aircraft Regiment RCA, under Headquarters St. John's Defences (Newfoundland).

Headquarters St. John's Defences (Newfoundland) was redesignated Headquarters Defended Port of St. John's, under General Order 206/44 (Effective 15th April 1944) and No. 5 Anti-Aircraft Gun Operation Room (Class B), RCA, Serial 1345, continued to serve under the headquarters until authorized to disband under General Order 305/45 (Effective 31st July 1945). Headquarters 25th Anti-Aircraft Regiment RCA, Serial 534, also disbanded at this time.

Headquarters, Defended Port of St. John's disbanded under General Order 379/45 (Effective 15th August 1945).

*   *   *

5th LAA Battery RCA, Montreal, P.Q. — Serial 141D — 1st Div

5th Light Anti-Aircraft Battery RCA, CASF, Serial 141A, and Headquarters, 2nd Light Anti-Aircraft Regiment RCA, CASF, Serial 141, mobilized under General Order 184/40 (Effective 24th May 1940), to become 1st Division Light Anti-Aircraft Unit.

5th Light Anti-Aircraft Battery RCA, CASF, departed for overseas 17th February 1941 on board the S.S. Dempo (Netherlands), and disembarked at Gourock, Scotland, 1st March 1941.

The Battery joined the regiment as it assembled at Colchester, Essex, prior to joining 1st Division in the field, and served with 1st Canadian Anti-Aircraft Brigade in the Air Defence of Great Britain (ADGB).

In a shuffle of Serial Numbers, 5th Light Anti-Aircraft Battery RCA was allotted Serial Number 141D, under General Order 54/42 (Effective 22nd December 1941). 2nd Light Anti-Aircraft Regiment RCA was allotted Serial Number 141, Headquarters, Serial 141A, 2nd Battery, Serial 141B, 4th Battery 141C, 5th Battery 141D, and 54th Battery, Serial 141E, in a four-battery regiment.

5th Light Anti-Aircraft Battery, 2nd Light Anti-Aircraft Regiment RCA sailed for the Mediterrranean 25th June 1943 and landed in Sicily on the 10th of July 1943 with the assaulting 1st Canadian Infantry Division, 30 British Corps, British Eighth Army.

With the fall of Sicily the battery and regiment moved under 13 British Corps for the assault on the Italian mainland and crossed the Strait of Messina, 4th September 1943.

Early 1944, 1st Canadian Infantry Division became a component of 1st Canadian Corps, upon the corps becoming operational and served with the corps in Italy until early 1945, then moved with the corps to NW Europe.

5th Battery sailed from Leghorn, Italy, to Marseilles, France, 7th March 1945, and joined the action in Holland 3rd April 1945 as a component of First Canadian Army.

5th Light Anti-Aircraft Battery RCA served until cessation of hostilities and received authorization to disband under General Order 401/45 (Effective 31st August 1945).

*   *   *

5th Special Mobile AA S/L Troop RCA — Serial 888 — Atlantic Comd

5th Special Mobile Anti-Aircraft Searchlight Troop RCA, Serial 888, mobilized under General Order 289/42 (Effective 10th June 1942) and served at Ives Point, Halifax, Nova Scotia, Debert, Nova Scotia, Penfield Ridge, New Brunswick, and the Greenwood, Nova Scotia, RCAF Station, in Atlantic Command.

5th Special Mobile Anti-Aircraft Searchlight Troop, RCA, Serial 888, received authorization to disband under General Order 18/46 (Effective 30th September 1945), the emergency having ended with cessation of hostilities in NW Europe and the Pacific.

*   *   *

6th AA Battery RCA, Yarmouth, N.S. — Serial 363 — N.S. & Goose Bay

84th Field Battery RCA (Howitzer) was redesignated 6th Anti-Aircraft Battery RCA under General Order 92/39 (Effective 1st June 1939), in Military District No. 6, in a reorganization of the Non-Permanent Active Militia.

6th Anti-Aircraft Battery RCA was localized at Yarmouth, Nova Scotia, under General Order 111/39 (Effective 1st June 1939).

"Details" of Serial 363, 6th Anti-Aircraft Battery RCA, CASF, became components of the Canadian Active Service Force under General Order 200/39 (Effective 1st September 1939), in Military District No. 6.

The CASF "Details" were absorbed into the battery, and Serial 363, 6th Anti-Aircraft Battery RCA was placed on Active Service under General Order 44/41 (Effective 1st January 1941), in Military District No. 6, under Headquarters Sydney-Canso Defences.

Serial 363, 6th Anti-Aircraft Battery RCA was redesignated 6th Anti-Aircraft

Battery (Type "H"), RCA, Serial 363, under General Order 297/41 (Effective 1st October 1941).

6th Anti-Aircraft Battery served with 23rd Anti-Aircraft Regiment RCA in the Sydney-Canso Defences, and also served at Goose Bay, Labrador, under Headquarters Goose Bay Defences.

Headquarters Sydney-Canso Defences was redesignated Headquarters Defended Port of Sydney, and Headquarters Goose Bay Defences was redesignated Headquarters Defended Area Goose Bay, under General Order 206/44 (Effective 15th April 1944).

Serial 363, 6th Anti-Aircraft Battery (Type "H") RCA received authorization to disband under General Order 208/45 (Effective 31st December 1944). Headquarters 23rd Anti-Aircraft Regiment RCA, Serial 530, also disbanded at that time.

Headquarters Defended Port of Sydney disbanded under General Order 379/45 (Effective 15th August 1945), and Headquarters Defended Area Goose Bay disbanded under General Order 18/46 (Effective 25th August 1945).

*   *   *

No. 6 AA GOR (Class B) RCA, Vancouver — Serial 1372 — 28 AA Regt

No. 6 Anti-Aircraft Gun Operation Room (Class B) RCA, Serial 1372, mobilized under General Order 437/42 (Effective 1st October 1942) and became a component of 28th Anti-Aircraft Regiment RCA, under Headquarters Vancouver Defences, Pacific Command.

No. 6 Anti-Aircraft Gun Operation Room (Class B) RCA, Serial 1372, received authorization to disband under General Order 208/45 (Effective 31st January 1945).

Headquarters Vancouver Defences disbanded under Genral Order 208/45 (Effective 15th February 1945), and Headquarters 28th Anti-Aircraft Regiment RCA disbanded under General Order 208/45 (Effective 31st December 1945).

Headquarters Pacific Command was redesignated Headquarters, Military District No. 11, under General Order 56/46 (Effective 23rd January 1946).

*   *   *

6th Light Anti-Aircraft Battery RCA — Serial 1413B — 7th Division

6th Light Anti-Aircraft Battery RCA, Serial 1413B, mobilized under General Order 309/42 (Effective 12th May 1942), to serve with 10th Light Anti-Aircraft

Regiment RCA, 7th Division, Home Defence, Eastern Canada. The battery was stationed at Petawawa, Ontario, Sussex, New Brunswick, Debert, Nova Scotia, and in June 1943 the Regiment visited the Tracadie, New Brunswick, Firing Camp.

6th Light Anti-Aircraft Battery on special assignment, proceeded to Quebec City to provide protection for the First Quebec Conference, 11th to 24th August 1943. Those in attendance included Prime Minister Winston Churchill, President Roosevelt and Prime Minister MacKenzie King.

6th Light Anti-Aircraft Battery RCA, Serial 1413B, was redesignated 96th Light Anti-Aircraft Battery RCA, Serial 1413B, under General Order 412/43 (Effective 1st September 1943), and remained a component of 10th Light Anti-Aircraft Regiment RCA.

The Battery under its new designation was to enjoy a rather short existence, however, as the run-down of 7th Division was soon begun.

*96th Light Anti-Aircraft Battery RCA, Serial 1413B (listed as Regiment), along with Headquarters 10th Light Anti-Aircraft Regiment RCA, received authorization to disband under General Order 15/44 (Effective 15th November 1943). 96th Battery and the Regiment supplied a cadre base for 1st Light Anti-Aircraft Training Battery RCA being formed at Debert, Nova Scotia.

Headquarters 7th Division disbanded under General Order 15/44 (Effective 15th October 1943). Headquarters Atlantic Command continued operational until receiving authorization to disband under General Order 305/45 (Effective 31st July 1945).

*Correction from "Regiment" to "Battery" is listed in General Order 336/44 (Effective 17th November 1944).

*   *   *

7th AA Bty RCA, Stellarton, N.S. — Serial 364 — Gander, "W" Force

83rd Field Battery RCA was redesignated 7th Anti-Aircraft Battery RCA under General Order 92/39 (Effective 1st June 1939), in a reorganization of the Non-Permanent Active Militia, in Military District No. 6 (Nova Scotia).

7th Anti-Aircraft Battery RCA, was localized at Stellarton, Nova Scotia, under General Order 111/39 (Effective 1st June 1939).

"Details" of Serial 364, 7th Anti-Aircraft Battery RCA, CASF, became components of the Canadian Active Service Force under General Order 200/39 (Effective 1st September 1939).

The CASF "Details" were absorbed into the Battery, and Serial 364, 7th Anti-Aircraft Battery RCA was placed on active service under General Order 44/41 (Effective 1st January 1941), in Military District No. 6.

Serial 364, 7th Anti-Aircraft Battery RCA, was redesignated 7th Anti-Aircraft Battery (Type "M") RCA, under General Order 297/41 (Effective 1st October 1941).

7th Anti-Aircraft Battery, Type M, RCA, Serial 364, was redesignated 7th Anti-Aircraft Battery, Type 2H, RCA, Serial 364, under General Order 257/42 (Effective 15th May 1942).

7th Anti-Aircraft Battery joined the original 26th Anti-Aircraft Regiment RCA, authorized under General Order 256/42 (Effective 1st June 1942) and served at Gander Lake, in the Gander Lake Area, Gander, Newfoundland Defences.

7th Anti-Aircraft Battery, Type 2H, RCA, Serial 364, received authorization to disband under General Order 432/44 (Effective 30th November 1943), upon the conversion of 26th Anti-Aircraft Regiment RCA to French speaking. The new Regiment and its French speaking batteries assumed the duties of the previous 26th Anti-Aircraft Regiment RCA in Newfoundland.

*   *   *

No. 7 AA GOR (Class B), RCA, Sydney-Canso, N.S. — Serial 1389

Mobilized as No. 7 Anti-Aircraft Gun Operations Room (Class B), Royal Canadian Artillery, Serial 1389, under General Order 103/43 (Effective 15th January 1943), and served with 23rd Anti-Aircraft Regiment RCA, under Headquarters Sydney-Canso Defences, and its later designation, Headquarters Defended Port of Sydney.

No. 7 AA GOR disbanded as No. 7 Anti-Aircraft Gun *Operation* Room (Class B), RCA, Serial 1389, under General Order 208/45 (Effective 31st December 1944). Headquarters 23rd Anti-Aircraft Regiment RCA Serial 530, also disbanded under General Order 208/45 (Effective 31st December 1944).

*   *   *

7th Light Anti-Aircraft Battery RCA — Serial 1413C — 7th Div

7th Light Anti-Aircraft Battery RCA, Serial 1413C, mobilized under General Order 309/42 (Effective 12th May 1942), to serve with 10th Light Anti-Aircraft Regiment RCA, 7th Division, Home Defence, Eastern Canada. The battery was stationed at Petawawa, Ontario, Sussex, New Brunswick, Debert, Nova Scotia, and visited the Firing Camp at Tracadie, New Brunswick.

10th Light Anti-Aircraft Regiment RCA of 7th Division trimmed to a three-battery regiment in June 1943 as infantry division light anti-aircraft regiments conformed to a new war establishment. 7th Light Anti-Aircraft Battery remained with 10th Light Anti-Aircraft Regiment RCA. 8th Battery moved to Coast Defence as 63rd Anti-Aircraft Battery Type 3L, RCA.

7th Light Anti-Aircraft Battery RCA, Serial 1413C, was redesignated 97th Light Anti-Aircraft Battery RCA, Serial 1413C, under General Order 412/43 (Effective 1st September 1943), and remained a component of 10th Light Anti-Aircraft Regiment RCA with 7th Division.

97th Light Anti-Aircraft Battery RCA, Serial 1413C was to enjoy a rather short existence however, as the run-down of 7th Division was begun. *97th Battery, listed as Regiment, along with Headquarters 10th Light Anti-Aircraft Regiment RCA, received authorization to disband under General Order 15/44 (Effective 15th November 1943).

97th Battery and the regiment supplied a cadre base for 1st Light Anti-Aircraft Training Battery RCA.

*Correction from "Regiment" to "Battery" is listed in General Order 336/44 (Effective 17th November 1944).

*   *   *

8th Anti-Aircraft Battery RCA, Saint John, N.B. — Serial 376

In the reorganization of the Royal Canadian Artillery in the Non-Permanent Active Militia under General Order 75/39, 106th Field Battery RCA (Howitzer) was converted to 8th Anti-Aircraft Battery RCA, in Military District No. 7 (Effective 15th May 1939).

8th Anti-Aircraft Battery RCA was localized at Saint John, New Brunswick, under General Order 78/39 (Effective 15th May 1939).

"Details" of Serial 376, 8th Anti-Aircraft Battery RCA, CASF, were authorized as components of the Canadian Active Service Force under General Order 200/39 (Effective 1st September 1939), in Military District No. 7.

The CASF "Details" were absorbed into the Battery and Serial 376, 8th Anti-Aircraft Battery RCA was placed on Active Service in Military District No. 7, under General Order 44/41 (Effective 1st January 1941).

8th Anti-Aircraft Battery RCA, Serial 376, was redesignated 8th Anti-Aircraft Battery (Type "H") RCA, Serial 376, under General Order 297/41 (Effective 1st October 1941).

Serial 376, 8th Anti-Aircraft Battery, Type H, RCA, was redesignated 8th Anti-Aircraft Battery, Type 2H, RCA, Serial 376, under General Order 257/42 (Effective 15th May 1942).

8th Anti-Aircraft Battery became a component of 22nd Anti-Aircraft Regiment RCA, and served under Headquarters Saint John Defences, and its later designation, Headquarters Defended Port of Saint John, New Brunswick, in Atlantic Command. The battery manned the Beaconsfield and Loch Lomond Sites.

8th Anti-Aircraft Battery, Type "H", RCA, Serial 376, along with Headquarters 22nd Anti-Aircraft Regiment RCA, Serial 528, were authorized to disband under General Order 208/45 (Effective 1st September 1944).

*   *   *

No. 8 AA GOR (Class B) RCA, Saint John, N.B. — Serial 1390

No. 8 Anti-Aircraft Gun Operations Room (Class B) Royal Canadian Artillery, Serial 1390, mobilized under General Order 103/43 (Effective 15th January 1943).

No. 8 Anti-Aircraft Gun Operations Room (Class B) Royal Canadian Artillery served with 22nd Anti-Aircraft Regiment RCA under Headquarters Saint John Defences, Saint John, New Brunswick, and its later designation, Headquarters Defended Port of Saint John.

Headquarters 22nd Anti-Aircraft Regiment RCA was authorized to disband under General Order 208/45 (Effective 1st September 1944).

No. 8 Anti-Aircraft Gun Operations Room (Class B), Royal Canadian Artillery, Serial 1390, continued to serve under Headquarters Defended Port of Saint John, Atlantic Command, until authorized to disband along with Headquarters Defended Port of Saint John, and Headquarters Atlantic Command, under General Order 305/45 (Effective 31st July 1945).

*   *   *

8th HAA Battery RCA, Charlottetown, P.E.I. — Serial 69B — Army Tps.

8th Heavy Anti-Aircraft Battery RCA, Serial 69B, mobilized as 8th Medium Battery (Howitzer) RCA, CASF, Serial 70, under General Order 135/39, 1st September 1939, with Headquarters of 2nd Medium Brigade RCA, CASF, Corps Troops mobilixing with 1st Division.

Headquarters of 2nd Medium Brigade RCA, CASF, was redesignated Headquarters of 2nd Medium Regiment RCA, CASF, and under the new organization batteries were paired in a two-battery regiment.

8th Medium Battery (H) RCA, CASF, Serial 70, combined with 11th Medium Battery (H) RCA, CASF, Serial 72, to become 8th/11th Medium Battery RCA, CASF, Serial 70, under General Order 123/40 (Effective 1st June 1940).

8th Battery regained individual identity as 8th Medium Battery RCA, Serial 70, and was redesignated 8th Heavy Anti-Aircraft Battery RCA, Serial 70, under General Order 149/41 (Effective 24th May 1941).

Headquarters 2nd Medium Regiment RCA was redesignated Headquarters 2nd Heavy Anti-Aircraft Regiment (Mobile) RCA, Serial 69, under General Order 149/41 (Effective 24th May 1941), and the battery remained with the regiment in its new role.

8th Heavy Anti-Aircraft Battery, 2nd Heavy Anti-Aircraft Regiment RCA, departed for overseas 19th September 1941 on board the Pasteur, and disembarked 26th September 1941 at Gourock, Scotland.

In a realignment of Serial Numbers within the Regiment, 8th Heavy Anti-Aircraft Battery RCA was allotted Serial Number 69B, under General Order 54/42 (Effective 22nd December 1941).

The Battery and Regiment joined 1st Canadian Anti-Aircraft Brigade in the Air Defence of Great Britain (ADGB) and remained with the Brigade until it disbanded under General Order 357/44 (Effective 1st March 1944).

8th Heavy Anti-Aircraft Battery with 2nd Heavy Anti-Aircraft Regiment RCA, Army Troops, landed in Normandy on the 6th of August 1944, with 107th British Anti-Aircraft Brigade — a component of First Canadian Army, and joined the action on the night of 8th/9th August 1944, in the Caen Sector.

8th Heavy Anti-Aircraft Battery RCA served in France, Belgium, Holland, and Germany, then with cessation of hostilities received authorization to disband under General Order 401/45 (Effective 7th September 1945).

*   *   *

8th Light Anti-Aircraft Battery RCA — Serial 1413D — 7th Div

8th Light Anti-Aircraft Battery RCA, Serial 1413D, mobilized under General Order 309/42 (Effective 12th May 1942), to serve with 10th Light Anti-Aircraft Regiment RCA, 7th Division, Home Defence, Eastern Canada. The battery was stationed at Petawawa, Ontario, Sussex, New Brunswick, Debert, Nova Scotia, and visited Tracadie, New Brunswick Firing Camp. Then came a change in the war establishment.

Four-battery Light Anti-Aircraft Regiments RCA mobilized with the infantry divisions were now to conform to Army Troops, Corps Troops, and Armoured Division Light Anti-Aircraft Regiments, each of which had mobilized as three-battery light anti-aircraft regiments. 10th Light Anti-Aircraft Regiment RCA of 7th Division trimmed to three batteries and 8th Light Anti-Aircraft Battery RCA became surplus, moving to coastal defence.

However, in its new role as an Anti-Aircraft Battery an 8th Anti-Aircraft Battery was already in existence and 8th Light Anti-Aircraft Battery RCA, Serial 1413D, was redesignated Serial 1338, 63rd Anti-Aircraft Battery Type 3L, RCA, under General Order 366/43 (Effective 15th June 1943).

63rd Anti-Aircraft Battery Type 3L, RCA, Serial 1338, was posted to 24th Anti-Aircraft Regiment RCA, and served at Arvida, Quebec, until authorized to disband along with Headquarters 24th Anti-Aircraft Regiment RCA, Serial 533, under General Order 208/45 (Effective 15th January 1945).

*   *   *

9th AA Battery RCA, Vancouver, British Columbia — Serial 418

68th Heavy Battery RCA was converted to 9th Anti-Aircraft Battery RCA, in the reorganization of Royal Canadian Artillery, Non-Permanent Active Militia in Military District No. 11, under General Order 75/39 (Effective 15th May 1939).

9th Anti-Aircraft Battery RCA is listed as a component of 1st Anti-Aircraft Regiment RCA, under General Order 76/39 (Effective 15th May 1939), and localized at Vancouver, British Columbia, under General Order 78/39 (Effective 15th May 1939).

Serial 418, 9th Anti-Aircraft Battery RCA, CASF (Details) became components of the Canadian Active Service Force under General Order 200/39 (Effective 1st September 1939), with 1st Anti-Aircraft Regiment RCA, CASF (Details), in Military District No. 11.

9th Anti-Aircraft Battery RCA, CASF, provided the nucleus for "A" Troop of 16th Light Anti-Aircraft Battery RCA, CASF, mobilized in Vancouver in 1940 for overseas service.

Serial 418, 9th Anti-Aircraft Battery RCA was placed on Active Service under General Order 44/41 (Effective 1st January 1941), with Headquarters 1st Anti-Aircraft Regiment RCA, Vancouver, British Columbia. The "Details" serving at this time were absorbed into the battery or the regiment.

In a general reorganization of Anti-Aircraft Units in Canada, a new 9th Anti-Aircraft Battery, Type "H", RCA, Serial 709, appeared on the scene and

9th Anti-Aircraft Battery RCA, Serial 418, received authorization to disband under General Order 183/42 (Effective 13th April 1942).

*   *   *

9th AA Battery RCA — Serial 709 — Pacific Command

9th Anti-Aircraft Battery, Type "H", RCA, Serial 709, mobilized under General Order 97/42 (Effective 17th February 1942).

9th Anti-Aircraft Battery Type H, RCA, Serial 709, was redesignated 9th Anti-Aircraft Battery Type 2H, RCA, under General Order 182/42 (Effective 13th April 1942). The previous 9th AA Battery, Serial 418, of 1st AA Regiment RCA, Vancouver, B.C. disbanded on this date.

9th Anti-Aircraft Battery, Serial 709, became a component of 27th Anti-Aircraft Regiment RCA and served under Headquarters Victoria and Esquimalt Fortress, prior to moving to Prince Rupert, British Columbia, under Headquarters Prince Rupert Defences.

9 Bty is listed with 27 AA Regt in Operational Units — Artillery — Cdn. Army North American Zone, 24 April 1943, Victoria & Esquimalt. (D. Hist., Ottawa).

War Diary — "11 Aug/43 "A" Tp at Pat Bay, "B" Tp at Bazan Bay — 13 Aug/43 "A" Tp & BHQ at Wilson Rd, "B" Tp at Bazan Bay. "A" Tp & BHQ moved to Macaulay and "B" Tp to Colwood".

Site Fighting Book, VH 2 Colwood, B.C., 27th AA Regt RCA, lists 9th AA Bty on Manning Duty 22 Aug/43 to 18 Sept/43.

War Diary HQ 27 AA Regt RCA, CA, Esq, B.C. — "Entire 9 AA Bty SOS 27 AA Regt on being placed under command of 29 AA Regt (Prince Rupert, B.C.) "B" Tp attached back to this Unit for a period of firing practice in Macaulay Camp. Part II Order #256 is created to attach 9th AA Bty to 29th AA Regt rather than as SOS 27th AA Regt 4th Dec/43".

Prince Rupert Defences came under command of 8th Division, 9th Oct/42, and 9th AA Bty joined 29th AA Regiment at Prince Rupert, 5th Oct/43. —(Order of Battle 8th Cdn Div, Public Archives Canada, Ottawa).

8th Canadian Division disbanded shortly after the arrival of 9th AA Battery, and the battery with 29th Anti-Aircraft Regiment RCA continued to serve under Headquarters Prince Rupert Defences, Pacific Command.

At Prince Rupert, in the Records of #1 CRLE Pacific Command Group AA Radars — Time in Op Condition Jan/44 — July 1945, "A" Tp 9th AA Bty is listed as manning PR H-2, Tobey Point Site, and "B" Tp 9th AA Bty manning PR H-1, 11th Ave Site under 29th AA Regiment.

9th Anti-Aircraft Battery, Type 2H, RCA, Serial 709, along with Headquarters 29th Anti-Aircraft Regiment RCA, received authorization to disband under General Order 305/45 (Effective 31st July 1945).

* * *

No. 9 AA GOR (Class B), RCA, Prince Rupert, B.C. — Serial 1391

No. 9 Anti-Aircraft Gun Operations Room (Class B), Royal Canadian Artillery, Serial 1391, mobilized under General Order 193/43 (Effective 15th January 1943), and served under Headquarters Prince Rupert Defences, Pacific Command.

No. 9 Anti-Aircraft Gun Operations Room joined 29th Anti-Aircraft Regiment RCA at Prince Rupert, British Columbia, March 1943 and with Prince Rupert Defences, served under 8th Canadian Division, Home Defence, Pacific Command, until 8th Division disbanded 15th October 1943.

No. 9 Anti-Aircraft Gun Operation Room (Class B), Royal Canadian Artillery, Serial 1391 continued to serve with 29th Anti-Aircraft Regiment RCA under Headquarters Prince Rupert Defences, Pacific Command, until receiving authorization to disband, along with Headquarters 29th Anti-Aircraft Regiment RCA, under General Order 305/45 (Effective 31st July 1945). Headquarters Prince Rupert Defences disbanded under General Order 18/46 (Effective 31st October 1945), and Headquarters Pacific Command was redesignated Headquarters, Military District No. 11, under General Order 56/46 (Effective 23rd January 1946).

* * *

9th Light Anti-Aircraft Battery RCA — Serial 1413E — 7th Div

9th Light Anti-Aircraft Battery RCA, Serial 1413E, mobilized as a component of 10th Light Anti-Aircraft Regiment RCA, 7th Division, Home Defence, under General Order 309/42 (Effective 12th May 1942), for service in Eastern Canada.

9th Battery was stationed at Petawawa, Ontario, Sussex, New Brunswick, Debert, Nova Scotia, and in June 1943 the Regiment visited the Tracadie New Brunswick Firing Camp.

Battery Headquarters and "F" Troop of 9th Light Anti-Aircraft Battery RCA, attached to 22nd Anti-Aircraft Regiment RCA, Saint John, New Brunswick, served under Headquarters Saint John Defences, Atlantic Command from June to September 1943.

9th Light Anti-Aircraft Battery RCA, Serial 1413E, was redesignated 99th Light Anti-Aircraft Battery RCA, Serial 1413E, under General Order 412/43 (Effective 1st September 1943), and remained a component of 10th Light Anti-Aircraft Regiment RCA.

*99th Light Anti-Aircraft Battery RCA, Serial 1413E enjoyed a rather short existence, however, as the run-down of 7th Division was soon begun. 99th Light Anti-Aircraft Battery RCA, Serial 1413E, listed as Regiment in error, along with Headquarters 10th Light Anti-Aircraft Regiment RCA, received authorization to disband under General Order 15/44 (Effective 15th November 1943). 99th Battery and the regiment supplied a cadre base for 1st Light Anti-Aircraft Training Battery RCA.

Headquarters 7th Division also disbanded under General Order 15/44, however the effective date was 15th October 1943.

Headquarters Atlantic Command continued operational until being authorized to disband under General Order 305/45 (Effective 31st July 1945).

*Correction from "Regiment" to "Battery" is listed in General Order 336/44 (Effective 17th November 1944).

*   *   *

10th AA Battery RCA, Vancouver, B.C. — Serial 419 — M.D. No. 11

10th Anti-Aircraft Battery, Royal Canadian Artillery, came into existence in Military District No. 11, authorized under General Order 75/39 (Effective 15th May 1939), a component of 1st Anti-Aircraft Regiment RCA, in the Non-Permanent Active Militia.

The composition of 1st Anti-Aircraft Regiment RCA was authorized under General Order 76/39 (Effective 15th May 1939), and 10th Anti-Aircraft Battery RCA was localized at Vancouver, British Columbia, under General Order 78/39 (Effective 15th May 1939).

Serial 419, 10th Anti-Aircraft Battery RCA, CASF (Details) became components of the Canadian Active Service Force under General Order 200/39 (Effective 1st September 1939), in Military District No. 11.

10th Anti-Aircraft Battery RCA, CASF, provided the nucleus for "B" Troop of 16th Light Anti-Aircraft Battery RCA, CASF, mobilized in Vancouver, September 1940, for overseas service.

Serial 419, 10th Anti-Aircraft Battery RCA, was placed on Active Service in Military District No. 11, under General Order 44/41 (Effective 1st January 1941). The "Details" were absorbed into the battery and the battery continued to serve in the Vancouver area until authorized to disband under General Order 183/42 (Effective 13th April 1942).

A general reorganization of anti-aircraft units at this time saw a number of anti-aircraft troops enlarged to batteries resulting in several duplications, which may have had some bearing in the phasing out of 1st Anti-Aircraft Regiment RCA and its component batteries.

*   *   *

10th AA Battery RCA, Victoria-Esquimalt, B.C. — Serial 710

10th Anti-Aircraft Battery RCA, Serial 710, mobilized as 10th Anti-Aircraft Troop, Type "L", RCA, Serial 710, under General Order 97/42 (Effective 17th February 1942).

10th Anti-Aircraft Troop Type L, RCA, Serial 710, was redesignated 10th Anti-Aircraft Battery Type 2L, RCA, Serial 710, under General Order 182/42 (Effective 13th April 1942). The previous 10th Anti-Aircraft Battery RCA, Serial 419, disbanded at this time.

War Diary — "The Bty formed at Macaulay Plains BHQ at Work Pt. Members of 10 AA Tp TOS. Took over 3 Bofors guns at Pat Bay from 2nd AA Bty, 1st May/42 & 12th May all personnel left Macaulay for Pat Bay on NE corner of Airport. 29th June/42 now part of 27 AA Regt".

10th Anti-Aircraft Battery (Type 2L) RCA, Serial 710, was redesignated 10th Anti-Aircraft Battery (Type 3L) RCA, Serial 710, under General Order 348/42 (Effective 15th July 1942).

January 1943, the battery visited Boundary Bay LAA Firing Practice Camp. (Vancouver Defences).

10th Bty is listed as a component of 27th AA Regiment, Victoria & Esquimalt, Pacific Command, in "Operational Units — Artillery — Cdn Army North American Zone, 24 April, 1943". — (D. Hist, Ottawa).

10th Anti-Aircraft Battery, Type 3L, RCA, Serial 710, continued to serve with 27th Anti-Aircraft Regiment RCA under Headquarters Victoria and Esquimalt Fortress and its later designation Headquarters Esquimalt Fortress, authorized under General Order 517/44 (Effective 8th August 1944).

10th Anti-Aircraft Battery's service with the headquarters under its new designation was of short duration however, upon Serial 710, 10th Anti-Aircraft Battery, Type 3L, RCA receiving authorization to disband under General Order 208/45 (Effective 1st September 1944).

Headquarters 27th Anti-Aircraft Regiment RCA, and Headquarters Esquimalt Fortress remained operational until disbanding under General Order 18/46 (Effective 31st October 1945).

*   *   *

No. 10 AA GOR (Class B) RCA — Serial 1552 — Goose Bay

No. 10 Anti-Aircraft Gun Operations Room (Class B) RCA, Serial 1552, mobilized under General Order 199/43 (Effective 1st April 1943) and served under Headquarters Goose Bay Defences.

No. 10 Anti-Aircraft Gun Operation Room (Class B) RCA, Serial 1552, continued to serve under the Headquarters upon it being redesignated Headquarters Defended Area Goose Bay in April 1944.

No. 10 Anti-Aircraft Gun Operation Room (Class B) RCA, Serial 1552, received authorization to disband under General Order 208/45 (Effective 15th November 1944).

Headquarters Defended Area Goose Bay, Serial 2940, remained operational until authorized to disband under General Order 18/46 (Effective 25th August 1945).

*   *   *

11th AA Battery RCA, Vancouver, B.C. — Serial 419A — M.D. No. 11

In a reorganization of the Non-Permanent Active Militia in Military District No. 11, 5th Medium Battery RCA was redesignated 11th Anti-Aircraft Battery RCA, to form part of 1st Anti-Aircraft Regiment RCA, authorized under General Order 92/39 (Effective 15th May 1939).

11th Anti-Aircraft Battery RCA, Non-Permanent Active Militia, was localized at Vancouver, British Columbia, in Military District No. 11, under General Order 111/39 (Effective 15th May 1939).

Serial 419a, 11th Anti-Aircraft Battery RCA, CASF (Details), and Headquarters 1st Anti-Aircraft Regiment RCA, CASF (Details), Serial 417, became components of the Canadian Active Service Force under General Order 200/39 (Effective 1st September 1939), in Military District No. 11.

Serial 419A, 11th Anti-Aircraft Battery RCA was placed on Active Service with Headquarters 1st Anti-Aircraft Regiment RCA, under General Order 44/41 (Effective 1st January 1941), at Vancouver, British Columbia, and the "Details" were absorbed into the regiment and battery.

11th Anti-Aircraft Battery RCA, Serial 419A, received authorization to disband under General Order 183/42 (Effective 13th April 1942).

*   *   *

11th Anti-Aircraft Battery RCA — Serial 711 — Pacific Command

11th Anti-Aircraft Battery RCA, Serial 711, mobilized as 11th Anti-Aircraft Troop, Type "L" RCA, Serial 711, under General Order 97/42 (Effective 17th February 1942).

11th Anti-Aircraft Troop Type L RCA, Serial 711, was redesignated 11th Anti-Aircraft Battery Type 2L RCA, Serial 711, under General Order 182/42 (Effective 13th April 1942), the same date the previous 11th Anti-Aircraft Battery RCA, Serial 419A, was authorized to disband.

War Diary — "11th AA Tp enlarged to Bty. Bty formed at Esquimalt. Moved to Sea Island under Cmd Officer Cmding Van Def 20 May/42 less 40 ORs posted to 10th AA Bty, Pat Bay".

43rd AA Bty War Diary — "On 6th June 1942, the 43rd, 21st, 31st, 11th & 47th Btys were placed in the 28th AA Regt RCA".

11th Anti-Aircraft Battery (Type 2L) RCA, Serial 711, was redesignated 11th Anti-Aircraft Battery (Type 3L) RCA, Serial 711, under General Order 386/42 (Effective 1st September 1942).

11th Bty is listed as a component of 28th AA Regiment RCA, in "Operational Units — Artillery — Cdn Army — North American Zone, 24 April, 1943". (D. Hist, Ottawa).

11th AA Bty joined 29 AA Regt Prince Rupert 19 Sept/43 — (Order of Battle 8th Cdn Div — Public Archives of Canada, Ottawa).

11th Anti-Aircraft Battery (Type 3L) RCA, Serial 711, was redesignated 11th Anti-Aircraft Battery (Type 4L) RCA, Serial 711, under General Order 79/44 (Effective 31st December 1943).

War Diary — "The Bty dep. Pr Rupert 11 Sept/45 arr Colwood Camp, Victoria, 14 Sept/45".

11th Anti-Aircraft Battery (Type 4L) RCA, Serial 711, received authorization to disband under General Order 18/46 (Effective 31st October 1945), at Colwood Camp.

Headquarters 27th Anti-Aircraft Regiment RCA, and Headquarters Esquimalt Fortress, also disbanded under General Order 18/46 (Effective 31st October 1945).

*   *   *

11th HAA Battery RCA, Winnipeg, Manitoba — Serial 69D — Army Tps.

11th Heavy Anti-Aircraft Battery RCA, Serial 69D, mobilized as 11th Medium Battery (Howitzer) RCA, CASF, Serial 72, under General Order 135/39, 1st September 1939, with Headquarters of 2nd Medium Brigade RCA, CASF, Corps Troops mobilizing with 1st Division.

Headquarters of 2nd Medium Brigade RCA, CASF, was redesignated Headquarters of 2nd Medium Regiment RCA, CASF, and Batteries were paired in a two-battery regiment.

11th Medium Battery (H) RCA, CASF, Serial 72 combined with 8th Medium Battery (H) RCA, CASF, Serial 70, to become 8th/11th Medium Battery RCA, CASF, Serial 70, under General Order 123/40 (Effective 1st June 1940).

11th Battery regained individual identity as 11th Medium Battery RCA, Serial 72 and was redesignated 11th Heavy Anti-Aircraft Battery RCA, Serial 72, under General Order 149/41 (Effective 24th May 1941).

Headquarters 2nd Medium Regiment RCA, Serial 69, was redesignated Headquarters, 2nd Heavy Anti-Aircraft Regiment (Mobile) RCA, Serial 69, under General Order 149/41 (Effective 24th May 1941), and the battery remained with the regiment in its new role.

11th Heavy Anti-Aircraft Battery, 2nd Heavy Anti-Aircraft Regiment RCA, departed for overseas 19th September 1941 on board the Pasteur, and disembarked 26th September 1941, at Gourock, Scotland.

In a realignment of Serial Numbers within the Regiment, 11th Heavy Anti-Aircraft Battery RCA was allotted Serial Number 69D, under General Order 54/42 (Effective 22nd December 1941).

The Battery and Regiment joined 1st Canadian Anti-Aircraft Brigade in the Air Defence of Great Britain (ADGB) and served with the brigade until its disbandment, authorized under General Order 357/44 (Effective 1st March 1944).

11th Heavy Anti-Aircraft Battery RCA, with 2nd Heavy Anti-Aircraft Regiment RCA, Army Troops, landed in Normandy on the 6th of August 1944 with 107th British Anti-Aircraft Brigade, which had replaced 1st Canadian Anti-Aircraft Brigade in First Canadian Army. 11th Battery joined the action with First Canadian Army the night of 8th/9th August 1944, in the Caen Sector.

11th Heavy Anti-Aircraft Battery RCA served in France, Belgium, Holland, and Germany, then with cessation of hostilities received authorization to disband under General Order 401/45 (Effective 7th September 1945).

*   *   *

12th AA Battery RCA — Serial 883 — Arvida, P.Q. Defences

12th Anti-Aircraft Battery RCA mobilized as No. 3 Anti-Aircraft Machine Gun Troop RCA, Serial 883, under General Order 306/41 (Effective 10th October 1941).

No. 3 Anti-Aircraft Machine Gun Troop RCA, Serial 883, was redesignated 12th Anti-Aircraft Troop (Type L) RCA, Serial 883, under General Order 26/42 (Effective 12th December 1941).

12th Anti-Aircraft Troop Type L, RCA, Serial 883, was redesignated 12th Anti-Aircraft Battery Type 4L RCA, Serial 883, under General Order 182/42 (Effective 13th April 1942).

12th Anti-Aircraft Battery Type "4L", RCA, Serial 883, was redesignated 12th Anti-Aircraft Battery Type "3L" RCA, Serial 883, under General Order 366/43 (Effective 15th June 1943).

12th Anti-Aircraft Battery Type "3L" RCA, Serial 883, was redesignated 12th Anti-Aircraft Battery (Type 2L) RCA, Serial 883, under General Order 493/43 (Effective 15th October 1943).

The Battery served with 24th Anti-Aircraft Regiment RCA, in the Arvida Defences, Arvida, P.Q.

12th Anti-Aircraft Battery Type 2L RCA, Serial 883, received authorization to disband under General Order 208/45 (Effective 15th January 1945). Headquarters 24th Anti-Aircraft Regiment RCA, Serial 533, also disbanded under General Order 208/45 (Effective 15th January 1945).

*   *   *

13th AA Battery RCA, Victoria-Esquimalt, B.C. — Serial 712

13th Anti-Aircraft Battery RCA Type "2L" RCA, Serial 712, mobilized under General Order 97/42 (Effective 17th February 1942).

13th Anti-Aircraft Battery Type 2L RCA, Serial 712, was redesignated 13th Anti-Aircraft Battery Type 3L RCA, Serial 712, under General Order 182/42 (Effective 13th April 1942).

War Diary — "The Battery was formed at Esquimalt, and 26 Apr/42 guns were placed in temporary locations, 1 at Colwood, 1 at Esquimalt drydock and 2 at Rodd Hill.

27th Apr. 2 guns taken over from 2 AA Bty at Esq drydock — 6 guns in action.

4th May/42 — 3 guns in Rodd Hill area & 3 guns at Drydock.

5th June/42 — new gun site at Signal Hill — Two new guns were put in action during the day 6th June/42.

1st July/42 — 4 guns of Bty (2 Rodd Hill, 1 Lang's Cove, 1 Macaulay Plain) moved to Pat Bay to man 10th AA Bty "C" positions and returned to Macaulay, Ogden Pt, Shoal Pt & Lang's Cove, 14th Aug/42.

7th Sept/42 — Tyee Rd Gunsite is referred to, and 22nd Sept/42 Football field Site is also mentioned.

13th AA Battery attended a LAA Firing Camp at Boundary Bay, with "D" Tp left at Tyee Rd, Vic West".

An excerpt from the War Diary of 44th AA Battery — "44th AA Bty took over RCA Camp Macaulay Plains for admin purposes, personnel of 44th, 47th, 58th and 13th AA Btys being att for R & Q, 7th Sept/42."

59th AA Bty War Diary — "Arrangements were made with 13th AA Bty for men of 59th AA Bty to take over two guns at Rodd Hill in an operational & training role under the guidance of 13th AA Bty, 5th to 19th Oct/42".

13 Bty is listed as a component of 27 AA Regt, Victoria-Esquimalt, Pacific Command, in Operational Units — Artillery — Cdn Army North American Zone, 24 April 1943. (D Hist, Ottawa).

13th Anti-Aircraft Battery Type "3L" RCA, Serial 712, was redesignated 13th Anti-Aircraft Battery Type "4L" RCA, Serial 712, under General Order 366/43 (Effective 15th June 1943).

The Fort Record Book of Fort Black Rock, 8th Nov/43, notes that — "adjacent to Belmont Fort the 13th L.A.A. Battery have four 40mm Bofors sited".

13th Battery served under Headquarters Victoria and Esquimalt Fortress and its later designation Headquarters Esquimalt Fortress, authorized under General Order 517/44 (Effective 8th August 1944).

However, almost coincidentally, 13th Anti-Aircraft Battery Type 4L RCA, Serial 712, received authorization to disband under General Order 208/45 (Effective 1st September 1944).

*   *   *

14th AA Battery RCA — Serial 129 — 2nd, 25th and 21st AA Regiments.

14th AA Battery mobilized as 14th Anti-Aircraft Battery RCA, CASF, Serial 129, under General Order 135/39, 1st September 1939, with Headquarters 2nd

Anti-Aircraft Regiment RCA, Canadian Active Service Force, Army Troops mobilizing with 1st Division.

The component Batteries of 2nd Anti-Aircraft Regiment RCA, CASF, were diverted to other Units and 14th Anti-Aircraft Battery RCA, Serial 129, was redesignated 14th Anti-Aircraft Battery (Type "M") RCA, Serial 129, under General order 297/41 (Effective 1st October 1941).

14th Anti-Aircraft Battery Type "M", RCA, Serial 129, was redesignated 14th Anti-Aircraft Battery Type "H", RCA, Serial 129, under General Order 98/42 (Effective 17th February 1942).

14th Battery served with 25th Anti-Aircraft Regiment RCA, under Headquarters St. John's Defences (Newfoundland), at St. John's-Torbay, Newfoundland, "W" Force.

In February 1944, 49th Anti-Aircraft Battery of 21st Anti-Aircraft Regiment RCA, Halifax, exchanged locations with 14th Anti-Aircraft Battery at Torbay, under 25th Anti-Aircraft Regiment RCA. 14th Battery moved to 21st Anti-Aircraft Regiment RCA, Headquarters Halifax Fortress and manned the McNab Island Site.

14th Anti-Aircraft Battery Type H, RCA, Serial 129, served with 21st Anti-Aircraft Regiment RCA until authorized to disband under General Order 305/45 (Effective 31st July 1945). Headquarters 21st Anti-Aircraft Regiment RCA, Serial 527, also disbanded under General Order 305/45 (Effective 31st July 1945).

* * *

15th Anti-Aircraft Battery RCA, CASF — Serial 130 — 2nd AA Regt

15th Anti-Aircraft Battery RCA, CASF, Serial 130, mobilized with Headquarters 2nd Anti-Aircraft Regiment RCA, CASF, Army Troops mobilizing with 1st Division, under General Order 135/39, 1st September 1939.

Three of four batteries listed to comprise 2nd Anti-Aircraft Regiment RCA, CASF, Serial 127, were diverted to other units. 4th Anti-Aircraft Battery RCA, CASF, Serial 128, moved to 2nd Light Anti-Aircraft Regiment, then to 11th Light Anti-Aircraft Regiment RCA. 14th Anti-Aircraft Battery Serial 129, served with 25th and 21st Anti-Aircraft Regiments, Serial 131, 1st (Yorkton) Light Anti-Aircraft Battery RCA, CASF, served as 2nd (Yorkton) Light Anti-Aircraft Battery in 2nd Light Anti-Aircraft Regiment RCA, 1st Division. 15th Battery was left without a task and became expendable.

15th Anti-Aircraft Battery RCA, Serial 130, was authorized to disband under General Order 183/42 (Effective 13th April 1942).

* * *

15th Anti-Aircraft Battery RCA — Serial 721 — Atlantic Command

15th Anti-Aircraft Battery mobilized as 15th Anti-Aircraft Battery Type "H", RCA, Serial 721, under General Order 97/42 (Effective 17th February 1942).

15th Anti-Aircraft Battery served outside regimental organization at Goose Bay, Labrador, July 1942 to July 1943, under Headquarters Goose Bay Defences.

Goose Bay Defences became the responsibility of Military Districts No. 6 and 7, and Batteries of 21st, 22nd and 23rd Anti-Aircraft Regiments RCA exchanged locations periodically with this outpost.

6th Anti-Aircraft Battery relieved 15th Battery at Goose Bay and 15th Battery moved to the Westmount Site under 23rd Anti-Aircraft Regiment RCA, Headquarters Sydney-Canso Defences, and its later designation, Headquarters Defended Port of Sydney, Nova Scotia.

15th Anti-Aircraft Battery, Type H, RCA, Serial 721, received authorization to disband under General Order 208/45 (Effective 15th November 1944).

*   *   *

15th LAA Bty RCA, Winnipeg — Serial 142-A & 38th LAA Bty — 2 Div

15th Light Anti-Aircraft Battery RCA, CASF, Serial 142-A, mobilized under General Order 243/40 (Effective 28th September 1940), with Headquarters 3rd Light Anti-Aircraft Regiment RCA, CASF, Serial 142.

3rd Light Anti-Aircraft Regiment was to serve as 2nd Canadian Infantry Division Light Anti-Aircraft Regiment.

15th Light Anti-Aircraft Battery, 3rd Light Anti-Aircraft Regiment RCA, remained in Winnipeg until receiving notice to proceed overseas. The Battery entrained for Halifax, where, on board the Warwick Castle in convoy, 15th Battery departed for overseas 20th February 1941, and disembarked at Gourock, Scotland, 1st March 1941.

Shortly after arriving overseas, 15th Light Anti-Aircraft Battery RCA, Serial 142-A, was redesignated 38th Light Anti-Aircraft Battery RCA, Serial 142-A, under General Order 112/41 (Effective 1st January 1941) — (Back-dated).

In a shuffle of Serial Numbers within the Regiment, 3rd Light Anti-Aircraft Regiment RCA was allotted Serial 142, Headquarters 3rd Light Anti-Aircraft Regiment RCA assumed Serial 142A and 38th Light Anti-Aircraft Battery RCA changed to Serial 142B, under General Order 54/42 (Effective 22nd December 1941).

The Regiment concentrated at Colchester, Essex, under 1st Canadian Anti-Aircraft Brigade for duty and training.

38th Light Anti-Aircraft Battery manned Sites at Farnborough and Bromley in the Air Defence of Great Britain (ADGB), August 1941 to February 1942, then returned to Colchester.

On the 19th March 1942, the Regiment moved to 2nd Division Defence area where the battery manned sites on the coast and trained with the division.

38th Light Anti-Aircraft Battery, 3rd Light Anti-Aircraft Regiment RCA accompanied other Units of 2nd Division on the Dieppe Raid, 19th August 1942, and upon its return the Battery resumed its role on the coast, guarding against hit-and-run raiders.

38th Battery once again crossed the Channel, this time however, the battery avoided the high cliffs and hazards of a defended port and landed on the Normandy beaches, 7th July 1944. The Regiment moved into position near Carpiquet Airfield, with 2nd Canadian Infantry Division.

As a component of 2nd Canadian Corps, the Division, Regiment, and 38th Battery served with Second British Army, then moved to First Canadian Army, 31st July 1944, on the Caen Front.

The regiment participated in the fierce fighting in the breakout from Caen, and the closing of the Falaise Gap. The Division then moved on to Dieppe, where on the 3rd of September 1944, following the capture of the City the Units paused for a Service of Remembrance in the cemetery in honour of those lost in the raid two years previous, and 38th Battery paraded with the division through the streets of the City.

38th Battery with the Regiment and 2nd Canadian Infantry Division, rejoined the action with First Canadian Army and served in France, Belgium, Holland, and Germany.

38th Light Anti-Aircraft Battery RCA served until cessation of hostilities and received authorization to disband under General Order 52/46 (Effective 23rd September 1945).

*   *   *

16th Anti-Aircraft Battery RCA — Serial 722 — Disbanded

16th Anti-Aircraft Battery Type "H", RCA, Serial 722, mobilized under General Order 97/42 (Effective 17th February 1942).

The battery however found itself without a role and in less than three months,

16th Anti-Aircraft Battery Type H, RCA, Serial 722, received authorization to disband under General Order 258/42 (Effective 15th May 1942).

* * *

16th AA (MG) Battery (CD) RCA — Serial 434 — "W" Force

16th Anti-Aircraft (M.G.) Battery (C.D.) RCA, Serial 434, mobilized under General Order 155/41 (Effective 22nd March 1941), and served with 25th Anti-Aircraft Regiment RCA in Newfoundland, under Headquarters St. John's Defences (Newfoundland), "W" Force, Atlantic Command.

War Diary — "HQ Troop & BHQ Gander Newf — "A" Det St. John's Newf. 1941. "B" Det. St. John's Newf. 1941.

BHQ, St. John's Jan/42 — Bty dispositions as follows — (3) — .50 Cal four (4) gun Tps at Gander Airport. 1 four gun Tp at Torbay Airport, with two of their four guns loaned to the Navy. One S/L Tp of five S/L Det, Tp HQ at Mundy's Pond, St. John's Newf. BHQ of 1 Off, 1 clerk 2 Gnrs at Mundy's Pond. Total —Ten Off & 284 ORs. Tps alternated between Gander & Torbay".

After almost 20 months of service, 16th Anti-Aircraft (MG) Battery (CD) RCA, Serial 434, received authorization to disband under General Order 19/43 (Effective 15th November 1942).

"A few ORs transferred to 25th Anti-Aircraft Regiment the remainder SOS to AA Arty Reinforcement Camp, Bedford, N.S.".

Headquarters 25th Anti-Aircraft Regiment RCA disbanded under General Order 305/45 (Effective 31st July 1945), and Headquarters Defended Port of St. John's was authorized to disband under General Order 379/45 (Effective 15th August 1945).

* * *

No. 16 AA Operations Room RCA — Serial 1746 — Army Troops

No. 16 Anti-Aircraft Operations Room RCA, Serial 1746, mobilized under General Order 371/43 (Effective 23rd June 1943) to serve as a component of 1st Canadian Anti-Aircraft Brigade. However, upon the disbanding of 1st Canadian Anti-Aircraft Brigade Headquarters, under General Order 357/44 (Effective 1st March 1944), No. 16 Anti-Aircraft Operations Room RCA was placed under command of 107th British Anti-Aircraft Brigade, along with 109th Heavy Anti-Aircraft Regiment, Royal Artillery, and 2nd Heavy Anti-Aircraft Regiment, Royal Canadian Artillery.

As a component of First Canadian Army, this formation landed in Normandy on the 6th of August 1944 and joined the action 8th/9th August 1944 on the Caen Front.

No. 16 AA Operations Room RCA assumed its duty of coordinating the Army Anti-Aircraft defences with the Royal Air Force, and the Royal Canadian Air Force, and served in France, Belgium, Holland, and Germany.

No. 16 Anti-Aircraft Operations Room RCA, Serial 1746, served until cessation of hostilities and received authorization to disband under General Order 321/45 (Effective 21st June 1945), as the run-down of Canadian Units in NW Europe was begun.

Personnel proceeded to the Canadian Army Pacific Force (CAPF), the Canadian Army Occupational Force (CAOF), for occupational duty in Germany, or were posted to divisional units from the Military District of their enlistment, for the return to Canada.

* * *

16th LAA Battery RCA, Vancouver, B.C. — Serial 142C — 2nd Div

16th Light Anti-Aircraft Battery RCA, CASF, Serial 142-B, with Headquarters 3rd Light Anti-Aircraft Regiment RCA, CASF, Serial 142, mobilized under General Order 243/40 (Effective 28th September 1940), to serve with 2nd Division, CASF.

The disbanding 1st Anti-Aircraft Regiment of Vancouver and its three Batteries supplied a firm foundation for 16th Light Anti-Aircraft Battery RCA, CASF, as 9th AA Battery provided the nucleus for "A" Troop, 10th AA Battery for "B" Troop, and 11th AA Battery for "C" Troop.

2nd Anti-Aircraft Battery from Victoria-Esquimalt Fortress also provided a number of volunteers for the overseas bound 16th Light Anti-Aircraft Battery.

Regimental Headquarterss, 3rd Light Anti-Aircraft Regiment RCA, CASF, also came from the Victoria-Esquimalt Fortress, led by Lt-Colonel B.R. Ker, from Headquarters 5th (B.C.) Coast Brigade RCA, Fort Mary Hill.

16th Light Anti-Aircraft Battery RCA, CASF, assembled at Seaforth Armouries in Vancouver, under Major E.J.D. Edmonds, and on the 24th of September 1940 moved to Windsor, Ontario, where its proximity to Detroit proved extremely popular as the US was still not at war.

16th Battery headed East again 8th February 1941, and at Halifax boarded the Orontes, only to encounter an outbreak of German Measles and quaranteen aboard ship. The convoy with the remainder of the Regiment (less 53rd Battery), sailed overseas without them.

16th Battery disembarked, and proceeded to Debert, Nova Scotia, to await another sailing, then 10th April 1941 departed for overseas on board the Batory and disembarked at Gourock, Scotland, on the 19th of April 1941.

The Regiment with its four component batteries joined 1st Canadian Anti-Aircraft Brigade at Colchester, Essex, and it was while on a night deployment at Walton-on-Naze that 16th Battery shot down its first enemy plane.

The training session at Colchester was followed by the responsibility of manning Air Defence of Great Britain (ADGB) sites at Gatwick and Red Hill in the South of England, from August 1941 to February 1942.

In a shuffle of Serial Numbers within the Regiment, 16th Light Anti-Aircraft Battery assumed Serial Number 142C, authorized under General Order 54/42 (Effective 22nd December 1941).

3rd Light Anti-Aircraft Regiment RCA returned to Colchester and 1st Anti-Aircraft Brigade from 9th February 1942 to 19th March 1942, then moved to 2nd Canadian Division Area on the South Coast to participate in divisional training and provide protection to the division area.

On the 18th August 1942 as darkness closed in, crews not employed on gun sites found themselves on board landing craft bound for the shores of France. Before noon on the 19th August 1942, the 4th and 6th Brigades of 2nd Canadian Division had been decimated at Dieppe.

Two Officers and twenty-four Other Ranks of 16th Light Anti-Aircraft Battery, 3rd Light Anti-Aircraft Regiment RCA, 2nd Division, landed with the Royal Regiment of Canada on the left flank, and of this party two officers and seventeen other ranks were reported missing. Seven other ranks returned to England, three of which were wounded.

Casualties listed in the Regimental History, May 1945, show one officer killed and one wounded and taken prisoner, eight other ranks killed and five of the nine taken prisoner were wounded.

This was the only group of 3rd Light Anti-Aircraft Regiment RCA to suffer casualties.

Returning to England, 16th Light Anti-Aircraft Battery RCA resumed its duty in the divisional area on the coast, guarding against tip-and-run raiders, and prepared for a return to the Continent.

Changes in War Establishment during 1943 and 1944 had a noticeable effect on the regiment as 53rd Battery moved to 11th Light Anti-Aircraft Regiment RCA and each remaining troop added two guns, one troop became self-propelled. In March 1944, a 20mm troop for each battery arrived from the disbanded 7th and 11th Light Anti-Aircraft Regiments RCA. Several members of the disbanded 53rd Light Anti-Aircraft Battery RCA returned to the regiment at this time.

After almost two years 2nd Div returned to France, however, this time they skirted the defended ports to enter the bridgehead in the Canadian Sector established by 3rd Canadian Infantry Division, 2nd Canadian Armoured Brigade and 19th Army Field Regiment RCA, aided by 1 Canadian Parachute Battalion, the Royal Canadian Navy and the Royal Canadian Air Force.

16th Battery, 3rd Light Anti-Aircraft Regiment RCA landed in Normandy 7th July 1944 and moved into position near Carpiquet, with 2nd Canadian Infantry Division, 2nd Canadian Corps, under Second British Army, then moved to First Canadian Army 31st July 1944, on the Caen Front.

In August the battery fired directional tracer marking the line of advance in the breakout from Caen, and with the capture of Dieppe, 16th Battery returned for a memorial service in the cemetery, 3rd September 1944, followed by a divisional parade through the city, then returned to action with First Canadian Army.

The 20mm troop was phased out, and during September the battery was trimmed to two troops equipped with Bofors, one self-propelled, and one semi-mobile, one troop to operate with the field regiment and one with the brigade.

The battery successfully undertook a number of ground tasks, clearing enemy strong-points, performed as infantry, reconnaissance, field artillery, and fired a number of "Pepperpots" with massed artillery, in addition to its Anti-Aircraft role when required.

16th Light Anti-Aircraft Battery RCA served in France, Belgium, Holland, and Germany, preceded by service on the Dieppe Raid in 1942. Service at Dieppe was included in qualifying for the 1939-1943 Star, which was later changed to the 1939-1945 Star.

16th Battery served until cessation of hostilities and received authorization to disband under General Order 52/46 (Effective 24th September 1945).

*   *   *

17th AA Battery RCA — Serial 882 — Arvida, P.Q. & Gander, Nfld.

17th Anti-Aircraft Battery (Type "M") RCA, Serial 882, mobilized under General Order 306/41 (Effective 10th October 1941).

The battery was posted to Arvida, P.Q. to man four 3-inch anti-aircraft guns in the Arvida Defences. The 3-inch guns were later exchanged for 3.7 inch anti-aircraft guns.

Headquarters 24th Anti-Aircraft Regiment RCA was authorized to mobilize under General Order 256/42 (Effective 1st June 1942), to encompass the Anti-Aircraft Units in the Arvida Defences and 17th Battery became a component.

17th Anti-Aircraft Battery Type "M", RCA, Serial 882, was redesignated 17th Anti-Aircraft Battery Type "2H", RCA, Serial 882, under General Order 366/43 (Effective 15th June 1943), and 17th Battery remained with 24th Anti-Aircraft Regiment RCA, in the Arvida Defences.

The responsibility of 24th Anti-Aircraft Regiment RCA was enlarged to include all anti-aircraft units in military district No. 5, in July 1943. The batteries at Quebec city and Gaspe, came under command.

On the 25th October 1943, 17th Anti-Aircraft Battery (2H) RCA, Serial 882, embarked at Halifax for St. John's, Newfoundland to join 26th Anti-Aircraft Regiment RCA at Gander, upon conversion of 26th Anti-Aircraft Regiment RCA to French Speaking. 17th Battery manned sites at North Camp and South Camp, under 26th Anti-Aircraft Regiment RCA.

17th Anti-Aircraft Battery (Type 2H) RCA, Serial 882, served at Gander until authorized to disband under General Order 213/45 (Effective 15th April 1945).

*   *   *

17th LAA Battery RCA, Calgary, Alberta — Serial 142D — 2nd Div.

17th Battery perpetuated the 93rd Battery of Macleod, Alberta, and mobilized in Calgary as 17th Light Anti-Aircraft Battery RCA, CASF, Serial 142-C, under General Order 230/40 (Effective 28th September 1940), with Headquarters 3rd Light Anti-Aircraft Regiment RCA, CASF, Serial 142, to serve with 2nd Division, CASF.

17th Light Anti-Aircraft Battery, 3rd Light Anti-Aircraft Regiment RCA, sailed overseas from Halifax, 17th February 1941 on board the Duchess of York, and disembarked at Gourock, Scotland, on the 28th February — (War Diary date).

The Regiment concentrated at Colchester, Essex, under 1st Canadian Anti-Aircraft Brigade for duty and training, then from August 1941 to February 1942, the battery manned sites at Kenley and Tolworth, in the Air Defence of Great Britain (ADGB). It was during this period that the Battery Serial Number was changed to 142D, under General Order 54/42 (Effective 22nd December 1941), in a shuffle of Serial Numbers within the Regiment.

17th Light Anti-Aircraft Battery RCA returned to Colchester in February, following duty at ADGB Sites, remaining until 19th March 1942, when the

regiment moved from Colchester to 2nd Division Defence area, where the
battery took part in divisional training, and manned sites on the coast.

3 officers and 54 other ranks of 17th Light Anti-Aircraft Battery, 3rd Light
Anti-Aircraft Regiment RCA accompanied other units of 2nd Canadian Division on the Dieppe Raid, 19th August 1942, and upon returning to England the
gunners continued guarding the coast against hit-and-run raiders.

17th Light Anti-Aircraft Battery with the regiment returned to France, landing
in Normandy on the 7th of July 1944, and moved into position near Carpiquet
Airfield, with 2nd Canadian Infantry Division.

As a component of 2nd Canadian Corps, the Regiment served with Second
British Army, then moved to First Canadian Army 31st July 1944 on the Caen
Front.

Following the capture of Dieppe, 17th Battery, with the Regiment, paused for a
memorial service at the cemetery, 3rd September 1944, then paraded with the
division through the streets of the city. 17th Battery rejoined the action under
First Canadian Army and served in France, Belgium, Holland, and Germany.

17th Light Anti-Aircraft Battery RCA served until the cessation of hostilities,
and received authorization to disband under General Order 52/46 (Effective
24th September 1945).

*   *   *

18th Anti-Aircraft Battery RCA — Serial 723 — Halifax and Arvida

18th Anti-Aircraft Battery Type "H", RCA, Serial 723, mobilized under General Order 97/42 (Effective 17th February 1942), for duty at the East Coast.

18th Anti-Aircraft Battery, Type H, RCA, Serial 723, was redesignated 18th
Anti-Aircraft Battery, Type 2H, RCA, Serial 723, under General Order 257/42
(Effective 15th May 1942).

18th Anti-Aircraft Battery RCA served with 21st Anti-Aircraft Regiment RCA
of Halifax, and following a short tour of duty at Arvida, P.Q., returned to
Halifax to serve at Rockhead and Purcell's Cove in the Halifax defences, under
Headquarters Halifax Fortress.

18th Anti-Aircraft Battery Type 2H, RCA, Serial 723, received authorization
to disband, along with Headquarters 21st Anti-Aircraft Regiment RCA, under
General Order 305/45 (Effective 31st July 1945).

*   *   *

19th Anti-Aircraft Battery RCA, Halifax, Nova Scotia — Serial 724

19th Anti-Aircraft Battery Type "H", RCA, Serial 724, mobilized under General Order 97/42 (Effective 17th February 1942).

19th Anti-Aircraft Battery Type H, RCA, Serial 724, was redesignated 19th Anti-Aircraft Battery, Type 2H, RCA, Serial 724, under General Order 257/42 (Effective 15th May 1942).

19th Anti-Aircraft Battery served continuously at Halifax with 21st Anti-Aircraft Regiment RCA in the Halifax defences at Navy Island Cove and Prince's Lodge, under Headquarters Halifax Fortress, Atlantic Command.

19th Anti-Aircraft Battery Type 2H, RCA, Serial 724, received authorization to disband under General Order 305/45 (Effective 31st July 1945). Headquarters Halifax Fortress was authorized to disband under General Order 85/46 (Effective 29th November 1945).

*   *   *

20th AA Battery RCA — Serial 725 — Atlantic Command

20th Anti-Aircraft Battery, Type "H", RCA, Serial 725, mobilized under General Order 97/42 (Effective 17th February 1942).

20th Anti-Aircraft Battery, Type "H", RCA, Serial 725, was redesignated 20th Anti-Aircraft Battery Type "2H", RCA, Serial 725, under General Order 366/43 (Effective 15th June 1943).

1st Anti-Aircraft Battery went to Goose Bay, Labrador, in June 1943, and was replaced in 21st Anti-Aircraft Regiment RCA by 20th Anti-Aircraft Battery RCA.

Upon the return of 1st Anti-Aircraft Battery to the Regiment, 20th Anti-Aircraft Battery RCA moved to Goose Bay in July 1944, as Batteries from Nova Scotia and New Brunswick shared the responsibility of the Goose Bay Defences.

Following service in Atlantic Command with 21st Anti-Aircraft Regiment RCA at Halifax under Headquarters Halifax Fortress, at Russell Lake and Morris Lake, and at Goose Bay, 20th Anti-Aircraft Battery, Type 2H, RCA, Serial 725, received authorization to disband under General Order 208/45 (Effective 15th November 1944), at Bedford, Nova Scotia.

Headquarters Atlantic Command and Headquarters 21st Anti-Aircraft Regiment RCA disbanded 31st July 1945, Headquarters Defended Area Goose Bay disbanded 25th August 1945 and Headquarters Halifax Fortress disbanded 29th November 1945.

*   *   *

21st AA Battery RCA — Serial 729 — Vancouver Defences

21st Anti-Aircraft Battery Type "H", RCA, Serial 729, mobilized under General Order 97/42 (Effective 17th February 1942).

21st Anti-Aircraft Battery Type H, RCA, Serial 729, was redesignated 21st Anti-Aircraft Battery Type 2H, RCA, under General Order 182/42 (Effective 13th April 1942).

War Diary 43rd AA Bty notes — "On 6th June 1942, the 43rd, 21st, 31st, 11th & 47th Btys were placed in the 28th AA Regt RCA, CA".

21st Bty is listed as a component of 28th AA Regiment, Vancouver Defences, Pacific Command, in "Operational Units — Artillery — Cdn Army North American Zone, 24 April, 1943". (D. Hist, Ottawa).

In the Record Book of #1 CRLE — Pacific Command Group — AA Radars — Time in Op Condition Jan 1944 — July 1945 — 21st Bty "A" Troop is listed on manning duty at Van H-1 Ambleside under 28 AA Regiment, Vancouver Defences, with "B" Troop, 21st Bty manning Van H-2 Lynnmour, under 28 AA Regiment, Vancouver Defences.

Headquarters 28th Anti-Aircraft Regiment RCA, Serial 539, received authorization to disband under General Order 208/45 (Effective 31st December 1944), 21st Anti-Aircraft Battery, Type 2H, RCA, Serial 729, received authorization to disband under the same General Order, (Effective 31st January 1945). Serial 2919 Headquarters Vancouver Defences also disbanded under General Order 208/45, however, the effective date was the 15th of February 1945.

*   *   *

22nd AA Battery RCA — Serial 735 — Pacific Command & 6 Div

22nd Anti-Aircraft Battery (Type H) RCA, Serial 735, mobilized under General Order 97/42 (Effective 17th February 1942).

22nd Anti-Aircraft Battery (Type H) RCA, Serial 735, was redesignated 22nd Anti-Aircraft Battery Type 2H, RCA, Serial 735, under General Order 400/42 (Effective 1st August 1942).

22nd Battery became a component of 29th Anti-Aircraft Regiment RCA, and served in the Prince Rupert Defences. Mid-September 1942, one troop of 22nd Anti-Aircraft Battery moved from Prince Rupert, B.C. to Annette Island,

Alaska, to provide heavy anti-aircraft defence to 115 and 118 Fighter Squadrons, Royal Canadian Air Force, operating from the airfield.

On the 9th of October 1942 the Prince Rupert Defences came under the command of 8th Division and 22nd Anti-Aircraft Battery with the Regiment, served in that capacity until September 1943. The detached Troop had returned to Prince Rupert from Annette Island, Alaska, in May 1943.

The Battery is listed with 29th Anti-Aircraft Regiment, Prince Rupert Defences until 11th September 1943, in Order of Battle 8th Canadian Division. — (Public Archives Canada, Ottawa). 8th Division disbanded the following month.

War Diary — "One Troop of 22 AA Bty RCA, CA arrive in Victoria and occupy Colwood Transit Camp 18 Sep/43. "B" Tp arrive in Victoria and occupy Colwood Transit Camp 10 Oct/43".

Site Fighting Book, VH 2 Site Colwood, B.C., under 27th Anti-Aircraft Regiment, lists 22nd Anti-Aircraft Battery "A" Troop, manning the Site 18 September to 11 October 1943 and "B" Troop on manning duty 11 October to 27 October 1943.

War Diary — "HQ & "A" Tp of 22 AA Bty arrive from Van & proceed to Pat Bay (Mills Rd). The Bty ceased to be att to 27 AA Regt except for pay 22 Dec/43 upon being placed under comd of HQ Esq Fortress".

22nd Anti-Aircraft Battery (2H), RCA, Serial 735, was redesignated 22nd Heavy Anti-Aircraft Battery (Mobile), RCA, Serial 735, under General Order 147/44 (Effective 15th February 1944).

6th Cdn Div Components — Public Archives Canada, Ottawa — "16th Oct/43, 6th Div reorganized to comprise Div HQ & three Brigade Groups, the 13th, 14th & 15th. 22nd HAA Bty (Mobile) joined the Div Troops 1st Feb 1944 and remained a component until 22nd Battery and the division disbanded."

Records of #1 CRLE — Pacific Command Group — AA Radars — Time in Op Condition Jan 1944 — July 1945, Victoria-Esquimalt Fortress, 27 AA Regt —lists 22 AA Battery "A" Troop on manning duty at SH 1, Wilson Rd Site and 22 AA Battery "B" Troop manning SH 2, Bazan Bay Site.

Headquarters 6th Division, Headquarters 6th Divisional Artillery RCA, and 22nd Heavy Anti-Aircraft Battery (Mobile) RCA, Serial 735, received authorization to disband under General Order 208/45 (Effective 31st January 1945).

*   *   *

23rd AA Battery RCA — Serial 736 — Pacific Command

23rd Anti-Aircraft Battery, Type "H", RCA, Serial 736, mobilized under General Order 97/42 (Effective 17th February 1942).

23rd AA Bty RCA, CA, War Diary excerpts — "Esquimalt, B.C., 1st May 1942 — Major A.A. Ransom former Officer Commanding 4th AA S/L Bty was appointed to command 23rd AA Bty with 4th AA S/L Bty upon its disbandment providing the majority of personnel. Unit H.Q. located at Bay St. Armoury, Victoria, B.C.

14th May — battery headquarters moved from Bay Street Armoury to Macaulay. Men under canvas, orderly room and qm stores allotted one house at the foot of Anson Street, Harrison Point.

The battery personnel moved from a tent camp to huts, 12th Aug, having been in tents since 14th May.

Approval was received from NDHQ for the former 4th AA S/L Bty red & blue lanyard to be worn as the official lanyard for 23rd AA Bty as the Officer Commanding and personnel are now with that battery.

9th Sept. — 23rd AA Bty & 33rd AA Bty stores & equip. and personnel proceeded by E & N Railway to Port Alberni, then boarded the CPSS "Maquinna" and arrived at Ucluelet at 0900 hrs, 10th Sept/42. A tent camp was erected at Long Beach, Tofino, B.C. 11th Sept/42, where 23rd & 33rd AA Btys were in telephone communication with 18th Inf Bde, and Radio communication with RCAF at Ucluelet.

1st Oct. 1942, two 3.7" AA guns arrive for the Bty. The guns & ammo were hauled by barge from Port Alberni to RCAF Station at Ucluelet and by bty. transport to Tofino Airfield. The bty. came under jurisdiction of 6th Div.

19th Oct. — Two more 3.7" AA guns arrive.

17th Apr/43 — The main body of the bty. embussed and proceeded to Ucluelet where they boarded the Lady Rose for Port Alberni where M.T. carried the unit to Nanaimo & CPR boat to the mainland. 23rd Bty. arrived at Hastings Park, Vancouver at 1715 hrs where they became part of 28th AA Regt".

23rd Anti-Aircraft Battery, Type "H", RCA, Serial 736, was redesignated 23rd Anti-Aircraft Battery, Type "2H", RCA, Serial 736, under General Order 366/43 (Effective 15th June 1943).

An excerpt from 44 AA Battery War Diary notes — "Prior to departure from Vancouver for Prince Rupert, 16th July/43, 44 AA Bty turned guns, ammo and stores over to 23 AA Bty".

Later in the year 23rd Battery returned to the Island as the troops in turn moved to Colwood Transit Camp.

War Diary — "A" Tp proceeded to Colwood Camp for manning duty 27 Oct/43 to 24 Nov/43, then moved to Macaulay Camp for four weeks of intensive AA trg. Bty HQ remained at Colwood & "B" Tp arrived from Hastings Park and assumed manning duty at Colwood Site 24th Nov/43".

Site Fighting Book of VH 2, Colwood, B.C., 27th AA Regiment, lists 23rd Battery "A" Troop on manning duty, 27 Oct/43 to 24 Nov/43 and "B" Troop manning the Site 24 Nov/43 to 6 Jan/44, being relieved by 43 AA Bty.

23rd AA Battery War Diary — "The Bty received movement orders from 27 AA Regt to move from Colwood & Macaulay to Lulu Island, Vancouver 6 Jan/44".

#1 CRLE Pacific Command Group — AA Radars — Time in Op Condition Jan 1944 — July 1945, Vancouver Defences, 28 AA Regiment, lists "B" Troop 23rd Battery manning VAN H-4 Little Mountain Site, and "A" Troop 23rd Battery on duty at VAN H-5 Lulu Island Site.

23rd Anti-Aircraft Battery, Type 2H, RCA, Serial 736, received authorization to disband under General Order 208/45 (Effective 31st January 1945). 23rd AA Battery had served as an Independent Battery, as part of 28th Anti-Aircraft Regiment RCA and as a part of 27th Anti-Aircraft Regiment RCA in Pacific Command.

*   *   *

24th AA Battery RCA - Serial 737 — Sydney-Canso

24th Anti-Aircraft Troop, Type "L", RCA, Serial 737, mobilized under General Order 97/42 (Effective 17th February 1942).

24th Anti-Aircraft Troop, Type "L", RCA, Serial 737, was redesignated 24th Anti-Aircraft Battery Type 4L, RCA, Serial 737, under General Order 182/42 (Effective 13th April 1942).

24th Anti-Aircraft Battery Type 4L, RCA, Serial 737, was redesignated 24th Anti-Aircraft Battery (Type 3L), RCA, Serial 737, under General Order 494/43 (Effective 15th October 1943), in a general reduction of units on the Home Front.

Following service with 23rd Anti-Aircraft Regiment RCA at Sydney, Nova Scotia, under Headquarters Sydney-Canso Defences, and its later designation, Headquarters Defended Port of Sydney, 24th Anti-Aircraft Battery Type 3L,

RCA, Serial 737, received authorization to disband under General Order 305/45 (Effective 31st July 1945).

* * *

25th AA Battery RCA — Serial 738 — Atlantic Command

25th Anti-Aircraft Troop, Type "L", RCA, Serial 738, mobilized under General Order 97/42 (Effective 17th February 1942).

25th Anti-Aircraft Troop, Type "L", RCA, Serial 738, was redesignated 25th Anti-Aircraft Battery Type 2L, RCA, Serial 738, under General Order 257/42 (Effective 15th May 1942).

Headquarters 22nd Anti-Aircraft Regiment RCA, Serial 528, mobilized under General Order 256/42 (Effective 1st June 1942), to encompass all anti-aircraft units serving under Headquarters Saint John Defences (New Brunswick).

25th Anti-Aircraft Battery became a component of 22nd Anti-Aircraft Regiment RCA, and served at Saint John, New Brunswick. A Troop of 25th Battery did rotation duty at Goose Bay, Labrador, beginning July 1943.

25th Anti-Aircraft Battery, Type "3L", RCA, Serial 738, was redesignated 125th Anti-Aircraft Battery (Type 3L) RCA, Serial 738, under General Order 412/43 (Effective 1st September 1943).

125th Anti-Aircraft Battery, Type 3L, RCA, Serial 738, received authorization to disband under General Order 208/45 (Effective 20th February 1945).

* * *

25th LAA Battery RCA, Ottawa, Ontario — Serial 813D — 6th Division.

25th Light Anti-Aircraft Battery RCA, Serial 813D, mobilized as a component of 9th Light Anti-Aircraft Regiment RCA, under General Order 147/42 (Effective 18th March 1942) to serve with 6th Division Home Defence.

The Regiment concentrated at Camp Petawawa and 25th Battery arrived on the 29th June 1942, to join the regiment and continue training. A number of 25th Battery personnel transferred to 6th Light Anti-Aircraft Regiment RCA prior to its departure overseas in October 1942.

25th Battery with the Regiment departed from Petawawa by train on the 3rd of October 1942, and arrived at Hastings Park, Vancouver, British Columbia, 7th October 1942, to provide Anti-Aircraft protection for the infantry brigades and Headquarters of 6th Division.

Early January 1943, 25th Battery crossed to Vancouver Island to join 18th

Infantry Brigade, now a component of 6th Division and stationed at Port Alberni, British Columbia. Headquarters 9th Light Anti-Aircraft Regiment RCA was authorized to disband in May 1943, and the batteries operated with their respective infantry brigade.

18th Infantry Brigade and 25th Light Anti-Aircraft Battery RCA returned to the mainland, and while at Wainwright the formation was placed under Headquarters Prince Rupert Defences, 8th Division, from 2nd September to 15th October 1943, on which date 8th Div disbanded. — (Order of Battle 8th Canadian Division — Public Archives Canada, Ottawa).

On the 16th of October 1943, 6th Division reorganized the comprise 13th (at Kiska), 14th and 15th Brigade Groups. 25th Battery now aligned with 15th Brigade Group, and while on the mainland, visited Wainwright, Alberta, Terrace, British Columbia, Jasper, Alberta, Prince George, British Columbia, then back to Port Alberni with 15th Brigade Group, 31st January 1944.

Attached to 20th Field Regiment RCA, 25th Battery crossed to the mainland and proceeded by road to Wainwright Camp, 18th May 1944.

25th Light Anti-Aircraft Battery RCA, Serial 813D, moved by train to Prince George, British Columbia, 7th October 1944 and remained until receiving authorization to disband under General Order 208/45 (Effective 31st January 1945).

*   *   *

26th AA Troop RCA — Serial 739 — Atlantic Command

26th Anti-Aircraft Troop, Type "L", RCA, Serial 739, mobilized under General Order 97/42 (Effective 17th February 1942).

26th Anti-Aircraft Troop served in the Shelburne, Nova Scotia Defences and disbanded as 26th Anti-Aircraft Troop, Type "L", RCA, Serial 739, under General Order 498/43 (Effective 1st November 1943).

*   *   *

27th AA Battery RCA — Serial 745 — "W" Force

27th Anti-Aircraft Troop, Type "L", RCA, Serial 745, mobilized under General Order 97/42 (Effective 17th February 1942).

27th Anti-Aircraft Troop, Type "L", RCA, Serial 745, was redesignated 27th Anti-Aircraft Battery Type 4L, RCA, Serial 745, under General Order 182/42 (Effective 13th April 1942).

27th Anti-Aircraft Battery Type 4L, RCA, Serial 745, was redesignated 27th Anti-Aircraft Battery, Type 2L, RCA, Serial 745, under General Order 235/42 (Effective 1st May 1942).

27th Battery served with 25th Anti-Aircraft Regiment RCA in the St. John's-Torbay area, under Headquarters St. John's Defences (Newfoundland), and its later designation Headquarters Defended Port of St. John's.

27th Anti-Aircraft Battery, Type 2L, RCA, Serial 745, received authorization to disband under General Order 208/45 (Effective 31st December 1944).

* * *

28th AA Battery RCA — Serial 746 — "W" Force

28th Anti-Aircraft Troop, Type "L", RCA, Serial 746, mobilized under General Order 97/42 (Effective 17th February 1942).

28th Anti-Aircraft Troop, Type "L", RCA, Serial 746, was redesignated 28th Anti-Aircraft Battery, Type 2 "L", RCA, Serial 746, under General Order 370/42 (Effective 15th August 1942).

The Battery served with the original 26th Anti-Aircraft Regiment RCA at Botwood, in the Newfoundland Defences and was authorized to disband under General Order 80/44 (Effective 25th January 1944), as 28th Anti-Aircraft Battery Type 2 "L", RCA, Serial 746, upon the conversion of 26th Anti-Aircraft Regiment RCA to French speaking.

* * *

29th AA Troop LS, RCA — Serial 747 — "W" Force

29th Anti-Aircraft Troop, Type "L", RCA, Serial 747, mobilized under General Order 97/42 (Effective 17th February 1942).

29th Anti-Aircraft Troop, Type "L", RCA, Serial 747, was redesignated 29th Anti-Aircraft Troop Type "LS", RCA, Serial 747, under General Order 366/43 (Effective 15th June 1943).

The Troop served with the original 26th Anti-Aircraft Regiment RCA, at Lewisporte, in the Newfoundland Defences.

29th Anti-Aircraft Troop (LS), RCA, Serial 747, was converted to French speaking, 15th October 1943, and served with the new 26th Anti-Aircraft Regiment RCA, (FS), at Lewisporte, Newfoundland.

29th Anti-Aircraft Troop LS, RCA, Serial 747 was authorized to disband under General Order 208/45 (Effective 30th November 1944).

* * *

30th Anti-Aircraft Battery RCA — Serial 748 — Atlantic Command

30th Anti-Aircraft Troop, type "L", RCA, Serial 748, mobilized under General Order 97/42 (Effective 17th February 1942).

30th Anti-Aircraft Troop, Type L, RCA, Serial 748, was redesignated 30th Anti-Aircraft Battery, Type 2L, RCA, Serial 748, under General Order 183/42 (Effective 13th April 1942).

30th Anti-Aircraft Battery, Type 2L, RCA, Serial 748, was redesignated 30th Anti-Aircraft Battery, Type "3L", RCA, Serial 748, under General Order 366/43 (Effective 15th June 1943).

30th Battery served independently in the Goose Bay, Labrador, Defences, in defence of the airport.

30th Anti-Aircraft Battery, Type "3L", RCA, Serial 748, received authorization to disband under General Order 305/45 (Effective 31st July 1945). Headquarters Atlantic Command also disbanded at this time.

* * *

30th LAA Battery RCA, Toronto, Ont. — Serial 991D — 2nd Corps

30th Field Battery of Toronto mobilized as 30th Light Anti-Aircraft Battery RCA, Serial 991D, under General Order 240/41 (Effective 5th September 1941), with 6th Light Anti-Aircraft Regiment RCA, to serve as 4th Division Light Anti-Aircraft Regiment.

30th Light Anti-Aircraft Battery RCA proceeded to Petawawa where the Regiment concentrated in February 1942.

A composite troop was posted to Prince Rupert, British Columbia, 4th March 1942, and on the 6th June 1942, 30th Light Anti-Aircraft Battery moved to the West Coast to serve on Vancouver Island in the Victoria-Esquimalt Fortress, and on Yorke Island.

112th Battery also moved West to serve at Prince Rupert, British Columbia, and Annette Island, Alaska.

The Regiment assembled at Petawawa in September 1942, then proceeded to Halifax to board the Queen Elizabeth, departed overseas 30th October 1942, and disembarked at Gourock, Scotland, on the 5th of November 1942.

6th Light Anti-Aircraft Regiment RCA joined 2nd Canadian Corps as Corps Light Anti-Aircraft Regiment, 16th February 1943.

30th Light Anti-Aircraft Battery, 6th Light Anti-Aircraft Regiment RCA proceeded to Normandy, 8th July 1944 with 2nd Canadian Corps and with 2nd Canadian Corps came under command Second British Army, 11th July.

First Canadian Army entered the fray on the 23rd of July 1944, and 2nd Canadian Corps became a component 31st July 1944, on the Caen Front.

30th Battery participated in the vicous fighting in the breakout from Caen and the closing of the Falaise Gap, continuing in action in France, Belgium, Holland, and Germany.

6th Light Anti-Aircraft Regiment RCA and its Batteries assumed a variety of roles in action. In one such role, 30th Battery manned the rocket launchers of 1st Rocket Battery RCA in January 1945, returning to an Anti-Aircraft role for the drive into Germany.

30th Light Anti-Aircraft Battery RCA, Serial 991D, served until the cessation of hostilities and received authorization to disband in NW Europe, under General Order 321/45 (Effective 24th June 1945).

Personnel proceeded to the Canadian Army Pacific Force (CAPF), the Canadian Army Occupational Force (CAOF), for occupational duty in Germany, or were posted to divisional units nearest the Military District of their enlistment, for the return to Canada.

*   *   *

31st AA Battery RCA — Serial 749 — Pacific Command

31st Anti-Aircraft Troop Type "L", RCA, Serial 749, mobilized under General Order 97/42 (Effective 17th February 1942).

31st Anti-Aircraft Troop Type "L", RCA, Serial 749, was redesignated 31st Anti-Aircraft Battery Type 3L RCA, Serial 749, under General Order 182/42 (Effective 13th April 1942).

War Diary — "Officers & NCOs were formed into a Cadre, taken on strength 31 AA Tp, attached to V & E Fortress for all purposes.

The Bty ceased to be attached to HQ V & E Fortress Area & moved to Vancouver 2nd May/42 to Vancouver Barracks.

The Bty manned two 40mm guns at Narrows North in defence of First Narrows bridge 23 May/42.

25th June/42, 28th AA Regt formed to comprise 31st, 11th, 21st, 43rd & 47th AA Btys". — (Vancouver Defences).

31st Bty is listed as a component of 28 AA Regt Pacific Command, in Operational Units — Artillery — Cdn Army North American Zone, 24 April 1943. — (D. Hist, Ottawa).

Following service under Headquarters Vancouver Defences, Pacific Command, 31st Anti-Aircraft Battery, Type 3L, RCA, Serial 749, and Headquarters 28th Anti-Aircraft Regiment RCA, Serial 539, received authorization to disband under General Order 208/45 (Effective 31st January 1945).

*   *   *

32nd AA Battery RCA — Serial 755 — Pacific Command

32nd Anti-Aircraft Battery RCA mobilized as 32nd Anti-Aircraft Troop Type "L", RCA, Serial 755, under General Order 97/42 (Effective 17th February 1942).

War Diary — "32 AA Tp formed at Esq B.C., V & E Fortress. Tp HQ at Work Pt Barracks Esq".

32nd Anti-Aircraft Troop Type L RCA, Serial 755, was redesignated 32nd Anti-Aircraft Battery Type 2L RCA, Serial 755, under General Order 182/42 (Effective 13th April 1942).

War Diary — "Personnel absorbed by 32 AA Bty V & E Fortress. The Bty became self-accounting & est. a camp on Macaulay Plains for drafts of recruits for AA Btys.

BHQ moved to house corner of Anson & Bewdley Ave Esq.

1 June/42, Advance party left for Pr. Rupt. BHQ & Bty sailed 8 June/42. Arrived 10 June & att to 112 Bty for R & Q and billeted in US Army huts on Acropolis".

32nd Anti-Aircraft Battery Type "2L", RCA, Serial 755, was redesignated 32nd Anti-Aircraft Battery Type "3L", RCA, Serial 755, under General Order 366/43 (Effective 15th June 1943).

32nd Battery served with 29th Anti-Aircraft Regiment RCA, under Headquarters Prince Rupert Defences, Pacific Command.

Prince Rupert Defences came under Cmd of 8th Division, 9th Oct/42, and as a component of 29th Anti-Aircraft Regiment RCA, 32nd Anti-Aircraft Battery

RCA served under 8th Division until 11th Sept/43. (Order of Battle 8th Cdn Div), Public Archives Canada, Ottawa.

32nd Anti-Aircraft Battery, Type "3L", RCA, Serial 755, continued to serve until authorized to disband under General Order 208/45 (Effective 31st January 1945).

* * *

32nd (Kingston) LAA Bty RCA, Kingston, Ont. — Serial 449D — 3rd Div.

The combined 32nd/34th Field Battery RCA, CASF, Serial 707B, mobilized as a component of 14th Field Regiment RCA, CASF, 3rd Division, CASF, authorized under General Order 184/40 (Effective 24th May 1940).

14th Field Regiment concentrated at Camp Petawawa, Ontario, on the 22nd of September 1940, and shortly after its arrival at Petawawa the regiment reorganized to comprise three Field Batteries RCA.

32nd Battery regained individual identity as 32nd (Kingston) Field Battery RCA, Serial 452, under General Order 45/41 (Effective 1st January 1941).

32nd (Kingston) Field Battery RCA, Serial 452, was converted to Light Anti-Aircraft and redesignated 32nd (Kingston) Light Anti-Aircraft Battery RCA, Serial 452, under General Order 74/41 (Effective 1st January 1941), joining the recently authorized 4th Light Anti-Aircraft Regiment RCA, 3rd Division.

4th Light Anti-Aircraft Regiment RCA with its four batteries concentrated at Camp Sussex, New Brunswick, 27th July 1941, and departed for overseas in two sailings before the end of the year.

32nd Light Anti-Aircraft Battery RCA with the Regiment (less 100th Light Anti-Aircraft Battery RCA), sailed on the Stratheden, 25th August 1941, and disembarked at Glasgow, Scotland, 2nd September 1941.

In an alignment of Serial Numbers within the Regiment, 32nd (Kingston) Light Anti-Aircraft Battery RCA was allotted Serial Number 449D, under General Order 54/42 (Effective 22nd December 1941).

During its stay in England the Battery manned Air Defence of Great Britain (ADGB) sites and deployed guns along the coast, guarding against hit-and-run raiders.

3rd Canadian Infantry Division was selected to land in the assault on the coast of Normandy on D-Day, 6th June 1944, and 4th Light Anti-Aircraft Regiment RCA was represented by 32nd Light Anti-Aircraft Battery RCA. Once ashore the battery deployed to protect two vital bridges and Headquarters, 3rd Canadian Infantry Division.

3rd Canadian Infantry Division served with 1 British Corps and 2nd Canadian Corps under Second British Army, then with 2nd Canadian Corps, became a component of First Canadian Army on the 31st of July 1944, on the Caen Front.

32nd (Kingston) Light Anti-Aircraft Battery RCA, served in France, Belgium, Holland, and Germany, then with cessation of hostilities received authorization to disband under General Order 52/46 (Effective 13th November 1945).

A reconstituted Battery mobilized as 2nd 32nd Light Anti-Aircraft Battery RCA, under General Order 319/45 (Effective 1st June 1945), to serve with 2nd 4th Light Anti-Aircraft Regiment RCA, in the Canadian Army Occupational Force In Germany and disbanded under General Order 162/46 (Effective 4th April 1946).

*   *   *

33rd AA Battery RCA — Serial 757 — Vancouver Island, B.C.

33rd Anti-Aircraft Troop, Type "L", RCA, Serial 757, mobilized under General Order 97/42 (Effective 17th February 1942).

33rd Anti-Aircraft Troop, Type L RCA, Serial 757, was redesignated 33rd Anti-Aircraft Battery Type 2L, RCA, Serial 757, under General Order 182/42 (Effective 13th April 1942).

Early 1943, the battery manned sites at Long Beach Camp, Tofino, Vancouver Island, British Columbia, being relieved by 59th Anti-Aircraft Battery, 23rd February 1943.

33rd Battery in turn relieved 59th Anti-Aircraft Battery at RCA Camp, Tofino, 1st July 1943.

The composition of 30th Anti-Aircraft Regiment was finalized at this time and 33rd Anti-Aircraft Battery became a component, being enlarged to 4L from 2L. Regimental Headquarters was located at Port Alberni, and the duty of the regiment was to protect the outlying areas and defences of Vancouver Island, British Columbia.

33rd Anti-Aircraft Battery Type "2L", RCA, Serial 757, was redesignated 33rd Anti-Aircraft Battery Type "4L", RCA, Serial 757, under General Order 366/43 (Effective 15th June 1943).

In the Organization Order 30th Anti-Aircraft Regiment RCA (Serial 1347), the Battery is listed as located at Tofino & Ucluelet. — (D. Hist, Ottawa). .

Headquarters 30th Anti-Aircraft Regiment RCA enjoyed a rather short existence, however, receiving authorization to disband under General Order 80/44, the effective date being the 31st December 1943. The batteries in some cases became self-accounting.

Fort Record Book Belmont Battery, Preface, 14 Aug. 44 notes — "The AA Defence of Fort Belmont consists of two 40 mm Bofors manned by the Detachment of the 33rd AA Bty and one Bren Machine Gun. The Bofors may be used as a secondary C.D. armament".

Fort Record Book Fort Duntze Head, 19 Dec/44 also mentions — "Adjacent to Belmont Fort the 33rd AA Bty RCA, CA., have sited one 40 mm Bofors light A.A. Gun, which could be used in a Close Defence Role".

33rd Anti-Aircraft Battery, Type "4L", RCA, was redesignated 129th Light Anti-Aircraft Battery RCA, under General Order 138/46 (Effective 1st March 1946).

129th Light Anti-Aircraft Battery RCA, became a component of the Postwar Permanent Force, under General Order 158/46 (Effective 27th June 1946).

* * *

34th AA Battery RCA — Serial 758 — Pacific Command

34th Anti-Aircraft Troop, Type "L", RCA, Serial 758, mobilized under General Order 97/42 (Effective 17th February 1942).

34th Anti-Aircraft Troop Type "L", RCA, Serial 758, was redesignated 34th Anti-Aircraft Battery Type 2L, RCA, Serial 758, under General Order 182/42 (Effective 13th April 1942).

War Diary — "115 & 118 RCAF Sqns were stationed on Annette Island, Alaska, early 1942, 112 LAA Bty, 6th LAA Regt RCA provided LAA protection for the airfield.

Mid Sept/42, 34th AA Bty took over the Bofors sites from 112th LAA Bty".

34th AA Bty is listed as a component of 29th AA Regiment, Prince Rupert Defences, and Prince Rupert Defences came under command of 8th Division on the 9th October 1942, remaining under command until 15th October 1943, when 8th Div disbanded. — (Order of Battle 8th Cdn Div, Public Archives Canada, Ottawa).

War Diary — "In Nov/43 the Air Station on Annette Island was closed down and 34th AA Bty moved to Pat Bay on Vancouver Island".

With the arrival of the Canadian-US "Greenlight" Force at Kiska in the

Aleutian Islands, August 1943 to find the Japanese invaders had withdrawn from the Islands, and the presence of a larger US Force in the area, the run-down of Canadian units was begun. 34th Anti-Aircraft Battery became expendable at this time. Headquarters 30th Anti-Aircraft Regiment RCA too, was phased out.

34th Anti-Aircraft Battery Type 2L, RCA, Serial 758, received authorization to disband under General Order 80/44 (Effective 31st December 1943).

*   *   *

35th AA Troop RCA — Serial 759 — Pacific Command

35th Anti-Aircraft Section, Type "L", RCA, Serial 759, mobilized under General Order 97/42 (Effective 17th February 1942).

Headquarters 58 Special Anti-Aircraft Battery (Type L), RCA, Serial 756, mobilized under General Order 256/42 (Effective 1st May 1942), to comprise 5 Special Sections RCA, including 35th Anti-Aircraft Section, Type "L" RCA, Serial 759, and a Headquarters.

Mobilized at Macaulay Camp, Victoria-Esquimalt Fortress, the battery was to defend the advanced air bases at Alliford Bay, Ucluelet, Bella Bella and Coal Harbour, with two 40mm Bofors at each location. The battery assumed the duty of manning the 75mm field guns at each location and absorbed the personnel of the Sections presently manning the guns.

35th Anti-Aircraft Section, Type "L", RCA, Serial 759, was redesignated 35th Anti-Aircraft Troop, Type "L", RCA, Serial 759, under General Order 366/43 (Effective 15th June 1943) and served with 29th Anti-Aircraft Regiment RCA, in the Prince Rupert, B.C. Defences.

Prince Rupert Defences came under command of 8th Division, Pacific Command, 9th October 1942, and remained so aligned until the disbandment of 8th Division under General Order 15/44 (Effective 15th October 1943).

35th Anti-Aircraft *Section*, Type "L", RCA, Serial 759, disbanded under General Order 80/44 (Effective 31st December 1943).

*   *   *

35th LAA Battery RCA, Sherbrooke, P.Q. — Serial 505B — 1st Corps

In the Canadian Active Service Force Mobilization Order, General Order 135/39, 1st September 1939, 35th Battery is listed as 35th Field Battery (H), RCA, CASF, Serial 164, with Headquarters of 5th Field Brigade RCA, CASF, 2nd Division, CASF.

However, 35th Field Battery (H), RCA, CASF, adopted Serial Number 14, with 2nd Field Brigade RCA, CASF, 1st Division, CASF, under General Order 206/39 (Effective 1st September 1939), in an exchange with 73rd Field Battery (H) RCA, CASF.

35th Field Battery, under Headquarters of 2nd Field Brigade RCA, CASF, departed for overseas 10th December 1939 on board the Empress of Britain, with the 1st Flight, and disembarked on the 18th of December 1939, at Gourock, Scotland.

Field brigades became field regiments. Headquarters of 2nd Field Brigade RCA, CASF, was redesignated Headquarters 2nd Field Regiment RCA, CASF, now to comprise two combined Field Batteries.

35th Field Battery (H), RCA, CASF, Serial 14, combined with 7th Field Battery RCA, CASF, Serial 12, to become 7th/35th Field Battery RCA, CASF, Serial 12, under General Order 44/40 (Effective 21st December 1939), remaining with 2nd Field Regiment RCA, CASF, 1st Division, CASF.

The combined 7th/35th Field Battery served with 7th Corps and the Canadian Corps in the Defence of England.

35th Battery regained individual identity as 35th Field Battery RCA, Serial 14, under General Order 45/41 (Effective 1st January 1941), as the regiment reorganized to comprise three Field Batteries RCA. 35th Battery became expendable.

35th Field Battery RCA, Serial 14, was redesignated 35th Light Anti-Aircraft Battery RCA, Serial 14, under General Order 57/41 (Effective 1st January 1941), and became a component of 1st Light Anti-Aircraft Regiment RCA, destined to become 1st Canadian Corps LAA Regiment.

Headquarters 1st Light Anti-Aircraft Regiment RCA, Serial 505, was authorized under General Order 56/41 (Effective 1st February 1941), and in an alignment of Serial Numbers, 35th Light Anti-Aircraft Battery RCA was allotted Serial Number 505B, under General Order 54/42 (Effective 22nd December 1941).

The Regiment congregated at Colchester, Essex, under 1st Canadian Anti-Aircraft Brigade for training, followed by duty on Air Defence of Great Britain (ADGB) Sites, interspersed with training. 35th Battery remained in England until late 1943, then proceeded to the Mediterranean Theatre of Operations.

35th Light Anti-Aircraft Battery, 1st Light Anti-Aircraft Regiment RCA, 1st Canadian Corps, departed from Gourock, Scotland, on the Edmund B. Alexander, 27th October 1943, on operation "Timberwolf", and disembarked at Augusta, Sicily, 8th November 1943. 1st Light Anti-Aircraft Regiment RCA crossed to the Italian mainland on the 8th of January 1944 to assume its duty as 1st Canadian Corps Light Anti-Aircraft Regiment.

In July 1944, 1st Light Anti-Aircraft Regiment RCA was converted to an infantry battalion and 35th Battery assumed traffic control duties.

The 89/109 Infantry Battalion, or 1 LAA Infantry Battalion, with the newly formed 12th Infantry Brigade in 5th Canadian Armoured Division, fought its initial battle, 1/2 September 1944.

Headquarters 1st Light Anti-Aircraft Regiment RCA and its three Batteries, including 35th Light Anti-Aircraft Battery RCA, Serial 505B, became "The Lanark and Renfrew Scottish Regiment", CIC, under General Order 18/45 (Effective 13th July 1944).

The Lanark and Renfrew Scottish Regiment, 12th Canadian Infantry Brigade, 5th Canadian Armoured Division, 1st Canadian Corps, served in Italy until early 1945.

The Regiment departed from Italy via Leghorn, on the 3rd of March 1945 and disembarked at Marseilles, France, on the 5th of March.

Upon arrival in NW Europe, 12th Canadian Infantry Brigade ceased to exist and the Lanark and Renfrew Scottish Regiment, Canadian Infantry Corps, became 1st Light Anti-Aircraft Regiment (Lanark and Renfrew Scottish Regiment) RCA, under General Order 295/45 (Effective 15th March 1945).

35th Anti-Aircraft Battery RCA resumed its duties with 1st Light Anti-Aircraft Regiment RCA, 1st Canadian Corps Troops, however, 1st Canadian Corps was now with First Canadian Army. 35th Light Anti-Aircraft Battery RCA served until cessation of hostilities and received authorization to disband in NW Europe, under General Order 321/45 (Effective 29th June 1945).

*   *   *

36th AA Troop RCA — Serial 764 — Pacific Command

36th Anti-Aircraft Section, Type "L", RCA, Serial 764, mobilized under General Order 97/42 (Effective 17th February 1942), at Macaulay Camp, Victoria-Esquimalt Fortress.

Headquarters 58 Special Anti-Aircraft Battery (Type L), RCA, Serial 756, mobilized under General Order 256/42 (Effective 1st May 1942), to comprise 5 Special Sections RCA, including 36th Anti-Aircraft Section, Type "L", RCA, Serial 764, and a Headquarters.

The Battery assumed the duty of manning the 75mm Field guns and the two 40mm AA guns in defence of the advanced air bases at Alliford Bay, Ucluelet, Bella Bella and Coal Harbour.

Order of Battle 8th Cdn Div, Public Archives Canada, Ottawa, lists 36th AA Section, 58 Special AA Bty RCA serving in the Prince Rupert Defences, British Columbia, under command of 8 Div, October 1942 to early 1943.

36th Anti-Aircraft Section of 58th Special Anti-Aircraft Battery was redesignated 36th Anti-Aircraft Troop (Type L) RCA, Serial 764, under General Order 366/43 (Effective 15th June 1943).

Headquarters, 58th Special Anti-Aircraft Battery, Type "L", RCA, disbanded under General Order 367/43 (Effective 15th June 1943), and personnel absorbed by Serial 764, 36th Anti-Aircraft Troop RCA.

36th Anti-Aircraft Troop (Type L), RCA, Serial 764, was posted to 30th Anti-Aircraft Regiment RCA, Port Alberni, British Columbia, 15th June 1943, and served at Comox, British Columbia, on Vancouver Island.

36th Anti-Aircraft Section, Type "L", RCA, Serial 764, is listed as disbanding under General Order 80/44 (Effective 31st December 1943), and should no doubt read "36th Anti-Aircraft *Troop* (Type L), RCA".

Headquarters 30th Anti-Aircraft Regiment RCA, Serial 1347, also disbanded at that time.

*   *   *

37th AA Section RCA — Serial 765 — Pacific Command

37th Anti-Aircraft Section, Type "L", RCA, Serial 765, mobilized under General Order 97/42 (Effective 17th February 1942), at Macaulay Camp, Victoria-Esquimalt Fortress, and served as 37th Anti-Aircraft Section of 58th Special Anti-Aircraft Battery RCA.

Headquarters 58 Special Anti-Aircraft Battery (Type L), RCA, Serial 756, mobilized under General Order 256/42 (Effective 1st May 1942), to comprise 5 Special Sections RCA, including 37th Anti-Aircraft Section Type "L", RCA, Serial 765, and a Headquarters.

58 Special Anti-Aircraft Battery assumed the duty of manning the 75mm Field guns and the two Bofors 40mm AA guns in defence of the advanced air bases at Alliford Bay, Ucluelet, Bella Bella, and Coal Harbour.

37th Anti-Aircraft Section, Type "L", RCA, Serial 765, received authorization to disband under General Order 367/43 (Effective 15th June 1943), and personnel posted to 33rd Anti-Aircraft Battery, 30th Anti-Aircraft Regiment RCA, Port Alberni, British Columbia, serving at Tofino and Ucluelet, on Vancouver Island, British Columbia.

Headquarters 58th Special Anti-Aircraft Battery, Type "L", RCA Serial 756, also disbanded under the same General Order.

*   *   *

38th AA Section RCA — Serial 770 — Pacific Command.

38th Anti-Aircraft Section, Type "L", RCA, Serial 770, mobilized under General Order 97/42 (Effective 17th February 1942), at Macaulay Camp, Victoria-Esquimalt Fortress, and served as 38th Anti-Aircraft Section of 58 Special Anti-Aircraft Battery RCA.

Headquarters 58 Special Anti-Aircraft Battery (Type L), RCA, Serial 756, mobilized under General Order 256/42 (Effective 1st May 1942), to comprise 5 Special Sections RCA, including 38th Anti-Aircraft Section Type "L", RCA, Serial 770, and a Headquarters.

58 Special Anti-Aircraft Battery manned two Bofors 40mm AA guns and 75mm field guns in defence of the advanced air bases at Coal Harbour, Ucluelet, Alliford Bay and Bella Bella.

38th Anti-Aircraft Section, Type "L", RCA, Serial 770, continued to serve as a component of 58th Special Anti-Aircraft Battery Type "L" RCA, Serial 756, until the Section and Battery were authorized to disband under General Order 367/43 (Effective 15th June 1943). Personnel of 38th Anti-Aircraft Section were posted to 59th Anti-Aircraft Battery, 30th Anti-Aircraft Regiment RCA of Port Alberni, British Columbia, and served at Port Hardy and Coal Harbour, on Vancouver Island, British Columbia.

*   *   *

38th LAA Battery RCA, Winnipeg, Manitoba — Serial 142B — 2nd Div.

38th Light Anti-Aircraft Battery RCA mobilized as 15th Light Anti-Aircraft Battery RCA, CASF, Serial 142-A, under General Order 230/40 (Effective 28th September 1940), with Headquarters 3rd Light Anti-Aircraft Regiment RCA, CASF, Serial 142, for service with 2nd Division, CASF.

15th Light Anti-Aircraft Battery, 3rd Light Anti-Aircraft Regiment RCA departed for overseas 20th February 1941 on board the Warwick Castle, and disembarked at Gourock, Scotland, 1st March 1941.

Shortly after arriving overseas, 15th Light Anti-Aircraft Battery RCA, Serial 142-A, was redesignated 38th Light Anti-Aircraft Battery RCA, Serial 142-A, under General Order 112/41 (Effective 1st January 1941) — (Back-dated).

In a shuffle of serial numbers within the Regiment, 3rd Light Anti-Aircraft Regiment RCA was allotted Serial Number 142, Headquarters 3rd Light Anti-Aircraft Regiment RCA assumed Serial Number 142A, 38th Light Anti-Aircraft Battery RCA changed to Serial Number 142B, under General Order 54/42 (Effective 22nd December 1941).

The regiment concentrated at Colchester, Essex, under 1st Canadian Anti-Aircraft Brigade for duty and training.

38th Light Anti-Aircraft Battery RCA manned Sites at Farnborough and Bromley in the Air Defence of Great Britain (ADGB), August 1941 to February 1942, then returned to Colchester.

On the 19th March 1942, the Regiment moved to 2nd Division Defence area where the Battery manned sites on the coast and trained with the division.

One officer and 51 other ranks from 38th Light Anti-Aircraft Battery, 3rd Light Anti-Aircraft Regiment RCA aboard the tank landing craft with the Calgary Tank Regiment, accompanied Units of 2nd Division on the Dieppe Raid, 19th August 1942, and upon its return to England the Battery continued its role on the coast, guarding against hit-and-run raiders.

38th Battery once again crossed the Channel, this time however, the battery avoided the high cliffs and hazards of a defended Port and landed in Normandy on the 7th of July 1944. 2nd Canadian Infantry Division moved into the bridgehead alongside 3rd Canadian Infantry Division and the regiment moved into position near the Carpiquet Airfield.

2nd Canadian Corps now became operational and as a component 2nd Canadian Infantry Division served with Second British Army, then moved to First Canadian Army, 31st July 1944, on the Caen Front.

38th Battery with the regiment, participated in the fierce fighting in the breakout from Caen and the closing of the Falaise Gap. The division then moved on to Dieppe, where following the capture of the city 2nd Division units paused for a service of remembrance in the cemetery and a divisional parade through the streets of the city, on the 3rd of September 1944.

38th Battery with the regiment and 2nd Canadian Infantry Division, rejoined the action with First Canadian Army and served in France, Belgium, Holland, and Germany.

38th Light Anti-Aircraft Battery RCA served until cessation of hostilities and received authorization to disband under General Order 52/46 (Effective 23rd September 1945).

*   *   *

39th AA Troop Type "L", RCA — Serial 771 — Pacific Command

39th Anti-Aircraft Section, Type "L", RCA, Serial 771, mobilized under General Order 97/42 (Effective 17th February 1942), at Macaulay Camp, Victoria-Esquimalt Fortress, and served as 39th Anti-Aircraft Section of 58 Special Anti-Aircraft Battery RCA.

Headquarters 58 Special Anti-Aircraft Battery (Type L), RCA, Serial 756, mobilized under General Order 256/42 (Effective 1st May 1942), to comprise 5 Special Sections RCA, including 39th Anti-Aircraft Section Type "L", RCA, Serial 771, and a Headquarters.

58 Special Anti-Aircraft Battery manned two Bofors 40mm AA guns and 75mm field guns in defence of the advanced air bases at Coal Harbour, Ucluelet, Alliford Bay, and Bella Bella.

39th Anti-Aircraft Section, Type "L", RCA, Serial 771, continued to serve as a component of 58th Special Anti-Aircraft Battery Type "L" RCA, Serial 756, until the 15th of June 1943.

39th Anti-Aircraft Section Type "L" RCA, Serial 771, of 58 Special Anti-Aircraft Battery RCA, was redesignated 39th Anti-Aircraft Troop, Type "L", RCA, Serial 771, under General Order 366/43 (Effective 15th June 1943).

58th Special Anti-Aircraft Battery Type "L" RCA, received authorization to disband under General Order 367/43 (Effective 15th June 1943). 39th Anti-Aircraft Troop RCA was posted to 30th Anti-Aircraft Regiment RCA of Port Alberni, British Columbia, and served at Bella Bella.

39th Anti-Aircraft Troop Type "L", RCA, Serial 771, received authorization to disband under General Order 498/43 (Effective 1st November 1943).

Headquarters 30th Anti-Aircraft Regiment RCA, Serial 1347, was authorized to disband under General Order 80/44 (Effective 31st December 1943).

*   *   *

40th AA Battery RCA — Serial 885 — Sault Ste Marie

40th Anti-Aircraft Battery (Type "H"), RCA, Serial 885, mobilized under General Order 118/42 (Effective 10th March 1942).

40th Anti-Aircraft Battery trained at Halifax, then was placed under the

Commanding General, US Military District of Sault Ste. Marie, Michigan and manned gunsites at Sault Ste. Marie locks until close of navigation in 1943.

40th Anti-Aircraft Battery (Type "H") RCA, Serial 885, received authorization to disband under General Order 498/43 (Effective 15th December 1943).

*   *   *

41st AA Battery RCA — Serial 779 — Arvida, P.Q.

41st Anti-Aircraft Battery, Type 2H, RCA, Serial 779, mobilized under General Order 181/42 (Effective 13th April 1942).

Headquarters 24th Anti-Aircraft Regiment RCA, Serial 533, was authorized to mobilize under General Order 256/42 (Effective 1st June 1942), to encompass the anti-aircraft units serving in the Arvida Defences, and 41st Anti-Aircraft Battery became a component.

41st Anti-Aircraft Battery, Type 2H, RCA, Serial 779, served continuously at Arvida, and received authorization to disband along with Headquarters 24th Anti-Aircraft Regiment RCA, Serial 533, under General Order 208/45 (Effective 15th January 1945).

*   *   *

41st LAA Battery RCA, Simcoe, Ontario — Serial 454B — 5th Div.

The combined 41st/102nd Field Battery RCA, CASF, Serial 905B, mobilized with 15th Field Regiment RCA, CASF, 4th Division, CASF, under General Order 184/40 (Effective 24th May 1940).

41st Battery regained individual identity as 41st Field Battery RCA, Serial 455, under General Order 85/41 (Effective 1st January 1941).

Headquarters 5th Light Anti-Aircraft Regiment RCA, Serial 454, was placed on active service and 41st Field Battery RCA, Serial 455, was redesignated 41st Light Anti-Aircraft Battery RCA, Serial 455, under General Order 85/41 (Effective 27th February 1941).

41st Light Anti-Aircraft Battery RCA was allotted Serial Number 454B, in an alignment of serial numbers with 5th Light Anti-Aircraft Regiment RCA, authorized under General Order 54/42 (Effective 22nd December 1941).

41st Light Anti-Aircraft Battery, 5th Light Anti-Aircraft Regiment RCA, 5th Canadian (Armoured) Division departed for overseas 19th September 1941 on board the Pasteur, and disembarked on the 27th of September 1941, at Greenock, Scotland.

41st Battery, with the regiment, came under command of 1st Canadian Anti-Aircraft Brigade at Colchester, Essex, for training, then moved to the South of England to man gunsites in the Air Defence of Great Britain (ADGB) and to participate in divisional training.

Transfer of 1st Canadian Corps to the Mediterranean Theatre of Operations saw Headquarters 1st Canadian Corps, Corps Troops, 5th Canadian Armoured Division, and 1st Canadian AGRA depart from England to join 1st Canadian Infantry Division and 1st Canadian Armoured Brigade presently serving with Eighth Army in Italy.

41st Battery boarded the John Ericsson at Liverpool, 27th October 1943 on operation "Timberwolf", then sailed to join the convoy off Scotland and proceeded directly to Naples, Italy, disembarking on the 8th of November 1943.

The Battery deployed in an Anti-Aircraft role near Gravina, 16th December 1943. 1st Canadian Corps became operational early in the New Year and as a component, 41st Battery, the regiment and 5th Canadian Armoured Division served in Italy until the Corps moved to NW Europe in 1945 to join First Canadian Army.

41st Battery departed from Italy via Leghorn, 28th February 1945, disembarked at Marseilles, France on the 1st of March 1945, and joined the action as a component of First Canadian Army on the 3rd of April 1945, near Elst, Holland, in the Arnhem Sector.

41st Light Anti-Aircraft Battery RCA served until cessation of hostilities and received authorization to disband under General Order 71/46 (Effective 27th November 1945).

* * *

42nd AA Battery RCA — Serial 780 — Pacific Command

42nd Anti-Aircraft Battery, Type 2H, RCA, Serial 780, mobilized under General Order 181/42 (Effective 18th April 1942).

War Diary — "The Bty to concentrate at Macaulay Plains with BHQ at Buxton House, Macaulay Plains, Esquimalt, B.C. BHQ moved to Fort Rodd Hill 2nd July/42. The Orderly Room & QM Stores located in the old lower fort".

The Battery assumed manning duties at VH 2, Colwood, B.C. Site, 11th Nov/42, under 27th AA Regiment, with Bty HQ moving to New Colwood Camp, Esquimalt Fortress Area 18 Apr/43.

42nd Bty is listed with 27 AA Regiment, Victoria & Esquimalt, Pacific Command, in Operational Units — Artillery — Cdn Army, North American Zone, 24 April 1943. — (D. Hist, Ottawa).

42nd Anti-Aircraft Battery also manned guns at Tillicum, Bazan Bay, and Wilson Rd Sites.

The Site Fighting Book of VH 2, Colwood, B.C., lists 9th AA Bty taking over manning duties from "A" & "B" Troops 42nd AA Bty 22nd August/43 "B" Troop returned for duty from 2nd March/44 to 20th April/44, then "A" Troop manned the Site until 6th Nov/44, when "B" Troop relieved "A" Troop. The Battery turned over the Site to 2nd AA Battery, 19th February 1945.

42 Bty "B" Tp, 27 AA Regt is listed on duty at VH 1, Macaulay Site and "A" Tp manning VH 2, Colwood Site, Victoria-Esquimalt Fortress, in the Record Book of #1 CRLE Pacific Command Group — AA Radars — Time in Op Condition Jan 1944 — July 1945.

42nd Anti-Aircraft Battery, Type 2H, RCA, Serial 780, was converted and redesignated 42nd Composite Anti-Aircraft Battery (Type 1H and 1L), RCA, under General Order 352/45 (Effective 15th September 1945).

War Diary — "The Bty took over Regtl Officers Quarters and kitchen, Clent Street, 1st Oct/45 & on 2nd & 3rd men & stores moved to New Colwood Camp.

BHQ moved from Harrison Pt to Colwood Camp 29 Oct/45 and 31 Oct/45 with the disbandment of 27th AA Regt, the Bty continued under HQ Fixed Def West Coast RCA.*

The Bty moved from Colwood Camp to Macaulay Camp between 26 & 29 Nov/45.

42nd CAA Bty took part in operation "Re-tree" during March 1946, att to Victoria Logging Co for R & Q".

42nd Composite Anti-Aircraft Battery (Type 1H and 1L) RCA — no listed Serial Number — received authorization to disband under General Order 205/46 (Effective 29th April 1946).

*HQ, Fixed Defences, West Coast, RCA was placed on Active Service under General Order 351/45 (Effective 15th September 1945).

HQ Esquimalt Fortress and HQ 27 AA Regiment RCA, disbanded under General Order 18/46 (Effective 31st October 1945).

HQ Pacific Command was placed on Active Service under General Order 264/43 (Effective 2nd December 1940), and was redesignated HQ Military

District No. 11, under General Order 56/46 (Effective 23rd January 1946).

*   *   *

42nd LAA Battery RCA, Delhi, Ontario — Serial 458D — Army Tps.

42nd Light Anti-Aircraft Battery RCA, Serial 461, mobilized as a component of 7th Light Anti-Aircraft Regiment RCA, under General Order 149/41 (Effective 24th May 1941).

The Battery proceeded to Niagara-on-the-Lake Camp, 13th August 1941, and in September moved to Petawawa to join the regiment.

42nd Battery, 7th Light Anti-Aircraft Regiment RCA, departed for overseas 13th November 1941 on board the Durban Castle, and disembarked at Gourock, Scotland, 22nd November 1941.

Colchester, Essex, was home base until December 1941, when the Regiment boarded ship at Stranraer, for Larne, Ireland, enroute to Ballykinler Camp, N. Ireland.

42nd Light Anti-Aircraft Battery RCA was allotted Serial Number 458D, under General Order 54/42 (Effective 22nd December 1941), in an alignment of Serial Numbers with 7th Light Anti-Aircraft Regiment RCA, Serial 458.

42nd Battery with the regiment returned to Colchester from Ireland on the 9th of May and resumed its air defence duty with 1st Canadian Anti-Aircraft Brigade.

The battery and regiment moved from Colchester, 16th July 1942, and at Haywards Heath, assumed its intended role of providing protection for Army Troops, First Canadian Army.

Headquarters 1st Canadian Anti-Aircraft Brigade and the two Army Troops Light Anti-Aircraft Regiments, 11th Light Anti-Aircraft Regiment RCA and 7th Light Anti-Aircraft Regiment RCA, which included 42nd Light Anti-Aircraft Battery RCA, Serial 458D, were authorized to disband under General Order 357/44 (Effective 1st March 1944), in England.

British units replaced the disbanded units in First Canadian Army to help ease the manpower shortage and served until the cessation of hostilities in NW Europe.

*   *   *

43rd AA Battery RCA — Serial 781 — Pacific Command

43rd Anti-Aircraft Battery, Type 2H, RCA, Serial 781, mobilized under General Order 181/42 (Effective 13th April 1942).

War Diary — "The Bty was formed at Esquimalt with the Orderly Room in Work Point Barracks. The Bty was to concentrate at Macaulay Camp and when organization completed and personnel trained the Bty will be stationed in the Van-New Westminster area.

On 6th June 1942, the 43rd, 21st, 31st, 11th & 47th Btys were placed in the 28th AA Regt RCA, CA" — (Vancouver).

"B" Troop returned to Vancouver Island in January 1944 to man VH 2 Site under 27 AA Regt at Colwood, B.C., and "A" Troop manned the Site during February 1944. They in turn were relieved by 42nd AA Bty. — (Site Fighting Book).

43rd Bty "B" Tp, 28 AA Regt is listed on duty at Van H-3, Burnaby Site and "A" Tp manning Van H-6, Point Grey Site, Vancouver Defences, in the Record Book of #1 C.R.L.E. Pacific Command Group — AA Radars — Time in Op Condition Jan 1944 — July 1945.

43rd Anti-Aircraft Battery Type 2H, RCA, Serial 781, received authorization to disband under General Order 208/45 (Effective 31st January 1945).

* * *

44th AA Battery RCA — Serial 782 — Pacific Command

44th Anti-Aircraft Battery, Type H, RCA, Serial 782, mobilized under General Order 181/42 (Effective 13th April 1942).

War Diary of 44th AA Bty RCA, CA (A) notes — "The Bty was formed at Macaulay Camp with Orderly Room in Building 34 Work Point Barracks. The Bty remained at Macaulay Plains Esquimalt, B.C. and 7th Sept/42, took over RCA Camp (CA) for admin purposes, personnel of 44th, 47th, 58th & 13th AA Btys being att for R & Q".

44 Bty is listed as a component of 28th AA Regt (Vancouver), in Operational Units — Artillery — Cdn Army — North American Zone, 24th April 1943. — (D. Hist, Ottawa).

War Diary — "Guns, ammo & stores turned over to 23 AA Bty. 44th AA Bty dep from Vancouver 16 July/43 & arr Pr. Rupt. 18 July/43 to KORC Camp until 12 Aug & the site at Pillsbury Cove completed".

Headquarters 29th Anti-Aircraft Regiment RCA was authorized under General Order 208/43 (Effective 29th March 1943) to encompass all anti-aircraft units in the Prince Rupert, British Columbia, Defences and 44th Anti-Aircraft Battery RCA became a component.

Prince Rupert Defences came under command of 8th Canadian Division from the 9th of October 1942 to the 15th of October 1943, at which time 8th Canadian Division disbanded. 44th AA Bty (H) RCA under Headquarters 29th AA Regiment RCA served with 8th Division from the latter part of July to the 15th of October 1943. — (Order of Battle 8th Cdn Div, Public Archives Canada, Ottawa).

44th Anti-Aircraft Battery with the regiment continued to serve in the Prince Rupert Defences under Pacific Command until the emergency ended.

In the Record Book of #1 C.R.L.E. — Pacific Command Group — AA Radars — Time in Op Condition Jan 1944 — July 1945 — 44 Bty is listed on manning duty at PR H-3 Pillsbury Cove Site, Prince Rupert, under 29 AA Regiment.

44th Anti-Aircraft Battery, Type H, RCA, Serial 782, along with Headquarters, 29th Anti-Aircraft Regiment RCA, received authorization to disband under General Order 305/45 (Effective 31st July 1945). Headquarters Prince Rupert Defences disbanded under General Order 18/46 (Effective 31st October 1945).

*   *   *

45th AA Troop RCA — Serial 783 — Atlantic Command

45th Anti-Aircraft Troop, Type L, RCA, Serial 783, mobilized under General Order 181/42 (Effective 13th April 1942).

45th Anti-Aircraft Troop operated independent of regimental control, providing protection for the Royal Canadian Air Force Airfield at Yarmouth, Nova Scotia.

45th Anti-Aircraft Troop, Type "L", RCA, Serial 783, received authorization to disband under General Order 498/43 (Effective 1st November 1943), in a reduction of Units on the Home Front.

*   *   *

46th AA Battery RCA — Serial 784 — Atlantic Command

46th Anti-Aircraft Troop, Type L, RCA, Serial 784, mobilized under General Order 181/42 (Effective 13th April 1942).

46th Anti-Aircraft Troop served with 22nd Anti-Aircraft Regiment RCA, under Headquarters Saint John Defences, at Moncton, New Brunswick.

46th Anti-Aircraft Troop, Type L, RCA, Serial 784, was redesignated 46th Anti-Aircraft Battery Type "3L", RCA, Serial 784, under General Order 366/43 (Effective 15th June 1943).

46th Anti-Aircraft Battery, Type "3L", RCA, Serial 784, was redesignated 146th Anti-Aircraft Battery (Type 3L) RCA, Serial 784, under General Order 412/43 (Effective 1st September 1943), and became a component of 21st Anti-Aircraft Regiment RCA, under Headquarters Halifax Fortress.

146th Battery manned sites at Ocean Terminal, Dockyard, and Citadel Hill.

146th Anti-Aircraft Battery Type 3L, RCA, Serial 784, along with Headquarters 21st Anti-Aircraft Regiment RCA, Serial 527, received authorization to disband under General Order 305/45 (Effective 31st July 1945).

*   *   *

46th LAA Battery RCA, Simcoe, Ontario — Serial 813C — 6 Div, Kiska

46th Light Anti-Aircraft Battery RCA, Serial 813C, mobilized under General Order 147/42 (Effective 18th March 1942), to serve with 9th Light Anti-Aircraft Regiment RCA, 6th Division, Home Defence.

9th Light Anti-Aircraft Regiment concentrated at Petawawa, then proceeded to Vancouver, British Columbia, in October 1942 to provide Anti-Aircraft support for the three Brigade Groups of 6th Division in Pacific Command.

Headquarters 9th Light Anti-Aircraft Regiment RCA was authorized to disband under General Order 251/43 (Effective 15th May 1943), and the Batteries operated with the Brigade Groups of 6th Division.

46th Light Anti-Aircraft Battery RCA aligned with 13th Infantry Brigade Group, was selected to join the Canadian-US "Greenlight" Force in an attack on the Island of Kiska, in the Aleutian Chain.

On the 12th July 1943 the Battery sailed for Adak, in the Aleutians, enroute to Kiska, for further training and acclimatization.

46th Light Anti-Aircraft Battery RCA disembarked at Kiska on the 15th and 16th of August 1943, and as the enemy had abandoned the Island, the Battery performed Garrison Duty until the 31st of December 1943, then sailed for Vancouver to resume its Home Defence role with 13th Infantry Brigade Group, 6th Division.

One Troop of 46th Light Anti-Aircraft Battery RCA participated in exercise "Eskimo", January and February 1945, in a skeleton 13th Brigade Group and the Royal Canadian Air Force, testing equipment under dry cold conditions in Northern Saskatchewan.

46th Light Anti-Aircraft Battery RCA, Serial 813C, received authorization to disband under General Order 213/45 (Effective 31st March 1945).

Headquarters 20th Field Regiment RCA had disbanded 31st December 1944, Headquarters 6th Division, Headquarters 6th Divisional Artillery RCA, 48th and 25th Light Anti-Aircraft Batteries RCA disbanded 31st January 1945. The remainder of 6th Division Divisional Artillery RCA - 24th and 25th Field Regiments RCA and 46th Light Anti-Aircraft Battery RCA disbanded 31st March 1945.

*   *   *

47th AA Troop RCA — Serial 785 — Pacific Command

47th Anti-Aircraft Troop, Type L, RCA, Serial 785, mobilized under General Order 181/42 (Effective 13th April 1942).

47th Anti-Aircraft Troop (Type L), RCA, Serial 785 was authorized to disband under General Order 385/42 (Effective 1st September 1942).

However, the Unit War Diary states that — "47th AA Bty, formed in Esquimalt and following training moved to 28th AA Regiment, Vancouver Defences (New Westminster). 28th AA Regt to comprise 31 Bty Narrows N., 11 Bty Sea Isl., 21 Bty Vancouver, 43 Bty Vancouver, 47 Bty Vancouver".

43rd AA Bty War Diary notes — "On 6th June 1942, the 43rd, 21st, 31st, 11th & 47th Btys were placed in the 28th AA Regt RCA, CA".

44th AA Bty RCA, CA (A), War Diary also mentions 47th AA Bty — "The Bty (44th) was formed at Macaulay. The Bty remained at Macaulay Plains Esquimalt, B.C. and 7th Sept/42, took over RCA Camp (CA) for admin purposes, personnel of 44th, 47th, 58th & 13th AA Btys being att. for R & Q".

59th AA Bty War Diary mentions — "52 men TOS from 47th AA Tp. 29 Sept/42 Pt II Orders".

Normal procedure saw previously mobilized AA *Troops* enlarged to AA *Batteries* or absorbed into the authorized battery bearing the same number. Perhaps the 47th AA Troop became an AA Battery on paper only and was never officially authorized.

*   *   *

47th (Napanee) LAA Bty RCA, Napanee, Ont. — Serial 454C — 5 Div

The combined 3rd/47th Field Battery RCA, CASF, Serial 905C, mobilized with the original 15th Field Regiment RCA, 4th Division, CASF, under General Order 184/40 (Effective 24th May 1940).

47th Battery regained individual identity as 47th (Napanee) Field Battery RCA, Serial 456 then was redesignated 47th (Napanee) Light Anti-Aircraft

Battery RCA, Serial 456, under General Order 85/41 (Effective 27th February 1941).

Headquarters 5th Light Anti-Aircraft Regiment RCA also mobilized under General Order 85/41 and 47th Battery became a component of the Regiment, in 1st Canadian Armoured Division, which became 5th Canadian (Armoured) Division under General Order 135/41 (Effective 5th June 1941).

47th Battery, 5th Light Anti-Aircraft Regiment RCA, 5th Canadian (Armoured) Division departed for overseas 19th September 1941 on board the Pasteur, and disembarked at Greenock, Scotland, 27th September 1941. The regiment came under command of 1st Canadian Anti-Aircraft Brigade at Colchester, Essex, for training, and manned sites in the Air Defence of Great Britain (ADGB), then moved to the 5th Division area in the South of England.

47th (Napanee) Light Anti-Aircraft Battery RCA was allotted Serial Number 454C, under General Order 54/42 (Effective 22nd December 1941), in an alignment of serial numbers within the regiment.

Mediterranean bound on operation "Timberwolf", 5th Light Anti-Aircraft Regiment RCA boarded the John Ericsson, at Liverpool, 27th October 1943 and sailed directly to Naples, Italy, where 47th Battery disembarked on the 8th of November 1943.

The Regiment and 5th Canadian Armoured Division became components of 1st Canadian Corps, along with 1st Canadian Armoured Brigade and 1st Canadian Infantry Division, both veterans of the battles in Sicily.

1st Canadian Corps supported by 1st Canadian AGRA, became operational early in 1944 and served in Italy until early 1945, then moved to NW Europe to join First Canadian Army.

47th Battery departed from Italy via Leghorn, 28th February 1945, disembarked at Marseilles, France, 1st March 1945 and joined the action under First Canadian Army, 3rd April 1945 near Arnhem, Holland.

47th (Napanee) Light Anti-Aircraft Battery RCA served until the cessation of hostilities and received authorization to disband under General Order 71/46 (Effective 27th November 1945).

*   *   *

48th AA Battery RCA — Serial 787 — "W" Force

48th Anti-Aircraft Battery, Type 2L, RCA, Serial 787, mobilized under General Order 234/42 (Effective 1st May 1942).

48th Battery departed on the SS Lady Rodney, 15th December 1942 from Halifax, and disembarked 21st December 1942 at St. John's, Newfoundland.

The Battery became a component of 25th Anti-Aircraft Regiment RCA serving in the St. John's-Torbay Defences and manned the Campbell Avenue and Bell Island Sites.

48th Anti-Aircraft Battery, Type 2L, RCA, Serial 787, was redesignated 148th Anti-Aircraft Battery (Type 2L) RCA, Serial 787, under General Order 412/43 (Effective 1st September 1943).

148th Anti-Aircraft Battery, Type 2L, RCA, Serial 787, received authorization to disband under General Order 305/45 (Effective 31st July 1945). Headquarters, 25th Anti-Aircraft Regiment RCA and Headquarters Atlantic Command also disbanded at this time. "W" Force Brigade Headquarters disbanded the following July.

*   *   *

48th LAA Battery RCA, Watford, Ontario — Serial 813B — 6 Div

48th Light Anti-Aircraft Battery RCA, Serial 813B, mobilized under General Order 147/42 (Effective 18th March 1942) to serve as a component of 9th Light Anti-Aircraft Regiment RCA, in 6th Division, Home Defence.

The Regiment concentrated at Petawawa, then moved to Vancouver, October 1942 to provide Anti-Aircraft support for the three brigade groups of 6th Division, under Pacific Command.

48th Light Anti-Aircraft Battery RCA was posted to 8th Division on the 6th of January 1943, and during June and July 1943, served in the Prince Rupert Defences, under command of 8th Division.

48th Light Anti-Aircraft Battery served with 8th Division until the division disbanded, authorized under General Order 15/44 (Effective 15th October 1943).

Headquarters, 9th Light Anti-Aircraft Regiment RCA had disbanded earlier, under General Order 251/43 (Effective 15th May 1943), and the batteries operated with the brigade groups.

Upon the disbanding of 8th Division, 48th Light Anti-Aircraft Battery returned to the reorganized 6th Division, which once again comprised 13th, 14th and 15th Brigade Groups. 48th Battery joined 14th Brigade Group on the 16th October 1943 and served as a component until the end of January 1945.

48th Light Anti-Aircraft Battery RCA, Serial 813B, received authorization to disband under General Order 208/45 (Effective 31st January 1945). Headquarters 6th Division and Headquarters 6th Divisional Artillery RCA, also disbanded at this time.

*   *   *

49th AA Battery RCA — Serial 788 — Atlantic Command

49th Anti-Aircraft Battery, Type H, RCA, Serial 788, mobilized under General Order 256/42 (Effective 15th May 1942).

Headquarters 21st Anti-Aircraft Regiment RCA was authorized 1st June 1942 to encompass the anti-aircraft units under Headquarters Halifax Fortress and as a component 49th Battery served at the McNab Island Site.

In February 1944, 49th Anti-Aircraft Battery departed for Torbay, Newfoundland in an exchange with 14th Anti-Aircraft Battery and served with 25th Anti-Aircraft Regiment RCA under Headquarters St. John's Defences (Newfoundland) and its later designation, Headquarters Defended Port of St. John's.

49th Anti-Aircraft Battery, Type H, RCA, Serial 788, returned to 21st Anti-Aircraft Regiment RCA at Halifax, where authorization to disband was received, under General Order 305/45 (Effective 31st July 1945). Headquarters Atlantic Command along with Headquarters 25th Anti-Aircraft Regiment and Headquarters 21st Anti-Aircraft Regiment RCA, disbanded under the same General Order.

*   *   *

50th AA Battery RCA — Serial 789 — Atlantic Command

50th Anti-Aircraft Battery, Type 2H, RCA, Serial 789, mobilized under General Order 256/42 (Effective 15th May 1942).

Headquarters 23rd Anti-Aircraft Regiment RCA was authorized 1st June 1942 to encompass the anti-aircraft units under Headquarters Sydney-Canso Defences and 50th Anti-Aircraft Battery became a component.

50th Battery "B" Troop manned the South Bar Site and "A" Troop of 50th Battery manned the Cossitt Lake Site. Both sites were the responsibility of 23rd Anti-Aircraft Regiment RCA, under Headquarters Sydney-Canso Defences and its later designation, Headquarters Defended Port of Sydney.

50th Anti-Aircraft Battery, Type 2H, RCA, Serial 789, received authorization to disband under General Order 208/45 (Effective 31st December 1944).

*   *   *

51st AA Battery RCA — Serial 790 — Sydney, N.S.

51st Anti-Aircraft Battery, Type 2H, RCA, Serial 790, mobilized under General Order 256/42 (Effective 15th May 1942).

Headquarters 23rd Anti-Aircraft Regiment RCA, Serial 530, was authorized to mobilize under General Order 256/42 (Effective 1st June 1942), and 51st Anti-Aircraft Battey RCA became a component, serving in the Sydney-Canso Defences, Atlantic Command.

Headquarters Sydney-Canso Defences was redesignated Headquarters Defended Port of Sydney, under General Order 206/44 (Effective 15th April 1944) and 51st Battery, with the regiment continued to serve under the headquarters in its new designation.

Atlantic Command — AA Radars — Time in Operating Condition, Records of #1 C.R.L.E., January 1944 — July 1945, Headquarters Defended Port of Sydney, 51 Battery A Troop is listed on duty at Jacksonville Site and 51, B troop at Wireless Hill Site, under 23rd Anti-Aircraft Regiment RCA. These sites, however, were phased out before the end of 1944.

51st Anti-Aircraft Battery, Type 2H, RCA, Serial 790, received authorization to disband under General Order 208/45 (Effective 31st December 1944).

*   *   *

52nd AA Battery RCA — Serial 791 — Gaspe, P.Q. & Newfoundland

52nd Anti-Aircraft Troop, Type L, RCA, Serial 791, mobilized under General Order 256/42 (Effective 15th May 1942) as a component of 22nd Anti-Aircraft Regiment RCA, Saint John, New Brunswick, and served in a detached role in the Gaspe Defences, P.Q.

Effective 15th July 1943 all Active Anti-Aircraft Units located in Military District No. 5, which included Gaspe, Serial 791, 52nd Anti-Aircraft Troop, Type L, RCA was placed under command of Headquarters 24th Anti-Aircraft Regiment RCA for administration and training supervision.

52nd Anti-Aircraft Troop, Type L, RCA, Serial 791, was redesignated 52nd Anti-Aircraft Battery (Type 4L) RCA, Serial 791, under General Order 494/43 (Effective 1st October 1943).

Upon the conversion of 26th Anti-Aircraft Regiment RCA from English speaking to French speaking, 52nd Anti-Aircraft Battery moved from Gaspe to Valcartier, arriving on the 5th of November, 1943, as the new regiment assembled prior to replacing the original regiment in Newfoundland.

52nd Anti-Aircraft Battery (Type 4L) RCA, Serial 791, moved from Valcartier to Bedford, Nova Scotia, then sailed for Newfoundland, arriving on the 4th of

December 1943 and served in the Gander Defences until authorized to disband under General Order 305/45 (Effective 31st July 1945).

*   *   *

53rd AA Battery RCA — Serial 792 — 22nd AA Regiment RCA

53rd Anti-Aircraft Battery, Type H, RCA, Serial 792, mobilized under General Order 256/42 (Effective 15th May 1942), to serve with 22nd Anti-Aircraft Regiment RCA of Saint John, New Brunswick, Military District No. 7, and served in a detached role at Gaspe, in the Gaspe, P.Q. Defences.

53rd Anti-Aircraft Battery, Type "H", RCA, Serial 792, following an existence of thirteen months, received authorization to disband under General Order 367/43 (Effective 15th June 1943).

*   *   *

53rd LAA Battery RCA, Toronto — Serial 142E — 2nd Div & Army Tps

53rd Field Battery RCA, CASF, Serial 157, mobilized under General Order 135/39, 1st September 1939, with Headquarters of 4th Field Brigade RCA, CASF, 2nd Division, CASF.

53rd Battery remained in Toronto for the winter and on the 24th of May 1940 all four batteries of 4th Field Brigade RCA, CASF, converged on Petawawa Camp where reorganization to a two-battery field regiment was begun.

Headquarters of 4th Field Brigade RCA, CASF, Serial 155, was redesignated Headquarters of 4th Field Regiment RCA, CASF, Serial 155, and 53rd Field Battery RCA, CASF, Serial 157, combined with 26th Field Battery RCA, CASF, Serial 156, to become 26th/53rd Field Battery RCA, CASF, Serial 156, under General Order 123/40 (Effective 1st June 1940), in 4th Field Regiment RCA, CASF, 2nd Division.

26th/53rd Field Battery RCA, CASF, sailed overseas on board the Empress of Australia, 27th August 1940, and disembarked at Glasgow, Scotland, 4th September 1940.

53rd Battery once more regained individual identity as 53rd Field Battery RCA, Serial 157, under General Order 45/41 (Effective 1st January 1941).

53rd Field Battery RCA, Serial 157, was redesignated 53rd Light Anti-Aircraft Battery RCA, Serial 157, under General Order 57/41 (Effective 1st January 1941) and moved to 3rd Light Anti-Aircraft Regiment RCA, also with 2nd Division.

53rd Light Anti-Aircraft Battery joined 3rd Light Anti-Aircraft Regiment

RCA at Colchester, Essex, 13th March 1941, where the regiment came under command of 1st Canadian Anti-Aircraft Brigade for training and duty.

At Colchester the regiment began intensive training, deployed guns along the coast near Clacton-on-Sea overnight, mobile schemes were conducted and firing camps visited, with 53rd Battery proceeding to the Firing Camp at St. Agnes in Cornwall.

3rd Light Anti-Aircraft Regiment RCA returned to Colchester, then moved to Air Defence of Great Britain (ADGB) Sites South of London, with 53rd Battery manning gunsites at Croydon and Biggen Hill, August 1941 to February 1942, then returned to Colchester. Shortly before its return to Colchester, 53rd Light Anti-Aircraft Battery RCA, Serial 157, was allotted Serial Number 142E, under General Order 54/42 (Effective 22nd December 1941), in an alignment of serial numbers within the regiment.

The regiment ceased to be under command of 1st Canadian Anti-Aircraft Brigade 19th March 1942 and moved to 2nd Canadian Division Area at Bexhill-on-Sea, Sussex.

In August 1942, 53rd Battery's guns were deployed to protect the Selsey area from hit-and-run raiders.

On the 18th of August 1942, leaving minimum crews manning the gun sites at Selsey, 53rd Battery boarded a tank landing craft (TLC), (Later redesignated Landing Craft Tank), at Newhaven, along with members of the Calgary Tank Regiment and Toronto Scottish, bound for Dieppe with Canada's 2nd Division.

Nearing the French coast, the gunners fired furiously at the enemy planes with their Bren guns, however, finding it impossible to land the tanks, the tank landing craft withdrew, and returned to England via Portsmouth. In England 53rd Battery resumed its duty on the coast.

A new war establishment in an infantry division, saw four-battery Light Anti-Aircraft Regiments RCA reduced to three-battery Light Anti-Aircraft Regiments RCA and 53rd Battery was selected to move once again.

Headquarters 11th Light Anti-Aircraft Regiment RCA, Serial 1170A, was authorized under General Order 242/43 (Effective 6th March 1943) and 53rd Light Anti-Aircraft Battery RCA, along with 4th Light Anti-Aircraft Battery RCA from 1st Division, and 62nd Light Anti-Aircraft Battery RCA from 3rd Division, moved to the new regiment, to serve as army troops.

In an army troops role, 53rd Light Anti-Aircraft Battery, 11th Light Anti-

Aircraft Regiment RCA served with 1st Canadian Anti-Aircraft Brigade, First Canadian Army, in the defence of England.

Headquarters 1st Canadian Anti-Aircraft Brigade RCA, Headquarters 11th Light Anti-Aircraft Regiment RCA, its Batteries, including 53rd Light Anti-Aircraft Battery RCA, Serial 142E, along with 7th Light Anti-Aircraft Regiment RCA, Army Troops, were authorized to disband in England, under General Order 357/44 (Effective 1st March 1944). The Anti-Aircraft Brigade Headquarters and two light anti-aircraft regiments were replaced in First Canadian Army by similar British Units, to relieve the manpower shortage.

* * *

54th AA Battery RCA — Serial 793 — "W" Force

54th Anti-Aircraft Battery, Type 2H, RCA, Serial 793, mobilized under General Order 256/42 (Effective 15th May 1942) at Bedford, Nova Scotia.

54th Anti-Aircraft Battery RCA departed from Halifax 15th December 1942 on board the SS Lady Rodney and disembarked 21st December 1942 at St. John's Newfoundland. 54th Battery joined 25th Anti-Aircraft Regiment RCA and served in the St. John's-Torbay area under Headquarters St. John's Defences (Newfoundland).

54th Anti-Aircraft Battery, Type 2H, RCA, Serial 793, was redesignated 154th Anti-Aircraft Battery (Type 2H), RCA, Serial 793, under General Order 412/43 (Effective 1st September 1943). The Battery under its new designation continued to serve with 25th Anti-Aircraft Regiment under Headquarters St. John's Defences (Newfoundland), and its 1944 designation, Headquarters Defended Port of St. John's.

Records of #1 CRLE, Atlantic Command — AA Radars — Time in Operating Condition. January 1944 — July 1945, lists 154A at Pennywell Road, and 154B at South Side Hills, under command of 25th Anti-Aircraft Regiment, Headquarters Defended Port of St. John's (Newfoundland).

154th Anti-Aircraft Battery, Type 2H, RCA, Serial 793, along with Headquarters 25th Anti-Aircraft Regiment RCA, and Headquarters Atlantic Command, received authorization to disband under General Order 305/45 (Effective 31st July 1945).

Headquarters Defended Port of St. John's disbanded under General Order 379/45 (Effective 15th August 1945), and "W" Force Brigade Headquarters disbanded under General Order 227/46 (Effective 30th July 1946).

* * *

54th LAA Bty RCA, Brantford, Ontario — Serial 141E — 1st Div

54th Field Battery (H), RCA, CASF, Serial 9, mobilized under General Order 135/39, 1st September 1939, with Headquarters of 1st Field Brigade RCA, CASF, 1st Division, CASF.

54th Field Battery (H), RCA, CASF, Serial 9, a component of 1st Field Brigade RCA, CASF, departed for overseas 10th December 1939, on board the Empress of Britain in Troop Convoy No. 1, and disembarked 18th December 1939, at Gourock, Scotland.

Headquarters of 1st Field Brigade RCA, CASF, Serial 5, was redesignated Headquarters, 1st Field Regiment RCA, CASF, Serial 5, and batteries paired in a two-battery Regiment, under General Order 44/40 (Effective 21st December 1939).

54th Field Battery (H), RCA, CASF, Serial 9, combined with "C" Battery, RCHA, CASF, Serial 8, to become "C"/54th Field Battery RCA, CASF, Serial 8, with 1st Field Regiment RCA, CASF, 1st Division, CASF.

"C"/54th Field Battery journeyed to Brest, France, on the 13th June 1940 to join the British Expeditionary Force (BEF). The battery proceeded inland but due to the deteriorating situation, was withdrawn and returned to England, 18th June 1940.

In the defence of England, "C"/54th Field Battery RCA served with 7th Corps upon its forming 21st July 1940, until the 25th of December 1940, when the Canadian Corps was formed and 7th Corps disbanded.

54th Battery regained individual identity as 54th Field Battery RCA, Serial 9, under General Order 45/41 (Effective 1st January 1941), as the regiment reorganized to comprise three batteries, RCHA.

54th Field Battery RCA, Serial 9, was converted to LAA and redesignated 54th Light Anti-Aircraft Battery RCA, Serial 9, under General Order 57/41 (Effective 1st January 1941), to serve with 2nd Light Anti-Aircraft Regiment RCA, in 1st Division.

54th Battery joined 2nd Light Anti-Aircraft Regiment at Colchester, Essex, in March 1941. While at Colchester the regiment came under 1st Canadian Anti-Aircraft Brigade for training and duty, then moved to Air Defence of Great Britain Sites (ADGB).

The regiment proceeded to the divisional concentration area in the South of England and manned sites along the coast.

54th Light Anti-Aircraft Battery RCA was allotted Serial Number 141E, under

General Order 54/42 (Effective 22nd December 1941), in an alignment of serial numbers within the regiment.

54th Battery, 2nd Light Anti-Aircraft Regiment RCA, sailed for the Mediterranean, 25th June 1943 and landed in Sicily on the 10th of July 1943, with the assaulting 1st Canadian Infantry Division, 30 British Corps, British Eighth Army.

The battery and regiment with 1st Canadian Infantry Division moved to 13 British Corps for the assault on the Italian mainland, and crossed the Strait of Messina to Italy, 4th September 1943.

1st Canadian Infantry Division moved to 1st Canadian Corps early 1944 upon the Corps becoming operational, and served in Italy until March 1945 when the Corps, Division, Regiment, and 54th Light Anti-Aircraft Battery moved to NW Europe to join First Canadian Army.

54th Battery departed via Leghorn, 7th March 1945, to Marseilles, France, and joined the action on the 3rd of April 1945 in Holland, under First Canadian Army.

54th Light Anti-Aircraft Battery RCA served until cessation of hostilities and received authorization to disband under General Order 401/45 (Effective 6th September 1945).

* * *

55th AA Troop Type LS, RCA — Serial 794 — "W" Force

55th Anti-Aircraft Section (Type L) RCA, Serial 794, mobilized under General Order 247/42 (Effective 1st June 1942), at Bedford, Nova Scotia.

55th Anti-Aircraft Section departed from Halifax 15th December 1942 on board the SS Lady Rodney and disembarked 21st December 1942 at St. John's, Newfoundland, to serve with "W" Force, authorized under General Order 61/41 (Effective 31st October 1940).

55th Anti-Aircraft Section Type "L", RCA, Serial 794, was redesignated 55th Anti-Aircraft Troop, Type "LS", RCA, Serial 794, under General Order 366/43 (Effective 15th June 1943), and served with 25th Anti-Aircraft Regiment RCA at Bell Island and St. John's-Torbay, under Headquarters St. John's Defences (Newfoundland).

55th Anti-Aircraft Troop, Type LS, RCA, Serial 794, received authorization to disband under General Order 208/45 (Effective 31st October 1943).

* * *

56th AA Battery RCA — Serial 795 — Atlantic Command

56th Anti-Aircraft Battery (Type H) RCA, Serial 795, mobilized under General Order 247/42 (Effective 1st June 1942), to serve with 21st Anti-Aircraft Regiment RCA. The battery was formed at Bedford, Nova Scotia and moved to Newfoundland in 1943.

56th Anti-Aircraft Battery (Type H) RCA sailed on Canadian Army Transport No. 1, 21st August 1943, disembarked at St. John's, Newfoundland, 21st August 1943 and arrived at Gander on the 22nd August 1943.

56th Battery served with the original 26th Anti-Aircraft Regiment RCA at Gander and Botwood, in the Newfoundland Defences until the 12th of November 1943 at which time the battery sailed from St. John's for Halifax, arriving 15th November 1943 to be disbanded.

56th Anti-Aircraft Battery (Type H) RCA, Serial 795, received authorization to disband under General Order 432/44 (Effective 10th December 1943).

*   *   *

57th AA Battery RCA — Serial 796 — "W" Force (Newfoundland)

57th Anti-Aircraft Battery, Type H, RCA, Serial 796, mobilized under General Order 247/42 (Effective 1st June 1942).

The Battery served at Lewisporte, in the Newfoundland Defences and was Regimented under Headquarters, 26th Anti-Aircraft Regiment RCA.

57th Anti-Aircraft Battery, Type H, RCA, Serial 796, received authorization to disband under General Order 367/43 (Effective 15th June 1943), upon the conversion of 26th Anti-Aircraft Regiment RCA to French speaking.

*   *   *

57th LAA Battery RCA, Levis, P.Q. — Serial 458B — Army Troops

57th Medium Battery (H) RCA, CASF, Serial 71, mobilized with Headquarters of 2nd Medium Brigade RCA, CASF, Serial 69, Corps Troops mobilizing with 1st Division, under General Order 135/39, 1st September 1939.

Headquarters of 2nd Medium Brigade RCA, CASF, Serial 69, was redesignated Headquarters of 2nd Medium Regiment RCA, CASF, Serial 69, and the batteries paired in a two-battery medium regiment.

57th Medium Battery (H) RCA, CASF, Serial 71, combined with 1st Medium Battery RCA, CASF, Serial 73, to become 1st/57th Medium Battery RCA, CASF, Serial 71, under General Order 123/40 (Effective 1st June 1940).

57th Battery regained individual identity as 57th Medium Battery RCA, Serial 71, then converted to light anti-aircraft and redesignated 57th Light Anti-Aircraft Battery RCA, Serial 71, under General Order 149/41 (Effective 24th May 1941), becoming a component of 7th Light Anti-Aircraft Regiment RCA.

57th Light Anti-Aircraft Battery, 7th Light Anti-Aircraft Regiment RCA, departed for overseas 13th November 1941 on board the Durban Castle, and disembarked at Gourock, Scotland, 22nd November 1941, then moved to Colchester, Essex, under 1st Canadian Anti-Aircraft Brigade.

57th Light Anti-Aircraft Battery RCA was allotted Serial Number 458B, under General Order 54/42 (Effective 22nd December 1941), in a shuffle of serial numbers within the regiment.

As a component of 1st Canadian Anti-Aircraft Brigade, Army Troops, First Canadian Army, 57th Battery manned gun sites in the defence of England, and had the unique distinction of attending a firing camp in Northern Ireland.

57th Light Anti-Aircraft Battery RCA, Serial 458B, received authorization to disband in England, under General Order 357/44 (Effective 1st March 1944). Personnel were posted to other units or to No. 3 Canadian Artillery Reinforcement Unit (AA) and joined the reinforcement pool.

Headquarters 1st Canadian Anti-Aircraft Brigade RCA, and 11th Light Anti-Aircraft Regiment RCA, Army Troops Artillery, also disbanded at this time. The disbanded Canadian units were replaced with British units in First Canadian Army to help relieve the manpower shortage.

*   *   *

HQ 58 Special AA Bty RCA — Serial 756 — Pacific Command

Headquarters 58 Special Anti-Aircraft Battery (Type L), RCA, Serial 756, was authorized to mobilize under General Order 256/42 (Effective 1st May 1942).

Mobilized at Macaulay Camp, Victoria-Esquimalt Fortress, the Battery was to comprise 35th, 36th, 37th, 38th, 39th Sections, and Headquarters, and was to defend the advanced air bases at Alliford Bay, Bella Bella, Coal Harbour and Ucluelet, with two Bofors 40mm guns at each location. The Sections also assumed the duty of manning two 75mm field guns at each location, with the exception of Coal Harbour, which had a single 75.

War Diary — "A, B, C & D Shrapnel Sections which are manning the 75mm guns have been absorbed into the battery and we have obtained 77 N.C.O.'s and gunners in this way".

Headquarters 58th Special Anti-Aircraft Battery, Type"L", RCA Serial 756, was authorized to disband under General Order 367/43 (Effective 15th June 1943), and personnel were absorbed by 36th Anti-Aircraft Troop, now with 30th Anti-Aircraft Regiment RCA.

35th and 36th Sections were enlarged to Troops, 15th June 1943 and moved under command of 30th Anti-Aircraft Regiment RCA of Port Alberni, Vancouver Island, British Columbia.

37th Section and 38th Section disbanded with the Battery, 15th June 1943. 37th Section personnel were absorbed by 33rd Battery and 38th Section personnel moved to 59th Battery, 30th Anti-Aircraft Regiment RCA.

39th Section was enlarged to a troop with 30th Anti-Aircraft Regiment, 15th June 1943 and disbanded 1st November 1943.

35th and 36th Troops, along with Headquarters 30th Anti-Aircraft Regiment RCA were authorized to disband under General Order 80/44 (Effective 31st December 1943).

*   *   *

59th AA Battery RCA — Serial 797 — Pacific Command

59th Anti-Aircraft Battery Type 2L, RCA, Serial 797, mobilized under General Order 398/42 (Effective 1st August 1942) in the Victoria-Esquimalt Fortress.

War Diary — "52 men TOS from 47th AA Tp 29 Sept/42 Pt II Orders.

5 Oct/42, arrangements were made with 13th AA Bty for the men of 59 AA Bty to take over the two guns at Rodd Hill and for basic training of these men under own NCOs.

7 Oct/42, plans made for unit basic training at Rodd Hill in conjunction with carrying out an operational role while att to 13 AA Bty.

8 Oct, idea cancelled and 20 men sent to 27th AA Regt Basic Training Troop in the CAS of I, the remainder to carry on Op role at Rodd Hill and when off duty do basic training under 59th AA Bty instructors.

Men also trained at Albert Head attached to 56th Cst Bty.

19 Oct/42 men returned from duty at Rodd Hill under 13 AA Bty and were quartered at RCA Camp in marquees.

27/11/42, The 59th AA Bty, together with 44th will be attached for a/p to 27th AA Regt RCA, CA, since its ultimate destination, Port Hardy, will not be ready for another six months. Majority of 59th men will take up an operational role at Patricia Bay, while Bty HQ will remain at Work Point Barracks.

22nd Feb/43, 59th AA Bty departed from Esquimalt arrived at Long Beach Camp, Tofino, B.C. at 0130 hrs.

The Bty assumed the duty of manning the guns in relief of 33rd AA Bty.

The Battery located at RCA Camp, Tofino, 1st May 1943".

59th Anti-Aircraft Battery Type "2L", RCA, Serial 797, was redesignated 59th Anti-Aircraft Battery Type "3L", RCA, Serial 797, under General Order 366/43 (Effective 15th June 1943).

War Diary — "59th Bty relieved by 33rd Bty departed Tofino 1st July/43, arrived at RCA Camp Esquimalt later in the day.

The Battery was placed directly under 6th Div for admin whilst in this area pending final formation of 30th AA Regt.

An organization order from Headquarters, Pacific Command, Vancouver, B.C., 8th July, 43, authorized 30th AA Regt to comprise 33rd AA Bty, 59th AA Bty, 36 AA Tp and 39 AA Tp, and 25 LAA Bty also to be administered by the HQ, with effect 15 June 1943. — D. Hist, Ottawa.

Regimental Headquarters was located at Port Alberni, and the Regiment was responsible for the defence of the outlying areas of Vancouver Island.

"C" Troop departed for Coal Harbour 1st Oct/43 and arrived 3rd Oct".

59th Anti-Aircraft Battery Type "3L", RCA, Serial 797, was redesignated 59th Anti-Aircraft Battery (Type 2L), RCA, Serial 797, under General Order 493/43 (Effective 15th October 1943).

War Diary — "C" Troop rejoined the bty. at Port Hardy 19 Oct and the Coal Harbour position closed down.

The bty. complete settled in at Port Hardy 21 Oct/43".

59th Anti-Aircraft Battery (Type 2L), RCA, Serial 797, was redesignated 59th Anti-Aircraft Battery (Type 3L), RCA, Serial 797, under General Order 79/44 (Effective 31st December 1943).

Headquarters, 30th Anti-Aircraft Regiment RCA, Serial 1347, received Authorization to disband under General Order 80/44 (Effective 31st December 1943).

War Diary — "On 8th Jan/44, 59th AA Bty became self accounting.
Port Hardy B.C. 13 Apr/44, Warning order received for move of one Tp &
BHQ to Bella Bella to form a 2-L Bty".

59th Anti-Aircraft Battery (Type 3L), RCA, Serial 797, was redesignated 59th
Anti-Aircraft Battery (Type 2L), RCA, Serial 797, under General Order
216/44 (Effective 15th April 1944).

War Diary — "One Tp to Victoria & BHQ and accompanying Tp arr at Bella
Bella 30 Apr/44. The Bty also took over duties formerly performed by the
infantry on SHEERWATER ISLAND (Advanced Airdrome Defence)".

59th Anti-Aircraft Battery, Type 2L, RCA, Serial 797, received authorization
to disband under General Order 208/45 (Effective 1st September 1944).

*   *   *

60th AA Battery RCA — Serial 1128 — Levis, P.Q. & Newfoundland

60th Anti-Aircraft Battery, Type H, RCA, Serial 1128, mobilized under General Order 199/43 (Effective 16th October 1942).

60th Anti-Aircraft Battery, Type H, RCA, Serial 1128, was redesignated 60th
Anti-Aircraft Battery (Type 2H) RCA, Serial 1128, under General Order
494/43 (Effective 23rd March 1943), and under the same General Order, 60th
Anti-Aircraft Battery, Type 2H, RCA, Serial 1128, was redesignated 60th
Anti-Aircraft Battery (Type H), RCA, Serial 1128 (Effective 1st October 1943).

Previous to this latter designation, 60th Anti-Aircraft Battery, on duty at Levis,
had come under command of 24th Anti-Aircraft Regiment RCA (15th July
1943), and provided protection for the First Quebec Conference, 11th to 24th
August 1943.

60th Anti-Aircraft Battery moved from Levis to Valcartier, 4th November,
becoming a component of the New 26th Anti-Aircraft Regiment, upon the
conversion of the original 26th Anti-Aircraft Regiment RCA, to French
Speaking, 15th October 1943.

The new Regiment moved from Valcartier to Bedford, Nova Scotia on the 14th
of November, then late November and early December, set sail for Newfoundland, arriving at Gander 17th December 1943. In Newfoundland, the Regiment
manned sites at Gander, Botwood, and Lewisporte.

60th Anti-Aircraft Battery is listed as 60th Anti-Aircraft Battery (Type 2H)
RCA, Serial 1128, In General Order 213/45, authorizing the Battery to disband
(Effective 15th April 1945).

Headquarters 26th Anti-Aircraft Regiment RCA, Serial 537, was authorized to disband under General Order 379/45 (Effective 15th August 1945).

* * *

61st AA Battery RCA — Serial 1129 — Levis, P.Q. & Newfoundland

61st Anti-Aircraft Troop, Type L, RCA, Serial 1129, mobilized under General Order 199/43 (Effective 16th October 1942).

61st Anti-Aircraft Troop at Levis, came under command of 24th Anti-Aircraft Regiment RCA of the Arvida Defences on the 15th of July 1943.

61st Anti-Aircraft Troop, Type L, RCA, Serial 1129, was redesignated 61st Anti-Aircraft Battery (Type 2L), RCA, Under General Order 494/43 (Effective 1st October 1943).

61st Anti-Aircraft Battery (Type 2L) RCA, was posted to 26th Anti-Aircraft Regiment RCA, 1st October 1943, upon conversion of 26th Anti-Aircraft Regiment RCA to French speaking and 61st Battery departed Levis for Newfoundland.

The new 26th Anti-Aircraft Regiment arrived in Newfoundland, 17th December 1943, and served at Gander, Botwood, and Lewisporte.

61st Anti-Aircraft Battery, Type 2L, RCA, Serial 1129, received authorization to disband under General Order 208/45 (Effective 30th November 1944).

* * *

62nd AA Troop (Type LS) RCA — Serial 1180 — Whitehorse, Y.T.

62nd Anti-Aircraft Troop (Type LS) RCA, Serial 1180, mobilized under General Order 126/43 (Effective 1st March 1943) and served under Headquarters Prince Rupert Defences until Headquarters 29th Anti-Aircraft Regiment RCA was authorized 29th March 1943, to encompass all Anti-Aircraft Units in the Prince Rupert area.

62nd Anti-Aircraft Troop (Type LS) RCA, Serial 1180, manned six Bofors 40mm light anti-aircraft guns in defence of the Royal Canadian Air Force landing field at Whitehorse, Y.T., until receiving authorization to disband under General Order 430/43 (Effective 30th September 1943).

* * *

62nd LAA Bty RCA, Duncan, B.C. — Serial 449C — 3 Div & Army Tps

"Details" of 62nd Field Battery RCA, CASF, were named components of the CASF, under General Order 135/39, 1st September 1939, in Military District No. 11.

The combined 44th/62nd Field Battery RCA, CASF, Serial 706B, mobilized under General Order 184/40 (Effective 24th May 1940), to serve with 13th Field Regiment RCA, CASF, 3rd Division, CASF. The CASF "Details" were absorbed into the combined Battery.

Canada's 1st and 2nd Divisions comprised field artillery brigades of four individual field batteries upon mobilizing in September 1939, were now in the process of changing to field regiments of two combined field batteries, effected by pairing the original batteries. It was during this period of combined batteries that 3rd Division Artillery mobilized in the Canadian Active Service Force (CASF).

Changes in War Establishment were to haunt the battery throughout its existence, and early in the New Year 13th Field Regiment RCA, reorganized to comprise three field batteries, 22nd, 44th, and 78th Field Batteries RCA. 62nd Battery became expendable.

62nd Battery regained individual identity as 62nd Field Battery RCA, Serial 451, under General Order 45/41 (Effective 1st January 1941). 62nd Field Battery RCA, Serial 451, was redesignated 62nd Light Anti-Aircraft Battery RCA, Serial 451, under General Order 74/41 (Effective 1st January 1941), and joined 4th Light Anti-Aircraft Regiment RCA, also in 3rd Division.

62nd Light Anti-Aircraft Battery RCA began its organization and training in Queens Park Barracks, London, Ontario, then moved to Sussex Camp in New Brunswick, where the regiment concentrated on the 27th of July 1941.

62nd Light Anti-Aircraft Battery, 4th Light Anti-Aircraft Regiment RCA, moved to Halifax, 23rd August 1941, and boarded the Stratheden, a P and O liner. The convoy sailed 25th August for Glasgow, Scotland, where the Regiment (less 100th Battery), disembarked on the 2nd of September 1941, and proceeded to Colchester, Essex.

62nd Light Anti-Aircraft Battery RCA was allotted Serial Number 449C, under General Order 54/42 (Effective 22nd December 1941), in an alignment of Serial Numbers within the Regiment.

Following training at Colchester, under 1st Canadian Anti-Aircraft Brigade, 62nd Battery moved to the South of England for duty on Air Defence of Great Britain Sites (ADGB). The regiment moved into the divisional area to train with the division and manned guns protecting the coastal towns from hit-and-run raiders.

Light Anti-Aircraft Regiments reorganized to comprise three batteries, and 62nd Light Anti-Aircraft Battery became surplus to 4th Light Anti-Aircraft Regiment RCA, 3rd Canadian Infantry Division.

62nd Battery moved from 3rd Division Artillery to Army Troops Artillery, under Headquarters 11th Light Anti-Aircraft Regiment RCA, Serial 1170A, authorized under General Order 242/43 (Effective 6th March 1943). The new regiment was to comprise 4th Light Anti-Aircraft Battery RCA from 1st Div, 53rd Light Anti-Aircraft Battery RCA from 2nd Div, and 62nd Light Anti-Aircraft Battery RCA from 3rd Div.

62nd Light Anti-Aircraft Battery RCA, 11th Light Anti-Aircraft Regiment RCA, served with 1st Canadian Anti-Aircraft Brigade, First Canadian Army, and manned gun sites in the south of England.

1st Anti-Aircraft Brigade Headquarters, RCA, 7th Light Anti-Aircraft Regiment RCA, and 11th Light Anti-Aircraft Regiment RCA, which included 62nd Light Anti-Aircraft Battery RCA, Serial 449C, disbanded in England, authorized under General Order 357/44 (Effective 1st March 1944). The disbanded Canadian units were replaced with British units in First Canadian Army to help aleviate the manpower shortage.

*   *   *

63rd AA Battery RCA — Serial 1338 — 7th Div & 24 AA Regt

8th Light Anti-Aircraft Battery RCA, Serial 1413D, mobilized under General Order 309/42 (Effective 12th May 1942), to serve with 10th Light Anti-Aircraft Regiment RCA, 7th Division, Home Defence, Eastern Canada. The Battery was stationed at Petawawa, Ontario, Sussex, New Brunswick, Debert, Nova Scotia, and Tracadie, New Brunswick, then reorganization struck.

Light anti-aircraft regiments in an infantry division were now to conform to the organization of Army Troops, Corps Troops, and Armoured Division Light Anti-Aircraft Regiments RCA, by becoming three-battery regiments. 8th Light Anti-Aircraft Battery became surplus to 10th Light Anti-Aircraft Regiment RCA, in 7th Division.

8th Light Anti-Aircraft Battery RCA, Serial 1413D, was redesignated 63rd Anti-Aircraft Battery Type 3L, RCA, Serial 1338, under General Order 366/43 (Effective 15th June 1943), and was posted to 24th Anti-Aircraft Regiment RCA, serving at Arvida, P.Q., until receiving authorization to disband under General Order 208/45 (Effective 15th January 1945).

*   *   *

67th (Rosetown) LAA Battery RCA — Serial 458C — Army Troops

67th Light Anti-Aircraft Battery RCA, Serial 460, mobilized at Rosetown, Saskatchewan, under General Order 149/41 (Effective 24th May 1941), to serve with 7th Light Anti-Aircraft Regiment RCA.

67th Light Anti-Aircraft Battery joined 7th Light Anti-Aircraft Regiment at

Petawawa in September, then moved to the eastern seaboard early in November.

67th Light Anti-Aircraft Battery, 7th Light Anti-Aircraft Regiment RCA, departed for overseas 13th November 1941, on board the Durban Castle, and disembarked at Gourock, Scotland, 22nd November 1941.

The regiment travelled by train to the garrison town of Colchester, Essex, where its association with 1st Canadian Anti-Aircraft Brigade was begun. Both 1st Canadian Anti-Aircraft Brigade and 7th Anti-Aircraft Regiment RCA were to become Army Troops, First Canadian Army.

67th Light Anti-Aircraft Battery RCA was allotted Serial Number 458C, under General Order 54/42 (Effective 22nd December 1941), in an alignment of serial numbers within the regiment.

Following training at Colchester under 1st Canadian Anti-Aircraft Brigade, 67th Battery journeyed to N Ireland, March 1942, returned to Colchester in May 1942, then moved to the South of England to continue training and to man gun sites protecting important locations in the Air Defence of Great Britain (ADGB).

67 Battery attended Firing Camps at Clacton and Cark, carried out anti-tank shoots at Beachy Head visited the battle training school at Penybont in Wales.

1st Anti-Aircraft Brigade Headquarters RCA, along with 11th Light Anti-Aircraft Regiment RCA and 7th Light Anti-Aircraft Regiment RCA, which included 67th (Rosetown) Light Anti-Aircraft Battery RCA, Serial 458C, were authorized to disband in England, under General Order 357/44 (Effective 1st March 1944).

The disbanded Canadian units were replaced in First Canadian Army with British units to ease the manpower shortage.

*   *   *

69th LAA Battery RCA, Brantford, Ont. — Serial 449B — 3 Div

The combined 11th/69th Field Battery RCA, CASF, Serial 705C, mobilized under General Order 184/40 (Effective 24th May 1940), with 12th Field Regiment RCA, CASF, 3rd Division, CASF.

69th Battery regained individual identity as 69th Field Battery RCA, Serial 450, under General Order 45/41 (Effective 1st January 1941). The field regiments reorganized to comprise three field batteries and 69th Battery became surplus to 12th Field Regiment.

69th Field Battery RCA, Serial 450, was redesignated 69th Light Anti-Aircraft Battery RCA, Serial 450, under General Order 74/41 (Effective 1st January 1941), and joined 4th Light Anti-Aircraft Regiment RCA, also with 3rd Division.

69th Light Anti-Aircraft Battery RCA, 4th Light Anti-Aircraft Regiment RCA, departed for overseas 25th August 1941 on board the Stratheden, and disembarked at Glasgow, Scotland, on the 2nd of September 1941.

The Regiment concentrated at Colchester, Essex, under 1st Canadian Anti-Aircraft Brigade, for training and duty, followed by the manning of Air Defence of Great Britain Sites (ADGB) south of London.

69th Light Anti-Aircraft Battery RCA, was allotted Serial Number 449B, under General Order 54/42 (Effective 22nd December 1941), in an alignment of serial numbers within the regiment.

4th Light Anti-Aircraft Regiment moved to the division area in the south of England for divisional training and manned gun sites along the coast.

3rd Canadian Infantry Division was selected as an assault division for the Normandy invasion and 4th Light Anti-Aircraft Regiment RCA was represented by 32nd Light Anti-Aircraft Battery in the assault on D-Day, 6th June 1944. The main body of 69th Light Anti-Aircraft Battery RCA landed on the 12th of June and joined the action on the 13th of June 1944 in the beachhead.

The battery and regiment served with 1 British Corps, Second British Army, then moved to 2nd Canadian Corps, Second British Army. 3rd Canadian Infantry Division with 2nd Canadian Corps, came under command of First Canadian Army, 31st July 1944 and participated in the vicious fighting in the breakout from Caen and the closing of the Falaise Gap.

69th Light Anti-Aircraft Battery RCA served in France, Belgium, Holland, and Germany, then with cessation of hostilities received authorization to disband under General Order 52/46 (Effective 13th November 1945).

A reconstituted battery mobilized as 2nd 69th Light Anti-Aircraft Battery RCA, under General Order 319/45 (Effective 1st June 1945), with 2nd 4th Light Anti-Aircraft Regiment RCA, to serve under Headquarters RCA 3rd Canadian Infantry Division, CAOF.

2nd 69th Light Anti-Aircraft Battery RCA served with the Canadian Army Occupational Force (CAOF) in Germany, and received authorization to disband under General Order 162/46 (Effective 4th April 1946).

*   *   *

70th LAA Bty RCA, Brandon, Man. — Serial 1906B — 4th Cdn Armd Div

70th Light Anti-Aircraft Battery RCA mobilized as 70th Field Battery RCA, Serial 981, under General Order 160/41 (Effective 10th May 1941), with the reconstituted 16th Field Regiment RCA, 4th Division.

4th Division was converted to an armoured division, authorized under General Order 132/42 (Effective 26th January 1942). The armoured division required one field artillery regiment only, leaving a surplus of field regiments and batteries.

Headquarters 16th Field Regiment RCA was redesignated Headquarters 8th Light Anti-Aircraft Regiment RCA, and 70th Battery became 70th Light Anti-Aircraft Battery RCA, Serial 1906B, with 4th (Armoured) Divisional Support Group, under General Order 132/42 (Effective 26th January 1942).

70th Light Anti-Aircraft Battery RCA, 8th Light Anti-Aircraft Regiment RCA, departed for overseas 9th August 1942 on board the Capetown Castle, and disembarked at Liverpool, 18th August 1942.

The regiment proceeded to Colchester, Essex, for training under 1st Canadian Anti-Aircraft Brigade, then moved to the divisional area in the south of England for training and duty on gun sites.

70th Battery crossed the Channel and landed in Normandy on the 25th of July 1944, with the remainder of the Regiment arriving on the 27th of July 1944.

8th Light Anti-Aircraft Regiment RCA, with 4th Canadian Armoured Division, joined 2nd Canadian Corps on the Caen Front and deployed on the 29th of July 1944, coming under command of First Canadian Army 31st July 1944.

70th Light Anti-Aircraft Battery, 8th Light Anti-Aircraft Regiment RCA, 4th Canadian Armoured Division, with 2nd Canadian Corps, served under First Canadian Army in France, Belgium, Holland, and Germany.

70th Light Anti-Aircraft Battery RCA served in NW Europe until the cessation of hostilities and received authorization to disband under General Order 71/46 (Effective 12th December 1945).

*   *   *

79th LAA Battery RCA, Montreal — Serial 813E — 6th Div Redesignated 79th AA Battery Type "2L" RCA — Serial 1337 — Pacific Command

79th Light Anti-Aircraft Battery RCA, Serial 813E, mobilized with 9th Light Anti-Aircraft Regiment RCA, Under Headquarters 6th Divisional Artillery RCA, authorized in General Order 147/42 (Effective 18th March 1942).

War Diary — "79th LAA Bty — Mob in Montreal May/42 at the Armouries, Wellington St. — The Bty conc at Petawawa 19th May/42. Departed Petawawa by train 3rd Oct/42 with 48 Bty & RHQ pers. arr Hastings Park Camp Vancouver in the Van Exhibition Grounds & Amusement Park.

4th Jan/43 RHQ moved to Victoria, 25 Bty to Port Alberni & 46 Bty to Nanaimo.

48 Bty to Terrace 6th Jan/43".

Headquarters 9th Light Anti-Aircraft Regiment RCA received authorization to disband under General Order 251/43 (Effective 15th May 1943), and the Batteries came under control of 6th Division Mobile Brigade Groups.

War Diary — "79th Bty moved to Sea Island — "K" Tp 24th May — "L" & "M" Tps at Hastings Park.

"L" Tp moved to Sea Island, 14th June/43".

Infantry division light anti-aircraft regiments reorganized from four-battery regiments to three-battery regiments, and 9th Light Anti-Aircraft Regiment RCA of 6th Division was to conform. 79th Light Anti-Aircraft Battery RCA became surplus and joined Coastal Defence as an AA Battery.

Serial 813E, 79th Light Anti-Aircraft Battery RCA, was redesignated Serial 1337, 79th Anti-Aircraft Battery type "2L" RCA, under General Order 366/43 (Effective 15th June 1943). 79th Battery continued to serve in the Vancouver Defences, Pacific Command. The battery's role on Coast Defence was of rather short duration however due to the reduction of Units on Home Defence during 1943.

War Diary — "M" Tp moved to Sea Island, 17th June/43. On 18th arrangements were made to take over two guns from 11th LAA (Static) Bty who have gun sites near our camp.

16th July/43 — All available men in battery did march to 43rd AA Bty RCA Camp on Lulu Island.

31st Oct/43 — Disbandment proceedings".

79th Anti-Aircraft Battery Type "2L" RCA, Serial 1337, received authorization to disband under General Order 498/43 (Effective 1st November 1943).

*   *   *

88th LAA Battery RCA, Dartmouth, N.S. — Serial 454D — 5 Div

In a reorganization of the Non-Permanent Active Militia in Military District No. 6, the King's Canadian Hussars (Armoured Car) was converted to 87th and 88th Field Batteries RCA, to form part of 14th Field Brigade RCA, under General Order 116/39 (Effective 15th August 1939).

88th Field Battery RCA, Non-Permanent Active Militia, was localized at Windsor, Nova Scotia, in Military District No. 6, under General Order 119/39 (Effective 15th August 1939), then localized at Canning, Nova Scotia, from Windsor, in July 1940.

88th Battery mobilized for Active Service as a combined battery in a two-battery Field Regiment RCA, its designation being Serial 906C, 87th/88 Field Battery RCA, CASF, authorized under General Order 184/40 (Effective 24th May 1940). The combined battery was to serve with the original 16th Field Regiment RCA, CASF, under Headquarters 4th Division, CASF.

87th/88th Field Battery RCA was formed at Dartmouth of King's County personnel in "A" Troop, former 1st and 16th Coast Brigade "Z" Force volunteers contributed to "B" Troop, and Hants County personnel formed "C" Troop.

The Battery moved to Aldershot, Nova Scotia, then to Halifax in October, remaining until winter quarters became available in the Exhibition Building at Woodstock, New Brunswick, in December.

87th/88th Battery departed for Petawawa, to join 16th Field Regiment RCA on the 22nd February 1941. However, changes were imminent and the component batteries of 15th and 16th Field Regiments were diverted to other formations.

88th Battery regained individual identity to become 88th Field Battery RCA, Serial 457, and 88th Field Battery RCA, Serial 457, was redesignated 88th Light Anti-Aircraft Battery RCA, Serial 457, under General Order 85/41 (Effective 27th February 1941), to serve with 5th Light Anti-Aircraft Regiment RCA, 1st Canadian Armoured Division — redesignated 5th Canadian (Armoured) Division, under General Order 135/41 (Effective 5th June 1941).

88th Light Anti-Aircraft Battery, 5th Light Anti-Aircraft Regiment RCA, 5th Canadian Armoured Division, departed for overseas 19th September 1941, on board the Pasteur, and disembarked at Greenock, Scotland, 27th September 1941.

The battery entrained for its first home in England, the garrison city of Colchester, Essex, for a five month sojourn under Headquarters 1st Canadian Anti-Aircraft Brigade, then moved to the South of England for duty on Air Defence of Great Britain Sites, and training with the division.

During its stay in Colchester 88th Light Anti-Aircraft Battery Serial Number was changed to Serial Number 454D, under General Order 54/42 (Effective 22nd December 1941), in an alignment of serial numbers within the regiment.

The battery, regiment, and divison, along with Headquarters 1st Canadian Corps, were transferred to the Mediterranean Theatre of Operations, in operation "Timberwolf". 88th Battery on board the John Ericsson, departed from Liverpool, 27th October 1943, and sailed directly to Naples, Italy, disembarking 8th November 1943.

88th Battery's first deployment was to protect a field gun concentration area in December and remained deployed during Christmas 1943, their third Christmas overseas.

Toward the middle of January 1944, the regiment moved up to the 1st Div Sector with other Units of 5th Division, to thicken the line north of the Sangro River. In May one troop in each battery drew 40mm Self-Propelled equipment.

Cassino fell to the attacking troops, the Gustav and Hitler Lines were breached as 1st Canadian Corps, under Eighth Army, clawed its way up the Italian boot. The Gothic Line, San Giovanni, the Uso River, Cervia, San Pietro, Mezzano, and on to Ricione, January 1945, the last action for the Regiment in Italy.

Transfer of 1st Canadian Corps from Italy to NW Europe saw the regiment wend its way across Italy, to Leghorn. The batteries sailed 28th February on LSTs from Leghorn, and disembarked at Marseilles, France, on the 1st March 1945.

From Marseilles, the regimental convoy travelled six days through France into Belgium, to three villages near Ypres, and billets with local families.

On the 31st March 1945, 88th Battery equipped with new Canadian Bofors SPs, deployed in the Arnhem Sector to protect the gun area of 1 Canadian AGRA. First Canadian Army now had both 1st and 2nd Canadian Corps under its wing for the final blow.

5th Light Anti-Aircraft Regiment RCA continued in action until the cessation of hostilities and 88th Battery had the honour of being selected for the Canadian Berlin Brigade, however, the plan was cancelled after a month's preparation.

Volunteers from the battery proceeded to the Canadian Army Pacific Force (CAPF), others joined the Canadian Army Occupational Force (CAOF), or returned to Canada with the regiment.

88th Light Anti-Aircraft Battery RCA, received authorization to disband under General Order 71/46 (Effective 27th November 1945).

* * *

89th LAA Bty RCA, Woodstock, N.B. — Serial 505D — 1 Corps & 5 Div

89th (Woodstock) Field Battery RCA, CASF, Serial 163, mobilized under General Order 135/39, 1st September 1939, with Headquarters of 5th Field Brigade RCA, CASF, 2nd Division, CASF.

Headquarters of 5th Field Brigade RCA, CASF, was redesignated Headquarters of 5th Field Regiment RCA, CASF, to comprise two combined Batteries. 89th (Woodstock) Field Battery RCA, CASF, Serial 163, combined with 28th Field Battery RCA, CASF, Serial 162, to become 28th/89th Field Battery RCA, CASF, Serial 162, under General Order 123/40 (Effective 1st June 1940).

The combined 28th/89th Field Battery RCA, CASF, 5th Field Regiment RCA, CASF, sailed overseas 27th August 1940 on board the Empress of Australia, and disembarked at Glasgow, Scotland, 4th September 1940.

89th Battery regained individual identity as 89th Field Battery RCA, Serial 163, under General Order 45/41 (Effective 1st January 1941), and was redesignated 89th Light Anti-Aircraft Battery RCA, Serial 163, under General Order 57/41 (Effective 1st January 1941).

Headquarters 1st Light Anti-Aircraft Regiment RCA, Serial 505, was authorized under General Order 56/41 (Effective 1st February 1941), to serve as 1st Corps Light Anti-Aircraft Regiment.

The Regiment concentrated at Colchester, Essex, under 1st Canadian Anti-Aircraft Brigade for training, followed by duty on Air Defence of Great Britain (ADGB) Sites.

In an alignment of serial numbers within the regiment, authorized under General Order 54/42 (Effective 22nd December 1941), Headquarters assumed Serial Number 505A, and 89th Battery, 505D.

The regiment returned to Colchester for mobile training, then in May 1942, 1st Light Anti-Aircraft Regiment RCA came under command of 1st Canadian Corps and moved to gun sites on the South Coast of England.

89th Battery departed for the Mediterranean, 27th October 1943 from Gourock, Scotland, and disembarked at Augusta, Sicily, 8th November, then crossed to the Italian mainland with the Regiment on the 8th of January 1944 to serve as 1st Canadian Corps Light Anti-Aircraft Unit.

In July 1944 the regiment was converted to an infantry battalion, and as 89/109 Infantry Battalion, or 1 LAA Infantry Battalion in 12th Canadian Infantry Brigade, the new infantry battalion fought its initial engagement, 1/2 September 1944.

Officially, Headquarters 1st Light Anti-Aircraft Regiment RCA and its three batteries, including 89th Light Anti-Aircraft Battery RCA, Serial 505D, became The Lanark and Renfrew Scottish Regiment, CIC, under General Order 18/45 (Effective 13th July 1944).

The Lanark and Renfrew Scottish Regiment, 12th Canadian Infantry Brigade, 5th Canadian Armoured Division, with 1st Canadian Corps, served in Italy until early 1945, then with 1st Canadian Corps moved to NW Europe to join First Canadian Army.

The Lanark and Renfrew Scottish Regiment departed from Italy via Leghorn, 3rd March 1945 and disembarked at Marseilles, France, 5th March. Upon arrival in NW Europe, 5th Canadian Armoured Division reverted to the official War Establishment and 12th Canadian Infantry Brigade was disbanded.

The Lanark and Renfrew Scottish Regiment, CIC (Canadian Infantry Corps), was redesignated 1st Light Anti-Aircraft Regiment (Lanark and Renfrew Scottish Regiment) RCA, and 89th Battery once more became 89th Light Anti-Aircraft Battery RCA, under General Order 295/45 (Effective 15th March 1945).

89th Light Anti-Aircraft Battery RCA, 1st Light Anti-Aircraft Regiment (Lanark and Renfrew Scottish Regiment) RCA, 1st Canadian Corps, came under command of First Canadian Army in NW Europe and served in Holland until cessation of hostilities.

89th Light Anti-Aircraft Battery RCA received authorization to disband in NW Europe under General Order 321/45 (Effective 29th June 1945). Volunteers proceeded to the Canadian Army Pacific Force (CAPF), other personnel joined the Canadian Army Occupational Force (CAOF) for occupational duty in Germany, or were posted to divisional units from the military district of their enlistment, for the return to Canada.

*　　*　　*

96th LAA Battery RCA — Serial 1413B — 7 Div

96th Light Anti-Aircraft Battery RCA mobilized as Serial 1413B, 6th Light Anti-Aircraft Battery RCA, under General Order 309/42 (Effective 12th May 1942), with 10th Light Anti-Aircraft Regiment RCA, 7th Division, Home Defence, Eastern Canada.

6th Light Anti-Aircraft Battery RCA provided anti-aircraft protection for the First Quebec Conference in August 1943.

6th Light Anti-Aircraft Battery RCA, Serial 1413B, was redesignated 96th Light Anti-Aircraft Battery RCA, Serial 1413B, under General Order 412/43 (Effective 1st September 1943).

The run-down of Home Defence Units went into effect the latter part of 1943, and Headquarters 7th Division along with its components were authorized to disband during October and November 1943.

10th Light Anti-Aircraft Regiment RCA, Headquarters 10th Light Anti-Aircraft Regiment RCA, and its three batteries (listed as Regiments in error), were authorized to disband under General Order 15/44 (Effective 15th November 1943). The correction is listed in General Order 336/44 (Effective 17th November 1944).

*   *   *

97th LAA Battery RCA — Serial 1413C — 7 Div

97th Battery mobilized as 7th Light Anti-Aircraft Battery RCA, Serial 1413C, under General Order 309/42 (Effective 12th May 1942), with 10th Light Anti-Aircraft Regiment RCA, 7th Division, Home Defence, Eastern Canada.

The battery was stationed at Petawawa, Ontario, Sussex, New Brunswick, and Debert, Nova Scotia, training and supplying drafts.

7th Light Anti-Aircraft Battery RCA, Serial 1413C, was redesignated 97th Light Anti-Aircraft Battery RCA, Serial 1413C, under General Order 412/43 (Effective 1st September 1943). The battery remained a component of 10th Light Anti-Aircraft Regiment RCA.

97th Light Anti-Aircraft Battery RCA, Serial 1413C, received authorization to disband under General Order 15/44 (Effective 15th November 1943), with a correction listed in General Order 336/44 (Effective 17th November 1944).

*   *   *

99th LAA Battery RCA — Serial 1413E — 7 Div

99th Light Anti-Aircraft Battery RCA mobilized as 9th Anti-Aircraft Battery RCA, Serial 1413E, under General Order 309/42 (Effective 12th May 1942), with 10th Light Anti-Aircraft Regiment RCA, 7th Division, Home Defence, Eastern Canada.

9th Light Anti-Aircraft Battery RCA, Serial 1413E, was redesignated 99th Light Anti-Aircraft Battery RCA, Serial 1413E, under General Order 412/43 (Effective 1st September 1943).

In the run-down of Home Defence Units, 7th Division was authorized to disband.

99th Light Anti-Aircraft Battery RCA, Serial 1413E, along with Headquarters 10th Light Anti-Aircraft Regiment RCA, disbanded under General Order 15/44 (Effective 15th November 1943), with correction listed under General Order 336/44 (Effective 17th November 1943).

*   *   *

100th LAA Bty RCA, Listowel, Ont. — Serial 449E — 3rd Div.

100th Field Battery RCA, CASF, Serial 239, mobilized 1st September 1939, under General Order 135/39, with Headquarters of 5th Army Field Brigade RCA, CASF, Army Troops mobilizing with 2nd Division.

Headquarters of 5th Army Field Brigade RCA, CASF, was redesignated Headquarters of 21st Army Field Regiment RCA, CASF, to comprise two batteries. Batteries were paired, utilizing the original battery numbers.

100th Field Battery RCA, CASF, Serial 239, combined with 97th Field Battery (H), RCA, CASF, Serial 241, to become 97th/100th Field Battery RCA, CASF, Serial 241, under General Order 123/40 (Effective 1st June 1940).

21st Army Field Regiment RCA, CASF, was in turn redesignated 7th Army Field Regiment RCA, CASF, under General Order 195/40 (Effective 15th August 1940).

Field regiments reorganized to comprise three batteries and the combined batteries were given individual identity, resulting in one surplus battery in each regiment.

100th Battery regained individual identity as 100th Field Battery RCA, Serial 453, then redesignated 100th Light Anti-Aircraft Battery RCA, Serial 453, under General Order 74/41 (Effective 1st January 1941).

The battery became a component of 4th Light Anti-Aircraft Regiment RCA, and 100th Light Anti-Aircraft Battery RCA was allotted Serial Number 449E, under General Order 54/42 (Effective 22nd December 1941).

100th Light Anti-Aircraft Battery RCA, 4th Light Anti-Aircraft Regiment RCA, departed for overseas 13th November 1941 on board the Oronsay and disembarked at Liverpool, 23rd November 1941, then proceeded to Colchester to rejoin the regiment which had disembarked at Glasgow, Scotland, 2nd September.

100th Battery trained at Colchester, attended light anti-aircraft firing camps, manned Air Defence of Great Britain (ADGB) gunsites and participated in training with 3rd Canadian Infantry Division.

3rd Canadian Infantry Division was selected as an assault Division and landed on Juno Beach on the coast of Normandy on D-Day, 6th June 1944. 4th Light Anti-Aircraft Regiment RCA was represented by 32nd Light Anti-Aircraft Battery in the assault. 100th Light Anti-Aircraft Battery RCA landed 12th June, joining 32nd Battery in the Beachhead.

100th Battery, 4th Light Anti-Aircraft Regiment RCA, 3rd Canadian Infantry Division, served with 1 British Corps and 2nd Canadian Corps under Second British Army, then with 2nd Canadian Corps came under command of First Canadian Army 31st July 1944 on the Caen Front.

100th Light Anti-Aircraft Battery RCA served in France, Belgium, Holland, and Germany, then with cessation of hostilities received authorization to disband under General Order 52/46 (Effective 13th November 1945).

A reconstituted battery mobilized as 2nd 100th Light Anti-Aircraft Battery RCA, under General Order 319/45 (Effective 1st June 1945), with 2nd 4th Light Anti-Aircraft Regiment RCA, to serve under Headquarters RCA 3rd Canadian Infantry Division, CAOF.

2nd 100th Light Anti-Aircraft Battery RCA served with the Canadian Army Occupational Force (CAOF) in Germany, and received authorization to disband under General Order 162/46 (Effective 4th April 1946).

*   *   *

101st LAA Bty RCA, Moosomin, Sask. — Serial 1906D — 4th Div

101st Light Anti-Aircraft Battery RCA, Serial 991C, mobilized under General Order 240/41 (Effective 5th September 1941), with 6th Light Anti-Aircraft Regiment RCA, which at the time comprised four batteries, and slated to serve with 4th Infantry Division.

4th Division was converted to an Armoured Division in January 1942 and the reconstituted 16th Field Regiment RCA was converted to Light Anti-Aircraft, redesignated 8th Light Anti-Aircraft Regiment RCA, and replaced 6th Light Anti-Aircraft Regiment in 4th Division.

8th Light Anti-Aircraft Regiment RCA comprised three batteries in the armoured division. 6th Light Anti-Aircraft Regiment RCA, also became a three battery regiment at this time.

In the shuffle, 101st Light Anti-Aircraft Battery moved to 8th Light Anti-Aircraft Regiment RCA.

101st Light Anti-Aircraft Battery RCA was allotted Serial Number 1906D, under General Order 438/42 (Effective 12th February 1942), in an alignment of serial numbers with 8th Light Anti-Aircraft Regiment RCA, in 4th Canadian Armoured Division.

101st Light Anti-Aircraft Battery, 8th Light Anti-Aircraft Regiment RCA, 4th Canadian Armoured Division departed for overseas on board the Capetown Castle, 9th August 1942, and disembarked at Liverpool, England, 18th August 1942.

The Regiment proceeded to Colchester, Essex, for training, followed by visits to firing camps, duty on Air Defence of Great Britain (ADGB) sites, and divisional training.

Almost two years were to pass before the battery crossed the English Channel to France, landing in Normandy on the 27th of July 1944.

101st Battery with the regiment deployed 29th July 1944 on the Caen Front, then with 4th Canadian Armoured Division, 2nd Canadian Corps, First Canadian Army, served in France, Belgium, Holland, and Germany.

101st Light Anti-Aircraft Battery RCA served until the cessation of hostilities and received authorization to disband under General Order 71/46 (Effective 12th December 1945).

*   *   *

102nd LAA Battery RCA, Dundas, Ontario — Serial 1906C — 4 Div

102nd (Wentworth) Field Battery, Dundas, Ontario, mobilized with the original 15th Field Regiment RCA, CASF, as the combined 41st/102nd Field Battery RCA, CASF, Serial 905B, under General Order 184/40 (Effective 24th May 1940), a component of 4th Divisional Artillery, RCA, CASF.

Field regiments reorganized to comprise three batteries almost similtaneously with the forming of 1st Canadian Armoured Division and a number of 4th Division Units moved to the new formation.

102nd Battery regained individual identity as 102nd (Wentworth) Field Battery RCA, Serial 905B, under General Order 85/41 (Effective 27th February 1941), and joined 18th and 70th Batteries in the reconstituted 16th Field Regiment RCA, 4th Division.

Early 1942, 4th Division became an armoured division, requiring one field regiment only in its support group. 16th Field Regiment RCA was converted to Light Anti-Aircraft and redesignated 8th Light Anti-Aircraft Regiment RCA, to serve as 4th Canadian Armoured Division Light Anti-Aircraft Regiment.

102nd Field Battery RCA, Serial 905B was redesignated 102nd Light Anti-Aircraft Battery RCA, Serial 1906C, under General Order 132/42 (Effective 26th January 1942).

102nd Battery, 8th Light Anti-Aircraft Regiment RCA, 4th Canadian Armoured Division, departed for overseas 9th August 1942 on board the Capetown Castle, and disembarked at Liverpool, England on the 18th August 1942.

102nd Battery landed in Normandy 27th July 1944, then deployed with the Regiment and 4th Canadian Armoured Division under 2nd Canadian Corps, 29th July, on the Caen Front. 2nd Canadian Corps moved to First Canadian Army, 31st July 1944, and as a component 102nd Light Anti-Aircraft Battery RCA served in France, Belgium, Holland, and Germany.

102nd Light Anti-Aircraft Battery RCA served until the cessation of hostilities and received authorization to disband under General Order 71/46 (Effective 12th December 1945).

*   *   *

105th AA Battery RCA -- Serial 891 — Gander, "W" Force

5th Anti-Aircraft Battery (Type L) RCA, Serial 891, mobilized under General Order 25/42 (Effective 12th December 1941).

5th Anti-Aircraft Battery (Type L) RCA, Serial 891, was redesignated Type 2L, under General Order 235/42 (Effective 1st May 1942), then enlarged to Type "4L", under General Order 366/43 (Effective 15th June 1943).

5th Anti-Aircraft Battery Type "4L", RCA, Serial 891, was redesignated 105th Anti-Aircraft Battery (Type 4L) RCA, Serial 891, under General Order 412/43 (Effective 1st September 1943).

The battery served with the original 26th Anti-Aircraft Regiment RCA at Gander, in the Newfoundland Defences, then with the conversion of 26th Anti-Aircraft Regiment to French speaking, 105th Anti-Aircraft Battery disbanded.

105th Anti-Aircraft Battery, (Type 4L), RCA, Serial 891, received authorization to disband under General Order 432/44 (Effective 31st December 1943).

*   *   *

109th LAA Bty RCA, Trail, B.C. — Serial 505C — 1 Corps & 5 Div

109th Field Battery RCA, CASF, mobilized under General Order 135/39, 1st Septemer 1939, its intended Serial Number to be 167, aligned with 6th Field Brigade RCA, CASF, 2nd Division, CASF.

However, effective immediately, under General Order 220/39, 109th Battery of Trail, B.C. and 111th Battery of Nelson, B.C., were authorized to exchange Brigades and Serial Numbers. 109th Field Battery RCA joined 3rd Field Brigade RCA, CASF, 1st Division, CASF.

109th Field Battery RCA, CASF, Serial 17, with 3rd Field Brigade RCA, CASF, 1st Division, CASF, departed for overseas on board the Monarch of Bermuda in Troop Convoy 1, 10th December 1939, and disembarked at Gourock, Scotland, 18th December 1939.

Headquarters of 3rd Field Brigade RCA, CASF, was redesignated Headquarters 3rd Field Regiment RCA, CASF, and 109th Field Battery RCA, CASF, Serial 17, combined with 92nd Field Battery (H) RCA, CASF, Serial 19, to become 92nd/109th Field Battery RCA, CASF, Serial 17, under General Order 44/40 (Effective 21st December 1939), in a two-battery regiment. The four original batteries were paired to effect the new organization.

109th Battery regained individual identity as 109th Field Battery RCA, Serial 17, under General Order 45/41 (Effective 1st January 1941), and was redesignated 109th Light Anti-Aircraft Battery RCA, Serial 17, under General Order 57/41 (Effective 1st January 1941).

Headquarters 1st Light Anti-Aircraft Regiment RCA, Serial 505, was authorized under General Order 56/41 (Effective 1st February 1941), and 109th Light Anti-Aircraft Battery RCA became a component.

Headquarters 1st Light Anti-Aircraft Regiment RCA was allotted Serial Number 505A, and 109th Light Anti-Aircraft Battery RCA was allotted Serial Number 505C, under General Order 54/42 (Effective 22nd December 1941), in an alignment of serial numbers within the regiment.

1st Light Anti-Aircraft Regiment moved under Corps Headquarters and served as 1st Corps Light Anti-Aircraft Regiment.

The decision to transfer 1st Canadian Corps to the Mediterranean, saw 109th Light Anti-Aircraft Battery RCA board the Edmund B. Alexander at Gourock, Scotland, 27th October 1943, on operation "Timberwolf", and disembark at Augusta, Sicily, 8th November 1943.

1st Light Anti-Aircraft Regiment RCA crossed the Strait of Messina to the Italian mainland 8th January 1944 and assumed its role as 1st Canadian Corps Light Anti-Aircraft Regiment.

The Regiment was converted to an Infantry Battalion in July 1944, and as the 89/109 Infantry Battalion, or 1 LAA Infantry Battalion, with the newly formed 12th Infantry Brigade, fought its initial engagement 1/2 September 1944.

Officially, Headquarters 1st Light Anti-Aircraft Regiment RCA and its three Batteries, including 109th Light Anti-Aircraft Battery RCA, Serial 505C, became the Lanark and Renfrew Scottish Regiment, CIC, under General Order 18/45 (Effective 13th July 1944). In its new role the regiment moved from corps troops, to 5th Canadian Armoured Division.

The Lanark and Renfrew Scottish Regiment, 12th Canadian Infantry Brigade, 5th Canadian Armoured Division, under 1st Canadian Corps, served in Italy until 3rd March 1945, then departed Italy via Leghorn, and disembarked at Marseilles, France, 5th March 1945.

Upon arrival in NW Europe, 5th Canadian Armoured Division reverted to its official War Establishment and 12th Canadian Infantry Brigade was disbanded. The Lanark and Renfrew Scottish Regiment CIC, was redesignated 1st Light Anti-Aircraft Regiment (Lanark and Renfrew Scottish Regiment) RCA, and 109th Battery once more became 109th Light Anti-Aircraft Battery RCA, under General Order 295/45 (Effective 15th March 1945).

109th Light Anti-Aircraft Battery RCA resumed its duties with 1st Light Anti-Aircraft Regiment RCA, as 1st Canadian Corps Light Anti-Aircraft Regiment. Now, however, both 1st Canadian Corps and 2nd Canadian Corps, and all five Canadian divisions with their supporting units were in the same theatre of operations under First Canadian Army.

The battery and regiment served in NW Europe until cessation of hostilities, having had the unique distinction of serving in action as Corps Troops Artillery and as an Infantry Battalion in an Armoured Division.

109th Light Anti-Aircraft Battery RCA, along with Headquarters 1st Light Anti-Aircraft Regiment (Lanark and Renfrew Scottish Regiment) RCA, received authorization to disband under General Order 321/45 (Effective 29th June 1945), in NW Europe.

Personnel proceeded to the Canadian Army Pacific Force (CAPF), the Canadian Army Occupational Force (CAOF), or were posted to divisional units from the military district of their enlistment, for the return to Canada.

*   *   *

112th LAA Bty RCA, Lethbridge, Alta. — Serial 991B — 2 Corps

112th Field Battery (Details) was added to NPAM Units called out on Service in Military District No. 13, under General Order 136/39 (Effective 26th August 1939).

Serial 426, 112th Field Battery RCA, CASF (Details) is listed with the Canadian Active Service Force (CASF) under General Order 135/39, 1st September 1939, in Military District No. 13.

112th Light Anti-Aircraft Battery RCA, Serial 991B, received authorization to mobilize under General Order 240/41 (Effective 5th September 1941), with 6th Light Anti-Aircraft Regiment RCA, in 4th Division.

The Regiment, a four-battery regiment upon mobilizing, also included 101st Light Anti-Aircraft Battery RCA.

Upon conversion of 4th Division to 4th (Armoured) Division, 6th Light Anti-Aircraft Regiment RCA was replaced by 8th Light Anti-Aircraft Regiment RCA, in the Armoured Division.

101st Battery moved to 8th Light Anti-Aircraft Regiment RCA. 6th Light Anti-Aircraft Regiment RCA, which now comprised 1st, 30th, and 112th Light Anti-Aircraft Batteries RCA, assembled at Petawawa, Ontario, February 1942.

4th March 1942, a composite troop was posted to Prince Rupert, B.C., and on 5th June 1942, 112th Battery with the regiment's six Bofors guns, moved west to join the composite troop in the Prince Rupert Defences.

Shortly after arrival at Prince Rupert, the Battery moved to Annette Island, Alaska, to defend the Airfield from which the 115th and 118th RCAF Squadrons were operating.

30th Battery departed from Petawawa for British Columbia, 6th June 1942, and served on Vancouver Island and Yorke Island.

112th and 30th Light Anti-Aircraft Batteries were relieved of their duties at the Coast by home defence units and returned to Petawawa where the Regiment concentrated prior to going overseas. 112th Battery arrived at Petawawa on the 26th of September.

The regiment moved to Halifax 25th October 1942 and 112th Light Anti-Aircraft Battery, 6th Light Anti-Aircraft Regiment RCA boarded the "Queen Elizabeth", on the 27th.

The "QE" sailed 30th October 1942 and 112th Battery disembarked at Gourock, Scotland, 5th November 1942.

The regiment trained at Colchester, Essex, followed by duty on Air Defence of Great Britain (ADGB) sites and during this period became enshrined as 2nd Canadian Corps Light Anti-Aircraft Regiment.

112th Battery and 6th Light Anti-Aircraft Regiment RCA, with 2nd Canadian Corps, landed in Normandy 11th July 1944 and served under Second British Army until 31st July 1944, then moved under command of First Canadian

Army on the Caen Front, participating in the vicious fighting in the breakout from Caen and the closing of the Falaise Gap.

Early in 1944 a proposal was made to use anti-aircraft rockets in a counter-mortar role. Demonstrations in June and September of this Land Service Mattress in England was impressive and a cadre of instructors with ten launchers, crossed to the continent to join First Canadian Army.

112th Light Anti-Aircraft Battery RCA was selected to operate the rocket equipment, receiving instruction from the cadre upon their arrival 14th October 1944.

In November 1944 the rockets were fired in action in support of 52nd (Low-land) Division near Flushing, Holland, and in support of the 1st Polish Armoured Division 6th November 1944, near Moerdijk, Holland.

The Canadian Cadre trained personnel of 337th and 338th Light Anti-Aircraft Batteries, Royal Artillery, and 30th Light Anti-Aircraft Battery, Royal Canadian Artillery, in the use of the rocket launchers. The rocket unit continued in action as 1st Rocket Battery RCA.

112th Battery returned to 6th Light Anti-Aircraft Regiment RCA the end of November 1944 and served until cessation of hostilities.

112th Light Anti-Aircraft Battery RCA, Serial 991B, which had served in France, Belgium, Holland, and Germany in a variety of roles, now received authorization to disband in NW Europe, under General Order 321/45 (Effective 24th June 1945).

Battery personnel proceeded to the Canadian Army Pacific Force (CAPF), the Canadian Army Occupational Force (CAOF), or moved to divisional units from the military districts of their enlistment, for the return to Canada.

*   *   *

125th AA Battery RCA — Serial 738 — Atlantic Command

25th Anti-Aircraft Troop, Type "L", RCA, Serial 738, mobilized under General Order 97/42 (Effective 17th February 1942), for service in the Saint John, N.B. Defences, under Headquarters Saint John Defences.

25th Anti-Aircraft Troop, Type L, RCA, Serial 738, was redesignated 25th Anti-Aircraft Battery, Type 2L, RCA, Serial 738, under General Order 257/42 (Effective 15th May 1942).

25th Anti-Aircraft Battery Type "2L", RCA, Serial 738, was redesignated 25th Anti-Aircraft Battery Type "3L", RCA, Serial 738, under General Order 366/43 (Effective 15th June 1943).

25th Anti-Aircraft Battery Type "3L", RCA, Serial 738, was redesignated 125th Anti-Aircraft Battery (Type 3L), RCA, Serial 738, under General Order 412/43 (Effective 1st September 1943).

25th Battery and 125th Battery served with 22nd Anti-Aircraft Regiment RCA, under Headquarters Saint John Defences and its later designation, Headquarters Defended Port of Saint John, in Atlantic Command.

Headquarters 22nd Anti-Aircraft Regiment RCA disbanded under General Order 208/45 (Effective 1st September 1944). 125th Anti-Aircraft Battery, Type 3L, RCA, Serial 738, received authorization to disband under General order 208/45 (Effective 20th February 1945).

* * *

128th HAA Battery RCA — Postwar Permanent Force

The Battery mobilized as 103rd Heavy Battery RCA, Serial 430, under General Order 71/41 (Effective 15th January 1941), and was redesignated 103rd Coast Battery RCA, 1st June 1942.

The Battery manned the Forts at Cape Spear, Amherst and Chain Rock, in the St. John's Newfoundland Defences.

103rd Coast Battery RCA was redesignated 128th Heavy Anti-Aircraft Battery RCA, under General Order 138/46 (Effective 1st March 1946), and 128th Heavy Anti-Aircraft Battery RCA, was embodied in the Postwar Permanent Force, under General Order 158/46 (Effective 27th June 1946).

* * *

129th LAA Battery RCA — Postwar Permanent Force

33rd Anti-Aircraft Troop RCA, Serial 757, mobilized under General Order 97/42 (Effective 17th February 1942) and was redesignated 33rd Anti-Aircraft Battery the following April.

The battery served with 30th Anti-Aircraft Regiment RCA at Tofino and Ucluelet, Vancouver Island, then with the disbanding of Headquarters 30th Anti-Aircraft Regiment RCA, the battery manned sites at Fort Belmont, Esquimalt Fortress.

33rd Anti-Aircraft Battery, Type "4L", RCA, Serial 757, was redesignated 129th Light Anti-Aircraft Battery RCA, under General Order 138/46 (Effective 1st March 1946), and became a component of the Postwar Permanent Force, under General Order 158/46 (Effective 27th June 1946).

* * *

146th AA Battery RCA — Serial 784 — Atlantic Command

46th Anti-Aircraft Troop, Type L RCA, Serial 784, mobilized under General Order 181/42 (Effective 13th April 1942).

46th Anti-Aircraft Troop became a component of 22nd Anti-Aircraft Regiment RCA, serving at Moncton, under Headquarters Saint John Defences, in New Brunswick.

46th Anti-Aircraft Troop, Type L, RCA, Serial 784, was redesignated 46th Anti-Aircraft Battery Type "3L", RCA, Serial 784, under General Order 366/43 (Effective 15th June 1943).

46th Anti-Aircraft Battery Type "3L", RCA, Serial 784, was redesignated 146th Anti-Aircraft Battery (Type 3L), RCA, Serial 784, under General Order 412/43 (Effective 1st September 1943), and served with 21st Anti-Aircraft Regiment RCA, Halifax.

146th Anti-Aircraft Battery Type 3L, RCA, Serial 784, Headquarters 21st Anti-Aircraft Regiment RCA, Headquarters Defended Port of Saint John, and Headquarters Atlantic Command were authorized to disband under General Order 305/45 (Effective 31st July 1945).

*   *   *

148th AA Battery RCA — Serial 787 — "W" Force

48th Anti-Aircraft Battery, Type 2L, RCA, Serial 787, mobilized under General Order 234/42 (Effective 1st May 1942), and became a component of 25th Anti-Aircraft Regiment RCA upon its forming 1st June 1942.

The battery served at St. John's-Torbay, under Headquarters St. John's Defences (Newfoundland).

48th Anti-Aircraft Battery, Type 2L, RCA, Serial 787, was redesignated 148th Anti-Aircraft Battery (Type 2L), RCA, Serial 787, under General Order 412/43 (Effective 1st September 1943), and the battery continued to serve under Headquarters St. John's Defences and its later designation, Headquarters Defended Port of St. John's.

148th Anti-Aircraft Battery, Type 2L, RCA, Serial 787, received authorization to disband under General Order 305/45 (Effective 31st July 1945). Headquarters 25th Anti-Aircraft Regiment RCA also disbanded at this time, and "W" Force Brigade Headquarters disbanded under General Order 227/46 (Effective 30th July 1946).

*   *   *

154th AA Battery RCA — Serial 793 — St. John's, Nfld., "W" Force

54th Anti-Aircraft Battery, Type 2H, RCA, Serial 793, mobilized under General Order 256/42 (Effective 15th May 1942), and became a component of 25th Anti-Aircraft Regiment RCA upon its forming 1st June 1942.

54th Battery served at St. John's-Torbay, under Headquarters St. John's Defences (Newfoundland).

54th Anti-Aircraft Battery, Type 2H, RCA, Serial 793, was redesignated 154th Anti-Aircraft Battery (Type 2H), RCA, Serial 793, under General Order 412/43 (Effective 1st September 1943). The Battery continued to serve under Headquarters St. John's Defences, and its later designation, Headquarters Defended Port of St. John's.

"A" Troop, 154th Bty is listed on manning duty at Pennywell Rd Site, and "B" Troop, 154th Bty manning South Side Hills Site, under 25th AA Regiment, Defended Port of St. John's (Nfld), "W" Force, in Records of #1 CRLE — Atlantic Command — AA Radars — Time in Op Condition Jan 1944 — July 1945.

154th Anti-Aircraft Battery, Type 2H, RCA, Serial 793, along with Headquarters 25th Anti-Aircraft Regiment RCA, and Headquarters Atlantic Command, received authorization to disband under General Order 305/45 (Effective 31st July 1945).

*   *   *

SECTION II

ANTI-TANK ARTILLERY

Section II includes anti-tank batteries of 1st Canadian Corps, 2nd Canadian Corps, 1st, 2nd and 3rd Canadian Infantry Divisions, 4th and 5th Canadian Armoured Divisions, 6th and 7th Divisions, Home Defence, No. 1 Anti-Tank Training Battery, First Canadian Army 2 Pr. School, Beachy Head and Michel Dean Anti-Tank Ranges, the Anti-Tank Companies RCA with 6th Division, Canadian Army Pacific Force, the reconstituted anti-tank batteries of the Canadian Army Occupational Force, and 127th Anti-Tank Battery RCA of the Postwar Permanent Force.

3rd Anti-Tank Regiment RCA of 3rd Division became the first anti-tank regiment to mobilize with its own slate of four batteries. Headquarters of 1st and 2nd Anti-Tank Regiments RCA, CASF, of 1st and 2nd Divisions respectively, were authorized to mobilize as components of the Canadian Active Service Force under General Order 135/39, 1st September 1939, with no allotted batteries. Field batteries mobilized under Headquarters of 1st and 2nd Army Field Brigades RCA, CASF, 1st September 1939, were moved under the anti-tank regiment headquarters and redesignated anti-tank batteries.

4th Anti-Tank Regiment RCA, originally with 4th Division, moved to 1st (Redesignated 5th Canadian (Armoured) Division), in 1941, and 5th Anti-Tank Regiment RCA joined 4th Division later in the year. 4th Division was converted to an armoured division, January 1942, and required one field regiment only in its Support Group, creating a surplus of field regiments and batteries.

3rd Battery had mobilized as a hyphenated battery with 15th Field Regiment

RCA, 4th Division, CASF, then was given individual identity and later in the year joined 18th Field Regiment RCA, 4th Division. 18th Field Regiment RCA became 2nd Medium Regiment RCA and 3rd Field Battery became 3rd Anti-Tank Battery, 5th Anti-Tank Regiment RCA in 4th Division.

It is interesting to note that three regiments later, 3rd Battery was still with 4th Division.

6th Anti-Tank Regiment RCA serving as 6th Division Anti-Tank Regiment, Home Defence, shed its Home Defence role and arrived overseas 1st September 1943, to serve as 2nd Canadian Corps Anti-Tank Regiment.

7th Anti-Tank Regiment RCA was formed in England in 1941, utilizing battery numbers left surplus upon the War Establishment of field regiments being changed from hyphenated batteries to three batteries. 7th Anti-Tank Regiment RCA served as 1st Canadian Corps Anti-Tank Regiment in Italy and NW Europe.

8th Anti-Tank Regiment RCA mobilized as 7th Division Anti-Tank Regiment, Home Defence, in May 1942 and served until May 1943, then was redesignated 28th Field Regiment RCA, remaining with 7th Division.

Of the three home defence divisions, 8th Division differed in that the division mobilized without an anti-tank regiment and served throughout without this anti-tank support. However, the conversion of 8th Anti-Tank Regiment RCA to 28th Field Regiment RCA in May 1943 and the departure overseas of 6th Anti-Tank Regiment RCA toward the end of August, all home defence divisions were without anti-tank regiments.

No. 1 Anti-Tank Training Battery RCA was formed as a component of 1 Canadian Training Brigade Group at Debert, Nova Scotia, to upgrade the general standard of reinforcements before proceeding overseas.

An Anti-Tank Company RCA mobilized with 1st, 2nd and 3rd Infantry Regiments of 6th Division, Canadian Army Pacific Force (CAPF). "VJ" Day intervened, and the CAPF disbanded.

Anti-tank batteries also served with the reconstituted 3rd Division, Canadian Army Occupational Force (CAOF) June 1945 to May 1946, in Germany

*   *   *

No. 1 Anti-Tank Training Battery RCA — Debert, N.S.

No. 1 Anti-Tank Training Battery RCA, mobilized under General Order 419/44 (Effective 1st October 1943).

The battery was formed as a component of 1 Canadian Training Brigade Group at Debert to upgrade the general standard of reinforcements before proceeding overseas.

Anti-tank training was carried out to the battery level beginning with detachment training in Phase I, troop training in Phase II and Phase III, culminating with battery training in Phase IV.

The training was as close to battle conditions as possible in his own corps and designed to acquaint the reinforcement with the overall picture in battle.

No. 1 Anti-Tank Training Battery RCA, disbanded under General Order 425/45 (Effective 14th December 1945).

* * *

Anti-Tank Companies RCA — CAPF

An Anti-Tank Company RCA mobilized with 1st, 2nd and 3rd Canadian Infantry Regiments, 6th Canadian Infantry Division, Canadian Army Pacific Force (CAPF).

With the arrival of "VJ" Day, the Anti-Tank Companies RCA of 1st, 2nd and 3rd Canadian Infantry Regiments were authorized to disband under General Order 425/45 (Effective 1st November 1945).

* * *

Anti-Tank Batteries RCA — CAOF

Reconstituted Anti-Tank Batteries RCA of the reconstituted 3rd Canadian Infantry Division mobilized for service with the Canadian Army Occupational Force (CAOF) in Germany following the cessation of hostilities in NW Europe.

2nd 4th Anti-Tank Battery, 2nd 52nd Anti-Tank Battery, 2nd 94th Anti-Tank Battery and 2nd 105th Anti-Tank Battery comprised 2nd 3rd Anti-Tank Regiment RCA, authorized under General Order 319/45 (Effective 1st June 1945), and disbanded under General Order 201/46 (Effective 14th May 1946).

* * *

First Canadian Army 2 Pr. School, Cdn Army (Overseas)

War Diary — "Approval was granted for the formation, on a temporary basis, of this Unit, effective 18 Jun 42 for training of personnel of Infantry and Motor Bns and Recce Regiments in the handling of the 2 pr A/Tk Gun". Personnel, 9 officers and 51 other ranks, were drawn from Reinforcements and Field Units RCA.

The school operated on a Field Return basis under command CCRA, 1 Cdn Corps for all purposes. The school was located at Birling Gap Hotel, Sussex.

First Canadian Army 2 Pr. School officially closed 17th October 1942 upon receiving a letter from H.Q. First Canadian Army authorizing its discontinuance.

* * *

Beachy Head & Michel Dean A. Tk Ranges

Beachy Head & Michel Dean A. Tk Ranges began operating 1st June/43, however, the official date was 14th Jan/43. 2 Pdr, 6 Pdr, 25 Pdr guns were fired on the Range with Inf Bns, Arty Regts, Armd Units.

Beachy Head & Michel Dean A/T Ranges were redesignated Beachy Head Ranges 7th May/43 to include 25 pdr, 17 pdr, 6 pdr, 2 pdr, Dive Bomber & Sub Calibre Range. Beachy Head Ranges operated until 31 July/43.

The following is an excerpt from the unpublished History of 1 Canadian School of Artillery (Overseas), 21 Nov 1942 to 21 June 1945 — "Beachy Head Ranges was actually composed of three Ranges: Michel Dean, Belle Toute and Shooters Bottom.

The Range started life in the Fall of 1942 as a 2 pr. School. Between the Fall of 1942 and Aug 1943 the Range was operated by H.Q. RCA First Cdn Army. It was a responsibility which this H.Q. was not equipped to handle and therefore it was handed over to the school on 10 Aug 43.

It was found that Michel Dean Range was no longer required after Shooters Bottom Range was completed in July 1944. The range was therefore closed as an A/Tk Range and converted into an infantry assault course".

* * *

3rd Anti-Tank Battery RCA, Gananoque — Serial 1992D — 4th Div

The combined 3rd/47th Field Battery RCA, CASF, Serial 905C, mobilized under General Order 184/40 (Effective 24th May 1940) with the original 15th Field Regiment RCA, CASF, 4th Division, CASF, in the era of combined battery field regiments.

3rd Battery regained individual identity under General Order 85/41 (Effective 27th February 1941), to become 3rd (Gananoque) Field Battery RCA, Serial 905C and joined 18th Field Regiment RCA in 4th Division. Field regiments had recently reorganized to comprise three field batteries.

Headquarters, 18th Field Regiment RCA, Serial 982, mobilized under General

Order 160/41 (Effective 10th May 1941) and replaced 17th Field Regiment RCA in 4th Division.

18th Field Regiment RCA and its three batteries congregated at Camp Sussex, New Brunswick, with 3rd Field Battery arriving early November 1941 to join the regiment.

4th Division was converted to an armoured division, authorized under General Order 132/42 (Effective 26th January 1942). The armoured division required one field regiment only in the Support Group and 15th Field Regiment RCA remained with the division. 16th Field Regiment RCA and 18th Field Regiment RCA became expendable.

3rd (Gananoque) Field Battery RCA, Serial 905C, was redesignated 3rd Anti-Tank Battery RCA, Serial 1992D, under General Order 132/42 (Effective 26th January 1942). The battery joined 5th Anti-Tank Regiment RCA, and continued to serve with 4th Division in its armoured role.

5th Anti-Tank Regiment RCA assembled at Sussex, New Brunswick in early March 1942, and remained until the end of June when the regiment departed Sussex for Halifax, Nova Scotia.

3rd Anti-Tank Battery, 5th Anti-Tank Regiment RCA, 4th (Armoured) Division, departed for overseas 3rd June 1942 on board the Duchess of York, and disembarked at Liverpool, England, 13th June 1942.

3rd Anti-Tank Battery with 5th Anti-Tank Regiment RCA landed in Normandy on the 26th and 27th of July 1944, then with 4th Canadian Armoured Division under 2nd Canadian Corps, moved to the Caen sector on the 30th of July. On the 31st of July 1944, 2nd Canadian Corps and its components came under command of First Canadian Army.

3rd Anti-Tank Battery RCA, equipped with 17 pounder towed anti-tank guns, served in France, Belgium, Holland, and Germany, then with cessation of hostilities, received authorization to disband under General Order 71/46 (Effective 10th December 1945).

*   *   *

4th Anti-Tank Battery RCA, Peterborough — Serial 708B — 3rd Div

4th Anti-Tank Battery RCA, CASF, Serial 708B, mobilized with 3rd Anti-Tank Regiment RCA, CASF, Headquarters 3rd Division, CASF, under General Order 184/40 (Effective 24th May 1940).

4th Anti-Tank Battery remained six weeks at Peterborough, then moved to the

Armouries at Lindsay, Ontario, where the battery remained until proceeding to Debert, Nova Scotia, where the Regiment assembled on the 12th of February 1941.

4th Anti-Tank Battery, 3rd Anti-Tank Regiment RCA, departed for overseas 9th October 1941 on board the Andes, and disembarked at Liverpool, England, 18th October 1941.

"C" Troop, 4th Anti-Tank Battery landed in Normandy on D-Day, 6th June 1944, with the assaulting 3rd Canadian Infantry Division, attached to 1 British Corps, Second British Army.

"C" Troop, the self-propelled troop, attached to 105th Anti-Tank Battery, 3rd Anti-Tank Regiment RCA, landed in support of 9th Canadian Infantry Brigade, 3rd Canadian Infantry Division, and the towed troops of the battery landed the following evening.

On the 30th June 1944, with the bridgehead secure, troops returned to their respective batteries and the regiment resumed normal organization.

3rd Canadian Infantry Division moved to 2nd Canadian Corps upon the Corps assuming an operational role, then with 2nd Canadian Corps, came under command of First Canadian Army on the 31st of July 1944, and served in France, Belgium, Holland, and Germany.

4th Anti-Tank Battery, RCA served until cessation of hostilities and received authorization to disband under General Order 52/46 (Effective 14th November 1945).

A reconstituted battery, the 2nd 4th Anti-Tank Battery RCA, 2nd 3rd Anti-Tank Regiment RCA, mobilized with the reconstituted 3rd Canadian Infantry Division, under General Order 319/45 (Effective 1st June 1945), for service with the Canadian Army Occupational Force (CAOF), and following occupational duty in Germany with 30 British Corps, 2nd 4th Anti-Tank Battery RCA was authorized to disband under General Order 201/46 (Effective 14th May 1946).

*   *   *

10th Anti-Tank Battery RCA — Serial 1414B — 7th Division

A cadre of NCOs reported to Hamilton from Military District No. 2, the Lincoln and Welland Regiment and 8th Field Brigade RCA, to form 10th Anti-Tank Battery RCA, Serial 1414B.

10th Anti-Tank Battery RCA, Serial 1414B, mobilized under General Order

309/42 (Effective 12th May 1942), to serve with 8th Anti-Tank Regiment RCA, 7th Division, Home Defence, Eastern Canada, and served at Petawawa and Sussex.

10th Anti-Tank Battery RCA, Serial 1414B, received authorization to disband under General Order 292/43 (Effective 15th May 1943), upon 8th Anti-Tank Regiment RCA being redesignated 28th Field Regiment RCA. — (War Diary 28th Field Regiment RCA).

* * *

11th Anti-Tank Battery RCA — Serial 1414C — 7th Division.

A cadre of NCOs reported to Montreal from Military District No. 4 to form 11th Anti-Tank Battery RCA.

The Battery mobilized under General Order 309/42 (Effective 12th May 1942), with 8th Anti-Tank Regiment RCA, 7th Division, Home Defence, Eastern Canada, and served at Petawawa, Ontario, and Sussex, New Brunswick.

11th Anti-Tank Battery RCA, Serial 1414C, received authorization to disband under General Order 292/43 (Effective 15th May 1943), upon 8th Anti-Tank Regiment RCA being redesignated 28th Field Regiment RCA. — (28th Field Regiment RCA War Diary).

* * *

12th Anti-Tank Battery RCA — Serial 1414D — 7th Division

A cadre of NCOs reported to Simcoe from Military District No. 2, the Algonquin Regiment and 25th Field Brigade, to form 12th Anti-Tank Battery RCA, Serial 1414D, authorized to mobilize under General Order 309/42 (Effective 12th May 1942).

12th Anti-Tank Battery served with 8th Anti-Tank Regiment RCA, 7th Division, Home Defence, Eastern Canada, and was stationed at Petawawa Camp, Ontario, and Sussex Camp, New Brunswick.

12th Anti-Tank Battery RCA, Serial 1414D, received authorization to disband Under General Order 292/43 (Effective 15th May 1943), and the regiment became 28th Field Regiment RCA.

* * *

13th Anti-Tank Battery RCA — Serial 1414E — 7th Division

A cadre of NCOs from Military District No. 2, The Dufferin & Haldimand Rifles and 8th Field Brigade RCA, proceeded to Hamilton to form 13th Anti-Tank Battery RCA.

The battery mobilized under General Order 309/42 (Effective 12th May 1942), with 8th Anti-Tank Regiment RCA, 7th Division, Home Defence, Eastern Canada, and served at Petawawa and Sussex.

13th Anti-Tank Battery RCA, Serial 1414E, received authorization to disband under General Order 292/43 (Effective 15th May 1943), and the regiment became 28th Field Regiment RCA.

*　　*　　*

14th A/T Battery RCA — Serial 1992E — Formed in England — 4 Div

The number of anti-tank batteries in an armoured division anti-tank regiment was increased to four from three and the new anti-tank battery formed in England to serve with 5th Anti-Tank Regiment RCA, 4th Canadian Armoured Division was designated 14th Anti-Tank Battery RCA.

14th Anti-Tank Battery RCA, Serial 1992E, mobilized in England, was authorized under General Order 333/43 (Effective 1st January 1943). The new battery which was often referred to as the "Rainbow" Battery due to the variety of patches worn by personnel transferred from other formations, became a 17 pounder battery and the three established batteries retained their 6 pounders.

During August 1943, 14th and 96th Batteries were designated Self-Propelled and US M-10, 3 inch SPs began to arrive. The regiment now comprised two self-propelled batteries and two towed 6 pounder equipped batteries. The 6 pounders were exchanged for 17 pounder towed guns later in the year.

Early in July 1944 the Self-Propelled batteries exchanged the 3 inch SPs for 17 pounder equipped Self-Propelled M-10s, and went into action so-equipped.

14th Anti-Tank Battery, 5th Anti-Tank Regiment RCA, 4th Canadian Armoured Division, landed in Normandy 23rd July 1944 and moved into the line under 2nd Canadian Corps, south of Caen on the 29th of July.

The battery, regiment, and 4th Canadian Armoured Division along with 2nd Canadian Corps, moved under command of First Canadian Army on the 31st of July 1944.

14th Anti-Tank Battery RCA served in France, Belgium, Holland, and Germany, then with the cessation of hostilities received authorization to disband under General Order 71/46 (Effective 10th December 1945).

*　　*　　*

15th A/T Battery RCA, Toronto — Serial 506D — 1st Cdn Corps

15th Anti-Tank Battery RCA of Toronto, mobilized as 15th Field Battery

RCA, CASF, Serial 211, with Headquarters of 3rd Army Field Brigade RCA, CASF, under General Order 135/39, 1st September 1939.

15th Field Battery RCA, CASF, with Headquarters of 3rd Army Field Brigade RCA, CASF, departed for overseas 30th January 1940 on the Aquitania, in the 3rd Flight and disembarked at Gourock, Scotland, 8th February 1940.

Headquarters of 3rd Army Field Brigade RCA, CASF, was redesignated Headquarters, 11th Army Field Regiment RCA, CASF, under General Order 44/40 (Effective 12th February 1940), and 15th Field Battery RCA, CASF, Serial 211, combined with 9th (Toronto) Field Battery (H) RCA, CASF, Serial 213, to become 9th/15th Field Battery RCA, CASF, Serial 210, in a two battery regiment.

11th Army Field Regiment reorganized to comprise three batteries and 15th Battery regained individual identity as 15th Field Battery RCA under General Order 45/41 (Effective 1st January 1941).

15th Field Battery RCA, Serial 211, was redesignated 15th Anti-Tank Battery RCA, Serial 211, under General Order 57/41 (Effective 1st January 1941) and was posted to 7th Anti-Tank Regiment RCA, upon its forming on the 25th July 1941 to serve as 1st Canadian Corps Anti-Tank Regiment.

15th Anti-Tank Battery RCA was allotted Serial Number 506D in an alignment of Serial Numbers with 7th Anti-Tank Regiment RCA, Serial 506, under General Order 54/42 (Effective 22nd December 1941).

Early September 1943 the battery was issued twelve Self-Propelled 3 inch M 10s and served as an SP battery throughout.

15th Anti-Tank Battery sailed for the Mediterranean on board the Scythia, from Avonmouth near Bristol, 12th November 1943, and disembarked at Algiers, N. Africa, 21st November 1943.

On the 4th of December 1943, 15th Battery embarked at Algiers and disembarked at Catania, Sicily, 8th December 1943, then crossed to the Italian mainland on the 3rd of January 1944 to begin its role with 1st Canadian Corps in battle.

7th Anti-Tank Regiment RCA served in Italy as Corps Anti-Tank Regiment until early 1945, then transferred with 1st Canadian Corps to NW Europe.

15th Anti-Tank Battery RCA departed from Italy via Naples, 25th February 1945 on board the Empire Pride and disembarked 27th February 1945 at Marseilles, France.

15th Battery joined the action with First Canadian Army in NW Europe, 7th April 1945 near Arnhem, Holland. First Canadian Army now had both 1st Canadian Corps and 2nd Canadian Corps under its wing for the knock-out blow.

15th Anti-Tank Battery RCA, Serial 506D, served until cessation of hostilities and received authorization to disband under General Order 321/45 (Effective 27th June 1945). Volunteers for the Canadian Army Pacific Force (CAPF) departed for Canada, other personnel were posted to divisional units from the Military Districts of their enlistment for the return to Canada, or proceeded to the Canadian Army Occupational Force (CAOF), to remain on the Continent until 1946.

*   *   *

16th A/T Battery RCA - Serial 908F — Formed in England — 5 Div

A new War Establishment increased to four from three the number of batteries in an armoured division anti-tank regiment.

The new battery in 4th Anti-Tank Regiment RCA, 5th Canadian Armoured Division was designated 16th Anti-Tank Battery RCA.

16th Anti-Tank Battery RCA, Serial 908F, mobilized in England, under General Order 333/43 (Effective 1st January 1943), and was to serve as a towed battery equipped with 6 pounder and 17 pounder anti-tank guns in 4th Anti-Tank Regiment RCA, 5th Canadian Armoured Division.

16th Anti-Tank Battery, 4th Anti-Tank Regiment RCA, 5th Canadian Armoured Division, boarded the Samaria, at Avonmouth, near Bristol, upon the transfer of Headquarters 1st Canadian Corps, Corps Troops, 5th Canadian Armoured Division, and 1st Canadian AGRA to the Mediterranean Theatre of Operations.

The Samaria sailed 15th November 1943 and docked at Algiers on the 26th November, where the regiment disembarked. The self-propelled batteries remained at Algiers, the two towed batteries — the 16th and 49th, reembarked for Phillipville, Algeria, on the Ville D Oran, then reembarked on the Cameronia, to disembark at Naples, Italy on the 1st of December 1943.

1st Canadian Corps became operational early 1944 in Italy and 16th Anti-Tank Battery joined the action, 5th February 1944. The division, regiment and 16th Battery served in Italy with 1st Canadian Corps until early 1945, then moved with the Corps to join First Canadian Army in NW Europe.

16th Anti-Tank Battery RCA departed from Italy via Leghorn on the 22nd of February 1945 and arrived at Marseilles, France, on the 25th of February 1945.

16th Battery joined First Canadian Army, 6th April, in NW Europe and participated in the action in Holland, 16th April 1945, in the Arnhem-Apeldoorn area. The battery also assumed an infantry role when required.

16th Anti-Tank Battery RCA served until cessation of hostilities and received authorization to disband under General Order 71/46 (Effective 28th November 1945).

*   *   *

18th Anti-Tank Battery RCA, Regina, Sask — Serial 170B — 2nd Division

18th Field Battery RCA, CASF, Serial 80, mobilized with Headquarters of 2nd Army Field Brigade RCA, CASF, Serial 79, Corps Troops mobilizing with 1st Division, under General Order 135/39, 1st September 1939.

Headquarters 2nd Army Field Brigade RCA, Serial 79, assumed the title and Serial Number of 2nd Anti-Tank Regiment RCA, CASF, Serial 170, under General Order 201/39 (Effective 1st October 1939), to serve with 2nd Division, CASF.

18th Field Battery was redesignated 18th Anti-Tank Battery RCA, under General Order 75/40 (Effective 1st December 1939). The batteries converged on Camp Shilo, Manitoba in May 1940, where 2nd Anti-Tank Regiment came into being.

18th Anti-Tank Battery, 2nd Anti-Tank Regiment RCA, departed for overseas 27th August 1940 on board the Duchess of York, and disembarked at Gourock, Scotland, 4th September 1940.

18th Anti-Tank Battery RCA retained Serial Number 80, under General Order 230/40, October 1940, then under General Order 54/42 (Effective 22nd December 1941), 18th Anti-Tank Battery RCA was allotted Serial Number 170B, with 2nd Anti-Tank Regiment RCA.

18th Anti-Tank Battery landed in Normandy on the 7th of July 1944 with 2nd Anti-Tank Regiment RCA, 2nd Canadian Infantry Division and moved to the Caen front with 2nd Canadian Corps.

Headquarters First Canadian Army became operational on the 23rd of July 1944, and on the 31st of July 1944, the division, regiment, and 18th Battery with 2nd Canadian Corps, moved under command.

On the 3rd of September, following the capture of Dieppe, 2nd Canadian Infantry Division paused for a memorial service in the cemetery and 18th Anti-Tank Battery paraded with the division through the streets of the city, then rejoined the action under First Canadian Army, serving in France, Belgium, Holland, and Germany.

18th Anti-Tank Battery RCA served until cessation of hostilities and received authorization to disband under General Order 52/46 (Effective 22nd September 1945).

*   *   *

20th Anti-Tank Battery RCA, Lethbridge, Alta. — Serial 170C — 2 Div

20th Anti-Tank Battery RCA, mobilized as 20th Field Battery RCA, CASF, Serial 81, with Headquarters of 2nd Army Field Brigade RCA, CASF, under General Order 135/39, 1st September 1939.

Headquarters of 2nd Army Field Brigade RCA, CASF, Serial 79, assumed the title and Serial Number of 2nd Anti-Tank Regiment RCA, CASF, Serial 170, under General Order 201/39 (Effective 1st October 1939).

2nd Anti-Tank Regiment, less batteries, had received authorization to mobilize with the Canadian Active Service Force (CASF) under General Order 135/39, 1st September 1939.

20th Field Battery RCA, was redesignated 20th Anti-Tank Battery RCA, under General Order 75/40 (Effective 1st December 1939).

20th Anti-Tank Battery, now with 2nd Anti-Tank Regiment RCA, CASF, 2nd Division, CASF, concentrated at Camp Shilo, Manitoba, in May 1940, then moved eastward to board the Duchess of York at Halifax. The convoy sailed 27th August 1940 and the regiment disembarked at Gourock, Scotland, 4th September 1940.

Serial Number 81 was confirmed for 20th Anti-Tank Battery RCA, CASF, under General Order 230/40, 15th October 1940, however, under General Order 54/42 (Effective 22nd December 1941), the battery Serial Number was changed to 170C.

20th Anti-Tank Battery landed in Normandy, 7th July 1944, with 2nd Anti-Tank Regiment RCA, 2nd Canadian Infantry Division, and moved to the Carpiquet area under 2nd Canadian Corps, then as a component of 2nd Canadian Corps, came under command of First Canadian Army, 31st July 1944 on the Caen front.

2nd Canadian Infantry Division took part in the vicious fighting in the breakout from Caen, and the closing of the Falaise Gap, then with the capture of Dieppe, the Division paused for a service of remembrance in the cemetery, 3rd September 1944, followed by a divisional parade through the streets of the city.

20th Anti-Tank Battery RCA, with the Regiment, rejoined the action under First Canadian Army and served in France, Belgium, Holland, and Germany.

20th Anti-Tank Battery RCA served until cessation of hostilities and received authorization to disband under General Order 52/46 (Effective 22nd September 1945).

*   *   *

23rd Anti-Tank Battery RCA, Calgary, Alta. — Serial 170E — 2 Div.

23rd Field Battery (H), RCA, CASF, Serial 83, with Headquarters of 2nd Army Field Brigade RCA, CASF, Serial 79, mobilized under General Order 135/39, 1st September 1939.

Headquarters of 2nd Army Field Brigade RCA, CASF, Serial 79, assumed the title and Serial Number of 2nd Anti-Tank Regiment RCA, CASF, Serial 170, under General Order 201/39 (Effective 1st October 1939). The batteries remained designated Field Batteries with 2nd Anti-Tank Regiment RCA, CASF.

2nd Anti-Tank Regiment RCA, CASF, less batteries had mobilized as a component of the Canadian Active Service Force (CASF) under General Order 135/39, 1st September 1939. The batteries of 2nd Army Field Brigade remained field batteries with 2nd Anti-Tank Regiment RCA, CASF, until redesignated anti-tank batteries under General order 75/40 (Effective 1st December 1939).

23rd Anti-Tank Battery, now with 2nd Anti-Tank Regiment RCA, CASF, 2nd Division, CASF, concentrated at Camp Shilo, Manitoba, in May 1940, then moved eastward to board the Duchess of York at Halifax. The convoy sailed 27th August 1940 and the regiment disembarked at Gourock, Scotland, on the 4th of September 1940.

Serial Number 83 was confirmed for 23rd Anti-Tank Battery RCA, CASF, under General Order 230/40, 15th October 1940, then the Serial Number was changed to 170E, under General Order 54/42 (Effective 22nd December 1941).

23rd Anti-Tank Battery landed in Normandy, 7th July 1944, with 2nd Anti-Tank Regiment RCA, 2nd Canadian Infantry Division and moved to the Carpiquet area with 2nd Canadian Corps. The corps, division, regiment and battery moved under command of First Canadian Army on the Caen front, 31st July 1944.

With the breakout from Caen effected, and the closing of the Falaise Gap, 2nd Canadian Division moved on to Dieppe, where on the 3rd of September 1944, following the capture of the city, the division paused for a service of remembrance. 23rd Battery participated in the divisional parade through the streets of the city, then with the division returned to action under First Canadian Army and served in France, Belgium, Holland, and Germany.

23rd Anti-Tank Battery RCA served until cessation of hostilities and received authorization to disband under General Order 52/46 (Effective 22nd September 1945).

*   *   *

24th A/T Battery RCA, Toronto — Serial 908C — 5th Armd Division

24th Medium Battery RCA of Toronto, mobilized as 24th Anti-Tank Battery RCA, with 4th Anti-Tank Regiment RCA, CASF, 4th Division, CASF, under General Order 184/40 (Effective 24th May 1940).

From Toronto, the Battery moved to Hamilton, Listowel, and on to Petawawa Camp where the batteries were regimented, April 1941, following the transfer of 4th Anti-Tank Regiment RCA to 1st Canadian Armoured Division. 1st Canadian Armoured Division was authorized under General Order 88/41 (Effective 27th February 1941), and was redesignated 5th Canadian (Armoured) Division under General Order 135/41 (Effective 5th June 1941).

24th Anti-Tank Battery, 4th Anti-Tank Regiment RCA, 5th Canadian (Armoured) Division, sailed overseas on board the Aorangi, 7th October 1941, and disembarked at Glasgow, Scotland, on the 17th of October 1941).

Shortly after the regiment arrived overseas, 49th Anti-Tank Battery RCA adopted Serial Number 908C, and replaced 24th Anti-Tank Battery in the regiment, authorized under General Order 274/41 (Effective 14th September 1941) — (Back-Dated).

49th Anti-Tank Battery, 4th Anti-Tank Regiment RCA, 5th Canadian Armoured Division, sailed on the Samaria, from Avonmouth, near Bristol, bound for the Mediterranean, 15th November 1943, on operation "Timberwolf II."

The battery disembarked at Algiers, North Africa, reembarked for Phillipville, on the Ville de Oran, then reembarked on the Cameronian, disembarking at Naples, Italy, 1st December 1943.

49th Battery served as a towed battery with the regiment in Italy until early 1945, during which time 5th Canadian Armoured Division served as a component of 1st Canadian Corps.

Transfer of 1st Canadian Corps to NW Europe saw 49th Anti-Tank Battery depart from Italy via Leghorn, 23rd February 1945 and arrive at Marseilles, France, 25th February 1945.

The battery joined the action with First Canadian Army in NW Europe, 1st April 1945, in support of 11th Canadian Infantry Brigade, near Nijmegen, Holland.

49th Anti-Tank Battery RCA served until cessation of hostilities and received authorization to disband under General Order 71/46 (Effective 28th November 1945).

*   *   *

27th Anti-Tank Battery RCA, Montreal — Serial 20D — 1st Division

27th Field Battery (H), RCA, CASF, Serial 77, mobilized with Headquarters of 1st Army Field Brigade RCA, Corps Troops mobilizing with 1st Division, under General Order 135/39, 1st September 1939.

The field batteries of Headquarters of 1st Army Field Brigade RCA, CASF, Serial 74, were moved to 1st Anti-Tank Regiment RCA, CASF, Serial 20, under General Order 201/39 (Effective 1st October 1939).

The batteries remained designated field batteries until authorized to become anti-tank batteries under General Order 75/40 (Effective 1st December 1939).

27th Anti-Tank Battery RCA, CASF, was allotted Serial Number 77, with 1st Anti-Tank Regiment RCA, CASF, Serial 20, under General Order 230/40, 15th October 1940.

The batteries and headquarters remained at their home stations until receiving embarkation notices, at which time personnel proceeded to Halifax to board the ships, 27th Battery the Orama, Headquarters with 51st Battery, the Almanzora, 57th and 90th Batteries, the Reina del Pacifico. The regiment was not to come together until its arrival overseas. The convoy, Troop Convoy 2, sailed 22nd December 1939, and the regiment disembarked on the 30th of December 1939 at Gourock, Scotland.

27th Battery again boarded ship and sailed for Brest, France, on the 14th of June 1940, but due to the deteriorating situation in France, returned to England the following day. In England, 1st Division, the regiment and 27th Battery served with 7th Corps, the Canadian Corps, and 1st Canadian Corps.

In a shuffle of serial numbers within the regiment, 27th Battery Serial Number was changed from 77, to 20D, under General Order 54/42 (Effective 1st January 1941).

27th Anti-Tank Battery, 1st Anti-Tank Regiment RCA, sailed for the Mediterranean, 28th June 1943 and landed in Sicily on the 10th of July 1943, with the assaulting 1st Canadian Infantry Division, 30 British Corps, British Eighth Army.

With the fall of Sicily the battery crossed to the Italian mainland, 5th September 1943, moving from 30 Corps to 13 British Corps, then joined 1st Canadian Corps upon the Corps becoming operational in 1944.

27th Battery departed from Italy via Leghorn and the regiment sailed at intervals beginning 9th March 1945, arriving at Marseilles, France, on the 11th of March 1945.

1st Anti-Tank Regiment RCA, 1st Canadian Infantry Division, with 1st Canadian Corps, joined the action in NW Europe under the command of First Canadian Army in Holland, 11th April 1945, and served until cessation of hostilities.

27th Anti-Tank Battery RCA received authorization to disband under General Order 401/45 (Effective 28th August 1945).

*   *   *

33rd A/T Battery RCA, Simcoe, Ontario — Serial 814B — 2nd Corps

33rd Anti-Tank Battery RCA, Serial 814B, mobilized under General Order 147/42 (Effective 18th March 1942), with 6th Anti-Tank Regiment RCA, 6th Division, Home Defence.

6th Anti-Tank Regiment RCA with its four component batteries assembled at Petawawa in April 1942. In January 1943 the regiment was selected for overseas service and moved to Debert, Nova Scotia, on the 26th of May 1943, prior to going overseas.

33rd Battery departed for overseas 27th August 1943 on board the Queen Mary, and disembarked at Gourock, Scotland, on the 1st of September 1943.

6th Anti-Tank Regiment RCA joined 2nd Canadian Corps as Corps Anti-Tank Regiment, and 33rd Battery became an (SP) Self-Propelled battery.

33rd Battery, 6th Anti-Tank Regiment RCA landed in Normandy on the 9th and 10th of July 1944 to assume its role with 2nd Canadian Corps in action. 33rd Battery deployed with 6th Canadian Infantry Brigade of 2nd Canadian Infantry Division, near the village of Ifs, on the 20th of July 1944. 2nd Canadian Corps at that time was under Second British Army.

2nd Canadian Corps came under command of First Canadian Army on the 31st of July 1944, and as components, 33rd Battery and the regiment served in France, Belgium, Holland, and Germany, culminating in the cessation of hostilities. The 8th of May 1945 was designated "VE" Day and the Canadian units prepared for the return to Canada.

33rd Battery saw service with 2nd Canadian Infantry Division, 3rd Canadian Infantry Division, 51st (Highland) Division, and was attached to 1st Anti-Tank Regiment RCA of 1st Canadian Infantry Division upon its arrival in NW Europe from Italy.

33rd Anti-Tank Battery RCA, Serial 814B, received authorization to disband under General Order 321/45 (Effective 23rd June 1945), in NW Europe.

*   *   *

49th Anti-Tank Battery RCA — Serial 908C — 5th Cdn Armoured Div.

24th Medium Battery RCA of Toronto, mobilized as 24th Anti-Tank Battery RCA, CASF, Serial 908C, under General Order 184/40 (Effective 24th May 1940), to serve with 4th Anti-Tank Regiment RCA, CASF, 4th Division, CASF.

4th Division units were diverted to 1st Canadian Armoured Division, redesignated 5th Canadian (Armoured) Division under General Order 135/41 (Effective 5th June 1941). 4th Anti-Tank Regiment RCA and 24th Anti-Tank Battery moved to the new formation.

24th Anti-Tank Battery, 4th Anti-Tank Regiment RCA, 5th Canadian (Armoured) Division, departed for overseas 7th October 1941 on board the Aorangi, and disembarked at Glasgow, Scotland, on the 17th of October 1941.

Two months after arriving overseas, 24th Anti-Tank Battery RCA, Serial 908C, was redesignated 49th Anti-Tank Battery RCA, Serial 908C, under General Order 274/41 (Effective 14th September 1941) — (Back-Dated). 49th Anti-Tank Battery served as a towed battery with 4th Anti-Tank Regiment RCA.

49th Battery sailed from Avonmouth 15th November 1943 on board the Samaria, bound for the Mediterranean on operation "Timberwolf II".

The Regiment disembarked at Algiers, N. Africa, 26th November 1943. Headquarters and the two towed batteries boarded the Ville de Oran to Phillipville, then reembarked on the Cameronian for Naples, Italy, where 49th Anti-Tank Battery disembarked on the 1st of December 1943.

The two self-propelled batteries arrived from North Africa to rejoin the regiment in Italy early in 1944.

49th Battery, with 4th Anti-Tank Regiment RCA, 5th Canadian Armoured Division, served in Italy until early 1945 as a component of 1st Canadian Corps, then moved with the corps to NW Europe.

On the 23rd of February 1945, 49th Battery departed Italy via Leghorn, and disembarked at Marseilles, France, on the 25th of February 1945.

The battery joined the action under First Canadian Army in NW Europe, in support of 11th Canadian Infantry Brigade of 5th Canadian Armoured Division, near Nijmegen, Holland, 1st April 1945, and served until cessation of hostilities.

49th Anti-Tank Battery RCA received authorization to disband under General Order 71/46 (Effective 28th November 1945).

*   *   *

51st A/T Battery RCA, Ottawa — Serial 20B — 1st Cdn Inf Div.

51st Field Battery RCA, CASF, Serial 75, mobilized with Headquarters of 1st Army Field Brigade RCA, CASF, Corps Troops mobilizing with 1st Division, under General Order 135/39, 1st September 1939.

The field batteries of Headquarters of 1st Army Field Brigade RCA, CASF, Serial 74, were aligned with 1st Anti-Tank Regiment RCA, CASF, Serial 20, under General Order 201/39 (Effective 1st October 1939).

51st Field Battery RCA was redesignated 51st Anti-Tank Battery RCA, under General Order 75/40 (Effective 1st December 1939). — (No Serial Number listed).

51st Anti-Tank Battery RCA, CASF, and Regimental Headquarters, 1st Anti-Tank Regiment RCA, CASF, 1st Division, CASF, departed for overseas 22nd December 1939 on board the Almanzora, in Troop Convoy 2, and disembarked at Greenock, Scotland, 30th December 1939. The regiment proceeded by train to the south of England and following a march from North Camp Station, Farnborough, Hampshire, RHQ and 51st Battery settled in at Lille Barracks.

As part of the 2nd British Expeditionary Force following the Dunkirk evacuation, 1st Canadian Division's 1st Brigade Group of which 51st Battery was a part, crossed the English Channel to Brest, France, between 11th and 14th June 1940. However, due to the deteriorating situation in France, the battery reembarked the following day and returned to England to prepare for the expected invasion.

In England the battery, regiment, and 1st Division served with 7th Corps, the Canadian Corps, and 1st Canadian Corps.

51st Battery Serial Number was changed from 75, to Serial 20B, under General Order 54/42 (Effective 1st January 1941), completing the transition to 1st Anti-Tank Regiment RCA.

51st Anti-Tank Battery, 1st Anti-Tank Regiment RCA sailed for the Mediterranean Theatre of Operations on the 28th of June 1943, and landed in Sicily with the assaulting 1st Canadian Infantry Division, 30 British Corps, British Eighth Army.

With the fall of Sicily 51st Battery crossed the Strait of Messina to the Italian mainland on the 5th of September 1943, moving from 30 Corps to 13 British Corps, British Eighth Army.

51st Anti-Tank Battery and 1st Anti-Tank Regiment RCA, with 1st Canadian Infantry Division, joined 1st Canadian Corps upon the corps becoming operational early 1944, in Italy, and served as a component until early 1945, then moved with the corps to NW Europe.

51st Battery departed from Italy via Leghorn, as the regiment sailed at intervals beginning 9th March 1945, arriving at Marseilles, France, on the 11th of March 1945.

The regiment joined the action in NW Europe under First Canadian Army in Holland, 11th April 1945, and served until the cessation of hostilities.

51st Anti-Tank Battery RCA received authorization to disband under General Order 401/45 (Effective 28th August 1945).

*   *   *

52nd A/T Battery RCA, Weymouth, N.S. — Serial 708D — 3rd Cdn Inf Div.

"Details" of 52nd Field Battery RCA, CASF, of Weymouth, Nova Scotia, were placed on Active Service in the Canadian Active Service Force, under General Order 142/39 (Effective 1st September 1939), for duty in Military District No. 6.

These "Details" were absorbed into the battery and 52nd Battery mobilized as 52nd Anti-Tank Battery RCA, CASF, Serial 708D, under General Order 184/40 (Effective 24th May 1940), with 3rd Anti-Tank Regiment RCA, CASF, 3rd Division, CASF.

The battery concentrated at Aldershot, Nova Scotia, from June until October 1940, then following several delays moved to Debert, Nova Scotia to spend the winter. The remainder of the regiment arrived at Debert in February 1941.

52nd Anti-Tank Battery, 3rd Anti-Tank Regiment RCA, 3rd Division, departed for overseas on board the Andes, 9th October 1941, and disembarked at Liverpool, England, 18th October 1941.

52nd Battery with the regiment landed in Normandy on D-Day, 6th June 1944 with the assaulting 3rd Canadian Infantry Division, 1 British Corps, Second British Army.

The two towed troops of 52nd Battery were joined by a towed troop of 6 pounders from 105th Battery and landed in support of 8th Canadian Infantry Brigade in the assault on the beaches.

The self-propelled troop of 52nd Battery was attached to 105th Battery and landed in support of 9th Brigade.

This organization remained until the end of June when the bridgehead was secure, enabling the troops to return to their respective batteries.

The division, regiment and battery joined 2nd Canadian Corps and on the 31st July 1944, 2nd Canadian Corps and its components came under command of First Canadian Army.

52nd Anti-Tank Battery RCA served in France, Belgium, Holland, and Germany until the cessation of hostilities and received authorization to disband under General Order 52/46 (Effective 14th November 1945).

A reconstituted 52nd Battery mobilized as 2nd 52nd Anti-Tank Battery RCA, with 2nd 3rd Anti-Tank Regiment RCA, in the reconstituted 3rd Canadian Infantry Division, authorized under General Order 319/45 (Effective 1st June 1945), and following service with the Canadian Army Occupational Force (CAOF) in Germany, 2nd 52nd Anti-Tank Battery RCA was authorized to disband under General Order 201/46 (Effective 14th May 1946).

*   *   *

56th A/T Battery RCA, Lindsay, Ontario — Serial 814D — 2nd Corps

56th Anti-Tank Battery RCA, Serial 814D, mobilized under General Order 147/42 (Effective 18th March 1942), with 6th Anti-Tank Regiment RCA, 6th Division, Home Defence.

The regiment assembled at Petawawa, then in January 1943, 6th Anti-Tank Regiment was selected for overseas service and the move to Debert, Nova Scotia, was completed 26th May.

56th Anti-Tank Battery, 6th Anti-Tank Regiment RCA, departed for overseas on board the Queen Mary, 27th August 1943, and disembarked 1st September 1943, at Gourock, Scotland.

6th Anti-Tank Regiment RCA, became Corps Anti-Tank Regiment, 2nd Canadian Corps, and upon going into action, comprised two towed batteries and two self-propelled batteries.

56th Battery equipped with twelve 3 inch M 10 Self-Propelled Anti-Tank guns, landed in Normandy with the regiment and 2nd Canadian Corps, 9th and 10th of July 1944, then moved to the concentration area, 12th July.

56th Battery joined the action on the Caen front, 30th July 1944, under command of 2nd Canadian Infantry Division, 2nd Canadian Corps.

2nd Canadian Corps moved under First Canadian Army, 31st July 1944 and 6th Anti-Tank Regiment RCA took part in the vicious fighting in the breakout from Caen, and the closing of the Falaise Gap.

Toward the end of August, 17 pounder SPs began arriving to replace the 3 inch M 10s. 56th Battery accompanied 3rd Canadian Infantry Division in the drive across France and on the 5th September joined 7th Recce Regiment in a drive for the Channel Ports, then assisted the division in the assaults on Boulogne, Cap Gris Nez and Calais. On the 7th of October the battery moved into Belgium, as 6th Anti-Tank Regiment prepared for the battle of the Scheldt.

During its time in action on the Continent, 56th Battery came under command of 2nd, 3rd Canadian Infantry Divisions, 4th Canadian Armoured Division, 51st (Highland) Division, 53rd (Welsh) Division, and Christmas 1944, came under command of the U.S. First Army during the Ardennes battle.

56th Anti-Tank Battery RCA served in France, Belgium, Holland, and Germany, then with cessation of hostilities received authorization to disband under General Order 321/45 (Effective 23rd June 1945), in NW Europe.

*   *   *

57th Anti-Tank Battery RCA, Quebec, P.Q. — Serial 20C — 1st Div.

57th Field Battery RCA, CASF, Serial 76, mobilized with Headquarters of 1st Army Field Brigade RCA, CASF, Corps Troops mobilizing with 1st Division, under General Order 135/39, 1st September 1939.

The field batteries of Headquarters of 1st Army Field Brigade RCA, CASF, Serial 74, aligned with 1st Anti-Tank Regiment RCA, CASF, Serial 20, under General Order 201/39 (Effective 1st October 1939).

57th Field Battery RCA, was redesignated 57th Anti-Tank Battery RCA, under General Order 75/40 (Effective 1st December 1939). — (The Serial Number was not listed).

The batteries remained in their respective cities until moving to the port of embarkation. 57th Anti-Tank Battery, 1st Anti-Tank Regiment RCA, 1st Division, CASF, boarded the Reina del Pacifico in Troop Convoy 2, and departed for overseas 22nd December 1939. 57th Battery disembarked at Greenock, Scotland, 30th December 1939 and proceeded South by train to the Aldershot area, Hampshire.

57th Battery sailed for Brest, France, 14th June 1940, but due to the deteriorating situation in France, returned to England the following day. In England the regiment served with 7th Corps, the Canadian Corps and 1st Canadian Corps.

In an alignment of serial numbers within the Regiment, 57th Battery Serial Number was changed from 76, to 20C, under General Order 54/42 (Effective 1st January 1941).

57th Anti-Tank Battery, 1st Anti-Tank Regiment RCA sailed for the Mediterranean on the 28th June 1943, and on the 5th of July the transport CC-1 was torpedoed and sunk with 57th Battery suffering casualties in killed and wounded.

On the 10th of July 1943, 1st Canadian Infantry Division, 30 Corps, British Eighth Army, landed in the assault on the Island of Sicily, with 1st Anti-Tank Regiment RCA going ashore on the Pachino Peninsula.

With the fall of Sicily, 57th Battery crossed to the Italian mainland, 5th September 1943, moving from 30 Corps to 13 British Corps, British Eighth Army.

The regiment, with the division, joined 1st Canadian Corps upon the corps becoming operational in 1944, and as a component, served in Italy until early 1945, then moved with the corps to NW Europe.

57th Battery departed from Italy via Leghorn, and the regiment sailed at intervals beginning 9th March, arriving at Marseilles, France, 11th March 1945.

1st Anti-Tank Regiment RCA joined the action in NW Europe under First Canadian Army in Holland, 11th April 1945, and served until cessation of hostilities.

57th Anti-Tank Battery RCA, received authorization to disband under General Order 401/45 (Effective 28th August 1945).

*   *   *

65th A/T Battery RCA, Grenfell — Serial 1992C — 4th Cdn Armd Div

65th Field Battery RCA of Grenfell, Saskatchewan, was converted to anti-tank and mobilized as 65th Anti-Tank Battery RCA, Serial 992C, under General Order 240/41 (Effective 5th September 1941), to serve with 5th Anti-Tank Regiment RCA, 4th Division.

Headquarters 4th Division was redesignated Headquarters 4th (Armoured) Division, under General Order 132/42 (Effective 26th January 1942), and 5th Anti-Tank Regiment joined the Armoured Division Support Group.

5th Anti-Tank Regiment RCA concentrated at Sussex, New Brunswick, in March 1942, prior to proceeding overseas.

65th Anti-Tank Battery RCA, with the regiment, departed for overseas, 3rd June 1942 on board the Duchess of York, and disembarked at Liverpool, England, on the 13th of June 1942.

5th Anti-Tank Regiment RCA proceeded to Dunley Hill, Surrey, under Headquarters Medium Artillery, pending the arrival of the remainder of 4th Armoured Division, and with the arrival of the division the regiment moved to Aldershot. In February 1943, 14th Anti-Tank Battery RCA was welcomed to the regiment.

65th Battery equipment graduated from 2 pounder to 6 pounder, and upon entering the conflict on the Continent, the battery was equipped with towed 17 pounders.

65th Anti-Tank Battery, 5th Anti-Tank Regiment RCA, 4th Canadian Armoured Division, landed in Normandy on the 23rd of July 1944 and joined 2nd Canadian Corps in the Caen sector.

2nd Canadian Corps with the division, regiment, and 65th Battery as components, moved under Headquarters First Canadian Army 31st July 1944, and served in France, Belgium, Holland, and Germany.

65th Anti-Tank Battery RCA served until cessation of hostilities and received authorization to disband under General Order 71/46 (Effective 10th December 1945).

* * *

74th A/T Battery RCA, Rock Island, P.Q. — Serial 814C — 2nd Corps

74th Anti-Tank Battery RCA, Serial 814C, mobilized under General Order 147/42 (Effective 18th March 1942), with 6th Anti-Tank Regiment RCA, 6th Division, Home Defence.

6th Anti-Tank Regiment RCA assembled at Petawawa in April 1942 to prepare for its home defence role. However, in January 1943, 74th Battery with the regiment was selected for overseas service and moved to Debert, Nova Scotia on the 26th of May 1943, prior to going overseas.

74th Anti-Tank Battery RCA departed for overseas 27th August 1943, on board the Queen Mary, and disembarked at Gourock, Scotland, 1st September 1943.

6th Anti-Tank Regiment RCA joined 2nd Canadian Corps as Corps Anti-Tank Regiment, and 74th Battery was to be equipped with towed 17 pounders.

74th Battery, 6th Anti-Tank Regiment RCA landed in Normandy on the 9th and 10th of July 1944 with 2nd Canadian Corps, and 74th Battery deployed with 7th Canadian Infantry Brigade of 3rd Canadian Infantry Division, 19th July 1944 on the Caen front.

2nd Canadian Corps moved to First Canadian Army, 31st July 1944, and as a component 74th Anti-Tank Battery RCA served in France, Belgium, Holland, and Germany.

74th Battery saw service with 2nd, 3rd and 5th Canadian Divisions, 49th British Division, 101st US Airborne Division, and came under command 1st Canadian Armoured Car Regiment of 1st Canadian Corps.

The Battery served as infantry when required and the Ram towers of the battery were utilized as Kangaroos to transport 3rd and 4th Canadian Division units into battle.

74th Anti-Tank Battery RCA, Serial 814C, served until cessation of hostilities and received authorization to disband under General Order 321/45 (Effective 23rd June 1945), as the run-down of Corps Troops and Army Troops was begun in NW Europe.

*   *   *

82nd (Gaspe) A/T Battery RCA, Gaspe, P.Q. — Serial 908D — 5 Div.

82nd Anti-Tank Battery RCA, CASF, Serial 908D, mobilized under General Order 184/40 (Effective 24th May 1940), with 4th Anti-Tank Regiment RCA, CASF, Headquarters 4th Division, CASF.

The battery is reported to have formed a 2 Pounder Anti-Motor Torpedo Boat Battery at an earlier date.

82nd Anti-Tank Battery RCA was redesignated 82nd (Gaspe) Anti-Tank Battery RCA, under General Order 47/41 (Effective 1st February 1941), retaining Serial Number 908D.

The battery and regiment transferred to 1st Canadian Armoured Division, which was redesignated 5th Canadian (Armoured) Division, under General Order 135/41 (Effective 5th June 1941). Headquarters, 1st Canadian Armoured Division had been authorized under General Order 88/41 (Effective 27th February 1941).

82nd (Gaspe) Anti-Tank Battery, 4th Anti-Tank Regiment RCA, 5th Canadian Armoured Division departed for overseas 7th October 1941 on board the Aorangi, and disembarked at Glasgow, Scotland, on the 17th of October 1941.

In January 1943 a fourth battery, designated 16th Anti-Tank Battery RCA, was added to 4th Anti-Tank Regiment RCA, and in late 1943, 82nd Anti-Tank Battery RCA received authorization to draw Self-Propelled equipment.

82nd Battery sailed for the Mediterranean on the Samaria, 15th November 1943 from Liverpool, on operation "Timberwolf", and disembarked at Algiers, North Africa, 26th November 1943.

The two Self-Propelled batteries, one of which was 82nd Battery, moved to a nearby Staging Camp and rejoined the regiment in Italy on the 2nd of January 1944. In Italy the battery, regiment and division served with 1st Canadian Corps, under British Eighth Army until early 1945.

Transfer of 1st Canadian Corps to NW Europe, saw 82nd Battery depart from Italy via Leghorn, 23rd February 1945 and disembark at Marseilles, France, on the 25th of February 1945.

The battery joined First Canadian Army 6th April 1945 and participated in the action, 16th April 1945 in Holland, and served until the cessation of hostilities.

82nd (Gaspe) Anti-Tank Battery RCA received authorization to disband under General Order 71/46 (Effective 28th November 1945).

*   *   *

90th A/T Battery RCA, Fredericton, N.B. — Serial 20E — 1st Division

90th Field Battery (H) RCA, CASF, Serial 78, mobilized under General Order 135/39, 1st September 1939, with Headquarters of 1st Army Field Brigade RCA, CASF, Corps Troops mobilizing with 1st Division.

The four field batteries of Headquarters of 1st Army Field Brigade RCA, CASF, Serial 74, were aligned with 1st Anti-Tank Regiment RCA, CASF, Serial 20, under General Order 201/39 (Effective 1st October 1939).

90th Field Battery RCA was redesignated 90th Anti-Tank Battery RCA, under General Order 75/40 (Effective 1st December 1939) — (No Serial Number).

90th Anti-Tank Battery RCA, CASF, is listed with Serial Number 78, in an allottment of Serial Numbers with 1st Anti-Tank Regiment RCA, CASF, Serial 20, in General Order 230/40, dated 15th October 1940.

90th Anti-Tank Battery, 1st Anti-Tank Regiment RCA, CASF, departed for overseas 22nd December 1939 on board the Reina del Pacifico in Troop Convoy 2 and disembarked at Greenock, Scotland, on the 30th of December 1939.

90th Battery sailed for Brest, France, on the 14th of June 1940, but due to the deteriorating situation in France, returned to England the following day.

In England the battery, regiment, and 1st Division served with 7th Corps, the Canadian Corps, and 1st Canadian Corps.

90th Battery Serial Number was changed from 78 to 20E, under General Order 54/42 (Effective 1st January 1941), completing the transition to 1st Anti-Tank Regiment RCA.

90th Anti-Tank Battery, 1st Anti-Tank Regiment RCA sailed for the Mediterranean, 28th June 1943, and landed in Sicily on the 10th of July 1943, with the assaulting 1st Canadian Infantry Division, 30 Corps, British Eighth Army.

With the fall of Sicily the battery crossed to the Italian mainland 5th September 1943, moving from 30 British Corps to 13 British Corps, British Eighth Army.

The Division, Regiment and Battery joined 1st Canadian Corps upon the corps becoming operational in 1944, and served as a component in Italy until early 1945.

90th Battery departed from Italy via Leghorn and the regiment sailed at intervals in Liberty ships and LSTs, beginning 9th March 1945, then following a 28 hour journey by sea, disembarked at Marseilles, France.

During the latter part of 1944 the battery had been using 2 pounder guns with a choke bore "Little John" adapter, now upon arrival in NW Europe the battery was to become an SP Battery, equipped with 17 pounder Valentines.

1st Anti-Tank Regiment RCA joined the action with First Canadian Army on the 11th of April 1945, in Holland, and served in NW Europe until the cessation of hostilities.

The 8th of May 1945 was designated "VE" Day and the regiment assumed the duty of disarming the German armies in Holland, and guarding equipment dumps.

90th Anti-Tank Battery RCA turned in the Self-Propelled Valentines, 28th June 1945, and received authorization to disband under General Order 401/45 (Effective 28th August 1945).

*   *   *

94th A/T Battery RCA, Quebec, P.Q. — Serial 708C — 3rd Cdn Inf Div.

94th Field Battery RCA is listed with Non-Permanent Active Militia Units called out on service in Military District No. 5, under General Order 124/39 (Effective 26th August 1939).

"Details" of 94th Field Battery RCA, CASF, Serial 321, mobilized in Military District No. 5, under General Order 135/39, 1st September 1939, and served in an Examination Battery role along the St. Lawrence River below Quebec City.

The battery mobilized for Active Service as 94th Anti-Tank Battery RCA, CASF, Serial 708C, under General Order 184/40 (Effective 24th May 1940), with 3rd Anti-Tank Regiment RCA, CASF, 3rd Division.

In February 1941, the regiment concentrated at Debert, Nova Scotia, where it remained until October and the move overseas was begun.

94th Anti-Tank Battery, 3rd Anti-Tank Regiment RCA departed for overseas 9th October 1941 on board the Andes, and disembarked at Liverpool, England, on the 18th of October 1941.

94th Battery landed in Normandy on D-Day, 6th June 1944, in support of 7th Canadian Infantry Brigade of the assaulting 3rd Canadian Infantry Division, 1 British Corps, Second British Army. 94th Battery suffered heavy casualties in helping secure the beachhead.

The division, regiment, and 94th Battery joined 2nd Canadian Corps, then with 2nd Canadian Corps, came under command of First Canadian Army on the 31st of July 1944, and served in France, Belgium, Holland and Germany.

Battery equipment ranged from 2 pounder to 6 pounder and 17 pounder towed guns, to M 10 SPs and 17 pounder Valentine SPs.

94th Anti-Tank Battery RCA served until cessation of hostilities and received authorization to disband under General Order 52/46 (Effective 14th November 1945).

A reconstituted 94th Battery mobilized as 2nd 94th Anti-Tank Battery RCA, under General Order 319/45 (Effective 1st June 1945), with 2nd 3rd Anti-Tank Regiment RCA, to serve in the reconstituted 3rd Canadian Infantry Division of the Canadian Army Occupational Force (CAOF).

Following service with the Canadian Army Occupational Force in Germany, 2nd 94th Anti-Tank Battery RCA received authorization to disband under General Order 201/46 (Effective 14th May 1946).

* * *

96th A/T Battery RCA, Edmonton — Serial 1992B — 4th Cdn Armd Div.

96th Field Battery was converted to anti-tank and mobilized as 96th Anti-Tank Battery RCA, Serial 992B, under General Order 240/41 (Effective 5th September 1941), with 5th Anti-Tank Regiment RCA, 4th Division, at that time an

Infantry Division. 5th Anti-Tank Regiment mobilized to replace 4th Anti-Tank Regiment RCA upon its departure to 1st (5th) Canadian Armoured Division.

4th Division also became an armoured division, authorized under General Order 132/42 (Effective 26th January 1942). The change in designation brought a change in serial number and 96th Anti-Tank Battery RCA assumed Serial Number 1992B, under General Order 438/42 (Effective 12th February 1942).

96th Battery departed for overseas 3rd June 1942 on board the Duchess of York and disembarked at Liverpool, England, 13th June 1942.

The battery was issued self-propelled equipment during August and September 1943, as the Regiment reorganized to comprise two towed batteries, and two self-propelled batteries.

96th Anti-Tank Battery, 5th Anti-Tank Regiment RCA, 4th Canadian Armoured Division, landed in Normandy 23rd July 1944 and moved into the line on the 29th July, in the Caen sector.

4th Canadian Armoured Division, with 2nd Canadian Corps, came under command of First Canadian Army, 31st July 1944, and served in France, Belgium, Holland, and Germany.

96th Anti-Tank Battery RCA served until cessation of hostilities and received authorization to disband under General Order 71/46 (Effective 10th December 1945).

*   *   *

98th (Bruce) A/T Battery RCA, Port Elgin — Serial 908B — 5 Div.

98th (Bruce) Anti-Tank Battery RCA, CASF, Serial 908B, mobilized under General Order 184/40 (Effective 24th May 1940), with 4th Anti-Tank Regiment RCA, CASF, Headquarters 4th Division, CASF. The regiment was to comprise four batteries in the Infantry Division.

1st Canadian Armoured Division received authorization to mobilize under General Order 88/41 (Effective 27th February 1941), then under General Order 135/41, was redesignated 5th Canadian (Armoured) Division (Effective 5th June 1941). To speed its forming and departure overseas, previously mobilized regiments and batteries were diverted to the armoured formation. 4th Anti-Tank Regiment RCA now to comprise three batteries, 24th, 82nd and 98th (Bruce) Anti-Tank Batteries moved to the new armoured division. 104th Battery became an independent battery.

98th (Bruce) Anti-Tank Battery, 4th Anti-Tank Regiment RCA, 5th Canadian (Armoured) Division, departed for overseas 9th October 1941 on board the Aorangi, and disembarked 17th October 1941 at Glasgow, Scotland.

Shortly after its arrival overseas 24th Battery was redesignated 49th Battery, then in January 1943, 16th Battery joined the regiment, and later in the year 98th Battery and 82nd Battery becamed Self-Propelled.

Transfer of Headquarters 1st Canadian Corps, Corps Troops, Army Troops, and 5th Canadian Armoured Division to the Mediterranean, saw 98th Battery with the regiment board the Samaria and sail from Liverpool, 15th November 1943, on operation "Timberwolf". The two self-propelled batteries disembarked at Algiers, North Africa, 26th November and moved to a nearby staging camp, rejoining the regiment early January 1944, in Italy.

In Italy, while awaiting the arrival of its self-propelled equipment the battery fell heir to towed 6 pounder and 17 pounder anti-tank guns left behind by the U.K. bound 7th Armoured Division (The Desert Rats), equipment on which the Desert battles and Desert sand had taken its toll.

49th Battery of the regiment moved into position north of Ortona, 14th January 1944 with 11 Brigade Group. 11th Canadian Infantry Brigade of 5th Canadian Armoured Division launched an attack 17th January 1944 with 49th Battery firing in support. 4th Anti-Tank Regiment RCA then moved to the Arielli river area opposite Orsogna, with 49th and 16th Batteries involved in the action.

98th Battery's chance to man the anti-tank defences came early in February farther along the Arielli, opposite Chietti, and toward the end of the month the battery received its M 10 Self-Propelled anti-tank guns.

In May, 98th Battery took part in an attack on the Gustav Line, then as part of an armoured force which included the British Columbia Dragoons, exploited the breakthrough and knocked out its first enemy tank. The Hitler Line was next to fall, then the Gothic Line.

12th Canadian Infantry Brigade was added to the division in July 1944 and 98th Battery supported units of both 11th and 12th Brigades until their departure from Italy in 1945.

Transfer of 1st Canadian Corps to NW Europe early 1945 saw the regiment depart from Leghorn, Italy, beginning 22nd February 1945 and arrive at Marseilles, France three days later.

The regiment concentrated in Belgium where the 3 inch M 10 SPs were exchanged for 17 pounder self-propelled equipment.

12th Canadian Infantry Brigade was disbanded as the division reorganized to conform to Armoured Division War Establishment. 11th Brigade was now the lone infantry brigade in the division.

4th Anti-Tank Regiment joined First Canadian Army in NW Europe, 6th April 1945 at Nijmegen, Holland, and 98th Battery joined the action in Holland on the 16th of April 1945.

98th (Bruce) Anti-Tank Battery RCA served until the cessation of hostilities and received authorization to disband under General Order 71/46 (Effective 28th November 1945).

*   *   *

103rd A/T Battery RCA, Campbellton, N.B. — Serial 814E — 2nd Corps

103rd Anti-Tank Battery RCA, Serial 814E, mobilized under General Order 147/42 (Effective 18th March 1942), with 6th Anti-Tank Regiment RCA, 6th Division, Home Defence.

6th Anti-Tank Regiment assembled at Petawawa in April 1942 to prepare for its home defence role. However, in January 1943, 103rd Battery, with the regiment, was selected for overseas service and moved to Debert, Nova Scotia, on the 26th of May 1943, prior to going overseas.

103rd Anti-Tank Battery RCA departed for overseas 27th August 1943, on board the Queen Mary, and disembarked 1st September 1943, at Gourock, Scotland.

6th Anti-Tank Regiment RCA joined 2nd Canadian Corps, as Corps Anti-Tank Regiment, and 103rd Anti-Tank Battery RCA was to be equipped with towed 17 pounders.

103rd Battery, 6th Anti-Tank Regiment RCA landed in Normandy on the 9th and 10th of July 1944 with 2nd Canadian Corps, and 103rd Battery deployed its guns north of Carpiquet Airfield in support of 3rd Canadian Infantry Division, under Second British Army.

2nd Canadian Corps moved to First Canadian Army, on the 31st of July 1944, and as a component, 103rd Anti-Tank Battery RCA served in France, Belgium, Holland, and Germany.

103rd Battery served with 3rd, 4th and 5th Canadian Divisions, 50 British Division, 51 (Highland) Division, 104 US Division, and came under command of 1st Canadian Armoured Car Regiment (RCD), 1st Canadian Corps.

The battery served as infantry when required and the Ram towers of the battery were utilized as Kangaroos to transport 3rd and 4th Canadian Division units into battle.

103rd Anti-Tank Battery RCA, Serial 814E, served until cessation of hostilities and received authorization to disband under General Order 321/45 (Effective 23rd June 1945), in NW Europe. Personnel proceeded to the Canadian Army Pacific Force, the Canadian Army Occupational Force, or were posted to divisional units for the return to Canada.

*   *   *

104th A/T Battery RCA, Fredericton, N.B. — Serial 506E — 1st Corps

104th Anti-Tank Battery RCA, CASF, Serial 908E, mobilized with 4th Anti-Tank Regiment RCA, CASF, Headquarters 4th Division, CASF, under General Order 184/40 (Effective 24th May 1940).

4th Division mobilized as an infantry division which required a four-battery anti-tank regiment in the divisional artillery.

Headquarters 1st Canadian Armoured Division was authorized under General Order 88/41 (Effective 27th February 1941), and its designation changed to 5th Canadian (Armoured) Division, under General Order 135/41 (Effective 5th June 1941).

4th Anti-Tank Regiment RCA moved to the new armoured division which required three anti-tank batteries only at this early date and 104th Anti-Tank Battery RCA became surplus.

104th Anti-Tank Battery RCA, however, departed for overseas as an independent battery, 10th April 1941, on board the Georgic, and disembarked at Gourock, Scotland, 19th April 1941.

7th Anti-Tank Regiment RCA was formed in England on the 25th of July 1941 to serve as 1st Canadian Corps Anti-Tank Regiment, and 104th Anti-Tank Battery RCA became a component.

In an alignment of Serial Numbers with 7th Anti-Tank Regiment RCA, 104th Anti-Tank Battery RCA Serial Number was changed from 908E, to 506E, under General Order 54/42 (Effective 22nd December 1941).

104th Anti-Tank Battery, 7th Anti-Tank Regiment RCA, 1st Canadian Corps, boarded the Scythia, 12th November 1943 at Bristol, bound for the Mediterranean on operation "Timberwolf II".

The ship rendezvoused with the convoy off Scotland, 15th November 1943 and 104th Battery disembarked at Algiers, North Africa, 25th November 1943.

104th Battery departed from Algiers, North Africa, 4th December on board the Chantilly and disembarked at Catania, Sicily, 8th December 1943.

7th Anti-Tank Regiment RCA crossed the Strait of Messina to the Italian mainland with 1st Canadian Corps, 3rd January 1944, and joined the action in support of 1st Canadian Infantry Division's attack on the Hitler Line in May 1944. The regiment served in Italy until early 1945, then with Headquarters 1st Canadian Corps and its Canadian components, moved to NW Europe.

104th Battery with 7th Anti-Tank Regiment RCA departed from Italy via Naples on board the Empire Pride, 25th February 1945 and disembarked at Marseilles, France, 27th February 1945.

The battery with its towed 17 pounder anti-tank guns, joined the action 7th April 1945 in Holland under First Canadian Army and served until cessation of hostilities.

104th Anti-Tank Battery RCA, Serial 506E, received authorization to disband under General Order 321/45 (Effective 27th June 1945). Personnel departed for the Canadian Army Pacific Force, the Occupational Force, or were posted to divisional units for the return to Canada as the run-down of Canadian units in NW Europe was begun.

*   *   *

105th A/T Battery RCA, St. George, N.B. — Serial 708E — 3rd Division

105th Anti-Tank Battery RCA, CASF, Serial 708E, mobilized under General Order 184/40 (Effective 24th May 1940), with 3rd Anti-Tank Regiment RCA, CASF, Headquarters 3rd Division, CASF.

105th Anti-Tank Battery RCA sailed overseas 9th October 1941 on board the Andes, and disembarked at Liverpool, England, on the 18th of October 1941.

Equipment ranged from 2 pounder, 6 pounder, 17 pounder towed anti-tank guns, then in 1944 the battery was equipped with Self-Propelled M 10s in one troop and towed 6 pounders in two troops.

105th Anti-Tank Battery RCA, 3rd Anti-Tank Regiment RCA, landed in Normandy on D-Day, 6th June 1944, with the assaulting 3rd Canadian Infantry Division.

One troop of towed guns landed with 7th Canadian Infantry Brigade and the other troop of towed guns landed with 8th Canadian Infantry Brigade, attached to 94th Anti-Tank Battery and 52nd Anti-Tank Battery, respectively.

The M 10 Self-Propelled Troop of 4th Battery, 52nd Battery, and 94th Battery, along with the Self-Propelled Troop of 105th Battery, were grouped under 105th Battery and landed on D-Day in support of 9th Canadian Infantry Brigade of 3rd Canadian Infantry Division.

This arrangement continued until the end of June when the bridgehead was secure and the troops returned to their respective batteries.

105th Battery served under 1 British Corps, Second British Army, 2nd Canadian Corps, Second British Army, then on the 31st of July 1944, with 2nd Canadian Corps, moved to First Canadian Army on the Caen front, and as a component of First Canadian Army served in France, Belgium, Holland, and Germany.

In April 1945, 105th Anti-Tank Battery RCA became an SP battery, equipped with 17 pounder Valentine Self-Propelled anti-tank guns and served as a self-propelled battery until cessation of hostilities.

105th Anti-Tank Battery RCA, as a SP battery, was selected as a component of the Canadian Berlin Brigade in mid-May, however, in early June 1945 the brigade was disbanded and the artillery batteries returned to their regiments.

105th Anti-Tank Battery RCA received authorization to disband under General Order 52/46 (Effective 14th November 1945).

2nd 105th Anti-Tank Battery RCA, 2nd 3rd Anti-Tank Regiment RCA, mobilized with the reconstituted 3rd Canadian Infantry Division under General Order 319/45 (Effective 1st June 1945), and following service with the Canadian Army Occupational Force in Germany, 2nd 105th Anti-Tank Battery RCA received authorization to disband under General Order 201/46 (Effective 14th May 1946).

*   *   *

108th A/T Battery RCA, Kimberley, B.C. — Serial 170D — 2nd Division

108th Field Battery (H), RCA, CASF, Serial 82, mobilized under General Order 135/39, 1st September 1939, with Headquarters of 2nd Army Field Brigade RCA, CASF, Serial 79.

Headquarters 2nd Army Field Brigade RCA, Serial 79, became 2nd Anti-Tank Regiment RCA, CASF, Serial 170, incorporating the four field batteries of 2nd Army Field Brigade, under General Order 201/39 (Effective 1st October 1939).

108th Field Battery RCA was redesignated 108th Anti-Tank Battery RCA, under General Order 75/40 (Effective 1st December 1939).

108th Anti-Tank Battery, 2nd Anti-Tank Regiment RCA, a component of 2nd

Infantry Division, departed for overseas 27th August 1940, on board the Empress of Australia, and disembarked at Gourock, Scotland, on the 4th of September 1940.

108th Battery Serial Number was changed from 82, to Serial 170D, under General Order 54/42 (Effective 22nd December 1941), completing the transition from 2nd Army Field Brigade RCA, to 2nd Anti-Tank Regiment RCA.

108th Anti-Tank Battery, 2nd Anti-Tank Regiment RCA, 2nd Canadian Infantry Division, landed in Normandy on the 7th of July 1944 and moved to the Carpiquet area where heavy mortar-fire by the enemy caused the battery to suffer its first casualty on the 12th July.

The battery, regiment, and division, with 2nd Canadian Corps became operational under Second British Army, then moved to First Canadian Army, 31st July 1944, on the Caen front.

2nd Canadian Corps took part in the vicious fighting in the breakout from Caen, and the closing of the Falaise Gap. 2nd Canadian Infantry Division moved on to Dieppe, where, upon capture of the city the division paused for a service of remembrance in the cemetery, 3rd of September 1944, and 108th Battery participated in the divisional parade through the streets of the city, with General Crerar taking the salute. Two years had passed since that fateful 19th of August Raid.

2nd Canadian Infantry Division rejoined the action under First Canadian Army, and 108th Anti-Tank Battery RCA, 2nd Anti-Tank Regiment RCA served in France, Belgium, Holland, and Germany.

108th Anti-Tank Battery RCA served until cessation of hostilities and received authorization to disband under General Order 52/46 (Effective 23rd September 1945).

*   *   *

111th (Nelson) A/T Bty RCA, Nelson, B.C. — Serial 506B — 1st Corps

111th Field Battery RCA, CASF, Serial 17, was listed as a component of Headquarters of 3rd Field Brigade RCA, CASF, 1st Division, CASF, under General Order 135/39, 1st September 1939, however, effective the same date, 111th Battery and 109th Battery exchanged units and serial numbers, authorized under General Order 220/39 (Effective 1st September 1939).

111th Field Battery RCA, CASF, now assumed Serial Number 167, with 6th Field Brigade RCA, CASF, 2nd Division, CASF.

Headquarters of 6th Field Brigade RCA, CASF, was redesignated Headquarters of 6th Field Regiment RCA, CASF, in a two battery organization and 111th Field Battery RCA, CASF, Serial 167, combined with 91st Field Battery RCA, CASF, Serial 168, to become 91st/111th Field Battery RCA, Serial 167, under General Order 123/40 (Effective 1st June 1940).

The combined 91st/111th Field Battery departed for overseas on board the Oronsay, 27th August 1940, and disembarked at Gourock, Scotland, 5th September 1940.

111th Battery regained individual identity as 111th (Nelson) Field Battery RCA, Serial 167, under General Order 45/41 (Effective 1st January 1941). 6th Field Regiment reorganized to become a three battery field regiment at this time and 111th Field Battery RCA became surplus to the regiment and departed 2nd Division.

111th (Nelson) Field Battery RCA, Serial 167, was redesignated 111th (Nelson) Anti-Tank Battery RCA, Serial 167, under General Order 57/41 (Effective 1st January 1941).

Headquarters 7th Anti-Tank Regiment RCA was authorized under General Order 56/41 (Effective 1st February 1941) and came into being 25th July 1941, in England. 111th Battery became a component.

111th (Nelson) Anti-Tank Battery RCA Serial Number was changed from 167, to 506B, under General Order 54/42 (Effective 22nd December 1941), in an alignment with 7th Anti-Tank Regiment RCA.

The battery graduated from 2 pounder to 6 pounder to 17 pounder, then August 1943 received twelve 3 inch M 10s (Self-Propelled), and went into action so-equipped.

111th Anti-Tank Battery, 7th Anti-Tank Regiment RCA, 1st Canadian Corps Anti-Tank Regiment, boarded the Scythia at Avonmouth, near Bristol, rendezvoused with the convoy off Scotland 15th November 1943 and sailed for the Mediterranean on operation "Timberwolf II".

111th Battery disembarked at Algiers, North Africa, 25th November 1943, departed 4th December 1943 and arrived at Catania, Sicily, 8th December 1943.

With the arrival of 113th Battery from North Africa, 31st December, the regiment intact, crossed the Strait of Messina to the Italian mainland, 3rd January 1944, and with 1st Canadian Corps, served in Italy until early 1945.

The decision to transfer 1st Canadian Corps to NW Europe, saw 111th Battery with the regiment depart from Italy via Naples on the 25th February 1945 and disembark at Marseilles, France, 27th February.

111th Battery was issued M 10, 17 pounder Self-Propelled guns in March 1945 and entered the line with First Canadian Army in NW Europe 7th April 1945 near Arnhem, Holland.

111th (Nelson) Anti-Tank Battery RCA, Serial 506B, served until cessation of hostilities and received authorization to disband under General Order 321/45 (Effective 27th June 1945). Personnel proceeded to the Canadian Army Pacific Force, the Canadian Army Occupational Force, or were posted to divisional units for the return to Canada.

*   *   *

113th A/T Battery RCA, Regina, Sask. — Serial 506C — 1st Cdn Corps

113th Battery mobilized as 113th Field Battery (H), RCA, CASF, Serial 217, under General Order 135/39, 1st September 1939, with Headquarters of 4th Army Field Brigade RCA, CASF, Corps Troops mobilizing with 2nd Division.

113th Field Battery (H) RCA, CASF, with Headquarters of 4th Army Field Brigade RCA, CASF, departed for overseas 28th January 1940 on board the Monarch of Bermuda in Troop Convoy 3, and disembarked at Greenock, Scotland, on the 8th of February 1940.

Headquarters of 4th Army Field Brigade RCA, CASF, Serial 214, was redesignated Headquarters, 8th Army Field Regiment RCA, CASF, Serial 214, under General Order 44/40 (Effective 12th February 1940), and 113th Field Battery (H) RCA, CASF, Serial 217, combined with 71st Field Battery (H) RCA, CASF, Serial 218, to become 71st/113th Field Battery RCA, CASF, Serial 217, in a two-battery regiment.

The combined 71st/113th Field Battery with 8th Army Field Regiment RCA, served with 7 Corps and the Canadian Corps in the defence of England.

Reorganization to a three-battery regiment, authorized under General Order 45/41 (Effective 1st January 1941), saw the batteries regain individual identity, resulting in 113th Battery being surplus to the regiment.

113th Field Battery RCA, Serial 217, was redesignated 113th Anti-Tank Battery RCA, Serial 217, under General Order 57/41 (Effective 1st January 1941), and joined 7th Anti-Tank Regiment RCA, upon its forming 25th July 1941 in England, as 1st Canadian Corps Anti-Tank Regiment.

Headquarters 7th Anti-Tank Regiment RCA, Serial 506, was authorized under General Order 56/41 (Effective 1st February 1941).

113th Anti-Tank Battery RCA was allotted Serial Number 506C, under General Order 54/42 (Effective 22nd December 1941), in an alignment of serial numbers within the regiment.

Mediterranean bound on operation "Timberwolf II" with 1st Canadian Corps, 113th Anti-Tank Battery boarded the Scythia, 12th November 1943 at Avonmouth and disembarked at Algiers, North Africa, 25th November 1943.

The regiment boarded ship at Algiers, however, due to overcrowding 113th Battery was taken ashore and the regiment sailed 4th December, arriving at Catania, Sicily, 8th December 1943.

113th Battery rejoined the regiment in Sicily on the 31st December 1943, and on the 3rd of January 1944 the regiment intact crossed the Strait of Messina to the Italian mainland.

113th Anti-Tank Battery RCA served in Italy until early 1945 as a component of 7th Anti-Tank Regiment RCA, in its role of Corps Anti-Tank Regiment, 1st Canadian Corps.

Upon the transfer of 1st Canadian Corps to NW Europe, 113th Battery departed from Italy via Naples, 26th February 1945 and disembarked at Marseilles, France, 28th February 1945.

With 1st Canadian Corps, 7th Anti-Tank Regiment RCA joined First Canadian Army in NW Europe. 113th Battery entered the battle near Arnhem, Holland, 1st week in April 1945, and served until cessation of hostilities.

113th Anti-Tank Battery RCA, Serial 506C, received authorization to disband under General Order 321/45 (Effective 27th June 1945), in NW Europe. Personnel departed to the Canadian Army Pacific Force (CAPF), the Canadian Army Occupational Force (CAOF), or to divisional units from the Military District to their enlistment, for the return to Canada.

Headquarters of 1st Canadian Corps, Headquarters 2nd Canadian Corps, Corps Troops, and a number of Army Troops units were dispersed in this manner as the run-down of Canadian units in NW Europe was begun.

*   *   *

127th Anti-Tank Battery RCA — Postwar Permanent Force

122nd Field Battery RCA, Serial 1612D, mobilized under General Order 309/42 (Effective 12th May 1942), as a component of 27th Field Regiment RCA, 8th Division, Home Defence.

8th Division Headquarters and the bulk of the division concentrated in the area encompassing Pacific Command, however, in its role of mobile reserve for Eastern Canada, 122nd Battery with the regiment, remained in the East.

122nd Field Battery RCA did not disband along with Headquarters 27th Field Regiment RCA, 120th, and 121st Field Batteries RCA, but was redesignated

127th Anti-Tank Battery RCA, under General Order 138/46 (Effective 1st March 1946).

127th Anti-Tank Battery RCA was permanently embodied in the Postwar Permanent Force, under General Order 158/46 (Effective 27th June 1946).

*   *   *

SECTION III

COAST ARTILLERY

Non-Permanent Active Militia members of the coast brigades were called out on service to man the local forts and guard vulnerable locations on the 26th of August 1939. These units became components of the Canadian Active Service Force (CASF) and continued to serve in the forts, which became the first line of defence.

In British Columbia, 5th (British Columbia) Coast Brigade RCA was redesignated 5th (B.C.) Coast Regiment RCA and manned the defences under Headquarters Victoria and Esquimalt Fortress, and its later designation, Headquarters Esquimalt Fortress. 15th (Vancouver) Coast Brigade, redesignated Regiment, served under Headquarters Vancouver Defences, with guns in the Vancouver area and Yorke Island. 17th (N.B.C.) Coast Regiment RCA served under Headquarters Prince Rupert Defences which in turn came under command of 8th Division during 1942-1943. All of which came under Headquarters Pacific Command.

1st (Halifax) Coast Regiment RCA served under Headquarters Halifax Fortress, 3rd (New Brunswick) Coast Regiment RCA served under Headquarters Saint John, New Brunswick Defences and Headquarters Defended Port of Saint John. 16th Coast Regiment RCA served under Headquarters Sydney-Canso and Headquarters Defended Port of Sydney. An independent coast battery served under Headquarters Shelburne Defences, Nova Scotia and Headquarters Defended Port of Shelburne.

Coast batteries also served under Headquarters St. John's Defences (Newfoundland) and it later designation Headquarters Defended Port of St. John's,

Headquarters Botwood Defences (Newfoundland), Headquarters Defended Port of Botwood, and at Lewisporte, in the Gander area defences. 108th Coast Battery served at Fort Rigolet, Labrador under Headquarters Goose Bay Defences which in turn was redesignated Headquarters Defended Area Goose Bay.

Canadian units serving in Newfoundland became part of "W" Force, and with coast defence batteries in Military Districts 6 and 7, plus the Gaspe Defences, came within the boundaries of Atlantic Command. The Quebec City Defences, including Fort La Martiniere, in Military District No. 5, served outside Atlantic Command.

Coast batteries assumed the searchlight manning duties following the disbanding of coast defence searchlight batteries early 1942, and also manned Bofors 40mm light anti-aircraft guns at the forts.

*   *   *

S 1 Coast and Anti-Aircraft Artillery School — Serial 489 — Esquimalt

Serial 489, Coast Artillery School of Instruction, mobilized under General Order 97/42 (Effective 1st January 1942) at Fort Macaulay, Esquimalt, British Columbia, under Headquarters Victoria-Esquimalt Defences.

War Diary Coast Artillery School of Instruction, Serial 489 — "The CAS of I was enlarged 1st Aug/42 to train a large number of HD recruits embarked on a 4 weeks training period consisting of basic & Arty trg.

3rd Aug/42 — The 2-13 pdr AA guns at Macaulay were dismantled under the direction of BSM (IG) Williams. Personnel were supplied from 60th Coast Bty.

5th Aug/42 "D" Wing was authorized to train 500 "R" recruits — "A" Bty for HAA and "B" Bty for LAA.

Occupation of Work Pt. Barracks was completed 10th Aug/42 from temporary location on Macaulay Plains with temp. offices located in Rm 1 RCSA building at Fort Macaulay.

14th Aug/42 the CAS of I reorg. to "A" Wing Cst Arty, "B" Wing S/L and "C" Wing L & HAA.

26th Aug 21 Fd fired 25 pdrs at targets of floats towed at sea at Jordan River and Otter Point" — (under the guidance of the CAS of I).

Coast Artillery School of Instruction, Serial 489, was redesignated S 1 Canadian Coast Artillery School, Serial 489, under General Order 29/43 (Effective 1st November 1942).

S 1 Canadian Coast Artillery School, Serial 489, was redesignated S 1 Canadian Coast and Anti-Aircraft Artillery School, Serial 489, under General Order 139/43 (Effective 1st March 1943).

S 1 Canadian Coast and Anti-Aircraft Artillery School, Serial 489, continued to operate under Headquarters Victoria and Esquimalt Fortress, and its later designation, Headquarters Esquimalt Fortress, until authorized to disband under General Order 18/46 (Effective 15th July 1945).

*   *   *

1st S/L Battery RCA — Serial 419C — Vancouver, B.C.

In a reorganization of the Royal Canadian Artillery in the Non-Permanent Active Militia in Military District No. 11, "B" Squadron of the British Columbia Hussars (Armoured Car) was converted, and redesignated 1st Searchlight Battery RCA, under General Order 75/39 (Effective 15th May 1939).

1st Searchlight Battery RCA became a component of 1st Searchlight Regiment RCA under General Order 77/39 (Effective 15th May 1939), and localized at Vancouver, British Columbia, under General Order 78/39 (Effective 15th May 1939).

Serial 419c, 1st Searchlight Battery RCA, CASF (Details) became a component of the Canadian Active Service Force, with Headquarters 1st Searchlight Regiment RCA, CASF (Details), under General Order 200/39 (Effective 1st September 1939).

1st Searchlight Battery RCA, Serial 419C, was placed on active service in Military District No. 11, under General Order 44/41 (Effective 1st January 1941). The CASF "Details" were absorbed into the battery.

This seems to have been a paper transaction only as personnel were absorbed by 16th Light Anti-Aircraft Battery RCA, 3rd Light Anti-Aircraft Regiment RCA, mobilized for service overseas with 2nd Canadian Infantry Division.

1st Searchlight Battery RCA, Serial 419C, received authorization to disband under General Order 314/44 (Effective 31st August 1940).

*   *   *

1st S/L Battery (CD) RCA, Saint John, N.B. — Serial 367 — MD 7

The organization of 1st Searchlight Battery RCA, Coast Defence (CD), in Military District No. 7, was authorized under General Order 60/39 (Effective 1st March 1939). Effective the same date, under General Order 61/39, 1st Searchlight Battery RCA (CD), Non-Permanent Active Militia, was attached to 3rd (New Brunswick) Coast Brigade RCA.

1st Searchlight Battery RCA (CD) was localized at Saint John, New Brunswick, Military District No. 7, under General Order 64/39 (Effective 1st March 1939).

1st Searchlight Battery (CD) RCA was called out on service with NPAM units in Military District No. 7, under General Order 124/39 (Effective 26th August 1939).

"Details" of 1st Searchlight Battery (CD) RCA, Serial 367, were authorized as components of the Canadian Active Service Force, 1st September 1939, under General Order 135/39, and the battery continued its duties at the forts.

Serial 367, 1st Searchlight Battery (CD) RCA, was placed on active service under General Order 44/41 (Effective 1st January 1941), attached to 3rd (New Brunswick) Coast Brigade RCA and served in Military District No. 7, under Headquarters Saint John Defences, Atlantic Command.

Headquarters 3rd (New Brunswick) Coast Brigade RCA, was redesignated Headquarters 3rd (N.B.) Coast Regiment RCA, under General Order 37/43 (Effective 1st August 1942). Its component Heavy Batteries RCA, were redesignated Coast Batteries, 4th Battery, under General Order 386/42 (Effective 1st August 1942), and 15th Battery under General Order 37/43 (Effective 1st September 1942).

Other changes at this time included the disbanding of coast defence searchlight batteries. 1st Searchlight Battery (CD) RCA, received authorization to disband under General Order 86/43 (Effective 1st September 1942). Personnel were absorbed by the coast batteries and the coast batteries assumed the searchlight manning duties.

*   *   *

2nd S/L Battery (CD) RCA — Serial 394 — Prince Rupert, B.C.

In a reorganization of the Royal Canadian Artillery, Non-Permanent Active Militia, authority was granted for the forming of 2nd Searchlight Battery (CD) Royal Canadian Artillery in Military District No. 11, under General Order 75/39 (Effective 15th May 1939).

2nd Searchlight Battery (CD) RCA was localized at Prince Rupert, British Columbia, Military District No. 11, under General Order 78/39 (Effective 15th May 1939).

2nd Searchlight Battery (CD) RCA is listed with NPAM units called out on service in Military District No. 11, under General Order 124/39 (Effective 26th August 1939), for duty in the Prince Rupert, British Columbia, defences.

"Details" of 2nd Searchlight Battery (CD) RCA, CASF, Serial 394, were authorized as components of the Canadian Active Service Force, in Military District No. 11, under General Order 135/39, 1st September 1939.

2nd Searchlight Battery (CD) RCA, Serial 394, was placed on active service and the CASF "Details" absorbed into the battery, under General Order 44/41 (Effective 1st January 1941), and 2nd Searchlight Battery continued to serve under Headquarters Prince Rupert Defences, in Military District No. 11.

Prince Rupert Defences reorganized and Headquarters 17th (N.B.C.) Coast Regiment RCA was formed, comprising 102nd Coast Battery RCA, and 9th Coast Battery RCA.

2nd Searchlight Battery (CD) RCA, Serial 394, was authorized to disband at this time, under General Order 312/42 (Effective 1st May 1942). The coast batteries assumed the searchlight manning duties and personnel of the searchlight battery were absorbed by Headquarters 17th (N.B.C.) Coast Regiment, 102nd Coast Battery, and 9th Coast Battery, at Prince Rupert, British Columbia, Pacific Command.

*   *   *

3rd S/L Battery (CD) RCA — Serial 393 — Vancouver, B.C.

In a reorganization of the Royal Canadian Artillery in the Non-Permanent Active Militia, The British Columbia Hussars (A.C.) was converted to 1st Searchlight Regiment RCA, with Headquarters, and "B" & "C" Squadron becoming, Headquarters, 1st Searchlight Regiment RCA, 1st Searchlight Battery RCA, and 3rd Searchlight Battery (CD) RCA, respectively, authorized in Military District No. 11, under General Order 75/39 (Effective 15th May 1939).

The composition of 1st Searchlight Regiment RCA, was authorized as Regimental Headquarters, 1st Searchlight Battery RCA, and 3rd Searchlight Battery (CD) RCA, under General Order 77/39 (Effective 15th May 1939). The regiment, its headquarters and the two batteries were localized at Vancouver, B.C., under General Order 78/39 (Effective 15th May 1939).

3rd Searchlight Battery (CD) RCA, was called out on service in Military District No. 11, under General Order 124/39 (Effective 26th August 1939), and "Details" of 3rd Searchlight Battery (CD) RCA, CASF, Serial 393, were authorized as components of the Canadian Active Service Force, under General Order 135/39, 1st September 1939.

"Details" of Headquarters, 1st Searchlight Regiment RCA, CASF, Serial

419b, and 1st Searchlight Battery RCA, CASF (Details), Serial 419c, were authorized as components of the Canadian Active Service Force, under General Order 200/39 (Effective 1st September 1939).

Serial 393, 3rd Searchlight Battery (CD), RCA, CASF (Details) was placed on active service under General Order 44/41 (Effective 1st January 1941), and the CASF "Details" were absorbed by the battery.

3rd Searchlight Battery (CD) RCA, Serial 393, continued to serve under Headquarters Vancouver Defences until authorized to disband under General Order 314/44 (Effective 18th July 1942), at which time the coast batteries assumed the searchlight manning duties and absorbed the personnel of 3rd Searchlight Battery (CD) RCA.

The remainder of the regiment too had been phased out, Serial 419C, 1st Searchlight Battery RCA, under General Order 314/44 (Effective 31st August 1940), and Serial 419B, Headquarters 1st Searchlight Regiment RCA, Under General Order 314/44 (Effective 10th September 1940).

*   *   *

4th Coast Battery RCA — Serial 366 — Saint John, New Brunswick

4th Medium Battery (Howitzer) RCA was converted to a Heavy Battery RCA and designated 4th Heavy Battery RCA, under General Order 46/39 (Effective 1st March 1939).

The battery ceased to be attached to, and made a unit of 3rd (New Brunswick) Coast Brigade RCA (The Loyal Company of Artillery), localized at Saint John, New Brunswick, under General Order 47/39 (Effective 1st March 1939).

4th Heavy Battery RCA, Non-Permanent Active Militia, was called out on service in Military District No. 7, with Headquarters 3rd (New Brunswick) Coast Brigade RCA, Non-Permanent Active Militia, under General Order 124/39 (Effective 26th August 1939), for duty at the local forts.

Serial 366, 4th Heavy Battery RCA, CASF (Details), with Serial 365, Headquarters 3rd (New Brunswick) Coast Brigade RCA, CASF (Details) were authorized as components of the Canadian Active Service Force under General Order 135/39, 1st September 1939, in Military District No. 7.

4th Heavy Battery RCA, Serial 366, was placed on active service under General Order 44/41 (Effective 1st January 1941), and the CASF "Details" were absorbed into the battery. 4th Heavy Battery RCA continued to serve with 3rd (New Brunswick) Coast Brigade RCA, under Headquarters Saint John Defences.

Serial 366, 4th Heavy Battery RCA was redesignated Serial 366, 4th Coast Battery RCA under General Order 386/42 (Effective 1st August 1942).

Headquarters 3rd (New Brunswick) Coast Brigade RCA was redesignated Headquarters 3rd (N.B.) Coast Regiment RCA under General Order 37/43 (Effective 1st August 1942).

Headquarters Saint John Defences was redesignated Headquarters Defended Port of Saint John, under General Order 206/44 (Effective 15th April 1944), and 4th Coast Battery RCA, Serial 366, continued to serve with Headquarters 3rd (NB) Coast Regiment RCA, Serial 365, until authorized to disband under General Order 55/45 (Effective 1st September 1944).

*   *   *

6th Coast Battery RCA — Serial 336 — Sydney, Nova Scotia

6th Heavy Battery RCA, with Headquarters, 16th Coast Brigade RCA, Military District No. 6, is included in the list of Non-Permanent Active Militia units called out on service under General Order 124/39 (Effective 26th August 1939), to man the forts in the Sydney-Canso Defences.

Serial 336, 6th Heavy Battery RCA, CASF (Details), with (Details) of Headquarters, 16th Coast Brigade RCA, CASF, were authorized as components of the Canadian Active Service Force, under General Order 135/39, 1st September 1939.

6th Heavy Battery RCA, Serial 336, was placed on active service under General Order 44/41 (Effective 1st January 1941), and the CASF "Details" were absorbed into the battery.

Serial 336, 6th Heavy Battery RCA was redesignated Serial 336, 6th Coast Battery RCA, and Headquarters 16th Coast Brigade RCA was redesignated Headquarters 16th Coast Regiment RCA, under General Order 399/42 (Effective 1st August 1942).

Headquarters Sydney-Canso Defences was redesignated Headquarters Defended Port of Sydney, under General Order 206/44 (Effective 15th April 1944) and remained operational until authorized to disband under General Order 379/45 (Effective 15th August 1945).

Headquarters, 16th Coast Regiment RCA disbanded under General Order 18/46 (Effective 15th August 1945), and 6th Coast Battery RCA, Serial 336, received authorization to disband under General Order 18/46 (Effective 30th September 1945).

*   *   *

9th Coast Battery RCA — Serial 343 — Halifax and Prince Rupert

9th Heavy Battery RCA, Non-Permanent Active Militia, was called out on service in Military District No. 6, with Headquarters, 1st (Halifax) Coast Brigade RCA, Non-Permanent Active Militia, under General Order 124/39 (Effective 26th August 1939).

9th Battery was allotted Serial Number 343, and designated 9th Heavy Battery (Howitzer) RCA, CASF (Details), in the Canadian Active Service Force, under General Order 135/39, 1st September 1939.

9th Coast Battery War Diary — "Reported to Halifax Armouries 1/9/39 and proceeded to Fort Sandwich for manning duty at Sandwich Bty, Halifax Fortress." The Battery was allotted F-21250 — F-22249 Regimental Numbers.

"18 Sep moved to Fort Connaught, emplacements for three 6 inch guns, facing the outer reaches of Halifax Harbour.

The Bty moved to new positions at East Lawrencetown, Porter's Lake. The Two B.L. 8″ Mk. VII-A Howitzers were moved from the Halifax Armoury to the new position".

The CASF "Details" were absorbed by the battery, and 9th Heavy Battery (H) RCA, Serial 343, was placed on Active Service under General Order 44/41 (Effective 1st January 1941), under Headquarters Halifax Fortress, in Military District No. 6.

War Diary — "The Bty departed Porter's Lake, N.S. 18 Mar/42 for Wellington Barracks, Halifax. Boarded the train 21 Mar/42.

Arrived at Pr Rupert, B.C. 26 Mar/42. The new guns are 8″ Railway Mounted. Men quartered in railway cars & eat at Ed Fus Barracks."

9th Heavy Battery (H) RCA, was redesignated 9th Coast Battery RCA, Serial 343, under General Order 311/42 (Effective 1st May 1942), and joined 17th (North British Columbia) Coast Regiment RCA at Prince Rupert, British Columbia.

9th Coast Battery, 17th (NBC) Coast Regiment RCA, and Prince Rupert Defences came under command 8th Division, Home Defence, Pacific Command from the 9th of October 1942, to the 15th of October 1943, at which time Headquarters 8th Division disbanded.

9th Battery manned two 8 inch guns mounted on railway carriages, and a light anti-aircraft section, at Fairview Point, two 12 pounder guns at Frederick

Point, and one 6 pounder gun at Casey Point, under Headquarters Prince Rupert Defences.

Personnel of 9th Coast Battery RCA from the railway mounted 8 inch guns at Fairview Point, Prince Rupert, rotated with personnel of 68th Coast Battery RCA, manning the two dismounted 8 inch railway guns at Christopher Point, Victoria-Esquimalt, on Vancouver Island. The exchange took place in August 1943, the battery designation however did not change.

9th Coast Battery RCA, Serial 343, served at Prince Rupert, British Columbia, until cessation of hostilities, and received authorization to disband under General Order 18/46 (Effective 31st October 1945).

*   *   *

9th S/L Battery (CD) RCA — Serial 345 — Glace Bay, Nova Scotia

The organization of 9th (Cape Breton) Searchlight Battery RCA (CD) in Military District No. 6, was authorized under General Order 60/39 (Effective 1st March 1939). The searchlight battery was attached to 16th Coast Brigade RCA, under General Order 61/39 (Effective 1st March 1939).

Both these 1st March dates were amended to read "(Effective 15th May 1939)", in General Order 174/39, 27th September 1939.

9th (Cape Breton) Searchlight Battery RCA (CD) was localized at Glace Bay, Nova Scotia, Military District No. 6, under General Order 64/39 (Effective 1st march 1939).

9th Searchlight Battery (CD) RCA is included in the NPAM units called out on service in Military District No. 6, under General Order 124/39 (Effective 26th August 1939).

Composition of the Canadian Active Service Force authorized under General Order 135/39, 1st September 1939, includes the battery, listed as Serial 345, 9th Searchlight Battery (CD) RCA, CASF (Details) and the battery continued its manning duties at the forts.

9th Searchlight Battery (CD) RCA, Serial 345, was placed on Active Service under General Order 44/41 (Effective 1st January 1941). The CASF "Details" were absorbed into the battery and continued to serve attached to 16th Coast Brigade RCA, under Headquarters Sydney-Canso Defences, in Military District No. 6, Atlantic Command.

Headquarters 16th Coast Brigade RCA was redesignated Headquarters 16th Coast Regiment RCA, and its three component Heavy Batteries RCA were redesignated Coast Batteries under General Order 399/42 (Effective 1st August 1942).

Serial 345, 9th Searchlight Battery (CD) RCA received authorization to disband at this time, under General Order 399/42 (Effective 1st August 1942). The coast batteries assumed the searchlight manning duties, and absorbed the personnel of 9th Searchlight Battery (CD) RCA.

*   *   *

10th S/L Battery (CD) RCA — Serial 346 — Halifax, Nova Scotia

The organization of 10th Searchlight Battery RCA (CD) in Military District No. 6, was authorized under General Order 60/39 (Effective 1st March 1939).

The searchlight battery was attached to 1st (Halifax) Coast Brigade RCA, under General Order 61/39 (Effective 1st March 1939). Both these 1st March dates were amended to read — "(Effective 15th May 1939)", in General Order 174/39, 27th September 1939.

10th Searchlight Battery RCA (CD) was localized at Halifax, Nova Scotia, in Military District No. 6, under General Order 64/39 (Effective 1st March 1939).

10th Searchlight Battery (CD) RCA is included in the NPAM units called out on service in Military District No. 6, under General Order 124/39 (Effective 26th August 1939).

Composition of the Canadian Active Service Force authorized 1st September 1939, under General Order 135/39, lists the battery as, Serial 346, 10th Searchlight Battery (CD) RCA, CASF (Details). The battery continued its manning duties at the local forts.

10th Searchlight Battery (CD) RCA, Serial 346, was placed on active service under General Order 44/41 (Effective 1st January 1941). The CASF "Details" were absorbed into 10th Searchlight Battery (CD) RCA, which remained attached to 1st (Halifax) Coast Brigade RCA, and continued to serve under Headquarters Halifax Fortress, Military District No. 6, Atlantic Command.

Headquarters 1st (Halifax) Coast Brigade RCA, was redesignated Headquarters 1st (Halifax) Coast Regiment RCA, and its component Heavy Batteries were redesignated Coast Batteries, under General Order 386/42 (Effective 1st August 1942).

Serial 346, 10th Searchlightd Battery (CD) RCA received authorization to disband at this time, under General Order 385/42 (Effective 1st August 1942). The coast batteries assumed the searchlight manning duties, and absorbed the personnel of 10th Searchlight Battery (CD) RCA.

*   *   *

15th Coast Battery RCA — Serial 378 — Saint John, New Brunswick

Serial 378, 15th Heavy Battery RCA, CASF (Details) was authorized as a component of the Canadian Active Service Force under General Order 45/40 (Effective 1st September 1939), for duty at the forts in Military District No. 7

15th Heavy Battery RCA, Serial 378, was placed on Active Service under General Order 44/41 (Effective 1st January 1941), and the CASF "Details" were absorbed into 15th Heavy Battery RCA.

15th Heavy Battery RCA served with 3rd (New Brunswick) Coast Brigade RCA, under Headquarters Saint John Defences.

Serial 378, 15th Heavy Battery RCA was redesignated 15th Coast Battery RCA, Serial 378, and Headquarters 3rd (New Brunswick) Coast Brigade RCA was redesignated Headquarters 3rd (N.B.) Coast Regiment RCA, under General Order 37/43 (Effective 1st August 1942), for Headquarters, and (Effective 1st September 1942), for 15th Battery.

Headquarters Saint John Defences was redesignated Headquarters Defended Port of Saint John, under General Order 206/44 (Effective 15th April 1944), and 15th Battery continued to serve with 3rd (N.B.) Coast Regiment RCA, under Headquarters Defended Port of Saint John, in Atlantic Command.

Headquarters 3rd (NB) Coast Regiment RCA received authorization to disband under General Order 55/45 (Effective 1st September 1944).

Headquarters Defended Port of Saint John, and Headquarters Atlantic Command, disbanded under General Order 305/45 (Effective 31st July 1945).

Serial 378, 15th Coast Battery RCA, received authorization to disband under General Order 18/46 (Effective 15th August 1945), the emergency having ended and the Japanese surrender imminent.

* * *

17th Searchlight Battery (CD) RCA — Serial 395 — Esquimalt, B.C.

The organization of 17th Searchlight Battery RCA (CD) in Military District No. 11, was authorized under General Order 60/39 (Effective 1st March 1939).

17th Searchlight Battery RCA (CD), Non-Permanent Active Militia, was attached to 5th (British Columbia) Coast Brigade RCA of the Non-Permanent Active Militia, under General Order 61/39 (Effective 1st March 1939), and under General Order 64/39 (Effective 1st March 1939), 17th Searchlight Battery RCA (CD) was localized at Esquimalt, British Columbia.

17th Searchlight Battery (CD) RCA is included in the NPAM Units called out on service in Military District No. 11, under General Order 124/39 (Effective 26th August 1939).

Volunteers of 17th Searchlight Battery (CD) RCA, NPAM, assembled at Bay Street Armoury, Victoria, British Columbia, 26th August 1939, then proceeded to Fort Macaulay and Fort Rodd Hill for duty on the searchlights in the Victoria-Esquimalt Defences.

Composition of the Canadian Active Service Force authorized 1st September 1939, under General Order 135/39, included Serial 395, 17th Searchlight Battery (CD) RCA, CASF (Details).

The battery continued its duty at the forts, with battery headquarters located at Rodd Hill 26th August 1939, Belmont 5th September 1939 to 14th February 1940, Rodd Hill to May 1940, Macaulay Fort 16th May 1940 to 11th July 1940, Fort Mary Hill 11th July to 11th November 1940, returning to Fort Rodd Hill at that time.

Detachments served at Rodd Hill, Black Rock, Ogden Point, Breakwater, McLaughlin Point, Albert Head, Duntze Head, Fort Macaulay, Mary Hill, Clover Point, Holland Point, and William Head.

"Details" were absorbed into the battery as Serial 395, 17th Searchlight Battery (CD) RCA was placed on active service under General Order 44/41 (Effective 1st January 1941), in Military District No. 11, and the battery continued to serve under Headquarters Victoria and Esquimalt Fortress.

From a total of 101 All Ranks, 31st December 1939, the battery grew to almost 300 during 1941, upon the posting of Home Defence troops for training.

Serial 395, 17th Searchlight Battery (CD) RCA, received authorization to disband under General Order 276/42 (Effective 1st May 1942). The coast batteries absorbed the officers and men of the searchlight battery and assumed the searchlight manning duties.

*   *   *

A 23 Coast and Anti-Aircraft Training Centre — Serial 1223 — Halifax

A 23 Coast and Anti-Aircraft Artillery Training Centre, Serial 1223, was called out on active service under General Order 250/41 (Effective 15th February 1941), at Halifax, Nova Scotia.

The training centre trained Cadres for coast artillery units and anti-aircraft units. Facilities were taxed to the limit during 1942 with the forming of the majority of anti-aircraft units for duty on the East Coast.

A 23 Coast and Anti-Aircraft Artillery Training Centre was redesignated The Royal Canadian School of Artillery (Anti-Aircraft) in Supplement to Canadian Army Orders 1947, No. 30, 28th July 1947 (Effective 1st October 1946).

* * *

31st Coast Battery RCA — Serial 388 — Vancouver, British Columbia

31st Heavy Battery RCA, 15th (Vancouver) Coast Brigade RCA, is listed with NPAM units called out on service in Military District No. 11, under General Order 124/39 (Effective 26th August 1939), to man the guns at Narrows North and Stanley Park, Vancouver Defences.

Serial 388, 31st Heavy Battery RCA, CASF (Details) and Headquarters 15th (Vancouver) Coast Brigade RCA, CASF (Details), became components of the Canadian Active Service Force in Military District No. 11, under General Order 135/39, 1st September 1939.

The "Details" were absorbed into the battery, as Serial 388, 31st Heavy Battery RCA was placed on active service under General Order 44/41 (Effective 1st January 1941).

Serial 388, 31st Heavy Battery RCA, was redesignated Serial 388, 31st Coast Battery RCA, and Headquarters 15th (Vancouver) Coast Brigade RCA, was redesignated Headquarters 15th (Vancouver) Coast Regiment RCA, under General Order 37/43 (Effective 1st June 1942).

31st Coast Battery manned one 18 pounder gun at Point Atkinson in an Examination role, two 12 pounder guns at Narrows North, and, originally, two 6 inch guns at Stanley Park, which were exchanged for two Yorke Island 4.7 inch guns in mid-1942. These forts were the responsibility of 15th (Vancouver) Coast Regiment RCA, under Headquarters Vancouver Defences, Pacific Command.

Following the disbandment of 3rd Searchlight Battery (Coast Defence) RCA in July 1942, the coast batteries assumed the searchlight manning duties, and absorbed the personnel of the searchlight battery.

31st Coast Battery RCA, Serial 388, and Headquarters 15th (Vancouver) Coast Regiment RCA, received authorization to disband under General Order 149/44. (Effective 1st March 1944). 85th Battery remained at Yorke Island. 58th Battery added Point Atkinson and Narrows North to its responsibilities. The two batteries continued to serve as Independent Batteries under Headquarters Vancouver Defences, Pacific Command.

* * *

36th Coast Battery RCA — Serial 337 — Sydney Mines, Nova Scotia

36th Heavy Battery RCA, Non-Permanent Active Militia, was called out on service in Military District No. 6, with Headquarters 16th Coast Brigade RCA, under General Order 124/39 (Effective 26th August 1939), for duty in the Sydney-Canso Defences.

Serial 337, 36th Heavy Battery RCA, CASF (Details) and Headquarters 16th Coast Brigade RCA, CASF (Details) were named components of the Canadian Active Service Force, under General Order 135/39, 1st September 1939.

36th Heavy Battery RCA, Serial 337, was placed on active service under General Order 44/41 (Effective 1st January 1941), and the CASF "Details" were absorbed into the battery.

Serial 337, 36th Heavy Battery RCA was redesignated Serial 337, 36th Coast Battery RCA, and Headquarters 16th Coast Brigade RCA was redesignated Headquarters 16th Coast Regiment RCA, under General Order 399/42 (Effective 1st August 1942).

36th Battery served with 16th Coast Regiment RCA as Examination Battery at Chapel Point, under Headquarters Sydney-Canso Defences, and its later designation — Headquarters Defended Port of Sydney.

36th Coast Battery RCA, Serial 337, received authorization to disband under General Order 208/45 (Effective 1st September 1944).

*   *   *

51st Coast Battery RCA — Serial 340 — Halifax, Nova Scotia

51st Heavy Battery RCA, Non-Permanent Active Militia, was called out on service in Military District No. 6, with Headquarters 1st (Halifax) Coast Brigade RCA, under General Order 124/39 (Effective 26th August 1939), to serve in the local forts.

"Details" of Serial 340, 51st Heavy Battery RCA, CASF, and "Details" of Serial 339, Headquarters 1st (Halifax) Coast Brigade RCA, CASF, were named components of the Canadian Active Service Force under General Order 135/39, 1st September 1939, in Military District No. 6.

"The Details" were absorbed into the battery as 51st Heavy Battery RCA, Serial 340 was placed on active service under General Order 44/41, Schedule "B", (Effective 1st January 1941), with Headquarters 1st (Halifax) Coast Brigade RCA.

51st Heavy Battery RCA, Serial 340, was redesignated 51st Coast Battery RCA, Serial 340, and Headquarters 1st (Halifax) Coast Brigade RCA was redesignated Headquarters 1st (Halifax) Coast Regiment RCA, Serial 339, under General Order 386/42 (Effective 1st August 1942).

51st Coast Battery RCA, Serial 340, and Headquarters 1st (Halifax) Coast Regiment RCA, Serial 339, served under Headquarters Halifax Fortress until authorized to disband under General Order 18/46 (Effective 15th August 1945).

* * *

52nd Coast Battery RCA — Serial 341 — Halifax, Nova Scotia

52nd Heavy Battery RCA, Non-Permanent Active Militia, was called out on service in Military District No. 6, with Headquarters 1st (Halifax) Coast Brigade RCA, under General Order 124/39 (Effective 26th August 1939), to serve in the local forts.

"Details" of Serial 341, 52nd Heavy Battery RCA, CASF and "Details" of Serial 339, Headquarters 1st (Halifax) Coast Brigade RCA, CASF, were named components of the Canadian Active Service Force under General Order 135/39, 1st September 1939, in Military District No. 6.

The "Details" were absorbed into the battery as 52nd Heavy Battery RCA, Serial 341, was placed on active service under General Order 44/41, Schedule "B", (Effective 1st January 1941), with Headquarters 1st (Halifax) Coast Brigade RCA.

52nd Heavy Battery RCA, Serial 341, was redesignated 52nd Coast Battery RCA, Serial 341, and Headquarters 1st (Halifax) Coast Brigade RCA was redesignated Headquarters 1st (Halifax) Coast Regiment RCA, Serial 339, under General Order 386/42 (Effective 1st August 1942).

52nd Coast Battery RCA, Serial 341, and Headquarters 1st (Halifax) Coast Regiment RCA served under Headquarters Halifax Fortress until authorized to disband under General Order 18/46 (Effective 15th August 1945).

* * *

53rd Coast Battery RCA — Serial 342 — Halifax, Nova Scotia

53rd Heavy Battery RCA, Non-Permanent Active Militia, was called out on service in Military District No. 6, for duty at the forts in the Halifax area, with Headquarters 1st (Halifax) Coast Brigade RCA, authorized under General Order 124/39 (Effective 26th August 1939).

"Details" of Serial 342, 53rd Heavy Battery RCA, CASF, and "Details" of Serial 339, Headquarters 1st (Halifax) Coast Brigade RCA, CASF, were named components of the Canadian Active Service Force under General Order 135/39, 1st September 1939, in Military District No. 6.

The "Details" were absorbed into the battery, as Serial 342, 53rd Heavy Battery RCA was placed on Active Service under General Order 44/41, Schedule "B",

(Effective 1st January 1941), with Headquarters 1st (Halifax) Coast Brigade RCA. The battery and regiment continued to serve in the Halifax Defences under Headquarters Halifax Fortress.

53rd Coast Battery RCA, Serial 342, served in the Halifax area until authorized to disband under General Order 227/46 (Effective 31st July 1946). Headquarters 1st Halifax Coast Regiment RCA had disbanded earlier under General Order 18/46 (Effective 15th August 1945), and Headquarters Halifax Fortress followed headquarters of the regiment into disbandment under General Order 85/46 (Effective 29th November 1945).

* * *

54th Coast Battery RCA — Serial 893 — Halifax, Nova Scotia

54th Heavy Battery RCA, Serial 893, mobilized under General Order 164/42 (Effective 10th April 1942), for service in Military District No. 6.

54th Heavy Battery RCA, Serial 893, was redesignated 54th Coast Battery RCA, Serial 893, under General Order 37/43 (Effective 1st November 1942). The battery served in the Halifax Defences with 1st (Halifax) Coast Regiment RCA, under Headquarters Halifax Fortress, in Atlantic Command.

54th Coast Battery RCA, Serial 893, received authorization to disband under General Order 149/44 (Effective 1st March 1944).

* * *

55th Coast Battery RCA — Serial 384 — Victoria, British Columbia

55th Heavy Battery RCA, Non-Permanent Active Militia, was called out on service in Military District No. 11, with Headquarters 5th (British Columbia) Coast Brigade RCA, under General Order 124/39 (Effective 26th August 1939), for duty in the Victoria-Esquimalt Fortress.

4 Officers and 33 Other Ranks of 55th Heavy Battery RCA, NPAM, proceeded to Fort Mary Hill to man the three 6 inch guns of the fort on the 26th August 1939 and were joined by 10 ORs of 5th Heavy Battery RCA, Permanent Force, 4 ORs of 11th Fortress Signals Company RCCS, and 2 ORs of 13th Field Ambulance RCAMC.

Also on the 26th of August 1939, 2 Officers and 15 ORs of 55th Battery marched to Fort Macaulay and were transferred to Fort Black Rock, to man the two 12 pounders.

"Details" of Serial 384, 55th Heavy Battery RCA, CASF, with Serial 383, Headquarters 5th (British Columbia) Coast Brigade RCA, CASF (Details), were named components of the Canadian Active Service Force, under General Order 135/39, 1st September 1939, in Military District No. 11

The "Details" were absorbed into the battery, as Serial 384, 55th Heavy Battery RCA was placed on active service under General Order 44/41 (Effective 1st January 1941), with Headquarters, 5th (British Columbia) Coast Brigade RCA.

55th Heavy Battery RCA, Serial 384, was redesignated 55th Coast Battery RCA, Serial 384, and Headquarters 5th (British Columbia) Coast Brigade RCA was redesignated Headquarters 5th (B.C.) Coast Regiment RCA, under General Order 37/43 (Effective 1st May 1942).

The Fort Mary Hill Battery operated in a Counter Bombardment, Close Defence and Examination Battery role. 55th Battery also manned two Bofors 40mm light anti-aircraft guns and three coast defence searchlights, operated in conjunction with the fort.

The battery also manned the two 12 pounders at Golf Hill in an Anti-Motor Torpedo Boat role. These were the same guns the battery had manned at Fort Black Rock.

Golf Hill Battery, situated on the western shore of Victoria Harbour, commanded the entrance to Victoria Harbour and the immediate vicinity. The duty of the battery in conjunction with Macaulay and Ogden Point Batteries was to protect Victoria Harbour and industries located there.

55th Coast Battery RCA, Serial 384, received authorization to disband under General Order 227/46 (Effective 31st July 1946), the emergency having ended with cessation of hostilities.

*   *   *

56th Coast Battery RCA — Serial 385 — Victoria, British Columbia

56th Heavy Battery RCA, Non-Permanent Active Militia, was called out on service in Military District No. 11, with Headquarters 5th (British Columbia) Coast Brigade RCA, under General Order 124/39 (Effective 26th August 1939), to man the forts in the Victoria-Esquimalt Fortress.

5 Officers and 34 Other Ranks of 56th Heavy Battery RCA, NPAM, proceeded to Fort Albert Head, 26th August 1939, to man the two 9.2 inch guns. — (increased to three guns early in 1943).

"Details" of Serial 385, 56th Heavy Battery RCA, CASF, with "Details" of Serial 383, Headquarters 5th (British Columbia) Coast Brigade RCA, CASF, were named components of the Canadian Active Service Force, under General Order 135/39, 1st September 1939, in Military District No. 11.

In September 1940, 56th Heavy Battery RCA assumed the duty of manning the two 12 pounder guns at Fort Duntze Head from 60th Heavy Battery RCA.

The "Details" were absorbed into the battery, as Serial 385, 56th Heavy Battery RCA, was placed on active service under General Order 44/41 (Effective 1st January 1941), with Headquarters, 5th (British Columbia) Coast Brigade RCA.

56th Heavy Battery RCA, Serial 385, was redesignated 56th Coast Battery RCA, Serial 385, under General Order 37/43.

Headquarters 5th (British Columbia) Coast Brigade RCA, was redesignated Headquarters 5th (B.C.) Coast Regiment RCA, under General Order 37/43 (Effective 1st May 1942). The effective date for 56th Battery was also 1st May 1942. The battery and regiment continued to serve under Headquarters Victoria and Esquimalt Fortress.

The Albert Head Battery operated in a Close Defence, and Counter Bombardment role. 56th Coast Battery RCA also manned two Bofors 40mm light anti-aircraft guns and two coast defence searchlights.

The 12 pounders of the Fort Duntze Head Battery were replaced by a twin 6 pounder, which was reported in action in July 1943, and on the 15th of August 1943, 109th Coast Battery RCA assumed responsibility for the Duntze Head Battery. The battery operated in a Close Defence, Anti-Motor Torpedo Boat role.

Instructions for reductions in Coast Artillery Armament on the Pacific Coast, dated 25th August 1944, included orders to put Albert Head Battery in maintenance and 56th Coast Battery RCA, Serial 385, received authorization to disband under General Order 208/45 (Effective 1st September 1944).

*   *   *

58th Coast Battery RCA — Serial 389 — Vancouver, B.C.

58th Heavy Battery RCA, 15th (Vancouver) Coast Brigade RCA, is listed with NPAM units called out on service in Military District No. 11, under General Order 124/39 (Effective 26th August 1939), to serve in the Vancouver, British Columbia Defences.

"Details" of 58th Heavy Battery RCA, CASF, Serial 389, and "Details" of Headquarters 15th (Vancouver) Coast Brigade RCA, CASF, Serial 387, became components of the Canadian Active Service Force in Military District No. 11, under General Order 135/39, 1st September 1939.

The "Details" were absorbed into the battery, as Serial 389, 58th Heavy Battery RCA was placed on active service under General Order 44/41, Schedule "B" (Effective 1st January 1941).

Serial 389, 58th Heavy Battery RCA, was redesignated Serial 389, 58th Coast Battery RCA, and Headquarters 15th (Vancouver) Coast Brigade RCA, was redesignated Headquarters 15th (Vancouver) Coast Regiment RCA, Serial 387, under General Order 37/43 (Effective 1st June 1942).

58th Coast Battery RCA manned the three 6 inch guns at Point Grey and two 18 pounder field guns at Steveston, and assumed the duty of manning the coast defence searchlights upon the disbandment of 3rd Searchlight Battery (Coast Defence) RCA, authorized under General order 314/44 (Effective 18th July 1942). The batteries of 15th (Vancouver) Coast Regiment RCA absorbed the members of the searchlight battery. To help alleviate boredom in the isolated areas the gun crews were interchanged periodically.

Headquarters 15th (Vancouver) Coast Regiment RCA, Serial 387, and 31st Coast Battery RCA, Serial 388, were authorized to disband under General Order 149/44 (Effective 1st March 1944). 58th Coast Battery and 85th Coast Battery became independent Coast Batteries and continued to serve under Headquarters Vancouver Defences, in Pacific Command.

85th Battery remained at Yorke Island. 58th Battery retained the manning duty at Point Grey, and assumed the responsibility of Point Atkinson and Narrows North, however, 58th Battery too was phased out later in the year.

58th Coast Battery RCA, Serial 389, received authorization to disband under General Order 208/45 (Effective 1st September 1944). Headquarters Vancouver Defences disbanded in February 1945, and 85th Coast Battery RCA disbanded 31st October 1945.

*   *   *

59th Coast Battery RCA — Serial 322 — Quebec and Levis, P.Q.

59th Medium Battery (Howitzer) RCA, was redesignated 59th Heavy Battery RCA and attached to 6th (Quebec and Levis) Medium Brigade RCA, under General Order 59/39 (Effective 1st April 1939).

59th Heavy Battery RCA, Non-Permanent Active Militia, was called out on service in Military District No. 5, under General Order 124/39 (Effective 26th August 1939), to serve in the Coast Defences at Quebec, P.Q.

Serial 322, 59th Heavy Battery RCA, CASF (Details), became a component of the Canadian Active Service Force, authorized under General Order 135/39, 1st September 1939.

The "Details" were absorbed into the battery, as Serial 322, 59th Heavy Battery RCA, was placed on active service, under General Order 44/41, Schedule "B", (Effective 1st January 1941), in Military District No. 5.

59th Heavy Battery RCA, Serial 322, was redesignated 59th Coast Battery RCA, Serial 322, under General Order 361/42 (Effective 1st June 1942), and served at Fort La Martiniere, Lauzon, P.Q.

59th Coast Battery RCA, Serial 322, received authorization to disband under General Order 208/45 (Effective 15th February 1945).

*   *   *

60th Coast Battery RCA — Serial 386 — Victoria, British Columbia

60th Heavy Battery RCA, Non-Permanent Active Militia, was called out on service in Military District No. 11, with Headquarters 5th (British Columbia) Coast Brigade RCA, under General Order 124/39 (Effective 26th August 1939), to man the forts in the Victoria-Esquimalt Fortress.

Volunteers assembled at the Bay Street Armoury in Victoria at 1300 hours, 26th August 1939, where 6 Officers and 37 Other Ranks drew uniforms and proceeded to Belmont Fort.

"Details" of Serial 386, 60th Heavy Battery RCA, CASF, and Serial 383, Headquarters 5th (British Columbia) Coast Brigade RCA, CASF (Details), were named components of the Canadian Active Service Force in Military District No. 11, under General order 135/39, 1st September 1939.

60th Battery also manned guns on the Breakwater, and Golf Hill, then on the 8th of September 1939, 1 Officer and 20 ORs moved to Fort Macaulay.

The "Details" were absorbed into the battery, as Serial 386, 60th Heavy Battery RCA was placed on active service with Headquarters, 5th (British Columbia) Coast Brigade RCA, under General Order 44/41, Schedule "B", (Effective 1st January 1941).

Previous to mobilizing, "E" Troop manned Belmont Battery at Fort Rodd Hill, in an Anti-Motor Torpedo Boat (AMTB) role, "B" Troop manned two 6 inch guns in Macaulay Battery, in an Examination and Close Defence role, "F" Troop manned a 12 pounder gun at Ogden Pier, in an AMTB role.

60th Heavy Battery RCA, Serial 386, was redesignated 60th Coast Battery RCA, Serial 386, and Headquarters 5th (British Columbia) Coast Brigade was redesignated Headquarters 5th (B.C.) Coast Regiment RCA, under General Order 37/43 (Effective 1st May 1942).

The battery and regiment continued to serve under Headquarters Victoria and Esquimalt Fortress and its later designation, Headquarters Esquimalt Fortress.

With the arrival of "VJ" Day and the cessation of hostilities, 60th Coast Battery RCA, Serial 386, received authorization to disband under General Order 18/46 (Effective 31st October 1945). Serial 383, Headquarters 5th (B.C.) Coast Regiment RCA, and Serial 2918, Headquarters Esquimalt Fortress, also disbanded at this time.

*   *   *

68th Coast Battery RCA — Serial 382 — Victoria-Esquimalt, B.C.

68th Heavy Battery RCA of 15th (Vancouver) Coast Brigade RCA was redesignated 9th Anti-Aircraft Battery RCA in a reorganization of Royal Canadian Artillery, Non-Permanent Active Militia in Military District No. 11, under General Order 75/39 (Effective 15th May 1939).

9th Anti-Aircraft Battery RCA became a component of 1st Anti-Aircraft Regiment RCA, and was localized at Vancouver, British Columbia. 9th Anti-Aircraft Battery RCA, Serial 418, disbanded under General Order 183/42 (Effective 13th April 1942).

68th Heavy Battery RCA surfaced again when it was decided to mobilize a battery for the new fort at Christopher Point, in the Victoria-Esquimalt Fortress, under the command of 5th (British Columbia) Coast Brigade RCA.

68th Heavy Battery RCA, Serial 382, mobilized under General Order 155/41 (Effective 11th June 1941), with 5th (British Columbia) Coast Brigade RCA, to man the coastal guns at Christopher Point, South Vancouver Island, under Headquarters Victoria-Esquimalt Fortress.

Two U.S. 8 inch Railway guns (1888) without railway mountings were installed at Christopher Point during September 1941.

68th Heavy Battery RCA, Serial 382, was redesignated 68th Coast Battery RCA, Serial 382, and Headquarters 5th (British Columbia) Coast Brigade was redesignated Headquarters 5th (B.C.) Coast Regiment RCA, under General Order 37/43 (Effective 1st May 1942).

The following is an excerpt from 68th Coast Battery War Diary: "26th July 1943 — Parade of all ranks called by Major D.G. McGavin to tell them that they were going to Prince Rupert to become the 9th Coast Battery very soon.

1 officer and 66 men left for Fairview Battery Prince Rupert 9th August 1943.

1 officer and 68 men from 9 Coast Battery arrived 15th August 1943 at Christopher Point.

2 officers and 52 ORs in 2nd Draft, left for Prince Rupert 16th August 1943.

2nd Draft from Prince Rupert of 2 officers and 42 ORs arrived 22nd August 1943.

Christopher Point Battery remained designated 68th Coast Battery RCA."

30th Light Anti-Aircraft Battery of 6th Light Anti-Aircraft Regiment RCA, and 59th Anti-Aircraft Battery RCA provided protection from air attack, prior to 68th Coast Battery adding its own light anti-aircraft section.

The run-down of units on the west coast was begun following the Japanese evacuation of the Aleutian Islands the latter part of 1943 and 68th Coast Battery RCA, Serial 382, received authorization to disband under General Order 247/44 (Effective 20th April 1944). The guns were returned to the U.S. in January 1945.

*   *   *

85th Coast Battery RCA — Serial 390 — Vancouver, British Columbia

85th Heavy Battery RCA, 15th (Vancouver) Coast Brigade RCA, is listed with NPAM units called out on service in Military District No. 11, under General Order 124/39 (Effective 26th August 1939), to man the Yorke Island Defences.

"Details" of Serial 390, 85th Heavy Battery RCA, CASF, and "Details" of Headquarters 15th (Vancouver) Coast Brigade RCA, CASF, became components of the Canadian Active Service Force, in Military District No. 11, under General Order 135/39, 1st September 1939.

The "Details" were absorbed into the battery, as Serial 390, 85th Heavy Battery RCA was placed on active service under General Order 44/41 (Effective 1st January 1941).

Serial 390, 85th Heavy Battery RCA, was redesignated Serial 390, 85th Coast Battery RCA, and Headquarters 15th (Vancouver) Coast Brigade RCA, was redesignated Headquarters 15th (Vancouver) Coast Regiment RCA, under General Order 37/43 (Effective 1st April 1942, for 85th Battery, and Effective 1st June 1942), for Headquarters 15th (Vancouver) Coast Regiment RCA.

The two 4.7 inch guns of the Yorke Island Battery were exchanged for the two 6 inch guns of the Stanley Park Battery at Ferguson Point in mid-1942, and 85th Coast Battery continued its manning duty on Yorke Island with these longer range guns. The battery also manned the coast defence searchlights and one coast battery Bofors 40mm light anti-aircraft section of two guns.

Personnel from this isolated spot periodically exchanged duties and locations with personnel of 58th Coast Battery RCA at Point Grey, Vancouver Defences.

85th Coast Battery RCA, Serial 390, continued to serve at Yorke Island as an Independent Battery following the disbanding of Headquarters 15th (Vancouver) Coast Regiment RCA, 1st March 1944, and with the cessation of hostilities, 85th Coast Battery RCA was authorized to disband under General Order 18/46 (Effective 31st October 1945).

* * *

86th Coast Battery RCA — Serial 338 — Antigonish, Nova Scotia

86th Heavy Battery RCA, 16th Coast Brigade RCA, is listed with Non-Permanent Active Militia units called out on service in Military District No. 6, under General Order 124/39 (Effective 26th August 1939), for duty in the Sydney-Canso Defences.

"Details" of 86th Heavy Battery RCA, CASF, Serial 338, and "Details" of Headquarters 16th Coast Brigade RCA, CASF, Serial 335, became components of the Canadian Active Service Force (CASF) in Military District No. 6, under General Order 135/39, 1st September 1939.

The CASF "Details" were absorbed into the battery, as Serial 338, 86th Heavy Battery RCA was placed on Active Service under General Order 44/41 (Effective 1st January 1941).

Serial 338, 86th Heavy Battery RCA, was redesignated 86th Coast Battery RCA, Serial 338, and Headquarters 16th Coast Brigade RCA, Serial 335, was redesignated Headquarters 16th Coast Regiment RCA, Serial 335, under General Order 399/42 (Effective 1st August 1942).

86th Battery manned the guns at Fort Melford and Beacon, at the entrance to the Straits of Canso, under Headquarters Sydney-Canso Defences, Nova Scotia, and its later designation, Headquarters Defended Port of Sydney.

86th Coast Battery RCA, Serial 338, continued to serve in the forts until cessation of hostilities was imminent and received authorization to disband under General Order 198/46 (Effective 15th August 1945).

* * *

102nd Coast Battery RCA — Serial 391 — Prince Rupert, B.C.

102nd (North British Columbia) Heavy Battery RCA, NPAM, was called out on service in Military District No. 11, under General Order 124/39 (Effective 26th August 1939), to aid in the defence of the Prince Rupert area.

102nd (North British Columbia) Heavy Battery RCA, CASF, was allotted Serial Number 391, and "Details" of the battery were authorized as components of the Canadian Active Service Force (CASF), under General Order 135/39, 1st September 1939.

102nd (North British Columbia) Heavy Battery RCA, Serial 391, was placed on active service under General Order 44/41 (Effective 1st January 1941). The CASF "Details" were absorbed into the battery and the battery continued to serve under Headquarters Prince Rupert Defences.

Serial 560, Headquarters 17th (North British Columbia) Coast Regiment RCA, was placed on active service under General Order 309/42 (Effective 1st May 1942), at Prince Rupert, British Columbia.

102nd (North British Columbia) Heavy Battery RCA, Serial 391, was redesignated 102nd Coast Battery RCA, Serial 391, under General Order 311/42 (Effective 1st May 1942).

17th (North British Columbia) Coast Regiment RCA was to comprise Serial 391, 102nd Coast Battery RCA and Serial 343, 9th Coast Battery RCA.

The regiment also received instructions to absorb the personnel of 2nd Searchlight Battery (Coast Defence), authorized to disband at that time.

102nd Coast Battery RCA manned three 6 inch guns and a light anti-aircraft section at Barrett Point, and one 75mm gun at Dundas Point, plus the searchlight duties, in the Prince Rupert Defences.

Serial 1600, Headquarters 8th Canadian Division was authorized to mobilize under General Order 301/42 (Effective 15th June 1942) and on the 9th of October 1942 the Prince Rupert Defences came under command.

The Battery and regiment served under 8th Division, Home Defence, Pacific Command, until mid-October 1943, at which time 8th Canadian Division disbanded.

102nd Coast Battery RCA, Serial 391, with 17th (North British Columbia) Coast Regiment RCA, Serial 560, continued to serve under Headquarters Prince Rupert Defences, Serial 2917, in Pacific Command, until cessation of hostilities. 102nd Coast Battery RCA, the regiment, and Headquarters Prince Rupert Defences received authorization to disband under General Order 18/46 (Effective 31st October 1945).

*   *   *

103rd Coast Battery RCA — Serial 430 — "W" Force

103rd Heavy Battery RCA, Serial 430, mobilized under General Order 71/41 (Effective 15th January 1941), "incorporating "Q" Battery RCA, AF, which became "C" Troop". (War Diary).

103rd Heavy Battery RCA, Serial 430, was redesignated 103rd Coast Battery RCA, Serial 430, under General Order 361/42 (Effective 1st June 1942).

103rd Battery operated independently outside regimental control under Headquarters St. John's Defences (Newfoundland), and its later designation, Headquarters Defended Port of St. John's. The battery manned the guns at Cape Spear, Amherst, and Chain Rock, in the St. John's, Newfoundland, defences, "W" Force, Atlantic Command.

103rd Coast Battery RCA, was redesignated 128th Heavy Anti-Aircraft Battery RCA, under General Order 138/46 (Effective 1st March 1946).

128th Heavy Anti-Aircraft Battery RCA was embodied in the Postwar Permanent Force, under General Order 158/46 (Effective 27th June 1946).

*   *   *

104th Coast Battery RCA — Serial 431 — Shelburne, Nova Scotia

104th Heavy Battery RCA, Serial 431, mobilized under General Order 71/41 (Effective 15th January 1941).

104th Heavy Battery RCA, Serial 431, was redesignated 104th Coast Battery RCA, Serial 431, under General Order 37/43 (Effective 1st June 1942).

104th Coast Battery served in Atlantic Command and manned guns at Government Point, Sand Point, and Fort McNutt, in the Shelburne, Nova Scotia, defences, under Headquarters Shelburne Defences, and its later designation, Headquarters Defended Port of Shelburne.

Headquarters Defended Port of Shelburne disbanded under General Order 208/45 (Effective 30th September 1944). Headquarters Atlantic Command disbanded under General Order 305/45 (Effective 31st July 1945). 104th Coast Battery RCA, Serial 431, received authorization to disband under General Order 18/46 (Effective 15th August 1945).

*   *   *

105th Coast Battery RCA — Serial 432 — Gaspe, P.Q.

105th Heavy Battery RCA, Serial 432, mobilized under General Order 71/41 (Effective 15th January 1941).

105th Heavy Battery RCA, Serial 432, was redesignated 105th Coast Battery RCA, Serial 432, under General Order 37/43 (Effective 1st June 1942) and served under Headquarters Gaspe Defences, Quebec, and its later designation, Headquarters Defended Port of Gaspe.

105th Coast Battery RCA, Serial 432, received authorization to disband under General Order 18/46 (Effective 15th August 1945).

*   *   *

106th Coast Battery RCA — Serial 433 — Botwood, Newfoundland

106th Heavy Battery RCA, Serial 433, mobilized under General Order 71/41 (Effective 15th January 1941).

106th Heavy Battery RCA, Serial 433, was redesignated 106th Coast Battery RCA, Serial 433, under General order 334/42 (Effective 1st June 1942).

106th Coast Battery RCA, Serial 433, served under Headquarters Botwood Defences (Newfoundland), and its later designation, Headquarters Defended Port of Botwood, until 106th Battery and the Headquarters were authorized to disband under General Orders 213/45 (Effective 31st March 1945) for 106th Coast Battery RCA, and (Effective 15th April 1945) for Headquarters Defended Port of Botwood.

*   *   *

107th Coast Battery RCA — Serial 892 — Lewisporte, Newfoundland.

107th Heavy Battery RCA, Serial 892, mobilized under General Order 90/42 (Effective 10th January 1942).

107th Heavy Battery RCA, Serial 892, was redesignated 107th Coast Battery RCA, Serial 892, under General Order 334/42 (Effective 1st June 1942).

107th Battery served in "W" Force, under Atlantic Command, at Lewishporte, in the Gander, Newfoundland, Defences.

107th Coast Battery RCA, Serial 892, received authorization to disband under General Order 213/45 (Effective 31st March 1945). "W" Force Brigade Headquarters, Serial 1140, disbanded under General Order 227/46 (Effective 30th July 1946).

*   *   *

108th Coast Battery RCA - Serial 786 — Fort Rigolet, Labrador

108th Battery mobilized as 108th Heavy Battery RCA, Serial 786, under General Order 181/42 (Effective 18th April 1942).

108th Heavy Battery RCA, Serial 786, was redesignated 108th Coast Battery RCA, Serial 786, under General Order 37/43 (Effective 1st June 1942).

108th Battery served in Atlantic Command, at Fort Rigolet, Labrador, under Headquarters Goose Bay Defences, and its later designation, Headquarters Defended Area Goose Bay.

108th Coast Battery RCA, Serial 786, received authorization to disband under General Order 208/45 — the effective date is not listed.

*   *   *

109th Coast Battery RCA - Serial 1722 — Victoria-Esquimalt, B.C.

War Diary Excerpt — "Fort Belmont, August 15th 1943 — Effective this date the 109th Coast Battery RCA, CA, is formed under Authority of HQS, 20-4-12B (Mob 1 b) dated 14 July 1943.

This Battery is to have as its main armament 6 pdr Duplex guns mounted one each at Belmont Fort, Duntze Head Fort and Ogden Pier.

Personnel have been taken over from the batteries manning the various Forts as follows: Belmont, 60th Coast Battery, Duntze Head, 56th Coast Battery, Ogden Pier, Holland Point and Clover Point from 60th Coast Battery.

Battery Headquarters 109th Coast Battery at Belmont."

109th Coast Battery RCA, Serial 1722, was authorized to mobilize under General Order 298/43 (Effective 1st June 1943), with Battery Headquarters at Fort Rodd Hill.

The battery was formed to man new 6 pounder (Duplex) Armament, but manned two 12 pounders in Belmont Battery until 6th July 1944 when the 6 pounder was emplaced, following alterations to the Belmont Battery site.

109th Coast Battery served as a component of 5th (B.C.) Coast Regiment RCA at Fort Duntze Head, Fort Ogden Pier, and Fort Belmont in a Close Defence role, with Belmont primarily an anti-motor torpedo boat battery and as a supporting battery for the Examination Battery at Fort Macaulay.

109th Coast Battery RCA, Serial 1722, manned the forts under Headquarters Victoria and Esquimalt Fortress, and its later designation, Headquarters Esquimalt Fortress, until cessation of hostilities.

109th Coast Battery, the Regiment, and Headquarters Esquimalt Fortress were authorized to disband under General Order 18/46 (Effective 31st October 1945).

*   *   *

110th Coast Battery RCA — Serial 1723

110th Coast Battery RCA, Serial 1723, received authorization to mobilize under General Order 298/43 (Effective 1st June 1943).

A change in the Battery War Establishment is authorized in General Order 304/43 (Effective 1st June 1943).

110th Coast Battery RCA, Serial 1723, was authorized to disband under General Order 149/44 (Effective 1st March 1944).

*   *   *

FIELD ARTILLERY

Section IV includes field artillery batteries of First Canadian Army, 1st, 2nd, 3rd and 4th Infantry Divisions, 4th and 5th Canadian Armoured Divisions, 6th, 7th and 8th Infantry Divisions, Home Defence, and 3rd Canadian Infantry Division, Canadian Army Occupational Force.

During the precautionary period preceding World War II, batteries of the Non-Permanent Active Militia were called out on service in the Military Districts to protect armouries and vital establishments.

The Canadian Active Service Force plan of a corps headquarters and two infantry divisions with supporting units was instituted 1st September 1939. The composition of the CASF was to include the existing Permanent Force units.

Eleven field artillery units were authorized to mobilize with the CASF 1st September 1939. Six of the eleven units became components of 1st and 2nd Divisions and five mobilized as army field brigades. Army field brigades were redesignated army field regiments, and field brigades field regiments. 1st and 2nd Army Field Brigades became anti-tank regiments. 5th Army Field Brigade was redesignated 21st Army Field Regiment, then 7th Army Field Regiment, and finally, 7th Medium Regiment RCA. 4th Army Field Brigade became 8th Army Field Regiment RCA, CASF, and 3rd Army Field Brigade was redesignated 11th Army Field Regiment RCA, CASF.

12th, 13th and 14th Field Regiments RCA mobilized with 3rd Division, CASF, and 15th, 16th and 17th Field Regiments mobilized with 4th Division, CASF, in May 1940. 18th Field Regiment RCA replaced 17th Field Regiment and 17th

Field Regiment joined 1st Canadian Armoured Division (Redesignated 5th Canadian (Armoured) Division) February 1941. 19th, 20th and 21st Field Regiments RCA mobilized with 6th Division in 1941.

4th Division was redesignated 4th (Armoured) Division in January 1942, retaining 15th Field Regiment RCA only. 16th and 18th Field Regiments were redesignated and allotted new roles in the overseas force.

22nd, 23rd and 24th Field Regiments mobilized with 7th Division, and 25th, 26th and 27th Field Regiments mobilized with 8th Division, in 1942. The brigade groups were shuffled between the home defence divisions and the artillery regiment moved with its allotted brigade.

8th Division less one brigade was responsible for the defence of northern B.C. 7th Division was located in eastern Canada as general reserve for Atlantic Command and 28th Field Regiment joined the division in 1943.

6th Division served in Pacific Command and 24th Field Regiment RCA accompanied 6th Division's 13th Brigade Group to Kiska, in the Aleutians, August 1943, returning to duty in Canada at the end of the year.

8th Army Field Regiment was added to 5th Canadian Armoured Division late 1943, and as 8th Field Regiment (Self-Propelled) RCA served with the division in Italy and NW Europe. 11th Field Regiment RCA served with 5th Division in Italy in 1944 providing artillery support for 12th CIB.

21st Field Regiment RCA arrived overseas to disbandment the latter part of 1943. 23rd Field Regiment (Self-Propelled) RCA joined 4th Canadian Armoured Division and served in France, Belgium, Holland, and Germany.

19th Army Field Regiment RCA shared the honour of landing in Normandy on D-Day, 6th June 1944 with 3rd Canadian Infantry Division's 12th, 13th and 14th Field Regiments RCA. The four regiments fired their 105mm SPs from the landing craft prior to going ashore.

A number of field artillery personnel accompanied 2nd Canadian Infantry Division in the raid on Dieppe, France, 19th August 1942. 2nd Division returned to the Continent in July 1944 and on the 3rd September 1944, following the capture of Dieppe, the Division paused for a service of remembrance and a divisional parade through the streets of the city.

1st Field Regiment with 1st Division's 1st Brigade Group sailed from England to France and back in June 1940. The Mediterranean beckoned in 1943 and 1st Canadian Infantry Division landed in the assault on the Island of Sicily 10th July 1943 with 30 Corps, British Eighth Army. The Division crossed to the Italian mainland during the first week of September 1943, serving until early

1945, then with 1st Canadian Corps departed for NW Europe and served under First Canadian Army until the cessation of hostilities.

*   *   *

"A" Battery RCHA, Kingston, Ontario — Serial 5B — 1st Cdn Inf Div.

"A" Battery was struck off strength from the Permanent Active Militia (PF), allotted Serial Number 6, and taken on strength the Canadian Active Service Force (CASF) under General Order 135/39, 1st September 1939, to serve with Headquarters of 1st Field Brigade RCA, CASF, in Canada's 1st Division, Canadian Active Service Force.

"A" Battery departed for overseas on board the Empress of Britain 10th December 1939, in Troop Convoy 1, and disembarked at Gourock, Scotland, 18th December 1939.

Field brigades were redesignated field regiments and under the new organization the original batteries were paired in a two battery field regiment, authorized under General Order 44/40 (Effective 21st December 1939).

"A" Battery RCHA, CASF, Serial 6, combined with "B" Battery RCHA, CASF, Serial 7, to become "A"/"B" Field Battery RCA, CASF, Serial 6, with Headquarters of 1st Field Regiment RCA, CASF.

As part of the Second British Expeditionary Force (BEF), "A"/"B" Field Battery RCA landed at Brest, France, 13th June 1940, but due to the deteriorating situation in France the battery returned to England via Brest, on the 18th June 1940 with its guns.

In the defence of England "A"/"B" Field Battery served with 7th Corps upon its forming on the 21st of July 1940, until the 25th of December 1940, when the Canadian Corps was formed and 7th Corps disbanded.

The regiment reorganized to comprise three batteries, authorized under General Order 45/41 (Effective 1st January 1941). "A" Battery regained individual identity and remained with the regiment as "A" Battery RCHA, Serial 6, 1st Field Regiment RCHA.

In a shuffle of serial numbers within the regiment, "A" Battery was allotted Serial Number 5B, under General Order 54/42 (Effective 22nd December 1941).

1st Canadian Infantry Division proceeded to the Mediterranean Theatre of Operations and landed in the assault on the island of Sicily with 30 Corps, British Eighth Army, 10th July 1943.

The RCHA in support of 3rd Canadian Infantry Brigade in a follow-up role, sailed from Glasgow, Scotland, the night of 1st/2nd July 1943, less "B" Battery.

"A" Battery landed in Sicily on the 13th of July near Pachino, and joined the action with 30 Corps on the 18th July 1943, near Enna, in support of a successful attack by the Royal 22nd Regiment of 3rd Canadian Infantry Brigade.

With the fall of Sicily "A" Battery supported 3rd Canadian Infantry Brigade in the assault on the Italian mainland and landed on the 3rd of September 1943, with 13 Corps, British Eighth Army.

The regiment rejoined 1st Canadian Corps in Italy upon the corps becoming operational early in 1944, and served as a component in Italy until 1945, then with the corps moved to NW Europe to join First Canadian Army for the knock-out blow.

"A" Battery desparted from Italy 17th March 1945 via Leghorn and arrived at Marseilles, France, 19th March 1945.

The regiment moved into the line 7th April 1945, and fired its first rounds under First Canadian Army in NW Europe, in support of 3rd Canadian Infantry Division from positions near the village of Joppe, as the Regina Rifle Regiment of 7th Canadian Infantry Brigade moved up on Deventer, Holland.

"A" Battery then fired in support of 1st Canadian Infantry Division with firing being halted temporarily while food was taken into the occupied part of Holland. The regiment fired its last rounds in action in NW Europe, 3rd May 1945, from positions near Nijkerk, Holland, and the 8th of May 1945 was declared "VE" Day.

The regiment moved to an area South of Rotterdam and assisted in the return of the Germans to their homeland and the transfer of their equipment to concentration areas.

"A" Battery RCHA received authorization to disband under General Order 401/45 (Effective 25th August 1945). The battery surfaced again in the Postwar Permanent Force and further actions.

*   *   *

"B" Battery RCHA, Kingston, Ontario — Serial 5C — 1st Cdn Inf Div.

"B" Battery was SOS from the Permanent Active Militia (PF), allotted Serial Number 7, and TOS the Canadian Active Service Force (CASF), under General Order 135/39, 1st September 1939, to serve with Headquarters of 1st Field Brigade RCA, CASF, in Canada's 1st Division, Canadian Active Service Force.

"B" Battery departed for overseas on board the Empress of Britain 10th December 1939 in Troop Convoy 1, and disembarked at Gourock, Scotland, 18th December 1939.

Field brigades were redesignated field regiments and under the new organization the original batteries were paired in a two battery field regiment, authorized under General Order 44/40 (Effective 21st December 1939).

"B" Battery RCHA, CASF, Serial 7, combined with "A" Battery RCHA, CASF, Serial 6, to become "A"/"B" Field Battery RCA, CASF, Serial 6, with Headquarters of 1st Field Regiment RCA, CASF.

As part of the Second British Expeditionary Force (BEF), "A"/"B" Field Battery RCA landed at Brest, France, on the 13th of June 1940, but due to the deteriorating situation in France the battery returned to England via Brest, 18th June 1940.

In the defence of England "A"/"B" Field Battery served with 7th Corps upon its forming on the 21st July 1940, until the 25th of December 1940, when the Canadian Corps was formed and 7th Corps disbanded.

The regiment reorganized to comprise three batteries, authorized under General Order 45/41 (Effective 1st January 1941). "B" Battery regained individual identity and remained with the regiment as "B" Battery RCHA, Serial 7, 1st Field Regiment RCHA.

"B" Battery was allotted Serial Number 5C, under General Order 54/42 (Effective 22nd December 1941).

1st Canadian Infantry Division moved to the Mediterranean Theatre of Operations and on the 10th of July 1943 landed in the assault on the island of Sicily with 30 Corps, British Eighth Army.

"B" Battery set sail 17th August 1943 to join the division, and landed at Augusta, Sicily, 27th August 1943. "B" Battery caught up with the regiment in time to support 3rd Canadian Infantry Brigade in the assault on the Italian mainland by 13 Corps of British Eighth Army, 3rd September 1943.

The regiment with the division rejoined 1st Canadian Corps early 1944, upon the corps becoming operational in Italy, and moved to NW Europe with the corps in 1945.

"B" Battery departed from Italy 17th March 1945 via Leghorn and arrived at Marseilles, France, 19th March 1945.

The regiment moved into the line under First Canadian Army in NW Europe,

7th April 1945, and fired its first rounds in support of 3rd Canadian Infantry Division from positions near the village of Joppe, as the Regina Rifle Regiment of 7th Canadian Infantry Brigade moved up on Deventer, Holland.

"B" Battery then fired in support of 1st Canadian Infantry Division with firing being halted temporarily on the 28th April while food was taken into the occupied part of Holland. The regiment fired its last round in action in NW Europe, 3rd May 1945 from positions near Nijkerk, Holland, and the 8th of May 1945 was designated "VE" Day.

"B" Battery with the regiment moved to an area South of Rotterdam and assisted in the return of the Germans to their homeland, and the movement of their confiscated equipment to a concentration area.

The return to Canada of the Canadian Forces in NW Europe was begun and "B" Battery RCHA received authorization to disband along with Headquarters of 1st Divisional Artillery RCA and all artillery regiments of 1st Canadian Infantry Division, under General Order 401/45 (Effective 25th August 1945). "B" Battery surfaced again in the Postwar Permanent Force.

*   *   *

"C" Battery RCHA, Winnipeg, Manitoba — Serial 5D — 1st Cdn Inf Div.

"C" Battery was struck off strength from the Permanent Active Militia (PF), allotted Serial Number 8 and taken on strength the Canadian Active Service Force (CASF), under General Order 135/39, 1st September 1939, to serve with Headquarters of 1st Field Brigade RCA, CASF, in Canada's 1st Division, Canadian Active Service Force.

"C" Battery departed for overseas 10th December 1939 on board the Empress of Australia, and disembarked at Gourock, Scotland, on the 17th of December 1939.

Field brigades were redesignated Field regiments and under the new organization the original batteries were paired in a two battery field regiment, authorized under General Order 44/40 (Effective 21st December 1939).

"C" Battery RCHA, CASF, Serial 8, combined with 54th Field Battery (H) RCA, CASF, Serial 9, to become "C"/54th Field Battery RCA, CASF, Serial 8, with Headquarters of 1st Field Regiment RCA, CASF.

As part of the Second British Expeditionary Force, "C"/54th Field Battery RCA landed at Brest, France, 13th June 1940, but due to the deteriorating situation in France the battery returned to England via Brest, 18th June 1940. The regiment was fortunate in returning to England with its twenty-four 18/25 pounder guns, less gun tractors, which had been destroyed at Brest.

In the defence of England "C"/54th Field Battery served with 7th Corps upon its forming on the 21st July 1940, until the 25th of December 1940 when the Canadian Corps was formed and 7th Corps disbanded.

The regiment reorganized to comprise three batteries, authorized under General Order 45/41 (Effective 1st January 1941). "C" Battery regained individual identity and remained with the regiment as "C" Battery RCHA, Serial 8, 1st Field Regiment RCHA. 54th Battery moved to 2nd Light Anti-Aircraft Regiment RCA which was recently designated 1st Division Light Anti-Aircraft Regiment.

"C" Battery was allotted Serial Number 5D, under General Order 54/42 (Effective 22nd December 1941).

1st Canadian Infantry Division moved to the Mediterranean Theatre of Operations and on the 10th of July 1943 landed in the assault on the island of Sicily with 30 Corps, British Eighth Army.

The RCHA, less "B" Battery sailed from Glasgow, Scotland, the night of 1st/2nd July and "C" Battery landed in Sicily 13th July 1943, near Pachino. The regiment joined the action and fired its first rounds on the 18th of July in support of a successful attack by the R 22 R near Enna.

With the fall of Sicily "C" Battery supported 3rd Canadian Infantry Brigade in the assault on the Italian mainland and landed on the 3rd of September with 13 Corps, British Eighth Army.

1st Canadian Corps became operational in Italy in 1944, and as a component the regiment served in Italy until early 1945.

"C" Battery departed from Italy 17th March 1945 via Leghorn and arrived at Marseilles, France, 19th March 1945.

The regiment moved into the line under First Canadian Army and fired its first rounds in NW Europe 7th April 1945, in support of 3rd Canadian Infantry Division in an attack toward Deventer, Holland. "C" Battery then fired in support of 1st Canadian Infantry Division, with firing being halted temporarily 28th April while food was taken into the occupied part of Holland. The regiment fired its last round in action, 3rd May 1945 from positions near Nijkerk, Holland.

The 8th of May 1945 was designated "VE" Day and "C" Battery with the regiment moved to an area South of Rotterdam to aid in the return of the Germans to their homeland, and their equipment to designated areas.

The return to Canada of the Canadian Troops was begun and "C" Battery received authorization to disband under General Order 401/45 (Effective 25th August 1945).

* * *

2nd (Ottawa) Field Battery RCA — Serial 155B — 2nd Cdn Inf Div.

2nd (Ottawa) Field Battery (H) RCA, CASF, Serial 159, mobilized with Headquarters of 4th Field Brigade RCA, CASF, 2nd Division, CASF, under General Order 135/39, 1st September 1939.

Headquarters of 4th Field Brigade RCA, CASF, was redesignated Headquarters of 4th Field Regiment RCA, CASF, Serial 155, and the regiment was to comprise two combined field batteries. The original batteries were paired and 2nd (Ottawa) Field Battery (H), RCA, CASF, Serial 159, combined with 14th (Midland) Field Battery RCA, CASF, Serial 158, to become 2nd/14th Field Battery RCA, CASF, Serial 158, under General Order 123/40 (Effective 1st June 1940).

The combined 2nd/14th Field Battery, 4th Field Regiment RCA departed for overseas 27th August 1940 on board the Empress of Australia, and disembarked at Glasgow, Scotland, on the 4th of September 1940.

2nd Division joined with 1st Division and Canadian ancillary units to form the Canadian Corps on the 25th of December 1940, and as a component the battery served in an anti-invasion role in the South of England.

4th Field Regiment RCA reorganized to a three-battery regiment. 2nd Battery regained individual identity as 2nd (Ottawa) Field Battery RCA, Serial 159, under General Order 45/41 (Effective 1st January 1941), and remained with the regiment.

2nd (Ottawa) Field Battery RCA, Serial 159, in a realignment of serial numbers within the regiment, was allotted Serial Number 155B, under General Order 54/42 (Effective 22nd December 1941).

Three officers and twenty other ranks of the regiment took time off from their duty on the coast and accompanied other units of 2nd Canadian Division on the Dieppe Raid, 19th August 1942. The regiment suffered the loss of three killed and the remainder taken prisoner.

2nd Battery, 4th Field Regiment RCA with 2nd Canadian Infantry Division, returned to the Continent, landing in Normandy 7th July 1944, and fired its first rounds from positions near Carpiquet Airfield, 12th July 1944.

2nd Canadian Infantry Division with 2nd Canadian Corps came under the command of Second British Army, then on the 31st July 1944 the Canadian units moved under First Canadian Army. 2nd Battery with 4th Field Regiment RCA, aligned with 4th Canadian Infantry Brigade, participated in the fierce fighting in the breakout from Caen and the closing of the Falaise Gap.

On the 3rd of September 1944, following the capture of Dieppe, 2nd Canadian Infantry Division paused for a service of remembrance in the cemetery, in honour of members of the division lost during the 19th of August 1942 raid. Following the service, 2nd Battery paraded with the division through the streets of the city.

The battery, regiment and division returned to action under First Canadian Army and served in France, Belgium, Holland, and Germany until the cessation of hostilities.

2nd (Ottawa) Field Battery RCA, received authorization to disband under General Order 52/46 (Effective 19th September 1945).

*   *   *

3rd Field Bty RCA, MD No. 4 — Serial 1410B — Pacific Command

3rd Field Battery RCA, Serial 1410B, mobilized with 22nd Field Regiment RCA in Military District No. 4, under General Order 147/42 (Effective 18th March 1942), to serve with 7 Division, Home Defence, Eastern Canada.

7th Division was to comprise 16th, 17th and 18th Brigade Groups, and 3rd Battery with 22nd Field Regiment RCA was aligned with 16th Infantry Brigade Group. This organization remained until mid-June 1942 when Headquarters 7th Division and Headquarters 8th Division were formed. Infantry Brigades were shuffled between the three divisions on home defence and 7th Division was now to comprise 15th, 17th and 20th Infantry Brigades. Divisional Artillery was grouped under division headquarters.

Headquarters 8th Canadian Division was authorized to mobilize under General Order 301/42 (Effective 15th June 1942), and 16th Infantry Brigade became a component, 1st October 1942.

3rd Battery with 22nd Field Regiment RCA followed 16th Infantry Brigade to British Columbia and joined the Divisional Artillery of 8th Division, in Pacific Command.

Prince Rupert Defences came under command of 8th Division, 9th October 1942 and 3rd Battery in a detached role in support of 14th Infantry Brigade, served under Headquarters Prince Rupert Defences from 11th November 1942 to the 24th of July 1943. 3rd Battery was joined by the remainder of the regiment under Headquarters Prince Rupert Defences on the 5th June 1943 during the Aleutian fright and the regiment complete, returned to division on the 24th of July 1943.

16th Infantry Brigade moved to 6th Division on the 29th of July 1943 and on the 30th July 1943, 3rd Battery and 80th Battery of 22nd Field Regiment RCA followed 16th Brigade to 6th Division, Home Defence, returning to the regiment at Terrace, under 8th Division, 2nd October 1943.

The run-down of home defence units was begun and 3rd Field Battery RCA, Serial 1410B, Headquarters 22nd Field Regiment RCA, Headquarters 16th Infantry Brigade, Headquarters 7th Division and Headquarters 8th Canadian Division received authorization to disband under General Order 15/44 (Effective 15th October 1943).

*   *   *

5th (Westmount) Field Battery RCA — Serial 160B — 2nd Cdn Inf Div.

5th (Westmount) Field Battery RCA, CASF, Serial 161, mobilized with Headquarters of 5th Field Brigade RCA, CASF, 2nd Division, CASF, under General Order 135/39, 1st September 1939.

Headquarters of 5th Field Brigade RCA, CASF, was redesignated Headquarters of 5th Field Regiment RCA, CASF, and under the new organization the regiment was to comprise two batteries. The existing batteries were paired to utilize the battery numbers.

5th (Westmount) Field Battery RCA, CASF, Serial 161, combined with 73rd Field Battery (Howitzer), RCA, CASF, Serial 164, to become 5th/73rd Field Battery RCA, CASF, Serial 161, under General Order 123/40 (Effective 1st June 1940). 28th and 89th Batteries combined to form the second battery in the regiment.

5th/73rd Field Battery, 5th Field Regiment RCA, CASF, 2nd Division, CASF departed for overseas 27th August 1940 on board the Empress of Australia, and disembarked 4th September 1940 at Glasgow, Scotland.

On the 25th of December 1940, the combined battery, regiment, and 2nd Division joined with 1st Division and Canadian ancillary troops to form the Canadian Corps. The Canadian Corps replaced 7th Corps and assumed an anti-invasion role in the defence of England.

The regiment reorganized to comprise three batteries, and 5th Battery regained individual identity as 5th (Westmount) Field Battery RCA, Serial 161, under General Order 45/41 (Effective 1st January 1941).

In a shuffle of serial numbers within the regiment, 5th Battery was allotted Serial Number 160B, under General Order 54/42 (Effective 22nd December 1941).

5th (Westmount) Field Battery, 5th Field Regiment RCA, 2nd Canadian Infantry Division, landed in Normandy on the 8th and 9th of July 1944 and joined the action at Authie, 12th July, in support of 3rd Canadian Infantry Division.

The regiment also fired in support of 15th Scottish Division, then commencing 19th July, supported 2nd Canadian Infantry Division in all operations, with most of the direct support going to 5th Canadian Infantry Brigade.

On the 3rd of September 1944 following the capture of Dieppe the battery paused for a service of remembrance and a divisional parade through the streets of the city, then rejoined the action, serving in France, Belgium, Holland, and Germany with First Canadian Army.

5th (Westmount) Field Battery RCA served until cessation of hostilities and received authorization to disband under General Order 52/46 (Effective 21st September 1945).

*   *   *

6th Field Battery RCA, MD No. 4 — Serial 1410C — Pacific Command

6th Field Battery RCA, Serial 1410C, mobilized in Military District No. 4 as a component of 22nd Field Regiment RCA, to serve with 7th Division, Home Defence, Eastern Canada, authorized under General Order 147/42 (Effective 18th March 1942).

7th Division was to comprise 16th, 17th and 18th Brigade Groups and 6th Battery, with 22nd Field Regiment RCA was aligned with 16th Infantry Brigade Group. This organization remained until mid-June 1942 when Headquarters 7th Division, and Headquarters 8th Canadian Division came into being. Infantry brigades were shuffled between the three home defence divisions and 7th Division was now to comprise 15th, 17th and 20th Infantry Brigades. Divisional Artillery was grouped under division headquarters.

Headquarters 8th Canadian Division was authorized to mobilize under General Order 301/42 (Effective 15th June 1942), and 16th Infantry Brigade became a component on the 1st of October 1942.

6th Battery with 22nd Field Regiment RCA followed 16th Infantry Brigade to the west coast in November 1942 and come under command of 8th Division, Pacific Command.

Prince Rupert Defences came under command of 8th Division on the 9th of October 1942 and 3rd Battery in a detached role served under Headquarters

Prince Rupert Defences, in support of 14th Infantry Brigade, from 11th November 1942 to 24th July 1943. As Divisional Troops all three batteries of the regiment moved under Headquarters Prince Rupert Defences on the 5th of June 1943, returning to division on the 24th July 1943. 16th Infantry Brigades moved to 6th Division on the 29th July, remaining until disbandment in October 1943.

6th Field Battery RCA, Serial 1410C, disbanded under General Order 15/44 (Effective 15th October 1943), following service in Pacific Command at Terrace and Prince Rupert, British Columbia. Headquarters 8th Canadian Division, and Headquarters 8th Divisional Artillery also disbanded at this time.

*   *   *

7th (Montreal) Field Battery RCA — Serial 10D — 1st Cdn Inf Div.

7th Field Battery RCA, CASF, Serial 12, mobilized with Headquarters of 2nd Field Brigade RCA, CASF, 1st Division, CASF, under General Order 135/39, 1st September 1939.

7th Battery departed for overseas 10th December 1939 on board the Empress of Britain, in Troop Convoy 1, and disembarked at Gourock, Scotland, 18th December 1939.

Headquarters of 2nd Field Brigade RCA, CASF, was dedesignated Headquarters of 2nd Field Regiment RCA, CASF, to comprise two batteries. 7th Field Battery RCA, CASF, Serial 12, combined with 35th Field Battery (H) RCA, CASF, Serial 14, to become 7th/35th Field Battery RCA, CASF, Serial 12, under General Order 44/40 (Effective 21st December 1939), in 1st Division, Canadian Active Service Force.

7th/35th Field Battery, 2nd Field Regiment RCA, CASF, served with 7th Corps, and the Canadian Corps in an anti-invasion role in the South of England.

7th Battery regained individual identity as 7th (Montreal) Field Battery RCA, Serial 12, authorized under General Order 45/41 (Effective 1st January 1941), and remained with the regiment in a three battery organization.

7th (Montreal) Field Battery RCA was allotted Serial Number 10D, under General Order 54/42 (Effective 22nd December 1941), in a shuffle of serial numbers within 2nd Field Regiment RCA.

7th Battery with the regiment embarked at Gourock, Scotland, 28th June 1943, Mediterranean bound, and landed in Sicily on the 10th of July 1943 with the assaulting 1st Canadian Infantry Division, 30 Corps, British Eighth Army.

With the fall of Sicily the battery crossed to the Italian mainland under 13 British Corps, 3rd September 1943, then moved to 1st Canadian Corps upon the corps assuming an operational role in 1944. As a component of 1st Canadian Corps, 1st Canadian Infantry Division served in Italy until early 1945, then moved with the corps to NW Europe.

7th Battery, 2nd Field Regiment RCA, 1st Canadian Infantry Division, 1st Canadian Corps, departed from Italy, 8th and 9th March 1945, via Leghorn, and disembarked at Marseilles, France, 9th and 10th March 1945, upon the transfer of 1st Canadian Corps to NW Europe for the knock-out blow.

1st Canadian Corps joined First Canadian Army in NW Europe and 7th Battery fired its first rounds, 8th April 1945, in Holland.

7th (Montreal) Field Battery RCA served until the cessation of hostilities and received authorization to disband under General Order 401/45 (Effective 26th August 1945).

*   *   *

8th Field Bty RCA, Moncton, N.B. — Serial 10B — 1st Cdn Inf Div.

8th Field Battery RCA, CASF, Serial 13, mobilized with Headquarters of 2nd Field Brigade RCA, CASF, 1st Division, CASF, under General Order 135/39, 1st September 1939.

8th Battery departed for overseas 10th December 1939 on board the Empress of Britain in Troop Convoy 1, and disembarked at Gourock, Scotland, 18th December 1939.

Headquarters of 2nd Field Brigade RCA, CASF was redesignated Headquarters, 2nd Field Regiment RCA, CASF, and 8th Field Battery RCA, Serial 13, combined with 10th (St. Catharines) Field Battery RCA, Serial 11, to become 8th/10th Field Battery RCA, Serial 13, under General Order 44/40 (Effective 21st December 1939), in a two battery regiment.

8th/10th Field Battery, 2nd Field Regiment RCA served with 7th Corps and the Canadian Corps in England in an anti-invasion role.

8th Battery regained individual identity as 8th Field Battery RCA, Serial 13, under General Order 45/41 (Effective 1st January 1941) and remained with 2nd Field Regiment RCA as it reorganized to a three battery regiment.

8th Field Battery RCA was allotted Serial Number 10B, under General Order 54/42 (Effective 22nd December 1941).

8th Battery with 2nd Field Regiment RCA departed from Scotland 28th June

1943, Mediterranean bound, and landed in Sicily on the 10th of July 1943 with the assaulting 1st Canadian Infantry Division, 30 Corps, British Eighth Army.

With the fall of Sicily the battery crossed the Strait of Messina to the Italian mainland with 13 British Corps on the 3rd of September 1943, and continued to serve under Eighth Army.

1st Canadian Infantry Division joined 1st Canadian Corps upon the corps assuming an operational role early in 1944, and as a component the division, regiment, and 8th Battery served in Italy until early 1945, then moved with the corps to NW Europe.

8th Battery departed from Italy via Leghorn, 8th and 9th March and disembarked at Marseilles, France, 9th and 10th March 1945.

The regiment joined First Canadian Army in NW Europe and 8th Battery fired its first rounds 8th April 1945, in Holland.

8th Field Battery RCA served until cessation of hostilities and received authorization to disband under General Order 401/45 (Effective 26th August 1945).

*   *   *

9th (Toronto) Field Bty RCA — Serial 209B — Army Troops & 5th Div.

9th (Toronto) Field Battery (H) RCA, CASF, Serial 213, mobilized with Headquarters of 3rd Army Field Brigade RCA, CASF, Corps Troops mobilizing with 2nd Division, authorized under General Order 135/39, 1st September 1939.

9th Battery departed for overseas 30th January 1940 on board the Aquitania, in the Third Flight and disembarked 8th February 1940, at Gourock, Scotland.

Headquarters of 3rd Army Field Brigade RCA, CASF, was redesignated Headquarters 11th Army Field Regiment RCA, CASF, under General Order 44/40 (Effective 12th February 1940). 11th Army Field Regiment RCA, CASF, was to comprise two hyphenated batteries.

9th (Toronto) Field Battery (Howitzer) RCA, Serial 213, combined with 15th Field Battery RCA, Serial 211, to become 9th/15th Field Battery RCA, CASF, Serial 210, in the two battery, 11th Army Field Regiment RCA, CASF.

11th Army Field Regiment and its combined batteries served with 7th Corps and the Canadian Corps in England during 1940, in an anti-invasion role.

The regiment reorganized to comprise three batteries and 9th Battery regained individual identity as 9th (Toronto) Field Battery RCA, Serial 213, under

General Order 45/41 (Effective 1st January 1941), and remained with 11th Army Field Regiment RCA.

9th (Toronto) Field Battery RCA was allotted Serial Number 209B, under General Order 54/42 (Effective 22nd December 1941).

On the 24th October 1943, 9th (Toronto) Field Battery, 11th Army Field Regiment RCA boarded the Argentina at Liverpool, and departed for the Mediterranean Theatre, on operation "Timberwolf".

The ship joined the convoy off Scotland and proceeded to Augusta, Sicily, where the regiment disembarked on the 8th of November 1943. 9th Battery crossed to the Italian mainland with the regiment on the 7th of January 1944 as a component of 1st Canadian AGRA.

9th Battery joined the action under 1st Canadian AGRA in support of 5th Canadian Armoured Division, 15th February 1944.

11th Army Field Regiment RCA served as Army Troops with 1st Canadian AGRA until mid-July 1944, then moved to 5th Canadian Armoured Division to serve as Divisional Artillery.

12th Canadian Infantry Brigade was authorized under General Order 17/45 (Effective 13th July 1944), to serve as an extra infantry brigade in 5th Canadian Armoured Division.

11th Army Field Regiment RCA ceased to operate as an Army Field Regiment and moved to the Divisional Artillery of 5th Canadian Armoured Division to become artillery support for 12th Canadian Infantry Brigade in Italy. The new brigade fought its initial engagement on the 1st and 2nd of September 1944.

9th Battery, 11th Field Regiment RCA, 5th Canadian Armoured Division, served with 1st Canadian Corps in Italy until early 1945, then moved to NW Europe with 1st Canadian Corps to join First Canadian Army.

The regiment departed from Leghorn, Italy, between the 16th and 24th February 1945, arriving at Marseilles, France, between the 18th and 26th of February 1945.

12th Canadian Infantry Brigade became surplus upon arrival in NW Europe, upon being redesignated Headquarters 3 CBRG, under General Order 295/45 (Effective 13th March 1945), as the division reverted to the official armoured division war establishment, and the regiment once more became 11th Army Field Regiment RCA, 1st Canadian AGRA, Army Troops.

9th Battery, 11th Army Field Regiment RCA joined First Canadian Army in

NW Europe and fired in support of 3rd Canadian Infantry Division from positions near Cleve, Germany, on the 31st March 1945, to become the first regiment of 1st Canadian Corps to fight in Germany.

The regiment moved to Holland where 9th Battery continued to fire in support of various divisions of First Canadian Army until the cessation of hostilities.

9th (Toronto) Field Battery RCA received authorization to disband under General Order 401/45 (Effective 4th September 1945).

*   *   *

10th (St. Catharines) Fd Bty RCA — Serial 10C — 1st Cdn Inf Div.

10th (St. Catharines) Field Battery RCA, CASF, Serial 11, mobilized under General Order 135/39, 1st September 1939, with Headquarters of 2nd Field Brigade RCA, CASF, 1st Division, CASF.

10th Battery departed for overseas 10th December 1939 on board the Empress of Britain in Troop Convoy 1, and disembarked at Gourock, Scotland, on the 18th of December 1939.

Headquarters of 2nd Field Brigade RCA, CASF, was redesignated Headquarters, 2nd Field Regiment RCA, CASF, and 10th (St. Catharines) Field Battery RCA, Serial 11, combined with 8th Field Battery RCA, Serial 13, to become 8th/10th Field Battery RCA, CASF, Serial 13, under General Order 44/40 (Effective 21st December 1939), in a two battery regiment.

8/10th Field Battery, 2nd Field Regiment RCA, 1st Division, served with 7th Corps and the Canadian Corps in England, in an anti-invasion role.

10th Battery regained individual identity as 10th (St. Catharines) Field Battery RCA, Serial 11, under General Order 45/41 (Effective 1st January 1941), and remained with 2nd Field Field Regiment RCA as it reorganized to comprise three batteries.

In a shuffle of serial numbers within the regiment, 10th (St. Catharines) Field Battery RCA was allotted Serial Number 10C, under General Order 54/42 (Effective 22nd December 1941).

10th Battery sailed for the Mediterranean, 28th June 1943, and the ship the City of Venice, carrying "E" Troop was torpedoed enroute.

10th Battery, less "E" Troop, landed in Sicily with the assaulting 1st Canadian Infantry Division, 30 Corps, British Eighth Army, on the 10th of July 1943.

With the fall of Sicily the battery crossed to the Italian mainland with 13 British

Corps, 3rd September 1943, then moved to 1st Canadian Corps early in the new year, upon the corps assuming an operational role, and served with the corps in Italy until 1945, at which time the corps, division, regiment, and 10th Battery were transferred to NW Europe.

10th Battery departed from Italy via Leghorn, 8th and 9th March 1945 and disembarked at Marseilles, France, 9th and 10th March 1945, then fired its first round under First Canadian Army in NW Europe on the 8th of April 1945, in Holland.

10th (St. Catharines) Field Battery RCA served until cessation of hostilities and received authorization to disband under General Order 401/45 (Effective 26th August 1945).

* * *

11th (Hamilton) Field Bty RCA — Serial 705C — 3rd Cdn Inf Div.

The combined 11th/69th Field Battery RCA, CASF, Serial 705C, was authorized to mobilize with 12th Field Regiment RCA, CASF, 3rd Division, CASF, under General Order 184/40 (Effective 24th May 1940).

The batteries to comprise the regiment moved to Petawawa where the regiment was formed 6th September 1940. The regiment proceeded to Camp Sussex, New Brunswick, by road and rail on the 3rd of October 1940.

11th Battery regained individual identity as 11th (Hamilton) Field Battery RCA, Serial 705C, under General Order 45/41 (Effective 1st January 1941), and remained with 12th Field Regiment RCA in a three battery organization. 69th Battery moved to 4th Light Anti-Aircraft Regiment RCA, in 3rd Division.

11th Field Battery, 12th Field Regiment RCA departed for overseas 21st July 1941 on board the Duchess of York, and disembarked at Liverpool, England, 30th July 1941.

3rd Canadian Infantry Division was selected as an assault division for the Normandy invasion. 11th Battery fired its 105mm self-propelled guns from the assault craft in support of 7th Canadian Infantry Brigade of 3rd Canadian Infantry Division prior to landing on D-Day, 6th June 1944.

During the early days of the invasion 3rd Canadian Infantry Division served under 1 British Corps, Second British Army, then moved to 2nd Canadian Corps, Second British Army, and on the 31st of July 1944 the Canadian components came under command of First Canadian Army.

Conforming to infantry division field artillery, the 105mm self-propelled guns were exchanged for towed 25 pounders on the 1st of August 1944, and so-equipped, 11th Field Battery RCA served in France, Belgium, Holland, and Germany, then with the cessation of hostilities, received authorization to disband under General Order 52/46 (Effective 31st October 1945).

While units of the Division prepared for the return to Canada a reconstituted 3rd Canadian Infantry Division (CAOF) was formed for occupational duty in Germany.

A 2nd 11th Field Battery RCA, 2nd 12th Field Regiment RCA, mobilized with the Canadian Army Occupational Force (CAOF), under General Orders 319/45 (Effective 1st June 1945), and following service in Germany, received authorization to disband under General Order 201/46 (Effective 18th May 1946). The reconstituted 3rd Canadian Infantry Division, CAOF, was formed of personnel desiring to remain on the Continent, and low-point men recently arrived overseas.

*   *   *

13th (Winnipeg) Field Bty RCA — Serial 165B — 2nd Cdn Inf Div.

13th (Winnipeg) Field Battery RCA, CASF, Serial 166, mobilized with Headquarters of 6th Field Brigade RCA, CASF, 2nd Division, CASF, under General Order 135/39, 1st September 1939.

The four component batteries of 6th Field Brigade RCA, CASF, converged on Camp Shilo, Manitoba, 22nd May 1940 and reorganization set in almost immediately.

Headquarters of 6th Field Brigade RCA, CASF, was redesignated Headquarters of 6th Field Regiment RCA, CASF, and the regiment was to comprise two batteries, utilizing the present battery numbers.

13th (Winnipeg) Field Battery RCA, CASF, Serial 166, combined with 21st Field Battery (H) RCA, CASF, Serial 169, to become 13th/21st Field Battery RCA, CASF, Serial 166, under General Order 123/40 (Effective 1st June 1940).

13th/21st Field Battery, 6th Field Regiment RCA, CASF, departed for overseas 27th August 1940 on board the Oronsay, and disembarked at Gourock, Scotland, on the 5th of September 1940.

13th Battery regained individual identity as 13th (Winnipeg) Field Battery RCA, Serial 166, under General Order 45/41 (Effective 1st January 1941) and remained with 6th Field Regiment RCA in a three battery organization.

In a shuffle of serial numbers within the regiment, 13th (Winnipeg) Field Battery RCA was allotted Serial Number 165B, under General Order 54/42 (Effective 22nd December 1941).

13th Battery, 6th Field Regiment RCA, 2nd Canadian Infantry Division, landed in Normandy 8th July 1944, then deployed 13th July near Carpiquet Airfield, attached to Second British Army, and fired in support of 3rd Canadian Infantry Division.

As a component of 2nd Canadian Corps, the division, regiment and 13th Battery moved to First Canadian Army 31st July 1944 on the Caen Front.

Following the capture of Dieppe, 2nd Canadian Infantry Division paused for a service of remembrance, 3rd September 1944, and 13th Battery paraded with the division through the streets of the city.

2nd Division rejoined the action under First Canadian Army and 13th Battery served in France, Belgium, Holland, and Germany.

Upon the cessation of hostilities, 13th (Winnipeg) Field Battery RCA received authorization to disband under General Order 52/46 (Effective 23rd September 1945).

*   *   *

14th (Midland) Fd Bty RCA, Cobourg, Ont. — Serial 155C — 2nd Div.

14th (Midland) Field Battery RCA, CASF, Serial 158, mobilized with Headquarters of 4th Field Brigade RCA, CASF, 2nd Division, CASF, under General Order 135/39, 1st September 1939.

Headquarters of 4th Field Brigade RCA, CASF, was redesignated Headquarters of 4th Field Regiment RCA, CASF, Serial 155, and the regiment was to comprise two field batteries. The original batteries were paired and 14th (Midland) Field Battery RCA, CASF, Serial 158, combined with 2nd (Ottawa) Field Battery (H), RCA, CASF, Serial 159, to become 2nd/14th Field Battery RCA, CASF, Serial 158, under General Order 123/40 (Effective 1st June 1940).

The combined 2nd/14th Field Battery, 4th Field Regiment RCA departed for overseas 27th August 1940 on board the Empress of Australia, and disembarked at Glasgow, Scotland, 4th September 1940. The regiment proceeded by train to Aldershot, Hampshire, in the South of England.

4th Field Regiment RCA reorganized to a three battery regiment. 14th Battery regained individual identity as 14th (Midland) Field Battery RCA, Serial 158, under General Order 45/41 (Effective 1st January 1941) and remained with the regiment.

14th (Midland) Field Battery RCA, Serial 158, was allotted Serial Number 155C, under General Order 54/42 (Effective 22nd December 1941), in a realignment of serial numbers within the regiment.

14th Battery, with the regiment, under the Canadian Corps, alternated between training and duty on the South coast of England. 2nd Division at the peak of its training was rewarded by being selected as the main participant in the raid on Dieppe, France. 4th Field Regiment RCA was represented on the Raid, 19th August 1942, by three officers and twenty other ranks, suffering the loss of three killed and the remainder taken prisoner.

14th Battery, 4th Field Regiment RCA with 2nd Canadian Infantry Division, returned to the Continent, skirting the defended ports to land on the beaches of Normandy, 7th July 1944, and fired its first rounds from positions near the Carpiquet Airfield, 12th July 1944.

2nd Canadian Corps, of which 2nd Canadian Infantry Division was a component, came under command of Second British Army, then on the 31st of July 1944 the Canadian units moved under First Canadian Army.

14th Battery with 4th Field Regiment RCA, aligned with 4th Canadian Infantry Brigade of 2nd Canadian Infantry Division, participated in the fierce fighting in the breakout from Caen and the closing of the Falaise Gap.

On the 3rd of September 1944, following the capture of Dieppe, units of 2nd Canadian Infantry Division paused for a service of remembrance in the cemetery, and 14th Battery paraded with the division through the streets of the city.

The battery, regiment and division returned to action under First Canadian Army and served in France, Belgium, Holland and Germany until cessation of hostilities.

14th (Midland) Field Battery RCA received authorization to disband under General Order 52/46 (Effective 19th September 1945).

*   *   *

16th Field Battery RCA, Guelph, Ontario — Serial 705B — 3rd Division.

16th Field Battery RCA of Guelph, Ontario, mobilized as the combined 16th/43rd Field Battery RCA, CASF, Serial 705B, under General Order 184/40 (Effective 24th May 1940), to serve as a component of 12th Field Regiment RCA, CASF, 3rd Division, CASF.

The regiment assembled at Petawawa early in September, remaining until the 3rd of October 1940 at which time headquarters and the two combined field batteries left by road and rail for Sussex, New Brunswick.

16th Battery regained individual identity as 16th Field Battery RCA, Serial 705B, under General Order 45/41 (Effective 1st January 1941), and remained with 12th Field Regiment RCA, now to comprise three batteries.

16th Field Battery, 12th Field Regiment RCA departed for overseas 21st July 1941 on board the Duchess of York and disembarked at Liverpool, England, 30th July 1941.

In England the regiment prepared for the invasion of the Continent as 3rd Canadian Infantry Division was selected as an assault division for the Normandy landings.

16th Battery fired its 105mm self-propelled guns from the assault craft in support of 7th Canadian Infantry Brigade of 3rd Canadian Infantry Division prior to landing in Normandy on D-Day, 6th June 1944.

During the early days of the invasion 3rd Canadian Infantry Division served with 1 British Corps, Second British Army, then 2nd Canadian Corps under Second British Army, and on the 31st of July 1944, 2nd Canadian Corps and its components moved under command of First Canadian Army on the Caen Front.

Conforming to infantry division field artillery 1st August 1944, the 105mm self-propelled guns were exchanged for towed 25 pounders and so-equipped, 16th Field Battery RCA served in France, Belgium, Holland, and Germany, then with cessation of hostilities the battery received authorization to disband under General Order 52/46 (Effective 31st October 1945).

2nd 16th Field Battery RCA, 2nd 12th Field Regiment RCA mobilized under General Order 319/45 (Effective 1st June 1945), to serve with the reconstituted 3rd Canadian Infantry Division, Canadian Army Occupational Force.

2nd 16th Field Battery RCA received authorization to disband under General Order 201/46 (Effective 18th May 1946), following service with the Canadian Army Occupational Force (CAOF) in Germany.

* * *

17th Field Battery RCA, Winnipeg, Man. — Serial 1905D — 4th Division

17th Field Battery RCA, Serial 909D, mobilized under General Order 85/41 (Effective 1st January 1941), to serve with the reconstituted 15th Field Regiment RCA in 4th Division.

Regimental headquarters was formed at Camp Shilo, Manitoba in July 1941. However, the regiment did not congregate until all the components arrived at Debert, Nova Scotia in August 1941.

4th Division was converted to an Armoured Division under General Order 132/42 (Effective 26th January 1942), and 15th Field Regiment became the lone field artillery regiment in the Support Group of 4th (Armoured) Division.

The Serial Number of 17th Field Battery RCA was changed from 909D to 1905D, under General Order 438/42 (Effective 12th February 1942).

17th Field Battery, 15th Field Regiment RCA, 4th Canadian (Armoured) Division departed for overseas 9th August 1942 on board the Cameronia, and disembarked at Glasgow, Scotland, 19th August 1942.

17th Battery landed in Normandy 26th July 1944 with the regiment and moved to the Caen Sector under 2nd Canadian Corps, as 4th Canadian Armoured Division joined the action on the 29th of July, then with 2nd Canadian Corps moved under command of First Canadian Army 31st July 1944.

17th Field Battery RCA served in France, Belgium, Holland, and Germany, then with cessation of hostilities received authorization to disband under General Order 71/46 (Effective 12th December 1945).

*   *   *

19th Field Battery RCA, Winnipeg, Manitoba — Serial 15C — 1st Division.

19th Field Battery RCA, CASF, Serial 16, mobilized with Headquarters of 3rd Field Brigade RCA, CASF, 1st Division, CASF, under General Order 135/39, 1st September 1939.

19th Battery departed for overseas 10th December 1939 on board the Empress of Australia, in Troop Convoy 1, and disembarked at Gourock, Scotland, 18th December 1939.

Headquarters of 3rd Field Brigade RCA, CASF, was redesignated Headquarters 3rd Field Regiment RCA, CASF, and 19th Field Battery RCA, CASF, Serial 16, combined with 77th Field Battery RCA, CASF, Serial 18, to become 19th/77th Field Battery RCA, CASF, Serial 16, under General Order 44/40 (Effective 21st December 1939). The regiment was now to comprise two combined field batteries.

In England, the combined 19th/77th Field Battery RCA, the regiment and 1st Canadian Division, plus ancillary units, served as components of 7th Corps upon its forming 21st July 1940 until the 25th of December 1940 when the Canadian Corps was formed and 7th Corps disbanded.

19th Battery regained individual identity as 19th Field Battery RCA, Serial 16, under General Order 45/41 (Effective 1st January 1941), and remained with 3rd Field Regiment RCA, in a three-battery organization.

In a shuffle of serial numbers within the regiment, 19th Field Battery RCA was allotted Serial Number 15C, under General Order 54/42 (Effective 22nd December 1941).

19th Battery with the regiment sailed from Scotland 28th June 1943 and landed in Sicily on the 10th of July 1943 with the assaulting 1st Canadian Infantry Division, 30 Corps, British Eighth Army.

With the fall of Sicily the battery crossed the Strait of Messina to the Italian mainland on the 4th of September 1943, in support of 13 British Corps, Eighth Army.

The battery, regiment and division joined 1st Canadian Corps upon the corps becoming operational in Italy, early 1944, and served in Italy until early 1945, then with 1st Canadian Corps, moved to NW Europe to join First Canadian Army.

19th Battery, 3rd Field Regiment RCA, 1st Canadian Infantry Division, 1st Canadian Corps, sailed from Leghorn, 15th March 1945 and disembarked at Marseilles, France, 16th March 1945.

19th Battery joined the action with First Canadian Army in NW Europe and fired in support of 3rd Canadian Infantry Division in an attack on Deventer, Holland, 7th April 1945.

Returning to 1st Division, the battery fired in support of the Ijssel River crossing in Holland on the 11th April 1945, and continued in action until cessation of hostilities.

19th Field Battery RCA received authorization to disband under General Order 401/45 (Effective 27th August 1945).

* * *

21st Field Battery RCA, Saskatoon, Sask. — Serial 165D — 2nd Div.

Under General Order 136/39 (Effective 26th August 1939), 21st Field Battery (H) RCA (Details), was added to the list of Non-Permanent Active Militia Units Called Out On Service in Military District No. 12. These "Details" are listed under Serial 421 as components of the CASF, under General Order 135/39, 1st September 1939.

21st Field Battery (H) RCA, CASF, Serial 169, mobilized with Headquarters of 6th Field Brigade RCA, CASF, 2nd Division, CASF, under General Order 135/39, 1st September 1939.

The four component batteries converged on Camp Shilo, Manitoba, 22nd May 1940 and reorganization was at once begun.

Headquarters of 6th Field Brigade RCA, CASF, was redesignated Headquarters of 6th Field Regiment RCA, CASF, and the regiment was to comprise two combined batteries. The original batteries were paired and 21st Field Battery (H) RCA, CASF, Serial 169, combined with 13th (Winnipeg) Field Battery RCA, CASF, Serial 166, to become 13th/21st Field Battery RCA, CASF, Serial 166, under General Order 123/40 (Effective 1st June 1940). The regiment remained with 2nd Division in the Canadian Active Service Force.

13th/21st Field Battery, 6th Field Regiment RCA, CASF, departed for overseas 27th August 1940 on board the Oronsay, and disembarked at Gourock, Scotland, on the 5th of September 1940.

The arrival overseas of 2nd Canadian Division signalled the forming of the Canadian Corps which came into being 25th December 1940, with 1st Canadian Division, 2nd Canadian Division and Canadian ancillary units under command. The corps assumed an anti-invasion role in the South of England. The batteries alternated between training and duty on the Coast.

21st Battery regained individual identity as 21st Field Battery RCA, Serial 169, under General Order 45/41 (Effective 1st January 1941), and remained with 6th Field Regiment RCA, as the regiment reorganized to comprise three batteries.

In a shuffle of serial numbers within the regiment, 21st Battery was allotted Serial Number 165D, under General Order 54/42 (Effective 22nd December 1941).

21st Field Battery, 6th Field Regiment RCA, aligned with 6th Canadian Infantry Brigade, 2nd Canadian Infantry Division, landed in Normandy on the 8th of July 1944 and joined the action 13th July 1944, near Carpiquet Airfield, firing in support of 3rd Canadian Infantry Division.

During July, 2nd Division participated in the heavy fighting in the Caen Sector with 2nd Canadian Corps, and on the 31st of July 1944, 2nd Canadian Corps, the division, regiment, and 21st Battery moved under the command of First Canadian Army.

With the breakout from Caen effected and the closing of the Falaise Gap, 2nd Canadian Infantry Division moved on to Dieppe where on the 3rd of September 1944, following the capture of the city, a service of remembrance was observed, followed by a divisional parade through the streets of the city.

21st Battery with 6th Field Regiment RCA and 2nd Canadian Infantry Division rejoined the action under First Canadian Army, serving until the cessation of hostilities.

21st Field Battery RCA received authorization to disband under General Order 52/46 (Effective 23rd September 1945).

*   *   *

22nd Field Battery RCA, Gleichen, Alberta — Serial 706C — 3rd Div.

22nd/78th Field Battery RCA, CASF, Serial 706C, mobilized as a component of 13th Field Regiment RCA, CASF, 3rd Division, CASF, under General Order 184/40 (Effective 24th May 1940).

Headquarters 13th Field Regiment and its combined batteries congregated at Camp Shilo, Manitoba, in October 1940, then in November moved to winter quarters in Winnipeg.

22nd Battery regained individual identity as 22nd Field Battery RCA, Serial 706C, under General Order 45/41 (Effective 1st January 1941), and remained with 13th Field Regiment RCA as it reorganized to comprise three batteries.

13th Field Regiment RCA, which included 22nd Battery, moved to Debert, Nova Scotia in February 1941 and departed for overseas 4th November 1941 on board the Pasteur, disembarking on the 13th of November 1941 at Gourock, Scotland.

3rd Canadian Infantry Division was selected as an assault division for the Normandy invasion and 22nd Field Battery, 13th Field Regiment RCA fired its 105mm self-propelled guns from the assault craft in support of 7th Canadian Infantry Brigade, prior to landing on the beaches of Normandy on D-Day, 6th June 1944.

In the early days of the invasion the division served with 1 British Corps, Second British Army, then moved to 2nd Canadian Corps under Second British Army, then with 2nd Canadian Corps moved under command of First Canadian Army, 31st July 1944, on the Caen Front.

With the beachhead established the self-propelled 105mm guns were exchanged for towed 25 pounders, 1st August 1944, conforming to infantry division field artillery, and so-equipped, 22nd Battery served in France, Belgium, Holland and Germany, then with the cessation of hostilities 22nd Field Battery RCA received authorization to disband under General Order 52/46 (Effective 14th November 1945).

A reconstituted 3rd Canadian Infantry Division, CAOF) was formed for service with the Canadian Army Occupational Force (CAOF). 2nd 22nd Field Battery RCA, 2nd 13th Field Regiment RCA, mobilized as a component of the CAOF, under General Order 319/45 (Effective 1st June 1945), and following occupational duties in Germany, 2nd 22nd Field Battery RCA (CAOF) received authorization to disband under General Order 201/46 (Effective 13th April 1946).

*   *   *

24th (Shefford) Field Battery RCA, Granby, P.Q. — Serial 811B.

The combined 24th/75th Field Battery RCA, CASF, Serial 906B, mobilized with 16th Field Regiment RCA, CASF, 4th Division, CASF, under General Order 184/40 (Effective 24th May 1940).

In the reorganizing of 4th Division following the transfer of a number of units to 1st Armoured Division, 16th Field Regiment RCA was allotted three new batteries. 24th Battery regained individual identity as 24th (Shefford) Field Battery RCA, Serial 992D, under General Orderd 240/41, then under the same General Order was redesignated 24th Anti-Tank Battery RCA, Serial 992D (Effective 5th September 1941).

24th Anti-Tank Battery RCA, Serial 992D, was redesignated 24th Field Battery RCA and allotted Serial Number 811B, under General Order 104/42 (Effective 26th January 1942).

On the 7th of February 1942, 24th Battery moved to 20th Field Regiment RCA, 15th Brigade Group, 6th Division, Home Defence, replacing 58th Battery upon its departure to 4th Medium Regiment RCA, which was to proceed overseas before the end of the year.

24th Battery and 20th Field Regiment RCA moved from Valcartier, P.Q. to Debert, Nova Scotia, in June 1942 upon the transfer of 20th Field Regiment RCA and 15th Brigade to 7th Canadian Division, Home Defence, Eastern Canada. The battery and regiment served with 7th Division until the division was authorized to disband under General Order 15/44 (Effective 15th October 1943).

24th Battery accompanied 20th Field Regiment RCA and 15th Brigade Group to 6th Division in Pacific Command as 6th Division, Home Defence reorganized to comprise division headquarters and its three original brigade groups, 13th, 14th and 15th Brigade Groups.

24th Field Battery RCA, Serial 811B, served at Prince George, Vancouver and Nanaimo, British Columbia, and Wainwright, Alberta, then received authorization to disband under General Order 208/45 (Effective 31st December 1944).

*   *   *

26th (Lambton) Field Battery RCA, Sarnia, Ont. — Serial 155D — 2nd Div.

26th Field Battery RCA, CASF, Serial 156, mobilized with Headquarters of 4th Field Brigade RCA, CASF, 2nd Division, CASF, under General Order 135/39, 1st September 1939.

Headquarters of 4th Field Brigade RCA, CASF, was redesignated Headquarters of 4th Field Regiment RCA, CASF, and 26th Field Battery RCA, CASF, Serial 156, combined with 53rd Field Battery RCA, CASF, Serial 157, to become 26th/53rd Field Battery RCA, CASF, Serial 156, under General Order 123/40 (Effective 1st June 1940), in a two-battery field regiment.

26th/53rd Field Battery RCA, CASF, departed for overseas 27th August 1940 on board the Empress of Australia, and disembarked at Glasgow, Scotland, on the 4th of September 1940.

2nd Division joined with 1st Division and Canadian ancillary troops to form the Canadian Corps on the 25th of December 1940, and served in an anti-invasion role in the South of England.

26th Battery regained individual identity as 26th Field Battery RCA, Serial 156, under General Order 45/41 (Effective 1st January 1941), and remained with 4th Field Regiment RCA, now to comprise three batteries. 53rd Battery moved to 3rd Light Anti-Aircraft Regiment RCA, 2nd Division, and later moved to 11th Light Anti-Aircraft Regiment RCA, Army Troops.

26th (Lambton) Field Battery RCA was allotted Serial Number 155D, under General Order 54/42 (Effective 22nd December 1941), in a shuffle of serial numbers within the regiment.

Three officers and twenty other ranks of 4th Field Regiment RCA landed at Dieppe, France, 19th August 1942, with other units of 2nd Division and suffered the loss of three killed and the remainder taken prisoner.

26th Field Battery, 4th Field Regiment RCA with 2nd Canadian Infantry Division returned to the Continent in 1944. 26th Battery landed in Normandy on the 7th of July 1944 and joined the action near Carpiquet Airfield.

Forward Observation Officers moved forward with the regiments of 4th Canadian Infantry Brigade of 2nd Canadian Division, 2nd Canadian Corps, under Second British Army, 11th July and 4th Field Regiment RCA fired its first rounds on the 12th of July 1944, at enemy infantry.

The battery, regiment and division with 2nd Canadian Corps moved under command of First Canadian Army on the 31st July 1944 and participated in the fierce fighting in the breakout from Caen and closing of the Falaise Gap.

2nd Canadian Infantry Division paused for a service of remembrance and a divisional parade through the city of Dieppe, 3rd September 1944, following the capture of the city. The division returned to action under First Canadian Army and served in France, Belgium, Holland and Germany until the cessation of hostilities.

26th (Lambton) Field Battery RCA received authorization to disband under General Order 52/46 (Effective 19th September 1945).

*   *   *

28th (Newcastle) Field Battery RCA, Newcastle, N.B. — Serial 160C

28th (Newcastle) Field Battery RCA, CASF, Serial 162, mobilized with Headquarters of 5th Field Brigade RCA, CASF, 2nd Division, CASF, under General Order 135/39, 1st September 1939.

Headquarters of 5th Field Brigade RCA, CASF, was redesignated Headquarters of 5th Field Regiment RCA, CASF, and 28th Field Battery RCA, CASF, Serial 162, combined with 89th (Woodstock) Field Battery RCA, CASF, Serial 163, to become 28th/89th Field Battery RCA, CASF, Serial 162, under General Order 123/40 (Effective 1st June 1940).

The combined 28th/89th Field Battery RCA, CASF, sailed overseas 27th August 1940 on board the Empress of Australia, and disembarked at Glasgow, Scotland, on the 4th of September 1940.

2nd Division joined with 1st Division and Canadian ancillary units to form the Canadian Corps on the 25th of December 1940, and as a component the battery served in an anti-invasion role in the South of England.

28th Battery regained individual identity as 28th (Newcastle) Field Battery RCA, Serial 162, under General Order 45/41 (Effective 1st January 1941), as the regiment reorganized to comprise three batteries and 89th Battery moved to 1st Light Anti-Aircraft Regiment RCA, 1st Corps Troops.

28th Battery was allotted Serial Number 160C, under General Order 54/42 (Effective 22nd December 1941), with 5th Field Regiment RCA, 2nd Division.

The battery and regiment was aligned with 5th Infantry Brigade and as the Dieppe Raid August 19th 1942 was primarily a 4th and 6th Infantry Brigade show, the regiment remained in England.

2nd Canadian Infantry Division returned to the Continent in July 1944. 28th Battery with 5th Field Regiment RCA landed in Normandy on the 7th of July 1944 and joined the action at Authie, 12th July, firing in support of 3rd Canadian Infantry Division, then moved to positions near Carpiquet Airfield to fire in support of 15 Scottish Division.

The battery, regiment and division served with 2nd Canadian Corps under Second British Army and from the 19th of July on, aligned with 5th Canadian Infantry Brigade, 28th Battery with the regiment supported 2nd Canadian Infantry Division in all its operations.

2nd Canadian Corps and its components moved under command of First Canadian Army on the 31st of July 1944 and participated in the fierce fighting in the breakout from Caen and the closing of the Falaise Gap.

2nd Canadian Infantry Division moved on to Dieppe and following the capture of the city, paused for a service of remembrance and a divisional parade through the streets on the 3rd of September 1944. 28th Battery, the regiment and units of the division rejoined the action under First Canadian Army, serving in France, Belgium, Holland and Germany until cessation of hostilities.

28th (Newcastle) Field Battery RCA received authorization to disband under General Order 52/46 (Effective 21st September 1945).

*   *   *

29th Field Battery RCA, Guelph, Ontario — Serial 209C — Army Troops

29th Field Battery (H) RCA, CASF, Serial 212, was authorized to mobilize with Headquarters of 3rd Army Field Brigade RCA, CASF, under General Order 135/39, 1st September 1939.

29th Field Battery (H) RCA, CASF, 3rd Army Field Brigade RCA, CASF, sailed overseas 30th January 1940 on board the Aquitania in the 3rd Flight and disembarked at Gourock, Scotland, on the 8th of February 1940.

Headquarters of 3rd Army Field Brigade RCA, CASF, Serial 209, was redesignated Headquarters 11th Army Field Regiment RCA, CASF, Serial 209, under General Order 44/40 (Effective 12th February 1940) and batteries paired in a two-battery regiment.

29th Field Battery (Howitzer) RCA, CASF, Serial 212, paired with 40th Field Battery RCA, CASF, Serial 210, to become 29th/40th Field Battery RCA, CASF, Serial 212.

The combined 29th/40th Field Battery served with 7th Corps and the Canadian Corps in England in an anti-invasion role.

29th Battery regained individual identity as 29th Field Battery RCA, Serial 212, under General Order 45/41 (Effective 1st January 1941).

29th Field Battery RCA was allotted Serial Number 209C, under General Order 54/42 (Effective 1st January 1941).

Mediterranean bound, the regiment boarded the Argentina, 24th October 1943 at Liverpool, on operation "Timberwolf", and disembarked at Augusta, Sicily, on the 8th of November 1943, to serve with 1st Canadian AGRA in support of 1st Canadian Corps.

29th Battery crossed to the Italian mainland, 7th January 1944 and joined the action as a component of 1st Canadian AGRA in support of 5th Canadian Armoured Division, 15th February 1944.

12th Infantry Brigade was authorized under General Order 17/45 (Effective 13th July 1944) to serve as an extra infantry brigade in 5th Canadian Armoured Division during the Italian Campaign.

29th Battery with the regiment transferred from Army Troops Artillery to 5th Canadian Armoured Division to provide field artillery support for the newly formed 12th Canadian Infantry Brigade. The brigade fought its initial engagement on the 1st and 2nd of September 1944 and served in Italy until early 1945.

29th Field Battery departed from Italy via Leghorn, upon the transfer of 1st Canadian Corps to NW Europe. Members of the regiment departed between the 16th and 24th of February 1945 and arrived at Marseilles, France, 18th to 26th of February 1945.

12th Canadian Infantry Brigade was phased out shortly after its arrival in NW Europe, being redesignated Headquarters 3 CBRG, under General Order 295/45 (Effective 13th March 1945), and the regiment resumed its role as 11th Army Field Regiment RCA with 1st Canadian AGRA, Army Troops.

The battery and regiment joined First Canadian Army in NW Europe and fired in support of 3rd Canadian Infantry Division from positions near Cleve, Germany, on the 31st of March 1945, to become the first regiment of 1st Canadian Corps to fight in Germany.

29th Battery returned to Holland to fire in support of various divisions comprising the multi-national First Canadian Army, and served until cessation of hostilities.

29th Field Battery RCA received authorization to disband under General Order 401/45 (Effective 4th September 1945).

* * *

31st Field Battery (SP) RCA, Toronto, Ont. — Serial 1411B — 4th Div.

31st Field Battery RCA, Serial 1411B, mobilized under General Order 147/42 (Effective 18th March 1942), with 23rd Field Regiment RCA, 7th Division, Home Defence, Eastern Canada.

A self-propelled field regiment was added to the war establishment of an armoured division and 23rd Field Regiment RCA was selected for overseas service with 4th Canadian Armoured Division.

31st Field Battery RCA, Serial 1411B, was redesignated 31st Self-Propelled Battery RCHA, Serial 1411B, under General Order 328/43 (Effective 15th May 1943).

31st Battery sailed overseas 23rd July 1943 on board the Queen Elizabeth and disembarked at Gourock, Scotland, on the 28th of July 1943.

31st Self-Propelled Battery RCHA, was redesignated 31st Battery (Self-Propelled) RCA, Serial 1411B, under General Order 396/43 (Effective 15th August 1943).

31st Battery (Self-Propelled) RCA, Serial 1411B, was redesignated 31st Field Battery (Self-Propelled) RCA, Serial 1411B, under General Order 452/43 (Effective 1st September 1943).

31st Field Battery (SP), 23rd Field Regiment (SP) RCA, 4th Canadian Armoured Division landed in Normandy on the 26th of July 1944 and moved to the Caen Sector, 29th July 1944 with 2nd Canadian Corps.

2nd Canadian Corps and its components moved under command of First Canadian Army, 31st July 1944 and 31st Battery participated in the bitter fighting in the breakout from Caen and closing of the Falaise Gap.

31st Field Battery (Self-Propelled) RCA served in France, Belgium, Holland and Germany, then with the cessation of hostilities, received authorization to disband under General Order 71/46 (Effective 18th December 1945).

* * *

34th Field Battery RCA, Belleville, Ontario — Serial 707B — 3rd Div.

The combined 32nd/34th Field Battery RCA, CASF, Serial 707B, mobilized with 14th Field Regiment RCA, CASF, 3rd Division, CASF, under General Order 184/40 (Effective 24th May 1940).

The regiment concentrated at Petawawa Military Camp, Ontario, 22nd September 1940, and it was here that the regiment reorganized to comprise three batteries.

34th Battery regained individual identity as 34th Field Battery RCA, Serial 707B, under General Order 45/41 (Effective 1st January 1941) and remained with 14th Field Regiment RCA. 32nd Battery moved to 4th Light Anti-Aircraft Regiment RCA, 3rd Division.

14th Field Regiment moved to Debert, Nova Scotia, February 1941, and on the 21st of July 1941, proceeded overseas on board the Empress of Canada, disembarking 29th July 1941 at Gourock, Scotland.

3rd Canadian Infantry Division was selected as an assault division for the Normandy invasion and 34th Field Battery, 14th Field Regiment RCA fired its

105mm self-propelled field guns from the landing craft in support of 8th Canadian Infantry Brigade prior to landing on the Normandy beaches on D-Day, 6th June 1944.

34th Field Battery, 14th Field Regiment RCA, 3rd Canadian Infantry Division, served with 1 British Corps and 2nd Canadian Corps under Second British Army in the early days of the invasion, then moved to First Canadian Army on the 31st of July 1944.

With the beachhead established, 34th Battery exchanged the 105mm self-propelled guns for towed 25 pounders, 1st week of August 1944, conforming to infantry division field artillery, and returned to action on the 13th of August, on the Caen Front.

34th Battery shook off the effects of the August bombing, the fierce fighting in the breakout from Caen and the Falaise Pocket, then headed for Boulogne, Calais and Cap Gris Nez, on the Channel coast.

Crossing the Leopold Canal in Belgium was the next objective, and on into Holland for the clearing of the Scheldt, then across the border into Germany on the 9th of February 1945. 34th Battery fired in support of the Rhine crossing, 23rd March 1945, and continued in action until the cessation of hostilities.

34th Field Battery RCA received authorization to disband under General Order 52/46 (Effective 2nd November 1945).

A reconstituted Battery mobilized as 2nd 34th Field Battery RCA, with 2nd 14th Field Regiment RCA, under General Order 319/45 (Effective 1st June 1945), to serve with the reconstituted 3rd Canadian Infantry Division, Canadian Army Occupational Force (CAOF).

2nd 34th Field Battery RCA received authorization to disband under General Order 162/46 (Effective 28th March 1946), following service with the Canadian Army Occupational Force in Germany.

*　　*　　*

36th Field Battery (SP) RCA, Cobourg, Ont. — Serial 1411C — 4th Div.

36th Field Battery RCA, Serial 1411C, mobilized under General Order 147/42 (Effective 18th March 1942), with 23rd Field Regiment RCA, to serve with 7th Division, Home Defence, Eastern Canada.

A self-propelled field regiment was added to the war establishment of an armoured division and 23rd Field Regiment RCA was selected for overseas service with 4th Canadian Armoured Division.

36th Field Battery RCA, Serial 1411C, was redesignated 36th Self-Propelled Battery RCHA, Serial 1411C, under General Order 328/43 (Effective 15th May 1943).

36th Battery sailed overseas 23rd July 1943 on board the Queen Elizabeth and disembarked at Gourock, Scotland, on the 28th of July 1943.

36th Self-Propelled Battery RCHA, was redesignated 36th Battery (Self-Propelled) RCA, Serial 1411C, under General Order 396/43 (Effective 15th August 1943).

36th Battery (Self-Propelled) RCA, Serial 1411C, was redesignated 36th Field Battery (Self-Propelled) RCA, Serial 1411C, under General Order 452/43 (Effective 1st September 1943).

36th Field Battery (SP), 23rd Field Regiment (SP) RCA, 4th Canadian Armoured Division landed in Normandy on the 26th of July 1944 and moved to the Caen Sector, 29th July 1944 with 2nd Canadian Corps.

2nd Canadian Corps and its components moved under command of First Canadian Army on the 31st of July 1944 and 36th Battery participated in the bitter fighting in the breakout from Caen and the closing of the Falaise Gap.

36th Field Battery (Self-Propelled) RCA served in France, Belgium, Holland and Germany, then with the cessation of hostilities, received authorization to disband under General Order 71/46 (Effective 18th December 1945).

* * *

37th Field Bty RCA, Portage La Prairie, Man. — Serial 907C — 5th Div.

37th Battery is unique, in that it mobilized as an individual battery in the era of two combined-battery field regiments.

37th Battery mobilized as 37th Field Battery RCA, CASF, Serial 907C, under General Order 184/40 (Effective 24th May 1940), with 17th Field Regiment RCA, CASF, 4th Division, CASF.

Headquarters 1st Canadian Armoured Division, Serial 562, and Headquarters 1st Canadian Armoured Division Support Group, Serial 578, mobilized under General Order 88/41 (Effective 27th February 1941).

17th Field Regiment RCA moved to the new formation as the lone field regiment in the Armoured Division Support Group. The division was redesignated 5th Canadian (Armoured) Division under General Order 135/41 (Effective 5th June 1941).

37th Battery, 17th Field Regiment RCA, 5th Canadian Armoured Division departed for overseas 13th November 1941 on board the Oronsay, and disembarked at Liverpool, England, 23rd November 1941.

On the 27th of October 1943, 37th Battery with the regiment returned to Liverpool to embark as 5th Canadian Armoured Division moved to the Mediterranean Theatre on operation "Timberwolf" and disembarked at Naples, Italy, on the 8th of November 1943.

With the arrival of Headquarters 1st Canadian Corps in Italy, 5th Canadian Armoured Division, 1st Canadian Infantry Division, 1st Canadian Armoured Brigade and 1st Canadian AGRA came under command and served as components.

37th Battery joined the action in the Ortona Sector, 17th January 1944 and served with 1st Canadian Corps, British Eighth Army in Italy until early 1945.

Transfer of 1st Canadian Corps to NW Europe saw groups of the regiment depart from Leghorn between 22nd and 26th February 1945, assembling at Marseilles, France, 1st March 1945.

The corps, division, regiment and battery joined First Canadian Army in NW Europe, with the regiment going into action on the "Island" between Nijmegen and Arnhem, Holland, on the 29th March 1945.

37th Field Battery RCA served until cessation of hostilities and received authorization to disband under General Order 71/46 (Effective 29th November 1945).

*   *   *

39th Field Battery RCA, Lethbridge, Alberta — Serial 812D — 6th Div.

39th Field Battery RCA, Serial 812D, mobilized under General Orders 63/42 (Effective 29th July 1941), to serve with 21st Field Regiment RCA, 6th Division, Home Defence. 19th and 20th Field Regiments RCA, also mobilized at that time to comprise the Divisional Field Artillery.

39th Battery with 21st Field Regiment RCA became components of 13th Brigade Group, 6th Division, on the 10th of December 1941. The regiment assembled in Westminister Camp, British Columbia, with 39th Battery arriving at the west coast, 14th December 1941.

On the 13th March 1942, the regiment moved from New Westminster to Nanaimo tent camp. While at Nanaimo, troops rotated for duty at Detached Unit gun positions at Otter Point and Jordan River.

During 1942 the batteries also visited the Artillery Ranges at Camp Shilo, Manitoba. From the 15th of July 1942 to the 22nd of May 1943, all artillery of the division was grouped under division headquarters instead of the brigade groups.

21st Field Regiment RCA departed Nanaimo 1st March 1943 and arrived at Port Alberni, 2nd March, remaining until moving to Willows Camp, Victoria, on the 17th of April 1943.

The battery and regiment crossed from Victoria to the mainland, 22nd May and arrived at Petawawa, Ontario, 26th May 1943. The next move was to Debert, Nova Scotia, 12 August as the unit worked its way eastward.

39th Battery, 21st Field Regiment RCA moved from Debert to Halifax, 26th August and departed for overseas 27th August 1943, on board the Queen Mary, disembarking at Gourock, Scotland, 1st September 1943.

39th Field Battery RCA, Serial 812D, proceeded to Cobham Camp in Surrey on the 2nd of September 1943, where the regiment disbanded, its last War Diary entry dated the 4th of October 1943.

The regiment and its three component batteries received authorization to disband under General Order 149/44 (Effective 11th October 1943). 21st Field was not to fight as a regiment, however, personnel joined the reinforcement pool and represented their old unit well on all battle fronts.

*   *   *

40th Field Battery RCA, Hamilton, Ontario — Serial 209D — Army Tps.

40th Field Battery RCA, CASF, Serial 210, mobilized under General Order 135/39, 1st September 1939, with Headquarters of 3rd Army Field Brigade RCA, CASF, Corps Troops mobilizing with 2nd Division.

40th Field Battery RCA, CASF, 3rd Army Field Brigade RCA, CASF, departed for overseas 30th January 1940 with the 3rd Flight, on board the Aquitania, and disembarked at Gourock, Scotland on the 8th of February 1940.

Headquarters of 3rd Army Field Brigade RCA, CASF, was redesignated Headquarters, 11th Army Field Regiment RCA, CASF, and batteries paired in a two-battery regiment.

40th Field Battery RCA, CASF, Serial 210, combined with 29th Field Battery (H) RCA, CASF, Serial 212, to become 29th/40th Field Battery RCA, CASF, Serial 212, under General Order 44/40 (Effective 12th February 1940). The combined battery served with 7th Corps and the Canadian Corps in the defence of England.

40th Battery regained individual identity as 40th Field Battery RCA, Serial 210, under General Order 45/41 (Effective 1st January 1941).

40th Field Battery RCA, was then allotted Serial Number 209D, under General Order 54/42 (Effective 22nd December 1941).

11th Army Field Regiment Mediterranean bound, boarded the Argentina at Liverpool, 24th October 1943, on operation "Timberwolf". The ship rendez-voused with the convoy off Scotland and 40th Battery with the regiment disembarked at Augusta, Sicily, on the 8th of November 1943.

The battery crossed to the Italian mainland, 7th January 1944, and joined the action under 1st Canadian AGRA, in support of 5th Canadian Armoured Division, 15th February 1944.

12th Canadian Infantry Brigade was formed as an extra infantry brigade for 5th Canadian Armoured Division, authorized under General Order 17/45 (Effective 13th July 1944), and 40th Battery with the regiment, moved from 1st Canadian AGRA to 5th Canadian Armoured Division to supply field artillery support for the new infantry brigade in Italy.

Transfer of 1st Canadian Corps from Italy saw 40th Battery and members of the regiment depart from Leghorn between the 16th and 24th of February 1945, arriving at Marseilles, France, between the 18th and 26th of February 1945.

12th Canadian Infantry Brigade ceased to exist upon arrival in NW Europe, being redesignated Headquarters 3 CBRG, under General Order 295/45 (Effective 13th March 1945), and the regiment once more became 11th Army Field Regiment RCA, 1st Canadian AGRA, Army Troops.

40th Battery and the regiment joined First Canadian Army in NW Europe and fired in support of 3rd Canadian Infantry Division from positions near Cleve, Germany, on the 31st March 1945, to become the first Regiment of 1st Canadian Corps to fight in Germany.

The battery returned to Holland and continued to support the divisions comprising First Canadian Army, until cessation of hostilities.

The 8th of May 1945 was officially declared "VE" Day and the run down of Canadian units was begun. Volunteers departed for the Canadian Army Pacific Force, high-point members returned to Canada, personnel moved to the Canadian Army Occupational Force, and those remaining returned to Canada with the regiment.

40th Field Battery RCA received authorization to disband under General Order 401/45 (Effective 4th September 1945).

* * *

43rd Field Battery RCA, Guelph, Ontario — Serial 705D — 3rd Division

43rd Field Battery RCA of Guelph, Ontario, mobilized as the combined 16th/43rd Field Battery RCA, CASF, Serial 705B, under General Order 184/40 (Effective 24th May 1940), with 12th Field Regiment RCA, CASF, 3rd Division, CASF.

The regiment assembled at Petawawa early in September, remaining until the 3rd of October 1940 at which time headquarters and the two combined field batteries left by road and rail for Camp Sussex, New Brunswick.

43rd Battery regained individual identity as 43rd Field Battery RCA, Serial 705D, under General Order 45/41 (Effective 1st January 1941), and remained with 12th Field Regiment RCA, now to comprises three field batteries.

43rd Field Battery, 12th Field Regiment RCA departed for overseas 21st July 1941, on board the Duchess of York, and disembarked at Liverpool, England, on the 30th of July 1941.

In England the regiment prepared for the invasion of the Continent as 3rd Canadian Infantry Division was selected as an assaulting division for the Normandy landings.

43rd Battery fired its 105mm self-propelled guns from the assault craft in support of 7th Canadian Infantry Brigade, 3rd Canadian Infantry Division, prior to landing on the Normandy Beaches, on D-Day, 6th June 1944.

During the early days of the invasion the division served with 1 British Corps, Second British Army, then moved to 2nd Canadian Corps under Second British Army, and on the 31st of July 1944, 2nd Canadian Corps and its Canadian components came under command of First Canadian Army.

Conforming to infantry division field artillery, the 105mm self-propelled guns were exchanged for towed 25 pounders, 1st August 1944, and so-equipped 43rd Battery served in France, Belgium, Holland, and Germany.

Upon the cessation of hostilities, 43rd Field Battery RCA received authorization to disband under General Order 52/46 (Effective 31st October 1945).

A 2nd 43rd Field Battery RCA, 2nd 12th Field Regiments RCA mobilized under General Orders 319/45 (Effective 1st June 1945), and following service with the reconstituted 3rd Canadian Infantry Division in Germany with the Canadian Army Occupational Force, 2nd 43rd Field Battery RCA, received authorization to disband under General Order 201/46 (Effective 18th May 1946).

*   *   *

44th Field Battery RCA, Prince Albert, Sask. — Serial 706B — 3rd Div.

44th Field Battery RCA mobilized in the era of combined field batteries as 44th/62nd Field Battery RCA, CASF, Serial 706B, with 13th Field Regiment RCA, CASF, 3rd Division, CASF, under General Order 184/40 (Effective 24th May 1940).

44th Battery regained individual identity as 44th Field Battery RCA, Serial 706B, under General Order 45/41 (Effective 1st January 1941) and remained with 13th Field Regiment RCA. 62nd Battery regained individual identity and moved to 4th Light Anti-Aircraft Regiment RCA, 3rd Division.

44th Field Battery, 13th Field Regiment RCA departed for overseas on board the Pasteur, 1st November 1941, and disembarked at Gourock, Scotland, 13th November 1941.

3rd Canadian Infantry Division was selected as an assault division for the invasion of Normandy, France, and landed on the beach at Courseulles-sur-Mer, with 3 British Division on their left flank and 50 (Northumbrian) Division on the right.

44th Battery fired its 105mm self-propelled guns from the assault craft in support of 7th Canadian Infantry Brigade prior to landing in Normandy on D-Day, 6th June 1944.

The division, regiment, and 44th Battery served with 1 British Corps, Second British Army during the assault and in the early days of the invasion, then moved to 2nd Canadian Corps, Second British Army. 2nd Canadian Corps and its Canadian components came under command of First Canadian Army on the 31st of July 1944.

With the beachhead established the battery exchanged the 105mm self-propelled guns for towed 25 pounders, 1st August 1944, conforming to infantry division organization.

44th Field Battery RCA served in France, Belgium, Holland, and Germany, then with cessation of hostilities, received authorization to disband under General Order 52/46 (Effective 14th November 1945).

A reconstituted battery, the 2nd 44th Field Battery RCA, 2nd 13th Field Regiment RCA, mobilized under General Order 319/45 (Effective 1st June 1945), and following service with the reconstituted 3rd Canadian Infantry

Division in Germany with the Canadian Army Occupational Force (CAOF), received authorization to disband under General Order 201/46 (Effective 13th April 1946).

*　　*　　*

49th Field Battery RCA, Kenora, Ontario — Serial 1412B — Kiska.

49th Field Battery RCA, Serial 1412B, mobilized at Kenora, Ontario, with 24th Field Regiment RCA, 18th Brigade Group, 7th Division, Home Defence, under General Order 147/42 (Effective 18th March 1942).

The Regiment concentrated at Camp Shilo, Manitoba, in June 1942, and in a shuffle of Brigades, 18th Infantry Brigade moved to 6th Division.

24th Field Regiment RCA aligned with 18th Brigade, joined Headquarters 6th Divisional Artillery RCA on the 15th July 1942.

49th Battery, 24th Field Regiment RCA moved to Vancouver, British Columbia, October 1942 under 6th Division, Pacific Command, and in March 1943 moved to Nanaimo, on Vancouver Island.

A reconstituted 13th Infantry Brigade Group was selected from 6th Division to accompany the Canadian-U.S. "Greenlight" Force in an attack on the Japanese occupied Island of Kiska, in the Aleutian Chain. 49th Battery with the regiment was to provide the field artillery support.

49th Battery sailed from Nanaimo, 12th July 1943 for Adak in the Aleutians to undergo further training and to become acclimatized.

The regiment departed from Adak, 13th August 1943, and 49th Battery disembarked at Kiska on the 15th and 16th August 1943, equipped with four US 75mm pack Howitzers and four 25 pounders.

Finding the enemy had vacated the island the battery remained on Garrison duty until 31st December 1943. On the return journey the battery paused at Adak for New Year's dinner, 2nd January, then on to Dutch Harbour for a visit on the 4th, and arrived in Vancouver, British Columbia, on the 21st of January 1944.

7th and 8th Divisions disbanded the latter part of 1943 and 6th Division reorganized to comprise 13th, 14th and 15th Brigade Groups. 13th Brigade Group remained intact upon its return from Kiska, and resumed its Home Defence role with 6th Division.

49th Field Battery RCA, Serial 1412B, with 24th Field Regiment RCA, made stops at Vernon, British Columbia, Wainwright and Suffield, Alberta, then returned to Vernon, where authorization to disband was received, authorized under General Order 213/45 (Effective 31st March 1945).

*   *   *

55th Field Battery RCA, London. Ontario — Serial 810B — Army Troops.

55th Field Battery RCA, Serial 810B, mobilized under General Order 63/42 (Effective 29th July 1941), with 19th Field Regiment RCA, aligned with 14th Brigade Group in 6th Division, Home Defence.

14th Infantry Brigade became a component of 8th Division, Home Defence, Pacific Command. 55th Battery with 19th Field Regiment, followed the brigade to the west coast and served with 14th Brigade Group at Terrace, British Columbia, from June to November 1942.

55th Field Battery RCA, saw duty on No. 1 Armoured Train, operating along the Skeena River between Terrace, and Prince Rupert, British Columbia.

19th Field Regiment RCA was selected for overseas service, and on the 15th of November 1942 moved to Petawawa, Ontario.

55th Field Battery RCA, Serial 810B, was redesignated 55th Self-Propelled Battery RCHA, Serial 810B, under General Order 328/43 (Effective 15th May 1943).

55th Battery departed for overseas 23rd July 1943 on board the Queen Elizabeth, and disembarked at Gourock, Scotland, 28th July 1943.

55th Self-Propelled Battery RCHA, Serial 810B, was redesignated 55th Battery (Self-Propelled) RCA, Serial 810B, under General Order 396/43 (Effective 15th August 1943), and under General Order 452/43, was redesignated 55th Field Battery (Self-Propelled) RCA, Serial 810B (Effective 1st September 1943).

19th Field Regiment (Self-Propelled) RCA which included 55th Field Battery (Self-Propelled) RCA, served temporarily with 5th Canadian Armoured Division, the regiment, however, was replaced by 8th Army Field Regiment RCA, upon its conversion to an SP Regiment.

19th Field Regiment (Self-Propelled) RCA, Serial 810, was redesignated 19th Army Field Regiment RCA, Serial 810, and 55th Field Battery (Self-Propelled) RCA, Serial 810B, was redesignated 55th Field Battery RCA, Serial 810B, under General Order 134/44 (Effective 18th October 1943).

As an Army Field Regiment under 2nd Canadian AGRA, the unit was attached to 3rd Canadian Infantry Division which required an extra field artillery regiment for the invasion of Normandy. Each of the two assaulting infantry brigades were allotted two self-propelled regiments of field artillery to aid in for the initial assault and the advance inland.

55th Battery fired its 105mm self-propelled guns from the assault craft in support of 8th Canadian Infantry Brigade, prior to landing on the beaches of Normandy on D-Day, 6th June 1944.

The battery and regiment remained attached to 3rd Canadian Infantry Division, 1 British Corps, Second British Army, in the early days of the invasion, then moved to 2nd Canadian Corps under Second British Army, 11th July 1944. The Canadian units, with 2nd Canadian Corps, moved under command of First Canadian Army on the 31st of July 1944.

With the bridghead established, the 105mm self-propelled guns were exchanged for 25 Pounder SPs, 24th August 1944.

55th Battery served in France, Belgium, Holland, and Germany, lending fire support to the multi-national components of First Canadian Army and a large number of 21 Army Group units.

Following the cessation of hostilities, 55th Field Battery RCA received authorization to disband under General Order 52/46 (Effective 16th November 1945).

*   *   *

59th Field Battery RCA, Brandon, Manitoba — Serial 812B — 6th Div.

59th Field Battery RCA, Serial 812B, mobilized under General Order 63/42 (Effective 29th July 1941), to serve with 21st Field Regiment RCA, 6th Division, Home Defence. 19th and 20th Field Regiments RCA also mobilized to complete the field artillery componenents of 6th Division.

59th Battery with 21st Field Regiment RCA, joined 13th Brigade Group, 6th Division, on the 10th of December 1941, The regiment assembled in Westminster Camp, British Columbia. 59th Battery arrived at the west coast on the 15th December and remained at New Westminster until 13th March 1942, then crossed to Nanaimo on Vancouver Island.

The regiment settled in, in the tent camp at Nanaimo, and also manned Detached Unit gun positions at Otter Point and Jordan River, during 1942. The batteries also visited the Artillery Range at Camp Shilo, Manitoba in 1942. All artillery was grouped under headquarters of the division from 15th July 1942, to 22nd May 1943, altering the structure of the brigade groups.

21st Field Regiment departed from Nanaimo, 1st March 1943, arrived at Port Alberni, 2nd March and remained until moved to Willows Camp, Victoria, on the 17th April 1943.

The battery and regiment crossed from Victoria to the mainland 22nd May and arrived at Petawawa, Ontario, 26th May 1943. The next move began on the 12th of August, a two day journey to Debert, Nova Scotia, as the unit worked its way eastward.

59th Field Battery, 21st Field Regiment RCA, moved from Debert to Halifax, 26th August, and departed for overseas 27th August 1943 on board the Queen Mary, disembarking at Gourock, Scotland on the 1st of September 1943.

59th Field Battery RCA, Serial 812B, proceeded to Cobham Camp, Surrey, 2nd September 1943. The unit's last War Diary entry is dated the 4th of October 1943.

The regiment and its three component batteries received authorization to disband under General Order 149/44 (Effective 11th October 1943). Members of 59th Battery joined the reinforcement pool and served on the Italian Front and in NW Europe, making their contribution to the defeat of the enemy.

*   *   *

60th Field Battery RCA, Aneroid, Saskatchewan — Serial 907B

The combined 60th/76th Field Battery RCA, CASF, Serial 907B, mobilized under General Orderd 184/40 (Effective 24th May 1940), with 17th Field Regiment RCA, CASF, 4th Division, CASF.

60th Battery regained individual identity under General Order 85/41 (Effective 1st January 1941), to become 60th Field Battery RCA, Serial 907B, and remained with 17th Field Regiment RCA in 4th Division, as the regiment reorganized to comprise three field batteries.

Headquarters 1st Canadian Armoured Division, Serial 562, along with Headquarters 1st Canadian Armoured Division Support Group, Serial 578, mobilized under General Order 88/41 (Effective 27th February 1941), and 17th Field Regiment RCA moved to the new armoured division as the lone field regiment in the support group.

1st Canadian Armoured Division was redesignated 5th Canadian (Armoured) Division, under General Order 135/41 (Effective 5th June 1941).

60th Field Battery RCA, 17th Field Regiment RCA, 5th Canadian (Armoured) Division, departed for overseas, 13th November 1941 on the Oronsay, and disembarked 23rd November 1941, at Liverpool, England.

60th Battery returned to Liverpool 27th October 1943, to embark on operation "Timberwolf", transfer to the Mediterranean Theatre of Headquarters 1st Canadian Corps, Corps Troops, 1st Canadian AGRA, and 5th Canadian Armoured Division.

60th Battery with 17th Field Regiment RCA, disembarked at Naples, Italy, on the 8th of November 1943.

With the arrival in Italy of Headquarters 1st Canadian Corps, 5th Canadian Armoured Division, 1st Canadian Infantry Division, and 1st Canadian Armoured Brigade became components, supported by 1st Canadian AGRA.

60th Battery joined the action 17th January 1944 in the Ortona Sector and served with 1st Canadian Corps in Italy until early 1945.

The battery and regiment departed from Italy via Leghorn, with groups leaving between the 22nd and 26th of February 1945, to Marseilles, France, where the regiment assembled 1st March 1945.

Headquarters 1st Canadian Corps and its components joined First Canadian Army in NW Europe. 17th Field Regiment entered the fray on the "Island" between Nijmegen and Arnhem, Holland, 29th March 1945, and served in Holland until the cessation of hostilities.

60th Field Battery RCA received authorization to disband under General Order 71/46 (Effective 29th November 1945).

*   *   *

61st Field Battery (SP) RCA, Edmonton, Alberta — Serial 214B — 5th Div.

61st Field Battery RCA, CASF, Serial 215, mobilized under General Order 135/39, 1st September 1939, with Headquarters of 4th Army Field Brigade RCA, CASF, Corps Troops mobilizing with 2nd Division.

61st Field Battery RCA, CASF, sailed overseas 28th January 1940 on board the Monarch of Bermuda, in Troop Convoy 3, and disembarked at Gourock, Scotland, on the 8th of February 1940.

Headquarters of 4th Army Field Brigade RCA, CASF, was redesignated Headquarters 8th Army Field Regiment RCA, CASF, and the regiment was to comprise two field batteries. 61st Field Battery RCA, CASF, Serial 215, combined with 107th Field Battery RCA, CASF, Serial 216, to become 61st/107th Field Battery RCA, CASF, Serial 215, under General Order 44/40 (Effective 12th February 1940). 71st and 113th Batteries combined as 71st/113th Battery to complete the regiment.

61st/107th Field Battery RCA, CASF, 8th Army Field Regiment RCA, CASF, served with 7th Corps and the Canadian Corps, in an anti-invasion role.

61st Battery regained individual identity as 61st Field Battery RCA, Serial 215, under General Order 45/41 (Effective 1st January 1941), and remained with the regiment, now to comprise three batteries.

61st Field Battery RCA was allotted Serial Number 214B, under General Order 54/42 (Effective 22nd December 1941), in a shuffle of serial numbers within the regiment.

8th Army Field Regiment RCA was attached to 3rd Canadian Infantry Division for the invasion of Normandy in 1944, enabling the two assaulting infantry brigades to attack with the support of two field regiments to each brigade.

The decision to transfer Headquarters 1st Canadian Corps, Corps Troops, 1st Canadian AGRA, and 5th Canadian Armoured Division to the Mediterranean Theatre of Operations, brought about a number of changes, and the regiment was selected to join 5th Canadian Armoured Division as a self-propelled regiment RCA.

8th Army Field Regiment RCA was redesignated 8th Field Regiment (Self-Propelled) RCA, and 61st Field Battery RCA became 61st Field Battery (Self-Propelled) RCA, Serial 214B, under General Order 134/44 (Effective 18th October 1943).

During its stay in England the battery served under the command of 1st, 2nd and 3rd Canadian Infantry Divisions, 5th Canadian Armoured Division, Headquarters Corps Medium Artillery, 1st and 2nd Canadian AGRAs.

61st Field Battery (SP) RCA, 8th Field Regiment (SP) RCA departed for the Mediterranean on board the Scythia, from Bristol. 13th of November 1943, on operation "Timberwolf II". The ship joined the convoy off Greenock and continued the journey on the 15th of November.

Algiers was reached 26th November, where the batteries disembarked on the 27th and remained three weeks before sailing for Naples, rejoining the remainder of the regiment at Gravina, Italy on the 23rd of December 1943.

61st Battery moved to the Front, 9th February 1944, joining the action with 5th Canadian Armoured Division, 1st Canadian Corps and served in Italy until the following February when 1st Canadian Corps moved to NW Europe to join First Canadian Army.

The battery sailed from Leghorn, Italy aboard US Navy LSTs, 22nd February 1945, disembarking at Marseilles, France, on the 24th of February 1945.

61st Battery and the regiment under First Canadian Army, fired in support of the attack on Arnhem, Holland, 12th April 1945, and continued in action in Holland until the cessation of hostilities.

61st Field Battery (Self-Propelled) RCA, received authorization to disband under General Order 71/46 (Effective 27th November 1945).

* * *

63rd Field Battery RCA, Guelph, Ontario — Serial 810C — Army Troops.

63rd Field Battery RCA, Serial 810C, mobilized under General Order 63/42 (Effective 29th July 1941), to serve with 19th Field Regiment RCA, 14th Brigade Group, 6th Division, Home Defence.

The regiment concentrated at Camp Borden, Ontario, in December 1941. "C" Troop with four eighteen pounders was posted to Prince Rupert, British Columbia, in March 1942, to aid in the defence of the harbour. The remainder of the regiment departed Camp Borden in May, stopping at Camp Shilo, Manitoba, Artillery Range, and arrived at Terrace, British Columbia, 4th June 1942. While at the Coast the regiment manned the two 75mm guns on No. 1 Armoured Train, operating along the railway line skirting the Skeena River between Prince Rupert and Terrace, and manned two guns at Tyee, B.C., inland from Prince Rupert.

Prince Rupert Defences and 14th Brigade Group came under command of 8th Division, 1st October 1942. The regiment's stay was shortlived however, for in November, 19th Field Regiment RCA was selected for overseas service and on the 15th of November 1942 moved from the west coast to Petawawa, Ontario.

63rd Field Battery RCA, Serial 810C, was redesignated 63rd Self-Propelled Battery RCHA, Serial 810C, under General Order 328/43 (Effective 15th May 1943).

The battery departed for overseas 23rd July 1943, on board the Queen Elizabeth, and disembarked 28th July 1943, at Gourock, Scotland.

63rd Self-Propelled Battery RCHA, Serial 810C, was redesignated 63rd Battery (Self-Propelled) RCA, Serial 810C, under General Order 396/43 (Effective 15th August 1943), and under General Order 452/43, was redesignated 63rd Field Battery (Self-Propelled) RCA, Serial 810C (Effective 1st September 1943).

19th Field Regiment (Self-Propelled) RCA, including 63rd Field Battery (Self-Propelled) RCA, served with 5th Canadian Armoured Division temporarily, then exchanged Formations with 8th Army Field Regiment RCA upon its conversion to an SP Regiment.

19th Field Regiment (Self-Propelled) RCA, Serial 810, was redesignated 19th Army Field Regiment RCA, Serial 810, and 63rd Field Battery (Self-Propelled) RCA, was redesignated 63rd Field Battery RCA, Serial 810C, under General Order 134/44 (Effective 18th October 1943).

As an Army Field Regiment, 19th Army Field Regiment RCA was attached to 3rd Canadian Infantry Division for the invasion of Normandy in 1944. This arrangement provided the support of two field artillery regiments for each of the two assaulting infantry brigades.

63rd Battery fired its 105mm self-propelled guns from the assault craft in support of 8th Canadian Infantry Brigade prior to landing on the beaches of Normandy on D-Day, 6th June 1944.

63rd Battery remained attached to 3rd Canadian Infantry Division, 1 British Corps, Second British Army, in the early days of the invasion, then moved to 2nd Canadian Corps under Second British Army, and on the 31st of July 1944, 2nd Canadian Corps came under command of First Canadian Army.

The 105mm self-propelled guns were exchanged for 25 pounder self-propelled guns, 24th August 1944, with the beachhead established, and the Army Field Regiment assumed its role with 2nd Canadian AGRA, Army Troops, First Canadian Army.

63rd Battery with the regiment, fired in support of 2nd, 3rd, 4th Canadian Divisions, 3, 43, 49, 50, 51, 52, 53 Infantry Divisions, 7, 11, and Guards Armoured Divisions, 1st Polish Armoured Division, and other formations under 21 Army Group.

The regiment served in France, Belgium, Holland, and Germany, then with the cessation of hostilities 63rd Battery was selected as a representative of the Royal Canadian Artillery in the Canadian Berlin Brigade. After a month of preparation the plan was cancelled, the Berlin Brigade disbanded and the batteries returned to their regiments to await repatriation.

63rd Field Battery RCA received authorization to disband under General Order 52/46 (Effective 16th November 1945).

*   *   *

64th (Yorkton) Field Battery RCA, Yorkton, Sask. — Serial 812C.

64th (Yorkton) Field Battery RCA, Serial 812C, mobilized under General Order 63/42 (Effective 29th July 1941), to serve with 21st Field Regiment RCA, 6th Division, Home Defence. 19th and 20th Field Regiments RCA also mobilized at that time to comprise the Divisional Artillery of 6th Division.

64th Battery with the regiment became components of 13th Brigade Group, 6th Division, on the 10th of December 1941. The regiment assembled in Westminister Camp, British Columbia, with 64th Battery arriving at the west coast, 15th December 1941.

On the 13th March 1942, the regiment moved from New Westminister to Nanaimo tent camp. While at Nanaimo, on Vancouver Island, troops rotated for duty at Detached Unit gun positions at Otter Point and Jordan River. During 1942 the batteries also visited the Artillery Ranges at Camp Shilo, Manitoba.

The regiment departed Nanaimo 1st March 1943, arriving at Port Alberni, 2nd March, remaining until moved to Willows Camp, Victoria on the 17th April 1943.

The battery and regiment crossed from Victoria to the mainland on the 22nd of May and arrived at Petawawa, Ontario, 26th May 1943. The next move was to Debert, Nova Scotia, 12th August, as the unit worked its way eastward.

64th Battery, 21st Field Regiment RCA moved from Debert to Halifax on the 26th of August and departed for overseas 27th August 1943 on board the Queen Mary, disembarking at Gourock, Scotland on the 1st of September 1943.

64th (Yorkton) Field Battery RCA, Serial 812C, proceeded to Cobham Camp, Surrey, 2nd September 1943, where the regiment disbanded, its last War Diary entry dated the 4th of October 1943.

21st Field Regiment RCA, Serial 812, Headquarters 21st Field Regiment RCA, Serial 812A, 59th Battery RCA, Serial 812B, 64th (Yorkton) Field Battery RCA, Serial 812C, and 39th Field Battery RCA, Serial 812D, received authorization to disband under General Order 149/44 (Effective 11th October 1943).

*   *   *

66th Field Battery RCA, Montreal, P.Q. — Serial 707C — 3rd Cdn. Inf. Div.

The combined 66th/81st Field Battery RCA, CASF, Serial 707C mobilized as a component of 14th Field Regiment RCA, CASF, 3rd Division, CASF, under General Order 184/40 (Effective 24th May 1940).

The two combined batteries, 66th/81st, and 32nd/34th, moved to Petawawa in August 1940, and on the 22nd of September came under regimental command.

While still at Petawawa, the regiment reorganized to comprise three field batteries. 66th Battery regained individual identity as 66th Field Battery RCA, Serial 707C, under General Order 45/41 (Effective 1st January 1941), and remained with 14th Field Regiment RCA. The regiment moved to Debert, Nova Scotia, in the divisional concentration area, in February 1941.

66th Battery, with the regiment, departed for overseas 21st July 1941 on board the Empress of Canada, and disembarked at Gourock, Scotland, 29th July 1941. The regiment settled in at Ewshott, in the South of England, alternating between training and manning anti-invasion gun sites on the coast.

As the threat of invasion diminished, offensive training surfaced and 3rd Canadian Infantry Division was selected as an assault division for the D-Day landings in June 1944 on the Normandy coast of France.

66th Field Battery, 14th Field Regiment RCA landed in Normandy on D-Day, 6th June 1944, with the assaulting 3rd Canadian Infantry Division. The battery fired its 105mm self-propelled guns from the assault craft in support of 8th Canadian Infantry Brigade, prior to landing.

The division, regiment and battery served with 1 British Corps, Second British Army during the early days of the invasion, then moved to 2nd Canadian Corps, Second British Army. 2nd Canadian Corps and its components came under the command of First Canadian Army on the 31st of July 1944 and prepared for the breakout from Caen.

With the beachhead established the 105mm self-propelled guns were exchanged for towed 25 pounders, 1st August, conforming to infantry division field artillery organization.

The battery took part in the fierce fighting around Caen and the closing of the Falaise Gap, then moved on to the Channel Ports, crossed the border into Belgium, Holland and Germany.

66th Field Battery RCA served until the cessation of hostilities and received authorization to disband under General Order 52/46 (Effective 2nd November 1945).

A reconstituted 66th Battery mobilized as 2nd 66th Field Battery RCA, under General Order 319/45 (Effective 1st June 1945), with 2nd 14th Field Regiment RCA, to serve with the reconstituted 3rd Canadian Infantry Division, Canadian Army Occupational Force (CAOF).

2nd 66th Field Battery RCA received authorization to disband under General Order 162/46 (Effective 28th March 1946), following service in Germany with the Canadian Army Occupational Force.

*   *   *

71st Field Battery (SP) RCA, Brandon, Manitoba — Serial 214C — 5th Div.

71st Field Battery (H) RCA, CASF, Serial 218, mobilized under General Order 135/39, 1st September 1939, with Headquarters of 4th Army Field Brigade RCA, CASF, Corps Troops mobilizing with 2nd Division.

71st Field Battery (H) RCA, CASF, departed for overseas 28th January 1940 on board the Monarch of Bermuda in Troop Convoy 3, and disembarked at Gourock, Scotland, 8th February 1940.

Reorganization and 4th Army Field Brigade arrived at Bordon in the South of England, almost simultaneously. Headquarters of 4th Army Field Brigade was redesignated Headquarters 8th Army Field Regiment RCA, CASF, and the regiment was to comprise two batteries. 71st Field Battery (H) RCA, CASF, Serial 218, and 113th Field Battery (H) RCA, CASF, Serial 217 combined to become 71st/113th Field Battery RCA, CASF, Serial 217, under General Order 44/40 (Effective 12th February 1940).

71st/113th Field Battery RCA, CASF, 8th Army Field Regiment RCA, CASF, served with 7th Corps and the Canadian Corps in England in an anti-invasion role until the threat of invasion subsided.

The regiment reorganized to comprise three batteries and 71st Battery regained individual identity as 71st Field Battery RCA, Serial 218, under General Order 45/41 (Effective 1st January 1941). 71st Battery remained with 8th Army Field Regiment RCA and 113th Battery moved to 7th Anti-Tank Regiment RCA, 1st Canadian Corps.

71st Field Battery was alotted Serial Number 214C, under General Order 54/42 (Effective 22nd December 1941), in a shuffle of serial numbers within the regiment.

In August 1943, as an Army Field Regiment, 8th Army Field Regiment RCA was attached to 3rd Canadian Infantry Division, which required a fourth field regiment for the Normandy invasion in 1944.

8th Army Field Regiment RCA was redesignated 8th Field Regiment (Self-Propelled) RCA, and 71st Field Battery RCA became 71st Field Battery (Self-Propelled) RCA, Serial 214C, under General Order 134/44 (Effective 18th October 1943).

However, upon the transfer of 5th Canadian Armoured Division to the Mediterranean, 8th Field Regiment (Self-Propelled) RCA, was selected to join 5th Canadian Armoured Division as an SP Regiment, a recent addition to an armoured division war establishment.

During its stay in England the battery had served under 1st, 2nd and 3rd Canadian Infantry Divisions, 1st Corps Medium Artillery, 1st and 2nd Canadian AGRAs, and now 5th Canadian Armoured Division.

71st Field Battery (SP) RCA, 8th Field Regiment (SP) RCA, departed for the Mediterranean on board the Scythia, from Bristol, England, 13th November 1943, on operation "Timberwolf II".

The ship rendezvoused with the convoy off Greenock, Scotland, and resumed the journey on the 15th of November. Algiers was reached 26th November 1943, where the batteries disembarked on the 27th, to remain three weeks before sailing for Naples, Italy. In Italy the regiment concentrated at Gravina, 22nd December 1943.

71st Battery joined the action on the 9th of February 1944 with 5th Canadian Armoured Division, 1st Canadian Corps, and served in Italy until the following February, then accompanied 1st Canadian Corps to NW Europe.

71st Battery departed Italy via Leghorn, 22nd February 1945 on US Navy LSTs and arrived at Marseilles, France, 24th February 1945. The regiment concentrated at Comines, Belgium, and received its new complement of 25 pounder Sexton self-propelled guns during the second week of March. The new guns were tested by firing into the enemy held pocket at Dunkirk on the 23rd of March.

The regiment deployed on the Island near Nijmegen, Holland, on the 6th of April, and on the 12th of April fired in support of a diversionary attack on the West side of Arnhem. The regiment continued in action in Holland under First Canadian Army until the cessation of hostilities.

71st Field Battery (Self-Propelled) RCA, received authorization to disband under General Order 71/46 (Effective 27th November 1945).

*   *   *

72nd Field Battery RCA, Coaticook, P.Q. — Serial 811C — 6th Division.

72nd Field Battery RCA, Serial 811C, mobilized under General Order 63/42 (Effective 29th July 1941), with 20th Field Regiment RCA, aligned with 15th Brigade Group, 6th Division, Home Defence. 19th Field Regiment RCA, and 21st Field Regiment RCA, also mobilized with 6th Division at that time.

Reorganization of 20th Field Regiment RCA following the departure of 50th and 58th Batteries to 4th Medium Regiment RCA, saw 24th Field Battery RCA and 75th Field Battery RCA arrive as replacement batteries. 20th Field Regiment RCA now comprised 24th Field Battery RCA, 72nd Field Battery RCA, and 75th Field Battery RCA.

24th Battery and 75th Battery had mobilized as a combined field battery bearing the designation 24th/75th Field Battery RCA, CASF, with the original 16th Field Regiment, 4th Division, CASF, in 1940. 24th/75th Field Battery became surplus in an ensuing shuffle. The batteries regained individual identity as field batteries, then became anti-tank batteries until being posted to 20th Field Regiment at Valcartier, P.Q. as field batteries.

72nd Battery and 20th Field Regiment RCA, accompanied 15th Brigade Group to 7th Canadian Division, Debert, Nova Scotia, in June 1942 and served with 7th Division until the division received authorization to disband in October 1943.

Following the disbandment of 7th and 8th Divisions, 6th Division reorganized to its original brigade components. 72nd Battery and the regiment with 15th Brigade Group, returned to 6th Division, Home Defence, Pacific Command, and served at Prince George, Vancouver, and Nanaimo, British Columbia, and Wainwright, Alberta.

72nd Field Battery RCA, Serial 811C, along with Headquarters 20th Field Regiment RCA, 24th Field Battery RCA and 75th Field Battery RCA, returned to Valcartier, P.Q. where authorization was received to disband under General Order 208/45 (Effective 31st December 1944).

* * *

73rd Field Battery RCA, Magog, P.Q. — Serial 160D — 2nd Cdn Inf. Div.

73rd Field Battery (H) RCA, CASF, Serial 14, mobilized under General Order 135/39, 1st September 1939, with Headquarters of 2nd Field Brigade RCA, CASF, 1st Division, CASF, however, the Battery was transferred and came under Headquarters of 5th Field Brigade RCA, CASF, assuming Serial Number 164, under General Order 206/39 (Effective 1st September 1939).

Headquarters of 5th Field Brigade RCA, CASF, was redesignated Headquarters of 5th Field Regiment RCA, CASF, and 73rd Field Battery (H) RCA, CASF, Serial 164, combined with 5th (Westmount) Field Battery RCA, CASF, Serial 161, to become 5th/73rd Field Battery RCA, CASF, Serial 161, under General Order 123/40 (Effective 1st June 1940).

57th/73rd Field Battery, 5th Field Regiment RCA, CASF, 2nd Division, CASF, sailed overseas on board the Empress of Australia, 27th August 1940 and disembarked at Glasgow, Scotland on the 4th September 1940. The combined battery became a component of the Canadian Corps and served in an anti-invasion role in the South of England.

73rd Battery regained individual identity under General Order 45/41 (Effective 1st January 1941) and remained with the regiment as it reorganized to comprise three batteries. 73rd Battery was allotted Serial Number 160D, under General Order 54/42 (Effective 22nd December 1941).

73rd Battery, 5th Field Regiment RCA, 2nd Canadian Infantry Division, landed in Normandy on the 7th July 1944 and joined the action 12th July in support of 3rd Canadian Infantry Division, 1 British Corps, Second British

Army, then moved to 2nd Canadian Corps, Second British Army. 2nd Canadian Corps and its components came under the command of First Canadian Army, 31st July 1944. 73rd Battery supported 2nd Division in its operations with 5th Canadian Infantry Brigade receiving the majority of the direct support.

Following the capture of Dieppe, 73rd Battery with the regiment participated in the divisional parade through the streets of the city on the 3rd of September 1944, then rejoined the battle under First Canadian Army, serving in France, Belgium, Holland and Germany.

73rd Field Battery RCA served until the cessation of hostilities and received authorization to disband under General Order 52/46 (Effective 21st September 1945).

*   *   *

75th Field Battery RCA, Cowansville, P.Q. — Serial 811D — 6th Div.

75th Battery mobilized as the combined 24th/75th Field Battery RCA, CASF, Serial 906B, under General Order 184/40 (Effective 24th May 1940), with 16th Field Regiment RCA, CASF, 4th Division, CASF.

Following the reorganization of 4th Division, 16th Field Regiment RCA was allotted three new batteries, and under General Order 240/41 (Effective 5th September 1941) 75th Battery regained individual identity as 75th Field Battery RCA, Serial 992E, then under the same General Order was redesignated 75th Anti-Tank Battery RCA, Serial 992E.

75th Anti-Tank Battery RCA, Serial 992E, was redesignated 75th Field Battery RCA, Serial 811D, under General Order 104/42 (Effective 26th January 1942).

75th Battery replaced 50th Battery in 20th Field Regiment RCA, 15th Brigade Group, 6th Canadian Division, Home Defence, at Valcartier, on the 7th of February 1942. 50th Battery moved to 4th Medium Regiment RCA, slated for overseas service.

75th Battery and 20th Field Regiment RCA accompanied 15th Brigade Group to 7th Canadian Division at Debert, Nova Scotia, in June 1942, and served until 7th Division disbanded, authorized under General Order 15/44 (Effective 15th October 1943).

8th Division, Home Defence also disbanded and 6th Division reorganized to comprise 13th, 14th and 15th Brigade Groups, regaining its original brigade structure. 75th Battery accompanied the regiment and 15th Brigade Group to 6th Division in Pacific Command. The battery and regiment served at Prince George, Vancouver, and Nanaimo, British Columbia, and Wainwright, Alberta.

Serial 811D, 75th Field Battery RCA returned to Valcartier, P.Q. and received authorization to disband under General Order 208/45 (Effective 31st December 1944).

*   *   *

76th Field Battery RCA, Indian Head, Sask. — Serial 907D — 5th Div.

76th Battery mobilized as the combined 60th/76th Field Battery RCA, CASF, Serial 907B, with 17th Field Regiment RCA, CASF, 4th Division, CASF, under General Order 184/40 (Effective 24th May 1940).

76th Battery regained individual identity as 76th Field Battery RCA, Serial 907D, under General Order 85/41 (Effective 1st January 1941) and remained with 17th Field Regiment RCA.

The battery and regiment moved to the Support Group, 1st Canadian Armoured Division, authorized under General Order 88/41 (Effective 27th February 1941), and then redesignated 5th Canadian (Armoured) Division under General Order 135/41 (Effective 5th June 1941).

76th Field Battery, 17th Field Regiment RCA, 5th Canadian (Armoured) Division, departed for overseas 13th November 1941, on board the Oronsay, and disembarked on the 23rd of November 1941, at Liverpool, England.

76th Battery embarked from Liverpool on the 27th of October 1943, upon the transfer of 5th Canadian Armoured Division to the Mediterranean, on operation "Timberwolf", and with the regiment, disembarked at Naples, Italy, on the 8th of November 1943.

With the arrival of Headquarters 1st Canadian Corps in Italy, 5th Canadian Armoured Division joined 1st Canadian Infantry Division to form 1st Canadian Corps, supported by 1st Canadian Armoured Brigade and 1st Canadian AGRA.

76th Battery joined the action in the Ortona Sector, 13th January 1944 and served in Italy until early 1945 with 1st Canadian Corps, British Eighth Army.

Transfer of 1st Canadian Corps to NW Europe, saw 76th Battery depart from Italy via Leghorn, with groups leaving between 22nd and 26th February 1945, assembling at Marseilles, France, on the 1st of March 1945.

1st Canadian Corps, the division, regiment and 76th Battery joined First Canadian Army in NW Europe, with the regiment going into action on the "Island" between Nijmegen and Arnhem, Holland, on the 29th of March 1945.

76th Field Battery RCA served until the cessation of hostilities and received authorization to disband under General Order 71/46 (Effective 29th November 1945).

*   *   *

77th Field Battery RCA, Moose Jaw, Saskatchewan — Serial 15B — 1st Div.

77th Field Battery RCA, CASF, Serial 18, mobilized under General Order 135/39, 1st September 1939, with Headquarters of 3rd Field Brigade RCA, CASF, 1st Division, CASF.

77th Battery departed for overseas 10th December 1939 on board the Empress of Britain, in Troop Convoy 1 and disembarked at Gourock, Scotland, 18th December 1939.

Headquarters of 3rd Field Brigade RCA, CASF, was redesignated Headquarters, 3rd Field Regiment RCA, CASF, to comprise two batteries. The original batteries were paired and 77th Field Battery RCA, CASF, Serial 18, combined with 19th Field Battery RCA, CASF, Serial 16, to become 19th/77th Field Battery RCA, CASF, Serial 16, under General Order 44/40 (Effective 21st December 1939).

77th Battery regained individual identity as 77th Field Battery RCA, Serial 18, under General Order 45/41 (Effective 1st January 1941) and remained with the regiment, now to comprise three batteries.

In a shuffle of serial numbers, 77th Battery was allotted Serial Number 15B, under General Order 54/42 (Effective 22nd December 1941).

In England, the battery and regiment served with 7th Corps, the Canadian Corps, and 1st Canadian Corps.

77th Battery, 3rd Field Regiment RCA returned to Gourock, Scotland in June 1943 and departed for the Mediterranean Theatre of Operations to join the famous Eighth Army on active duty.

The battery landed in Sicily on the 10th of July 1943 with the assaulting 1st Canadian Infantry Division, 30 Corps, British Eighth Army, then crossed to the Italian mainland with 13 Corps, Eighth Army, 3rd September 1943.

Upon 1st Canadian Corps becoming operational early 1944 in Italy, 1st Division became a component and served until early 1945, then accompanied the corps to NW Europe to join First Canadian Army.

On the 15th March 1945, 77th Battery departed Italy via Leghorn, and arrived at Marseilles, France, 16th March 1945. The battery joined the action in support of 3rd Canadian Infantry Division, 7th April 1945, in an attack on

Deventer, in Holland, then returned to 1st Canadian Infantry Division for the Ijssel River crossing and served until cessation of hostilities.

77th Field Battery RCA received authorization to disband under General Order 401/45 (Effective 27th August 1945).

*   *   *

78th Field Battery RCA, Red Deer, Alberta — Serial 706D — 3rd. Div.

78th Battery mobilized with 13th Field Regiment RCA, CASF, under General Orders 184/40 (Effective 24th May 1940), as the combined 22nd/78th Field Battery RCA, CASF, Serial 706C, in Canada's 3rd Division, CASF.

78th Battery regained individual identity as 78th Field Battery RCA, Serial 706D, under General Order 45/41 (Effective 1st January 1941), and remained with 13th Field Regiment RCA as the regiment reorganized to comprise three batteries.

78th Battery departed for overseas 4th November 1941 on board the Pasteur, and disembarked at Gourock, Scotland on the 13th of November 1941.

78th Field Battery, 13th Field Regiment RCA, landed in Normandy on D-Day, 6th June 1944, with the assaulting 3rd Canadian Infantry Division, 1 British Corps, Second British Army.

The battery fired its 105mm self-propelled guns from the assault craft in support of 7th Canadian Infantry Brigade prior to landing on the Normandy beaches.

78th Battery with the regiment moved to 2nd Canadian Corps under Second British Army, then with 2nd Canadian Corps, became a component of First Canadian Army on the 31st of July 1944.

On the 1st of August 1944, with the beachhead established, the 105mm self-propelled guns were exchanged for towed 25 pounders, as the regiment conformed to infantry division organization.

78th Field Battery RCA served in France, Belgium, Holland, and Germany, then with cessation of hostilities, received authorization to disband under General Order 52/46 (Effective 14th November 1945).

A reconstituted Battery, the 2nd 78th Field Battery RCA, 2nd 13th field Regiment RCA, mobilized with the reconstituted 3rd Canadian Infantry Division, under General Order 319/45 (Effective 1st June 1945), for service with the Canadian Army Occupational Force (CAOF), and following occupational duty in Germany, 2nd 78th Field Battery RCA received authorization to disband under General Order 201/46 (Effective 13th April 1946).

* * *

80th Field Battery RCA, Quebec-Levis — Serial 1410D — 8th Division.

80th Field Battery RCA, Serial 1410D, mobilized with 22nd Field Regiment RCA, authorized under General Order 147/42 (Effective 18th March 1942), to serve with 7th Division, Home Defence, Eastern Canada.

7th Division was to comprise 16th, 17th and 18th Brigade Groups and 80th Battery with 22nd Field Regiment RCA was aligned with 16th Infantry Brigade Group. The organization remained until mid-June 1942 when Headquarters 7th Division and Headquarters 8th Division received authorization to mobilize. The infantry brigades were shuffled between the three home defence divisions and 7th Division was now to comprise 15th, 17th and 20th Infantry Brigades. The Divisional Artillery was grouped under headquarters of the division, rather than in brigade groups.

Headquarters 8th Canadian Division was authorized to mobilize under General Order 301/42 (Effective 15th June 1942), with 14th and 16th Infantry Brigades becoming components, 1st October 1942.

80th Battery with 22nd Field Regiment RCA followed 16th Infantry Brigade to British Columbia and joined the Divisional Artillery of 8th Division in Pacific Command.

Prince Rupert Defences came under command of 8th Division, 9th October 1942 and 3rd Battery in a detached role in support of 14th Infantry Brigade, served under Headquarters Prince Rupert Defences from 11th November 1942 to 24th of July 1943. 80th Battery with the remainder of the regiment joined 3rd Battery under Headquarters Prince Rupert Defences on the 5th of June 1943 during the Aleutian fright, and on the 24th of July 1943, the regiment complete, returned to division.

16th Infantry Brigade moved to 6th Division on the 29th of July 1943 and on the 30th of July, 80th Battery and 3rd Battery of 22nd Field Regiment RCA followed 16 Brigade to 6th Division, returning to the regiment at Terrace, British Columbia, under 8th Division on the 2nd of October 1943. 16th Infantry Brigade remained with 6th Division until disbanding in October 1943.

The threat of attack on the west coast lessened with the departure of the Japanese from the Aleutians and the run-down of the home defence units was begun. Headquarters 7th Division, Headquarters 8th Canadian Division, Headquarters of 16th, 18th, 19th, 20th, 21st Infantry Brigades, 22nd Field Regiment RCA, Headquarters 22nd Field Regiment RCA, 3rd Field Battery

RCA, 6th Field Battery RCA, and Serial 1410D, 80th Field Battery RCA, were authorized to disband under General Order 15/44 (Effective 15th October 1943).

*   *   *

81st Field Battery RCA, Shawinigan Falls, P.Q. — Serial 707D — 3rd Div.

The combined 66th/81st Field Battery RCA, CASF, Serial 707C mobilized as a component of 14th Field Regiment RCA, CASF, 3rd Division, CASF, under General Order 184/40 (Effective 24th May 1940).

The two combined batteries, 66th/81st, and 32nd/34th Field Batteries, moved to Petawawa in August 1940, and on the 22nd of September came under regimental command.

While still at Petawawa, the regiment reorganized to comprise three field batteries. 81st Battery regained individual identity as 81st Field Battery RCA, Serial 707D, under General Order 45/41 (Effective 1st January 1941), and remained with 14th Field Regiment RCA in 3rd Division. The regiment moved to the divisional concentration area at Debert, Nova Scotia, in February 1941.

81st Battery with the regiment, departed for overseas 21st July 1941 on board the Empress of Canada, and disembarked at Gourock, Scotland, 29th July 1941. The regiment settled in at Ewshott, in the South of England, alternating between training and manning anti-invasion gun sites on the coast.

As the threat of invasion diminished, offensive training began to predominate, and 3rd Canadian Infantry Division was selected as an assault division for the invasion of France in 1944. The assaulting field batteries were to be self-propelled.

81st Field Battery, 14th Field Regiment RCA landed in Normandy on D-Day, 6th June 1944 with the assaulting 3rd Canadian Infantry Division. The Battery fired its 105mm self-propelled guns from the assault craft in support of 8th Canadian Infantry Brigade, prior to landing.

The division, regiment and battery served with 1 British Corps, Second British Army during the early days of the invasion, then moved to 2nd Canadian Corps, Second British Army. 2nd Canadian Corps and its components came under command of First Canadian Army on the 31st of July 1944 and prepared for the breakout from Caen.

With the beachhead established, 81st Battery and all batteries of the Divisional Field Artillery exchanged the 105mm self-propelled guns for towed 25 pounders on the 1st of August 1944, conforming to infantry division field artillery organization.

The battery took part in the fierce fighting around Caen and the closing of the Falaise Gap, then moved on to the Channel Ports, followed by the task of dislodging the determined enemy from Belgium and Holland, culminating with crossing into Germany and the cessation of hostilities.

The 8th of May 1945 was designated "VE" Day, and 81st Field Battery RCA received authorization to disband under General Order 52/46 (Effective 2nd November 1945).

A reconstituted 81st Field Battery RCA mobilized with 2nd 14th Field Regiment RCA for service with the reconstituted 3rd Canadian Infantry Division, in the Canadian Army Occupational Force (CAOF) in Germany. The Unit War Diary continued to record the activities of 2nd *81st* Field Battery RCA, 2nd 14th Field Regiment RCA until the Force disbanded. However, in the General Order authorizing the mobilization and disbandment of the battery it is listed as 2nd *87th* Field Battery RCA.

Headquarters 2nd 14th Field Regiment RCA and its component batteries mobilized under General Order 319/45 (Effective 1st June 1945), and disbanded under General Order 162/46 (Effective 28th March 1946).

*   *   *

83rd Field Battery (SP) RCA, Niagara District, Ont. — Serial 1411D.

83rd Field Battery RCA, Serial 1411D, mobilized as a component of 23rd Field Regiment RCA in the Niagara District cities of Hamilton, Brantford, and St. Catharines, under General Order 147/42 (Effective 18th March 1942), for service with 7th Division, Home Defence.

23rd Field Regiment concentrated at Petawawa, Ontario, with 83rd Battery arriving in April 1942. 83rd Battery then moved with the regiment to Camp Sussex, New Brunswick, in August 1942.

A self-propelled field regiment was added to the war establishment of an armoured division and 23rd Field Regiment RCA was selected for overseas service with 4th Canadian Armoured Division.

83rd Field Battery RCA, Serial 1411D, was redesignated 83rd Self-Propelled Battery RCHA, Serial 1411D, under General Order 328/43 (Effective 15th May 1943).

83rd Battery departed for overseas on board the Queen Elizabeth, 23rd July 1943, and disembarked at Gourock, Scotland, on the 28th of July 1943.

83rd Self-Propelled Battery RCHA, Serial 1411D, was redesignated 83rd Battery (Self-Propelled) RCA, Serial 1411D, under General Order 396/43 (Effective 15th August 1943).

83rd Battery (Self-Propelled) RCA, Serial 1411D, was redesignated 83rd Field Battery (Self-Propelled) RCA, Serial 1411D, under General Orders 452/43 (Effective 1st September 1943).

83rd Field Battery (Self-Propelled) RCA, 23rd Field Regiment (Self-Propelled) RCA, 4th Canadian Armoured Division, landed in Normandy on the 26th of July 1944, and moved to the Caen Sector on the 29th of July 1944 with 2nd Canadian Corps.

2nd Canadian Corps and its components moved under command of First Canadian Army, 31st July 1944 and 83rd Battery participated in the bitter fighting in the breakout from Caen and closing of the Falaise Gap.

83rd Field Battery (Self-Propelled) RCA continued in action serving in France, Belgium, Holland and Germany, then with cessation of hostilities disbanded under General Order 71/46 (Effective 18th December 1945).

*   *   *

84th Field Battery RCA, Moosomin, Sask. — Serial 1412C — Kiska.

84th Field Battery RCA, Serial 1412C, mobilized at Moosomin, Saskatchewan, with 24th Field Regiment RCA, 18th Brigade Group, 7th Division, Home Defence, under General Order 147/42 (Effective 18th March 1942).

The regiment concentrated at Camp Shilo, Manitoba in June 1942, and in a shuffle of brigades in the three home defence divisions, 18th Infantry Brigade moved to 6th Division, in Pacific Command. 24th Field Regiment aligned with 18th Brigade, joined Headquarters 6th Divisional Artillery RCA, on the 15th of July 1942.

84th Battery, 24th Field Regiment RCA moved to Vancouver, October 1942 and crossed to Nanaimo, on Vancouver Island, in March 1943.

A reconstituted 13th Infantry Brigade Group was selected from 6th Division to accompany the Canadian-U.S. "Greenlight" Force in an attack on the Japanese occupied Island of Kiska, in the Aleutian Chain. 84th Battery with the regiment, was to provide the field artillery support.

24th Field Regiment sailed from Nanaimo on the 12th of July 1943 for Adak in the Aleutians, to undergo further training and to become acclimatized.

On the 13th of August 1943, 84th Battery departed from Adak and disembarked at Kiska on the 15th and 16th of August 1943, equipped with four U.S. 75mm pack Howitzers and four 25 pounders.

Finding the enemy had vacated the Island, 84th Battery remained on Garrison duty until the 31st of December 1943.

On the return journey the battery paused at Adak for New Year's dinner, 2nd January, then visited Dutch Harbour, 4th of January and arrived at Vancouver, British Columbia, on the 21st of January 1944.

During the absence of the regiment, 7th and 8th Divisions had disbanded and 6th Division had reorganized to comprise its original Brigades, 13th, 14th and 15th. 13th Brigade Group remained intact upon its return from Kiska, and resumed its Home Defence duties with 6th Division.

Serial 1412C, 84th Field Battery RCA moved to Vernon, British Columbia, Wainwright and Suffield, Alberta, then returned to Vernon, where the battery received authorization to disband under General Order 213/45 (Effective 31st March 1945).

*   *   *

85th Field Battery RCA, Calgary, Alta. — Serial 1412D — Kiska.

85th Field Battery RCA, Serial 1412D, mobilized at Calgary, with 24th Field Regiment RCA, 18th Brigade Group, 7th Division, Home Defence, under General Order 147/42 (Effective 18th March 1942).

The regiment concentrated at Camp Shilo, Manitoba, June 1942, and in a shuffle of brigades, 18th Infantry Brigade became a component of 6th Division. 24th Field Regiment moved under Headquarters 6th Divisional Artillery RCA on the 15th of July 1942.

85th Battery moved to Vancouver, British Columbia, in October 1942, and in March 1943 moved to Nanaimo, on Vancouver Island.

The battery and regiment became components of the reconstituted 13th Infantry Brigade Group, selected from 6th Division to accompany the Canadian-U.S. "Greenlight" Force in an attack on the Japanese occupied Island of Kiska, in the Aleutian Chain.

24th Field Regiment RCA was to provide the field artillery support and sailed from Nanaimo on the 12th of July 1943 for Adak in the Aleutians, to undergo further training and to become acclimatized.

On the 13th of August 1943, 85th Battery departed from Adak and disembarked at Kiska on the 15th and 16th of August 1943, equipped with four U.S. 75mm pack Howitzers and four 25 pounders.

Finding the enemy had vacated the Island, 85th Battery remained on Garrison duty until the 31st of December 1943.

On the return journey the battery paused at Adak for New Year's dinner on the

2nd of January, then visited Dutch Harbour on the 4th of January and arrived at Vancouver, British Columbia, on the 21st of January 1944.

During the absence of the regiment, 7th and 8th Divisions had been disbanded and 6th Division had reorganized to comprise its original Brigades, 13th, 14th and 15th. 13th Brigade Group remained intact upon its return from Kiska, and resumed its Home Defence duties with 6th Division.

Serial 1412D, 85th Field Battery RCA moved to Vernon, British Columbia, Wainwright and Suffield, Alberta, then returned to Vernon, where the Battery received authorization to disband under General Order 213/45 (Effective 31st March 1945).

*   *   *

91st Field Battery RCA, Calgary, Alberta — Serial 165C — 2nd Div.

91st Field Battery RCA, CASF, Serial 168, mobilized under General Order 135/39, 1st September 1939, with Headquarters of 6th Field Brigade RCA, CASF, 2nd Division, CASF.

Headquarters of 6th Field Brigade RCA, CASF, was redesignated Headquarters of 6th Field Regiment RCA, CASF, to comprise two batteries. 91st Field Battery RCA, CASF, Serial 168, combined with 111th Field Battery RCA, CASF, Serial 167, to become 91st/111th Field Battery RCA, CASF, Serial 167, under General Order 123/40 (Effective 1st June 1940).

The combined 91st/111th Field Battery RCA, CASF, departed for overseas 27th August 1940 on board the Oronsay, and disembarked at Gourock, Scotland, on the 5th of September 1940.

6th Field Regiment reorganized to comprise three batteries. 91st Battery regained individual identity as 91st Field Battery RCA, Serial 168, and remained with 6th Field Regiment RCA in 2nd Division, authorized under General Order 45/41 (Effective 1st January 1941). 111th Battery moved to 7th Anti-Tank Regiment RCA, 1st Canadian Corps Anti-Tank Regiment.

In a shuffle of serial numbers within the regiment 91st Battery was allotted Serial Number 165C, under General Order 54/42 (Effective 22nd December 1942).

91st Field Battery, 6th Field Regiment RCA, aligned with 6th Canadian Infantry Brigade, 2nd Canadian Infantry Division, landed in Normandy on the 8th of July 1944 and joined the action on the 13th of July 1944 near Carpiquet Airfield, firing in support of 3rd Canadian Infantry Division.

During July, 2nd Division participated in the heavy fighting in the Caen Sector with 2nd Canadian Corps, Second British Army, and on the 31st of July 1944, the components of 2nd Canadian Corps came under command of First Canadian Army.

In August, with the breakout from Caen effected, and the closing of the Falaise Gap, 2nd Canadian Infantry Division moved on to Dieppe where on the 3rd of September 1944 following the capture of the city, the division paused for a service of remembrance, followed by a parade through the city.

91st Battery with 6th Field Regiment RCA and 2nd Canadian Infantry Division, rejoined the action under First Canadian Army, serving in France, Belgium, Holland, and Germany until cessation of hostilities.

91st Field Battery RCA received authorization to disband under General Order 52/46 (Effective 23rd September 1945).

*   *   *

92nd Field Battery RCA, Edmonton, Alberta — Serial 15D — 1st Div.

92nd Field Battery (H) RCA, CASF, Serial 19, mobilized with Headquarters of 3rd Field Brigade RCA, CASF, 1st Division, CASF, under General Order 135/39, 1st September 1939.

92nd Field Battery (H) RCA, CASF, 3rd Field Brigade RCA, CASF, departed for overseas 10th December 1939 on board the Empress of Britain in Troop Convoy 1, and disembarked on the 18th of December 1939, at Gourock, Scotland.

Headquarters of 3rd Field Brigade RCA, CASF, Serial 15, was redesignated Headquarters 3rd Field Regiment RCA, CASF, Serial 15, to comprise two batteries. 92nd Field Battery (H) RCA, CASF, Serial 19, combined with 109th Field Battery RCA, CASF, Serial 17, to become 92nd/109th Field Battery RCA, CASF, Serial 17, under General Order 44/40 (Effective 21st December 1939).

3rd Field Regiment reorganized to comprise three batteries and 92nd Battery regained individual identity under General Order 45/41 (Effective 1st January 1941), remaining with 3rd Field Regiment RCA. 109th Battery moved to 1st Light Anti-Aircraft Regiment RCA, 1st Canadian Corps Light Anti-Aircraft Regiment.

92nd Field Battery, 3rd Field Regiment RCA, 1st Division, served with 7 Corps, the Canadian Corps, and 1st Canadian Corps, in the defence of England.

In a shuffle of serial numbers within the regiment, 92nd Field Battery RCA was allotted Serial Number 15D, under General Order 54/42 (Effective 22nd December 1941).

92nd Battery and the regiment with 1st Canadian Infantry Division, sailed for the Mediterranean on the 28th of June 1943, to join 30 British Corps, British Eighth Army, in the assault on the island of Sicily.

Enroute, on the 4th of July 1943, the Landing Ship BB-3, with 52 men, six guns of 92nd Battery, and a quarter of the regiment's transport, was torpedoed and sunk in the Mediterranean.

92nd Battery was without guns until some arrived from Africa toward the end of July, except for a few days earlier, when the battery manned captured horse drawn, Italian guns.

Aligned with 2nd Canadian Infantry Brigade, 92nd Battery and 3rd Field Regiment RCA crossed the Strait of Messina to the Italian mainland with 13 British Corps, on the 4th of September 1943.

The division, regiment and battery moved to 1st Canadian Corps upon the corps becoming operational early 1944, in Italy.

92nd Battery departed from Italy via Leghorn, 15th March 1945 and disembarked at Marseilles, France, 16th March 1945, upon the transfer of 1st Canadian Corps to NW Europe.

In NW Europe under First Canadian Army the regiment fired in support of 3rd Canadian Infantry Division, 7th April 1945, then returned to 1st Division and continued in action in Holland until the cessation of hostilities.

92nd Field Battery RCA received authorization to disband under General Order 401/45 (Effective 27th August 1945).

*   *   *

93rd Battery

The number 93 was not utilized in the mobilizing of the Royal Canadian Artillery Batteries during World War II. However, 93rd Field Battery RCA, of Macleod, Alberta, was represented in the Canadian Active Service Force by 17th Light Anti-Aircraft Battery RCA, 3rd Light Anti-Aircraft Regiment RCA.

*   *   *

95th Field Battery RCA, Calgary, Alberta — Serial 1905B — 4th Div.

95th Field Battery RCA, Serial 978, mobilized as a component of the reconstituted 15th Field Regiment RCA, 4th Division, under General Order 160/41 (Effective 10th May 1941).

Headquarters 4th Division was redesignated Headquarters 4th (Armoured)

Division, and Headquarters 4th Divisional Artillery, RCA, was redesignated Headquarters 4th (Armoured) Divisional Support Group, under General Order 132/42 (Effective 26th January 1942).

95th Battery was allotted Serial Number 1905B, under General order 438/42 (Effective 12th February 1942), and with 15th Field Regiment, became a component of 4th (Armoured) Divisional Support Group, which at that time required only one Field Regiment.

95th Field Battery, 15th Field Regiment RCA, 4th Canadian Armoured Division, departed for overseas 9th August 1942, on board the Cameronia, and disembarked at Glasgow, Scotland, on the 19th of August 1942.

95th Battery landed at Courseulles-sur-Mer, Normandy, 26th July 1944, with 15th Field Regiment RCA, 4th Canadian Armoured Division and deployed in the Caen Sector 30th July, under 2nd Canadian Corps, then with 2nd Canadian Corps moved under command of First Canadian Army on the 31st of July 1944.

95th Field Battery RCA served in France, Belgium, Holland, and Germany, then with the cessation of hostilities, received authorization to disband under General Order 71/46 (Effective 12th December 1945).

*   *   *

97th Field Battery RCA, Walkerton, Ontario — Serial 238C — Army Troops.

97th Field Battery (H) RCA, CASF, Serial 241, mobilized with Headquarters of 5th Army Field Brigade RCA, CASF, Army Troops mobilizing with 2nd Division, under General Order 135/39, 1st September 1939.

Headquarters of 5th Army Field Brigade RCA, CASF, was redesignated Headquarters of 21st Army Field Regiment RCA, CASF, to comprise two batteries. 97th Field Battery (H) RCA, CASF, Serial 241, combined with 100th Field Battery RCA, CASF, Serial 239, to become 97th/100th Field Battery RCA, CASF, Serial 241, under General Order 123/40 (Effective 1st June 1940).

21st Army Field Regiment RCA, CASF, was redesignated 7th Army Field Regiment RCA, CASF, under General Order 195/40 (Effective 15th August 1940).

7th Army Field Regiment reorganized to comprise three batteries and 97th Battery regained individual identity as 97th Field Battery RCA, Serial 241, under General Order 74/41 (Effective 1st January 1941), and remained with 7th Army Field Regiment. 100th Battery moved to 4th Light Anti-Aircraft Regiment RCA, 3rd Division.

97th Field Battery, 7th Army Field Regiment RCA departed for overseas 13th November 1941 on board the Duchess of Atholl, and disembarked at Gourock, Scotland, 21st November 1941.

97th Battery was allotted Serial Number 238C, under General Order 54/42 (Effective 22nd December 1941), replacing Serial Number 241.

The battery and regiment served under Headquarters, 1st Corps Medium Artillery, RCA, which was redesignated Headquarters No. 1 Artillery Group RCA, September 1942, then redesignated Headquarters No. 1 Army Group RCA in May 1943. The regiment also served with No. 2 Army Group RCA (2nd Canadian AGRA), Army Troops.

7th Army Field Regiment RCA was converted to a Medium Regiment of two Medium Batteries and 97th Battery became surplus.

97th Field Battery RCA, Serial 238C, received authorization to disband in England, under General Order 22/44 (Effective 21st November 1943).

*   *   *

99th Field Battery RCA, Wingham, Ontario — Serial 810D — Army Troops.

99th Field Battery RCA, Serial 810D, mobilized under General Order 63/42 (Effective 29th July 1941), to serve with 19th Field Regiment RCA, 14th Brigade Group, 6th Division, Home Defence.

The regiment concentrated at Camp Borden, Ontario, in December 1941. "C" Troop with four eighteen pounders was posted to Prince Rupert, British Columbia in March 1942, to aid in the defence of the harbour. The remainder of the regiment departed from Camp Borden in May, stopping at Camp Shilo, Manitoba Artillery Range, and arrived at Terrace, British Columbia, 4th June. While at the Coast the regiment manned the two 75mm guns on No. 1 Armoured Train, operating along the railway line skirting the Skeena River between Prince Rupert and Terrace, and manned two guns at Tyee, British Columbia, inland from Prince Rupert.

Prince Rupert Defences and 14th Brigade Group came under command of 8th Division, 1st October 1942. The regiment's stay was short lived however, for in November 19th Field Regiment RCA was selected for overseas service and on the 15th November moved from the west coast to Petawawa.

99th Field Battery RCA, Serial 810D was redesignated 99th Self-Propelled Battery RCHA, Serial 810D, under General Order 328/43 (Effective 15th May 1943).

The battery departed for overseas 23rd July 1943 on board the Queen Elizabeth and disembarked at Gourock, Scotland, on the 28th of July 1943.

99th Self-Propelled Battery RCHA, Serial 810D, was redesignated 99th Battery (Self-Propelled) RCA, Serial 810D, under General Order 396/43 (Effective 15th August 1943) and under General Order 452/43, was redesignated 99th Field Battery (Self-Propelled) RCA, Serial 810D (Effective 1st September 1943).

The regiment joined 5th Canadian Armoured Division. Fate intervened however, as the division was selected for service in Italy and 8th Army Field Regiment exchanged roles with 19th Field Regiment (Self-Propelled) RCA. 8th Field Regiment (Self-Propelled) RCA departed for the Mediterranean Theatre of operations in November 1943. 19th Army Field Regiment replaced 8th Army Field Regiment in 2nd Canadian AGRA, and participated in the greatest assault landing in history the following June.

19th Field Regiment (Self-Propelled) RCA was redesignated 19th Army Field Regiment RCA, and 99th Field Battery (Self-Propelled) RCA, was redesignated 99th Field Battery RCA, Serial 810D, under General Order 134/44 (Effective 18th October 1943).

12th, 13th and 14th Field Regiments RCA comprised the field artillery of 3rd Canadian Infantry Division. The division was to assault on a two brigade front and 19th Army Field Regiment, as an Army Field Regiment was attached to 3rd Division which required the support of two field regiments for each of the two assaulting infantry brigades.

The batteries of 19th Army Field Regiment RCA fired their 105mm self-propelled guns from the assault craft in support of 8th Canadian Infantry Brigade, prior to landing on the beaches of Normandy, on D-Day, 6th June 1944.

99th Battery remained attached to 3rd Canadian Infantry Division in the early days of the invasion, serving first under 1 British Corps, Second British Army, then 2nd Canadian Corps, Second British Army and on the 31st of July 1944, with 2nd Canadian Corps came under command of First Canadian Army.

On the 24th of August 1944 with the beachhead established 99th Battery exchanged its 105mm self-propelled guns for 25 pounder self-propelled guns and continued in action with First Canadian Army, adding its fire-power to a large number of 21 Army Group units in France, Belgium, Holland, and Germany.

Following the cessation of hostilities, 99th Field Battery RCA received authorization to disband under General Order 52/46 (Effective 16th November 1945).

*　　*　　*

107th Field Battery (SP) RCA, Cranbrook, B.C. — Serial 214D — 5th Div.

107th Field Battery RCA, CASF, Serial 216, mobilized under General Order 135/39, 1st September 1939, with Headquarters of 4th Army Field Brigade RCA, CASF, Corps Troops mobilizing with 2nd Division.

107th Field Battery RCA, CASF, 4th Army Field Brigade RCA, CASF, sailed overseas 28th January 1940 on board the Monarch of Bermuda in Troop Convoy 3, and disembarked at Gourock, Scotland, on the 8th of February 1940.

Headquarters of 4th Army Field Brigade RCA, CASF, was redesignated Headquarters, 8th Army Field Regiment RCA, CASF, Serial 214, to comprise two batteries and 107th Field Battery RCA, CASF, Serial 216, combined with 61st Field Battery RCA, CASF, Serial 215, to become 61st/107th Field Battery RCA, CASF, Serial 215, authorized under General Order 44/40 (Effective 12th February 1940).

61st/107th Field Battery RCA, CASF, 8th Army Field Regiment RCA, CASF, served with 7th Corps and the Canadian Corps in the defence of England.

8th Army Field Regiment reorganized to comprise three batteries. 107th Battery regained individual identity as 107th Field Battery RCA, Serial 216, under General Order 45/41 (Effective 1st January 1941), and remained with 8th Army Field Regiment RCA.

In a shuffle of serial numbers within the regiment 107th Field Battery RCA was allotted Serial Number 214D, under General Order 54/42 (Effective 22nd December 1941).

8th Army Field Regiment RCA moved to 2nd Canadian AGRA, Army Troops, First Canadian Army, and was slated to support 3rd Canadian Infantry Division in the Normandy landings. This plan was changed, however, and a new role awaited the regiment as the war establishment of an armoured division was altered to include a self-propelled regiment of field artillery.

8th Army Field Regiment RCA was redesignated 8th Field Regiment (Self-Propelled) RCA and joined 5th Canadian Armoured Division. 107th Field Battery RCA, Serial 214D, was redesignated 107th Field Battery (Self-Propelled) RCA, Serial 214D, under General Order 134/44 (Effective 18th October 1943).

Headquarters 1st Canadian Corps, Corps Troops, 5th Canadian Armoured Division, 1st Canadian AGRA, plus ancillary units, received orders to proceed to the Mediterranean Theatre in an operational role and sailed during October and November 1943.

Upon becoming operational in Italy 1st Canadian Corps would also include 1st Canadian Infantry Division and 1st Canadian Armoured Brigade, veteran units of the fighting in Sicily and Italy.

107th Field Battery (Self-Propelled) RCA, 8th Field Regiment (Self-Propelled) RCA, embarked from Bristol, England on board the Scythia, 12th November 1943 on operation "Timberwolf II", and arrived at Algiers, North Africa, 25th November 1943.

107th Battery arrived in Italy on the 19th of December 1943, and joined the action, 9th February 1944, with 5th Canadian Armoured Division, 1st Canadian Corps, British Eighth Army.

Transfer of 1st Canadian Corps to NW Europe, saw 107th Battery depart from Italy via Leghorn, 15th February 1945, and disembark at Marseilles, France, 16th February 1945.

The battery and regiment joined First Canadian Army in NW Europe on the 31st March 1945 and served in Holland until the cessation of hostilities. 107th Battery was selected for the Canadian Berlin Brigade during May and June and returned to the regiment upon the disbanding of the Brigade.

107th Field Battery (Self-Propelled) RCA received authorization to disband under General Order 71/46 (Effective 27th November 1945).

*   *   *

110th Field Battery RCA, Broadview, Sask. — Serial 1905C — 4th Division.

110th Field Battery RCA, Serial 979, mobilized under General Order 160/41 (Effective 10th May 1941) as a component of the reorganized 15th Field Regiment RCA, in 4th Division.

4th Division was converted to 4th (Armoured) Division under General Order 132/42 (Effective 26th January 1942), and 15th Field Regiment became the lone Field Artillery Regiment in the Support Group of the Armoured Division.

The Serial Number of 110th Field Battery RCA was changed to 1905C, under General Order 438/42 (Effective 12th February 1942).

110th Field Battery RCA, 15th Field Regiment RCA, 4th Canadian (Armoured) Division departed for overseas on board the Cameronia, 9th August 1942 and disembarked at Glasgow, Scotland, on the 19th of August 1942.

Headquarters 4th (Armoured) Divisional Support Group, Serial 904, was redesignated Headquarters 4th Armoured Divisional Artillery, Serial 904, under General Order 335/43 (Effective 1st January 1943).

110th Battery with 15th Field Regiment RCA remained equipped with towed 25 pounders, and welcomed 23rd Field Regiment (Self-Propelled) RCA to the Divisional Artillery later in the year.

4th Canadian Armoured Division crossed the English Channel and 110th Battery with 15th Field Regiment RCA landed in Normandy 26th July 1944. The division deployed on the Caen front with 2nd Canadian Corps and as a component of 2nd Canadian Corps came under command of First Canadian Army on the 31st of July 1944.

110th Battery participated in the vicious fighting in the breakout from Caen and the closing of the Falaise Gap. The regiment continued in action through France, Belgium, Holland, and Germany.

110th Field Battery RCA served until the cessation of hostilities and received authorization to disband under General Orderd 71/46 (Effective 12th December 1945).

*   *   *

114th Field Battery RCA, MD 13 — Serial 1610B — 6th Division.

114th Field Battery RCA, Serial 1610B, mobilized under General Order 309/42 (Effective 12th May 1942) with 25th Field Regiment RCA, to provide artillery support for 19th Infantry Brigade.

13th, 14th and 15th Infantry Brigades were allotted to 6th Division, however, on the 15th of July 1942, 18th and 19th Infantry Brigades replaced 14th and 15th Brigades in 6th Division, Home Defence, Pacific Command.

114th Battery with 25th Field Regimentd joined 6th Division Artillery at that time, and with the exception of the month of September 1943 in the Prince Rupert Defences, 114th Battery was with 6th Division.

On the 16th of October 1943, 13th, 14th and 15th Brigades once more became components of 6th Division and 114th Battery with 25th Field Regiment joined 14th Infantry Brigade Group and remained with 6th Division.

114th Field Battery RCA, Serial 1610B, received authorization to disband, along with Headquarters 25th Field Regiment RCA, under General Order 213/45 (Effective 31st March 1945).

*   *   *

115th Field Battery RCA, MD 10 — Serial 1610C — 6th Division.

115th Field Battery RCA, Serial 1610C, mobilized under General Order 309/42 (Effective 12th May 1942) with 25th Field Regiment RCA, to provide artillery support for 19th Infantry Brigade.

13th, 14th and 15th Infantry Brigades were allotted to 6th Division, Home Defence, and on the 15th of July 1942, 14th and 15th Infantry Brigades were replaced by 18th and 19th Infantry Brigades in 6th Division. 14th Brigade moved to 8th Division and 15th Brigade moved to 7th Division.

115th Battery with 25th Field Regiment RCA joined 6th Division Artillery at that time and with the exception of the month of September 1943 with the Prince Rupert Defences, 115th Battery was with 6th Division.

On the 16th of October 1943, 13th, 14th and 15th Brigades returned to 6th Division and 115th Battery with 25th Field Regiment RCA joined 14th Infantry Brigade Group.

115th Field Battery RCA, Serial 1610C, along with Headquarters 25th Field Regiment RCA, received authorization to disband under General Order 213/45 (Effective 31st March 1945).

*   *   *

116th Field Battery RCA, MD 12 — Serial 1610D — 6th Division.

116th Field Batterys RCA, Serial 1610D, mobilized under General Order 309/42 (Effective 12th May 1942) with 25th Field Regiment RCA, to provide artillery support for 19th Infantry Brigade.

13th, 14th and 15th Infantry Brigades were originally allotted to 6th Division, Home Defence, and on the 15th of July 1942, 14th and 15th Infantry Brigades were replaced by 18th and 19th Infantry Brigades in 6th Division.

Headquarters 19th Infantry Brigade was located at Vernon, British Columbia, and the brigade was held in Pacific Command reserve.

19th Infantry Brigade is listed as a component of 6th Canadian Division and 116th Battery, 25th Field Regiment RCA is listed with the divisional artillery, in "Components of 6th Canadian Division", Public Archives Canada, Ottawa, Ontario. With the exception of the month of September 1943 with Prince Rupert Defences, 116th Battery is listed with 6th Division.

6th Division reorganized upon the disbanding of 7th and 8th Divisions the latter part of 1943, 18th and 19th Infantry Brigades also disbanded. 6th Division components once more became 13th, 14th and 15th Infantry Brigades. 116th Battery with 25th Field Regiment RCA joined 14th Infantry Brigade Group.

116th Battery participated in Exercise "Eskimo", January and February 1945, in the skeleton 13th Brigade Group and Royal Canadian Air Force, testing equipment under dry cold conditions in Northern Saskatchewan.

116th Field Battery RCA, Serial 1610D, received authorization to disband under General Order 213/45 (Effective 31st March 1945).

* * *

117th Field Battery RCA, Toronto — Serial 1611B — 7th Division.

117th Field Battery RCA, Serial 1611B, mobilized under General Order 309/42 (Effective 12th May 1942), with 26th Field Regiment RCA, to provide artillery support for 20th Infantry Brigade, 7th Division, Home Defence, Eastern Canada.

20th Infantry Brigade moved to 6th Division, 20th July 1943, however, 117th Battery and 26th Field Regiment RCA remained with 7th Division.

117th Battery mobilized in Toronto and was stationed at Petawawa, Ontario, Debert, Nova Scotia, Tracadie and Sussex, New Brunswick.

117th Field Battery RCA, Serial 1611B, along with Headquarters 26th Field Regiment RCA, received authorization to disband under General Order 15/44 (Effective 15th November 1943).

* * *

118th Field Battery RCA, Toronto — Serial 1611C — 7th Division.

118th Field Battery RCA, Serial 1611C, mobilized under General Order 309/42 (Effective 12th May 1942), with 26th Field Regiment RCA, to provide artillery support for 20th Infantry Brigade, 7th Division, Home Defence, Eastern Canada.

20th Infantry Brigade moved to 6th Division, 20th July 1943, however, 118th Battery and 26th Field Regiment RCA remained with 7th Division.

Recruited in Toronto, 118th Battery received postings to Petawawa, Ontario, Debert, Nova Scotia, Tracadie and Sussex, New Brunswick.

118th Field Battery RCA, Serial 1611C, received authorization to disband along with Headquarters 26th Field Regiment RCA, undersd General Order 15/44 (Effective 15th November 1943).

* * *

119th Field Battery RCA, Toronto — Serial 1611D — 7th Division.

119th Field Battery RCA, Serial 1611D, mobilized under General Order 309/42 (Effective 12th May 1942), with 26th Field Regiment RCA, to provide artillery support for 20th Infantry Brigade, 7th Division, Home Defence, Eastern Canada.

20th Infantry Brigade moved to 6th Division, 20th July 1943, however, 119th Battery and 26th Field Regiment RCA remained with 7th Division.

Recruited in Toronto, 119th Battery was stationed at Petawawa, Ontario, Debert, Nova Scotia, Tracadie and Sussex, New Brunswick.

119th Field Battery RCA, Serial 1611D, along with Headquarters 26th Field Regiment RCA, received authorization to disband under General Order 15/44 (Effective 15th November 1943).

* * *

120th Field Battery RCA, Montreal — Serial 1612B — 8th Division.

120th Field Battery RCA, Serial 1612B, mobilized under General Order 309/42 (Effective 12th May 1942).

120th Battery mobilized as a component of 27th Field Regiment RCA, and served with a Brigade Group of 8th Division, Home Defence, as mobile reserve for Eastern Canada.

Following postings with 27th Field Regiment RCA to Petawawa, Ontario, Tracadie and Sussex, New Brunswick, 120th Field Battery RCA, Serial 1612B, received authorization to disband under General Order 15/44 (Effective 15th October 1943).

* * *

121st Field Battery RCA, Montreal — Serial 1612C — 8th Division.

121st Field Battery RCA, Serial 1612C, mobilized under General Order 309/42 (Effective 12th May 1942), with 27th Field Regiment RCA and served with a Brigade Group of 8th Division, Home Defence, as mobile reserve for Eastern Canada.

121st Battery was stationed at Petawawa, Ontario, Tracadie, New Brunswick, and Sussex, New Brunswick, in its mobile reserve role.

121st Field Battery RCA, Serial 1612C, received authorization to disband under General Order 15/44 (Effective 15th October 1943).

* * *

122nd Field Battery RCA, Montreal — Serial 1612D — 8th Division.

122nd Field Battery RCA, Serial 1612D, mobilized under General Orders 309/42 (Effective 12 May 1942).

122nd Battery mobilized as a component of 27th Field Regiment RCA, and served with a Brigade Group of 8th Division, Home Defence, as mobile reserve for Eastern Canada.

Following postings to Petawawa, Ontario, Tracadie and Sussex, New Brunswick, Headquarters 27th Field Regiment RCA, 120th Field Battery RCA and 121st Field Battery RCA were authorized to disband under General Order 15/44 (Effective 15th October 1943).

122nd Field Battery RCA, Serial 1612D, however, did not disband with the regiment but was redesignated 127th Anti-Tank Battery RCA, under General Orders 138/46 (Effective 1st March 1946).

127th Anti-Tank Battery RCA was permanently embodied in the Postwar Permanent Force, under General Order 158/46 (Effective 27th June 1946).

* * *

123rd Field Battery RCA — Serial 1814B — 7th Division.

"8th Anti-Tank Regiment was converted to Field Artillery and redesignated 28th Field Regiment RCA". (War Diary)

123rd Field Battery RCA, Serial 1814B, mobilized under General Order 289/43 (Effective 15th May 1943), with 28th Field Regiment RCA, 7th Division, Home Defence.

19th, 21st and 23rd Field Regiments RCA were added to the overseas force during 1943, depleting the ranks of the home defence divisions. 28th Field Regiment RCA and its component batteries mobilized, however, its existence was of rather short duration upon the disbanding of 7th and 8th Divisions before the end of the year.

123rd Field Battery RCA, Serial 1814B, received authorization to disband under General Order 15/44 (Effective 15th October 1943), and its personnel posted to 1 Training Field Regiment RCA.

* * *

124th Field Battery RCA — Serial 1814C — 7th Division.

"8th Anti-Tank Regiment RCA was converted to Field Artillery and redesignated 28th Field Regiment RCA". (War Diary 28th Field Regiment RCA).

124th Field Battery RCA, Serial 1814C, mobilized under General Order 289/43 (Effective 15th May 1943), with 28th Field Regiment RCA, 7th Division, Home Defence.

During the summer of 1943, 19th, 21st and 23rd Field Regiments departed for overseas, depleting the ranks of the home defence divisions.

28th Field Regiment RCA had earlier mobilized to lessen the blow. The existence of 28th Field Regiment RCA was of rather short duration however with 7th and 8th Divisions receiving authorization to disband before the year's end.

124th Field Battery RCA, Serial 1814C, was authorized to disband under General Order 15/44 (Effective 15th October 1943), and its personnel posted to 1 Training Field Regiment RCA.

*   *   *

125th Field Battery RCA — Serial 1814D — 7th Division.

"8th Anti-Tank Regiment was converted to Field Artillery and redesignated 28th Field Regiment RCA". (War Diary).

28th Field Regiment RCA was formed to help aleviate the shortage of field regiments in the home defence divisions. The shortage was created in 1943 by the addition of 19th, 21st and 23rd Field Regiments RCA to the overseas force.

125th Field Battery RCA, Serial 1814D, mobilized under General Order 289/43 (Effective 15th May 1943), with 28th Field Regiment RCA, 7th Division, Home Defence, for service in Eastern Canada.

28th Field Regiment RCA enjoyed a rather short existence however with the disbanding of 7th and 8th Divisions the latter part of 1943.

125th Field Battery RCA, Serial 1814D, received authorization to disband under General Order 15/44 (Effective 15th October 1943), and its personnel moved to 1 Training Field Regiment RCA.

*   *   *

SECTION V

MEDIUM ARTILLERY

Section V includes medium batteries serving with 1st Canadian AGRA and 2nd Canadian AGRA, and although the two Canadian AGRAs served on widely separated battlefields they remained Army Troops and wore the First Canadian Army artillery patch.

Two medium brigades mobilized with the Canadian Active Service Force 1st September 1939 and each medium brigade comprised four medium batteries. 3rd Medium Battery RCA of the Permanent Force became a component of 1st Medium Brigade RCA, CASF, along with 2nd, 7th and 23rd Medium Batteries RCA, CASF. The medium brigades were redesignated medium regiments and the batteries were paired in a two battery regiment.

The batteries of 1st Medium Regiment were given individual identity as the regiment reorganized to comprise two ordinary batteries. 2nd and 3rd Medium Batteries RCA remained components of the regiment and 7th and 23rd Batteries moved to 5th Medium Regiment RCA.

Headquarters of 2nd Medium Brigade RCA, CASF which had mobilized 1st September 1939 with four medium batteries became Headquarters 2nd Medium Regiment RCA, CASF with two hyphenated batteries in June 1940. Headquarters 2nd Medium Regiment RCA was redesignated 2nd Heavy Anti-Aircraft Regiment (Mobile) RCA in May 1941 and the batteries regained individual identity in a three battery regiment. 57th Battery joined 7th Light Anti-Aircraft Regiment RCA.

A new 2nd Medium Regiment was authorized and upon the conversion of 4th

Division to an armoured division 18th Field Regiment RCA became surplus. Headquarters 18th Field Regiment RCA was redesignated Headquarters 2nd Medium Regiment RCA in January 1942 and 25th Battery accompanied Headquarters 18th Field Regiment to 2nd Medium Regiment RCA. 18th Battery arrived from 16th Field Regiment RCA to complete the new regiment.

5th Medium Battery RCA of Vancouver and 87th Medium Battery of Nova Scotia, representing the west and east coast forts respectively, were brought together under Headquarters 3rd Medium Regiment RCA in January 1942. 3rd Medium Regiment RCA served as a component of 2nd Canadian AGRA, First Canadian Army from Normandy to Germany, July 1944 to "VE" Day, 8th May 1945.

50th and 58th Batteries had mobilized with 20th Field Regiment RCA, 6th Division, Home Defence, in July 1941. The batteries were redesignated medium batteries and given an overseas role with 4th Medium Regiment RCA in January 1942. The Regiment served with 2nd Canadian AGRA in France, Belgium, Holland, and Germany.

7th Medium Battery and 23rd Medium Battery, the two batteries of 1st Medium Regiment RCA left surplus when the regiment pared down to two batteries, became the nucleus of 5th Medium Regiment RCA, formed in England 1st February 1941. 5th Medium Regiment RCA served with 1st Canadian AGRA in Italy and NW Europe.

7th Medium Regiment RCA completed the Canadian medium components of the Canadian AGRAs. The Regiment mobilized as 5th Army Field Brigade RCA, CASF, 1st September 1939. Brigades became regiments and to eliminate confusion between field regiments and army field regiments the numerical designation of the Army Field Regiments was changed.

Headquarters of 5th Army Field Brigade RCA, CASF, was redesignated 21st Army Field Regiment RCA, CASF, in June 1940 and batteries were paired in a two battery regiment. 21st Army Field Regiment became 7th Army Field Regiment RCA, CASF, in August 1940, then in January 1941 the regiment reorganized to comprise three batteries.

7th Army Field Regiment RCA pared down to two batteries to become 7th Medium Regiment RCA in November 1943. 7th Medium Regiment RCA crossed the Channel to Normandy 11th July 1944 with 2nd Canadian AGRA in support of 2nd Canadian Corps. The Canadian units came under the command of First Canadian Army 31st July 1944 and served until cessation of hostilities in NW Europe, May 1945.

*   *   *

2nd Medium Battery RCA, Charlottetown, P.E.I. — Serial 64B — 1 CAG.

2nd Medium Battery (H) RCA, CASF, Serial 66, mobilized under General Order 135/39, 1st September 1939, with Headquarters of 1st Medium Brigade RCA, CASF, Headquarters 1st Corps Medium Artillery RCA, CASF.

2nd Medium Battery (H) RCA, CASF, 1st Medium Brigade RCA, CASF, departed for overseas 30th January 1940 on board the Aquitania, in Troop Convoy 3 and disembarked at Gourock, Scotland, 8th Febraury 1940.

Headquarters of 1st Medium Brigade RCA, CASF, was redesignated Headquarters 1st Medium Regiment RCA, CASF, and its component batteries were paired in a two battery regiment.

2nd Medium Battery (H) RCA, CASF, Serial 66, combined with 7th Medium Battery (H) RCA, CASF, Serial 65, to become 2nd/7th Medium Battery RCA, CASF, Serial 66, under General Order 44/40 (Effective 12th February 1940), with 1st Medium Regiment RCA, CASF.

2nd Battery regained individual identity as 2nd Medium Battery RCA, Serial 66, under General Order 45/41 (Effective 1st January 1941), and remained with 1st Medium Regiment as it reorganized to comprise two regular batteries. 7th Battery moved to 5th Medium Regiment RCA.

2nd Medium Battery RCA was allotted Serial Number 64B, under General Order 54/42 (Effective 22 December 1941), in a shuffle of serial numbers within the regiment.

2nd Medium Battery, 1st Medium Regiment RCA, boarded the E.B. Alexander at Greenock, Scotland, 24th October 1943, bound for the Mediterranean and disembarked at Augusta, Sicily 8th November 1943, to serve as a component of 1st Canadian AGRA.

1st Medium Regiment RCA crossed to the Italian mainland on the 19th of November 1943 and fired its first rounds in support of Fifth American Army 2nd of December 1943, becoming the first Canadian medium regiment in action.

2nd Battery and the regiment rejoined 1st Canadian AGRA and served in Italy until early 1945, supporting units of 1st Canadian Corps.

Transfer of 1st Canadian Corps to NW Europe saw 2nd Medium Battery depart from Naples, Italy, 11th March 1945 and disembark 13th March 1945 at Marseilles, France. 1st Canadian AGRA joined the action in NW Europe, 1st April 1945 in Holland, and with their counterparts 2nd Canadian AGRA, served as Army Troops, First Canadian Army, until cessation of hostilities.

2nd Medium Battery RCA received authorization to disband under General Order 401/45 (Effective 1st September 1945).

*   *   *

3rd Medium Battery RCA (PF), Kingston, Ont. — Serial 64C — 1 CAG.

A Permanent Force Battery, 3rd Medium Battery RCA, CASF, Serial 68 mobilized under General Order 135/39, 1st September 1939, with Headquarters of 1st Medium Brigade RCA, CASF, Headquarters 1st Corps Medium Artillery RCA, CASF, Corps Troops mobilizing with 1st Division.

3rd Medium Battery, 1st Medium Brigade RCA, CASF, departed for overseas, 30th January 1940 on board the Aquitania in Troop Convoy 3, and disembarked at Gourock, Scotland, 8th February 1940.

Headquarters of 1st Medium Brigade RCA, CASF, was redesignated Headquarters 1st Medium Regiment RCA, CASF, and batteries were paired in a two battery organization. 3rd Medium Battery RCA, CASF, Serial 68, combined with 23rd Medium Battery (H) RCA, CASF, Serial 67, to become 3rd/23rd Medium Battery RCA, CASF, Serial 65, under General Order 44/40 (Effective 12th February 1940).

With the fall of France in 1940, 3rd/23rd Medium Battery RCA, CASF, 1st Medium Regiment RCA, CASF, served in an anti-invasion role in support of 7 Corps and the Canadian Corps in the South of England.

3rd Battery regained individual identity as 3rd Medium Battery RCA, Serial 68, under General Order 45/41 (Effective 1st January 1941), and remained a component of 1st Medium Regiment RCA. The use of hyphenated batteries was discontinued in the Canadian Army and 1st Medium Regiment now comprised 2nd Medium Battery RCA, and 3rd Medium Battery RCA. 7th and 23rd Batteries moved to 5th Medium Regiment RCA.

3rd Medium Battery RCA was allotted Serial Number 64C, under General Order 54/42 (Effective 22nd December 1941), in an alignment of serial numbers within the regiment.

Headquarters 1st Corps Medium Artillery RCA, Serial 63, was redesignated Headquarters No. 1 Artillery Group RCA, Serial 63, under General Order 447/42 (Effective 7th September 1942) and then redesignated Headquarters No. 1 Army Group, RCA, Serial 63, under General Order 341/43 (Effective 20th May 1943).

3rd Medium Battery, 1st Medium Regiment RCA, 1st Canadian AGRA, boarded the E.B. Alexander at Greenock, Scotland, 24th October 1943 on operation "Timberwolf", and disembarked at Augusta, Sicily, 8th November 1943.

1st Medium Regiment RCA crossed to the Italian mainland, 19th of November 1943, and fired its first rounds 2nd of December 1943 in support of Fifth American Army, becoming the first Canadian medium regiment in action.

3rd Medium Battery and the regiment rejoined 1st Canadian AGRA and served in Italy until early 1945, supporting units of 1st Canadian Corps.

Transfer of 1st Canadian Corps to NW Europe saw 3rd Medium Battery depart from Naples, Italy, 11th March 1945 and disembark 13th March 1945 at Marseilles, France. 1st Canadian AGRA joined the action in NW Europe, 1st April 1945 in Holland, and with their counterparts 2nd Canadian AGRA, served with First Canadian Army as Army Troops until cessation of hostilities.

The battery had mobilized for active service 1st September 1939, now six years later, 3rd Medium Battery RCA received authorization to disband under General Order 401/45 (Effective 1st September 1945).

* * *

5th Medium Battery RCA, Vancouver, B.C. — Serial 1050C — 2 CAG.

5th Medium Battery RCA was redesignated 11th Anti-Aircraft Battery RCA, to form part of 1st Anti-Aircraft Regiment RCA, authorized under General Order 92/39 (Effective 15th May 1939), in a Non-Permanent Active Militia reorganization, and localized at Vancouver, British Columbia, Military District No. 11, under General Order 111/39 (Effective 15th May 1939).

5th Medium Battery RCA surfaced again, however, when the decision was made to form a medium regiment for overseas service representative of the West Coast forts and East Coast forts.

5th Medium Battery RCA, Serial 1050C, and Headquarters, 3rd Medium Regiment RCA mobilized under General Order 103/42 (Effective 26th January 1942).

5th Medium Battery RCA from British Columbia and 87th Medium Battery RCA from Nova Scotia, converged on Camp Petawawa in April 1942 to form 3rd Medium Regiment RCA.

5th Medium Battery, with 3rd Medium Regiment RCA, departed for overseas 16th June 1942 on board the Empress of Scotland (Formerly Empress of Japan), and disembarked at Gourock, Scotland, 24th June 1942.

3rd Medium Regiment RCA came under command Corps Medium Artillery, which became 1st Canadian AGRA, then late 1943 the regiment became a component of 2nd Canadian AGRA, to serve as Army Troops.

5th Medium Battery, 3rd Medium Regiment RCA, with 2nd Canadian AGRA, landed in Normandy on the 9th of July 1944 as support for 2nd Canadian Corps and fired its first rounds on the 13th of July 1944, from positions near Vieux Cairon.

The battery, regiment, and AGRA, with 2nd Canadian Corps came under command of First Canadian Army, 31st July 1944, and 5th Battery fired in support of the multi-national components of First Canadian Army in France, Belgium, Holland, and Germany.

5th Medium Battery served until cessation of hostilities in NW Europe and upon the 8th of May 1945 being designated "VE" Day, battery personnel proceeded to the Canadian Army Pacific Force (CAPF), the Canadian Army Occupational Force (CAOF), were posted to batteries from the military district of their enlistment, or remained with 5th Medium Battery for the return to Canada.

5th Medium Battery RCA received authorization to disband under General Order 52/46 (Effective 16th November 1945).

*   *   *

7th Medium Battery RCA, Montreal, P.Q. — Serial 507B — 1 CAG.

7th Medium Battery (H) RCA, CASF, Serial 65, was authorized to mobilize as a component of 1st Medium Brigade, RCA, CASF, under General Order 135/39, 1st September 1939, to serve under Headquarters 1st Corps Medium Artillery, RCA, CASF, Serial 63.

7th Medium Battery (H), 1st Medium Brigade RCA, CASF, departed for overseas 30th January 1940 on board the Aquitania, in Troop Convoy 3, and disembarked at Gourock, Scotland, on the 8th of February 1940.

Headquarters of 1st Medium Brigade RCA, CASF, was redesignated Headquarters of 1st Medium Regiment RCA, CASF, and the regiment was to comprise two batteries in the new war establishment.

7th Medium Battery (H) RCA, CASF, Serial 65, combined with 2nd Medium Battery (H) RCA, CASF, Serial 66, to become 2nd/7th Medium Battery RCA, CASF, Serial 66, under General Order 44/40 (Effective 12th February 1940).

7th Battery regained individual identity as 7th Medium Battery RCA, Serial 58, under General Order 45/41 (Effective 1st January 1941). The battery number was utilized in the forming of 5th Medium Regiment RCA, in England.

Headquarters 5th Medium Regiment RCA, Serial 507, was authorized under General Order 56/41 (Effective 1st February 1941), and "D" Troop, 1st

Medium Regiment RCA provided the nucleus for the new 7th Medium Battery, 5th Medium Regiment RCA.

7th Medium Battery Serial Number was changed from 58 to 507B, in an alignment of serial numbers within the regiment, authorized under General Order 54/42 (Effective 22nd December 1941).

7th Medium Battery, 5th Medium Regiment RCA, Mediterranean bound, embarked from Glasgow, Scotland, 25th October 1943, and disembarked at Palermo, Sicily, 8th November 1943.

As a component of 1st Canadian AGRA, 7th Battery with the regiment crossed to the Italian mainland on the 7th of January 1944, and joined the action on the 28th of February 1944 in the Lanciano campaign. 1st Canadian AGRA served in Italy until early 1945 in support of 1st Canadian Corps.

Transfer of 1st Canadian Corps to NW Europe saw 7th Battery depart from Italy via Naples, 11th March 1945, and disembark at Marseilles, France, 13th March 1945.

5th Medium Regiment RCA, 1st Canadian AGRA, joined the action in NW Europe as a component of First Canadian Army and 7th Battery fired in support of 49 British Infantry Division, 1st April 1945, near Nijmegen, Holland.

7th Medium Battery RCA, Serial 507B served until cessation of hostilities and received authorization to disband under General Order 321/45 (Effective 30th June 1945).

*   *   *

12th Medium Battery RCA, London, Ontario — Serial 238B — 2 CAG.

12th Medium Battery RCA, mobilized as 12th Field Battery RCA, CASF, Serial 240, with Headquarters of 5th Army Field Brigade RCA, CASF, Serial 238, Army Troops mobilizing with 2nd Division, authorized under General Order 135/39, 1st September 1939.

Headquarters of 5th Army Field Brigade RCA, CASF, Serial 238, was redesignated Headquarters of 21st Army Field Regiment RCA, CASF, Serial 238, under General Order 123/40 (Effective 1st June 1940), and 12th Field Battery RCA, CASF, Serial 240, combined with 45th Field Battery (H) RCA, CASF, Serial 242, to become 12th/45th Field Battery RCA, CASF, Serial 240, as the regiment was now to comprise two batteries.

21st Army Field Regiment RCA, CASF, was redesignated 7th Army Field Regiment RCA, CASF, under General Order 195/40 (Effective 15th August 1940).

12th Battery regained individual identity as 12th Field Battery RCA, Serial 240, under General Order 74/41 (Effective 1st January 1941), and remained with 7th Army Field Regiment RCA in a three battery regiment.

12th Field Battery, 7th Army Field Regiment RCA departed for overseas 13th November 1941 on board the Duchess of Atholl, and disembarked at Gourock, Scotland, 21st November 1941.

In a realignment of serial numbers within the regiment, 12th Field Battery RCA was allotted Serial Number 238B, under General Order 45/42 (Effective 22nd December 1941).

In England, 12th Field Battery, 7th Army Field Regiment RCA served with Headquarters 1st Corps Medium Artillery, which evolved into 1st Canadian AGRA, and upon the forming of No. 2 AGRA, the regiment moved to that formation.

7th Army Field Regiment RCA, Serial 238 was converted to medium artillery and redesignated Serial 238, 7th Medium Regiment RCA, to comprise Serial 238A, Headquarters 7th Medium Regiment RCA and two medium batteries, authorized under General Order 21/44 (Effective 21st November 1943).

12th Field Battery RCA, Serial 238B, was converted and redesignated 12th Medium Battery RCA, Serial 238B, under General Order 21/44 (Effective 21st November 1943).

12th Medium Battery, 7th Medium Regiment RCA, 2nd Canadian AGRA, landed in Normandy, 11th July 1944 and joined the action on the Caen Front with 2nd Canadian Corps.

The battery, regiment and AGRA with 2nd Canadian Corps, came under the command of First Canadian Army, 31st July 1944 and fired in support of the multi-national components of First Canadian Army in France, Belgium, Holland, and Germany.

12th Medium Battery RCA served until the cessation of hostilities and received authorization to disband under General Order 52/46 (Effective 25th September 1945).

*   *   *

18th Medium Battery RCA, Port Arthur — Serial 982B — 1 CAG.

18th Medium Battery RCA of Port Arthur, Ontario, mobilized as 18th Field Battery RCA, Serial 980, to serve with the reconstituted 16th Field Regiment RCA in 4th Division. Mobilization of 18th Field Battery was authorized under General Order 160/41 (Effective 10th May 1941).

4th Division was converted to an armoured division requiring one field regiment only in its support group. 16th Field Regiment RCA was redesignated 8th Light Anti-Aircraft Regiment RCA and remained with the division in its new role. 101st Light Anti-Aircraft Battery from 6th Light Anti-Aircraft Regiment RCA joined 8th Light Anti-Aircraft Regiment RCA and 18th Field Battery RCA moved to 2nd Medium Regiment RCA.

18th Field Battery RCA, Serial 980, previously a medium battery, became 18th Medium Battery RCA, Serial 982B, and Headquarters 18th Field Regiment RCA, also of 4th Division, was redesignated Headquarters 2nd Medium Regiment RCA, under General Order 104/42 (Effective 26th January 1942), the previous 2nd Medium Regiment had been redesignated 2nd Heavy Anti-Aircraft Regiment (Mobile) RCA.

The former 18th Field Battery RCA joined Headquarters of the former 18th Field Regiment RCA in the new 2nd Medium Regiment RCA.

18th Medium Battery departed Debert, Nova Scotia for Petawawa Camp, Ontario, where 2nd Medium Regiment RCA assembled in January 1942.

18th Medium Battery, 2nd Medium Regiment RCA departed for overseas 21st March 1942 on board the Aorangi, and disembarked at Glasgow, Scotland, 29th March 1942.

On the 24th of October 1943, Mediterranean bound, 2nd Medium Regiment RCA which comprised 18th and 25th Medium Batteries, boarded the Argentina at Liverpool, rendezvoused with the operation "Timberwolf" convoy off Scotland, and disembarked at Augusta, Sicily on the 8th of November 1943.

2nd Medium Regiment RCA crossed to the Italian mainland 5th January 1944, and under 1st Canadian AGRA, 18th Battery fired its first rounds near Ortona, 22nd February 1944.

18th Medium Battery served in Italy until 11th March 1945, then boarded the Ville D'Oran at Naples, sailed on the 12th of March and disembarked at Marseilles, France, 13th March 1945.

2nd Medium Regiment RCA, with 1st Canadian AGRA, joined First Canadian Army in NW Europe and 18th Battery moved into position on the 30th March 1945, in Holland.

18th Medium Battery RCA served until the cessation of hostilities and received authorization to disband under General Order 52/46 (Effective 3rd October 1945).

*   *   *

23rd Medium Battery RCA, Toronto, Ont. — Serial 507C — 1 CAG.

23rd Medium Battery (H) RCA, CASF, Serial 67, with Headquarters of 1st Medium Brigade RCA, CASF, Corps Troops mobilizing with 1st Division, was authorized to mobilize under General Order 135/39, 1st September 1939, to serve under Headquarters 1st Corps Medium Artillery RCA, CASF, Serial 63.

23rd Medium Battery (H) RCA, CASF, 1st Medium Brigade RCA, CASF, departed for overseas 30th January 1940 on board the Aquitania in Troop Convoy 3, and disembarked at Gourock, Scotland, on the 8th of February 1940.

Headquarters of 1st Medium Brigade RCA, CASF, was redesignated Headquarters 1st Medium Regiment RCA, CASF, and the existing four batteries were paired in a two battery regiment.

23rd Medium Battery (H) RCA, CASF, Serial 67, combined with 3rd Medium Battery RCA, CASF, Serial 68, to become 3rd/23rd Medium Battery RCA, CASF, Serial 65, under General Order 44/40 (Effective 12th February 1940).

Following the fall of France in 1940, 3rd/23rd Medium Battery RCA served in support of 7 Corps and the Canadian Corps in an anti-invasion role in the South of England.

23rd Battery regained individual identity as 23rd Medium Battery RCA, Serial 60, under General Order 45/41 (Effective 1st January 1941), and with "B" Troop forming the nucleus, 23rd Medium Battery RCA became a component of 5th Medium Regiment RCA.

Headquarters 5th Medium Regiment RCA, Serial 507, was authorized under General Order 56/41 (Effective 1st February 1941).

In an alignment of serial numbers with 5th Medium Regiment RCA, 23rd Medium Battery RCA was allotted Serial Number 507C, under General Order 54/42 (Effective 22nd December 1941).

23rd Medium Battery, 5th Medium Regiment RCA, Mediterranean bound, boarded the Sloterdijk, at Glasgow, Scotland, 25th October 1943, and disembarked at Palermo, Sicily, 8th November 1943.

5th Medium Regiment RCA crossed to the Italian mainland on the 7th January 1944, and as a component of 1st Canadian AGRA, 23rd Medium Battery RCA joined the action on the 28th of February 1944, in the Lanciano Campaign. 23rd Battery continued to support the units of 1st Canadian Corps in Italy until moving with the corps to NW Europe early 1945.

The departure of 1st Canadian Corps from Italy saw 23rd Battery sail from Naples, 11th March 1945, and disembark at Marseilles, France, 13th March 1945.

23rd Battery joined the action with First Canadian Army in NW Europe, firing in support of 49 British Infantry Division, 1st April 1945, near Nijmegen, Holland.

5th Medium Regiment RCA continued in action until cessation of hostilities and 23rd Medium Battery RCA, Serial 507C, received authorization to disband under General Order 321/45 (Effective 30th June 1945).

*   *   *

25th Medium Battery RCA, Toronto, Ont. — Serial 982C — 1 CAG.

25th Field Battery RCA, Serial 983, mobilized under General Order 160/41 (Effective 10th May 1941) as a component of 18th Field Regiment RCA, 4th Division. 18th Field Regiment RCA mobilized as a replacement for 17th Field Regiment RCA in 4th Division Divisional Artillery RCA.

16th and 18th Field Regiments RCA became surplus upon the conversion of 4th Division to an armoured division requiring one field regiment only (15th Field), in the support group.

Headquarters 18th Field Regiment RCA, Serial 982, was redesignated Headquarters 2nd Medium Regiment RCA, Serial 982A, under General Order 104/42 (Effective 26th January 1942). A previous Headquarters of 2nd Medium Regiment RCA, CASF, Serial 69, had been redesignated Headquarters 2nd Heavy Anti-Aircraft Regiment (Mobile), RCA, Serial 69, under General Order 149/41 (Effective 24th May 1941).

25th Field Battery RCA, Serial 983, was redesignated 25th Medium Battery RCA, Serial 982C, under General Order 104/42 (Effective 26th January 1942), and accompanied 18th Field Headquarters to 2nd Medium Regiment RCA. 18th Battery arrived from the former 16th Field Regiment to complete the new 2nd Medium Regiment RCA.

2nd Medium Regiment assembled at Petawawa, Ontario in January 1942, and on the 21st of March 1942, 25th Medium Battery with the regiment, departed for overseas on board the Aorangi, disembarking at Glasgow, Scotland, 29th March 1942.

Operation "Timberwolf" saw the battery embark for the Mediterranean on board the SS Argentina, 24th October 1943 from Liverpool, England, and disembark at Augusta, Sicily, 8th November 1943.

2nd Medium Regiment RCA crossed to the Italian mainland 5th January 1944 and as a component of 1st Canadian AGRA 25th Battery fired in support of 1st Canadian Corps during the Italian campaign.

25th Battery served in Italy until 11th March 1945, then on board the Ville D'Oran, sailed from Naples to Marseilles, France, disembarking 13th March, as 1st Canadian Corps moved to NW Europe.

25th Battery with 2nd Medium Regiment RCA joined First Canadian Army in Western Holland, 30th March 1945, and served until the cessation of hostilities.

2nd Medium Regiment, less 25th Medium Battery, received authorization to disband under General Order 52/46 (Effective 3rd October 1945).

25th Medium Battery RCA, was redesignated *68th Medium Battery RCA,* under General Order 138/46 (Effective 1st March 1946).

68th Medium Battery RCA, became part of the *Postwar Permanent Force,* authorized under General Order 158/46 (Effective 27th June 1946).

*   *   *

45th Medium Battery RCA, Lindsay, Ont. — Serial 238D — 2 CAG.

45th Medium Battery mobilized as 45th Field Battery (H) RCA, CASF, Serial 242, with Headquarters of 5th Army Field Brigade RCA, CASF, Serial 238, under General Order 135/39, 1st September 1939.

Headquarters of 5th Army Field Brigade RCA, CASF, Serial 238, was redesignated Headquarters of 21st Army Field Regiment RCA, CASF, Serial 238, under General Order 123/40 (Effective 1st June 1940).

The change in designation from Army Field Brigade to Army Field Regiment also brought organizational changes as the regiment was now to comprise two batteries. Batteries were paired, utilizing the four original battery numbers, and 45th Field Battery (H) RCA, CASF, Serial 242, combined with 12th Field Battery RCA, CASF, Serial 240, to become 12th/45th Field Battery RCA, CASF, Serial 240.

21st Army Field Regiment RCA, CASF, was redesignated 7th Army Field Regiment RCA, CASF, authorized under General Order 195/40 (Effective 15th August 1940).

45th Battery regained individual identity as 45th Field Battery RCA, Serial 242, under General Order 74/41 (Effective 1st January 1941), and remained with 7th Army Field Regiment RCA.

45th Field Battery, 7th Army Field Regiment RCA departed for overseas 13th November 1941 on board the Duchess of Atholl and disembarked at Gourock, Scotland, 21st November 1941.

In a realignment of serial numbers within the regiment, 45th Field Battery RCA was allotted Serial Number 238D, under General Order 54/42 (Effective 22nd December 1941).

In England, 45th Battery, 7th Army Field Regiment RCA served with Headquarters 1st Corps Medium Artillery, which evolved into 1st Canadian AGRA, and upon the forming of No. 2 AGRA, the regiment moved to that formation.

7th Army Field Regiment RCA, Serial 238, was converted to a Medium Regiment comprising Serial 238, 7th Medium Regiment RCA, Headquarters 7th Medium Regiment RCA, Serial 238A, 12th Medium Battery RCA, Serial 238B, and 45th Medium Battery RCA, Serial 238D, authorized under General Order 21/44 (Effective 21st November 1943). 97th Battery became surplus and was authorized to disband at that time.

45th Field Battery RCA, Serial 238D, was converted and redesignated 45th Medium Battery RCA, Serial 238D, under General Order 21/44 (Effective 21st November 1943).

45th Medium Battery, 7th Medium Regiment RCA, 2nd Canadian AGRA landed in Normandy, 11th July 1944 and joined the action on the Caen Front with 2nd Canadian Corps.

45th Battery, 7th Medium Regiment RCA, 2nd Canadian AGRA, with 2nd Canadian Corps, came under command of First Canadian Army on the 31st of July 1944, and fired in support of its multi-national components in France, Belgium, Holland, and Germany.

7th Medium Regiment RCA served until cessation of hostilities and following the designation of the 8th of May as "VE" Day, members of the Regiment departed to the Canadian Army Pacific Force (CAPF), the Canadian Army Occupational Force (CAOF), were posted to units from the military district of their enlistment, or prepared for the return to Canada with the regiment.

45th Medium Battery RCA received authorization to disband under General Order 52/46 (Effective 25th September 1945).

*   *   *

50th Medium Batterys RCA, Montreal, P.Q. — Serial 1051C — 2 CAG.

50th Field Battery RCA, Serial 811D, mobilized under General Order 63/42 (Effective 29th July 1941), with 20th Field Regiment RCA, to serve with 15th Brigade Group, 6th Division, Home Defence.

50th Battery was converted and redesignated 50th Medium Battery RCA, Serial 1051C, under General Order 104/42 (Effective 26th January 1942). 50th Battery and 58th Battery, also from 20th Field Regiment RCA, shed their Home Defence role and proceeded to Camp Petawawa. Ontario, to form overseas bound 4th Medium Regiment RCA.

50th Medium Battery, 4th Medium Regiment RCA departed for overseas 9th August 1942 on board the Capetown Castle, and disembarked 18th August 1942, at Liverpool, England.

The regiment proceeded to the South of England and under command of Headquarters Cdn. Corps Med. Arty. (HQ MA 1 Cdn Corps), which after several designations became 1st Canadian AGRA. By the end of September eight 6 inch Howitzers had arrived for training, with the 5.5s arriving mid-March 1943.

4th Medium Regiment RCA came under command of 2nd Canadian AGRA, 15th October 1943, and in July 1944 accompanied the AGRA to Normandy. Two ships, the Fort Brunswick and Fort Yale, carried the regiment to Normandy and 50th Battery RCA disembarked 9th July 1944.

50th Battery moved into position near the village of Rots, and under 2nd Canadian AGRA, fired its first rounds in action on the 13th of July 1944.

The battery, regiment, and 2nd Canadian AGRA with 2nd Canadian Corps, joined First Canadian Army on the 31st of July 1944 and served in France, Belgium, Holland, and Germany.

In action the regiment came under command of 2nd Canadian Corps, 1 British Corps, 30 British Corps, 2nd, 3rd and 4th Canadian Divisions, 1st Polish Armoured Division, 101 US Airborne Division, 49 (West Riding) Division, 53 (Welsh) Division, 15 (Scottish) Division and No. 4 Commando.

4th Medium Regiment RCA served until the cessation of hostilities, firing its last round 1st of May, and with the 8th of May 1945 designated "VE" Day, the regiment prepared for the return to Canada.

50th Medium Battery RCA received authorization to disband under General Order 52/46 (Effective 26th September 1945).

*　　*　　*

58th Medium Battery RCA, Quebec, P.Q. — Serial 1051B — 2 CAG.

58th Field Battery RCA, Serial 811B, mobilized under General Order 63/42 (Effective 29th July 1941), with 20th Field Regiment RCA, to serve with 15th Brigade Group, 6th Division, Home Defence.

58th Battery was converted, and redesignated 58th Medium Battery RCA, Serial 1051B, under General Order 104/42 (Effective 26th January 1942). 58th Battery, and 50th Battery, also from 20th Field Regiment RCA, proceeded to Camp Petawawa, Ontario, to form 4th Medium Regiment RCA.

58th Medium Battery, 4th Medium Regiment RCA, departed for overseas 9th August 1942 on board the Capetown Castle, and disembarked 18th August 1942 at Liverpool, England.

4th Medium Regiment RCA came under command of 2nd Canadian AGRA, 15th October 1943 and accompanied the AGRA to Normandy in July 1944. Two ships, the Fort Brunswick and Fort Yale, carried the regiment to the beaches of Normandy and 58th Battery disembarked on the 9th of July 1944.

58th Battery occupied gun positions near the village of Rots under 2nd Canadian AGRA, and fired its first rounds in action on the 13th of July 1944.

58th Battery, 4th Medium Regiment RCA and 2nd Canadian AGRA, under 2nd Canadian Corps, joined First Canadian Army, 31st July 1944 and served in France, Belgium, Holland, and Germany.

In action, the regiment came under command of 2nd Canadian Corps, 1 British Corps, 30 British Corps, 2nd, 3rd and 4th Canadian Divisions, 1st Polish Armoured Division, 101 US Airborne Division, No. 4 Commando, 15th (Scottish) Division, 49 (West Riding) Division and 53 (Welsh) Division.

58th Medium Battery RCA served until cessation of hostilities and received authorization to disband under General Order 52/46 (Effective 26th September 1945).

*   *   *

68th Medium Battery RCA — *Postwar Permanent Force*

68th Medium Battery RCA mobilized as 25th Field Battery RCA, Serial 983, under General Order 160/41 (Effective 10th May 1941), with 18th Field Regiment RCA, 4th Division. 4th Division was converted to an armoured division requiring one field regiment only and 25th Battery accompanied Headquarters 18th Field Regiment RCA to 2nd Medium Regiment RCA, upon both Headquarters and 25th Battery being designated Medium Artillery. 18th Battery from the former 16th Field Regiment RCA completed 2nd Medium's components.

25th Field Battery RCA, Serial 983, was redesignated 25th Medium Battery RCA, Serial 982C, under General Order 104/42 (Effective 26th January 1942).

25th Medium Battery, 2nd Medium Regiment RCA, departed for overseas on board the Aorangi, 21st March 1942, and disembarked at Glasgow, Scotland, 29th March 1942.

2nd Medium Regiment RCA departed for the Mediterranean 24th October 1943 aboard the SS Argentina, on operation "Timberwolf", and disembarked at Augusta, Sicily on the 8th of November 1943, then crossed to the Italian mainland, 5th January 1944 for service with 1st Canadian AGRA in support of 1st Canadian Corps.

Transfer of 1st Canadian Corps to NW Europe saw 25th Battery depart from Italy via Naples, 11th March 1945 on the Ville D'Oran, and disembark at Marseilles, France, 13th March 1945. 25th Battery moved to Western Holland, 30th March 1945 and served in action with First Canadian Army until cessation of hostilities.

The regiment, less 25th Medium Battery, received authorization to disband under General Order 52/46 (Effective 3rd October 1945).

25th Medium Battery RCA, was redesignated *68th Medium Battery RCA,* under General Order 138/46 (Effective 1st March 1946).

68th Medium Battery RCA, became part of the *Postwar Permanent Force,* under General Order 158/46 (Effective 27th June 1946).

*   *   *

87th Medium Battery RCA, Dartmouth, N.S. — Serial 1050B — 2 CAG.

In a reorganization of the Non-Permanent Active Militia in Military District No. 6, the King's Canadian Hussars (Armoured Car) was converted to 87th and 88th Field Batteries RCA, to form part of 14th Field Brigade RCA, under General Order 116/39 (Effective 15th August 1939).

87th Field Battery RCA of the Non-Permanent Active Militia, was localized at Kentville, Nova Scotia, in Military District No. 6, under General Order 119/39 (Effective 15th August 1939).

87th Battery mobilized for Active Service at Dartmouth, Nova Scotia, as the combined 87th/88th Field Battery RCA, CASF, Serial 906C, with the original 16th Field Regiment RCA, CASF, Headquarters 4th Division, CASF, under General Order 184/40 (Effective 24th May 1940).

87th Battery regained individual identity under General Order 85/41 (Effective 27th February 1941), to become 87th Field Battery RCA, Serial 906C, and was posted to 18th Field Regiment RCA. 18th Field Regiment RCA, had mobilized to replace 17th Field Regiment RCA in 4th Division.

With the conversion of 4th Division to an armoured division requiring one field regiment only in the armoured division support group, 18th Field Regiment RCA became surplus. Headquarters 18th Field Regiment RCA, became Headquarters 2nd Medium Regiment RCA, encompassing 18th and 25th Batteries.

87th Field Battery RCA, Serial 906C, was converted and redesignated 87th Medium Battery RCA, Serial 1050B, under General Order 104/42 (Effective 26th January 1942).

87th Medium Battery RCA, representative of the East Coast forts, and 5th Medium Battery RCA of Vancouver, representing the West Coast forts, converged on Camp Petawawa, Ontario, in April 1942 to form 3rd Medium Regiment RCA.

87th Medium Battery, 3rd Medium Regiment RCA, departed for overseas 16th June 1942 on board the Empress of Scotland, and on the 24th June 1942, disembarked at Gourock, Scotland. The regiment came under command Headquarters Medium Artillery, 1st Canadian Corps and moved to 2nd Canadian AGRA late 1943.

87th Battery, 3rd Medium Regiment RCA, a component of 2nd Canadian AGRA, Army Troops, landed in Normandy on the 9th of July 1944 and fired in support of 2nd Canadian Corps. The regiment and AGRA with 2nd Canadian Corps came under command of First Canadian Army 31st July 1944 and supported its multi-national components in France, Belgium, Holland, and Germany.

87th Medium Battery RCA served until the cessation of hostilities and received authorization to disband under General Order 52/46 (Effective 16th November 1945).

*   *   *

SECTION VI

SPECIALIZED UNITS

Section VI includes specialized units, units bearing the RCA title or were closely associated with the Royal Canadian Artillery during World War II.

Air observation post squadrons were formed to act as the "eyes" of the artillery in action. The three Canadian air observation post squadrons mobilized as No. 1, No. 2, and No. 3. Air Observation Post Squadrons RCA. No. 1 AOP Squadron became Canadian Army Component — 664 (RCAF) Air Observation Post Squadron, and remained so-designated. No. 2 and No. 3 Air Observation Post Squadrons RCA disbanded under their original designation although referred to as No. 665 and 666 (RCAF) (AOP) Squadrons, respectively. Canadian Army Component — 664 (RCAF) Air Observation Post Squadron served with the Canadian Army Occupational Force following cessation of hostilities.

The artillery training centres and Canadian artillery schools in Canada, along with No. 1 Canadian School of Artillery (Overseas), No. 1, No. 2 and No. 3 Canadian Artillery Reinforcement Units in the south of England, all played an important role.

Second Meteorological Section became 1st Corps Meteorological Section RCA and assumed the meteorological duties from the Royal Air Force. Upon the forming of 2nd Canadian Corps and Headquarters First Canadian Army the section grew into an army meteorological group. The change was hastened when it was decided to transfer part of First Canadian Army to the Mediterranean during 1943.

No. 1 Calibration Troop RCA provided a valuable service to assure the continuing accuracy of the guns. In England a permanent calibration range was established at Poling, Sussex, for the calibrating of field, medium and heavy guns. The troop calibrated Canadian, British and US guns, and the guns of 1 Belgian Battery. The troop moved to the continent and was in constant demand, calibrating guns of the units under Headquarters First Canadian Army.

Counter Battery Officers' Staff was added to the Canadian Corps in September 1941, then was redesignated 1st Counter Battery Officer's Staff RCA in September 1942 and remained with 1st Canadian Corps. 2nd Counter Battery Officers Staff RCA was authorized to mobilize at that time to serve with 2nd Canadian Corps.

A counter mortar officers staff was formed in each division during 1944, 1st and 5th Divisions in Italy, 2nd and 4th in England, and 3rd Canadian Infantry Division's CMO staff came into existence in Normandy as the division was battling for elbow room in the beachhead.

1st Radar Battery RCA and 1st Rocket Battery RCA came into being the latter part of 1944 in NW Europe. 1st Radar Battery RCA, Army Troops, proved invaluable in a counter mortar role. 1st Rocket Battery RCA, also an Army Troops unit, was staffed initially by personnel wearing the 2nd Canadian Corps artillery patch as 112th Battery and 30th Battery of 6th Light Anti-Aircraft Regiment RCA assumed the manning duties following instruction from the original cadre. Two British batteries also received instruction and assisted in manning the rockets of 1st Rocket Battery, Royal Canadian Artillery.

At the west coast the Armoured Train provided a mobile defence to an isolated area of northern British Columbia when the fear of attack was prevalent. The presence of the Japanese in the Aleutians from June 1942 to the summer of 1943 saw the greater part of two divisions stationed in British Columbia, under Headquarters Pacific Command.

In the early days of the war the Permanent Force batteries provided instructors and played an important role in preparing the recently mobilized NPAM batteries for an active service role. The field, medium and anti-aircraft Permanent Force batteries became part of the CASF with the RCHA being allotted to 1st Division, as was 4th Light Anti-Aircraft Battery RCA. Members of the Permanent Force coast batteries were assimilated into the coast batteries on the home front, or proceeded overseas during the course of the war to serve on distant battlefields.

"X" & "Y" Super Heavy Batteries RCA added to the history of the Royal Canadian Artillery in England and are included herein.

*   *   *

Cdn. Army Component — 664 (RCAF) AOP Sqn — Serial 2391 — Army Tps.

1st Air Observation Post Squadron RCA, was authorized under General Order 493/44 (Effective 4th May 1944). The Squadron, composed of both Army and RCAF personnel, mobilized at RAF Station, Andover, Hampshire, England, and was to be equipped with Auster Aircraft.

1st Air Observation Post Squadron RCA, was redesignated Canadian Army Component — 664 (RCAF) Air Observation Post Squadron, under General Order 159/46 (Effective 9th December 1944). The Squadron completed mobilization 2nd February 1945 and moved to Penhurst, Kent, prior to proceeding overseas.

Canadian Army Component — 664 (RCAF) Air Observation Post Squadron became operational in Holland, March 1945 with 5th Canadian Armoured Division, under First Canadian Army. "B" Flight drew the assignment, followed by duty with 4th Canadian Armoured Division.

"A", "B" and "C" Flights later moved to 2nd Canadian Corps, aiding 4th Canadian Armoured Division, 2nd and 3rd Canadian Infantry Divisions respectively. The Squadron continued in action until cessation of hostilities and following "VE" Day, 8th May 1945, provided a number of valuable services prior to being assigned to the Occupational Force in September.

Canadian Army Component RCA — 664 (RCAF) Air OP Squadron Part II Orders issued by Canadian Section 2nd Echelon Headquarters, British Army of the Rhine, No. 12, 18 Sep. 45 — "Under Auth CMHQ Adm Order No. 111/45 Canadian Army Component RCA — 664 (RCAF) Air OP Squadron is Reallocated to CAOF wef 4 Sep. 45. This is the last Part II Order issued under present designation. Personnel were Struck off Strength and Taken on Strength the CAOF Unit".

Canadian Army Component RCA — 664 (RCAF) Air OP Squadron disbanded at Rostup, Germany, following service with the Canadian Army Occupational Force (CAOF). Its last War Diary entry listed the date as the 8th of May 1946. 120 Wing RCAF assumed flying control duties and responsibilities 21st May 1946. Disbandment was authorized under General Order 275/46 (Effective 1st July 1946).

*   *   *

No. 1 Armoured Train — Serial 1382 — Pacific Command

No. 1 Armoured Train mobilized under General Order 45/43 (Effective 1st December 1942).

The Armoured Train provided a mobile defence on the railway running along the Skeena River between Terrace and Prince Rupert, British Columbia, and made a return trip each 24 hours.

Gunners manned the two 75mm guns, four Bofors 40mm Light Anti-Aircraft guns and two searchlights on board the train.

The Armoured train also carried four platoons of Infantry and their weapons.

No. 1 Armoured Train, Serial 1382, received authorization to disband under General Order 378/44 (Effective 31st July 1944).

*   *   *

No. 1 Cdn Artillery Base Reinforcement Regiment, Type "B"

No. 1 Canadian Artillery Base Reinforcement Regiment, Type "B", mobilized under General Order 131/45 (Effective 27th January 1945).

No. 1 Canadian Artillery Base Reinforcement Regiment Type "B" received authorization to disband under General Order 296/45 (Effective 20th March 1945).

*   *   *

No. 1 Canadian Army Met Group — Serial 477 — Army Troops

Second Meteorological Section was authorized to mobilize under General Order 71/42 (Effective 24th December 1941). The Royal Air Force provided the Meteorological data for 7th Corps, and the Canadian Corps, previous to the Canadian Section being formed.

Second Meteorological Section, Serial 477, was redesignated 1st Corps Meteorological Section, RCA, Serial 477, under General Order 104/42 (Effective 26th January 1942).

1st Corps Meteorological Section RCA, Serial 477, was redesignated No. 1 Canadian Army Meteorological Group, Serial 477, under General Order 33/44 (Effective 18th October 1943). — (RCA was not included in the new designation).

No. 1 Canadian Army Meteorological Group, Serial 477, was to comprise:

477P HQ No. 1 Canadian Army Meteorological Group
477A No. 10 Cdn Met Section (Type "A") — 1st Corps
477B No. 11 Cdn Met Section (Type "A") — 2nd Corps
477C No. 12 Cdn Met Section (Type "B") — 1st Div
477D No. 13 Cdn Met Section (Type "B") — 2nd Div
477E No. 14 Cdn Met Section (Type "B") — 3rd Div

477F No. 15 Cdn Met Section (Type "B") — 4th A/Div
477G No. 16 Cdn Met Section (Type "B") — 5th A/Div
477H No. 17 Cdn Met Section (Type "C") — 1 AGRA
477J No. 18 Cdn Met Section (Type "C") — 2 AGRA
477K No. 19 Cdn Met Section (Type "D") — 1 Svy R
477L No. 20 Cdn Met Section (Type "D") — 2 Svy R
477M No. 21 Cdn Met Section (Type "E") — 1st Corps
477N No. 22 Cdn Met Section (Type "E") — 2nd Corps

Authorized under General Order 33/44 (Effective 18th October 1943).

Six Sections departed for the Mediterranean Theatre of operations the latter part of October 1943. Four of the Sections disembarked at Augusta, Sicily, 7th November, and crossed to the Italian mainland, 2nd January 1944. No. 12 Section (1st Div), and No. 16 Section (5th A/Div), proceeded directly to Italy from England.

The six Sections served in Italy until early 1945, then moved with 1st Candian Corps to NW Europe to join First Canadian Army and finish the war with all Sections of No. 1 Canadian Army Meteorological Group in the same Theatre of operations.

The remnants of No. 1 Canadian Army Meteorological Group left at Headly Court in England with Army Headquarters following the hasty departure of the Mediterranean bound Sections, began to form the Sections for 2nd Canadian Corps.

The Sections reported to their allotted Formations for the crossing to Normandy. No. 14 Section slated to land on D-Day, 6th June 1944, landed 8th June, Headquarters and the remaining Sections crossed the Channel during July and moved into the bridgehead. No. 11 Section accompanied Headquarters 2nd Canadian Corps, No. 13 Section, 2nd Canadian Infantry Division, No. 15 Section with 4th Canadian Armoured Division, No. 18 Section, 2nd Canadian AGRA, No. 20 Section with 2nd Survey Regiment RCA, and No. 22 Section, as 2nd Canadian Corps Mobile Section, moved with 2nd Corps.

Canadian Units came under command of First Canadian Army 31st July 1944 on the Caen Front and participated in the vicious fighting in the breakout from Caen and the closing of the Falaise Gap.

84 Group Met Office was responsible for the supply of all Met information required by General Staff of First Canadian Army.

Headquarters No. 1 Canadian Army Met Group supplied Met information of a climatological nature, had one Met Officer especially trained in CW available to advise on gas and smoke operations. This Section was also responsible for the technical guidance, supply of technical information and equipment, and the provision of relief personnel to all Met Sections.

All Sections below Army level were responsible for the computation of (Ground, AA, and calibration) Meteors for the Artillery, and for advice to staff of Units, Formations, and Air OP Squadrons on all weather data.

The use of Smoke Screens gained prominence during the drive into Germany in 1945, and the crossing of the Rhine River.

No. 1 Canadian Army Meteorological Group served until cessation of hostilities, work with the Air OP however continued until disbandment.

No. 1 Canadian Army Meteorological Group and Headquarters No. 1 Canadian Army Meteorological Group, received authorization to disband under General Order 388/45 (Effective 28th July 1945).

No. 10, No. 12, No. 16, No. 17, No. 19, and No. 21 Canadian Met Sections, following service in Italy and NW Europe, received authorization to disband under General Order 388/45 (Effective 8th August 1945).

No. 11, No. 13, No. 14, No. 15, No. 18, No. 20, and No. 22 Canadian Met Sections received authorization to disband under General Order 388/45 (Effective 8th August 1945), following service in France, Belgium, Holland, and Germany.

* * *

No. 1 CARU (Field) — Serial 292 — Bordon, Hants, England

No. 1 CARU mobilized in Canada as No. 1 Artillery Holding Unit, Canadian Active Service Force (CASF), Serial 292, under General Order 32/40 (Effective 1st September 1939).

No. 1 Artillery Holding Unit proceeded overseas in May 1940 and settled in at Bordon, Hampshire, in the South of England.

No. 1 Artillery Holding Unit, CASF, Serial 292, was redesignated No. 1 Canadian Artillery Holding Unit, Serial 292, under General Order 62/41 (Effective 18th September 1940).

No. 1 Canadian Artillery Holding Unit, Serial 292, was redesignated No. 1 Canadian Artillery Reinforcement Unit (Field), Serial 292. under General Order 290/42 (Effective 1st June 1942). However, this Designation and Effective date were cancelled and No. 1 Canadian Artillery Holding Unit, Serial 292, was redesignated No. 1 Canadian Artillery Reinforcement Unit (Field) under

General Order 127/43 (Effective 1st November 1941). The new General Order also corrected the alignment of Units listed in the cancelled General Order.

No. 1 Canadian Artillery Reinforcement Unit (Field), remained operational until cessation of hostilities in NW Europe, and when the demobilization of Canadian Units was begun, No. 1 CARU (Field), received authorization to disband under General Order 354/45 and also under General Order 359/45 (Effective 30th June 1945), in both General Orders.

* * *

A 1 Canadian Artillery Training Centre — Serial 1203 — Petawawa

A 1 Canadian Artillery Training Centre, Serial 1203, was placed on Active Service under General Order 250/41 (Effective 15th February 1941).

A Canadian Artillery Training Centre (Field & Anti-Tank) was formed in Kingston, Ontario, home of the Royal Canadian School of Artillery. The Training Centre was expanded and moved to Petawawa under the designation A 1 Canadian Artillery Training Centre in 1941 and remained operational until the war's end.

A 1 Canadian Artillery Training Centre, Serial 1203, received authorization to disband under General Order 18/46 (Effective 6th November 1945).

* * *

1st Canadian Centaur Battery — (Compiled from Unit History)

1st Canadian Centaur Battery was formed 6th August 1944 in Normandy, equipped with twelve 95mm Centaurs (Self-Propelled), and three Sherman Tank OPs.

The Battery served with 3rd Parachute Brigade, 1st Canadian Parachute Battalion, serving with 6th British Airborne Division.

6th British Airborne Division which had landed in Normandy the night 5th/6th June 1944 prior to the sea-borne landing, was withdrawn from 1 British Corps, 30th August 1944 and 1st Canadian Centaur Battery disbanded at that time.

* * *

No. 1 Canadian CMO Staff (Type A) RCA — Serial 2531 — 1st Div.

No. 1 Canadian Counter Mortar Officers Staff (Type A), mobilized under General Order 119/45 (Effective 15th July 1944). The Unit Serial Number is listed in the War Diary as Serial 2531.

The decision to form an organization to deal with enemy mortars saw the birth of Counter Mortar on the Ortona Front. Previous to this date locating mortars was left to chance or to individual FOOs to deal with and a Unit with specialized equipment became most desirable.

CBO Staff, with similar problems aided in the forming of the new Unit. CM detachments came under HQ RCA and were attached to the Support Battalion, with the 4.2″ mortar as the logical reprisal weapon in the deeply ravined Ortona country, with HAA airburst becoming popular.

CMO was moved from Div to Brigade HQ, speeding communications. Air OP ranging of 4.2″ mortars on targets proved very satisfactory.

The CMO Staff reorganized and early in May joined HQ RCA in readiness for the Hitler Line battle. Field Artillery, HAA airburst and 4.2″ mortars were used in the initial stages and following the main battle the CM duties were handled by the ACMOs at the Brigades as the Brigades outdistanced Div HQ.

At the end of August 1944, CMO accompanied the Div to the Florence Front, then moved up to the Gothic Line early in September and was joined by a 4-pen recorder section from 1st Canadian Survey Regiment, which was later put under command. CBO net provided valuable flash spotting and sound ranging information.

Late September 1944 a skeleton staff moved to HQ 1st Canadian Corps to form a Corps Counter Mortar Office, mainly to co-relate the two Divisional fronts and to work out a fire plan for the Corps Artillery, that was to precede the attack up the road to Cesena.

The Road to Bologna led to the Lamone River and the Winter Line, early in December 1944. In late December one Radar Battery joined CMO.

At the beginning of March 1945, 1st Canadian Infantry Division was relieved by 10 Indian Division. The CMO Staff moved down the Coast, joining 1st Anti-Tank Regiment RCA for the move to NW Europe. The Unit departed Italy via Leghorn, to Marseilles, France, then on to Belgium.

No. 1 Canadian Counter Mortar Officers Staff (Type A), was redesignated No. 1 Canadian Counter Mortar Officers Staff (Type A), RCA, under General Order 252/45 (Effective 31st March 1945).

The CMO Staff rejoined HQ RCA at Iteghem, Belgium, then moved to the Reichswald Forest, under 2nd Canadian Corps, later moving near Zutphen, Holland, where 1st Canadian Infantry Division was to attack and cross the Ijssel River. Moves to the Apeldoorn and Amersfoort areas in Holland followed and the Unit served until cessation of hostilities. The 8th of May 1945 was declared "VE" Day and the run-down of Canadian Units was begun.

No. 1 Canadian Counter Mortar Officers Staff (Type A), RCA, following service in Italy and NW Europe with 1st Canadian Infantry Division, received authorization to disband under General Order 321/45 (Effective 21st June 1945). The Canadian Army Pacific Force (CAPF) beckoned to a considerable number of the personnel.

*   *   *

No. 1 Calibration Troop RCA — Serial 257 — Army Troops

No. 1 Calibration Troop RCA, Serial 257, received authorization to mobilize under General Order 128/41 (Effective 16th April 1941).

The function of the Calibration Troop was the instrumental calibration of all Field, Medium and Heavy guns. The Troop mobilized under Headquarters Canadian Corps and was attached to 1st Canadian Survey Regiment RCA, and although a separate Unit its personnel were to be accounted for by 1st Canadian Survey Regiment.

A nucleus of personnel transferred from 1st Canadian Survey Regiment RCA, others were posted from the Artillery Holding Unit. The War Establishment called for a Troop of 2 Officers and 24 Other Ranks. All technical personnel were to be Surveyors RCA (A).

The Survey Regiment was at Dunley Hill, near Effingham in Surrey when the Calibration Troop mobilized. On 6th October 1941 the Troop visited Sennybridge, Wales, practice camp with two guns of 11th Army Field Regiment RCA to produce Muzzle Velocities.

Upon the return of the Troop from Wales the Regiment moved to the seaside resort of Worthing, Sussex, and in November calibrated the guns of a British Division at Poling, West of Worthing, firing into the sea. This area was later taken over as a permanent calibration range.

The Troop moved back to Sennybridge and calibrated various Regiments, mid-December until the first week of January. Returning to Poling, an intensive program was laid on for the Calibration of all Canadian guns, beginning 8th January 1942, and completed 13th February. The Troop, on loan to British Units often travelled to other areas to calibrate the Royal Artillery guns, and during this period calibrated 938 guns for Canadian Units and 192 guns for RA Units. Guns calibrated included 25 pounders, 25/18 pounders, 5.5 inch guns, two types of 6 inch guns, 7.2 inch, 8 inch, 9.2 inch and 12 inch Howitzers — (The latter Railway mounted). The Troop also enjoyed the pleasure of calibrating the new 7.2 inch Howitzers when they appeared. A Heavy Regiment of the Royal Artillery had been re-equipped with the new 7.2s.

On the 10th March 1942 the Troop was placed under Headquarters RCA Canadian Corps for employment and when dealing with technical matters, and when with the Survey Regiment the Troop was attached for rations, quarters and discipline only. Later 1st Survey Regiment became Corps Troops and the Calibration Troop was detached entirely and remained part of Army Troops directly under Headquarters RCA.

The Troop carried out tests using two cameras for calibration 26th April to 2nd May 1942 at the Poling range, assisted by one 25 pounder of 3rd Canadian Field Regiment. The two-camera method eliminated the use of heavy muzzle clamps and was adopted when muzzle brakes for 25 pounders was introduced.

13th Canadian Field Regiment supplied one 25 pounder for a shoot to determine the loss of Muzzle Velocity when using propellant charges exposed to varying degrees of moisture, and 5th Canadian Medium Regiment supplied a 5.5 inch gun to test air burst shooting with the new 222 fuze.

A graph for obtaining Muzzle Velocity was printed and first used 22nd February 1943 in calibrating guns of 7th Canadian Army Field Regiment, then in May and June 1943 the Calibration Troop proceeded to Scotland to calibrate the guns of 1st Canadian Infantry Division prior to their departure for the Sicilian campaign.

No. 1 Calibration Troop RCA returned to Poling, where in December a trial shoot for the U.S. 105mm guns was carried out. Self-Propelled 105mm equipments were issued to 12th, 13th, 14th Field Regiments of 3rd Canadian Infantry Division, and 19th Army Field Regiment RCA, delegated to take part in the Normandy assault. These SPs were calibrated by 1 Calibration Troop at Christchurch in February and March 1944. Fall of Shot was taken by Flash Spotting Troop of 9 British Survey Regiment.

An U.S. 155mm gun was calibrated by Fall of Shot and instrument early in 1944. A Canadian made P.E.C. Velocity measuring equipment was used in England for the first time during this shoot. Upon completion of this experiment practically all shoots were done with both camera MV, and P.E.C. (Use of Photo Electric Cells).

At Poling during the spring 1st Calibration Troop calibrated guns of 4th, 5th, and 6th Field Regiments RCA of 2nd Division, 15th Field Regiment RCA of 4th Division, 7th Canadian Medium Regiment, 15 British Medium Regiment and 1 British Heavy Regiment, recently equipped with 7.2 inch Howitzers Mk II. Later one half of 1 Heavy Regiment RA was equipped with 155mm guns.

119 Field Regiment RA, 120 Field Regiment RA and 1 Belgian Battery were calibrated in Kent and 23rd Canadian Field Regiment's Self-Propelled 25 pounders were calibrated at Alfriston.

Further trials for the P.E.C. were carried out at Larkhill and the P.E.C. received acceptance by U.S., British and Canadian Military.

Elements of five Medium Regiments of 9 British AGRA, 987 FA Bn equipped with 155mm SPs and 1 Heavy Regiment RA equipped with 155mm guns were calibrated, and the Troop's last Shoot was the 25 pounder guns of the Canadian School of Artillery at Seaford on the 4th June 1944.

No. 1 Calibration Troop RCA crossed the Channel, landing at Gold Beach Arromanches, 7th August 1944 and moved to the Army Troops area at Fontaine-Henry. Between 11th and 14th August the 25 pounder guns of 12th and 13th Field Regiments of 3rd Canadian Infantry Division were calibrated. These Regiments had just been issued towed 25 pounders in exchange for the 105mm SPs in use since D-Day. 14th Field Regiment's guns and the SPs of 19th Army Field Regiment RCA were calibrated at a later date.

On the 19th August 1944 the Calibration Troop joined 4 British AGRA under 1 British Corps and calibrated the Medium and Heavy guns when the opportunity presented itself. The calibrating of the 7.2 inch and 155mm guns was done at the gun locations, the lighter guns in most cases were brought to the calibrating location.

The Calibration Troop caught up with 2nd Canadian Infantry Division and calibrated 4th, 5th and 6th Field Regiments' 25 pounders near Dunkirk, 16th to 18th September 1944.

The Troop moved its base to Ghent in Belgium, but returned to Calais to calibrate the guns of 2nd Canadian AGRA, 1st to 3rd October, this phase was continued in Belgium.

Headquarters moved from Ghent to Antwerp, calibrating the guns of 49 (WR) Division, employing 21 Army Group Special Standard Guns, two 25 pounders calibrated by Fall of Shot at Larkhill. These guns were used to calibrate the guns of 2nd and 3rd Canadian Infantry Divisions near Nijmegen, Holland, 11th to 24th November 1944. Base for the Troop moved to Tilburg, then Boxtel, Holland for the winter.

The 25 pounder SPs of 19th Army Field Regiment RCA and 23rd Field Regiment (SP) RCA were given extensive tests the early part of December near s'Hertogenbosch, Holland, then between 17th December 1944 and 5th January 1945, 2nd Canadian AGRA guns were calibrated near Nijmegen with the aid of 2nd Canadian Survey Regiment. Later in January 1945, four Medium Regiments of 4 British AGRA were calibrated. The Troop moved to Mill for easier access to the Front.

Following the attack on the Reichswald Forest the Calibration Troop began to calibrate 5 AGRA's guns in Germany 11th to 13th February 1945, then calibrated 1 Heavy Regiment's 7.2 inch Howitzers of 2nd Canadian AGRA, and completed 5 AGRA guns 15th to 21st March.

A pleasant interlude followed as the Calibration Troop returned to the coast in Belgium to assist in the calibration of the guns of 1st Canadian Corps, recently arrived from Italy.

First Canadian Army now had both 1st Canadian Corps and 2nd Canadian Corps under its wing in NW Europe for the final blow.

No. 1 Canadian Calibration Troop RCA served in France, Belgium, Holland, and Germany, then with the cessation of hostilities received authorization to disband under General Order 201/46 (Effective 21st June 1945), in NW Europe.

*   *   *

No. 1 Canadian Radio Location Est. RCA — Serial 1363 — Cda. & Nfld.

No. 1 Canadian Radio Location Establishment RCA, Serial 1363, mobilized under General Order 161/43 (Effective 15th October 1942), to provide technical Officers and NCOs to act as advisors on Radar to GOCs (in C), Fortress commands, Regimental commands and Battery commands to provide 1st line maintenance on Radar equipments.

For administration, all Radar RCA personnel other than Operators Radar required for operational duty, were kept on strength 1 CRLE.

The RLE was attached to Coast and Anti-Aircraft Units in Canada, Newfoundland and Labrador.

No. 1 Canadian Radio Location Establishment RCA, Serial 1363, received authorization to disband under General Order 18/46 (Effective 14th November 1945).

*   *   *

No. 1 Canadian Radio Location Unit — Serial 852 (WD) — England

No. 1 Canadian Radio Location Unit is mentioned by Colonel C.P. Stacey in Six Years of War, page 246, Queen's Printer, Ottawa 1955, and in the History of The Royal Canadian Corps of Signals 1903-1961, page 112, written by Officers of the Corps and edited by John S. Moir, published by authority of the Corps Committee, Royal Canadian Corps of Signals, Ottawa, 1962.

No. 1 Canadian Radio Location Unit was formed in January 1942 and was intended to operate radar in conjunction with Anti-Aircraft for direction-finding purposes. After training, the Unit manned radar sets at points on the English South coast. The work became an Artillery responsibility and No. 1 Canadian Radio Location Unit, conforming to British War Establishment, disbanded early 1943.

War Diary — "Administrative Order No. 12, issued by Maj.-Gen. P.J. Montague, CMHQ authorizing formation of No. 1 Cdn Radio Location Unit with effect from 24 July 1941."

Initial concentration of the Unit began 26 Jan/42 at Quebec Barracks, Bordon, Hants and on 28th Jan/42 personnel of No. 1 Cdn Radio Location Unit concentrated at No. 1 Cdn Arty Reinforcement Unit in Quebec Barracks, Bordon, from operational gun sites. The Unit moved to Colchester, Essex during 1942 with detachments on manning duty on the coast.

No. 1 Canadian Radio Location Unit moved from Colchester to Aldershot 10 May/43 with quarters in E. Waterloo Barracks.

30-31 May 1943 — Under authority of Admin. Order #75, This Unit Ceases to Exist.

* * *

No. 1 Field Training Regiment RCA — Debert, Nova Scotia.

No. 1 Field Training Regiment RCA, mobilized under General Order 419/44 (Effective 1st October 1943).

No. 1 Field Training Regiment RCA was formed as a component of 1 Canadian Training Brigade Group at Debert, Nova Scotia, to upgrade the general standard of reinforcements before their departure overseas.

Field Artillery training was carried out to the Regimental level beginning with Detachment training in Phase I, Troop training in Phase II, Battery training in Phase III, graduating to Regimental training in Phase IV.

The training was as close to battle conditions as possible in his own Corps and designed to acquaint the reinforcement on his part in the overall picture in battle.

No. 1 Field Training Regiment RCA was authorized to disband under General Order 85/46 (Effective 14th December 1945).

* * *

No. 1 Canadian School of Artillery, Overseas — Seaford, England

The need for a Canadian School of Artillery was evident with insufficient vacancies on courses at the RA School of Artillery, Larkhill, the latter part of 1942.

Approval was granted for the formation of a Canadian School of Artillery (Overseas) wef 21st November 1942, using Canadian Instructors in Gunnery who had qualified in the War Gunnery Staff Courses at the RA School of Artillery, Larkhill.

The Canadian School, located in the Aldershot-Bordon, Hants, area, came under command HQ "C" Group, CRU for all purposes, with Headquarters in Pinewood at Whitehill, Hants. Facilities at the Canadian Artillery Reinforcement Units were utilized for training, rations and quarters.

On the 3rd of December 1942 the School was authorized to comprise Headquarters, and five Wings (Fd—Med—A Tk—AA—Svy). The Wings were to be adjuncts of the existing CARUs. A staff of twelve IsG and twenty AIsG had been assembled to instruct the first three courses 3rd January 1943.

The Field and Medium Wings had been combined into one Wing from the beginning, however, while in the Aldershot-Bordon area the Field Wing was at 1 CARU and the Medium Wing at 2 CARU. The peak period for the Wing was during 1943 when the Wing was servicing five Divisions and two AGRAs in addition to Courses at the School.

Authority was granted to operate as an independent Unit and the Canadian School of Artillery (Overseas) moved to the Seaford, Sussex, area, August 1943, assuming the administration of the Anti-Tank Ranges at Beachy Head, and the Field Ranges at Alfriston.

The selection of the Seaford College area for the Canadian School of Artillery (Overseas) was due to suitable accommodation for the School and the proximity of the Alfriston Range and the Beachy Head Ranges.

The Survey Wing of the Canadian School of Artillery (Overseas) also played an important role.

The Wing concentrated on Regimental Survey Officers Courses and upgrading Surveyors RCA during 1943.

In 1944 new types of Courses were introduced for both Canadian and British Units, with Regimental Survey parties reporting as a group for training on a Divisional level.

Two months prior to "D" Day British and Canadian Units kept the Beachy Head Ranges incessantly in operation.

At Seaford the School was placed under Headquarters "C" Group except for local administration when it came under command of 2nd Canadian Corps until April 1944, then returned to under command of Headquarters Canadian Reinforcement Units, and "C" Group.

Admin Order 113, 23 June 1944 (Appendix "H") placed the School under CMHQ (GS Branch) for training, and under command of Headquarters Canadian Reinforcement Units for all other purposes.

The School reverted to under command "C" Group HQ for all purposes upon the departure of First Canadian Army from England. 1944 also saw the task of the School changed to the training of Artillery reinforcements.

The Canadian School of Artillery (Overseas) despatched an IG to the Continent to assist with the command of an 95mm Centaur Battery to be taken over by First Canadian Army. The IG departed on the 5th August and returned 11th September, the Unit having disbanded when the equipment broke down and no replacements available.

The School successfully operated an Officers Training Wing 17th August to 31st October 1944 to accommodate a large reserve of Officers from 1 and 2 CARUs. An Infantry Battle School was also conducted by the School.

A four day firing practice on the Alfriston Range was held for British Air OP Courses under training at Larkhill.

The School wrote a Gun Drill book and trained a cadre of instructors in the use of the 20mm quad.

Admin. Order No. 185 granted the new designation of the School as No. 1 Canadian School of Artillery (Overseas) 22nd November 1944, and General Orders authorized the mobilization of No. 1 Canadian School of Artillery, Overseas, under General Order 113/45 (Effective 22nd November 1944).

The School undertook a number of specialized assignments which included an amendment to the 25 pounder Sexton on Ram Carriage, SP Gun Drill, conducted 40mm Bofors wire cutting trials, modifications to the Stiffkey Stick Bofors sight, produced a Bofors 40mm SP Gun Drill, produced a drill for indirect firing of Anti-Tank and Light Anti-Aircraft Guns.

Successful trials were conducted on Upper Register Shooting of 25 pounders. Land Mattress Rocket Equipment was improved upon, a cadre of instructors trained at the School, a Drill written and a method of producing meteor data devised. The 32 barreled adaption of the 1 ton trailer was adopted by the Canadian Army for issue to the Light Anti-Aircraft and proved succesful in action.

In February 1945 the School conducted a Layers Error Trial to determine the effect of fatigue on the accuracy of the gun layers.

One IG and three AIsG proceeded to NW Europe in March 1945 to direct the training of the re-formed 1st Light Anti-Aircraft Regiment, recently arrived from Italy.

In May 1945 a further British Course was started but this Course had to be returned to Larkhill before its completion due to the Canadian School of Artillery (Overseas) closing.

No. 1 Canadian School of Artillery (Overseas) received authorization to disband under General Order 52/46 (Effective 21st September 1945). The School had trained a large number of members of the RCA and added immeasurably to the success of the Royal Canadian Artillery in battle.

*   *   *

1st Counter Battery Officers Staff RCA — Serial 837 — 1st Corps

Formation of Counter Battery Officers' Staff, Serial 837, was authorized under General Order 273/41 (Effective 3rd September 1941).

The CBO Staff was formed in England, at Cobham, Surrey, with a War Establishment of four Officers and twenty-one Other Ranks, sharing the office and administration work with Corps Artillery Headquarters. The Unit moved to Turner's Hill mid November 1941 and in January and February 1942 participated in schemes with the Divisions to acquaint the troops with the function of Counter Battery.

Counter Battery Officers' Staff, Serial 837, was redesignated 1st Counter Battery Officer's Staff, RCA, Serial 837, under General Order 447/42 (Effective 7th September 1942).

The Staff moved from Turner's Hill to Horsham in October 1943, remaining a few days prior to going overseas.

1st Counter Battery Officer's Staff twenty-odd strong boarded the E.B. Alexander and on the 27th October 1943 departed Britain's shore for the Mediterranean. The CBO Staff disembarked on the 8th November 1943 at Augusta, Sicily, and moved to Taormina, 10th November. The Unit remained at this location until 1st January 1944 and during this period two members of the staff were attached to 5 British Corps CBO on the Eighth Army Front for two weeks to gain experience.

1st CBO Staff boarded LCTs, 2nd January 1944 at Messina, Sicily, and set sail for the Italian mainland early in the morning of 3rd January, arriving at the port of Reggio one and one-half hours later.

The CBO Staff proceeded to the concentration area on the Bari Road, East of Altamura and remained under canvas until the 15th January, then moved to the Ortona Front on the Adriatic Coast, 16th January 1944.

Quarters were found in the town of Lanciano alongside 1st Canadian AGRA with whom 1st Counter Battery Officer's Staff would be working.

By the 19th January the CBO Staff was fully operational and ready to take over. The Air Photo Interpreter and his Section had gone to the airfield at Vasto to take up duties with MAIU (West).

1st CBO Staff assumed responsibility for the counter-battery 21st January, although 1st Canadian Corps did not fully take over from 5 British Corps until midnight 2nd/3rd February 1944. This was the first employment in action of a Canadian CBO Staff in the war.

On 6th March 1944 the Unit moved back to Lanciano as 1st Canadian AGRA and 1st CBO Staff RCA relieved 6th British AGRA on the 5 British Corps Front, remaining until 27th March and 5 Corps CBO officially became responsible for counter-battery on the Eighth Army Front.

1st CBO Staff moved to Larino, Raviscano, then to Mignano on the 16th April under command of 1st Canadian AGRA, in readiness to take over from 13 Corps CBO upon 1st Canadian Corps exploiting the breakthrough in the German lines.

The Gustav Line battle opened 11th May preceded by a terrific Artillery program. On the 15th an Artillery program was fired to support the Polish Corps attack around Cassino.

The Hitler Line was the next objective for 1st Canadian Corps with 1st CBO Staff responsible for counter-battery. 1st Canadian Infantry Division was to make the breakthrough and 5th Canadian Armoured Division to exploit as far as the Melfa River.

It was decided to put 1st Canadian Infantry Division and 6 South African Division forward with 5th Canadian Armoured Division in reserve. The CBO detachment moved to 6 South African Division and 5th Division detachment moved to 1st Division.

AGRA Headquarters and CBO moved to Agnani on the 4th June and moved again 6th June through Rome and beyond. While on the move news of the Normandy landing was received.

13 Corps CBO took over the CBO responsibility for the Front on the 8th June.

1st CBO Detachments returned from 1st Canadian Infantry Division and 6 SA Division, the RAF operators returned to their airfield and the Air Photo Section rejoined CBO Staff in new quarters at San Salvatore (near Raviscanini).

The CBO Staff moved to Castel Ritaldi, near Spoleto 2nd August in readiness for the next operation. However, the operation was cancelled and the Unit remained in Castel Ritaldi until 16th August.

CBO Staff with AGRA Headquarters moved to the Jesi area 16th August for a four phase attack beginning with the crossing of the F. Metauro in Phase 1, Pursuit to the Gothic Line in Phase 2, Breaking through the Gothic Line in Phase 3 and the drive on Bologna in Phase 4. 1st Canadian Corps was again in the centre, 5 British Corps on the left and the Polish Corps on the right. 1st Canadian Counter Battery Officer's Staff was responsible for counter-battery along the whole Eighth Army Front.

The operation began 25th August. Two destroyers and a gun boat were placed at the disposal of Counter Battery on 1st September. The Metauro River was crossed and 1st Canadian Corps took over the Adriatic Sector from the Polish Corps. On the 3rd September CBO detachments moved to the Artillery Head-quarters at 1st and 5th Canadian Divisions.

In a combined operation CBO Staff called on fifteen Kittyhawk bombers, one Heavy Battery of 155s plus Navy guns controlled by the Air OP to silence an enemy coastal Battery firing on the Navy boats off shore in the Adriatic.

The Unit moved forward through the Gothic Line on the 4th September. Resistence stiffened around the Marano River and the Counter Battery Offic-er's Staff detachments were recalled from 1st and 5th Divisions. The enemy employed aircraft in counter-battery as light bombers hovered above the gun areas and dropped their anti-personnel bombs at the gun flashes.

During the operation 1st CBO Staff carried out a number of neutralizing shoots on enemy Anti-Aircraft guns while allied planes were over their lines. Shelling from roving Self-Propelled guns and mortaring by nebelwerfers was prominent at this time and it was suggested they be combatted with Self-Propelled guns and Counter Mortar.

5 British Corps mounted an attack 8th September, 4 British Division attacked along with 1st Canadian Infantry Division 18th September. CBO Staff moved to Riccione on the 19th and to Rimini on the 21st, then moved again 25th September North of Rimini.

A new development of counter-battery was the adoption of quick neutralizing programs for use by the Air OP. Also a radar experimental station was set up near 2nd Medium Regiment RCA for passing shelreps and locreps to CBO. Primarily designed for mortar locations, was also utilized to locate hostile guns within range limitations. Nebelwerfer locations with one or two nebelwerfers were to be handled by CMO and larger concentrations by CBO. On the 20th October CBO moved to a location near Gambolito and to a concentration and rest area near Cesenatico on the 28th.

CBO set up an office with Porter Force along with 2nd Canadian Medium Regiment 12th November and on 26th November moved to Coccolia and became operational on the 27th, then moved to Russi, 4th December. The weather cleared 10th December and the Air OP and Arty/R took full advantage.

A counter-battery neutralizing program was fired the same day in support of an attack by 1st Canadian Infantry Division. Rocket-firing fighter bombers were used by CBO against Harassing Batteries, 15th December 1944, for the first time.

The Unit remained in this location for eight weeks as winter set in and the Front became static. During this period the method of handling Arty/R shoots was changed and the shoots were to be handled direct from an VHF set at 17 Heavy Battery (155s).

During January 1945 the Italian Cremona Combat Group moved into the Front and a Battery of its guns were used in CB work. CBO 10 British Corps replaced 5 British CBO at this time.

The amount of air time supplied by the RAF was compacted with only 3 HBs per day outside the range of the guns where possible, grouped together in 100 yards and 50 yards accuracy fix. These targets were passed on to the Air Photo Interpreter at the airfield who plotted the location on large scale photos and the pilots to do the bombing were briefed by the ALO and the Photo Interpreter on large scale photos and maps. This procedure enabled the pilot to come as close to the target as possible without being able to see the enemy guns.

CBO moved to Godo on the 1st February 1945 and on the 5th February moved under the same roof as Headquarters 1st Canadian AGRA in Godo.

On the 10th February, 1st Canadian Counter Battery Officer's Staff turned over CB responsibility on the Corps Front to 5 Corps CBO and under command 1st Canadian Corps moved to a concentration area in Ravenna, remaining until 17th February, then following stops at Masserata, Torino, Lucera and Raviscanini, arrived at Naples.

On the 25th February, 1st Counter Battery Officer's Staff RCA boarded the SS Empire Pride and departed Italy, arriving at Marseilles, France on the 27th of February 1945.

The Unit reached Cambrai, Belgium, 8th March 1945, then was dispersed to Waereghem, Belgium, and set up an office. On 20th March 1st Canadian CBO Staff moved into Holland near the Grave Bridge in the Nijmegen area.

The CBO moved to the Island North of Nijmegen on 30th March in readiness for operation Destroyer, which began 2nd April 1945. On the 11th April an ACBO detachment departed to 1st Canadian Infantry Division near Zutphen, and another ACBO detachment proceeded to 5th Canadian Armoured Division, with main Headquarters remaining on the 49 (WR) Infantry Division Front.

The three-pronged attack advanced rapidly. 1st Canadian Infantry Division moved through Zutphen, Apeldoorn and towards Amersfoort. 5th Canadian Armoured Division went from Arnhem to Otterloo to Barneveld. 49 (WR) Division boarded boats and crossed the Neder Rijn around the left of Arnhem and proceeded West.

The ACBO at 5th Canadian Armoured Division was at Otterloo when a large number of enemy paratroops tried to break through the Canadian lines and ran into Headquarters 5th Canadian Armoured Division 16th April, and were repulsed following a vicious attack.

On 18th April CBO Main office and AGRA Headquarters moved up Maple Leaf Route through Arnhem to Otterloo. The ACBO detachments returned from 1st Canadian Infantry Division and 5th Canadian Armoured Division on 20th April and the Unit was once more intact.

CBO and the AGRA moved again 23rd April near Lunteren, West of Otterloo. It was at this location that the news of the ceasefire was received and 8th May 1945 was declared the official date.

The Unit left the AGRA and under command CCRA, moved to the outskirts of Apeldoorn, then moved to Hilversum on the 30th May.

On 8th June, 1st Canadian CBO Staff and all Corps Artillery Units came under command 1st Canadian AGRA. CBO remained at Hilversum where the rundown of Units was begun and the final parade held.

Volunteers proceeded to the Canadian Army Pacific Force and the Canadian Army Occupation Force. Personnel remaining were posted to Units originating in the Military District of their enlistment for the return to Canada.

1st Counter Battery Officers Staff, RCA, Serial 837, received authorization to disband under General Order 321/45 (Effective 4th July 1945).

*   *   *

1st Kinetheodolite Detachment RCA — Serial 1373 — M.D. No. 6

1st Kinetheodolite Detachment RCA, Serial 1373, mobilized under General Order 454/42 (Effective 16th September 1942).

One Officer and 19 Other Ranks of #12 Company Canadian Women's Army Corps, Ottawa were posted to the Kinetheodolite Detachment and served at Dartmouth, Nova Scotia.

The Detachment did calculations of Shot at Devil's Battery and Anti-Aircraft Battery Shoots.

Crews also served at Osborne Head, McNabs and Hartland Point.

1st Kinetheodolite Detachment, RCA, Serial 1373, received authorization to disband under General Order 280/45 (Effective 30th June 1945).

*   *   *

No. 1 Meteorological Section RCA — Serial 84A — Disbanded

No. 1 Meteorological Section RCA, Serial 84A, mobilized under General Order 155/41 (Effective 1st April 1941), presumably to serve with 1st Survey Regiment RCA, Serial 84. However, the composition of a Survey Regiment was in a state of flux and the Section was unwanted at that time.

No. 1 Meteorological Section RCA, Serial 84A, was authorized to disband under General Order 276/42 (Effective 10th March 1942).

*   *   *

No. 1 Proof Range Detachment RCA — Serial 876

No. 1 Proof Range Detachment RCA, Serial 876, mobilized under General Order 207/41 (Effective 1st April 1941).

No. 1 Proof Range Detachment RCA, Serial 876, received authorization to disband under General Order 87/43 (Effective 31st December 1942).

*   *   *

1st Radar Battery RCA — Army Troops, First Canadian Army

Trials in the use of Radar to locate enemy mortars proved successful and it was decided to form a Radar Battery for each Army in 21 Army Group.

The Battery mobilized as 1st Radar Battery RCA, under General Order 46/45 (Effective 22nd September 1944).

1st Radar Battery RCA formed under 107 British Anti-Aircraft Brigade and consisted of one Troop of three Sections per Corps, with Corps allotting one Section to each Division.

Early December 1944 "A" Troop deployed with 1 British Corps and "B" Troop deployed with 2nd Canadian Corps in Holland.

1st Radar Battery RCA served in Holland and Germany with these Units until March 1945 when 1st Canadian Corps arrived in NW Europe from Italy, replacing 1 British Corps in First Canadian Army.

"A" Troop moved from 1 British Corps to 1st Canadian Corps at that time and "B" Troop remained with 2nd Canadian Corps.

1st Radar Battery RCA served until the cessation of hostilities, and received authorization to disband under General Order 321/45 (Effective 21st June 1945).

*   *   *

No. 1 Radar Operating Unit — Serial 1348

No. 1 R.D.F. Operating Unit, Serial 1348, mobilized under General Order 208/43 (Effective 15th April 1943).

RCA Gunners performed the manning duties, but RCA is not included in the Unit title.

No. 1 R.D.F. Operating Unit, Serial 1348, was redesignated No. 1 Radar Operating Unit, Serial 1348, under General Order 34/44 (Effective 1st January 1944).

No. 1 Radar Operating Unit, Serial 1348, received authorization to disband under General Order 213/45 (Effective 30th April 1945).

*   *   *

1st Rocket Battery RCA — Army Troops, First Canadian Army

A Land Mattress Party was formed in England, June 1944 and crossed the Channel in October as instructors.

112th Light Anti-Aircraft Battery RCA of 6th Light Anti-Aircraft Regiment RCA, 2nd Canadian Corps Light Anti-Aircraft Regiment, was selected to operate the launchers and received instruction from the original cadre. The 32 barrelled adaption of the one ton trailer was adopted for use by the Unit.

112th Battery first fired the launchers 28th October 1944, then under command of 2nd Canadian AGRA, the Battery fired in support of 52nd (Lowland) Division in the attack on the Port of Flushing, 1st November 1944.

1st Rocket Battery moved to the 1st Polish Armoured Division sector and engaged targets in the area of Moerdijk, 6th to 8th of November 1944.

Following this operation 112th Battery personnel returned to their Anti-Aircraft role and 338th Light Anti-Aircraft Battery Royal Artillery and 337th Light Anti-Aircraft Battery Royal Artillery manned the projectors.

1st Rocket Battery RCA officially came into being under General Order 175/45 (Effective 23rd December 1944).

337th Light Anti-Aircraft Battery Royal Artillery was replaced by 30th Light Anti-Aircraft Battery of 6th Light Anti-Aircraft Regiment Royal Canadian Artillery on the 24th of January 1945.

The Rocket Battery supported the breaching of the Siegfried Line February 1945 and continued in action, firing its last salvo 2nd May 1945, near Oldenburg, Germany.

The run-down of Canadian Units was begun following cessation of hostilities and 1st Rocket Battery RCA received authorization to disband in NW Europe, under General Order 321/45 (Effective 21st June 1945).

*   *   *

1st Survey Battery RCA — Serial 84E — 1st Canadian Corps

1st Survey Regiment RCA mobilized in September 1939 and proceeded overseas in three groups to Gourock, Scotland, during 1940. The Survey Battery was the first to sail and disembarked at Gourock on the 9th of February.

When the Survey Battery departed overseas a nucleus of personnel remained in Montreal to form a Flash Spotting Battery and Regimental Headquarters. The Unit moved to Petawawa 24th May and toward the end of July a Sound Ranging Battery was added to the Regiment.

Flash Spotting Battery followed the Survey Battery overseas and disembarked on the 4th of September. With the arrival in Scotland of Regimental Headquarters and Sound Ranging Battery on the 26th of December, the Regiment was now complete.

A number of organizational changes were introduced and 1st Survey Regiment RCA became an Army Survey Regiment of five Batteries which included Sound Ranging Battery, A, B, C and D Survey Batteries. The Batteries were allotted to the Canadian Divisions in England.

This organization remained in effect until official notification was received of the transfer of Headquarters 1st Canadian Corps to the Mediterranean Theatre of Operations. Corps Troops, 5th Canadian Armoured Division and 1st Canadian AGRA were to accompany Corps Headquarters and they along with 1st Canadian Infantry Division and 1st Canadian Armoured Brigade, presently in action with British Eighth Army in Italy were to come under command 1st Canadian Corps.

1st Survey Regiment was split in two to form two Survey Regiments for the split First Canadian Army, one for 1st Canadian Corps and one for 2nd Canadian Corps. 1st Survey Regiment RCA which had been Army Troops, First Canadian Army, now became Corps Troops, 1st Canadian Corps.

"A" Survey Battery RCA, Serial 84E, was redesignated 1st Survey Battery RCA, Serial 84E, under General Order 486/43 (Effective 18th October 1943). The Battery, often referred to as "P" Battery, remained a component of 1st Survey Regiment RCA following the split.

1st Survey Battery, 1st Survey Regiment RCA, 1st Canadian Corps departed for the Mediterranean 13th November on board the Scythia from Avonmouth and rendezvoused with the convoy in the Clyde. The convoy sailed on the 14th and the Regiment disembarked at Algiers, N. Africa, 25th November 1943. The Battery departed Algiers on the Chantilly and arrived at Catania, Sicily, 8th December 1943.

1st Survey Regiment RCA crossed the Strait of Messina to the Italian mainland 4th January 1944 and moved to the Front 6th February in relief of 5 British Survey Regiment as they moved on to Anzio.

Slow progress in the Anzio beachhead required one Battery only of 5 Survey Regiment and the Regiment less one Battery returned to Ortona. The Canadian Corps was relieved of its duties on the Ortona Front at this time, however, 1st Survey Battery RCA came under the command of 5 Survey Regiment 6th March 1944, replacing the Battery detached at Anzio. 1st Survey Battery RCA remained under command of 5 British Survey Regiment until the first week of June.

1st Survey Battery RCA, returned to 1st Survey Regiment RCA and with 1st Canadian Corps served in Italy until early 1945, then with the other components of 1st Canadian Corps moved to NW Europe to join First Canadian Army.

The Regiment boarded the MS Empire Pride, 26th February 1945 at Naples and disembarked at Marseilles, France, 28th February, then proceeded to Belgium, where the Corps congregated.

1st Survey Battery moved from Belgium to Oss, Holland, 27th March, with C Troop relieving a Troop of 1 British Survey Regiment. The Battery's final action was the attack on Apeldoorn, Holland, followed by cessation of hostilities and the designation of the 8th of May 1945 as "VE" Day.

1st Survey Regiment RCA, Serial 84, received authorization to disband under General Order 321/45 (Effective 28th June 1945), the Batteries are not listed.

*   *   *

Permanent Active Militia Batteries RCA (PF) — Canada.

Prior to the War, Permanent Force Batteries provided instructors for Schools of Instruction, were attached to Non-Permanent Active Militia Units as advisers and instructors, and conducted summer camps for the Non-Permanent Active Militia Units on the East and West coasts, in Ontario and the Prairie Provinces.

1st Heavy Battery RCA and 2nd Heavy Battery RCA performed Yeoman duty at the Halifax Forts. 3rd Medium Battery of Kingston was responsible for the Medium Artillery Units. 4th Anti-Aircraft Battery RCA, Kingston, aided the Anti-Aircraft Units. "A" Battery RCHA and "B" Battery RCHA of Kingston and "C" Battery RCHA of Winnipeg passed their knowledge on to the Field Artillery Units in Eastern and Western Canada respectively. 5th Heavy Battery RCA (PF) guided the defenders of the West Coast Forts.

Following mobilization in 1939 Permanent Force Batteries made a major contribution to the Canadian Active Service Force and the Non-Permanent Active Militia by providing instructors at the Unit level and at the Training Centres.

"A", "B" and "C" Batteries RCHA served with 1st Field Regiment RCHA, 1st Canadian Infantry Division in Sicily, Italy and NW Europe. 3rd Medium Battery served in Italy and NW Europe with 1st Medium Regiment RCA, 1st Canadian AGRA, Army Troops, 4th Battery served as a Light Anti-Aircraft Battery with 2nd Light Anti-Aircraft Regiment RCA, 1st Division, and 11th Light Anti-Aircraft Regiment RCA, Army Troops, in England. A large number of Permanent Force personnel from the Coastal Forts departed for overseas as the need for reinforcements increased. Recruits called up for Home Defence arrived as replacements. A solid core of Coast Gunners remained however, and served in this first line of Defence until cessation of hostilities.

*   *   *

RCA Band

Royal Canadian Artillery Band mobilized under General Order 462/44 (Effective 10th June 1944).

Royal Canadian Artillery Band received authorization to disband under General Order 111/46 (Effective 15th February 1946)

*   *   *

Royal Canadian Artillery, CASF, Depot, Kingston, Ontario

Royal Canadian Artillery, CASF, Depot, Kingston, Ontario, was placed on Active Service under General Order 140/39 (Effective 2nd September 1939).

*   *   *

Royal Canadian Horse Artillery, CASF, Depot, Winnipeg, Man.

Royal Canadian Horse Artillery, CASF, Depot, Winnipeg, Manitoba, was placed on Active Service under General Order 140/39 (Effective 2nd September 1939).

*   *   *

A 2 Canadian Artillery Training Centre — Serial 1204 — Petawawa

A Canadian Artillery Training Centre (Field and Anti-Tank) was formed in Military District No. 3 under General Order 9/40 (Effective 1st December 1939).

The Training Centre was expanded and moved from Kingston to Petawawa under the designation A 2 Canadian Artillery Training Centre in 1941.

A 2 Canadian Artillery Training Centre, Serial 1204, was placed on Active Service under General Order 250/41 (Effective 15th February 1941).

A 2 Canadian Artillery Training Centre, Serial 1204, remained operational at Petawawa until receiving authorization to disband under General Order 153/45 (Effective 15th January 1945).

*   *   *

2nd Air OP Squadron RCA — Serial 2381 — Army Troops

2nd Air Observation Post Squadron RCA, was authorized under General Order 493/44 (Effective 4th May 1944).

2nd Air Observation Post Sqn RCA, Canadian Army Overseas, Part II Orders, Order No. 2, 12 Feb/45 excerpt — "authority is granted for the formation of 2nd Air Observation Post Squadron, RCA, wef 22 Jan. 45".

2nd Canadian Air OP Squadron (No. 665 (RCAF) (AOP) Squadron), mobilized 22nd January 1945 at RAF Station, Andover, Hampshire, England, comprising RCAF groundcrew and Army personnel, with the main body arriving 25th February 1945. The Unit was aided by 1st Canadian AOP Squadron (664 Sqn) during its forming.

1st Canadian AOP Squadron (No. 664 Sqn) moved to its new location 2nd February 1945 and 2nd Canadian AOP Squadron (No. 665 Sqn) was on its own. 2nd Canadian AOP Squadron (No. 665 Sqn) in turn aided in the forming of 3rd Canadian AOP Squadron (No. 666 Sqn).

Army personnel arrived from 1 CARU, 7th February 1945 to fill the Clerk, Driver Operator, Artillery Signallers and vehicle mechanic vacancies.

2nd AOP Squadron (No. 665 Sqn) had received its full complement of 16 Auster Aircraft by the 22nd February 1945 and the Squadron Commander was appointed. The "A", "B" and "C" Flight Commanders were appointed 28th February 1945.

Commencing in Part II Orders, Issue No. 5, 13 Mar/45, Part II Orders were issued under the designation, 2nd Cdn AOP Squadron (No. 665 (RCAF) (AOP) Sqn), Canadian Army Overseas.

The Squadron moved to Oatlands Hill, Wiltshire, 17th March 1945 for from two to three weeks of field exercises, with the three Flights departing at thirty minute intervals.

RAF Station Andover continued to be the Parent Station for the Unit and the Unit was to return to Andover before proceeding overseas.

Effective 15th April 1945 the Unit transferred from 70 Group HQ to 84 Group 2nd TAF for duty on the Continent. The Squadron departed Oatlands Hill 19th April 1945 for the marshalling area at Hornchurch where they embarked on 3 LSTs, set sail on the 20th and disembarked at Ostend, Belgium on the 21st. The Air Party arrived 25th April 1945.

The Squadron was to be located temporarily at Gilze, Holland. HQ 665 Air OP Squadron however, remained at Gilze Rijen, Holland under command First Canadian Army, its Flights scattered in three countries, "A" Flight in 2nd Canadian Corps area under command 2nd Canadian Corps for 1 Polish Armoured Division, "B" Flight at Dunkirk (France) under 21 Army Group, "C" Flight at Tilberg (Holland) under 1st Canadian Corps for Netherlands District, with one Section to North Beveland Island, relieving 652 AOP Sqn RAF in these locations. "C" Flight carried out the first operational sortie for the Squadron, 27th April.

On the 29th April "A" Flight departed for the Papenburg Area with the Polish Div, then to Moorburg, Germany, 4th May 1945, where news of the unconditional surrender was received, then on to Jeevers, Germany with communications flights carried out.

"B" Flight carried out sorties over Dunkirk, 5th May 1945. The 8th of May was designated "VE" Day. On the 21st of May the Flight aided in the rescue of four survivors of a capsized boat.

The Squadron congregated in Holland and during the month the Squadron changed from a specialized "AOP" Squadron to a mail service and communication Squadron.

Disbandment proceedings were begun and a number of personnel moved to 664 Air OP Squadron, Army and RCAF volunteers departed for the Canadian Army Pacific Force and Aircraft were transferred to other AOP Units, 9th July.

2nd Air Observation Post Squadron RCA received authorization to disband under General Order 388/45 (Effective 10th July 1945), in NW Europe.

*   *   *

No. 2 CARU — Serial 1132 (Med, A/Tk, Svy) — Bordon, England

No. 2 Canadian Artillery Holding Unit (No. 2 CAHU), Serial 1132, mobilized under General Order 61/41 (Effective 18th September 1940).

No. 2 Canadian Artillery Holding Unit, Serial 1132, was redesignated No. 2 Canadian Artillery Reinforcement Unit (Medium Anti-Tank Survey), Serial 1132, under General Order 290/42 (Effective 1st June 1942). However, this designation and effective date were cancelled and No. 2 Canadian Artillery Holding Unit, Serial 1132, was redesignated No. 2 Canadian Artillery Reinforcement Unit (Medium Anti-Tank Survey), Serial 1132, under General Order 127/43 (Effective 1st November 1941). The new General Order also corrected the alignment of Units listed in the cancelled General Order.

No. 2 CARU (Medium Anti-Tank Survey), was located at Bordon, Hampshire, England, and provided a ready supply of reinforcements to the Medium, Anti-Tank and Survey Regiments RCA.

No. 2 Canadian Artillery Reinforcement Unit (Medium Anti-Tank Survey), Serial 1132, received authorization to disband under General Order 321/45 (Effective 30th June 1945), as the run-down of Canadian Units in England and on the Continent was begun upon cessation of hostilities in NW Europe.

*   *   *

S 2 Canadian Artillery School — Serial 536 — Petawawa, Ontario

Canadian School of Artillery, Serial 536, mobilized under General Order 206/42, Part "A" (Effective 1st April 1942).

Canadian School of Artillery, Serial 536, was redesignated S 2 Canadian

Artillery School, Serial 536, under General Order 29/43 (Effective 1st November 1942).

S 2 Canadian Artillery School, Serial 536, received authorization to disband under General Order 18/46 (Effective 31st March 1945).

*   *   *

2nd Counter Battery Officers Staff RCA — Serial 1183 — 2nd Corps.

2nd Counter Battery Officers Staff RCA, Serial 1183, mobilized under General Order 446/42 (Effective 7th September 1942), to serve with 2nd Canadian Corps.

2nd Counter Battery Officers Staff RCA with a War Establishment of four Officers and eighteen Other Ranks assembled at Cobham, Surrey.

2nd Canadian Corps Headquarters moved to the Three Bridges area in October 1943 and 2nd Counter Battery Officers Staff moved to Lingfield. A steady stream of schemes followed from this location.

During February and March 1944 the War Establishment was increased by two Officers and four clerks, enabling the Unit to provide a detachment for the Air Photo Int. S. at the Tac R. Airfield.

In April 1944, 2nd CBO Staff moved from Lingfield to Eastling Wood, North of Dover. The invasion of Normandy began 6th June 1944 and the Unit awaited its turn to join 3rd Canadian Division in the beachhead.

A detachment of 2nd CBO Staff landed in Normandy with Headquarters 2nd Canadian Infantry Division, 5th July and received a warm reception at Carpiquet Airfield. The main party of 2nd Counter Battery Officers Staff RCA with Headquarters 2nd Canadian Corps, landed on the 7th July 1944 and were joined by the 2nd Division detachment at the main Counter Battery Headquarters.

The Headquarters joined the action for operation "Goodwood", to establish a bridgehead over the River Orne at Caen, and crossed the Orne on the 22nd July under command 1 British Corps, Second British Army.

2nd CBO Staff with Headquarters 2nd Canadian Corps, came under the command of First Canadian Army, 31st July 1944. The Unit was extremely busy during the vicious fighting in the breakout from Caen, with many locations supplied by Flash Spotting and Sound Ranging Troops of 2nd Canadian Survey Regiment. APIS gave plenty of air photo information and the Air OPs located and engaged harassing Batteries. The CBO Staff also dodged a considerable number of enemy mortars, shells and bombs, and Allied bombs as well.

With the closing of the Falaise Gap a detachment moved forward with 3rd Canadian Infantry Division and the remainder of the Unit moved with Headquarters 2nd Canadian Corps, crossing the River Seine and the River Somme, stopping South of Dunkirk to begin the battle of the Channel Ports.

A heavy bomber attack preceded the attack on Boulogne which began 17th September with three Heavy Regiments, two Heavy Anti-Aircraft Regiments and three Medium Regiments allotted, aided by C Flight 661 Air OP Squadron. Boulogne fell on the 19th and the attack on Calais was launched 27th September, ending on the 30th.

2nd CBO Staff moved on to Belgium and the Battle of the Scheldt with 2nd, 3rd and 4th Canadian Divisions and 52nd (Lowland) Division playing important roles. The Unit with 2nd Canadian Corps moved to the Nijmegen, Holland area in relief of 30 British Corps, 9th and 10th of November 1944.

The drive into Germany was begun 8th February 1945. The Reichswald Forest and Hochwald Forest were cleared, followed by the crossing of the River Rhine, 24th March.

During April 1945, 2nd Counter Battery Officers Staff provided Counter Battery for 2nd, 3rd and 4th Canadian Divisions and did the Counter Battery part of 1st Canadian Infantry Division's crossing of the Ijssel River in Holland, then turned the duties over to 1st Canadian Counter Battery Office.

"Cease Fire" was ordered 5th May, with the 8th of May 1945 being designated "VE" Day. 2nd CBO Staff moved back to Holland, 14th June, then on the 26th proceeded to 13 Canadian Base Reinforcement Group (CBRG), for disbandment. Personnel departed for the Canadian Army Pacific Force, the Canadian Army Occupational Force, or were posted to Units from the Military District of their enlistment for the return to Canada.

2nd Counter Battery Officers Staff RCA, Serial 1183, received authorization to disband under General Order 321/45 (Effective 27th June 1945).

*   *   *

2nd CMO Staff (Type A) RCA — Serial 2532 — 2nd Cdn. Inf. Div.

No. 2 Counter Mortar Officers Staff (Type "A"), mobilized under General Order 462/44 (Effective 6th June 1944).

No. 2 CMO Staff was organized in the Dover, Kent area, England, for service with 2nd Canadian Infantry Division, and carried out some preliminary training prior to crossing the Channel to France. Since no previous Counter Mortar Staff existed the Unit was patterned after the Counter Battery Officers Staff.

The Staff was divided into four detachments, with the CMO, ACMO and a small staff with Div HQ detachment, and ACMO and a small staff with each of the Brigade detachments at 4th Brigade HQ, 5th Brigade HQ and 6th Brigade HQ.

The Brigade detachments arrived in Normandy 8th July with their respective Brigades and the Div. detachment travelled with HQ RCA. The Staff ranks were sadly depleted on the second day with the loss of one OR killed and two ACMOs wounded.

It was soon realized that counter mortar would operate more successfully when centralized at Div HQ. Listening posts staffed by 3rd LAA Regiment RCA personnel were introduced to take bearings on enemy targets. The guns of the Division and 2nd Canadian AGRA were available to neutralize the weapons and activity was intense until the breakthrough at Falaise.

The CMO Staff also assumed CBO responsibilities during the dash across France where the fluid situation added to the difficulty of carrying out bombards.

A few targets were bombarded near Rouen, in August, then on to Dieppe, where on the 3rd September the Division paused for a Service of Remembrance and a Divisional parade through the city.

The Unit moved to Antwerp, Belgium and it was found more convenient to set up individual Counter Mortar and Counter Battery Offices.

No. 2 Counter Mortar Officers Staff (Type A), was redesignated 2nd Counter Mortar Officers Staff (Type A) RCA (Effective 22nd September 1944).

Following action in the Antwerp-Tournhout Canal battle, CMO Staff moved to the Hoogerheide sector, then South of Bergen Op Zoom, South Beveland and to the Nijmegen area at Groesbeek where the line was established and many bombards fired by the Toronto Scottish Heavy Mortar Company 4.2" mortars.

The Unit was joined by a detachment of the Mortar Location Troop of 2nd Canadian Survey Regiment with a four-pen recorder specially made to pick up the sound of enemy mortars. The four pens recorded the vibrations picked up by the microphones at the sound ranging base.

A Radar detachment from 1st Canadian Radar Battery was allotted the Unit at this time and the equipment proved extremely accurate. The Radar station always came under command while the Mortar Location Section was always in support.

In readiness for operation Veritable, the breakthrough to the Rhine via the Reichswald Forest, the CMO Stations on the 30 British Corps front were turned over to its Divisions 8th February 1945. Enemy mortars were quite active during the early stages of the operation, fading toward nightfall, and the CMO duties ended for the moment as 2nd Canadian Infantry Division troops completed their part of the operation with the capture of Wyler.

Following the capture of Cleve the Unit deployed in the area on the 17th February and on the 24th the Radar station was hit by enemy shelling killing two and wounding two.

In operation Blockbuster, clearing the Hochwald Forest, Germany, 1st March 1945, 2nd Div responsibility was clearing of the East section of the Forest.

The Division advanced from the Hochwald to Xanten, then on to Wesel. The Radar station and Mortar Location Section ceased to be under command 11th March 1945 and reverted to the command of 2nd Canadian Corps.

2nd Division held the line from Milligen to Emmerich for three weeks and crossed the Rhine at Rees, 31st March 1945, then headed due North with Groningen in NE Holland as the final objective.

On the 18th April 1945 the Division moved from Groningen to an area between Bremen, Germany and Oldenburg, where 2nd Canadian CMO Staff once again took over Counter Battery duties. The last bombard was fired from this location 2nd May 1945, then upon receiving the "Cease Fire" order and the designation of the 8th of May "VE" Day, the war in Europe had ended.

2nd Counter Mortar Officers Staff (Type A), RCA, served in France, Belgium, Holland, and Germany as a component of 2nd Canadian Infantry Division, 2nd Canadian Corps, under First Canadian Army until cessation of hostilities and received authorization to disband in NW Europe, under General Order 321/45 (Effective 21st June 1945).

*   *   *

2nd Survey Battery RCA — Serial 84F — 1st Canadian Corps

1st Survey Regiment RCA mobilized in September 1939 and proceeded overseas in three groups during 1940. The Survey Battery on board the Monarch of Bermuda arrived at Gourock, Scotland and disembarked 9th February 1940. Flash Spotting Battery disembarked from the Scythia at Gourock, 4th September 1940. Regimental Headquarters and Sound Ranging Battery sailed on the Pasteur and disembarked at Gourock on the 26th of December 1940. The Regiment complete, was now overseas.

Following a number of organizational changes 1st Survey Regiment RCA became an Army Survey Regiment with five Batteries, Sound Ranging Battery, A, B, C and D Survey Batteries. The Batteries were allotted to the Canadian Divisions in England.

This organization remained in effect until official notification was received of the transfer of Headquarters 1st Canadian Corps to the Mediterranean.

Accompanying Headquarters 1st Canadian Corps to the Mediterranean were Corps Troops of 1st Canadian Corps, 5th Canadian Armoured Division and 1st Canadian AGRA. In addition the Corps was to encompass 1st Canadian Infantry Division and 1st Canadian Armoured Brigades, both having seen action in Sicily and presently serving with British Eighth Army in Italy.

1st Survey Regiment was split in two to form two Survey Regiments, one for 1st Canadian Corps and one for 2nd Canadian Corps. 1st Survey Regiment RCA which had been Army Troops, First Canadian Army, now became Corps Troops, 1st Canadian Corps.

"B" Survey Battery RCA, Serial 84F, was redesignated 2nd Survey Battery RCA, Serial 84F, under General Order 486/43 (Effective 18th October 1943). The Battery, often referred to as "Q" Battery, remained a component of 1st Survey Regiment RCA following the split.

2nd Survey Battery, 1st Survey Regiment RCA, 1st Canadian Corps, departed for the Mediterranean 13th November on board the Scythia from Avonmouth and rendezvoused with the convoy in the Clyde. The convoy sailed on the 14th and the Regiment disembarked at Algiers, N. Africa, 25th November 1943. The Battery departed Algiers on the Chantilly and arrived at Catania, Sicily, 8th December 1943.

1st Survey Regiment RCA crossed the Strait of Messina to the Italian mainland 4th January 1944 and 2nd Battery became operational at Ortona on the 6th of February, as the Regiment relieved 5 British Survey Regiment upon their departure for Anzio.

Limited progress in the Anzio beachhead required one Battery only of 5 Survey Regiment and the British Regiment less one Battery returned to Ortona. The Canadian Corps was relieved of its duties at Ortona at this time, however, 1st Survey Battery RCA came under command of 5 Survey Regiment 6th March 1944, replacing the Battery detached at Anzio, and remained until the first week of June. RHQ, in the meantime moved to Palata, with 2nd Battery at Tavenna, then on to Telese and Raviscanini, in readiness for the Hitler Line Battle.

The 11th of May heralded the beginning of the Hitler Line Battle. 1st Canadian Infantry Division with a Troop of 2nd Survey Battery attached, crossed the

Rapido River on the 17th and entered the battle. 5th Canadian Armoured Division crossed the Melfa River where Major Mahoney of the Westminster Regiment won the Victoria Cross. Rome fell on the 4th of June 1944.

On the 6th of June the Regiment moved to the Corps rest area with personnel returning to the Regiment following duty with 3 Survey Regiment and 5 Survey Regiment.

The battle for the Gothic Line took place in August and the Po Valley Action in December. 5th Canadian Armoured Division cleared up to Lake Commachio in the Northern sector and turned the area over to an Italian Division. 3rd and 5th Survey Regiments relieved 1st Canadian Survey Regiments 10th February 1945 and the Regiment with 1st Canadian Corps prepared to move to NW Europe.

1st Survey Regiment RCA boarded the MS Empire Pride at Naples, 26th February and disembarked at Marseilles, France, 28th February 1945, then proceeded to Belgium, to the Corps concentration area.

2nd Survey Battery moved from Belgium to the Island in front of Nijmegen and by the 21st March had a Sound Ranging and a Flash Spotting base on the Island. Survey Troop and Battery Headquarters were billeted near 49 (WR) Infantry Division and continued with the Division.

E Troop was put in support of 5th Canadian Armoured Division 1st April and were in support during the 17th Field Regiment's famous battle of Otterloo.

2nd Survey Battery RCA served with 1st Survey Regiment RCA until cessation of hostilities. 1st Survey Regiment RCA, Serial 84, received authorization to disband under General Order 321/45 (Effective 28th June 1945), the Batteries, however, are not listed.

*   *   *

3rd Air OP Sqn RCA — Serial 2382 — 666 (RCAF) (AOP) Sqn — Army Tps

3rd Air Observation Post Squadron RCA was authorized under General Order 493/44 (Effective 4th May 1944). The mobilization of the Squadron however was held in abeyance.

On the 5th March 1945, RCAF personnel arrived from 665 (RCAF) (AOP) Squadron where they were being held for the forming of 666 (RCAF) (AOP) Squadron which commenced on that date at Andover, Hampshire, England. The main party of 76 Army Other Ranks arrived from No. 1 CARU, 12th March 1945.

Flight allocations were made 12th April 1945 with "A", "B" and "C" Flights being staffed, and a full complement of Auster Aircraft had been received. The Squadron departed Andover, Hampshire for Petworth Park, Friston, Sussex, 17th April 1945, arriving on the 18th and was billeted under canvas.

666 (RCAF) (AOP) Squadron Ground Party proceeded to the concentration area at RAF Station Hornchurch, 29th May 1945. The Air Party returned to Andover. The Ground Party boarded LSTs on the 30th and 31st May, arriving at Ostend, Belgium, on the 31st May and 1st June, and proceeded to Bruges, Belgium. The parties converged on Gilze Rijon, 2nd June and Air Party arrived 3rd June 1945.

Headquarters arrived at its destination, Hilversum, Holland, 6th June. "A" Flight was placed in support of 1st Canadian Infantry Division at Doerdrecht, "B" Flight with 1st Canadian AGRA at Maarsden and "C" Flight with 3rd Canadian Infantry Division at Hilversum.

On the 8th June "A" Flight was attached to 1st Canadian Division Artillery and officially took over all commitments of 657 Squadron which consisted of twice daily flights servicing 1st Division and 1 AGRA for ADIS.

The Flights moved to Apeldoorn, Holland, "C" Flight arrived 21st June with "A" and "B" Flights arriving 25th June. On the 27th June all flying duties were administered by 664 Squadron. Flights were broken up and came under Squadron Headquarters for administration.

666 (RCAF) (AOP) Squadron remained operational until 31st October 1945. Personnel were posted to 664 (RCAF) (AOP) Squadron, or moved to other Units for repatriation to Canada, others volunteered for further duty overseas.

3rd Air Observation Post Squadron RCA received authorization to disband under General Order 52/46 (Effective 31st October 1945).

*   *   *

No. 3 CARU (Anti-Aircraft) — Serial 1137 — Bramshott, Surrey

No. 3 Canadian Artillery Reinforcement Unit (Anti-Aircraft), Serial 1137, mobilized under General Order 289/42 (Effective 1st January 1942).

However, 4th Light Anti-Aircraft Regiment RCA Regimental History notes — "We dispatched a few trained officers and about 151 ORs to form a nucleus of a new holding unit known as 3 CAHU, the bulk leaving on 13 October" (1941).

Bramshott, Surrey, was the location selected for No. 3 Canadian Artillery Reinforcement Unit (Anti-Aircraft), and according to local residents the camp was built on the ashes of a Canadian First World War camp.

In a compacting of Reinforcement Units No. 2 CARU assumed the Anti-Aircraft responsibilities and No. 3 Canadian Artillery Reinforcement Unit (Anti-Aircraft), Serial 1137, was authorized to disband under General Order 464/44 (Effective 27th March 1944).

* * *

A 3 Cdn Artillery Training Centre — Serial 1205 — Shilo, Manitoba

A Canadian Artillery Training Centre (Field and Anti-Tank) was authorized in Military District No. 10, under General Order 57/40 (Effective 20th March 1940). The Training Centre was enlarged to A 3 at Shilo and A 4 Brandon.

A 3 Canadian Artillery Training Centre, Serial 1205, was called out on Active Service under General Order 250/41 (Effective 15th February 1941).

A 3 Canadian Artillery Training Centre remained operational at Camp Shilo, Manitoba, and was redesignated The Royal Canadian School of Artillery (Effective 1st October 1946), in Issue No. 30, 28th July 1947, Supplements to Canadian Army Orders 1947 (Issues No. 1 to No. 53 Inclusive).

* * *

3rd CMO Staff (Type "A") RCA — Serial 2533 — 3rd Cdn Inf Div.

3rd Counter Mortar Officers Staff (Type "A") RCA, Serial 2533, mobilized as No. 3 Canadian Counter Mortar Officers Staff (Type A) under General Order 119/45 (Effective 15th July 1944). The Unit was formed under battle conditions in the Field as a component of 3rd Canadian Infantry Division which had landed in Normandy with the assaulting Forces on D-Day, 6th June 1944.

The Liaison Officer at Headquarters RCA in cooperation with the Brigade Major Royal Artillery, devoted considerable time to counter mortar activities and even a rough location of hostile mortars brought a large concentration of fire from the Field Artillery Regiments of the Division.

In July a Counter Mortar Officer and an Assistant Counter Mortar Officer was appointed. A Headquarters Detachment was formed of two Officers and four Assistants, with an Assistant Counter Mortar Officer at each of the three Infantry Brigade Headquarters.

No. 3 Counter Mortar Officers Staff started to operate as a Unit south of Caen where mortars and "Moaning Minnies" (Nebelwerfers) were extremely active, and Field Artillery ammunition in good supply. Information came from Infantry Observation Posts and Artillery Forward Observation Officers.

After Falaise 3rd Canadian Infantry Division raced across France to the outskirts of Boulogne, Cap Gris Nez and Calais, in the battle of the Channel

Ports, where there was an absence of mortar fire due to the defenders being Coast Artillery and Marines.

No. 3 Canadian Counter Mortar Officers Staff (Type "A") was redesignated 3rd Counter Mortar Officers Staff (Type "A") RCA, Serial 2533, under General Order 146/45 (Effective 22nd September 1944).

7th Canadian Infantry Brigade of 3rd Canadian Infantry Division encountered concentrated mortar fire in crossing the Leopold Canal in the battle of the Scheldt and 7.2 inch heavy guns were used for the first time against enemy mortars. A 4 Pen Recorder for sound ranging also came into use on this Front.

On the static Nijmegen Front technical equipment proved invaluable under foggy conditions. The most satisfactory organization proved to be a Counter Mortar staffed Observation Post at each Brigade with one Section of Radar and one Mortar Location Section under command.

3rd Counter Mortar Officers Staff (Type A) RCA served with 3rd Canadian Infantry Division in France, Belgium, Holland, and Germany, then with cessation of hostilities received authorization to disband under General Order 321/45 (Effective 21st June 1945), in NW Europe.

*   *   *

A 4 Cdn Artillery Training Centre — Serial 1206 — Brandon, Man.

A Canadian Artillery Training Centre (Field and Anti-Tank) was authorized in Military District No. 10, under General Order 57/40 (Effective 20th March 1940). The Training Centre was enlarged to A 3 Shilo and A 4 Brandon.

A 4 Canadian Artillery Training Centre, Serial 1206, was called out on Active Service under General Order 250/41 (Effective 15th February 1941).

A 4 Canadian Artillery Training Centre moved into the buildings and camp formerly occupied by 101st Training Centre, Brandon.

101st NPAM Training Centre, Serial 1206 was authorized in M.D. 10 and came into being in August 1940 at Brandon, Manitoba, to train men called up under the NRM Act 1940. Eight training periods per year was projected with trainees posted to two Companies of 2nd Battalion Winnipeg Grenadiers, and two Companies TOS 2nd Battalion Royal Winnipeg Rifles.

The first group arrived the early part of October and following thirty days training were provided with transportation home. The name of the Training Centre was changed to 101st NPAM Training Centre, Fort Brandon Barracks.

101st NPAM Training Centre was redesignated No. 101 Reserve Training

Centre under General Order 273/40 (Effective 7th November 1940). Trainees reported the latter part of November 1940 and the third group in January 1941. At the conclusion of thirty days training for this group it was decided to lengthen the training period for the next group to four months.

Recruits were to train at Basic Training Centres for two months then move to an Advanced Training Centre for two months and it was at this time 101st Training Centre became A 4 Canadian Artillery Training Centre, Serial 1206, training both Volunteers and NRMA conscripts. The new system was implemented 20th March 1941.

A 4 Canadian Artillery Training Centre, Serial 1206, remained operational until receiving authorization to disband under General Order 296/44 Part "A" (Effective 1st June 1944).

* * *

4th CMO Staff (Type B) RCA — Serial 2534 — 4th Cdn Armd Div.

No. 4 Counter Mortar Officers Staff (Type "B"), mobilized under General Order 462/44 (Effective 6th June 1944).

No. 4 Counter Mortar Officers Staff (Type B) was redesignated 4th Counter Mortar Officers Staff (Type B) RCA, under General Order 54/45 (Effective 22nd September 1944).

4th Counter Mortar Officers Staff (Type B) RCA served as a component of 4th Canadian Armoured Division, 2nd Canadian Corps, First Canadian Army, in France, Belgium, Holland, and Germany, then with cessation of hostilities received authorization to disband under General Order 321/45 (Effective 21st June 1945), in NW Europe.

* * *

4th Searchlight Battery RCA, CASF — Serial 133 — No CASF role

4th Searchlight Battery RCA, CASF, Serial 133, was authorized as a component of 2nd Searchlight Regiment RCA, CASF, Army Troops mobilizing with 1st Division, under General Order 135/39, 1st September 1939.

4th Searchlight Battery RCA, CASF, Serial 133, along with Headquarters 2nd Searchlight Regiment RCA, CASF, Serial 132, were left without a role at this early date and authorized to disband under General Order 438/43 (Effective 1st September 1939).

* * *

No. 5 CCMO Staff (Type B) RCA — Serial 2535 — 5th Cdn Armd Div.

No. 5 Canadian Counter Mortar Officers Staff (Type B), mobilized under General Order 119/45 (Effective 15th July 1944).

No. 5 Canadian Counter Mortar Officers Staff (Type B), was redesignated No. 5 Canadian Counter Mortar Officers Staff (Type B), RCA, under General Order 252/45 (Effective 15th March 1945).

No. 5 Canadian Counter Mortar Officers Staff (Type B), RCA served with 5th Canadian Armoured Division in Italy and NW Europe, then with cessation of hostilities received authorization to disband under General Order 321/45 (Effective 21st June 1945).

* * *

5th Heavy Battery RCA — Permanent Active Militia (PF) — West Coast

Non-Permanent Active Militia Units, Royal Canadian Artillery, were called out on Service under General Order 124/39, 26th August 1939 for duty at the local Forts (Victoria and Esquimalt), under the guidance of 5th Heavy Battery RCA, Permanent Force (PF).

15 members of 5th Heavy Battery RCA, Permanent Force, were attached to 2nd Anti-Aircraft Battery RCA, Non-Permanent Active Militia, for Duty, Discipline, Rations and Quarters on the 26th August 1939, upon 2nd Anti-Aircraft Battery assuming the duty of manning the guns at Fort Macaulay, Victoria-Esquimalt Fortress. — (Part II Orders, 5th B.C. Coast Brigade, RCA, Fort Macaulay Detachment, Issue No. 1, Fort Macaulay, August 26, 1939).

10 members of 5th Heavy Battery RCA (PF) were attached to 55th Heavy Battery at Fort Mary Hill for Duty, Discipline, Rations and Quarters, 10 members of 5th Heavy Battery were attached to 60th Heavy Battery at Fort Rodd Hill, and one Permanent Force Officer was attached to Headquarters 5th (B.C.) Coast Brigade RCA on the 26th of August 1939.

The Permanent Force Gunners were transferred from Fort to Fort in the Victoria-Esquimalt Defences, performing a valuable service to the men in the Forts. In addition to its duties in the Vancouver Island Defences 5th Heavy Battery RCA (PF) also provided personnel for the Prince Rupert Defences and Vancouver Defences, British Columbia, which included Yorke Island.

Most of these men were assimilated into Units of the Active Force during the course of the War and the "P" Regimental Number of the 5th Permanent Force Battery was to be found on the nominal roll of most Canadian Army Units at home or overseas.

* * *

5th Survey Battery RCA — Serial 1790B — 2nd Canadian Corps

Regimental Headquarters and Sound Ranging Battery of 1st Survey Regiment RCA disembarked at Gourock, Scotland on the 26th December 1940 and the Regiment assembled in the South of England. Survey Battery and Flash

Spotting Battery had arrived at Gourock during February and September 1940, respectively.

Several organizational changes took place before 1st Survey Regiment RCA became an Army Survey Regiment of five Batteries which included Sound Ranging Battery, A, B, C and D Survey Batteries. The Batteries were allotted to the Canadian Divisions in England.

Exercise "Split" began when it was learned that 1st Canadian Corps was Mediterranean bound. 1st Survey Regiment RCA as Army Troops, was responsible for all Units of First Canadian Army, now became Corps Troops, 1st Canadian Corps and a second Survey Regiment was formed as Corps Troops, 2nd Canadian Corps. 1st Survey Regiment RCA was split in two, retaining A and B Batteries and C and D Batteries were allotted to the new Regiment.

C Survey Battery of 1st Survey Regiment RCA became P Battery or 5th Survey Battery of 2nd Survey Regiment RCA. The Battery was to comprise Battery Headquarters, A Flash Spotting Troop, C Sound Ranging Troop and X Survey Troop, with a Meteorological Section, Z Survey Troop, a Light Aid Detachment and Regimental Aid Post under Regimental Headquarters.

5th Survey Battery RCA, Serial 1790B, was authorized under General Order 485/43 (Effective 18th October 1943). Priorities were directed toward the Batteries bound for the Mediterranean after which time the new Regiment whipped itself into shape for the cross-channel invasion.

5th Survey Battery, 2nd Survey Regiment RCA, 2nd Canadian Corps landed in Normandy on the 9th of July 1944 and deployed in the area of Carpiquet Airfield 11th July with 2nd Canadian Corps under Second British Army.

The Regiment crossed the Orne River 21st July, then with 2nd Canadian Corps came under command of First Canadian Army 31st July and participated in the heavy fighting around Caen. 5th Battery suffered the loss of several Officers and Other Ranks in the bombing by the USAAF, 8th August and by the RAF on the 14th August.

With the breakout from Caen effected and the closing of the Falaise Gap the left Section of X Survey Troop, 5th Survey Battery, attached to 3rd Canadian Infantry Division raced across France to Boulogne, deploying 12th September, then moved to Calais 17th September. The right Section moved with 4th Canadian Armoured Division.

The Regiment moved to an area near Ghent, Belgium, 20th September and during the following week deployed on the Leopold Canal in readiness for the battle of the Scheldt Estuary, then on to Nijmegen, Holland, in relief of 4th British Survey Regiment on the 8th of November.

The Ardennes offensive in December slowed the date of the drive into Germany which began on the 8th of February 1945, heralded by the greatest gun barrage to date. The Battery moved to an area East of the Reichswald Forest 18th February, then to the Hochwald Forest 28th February. The assault on the Rhine River began 24th March and the Regiment complete, crossed 2nd April.

5th Survey Battery moved with 2nd Canadian Infantry Division for the drive into North Holland, then back into Germany to the outskirts of Emdem where the cease-fire was given. A Troop and X Troop ended the war at Oldenburg.

In action the Regiment also worked with 1st Polish Armoured Division, 11th Armoured Division, 49th (WR) Division, 51st (Highland) Division, 52nd (Lowland) Division and 101st US Airborne Division.

5th Survey Battery RCA received authorization to disband under General Order 238/46 (Effective 22nd June 1945), in NW Europe.

*   *   *

5th Searchlight Battery RCA, CASF — Serial 134 — Disbanded

5th Searchlight Battery RCA, CASF, Serial 134, received authorization to mobilize under General Order 135/39, 1st September 1939, with Headquarters of 2nd Searchlight Regiment RCA, CASF, Army Troops Mobilizing with 1st Division.

The services of 5th Searchlight Battery RCA, CASF, Serial 134, and Headquarters of 2nd Searchlight Regiment RCA, CASF, were not required at this time and disbanded under General Order 438/43 (Effective 1st September 1939).

*   *   *

6th Survey Battery RCA — Serial 1790C — 2nd Canadian Corps

1st Survey Regiment RCA assembled in the South of England following the arrival of Regimental Headquarters and Sound Ranging Battery in December 1940. Survey Battery and Flash Spotting Battery had arrived at Gourock, Scotland, in February and September, respectively.

Composite Batteries proved to be the most satisfactory organization and 1st Survey Regiment RCA reorganized to comprise Regimental Headquarters, Sound Ranging Battery, A and B Survey Batteries, in February 1942. C and D Batteries were formed later and each Battery consisted of Battery Headquarters, Survey Troop and Flash Spotting Troop. As Army Troops the Regiment served First Canadian Army and the composite Batteries were allotted to the Canadian Divisions in England.

1st Survey Regiment was split in two prior to proceeding to the Mediterranean Theatre of Operations. 2nd Survey Regiment RCA was formed to serve with 2nd Canadian Corps and 1st Survey Regiment changed from Army Troops to Corps Troops and accompanied Headquarters 1st Canadian Corps to the Mediterranean, retaining A and B Batteries. C and D Survey Batteries formed the new 5th (P) Battery and 6th (Q) Battery in 2nd Survey Regiment RCA. C and D Batteries with their Serial Numbers were phased out.

6th Survey Battery RCA, Serial 1790C, was authorized to mobilize under General Order 485/43 (Effective 18th October 1943).

6th Survey Battery, 2nd Survey Regiment RCA landed in Normandy 9th July 1944 and moved to the Carpiquet area with 2nd Canadian Corps, under Second British Army.

The Regiment crossed the Orne River 21st July, then with 2nd Canadian Corps came under command of First Canadian Army 31st July and participated in the heavy fighting around Caen where the Regiment suffered the loss of several officers and other ranks in the misdirected bombing.

With the breakout from Caen effected and the closing of the Falaise Gap, the Regiment joined in the race across France.

Y Survey Troop of 6th Survey Battery travelled with 2nd Division to Dieppe where they paused for a Service of Remembrance honouring members of the Division lost on the Dieppe Raid of 1942 and participated in a Divisional parade through the streets of the city.

The Troop moved on to Rouen, Dunkirk, then to Antwerp, Belgium, in support of D Troop and 2nd Division and were placed in support of 52nd Lowland Division on Zuid Beveland and Walcheren Island. The Troops returned to the Battery in time to move up to Nijmegen where the Battery took over the bases from 4 Survey Regiment on the 9th of November.

The Ardennes offensive delayed the attack into Germany in the area of the Reichswald Forest and the Siegfried Line. The greatest gun barrage to date heralded the attack on the 8th of February 1945. The barrage was interrupted for a period of ten minutes to permit Sound Ranging, Flash Spotting and Mortar Location units to locate retaliatory fire.

The Mortar Location Sections operated the 4-pen recorders as a component of the Survey Regiment and came under command the Counter Mortar Officers Staff in the Divisions.

6th Survey Battery moved forward 11th February to the Cleve area and Y Survey Troop was attached to 2nd Division for the complete operation.

By the 2nd of April all segments of 2nd Survey Regiment RCA had crossed the Rhine.

6th Battery was placed in support of 3rd Canadian Infantry Division in a dash into North Holland, the route running parallel to the 2nd Canadian Infantry Division route. The Battery then returned to Germany and was in the Emdem area when the cease-fire was received.

6th Survey Battery RCA had served in France, Belgium, Holland, and Germany, and with the cessation of hostilities received authorization to disband under General Order 238/46 (Effective 22nd June 1945), in NW Europe.

*   *   *

No. 61 Cdn Arty (Basic) Training Centre — Serial 1249

No. 61 Canadian Army (Basic) Training Centre, Serial 1249, was placed on Active Service under General Orders 250/41 (Effective 15th February 1941), and redesignated No. 61 Canadian Artillery (Basic) Training Centre, Serial 1249, under General Order 487/43 (Effective 15th November 1943).

No. 61 Canadian Artillery (Basic) Training Centre, Serial 1249, received authorization to disband under General Order 470/44 (Effective 30th September 1944).

*   *   *

No. 62 Cdn Artillery (Basic) Training Centre — Serial 1250

No. 62 Canadian Army (Basic) Training Centre, Serial 1250, was placed on Active Service under General Order 250/41 (Effective 15th February 1941), and redesignated No. 62 Canadian Artillery (Basic) Training Centre, Serial 1250, under General Order 487/43 (Effective 15th November 1943).

No. 62 Canadian Artillery (Basic) Training Centre, Serial 1250, received authorization to disband under General Order 347/45 (Effective 31st January 1945).

*   *   *

"Q" Battery RCA (AF) — "W" Force, Newfoundland

"Q" Battery RCA (AF), proceeded to Newfoundland and manned coastal guns in the St. John's area at Fort Amherst and Chain Rock, 14th June 1941, with "W" Force, Newfoundland.

"Q" Battery became "C" Troop, 103rd Heavy Battery RCA (AF), Serial 430, at Chain Rock, Newfoundland, 14th June 1941.

*   *   *

"X" Super Heavy Bty RCA — X & Y Battery Super Heavy Group RCA — England

"X" Super Heavy Battery RCA formed part of 3rd Super Heavy Regiment Royal Artillery, which also comprised 13th Super Heavy Battery RA, 4th Super Heavy Battery RA and "Y" Super Heavy Battery RCA.

Battery Headquarters of "X" Battery and Right Section proceeded to Littlestone, Kent. Left Section journeyed to Shorncliffe, then to Golden Wood. Calibration shoots were carried out during October 1940.

Battery Headquarters and Right Section moved to billets at Kingsworth 19th December 1940.

"X" Battery moved from Kingsworth, Kent, to Bordon, Hampshire, February 1941, upon being relieved by 15th Super Heavy Battery RA.

*   *   *

"Y" Super Heavy Battery RCA — X & Y Bty Super Heavy Group RCA — England

On the 4th of September 1940 orders were received to organize Y Super Heavy Railway Battery RCA at Banstead Wood, Headquarters of 11th Army Field Regiment RCA, where one officer and 14 ORs of 11th Army Field Regiment RCA transferred to the new unit.

The battery departed Banstead Wood for Shorncliffe, Kent, in convoy on the 8th of September. Guns were to be at Golden Wood, near Ashford, and at Bridge, near Canterbury. The guns were 23 miles apart and the battery, which formed part of 3rd Super Heavy Regiment Royal Artillery, came under CCMA 12 Corps, Eastern Command.

On the 10th of September, No. 1 and No. 2 Sections commenced training on the 9.2" B.L. gun of 4th Super Heavy Railway Battery RA, Hythe, in position at Hythe.

"Y" Super Heavy Battery RCA remained on duty in Kent until February 1941, then moved to Bordon, Hampshire, to the Canadian Artillery Holding Unit, where the battery was phased out.

*   *   *

81st, 103rd and 104th (Artillery) Reserve Companies Veterans Guard

The Veterans Home Guard was authorized as a corps of the Active Militia under General Order 112/40 (Effective 24th May 1940) and was redesignated Veterans Guard of Canada under General Order 188/40 (Effective 16th August 1940). The infantry reserve companies Veterans Guard of Canada in each Military District were designated numerically and localized under General Order 198/40 (Effective 24th May 1940). The arm of the service in brackets, inserted between the numeral and reserve, was authorized under General Order 255/40 (Effective 12th October 1940).

81st (Artillery) Reserve Company Veterans Guard, Toronto, 103rd (Artillery) Reserve Company Veterans Guard of Canada, Dauphin and Swan River, Manitoba, 104th (Artillery) Reserve Company Veterans Guard of Canada, Winnipeg, Manitoba, mobilized as Infantry Reserve Companies under General Order 198/40 (Effective 24th May 1940), and are included in a list of companies redesignated and localized under General Order 137/42 (Effective 1st April 1942).

No. 4 Platoon of No. 103 Infantry Reserve Company Veterans Guard of Canada was relocated at Swan River, Manitoba, from Dauphin, Manitoba, under General Order 115/42 (Effective 19th March 1942), and is listed as No. 4 Platoon, 103rd (Artillery) Reserve Company, Swan River, Manitoba, in General Order 137/42 (Effective 1st April 1942).

81st Company received authorization to disband under General Order 402/45 (Effective 31st October 1945), 103rd Company disbanded under General Order 453/44 (Effective 1st October 1944), and 104th Company disbanded under General Order 12/43 (Effective 29th October 1942).

*   *   *

HEADQUARTERS

Section VII includes Headquarters First Canadian Army, Headquarters 1st and 2nd Canadian Corps, 1st, 2nd and 3rd Canadian Infantry Divisions, 4th and 5th Canadian Armoured Divisions, 1st AA Brigade, 1st and 2nd Canadian AGRAs and the independent armoured brigades of the overseas force, Atlantic and Pacific Commands, fortresses, defended ports and defended areas on the east coast and at the west coast, along with 6th, 7th and 8th Divisions on the home front, "B" Force (Bermuda), "C" Force (Hong Kong), Force "G" (Goose Bay), "Greenlight" Force* (Kiska), "N" Force (Bahamas), "W" Force (Newfoundland), "Z" Force (Iceland), and Jamaica, outside Canada. The Canadian Army Occupational Force, the Canadian Army Pacific Force, Newfoundland Regiments Royal Artillery, Exercise "Eskimo", the postwar organization of commands, and 23rd Infantry Brigade Group of the Postwar Permanent Force are also included.

With the arrival in England of 2nd Canadian Infantry Division plus ancillary units during 1940 the force grew from one infantry division to a corps of two divisions. 3rd Canadian Infantry Division, 5th Canadian Armoured Division and 1st Canadian Army Tank Brigade arrived during 1941 and were joined by 4th Canadian Armoured Division in 1942. The two armoured divisions moved under command of Headquarters 2nd Canadian Corps upon its forming in January 1943.

Headquarters First Canadian Army was formed in April 1942 and General A.G.L. McNaughton prepared to lead his two-corps First Canadian Army in the cross-channel invasion of the Continent. This dream was suddenly shattered with the departure of 1st Canadian Infantry Division and 1st Canadian

Army Tank Brigade to the Mediterranean for the invasion of Sicily, 10th July 1943.

The ranks of First Canadian Army were further depleted with the departure to the Mediterranean of Headquarters 1st Canadian Corps, Corps Troops, 5th Canadian Armoured Division, supporting units and 1st Canadian AGRA, during October and November 1943.

1st Canadian Infantry Division returned to under command of 1st Canadian Corps as the corps became operational early 1944 in Italy. 1st Canadian Armoured Brigade was attached to 13 British Corps.

On the 16th of May 1944, 1st Canadian Corps in its first big battle directed 1st Canadian Infantry Division through 8th Indian Division's breach in the Gustav Line and the division battled fiercely to reach the Hitler Line which it penetrated on the 23rd of May. 5th Canadian Armoured Division entered 1st Division's breach in the Hitler Line and continued the advance into the Liri Valley. Rome fell 4th June 1944.

On the 6th of June the Allied invasion of Normandy was launched. 3rd Canadian Infantry Division with 2nd Canadian Armoured Brigade and 19th Army Field Regiment RCA representing 2nd Canadian Corps stormed ashore in Normandy on D-Day, 6th June 1944, along with two British Divisions and two US Divisions, aided by Canadian, British and US paratroopers.

Headquarters First Caadian Army, Headquarters 2nd Canadian Corps, 2nd Canadian Infantry Division, 4th Canadian Armoured Division and 2nd Canadian AGRA, entered the beachhead in July.

The Canadian units in Normandy came under command of First Canadian Army 31st July 1944 for the breakout from Caen, the army then moved to the left along the coast to clear the forts, capture the ports and eliminate the buzz-bomb launching sites. 2nd Div returned to Dieppe, 3rd September. First Canadian Army moved on to Belgium and Holland for the battle of the Scheldt, to clear the port of Antwerp to shipping, then moved to the Nijmegen salient in Holland.

First Canadian Army was given the honour of planning and executing the breakout from the Nijmegen salient into the Rhineland 8th February 1945. 2nd and 3rd Canadian Divisions were placed under 30 British Corps for the initial attack, then returned to 2nd Canadian Corps to begin a two-corps advance, cracking the Siegfried Line and closing to the River Rhine.

1st Canadian Corps arrived from Italy to join First Canadian Army and became operational in the Arnhem Sector on the left flank of 21 Army Group, 15th March 1945.

Upon crossing the Rhine 2nd Canadian Corps cleared NE Holland and a section of Germany as 1st Canadian Corps cleared western Holland, liberating its starving people.

While First Canadian Army was so-employed the "Cease Fire" was received 5th of May and the 8th of May 1945 was designated "VE" Day, ending the conflict in NW Europe.

*Operation "Cottage".

*   *   *

HQ First Canadian Army — Serial 1150 — 21 Army Group — NW Europe

Headquarters of an Army, Serial 1150, was authorized under General Order 131/42 (Effective 1st April 1942).

Headquarters of an Army, Serial 1150, was redesignated Headquarters First Canadian Army, Serial 1150, under General Order 471/42 (Effective 1st April 1942).

Four Canadians divisions, an army tank brigade and a number of ancillary units had arrived in England by the end of 1941 with another division slated to arrive in 1942, necessitating the forming of a larger headquarters to aid the overburdoned Canadian corps headquarters. Normal progression suggested the forming of a second corps headquarters and an army headquarters to command the two corps.

The existing Canadian corps became 1st Canadian Corps. The forming of Headquarters 2nd Canadian Corps however was delayed until January 1943, then both 1st Canadian Corps and 2nd Canadian Corps came under Headquarters First Canadian Army and prepared for the forthcoming cross-channel invasion.

This dream was suddenly shattered with the departure of 1st Canadian Infantry Division and 1st Canadian Army Tank Brigade to the Mediterranean for the assault on the island of Sicily, 10th July 1943, to be followed toward the end of the year by Headquarters 1st Canadian Corps, 5th Canadian Armoured Division, 1st Canadian AGRA, and ancillary units, to serve under British Eighth Army.

Headquarters First Canadian Army continued to exist with its limited Canadian content and now comprised 2nd Canadian Corps, 2nd Canadian Infantry Division, 3rd Canadian Infantry Division, 4th Canadian Armoured Division, 2nd Canadian Armoured Brigade, 2nd Canadian AGRA, plus ancillary units, to be supplemented by British and units of many nationalities.

Headquarters First Canadian Army prepared for the movement to the Continent of its headquarters, Army Troops, and 2nd Canadian Corps less 3rd Canadian Infantry Division and 2nd Canadian Armourd Brigade, attached to Second British Army for the D-Day landings.

The role assigned First Canadian Army now commanded by General A.D.G. Crerar was to follow Second British Army into the beachhead area, assume responsibility for the left sector and capture the ports of Le Havre and Rouen. 3rd Canadian Infantry Division and 2nd Canadian Armoured Brigade were to return under command. A British corps with its quota of Army Troops from Second British Army were to come under command in the bridgehead and 84 Group RAF Headquarters was to set up alongside army headquarters and provide tactical air support for First Canadian Army.

The army commander and a small tactical headquarters arrived in France the latter part of June awaiting room to deploy in the beachhead. Headquarters First Canadian Army with 1 British Corps replacing 1st Canadian Corps in the order of battle, became operational in Normandy on the 23rd of July 1944. 2nd Canadian Corps and the bulk of Canadian units came under command of First Canadian Army 31st July on the Caen Front.

First Canadian Army participated in the vicious fighting in the breakout from Caen and the closing of the Falaise Gap, which was effected 19th August when 1st Polish Armoured Division of First Canadian Army joined United States forces to complete the encirclement.

The dash for the River Seine was begun and the enemy resisted stubbornly at the river, particularly in the Forêt de la Londe area. Once across the Seine, First Canadian Army fanned out toward the channel ports to silence the cross-channel guns and open the ports to shipping. 1 British Corps captured Le Havre, 2nd Canadian Division of 2nd Canadian Corps returned to Dieppe, then aided in clearing the coastal belt.

3rd Canadian Infantry Division continued along the coast clearing Boulogne, Calais, and Cap Gris Nez. First Canadian Army Headquarters Defence Company (Royal Montreal Regiment) was attached to 7th Brigade of 3rd Canadian Infantry Division for the clearing of the forts at Cap Gris Nez and Calais, then moved with the brigade into Belgium. During the advance along the channel coast First Canadian Army units overran and destroyed the buzz-bomb launching sites.

A determined enemy controlled all approaches to the port of Antwerp and the need to open the port to shipping was given top priority. The task was delegated to First Canadian Army and 2nd Canadian Infantry Division of 2nd Canadian Corps was whisked away from responsibilities at Dunkirk, to Antwerp, establishing a bridgehead over the Albert canal and enlarging the bridgehead over the Antwerp-Turnhout canal. 1 British Corp's 49 (WR) Division of First Canadian Army assumed responsibility for the area to the right of 2nd Div and with 2nd Canadian Corps so widely dispersed 2nd Canadian Infantry Division was temporarily placed under 1 British Corps, as was 1st Polish Armoured Division as it moved into the area.

Toward the end of September 2nd Canadian Corps turned over Dunkirk containing force duties to Headquarters First Canadian Army and in October 1st Czechoslovak Independent Armoured Brigade Group assumed the containment duty under First Canadian Army, along with a French infantry battalion and units of the French Forces of the Interior (FFI). 2nd Canadian Heavy Anti-Aircraft Regiment also served with the force.

The Breskens Pocket and Walcheren became the next objectives for First Canadian Army. 3rd Canadian Infantry Division was to clear the Breskens pocket from the Leopold canal in Belgium to the West Scheldt in Holland. North of Antwerp an isthmus connected the peninsula of South Beveland with the mainland and a long narrow causeway led to Walcheren Island. First Canadian Army allotted the task of clearing South Beveland and the causeway to 2nd Canadian Infantry Division. 2nd Division returned to 2nd Canadian Corps from 1 British Corps 6th October.

3rd Canadian Infantry Division completed the task of clearing Calais 1st October and on the 6th of October made an assault crossing over the Leopold canal to begin clearing the Breskens pocket, with First Canadian Army Headquarters Defence Company (Royal Montreal Regiment) taking part. 9th Canadian Infantry Brigade attacked the pocket in an amphibious assault across the Braakman, and 3rd Canadian Infantry Division reported the Breskens operation completed 3rd November.

2nd Canadian Infantry Division began its operation against South Beveland 24th October and as 2nd Div approached the Beveland canal on the 26th of October 52 (Lowland) Division began an amphibious attack across the West Scheldt. The two divisions linked up on the 29th and South Beveland was cleared by the 31st. The narrow causeway to Walcheren now faced the units of 2nd Canadian Infantry Division, and as the infantry began the perilous crossing the division reconnaissance regiment cleared the neighbouring island of North Beveland with the assistance of the machine guns and heavy mortars of the Toronto Scottish. 52 (Lowland) Division assumed responsibility for the advance upon 2nd Division crossing the causeway, ending 2nd Division's participation in the Scheldt operation 3rd November.

Elements of 4 Special Service Brigade launched a seaborne attack at Westkapelle on Walcheren Island, and with a brigade of 52 (Lowland) Division also crossed the West Scheldt from Breskens in an amphibious attack at Flushing on Walcheren Island 1st November under 2nd Canadian Corps, First Canadian Army. Organized enemy resistance ended 8th November and the last pocket was cleared from Walcheren 10th November freeing the port of Antwerp. Supplies began to flow through the port on the 1st of December 1944, and Antwerp became the main supply port for the Allies in NW Europe.

4th Canadian Armoured Division moved to 1 British Corps, and 1 British Corps of First Canadian Army with 4th Canadian Armoured Division, 49 (West Riding) Division, 104 US Division and 1st Polish Armoured Division under command cleared up to the Hollandschdiep, the lower tributary of the Maas River. This and the clearing of the enemy from the approaches to Antwerp, ended the battle of the Scheldt. 104 US Division returned to under US command and 49 (WR) Division moved under command of Second British Army.

A static period ensued and First Canadian Army prepared to spend the winter on the Maas beginning 8th November 1944 and ending 8th February 1945 when the battle of the Rhineland was launched.

First Canadian Army assumed control of the Nijmegen bridgehead 9th November 1944. 1 British Corps held an extended section of the line and 2nd Canadian Corps took over the Nijmegen Sector from 30 Corps of Second British Army, with 2nd Canadian Infantry Division, 3rd Canadian Infantry Division, 50 (N) Division, 101 US Airborne Division and 82 US Airborne Division in the line. 3rd Canadian Infantry Division relieved 82 US Airborne Division, 49 (WR) Division and 51 (H) Division relieved 50 (N) Division and 101 US Airborne Division.

The static role was interrupted by the Ardennes offensive in December and the Corps alignment was adjusted as a precautionary measure. 30 Corps was placed under Second British Army temporarily and returned to under command First Canadian Army in readiness for the attack into Germany. Headquarters First Canadian Army was given responsibility for the offensive and 30 British Corps was to lead the attack with 51 (Highland) Division, 53 (Welsh) Division, 15 (Scottish) Division, 2nd and 3rd Canadian Infantry Divisions under command.

A week later 2nd Canadian Corps which had been protecting 30 Corps left flank, moved into the line and 2nd and 3rd Canadian Divisions returned to under command. 43 (Wessex) Division and 52 (Lowland) Division moved up to join the 30 Corps attack.

As 2nd Canadian Corps battled its way forward each brigade of 2nd and 3rd Canadian Infantry Divisions met fierce enemy resistance. The battalions of 7th Canadian Infantry Brigade took part in a bitter battle in clearing Moyland Wood, and in capturing the nearby Goch-Calcar road 4th Brigade of 2nd Division added to its battle honours. 5th and 6th Brigades of 2nd Canadian

Infantry Division, 8th and 9th Brigades of 3rd Canadian Infantry Division each successfully completed a phase of the operation against a determined enemy. The infantry divisions were ably assisted by tanks of 2nd Canadian Armoured Brigade. Sergeant Aubrey Cosens of the Queen's Own Rifles of Canada (3rd Div) was posthumously awarded the Victoria Cross for heroism in action 26th February 1945, and Major F. A. Tilston of 2nd Division's Essex Scottish was awarded the Victoria Cross for heroism 1st March 1945.

The junction of First Canadian Army and Ninth US Army was effected on the 3rd of March 1945. The Guards Armoured Division rejoined the battle on the 4th and 53 (Welsh) Division was relieved by 52 (Lowland) Division. The Corps front narrowed to a two division advance and as the line shortened 30 Corps Headquarters transferred its divisions to 2nd Canadian Corps, then on the 8th of March 30 Corps returned to under the command of Second British Army for future operations.

On the 9th March XVI US Corps came under First Canadian Army for the final drive to the Rhine at Wesel. Divisions were ordered to stand down as the bridgehead shrunk and the battle for the Rhineland ended 11th March 1945 with 21 Army Group's First Canadian Army and Ninth US Army along the Rhine from the German border near Nijmegen, to Dusseldorf. Organized German resistance west of the Rhine ended by the 25th March as First, Third and Seventh US Armies, and First French Army closed to the Rhine.

On the 21 Army Group sector it was Second British Army's turn to enter the offensive with First Canadian Army in a holding role during the initial operation. 9th Canadian Infantry Brigade (The Highland Brigade) of 3rd Canadian Infantry Division was given the honour of accompanying 51 (Highland) Division of Scotland in the Rhine crossing.

Crossings were made in the area of Wesel and Rees with Ninth US Army on the right and Second British Army on the left. Corporal F.G. Topham of 1st Canadian Parachute Battalion, 6th British Airborne Division was awarded the Victoria Cross for heroism 24th March 1945 beyond the Rhine.

2nd Canadian Corps under Second British Army was to play a role similar to the 30 Corps role with First Canadian Army in the Rhineland battle and moved into the left sector of the bridgehead across the Rhine where 3rd Canadian Infantry Division returned to under command. First Canadian Army prepared to enter the second phase of the attack.

Headquarters 1st Canadian Corps arrived from Italy and came under command Headquarters First Canadian Army 15th March 1945, with 49 (West Riding) Division as a component, and remained in the Arnhem area.

2nd Canadian Infantry Division moved into the bridgehead across the Rhine on the 28th and 29th March to spearhead 2nd Canadian Corps advance northward with 3rd Canadian Infantry Division on its left and 4th Canadian Armoured Division on the right.

Headquarters First Canadian Army took control of the 2nd Canadian Corps drive beyond the Rhine 1st April and 1st Canadian Corps also came under command replacing 1 British Corps which had served as a component of First Canadian Army since July 1944 in Normandy. The British Corps returned to Second British Army and First Canadian Army was now predominently Canadian in content.

Ninth US Army departed 21 Army Group, returning to under US command 3rd and 4th April 1945. 1st Polish Armoured Division returned to 2nd Canadian Corps 8th April for the drive to the North Sea and Special Air Service troops harassed the enemy in a number of areas. The Armoured Car Regiments of 1st and 2nd Canadian Corps and the reconnaissance regiments of the infantry divisions ranged far and wide, contributing greatly to the speed of the advance, as did the "Kangaroos" of 1st Canadian Armoured Personnel Carrier Regiment, the "Buffaloes" of 79 British Armoured Division, and "Rams" of 2nd Corps anti-tank regiment.

49 (WR) Division cleared the south-eastern end of the Nijmegen Island simultaneous with 3rd Canadian Infantry Division's operation east of the Rhine 2nd and 3rd April and 5th Canadian Armoured Division cleared the western section of the "Island". Upon completion of this phase of the operation 1st Canadian Corps was given the task of clearing the enemy from West Holland.

1st Canadian Infantry Division was temporarily placed under 2nd Canadian Corps for an attack across the Ijssel river 11th April to capture Apeldoorn and the high ground leading to Arnhem where 1st Canadian Corps with 49 (WR) Division under command, was ready to attack.

Supported by its own divisional Artillery, 1st Canadian AGRA medium regiments and 11th Army Field Regiment RCA, 1st Rocket Battery RCA and 1st Canadian Armoured Brigade, 49 (West Riding) Division crossed the Ijssel late on the 12th establishing a bridgehead which was enlarged and Arnhem captured on the 14th.

1st Canadian Infantry Division reverted to under command of 1st Canadian Corps 13th April and the Corps objective was revised to clearing the enemy from Western Holland between the Ijssel and the Grebbe Line. 1st Division advanced from the vicinity of Deventer to Apeldoorn and captured the city on the 17th March.

5th Canadian Armoured Division received orders to make a quick thrust north to the Ijsselmeer and the advance from Arnhem was begun 15th March, clearing Otterloo on the 16th. Division Headquarters moved to Otterloo and became involved in the "Battle of Otterloo" the night of the 17th when a group of Germans attempted an escape through the extended line of the Division at Otterloo. The Irish Regiment of Canada, Headquarter's tanks, 3rd Medium Regiment RA, and 17th Field Regiment RCA whose gunners fired the 25 pounders over open sights, repulsed the attack.

Barneveld was occupied on the 17th and 5th Canadian Armoured Division meeting stiff resistance enroute, reached the Ijsselmeer on the 18th to complete the operation and 1st Canadian Infantry Division assumed responsibility for the area on the 19th. 5th Division moved to the northeast for duty with 2nd Canadian Corps.

One brigade of 49 (WR) Division cleared a section of the main route from Arnhem to Zutphen to effect a junction with 1st Canadian Infantry Division. Two brigades advanced westward with support of 1st Canadian Armoured Brigade directed toward Ede, and along the bank of the Neder Rijn River. Ede, Bennekom and Wageningen were liberated on the 17th as the approaches to the Grebbe Line were reached.

Following its relief of 5th Canadian Armoured Division 19th April, 1st Canadian Infantry Division advanced from Barneveld toward Amersfoort, Nijkerk, and the Ijsselmeer, and was approaching the Eem River toward Hilversum on the 21st of April. Upon clearing the full length of the Grebbe Line 1st Canadian Corps advance ground to a halt to await further orders for the advance into Western Holland.

2nd Canadian Corps of First Canadian Army operating to the right of 1st Canadian Corps from north-eastern Netherlands to the Weser River below Bremen, continued its drive northward with 2nd, 3rd, 4th, 5th Canadian Divisions, 1st Polish Armoured Division and 3 British Division (from 28th April) under command, supported by 2nd Canadian Armoured Brigade and 4 British AGRA.

The relief of 3rd Canadian Infantry Division by 5th Canadian Armoured Division was completed on the 24th and 5th Canadian Armoured Division now with 2nd Canadian Corps, assumed responsibility for the provinces of Friesland, Groningen, Drenthe, and the northern portion of Overijssel to the Dutch-German border.

5th Division's 11th Infantry Brigade began to reduce the Delfzijl pocket with the aid of the division's armoured brigade and artillery. The attack on Delfzijl was coordinated with 3rd Canadian Infantry Division's attack on Emdem. Delfzijl was captured 1st May as 5th Canadian Armoured Division successfully completed its last major operation of the war.

3rd Canadian Infantry Division captured Leer then crossed the Ems and Leda rivers and advanced deep into the Emdem-Wilhelmshaven peninsula. 8th Brigade approached Aurich on the Ems-Jade canal 4th May when operations were suspended. 27th Armoured Regiment (The Sherbrooke Fusiliers Regiment) operated with the division during this operation.

1st Polish Armoured Division and 4th Canadian Armoured Division under First Canadian Army also penetrated deep into the Emdem-Wilhelmshaven peninsula over terrain most unsuitable for armoured vehicles. 1st Polish Armoured Division cleared to within two miles of Neuenburg 4th May. 4th Canadian Armoured Division advanced from its fiercely contested bridgehead over the Kusten canal and entered Bad Zwischenahn 30th April. By the 4th of May elements of the division had advanced to the outskirts of Beckenhausen, north of Oldenburg. A force under 2nd Canadian Armoured Brigade comprising 6th Armoured Regiment (1st Hussars), 1st Armoured Car Regiment (Royal Canadian Dragoons), 18th Armoured Car Regiment (12th Manitoba Dragoons), and the Belgian SAS serving with 4th Canadian Armoured Division reached Grabstede by the 4th of May.

2nd Canadian Infantry Division in its advance northward reached Groningen and on the 18th of April was whisked away to the right flank of First Canadian Army between 4th Canadian Armoured Division and 43 (W) Division of Second British Army for the advance toward Bremen. As 5th Canadian Infantry Brigade closed to the Weser River above Bremen 4th Brigade cleared Falkenburg, then with 6th Brigade which had captured Kirchhatten, advanced on Oldenburg. Oldenburg fell to 4th and 6th Brigades 3rd May and as the brigades advanced beyond the city on the following day operations were suspended with the "Cease Fire" imminent.

On the 1st Canadian Corps front operations had been temporarily suspended at the Grebbe Line as arrangements were being made to supply the starving people in the German occupied area of Western Holland. Meetings on the 28th April permitted food packages to be dropped by air immediately and the land delivery began 2nd May. Active operations for 1st Canadian Corps ended at the Grebbe Line. Active operations for First Canadian Army in NW Europe ended 5th May and the 8th of May 1945 was designated "VE" Day.

First Canadian Army had contributed greatly to the defeat of the enemy in NW Europe bringing honour to its multi-national components which included Canadian, British, Polish, US, Belgian, Czechoslovak, Netherlands, French, and Norwegian (the Norwegian troops had served with No. 10 (Inter-Allied) Commando).

The evacuation of the defeated enemy from the Netherlands to a concentration area in the Emdem-Wilhelmshaven peninsula was begun 25th May with Headquarters First Canadian Army administrative staff supervising, coordinating and controlling the evacuation, selecting routes, sites of transit camps along the way and providing stores.

5th Canadian Armoured Division supervised the march from the Ijsselmeer causeway to the German border where 2nd Canadian Corps took control. On the 15th of June Headquarters 2nd Canadian Corps was relieved of its duty by Headquarters 30 British Corps District.

During the early phase of disbandment British operational troops departed from under command of First Canadian Army and all Canadian units except the reconstituted 3rd Canadian Infantry Division, Canadian Army Occupational Force, concentrated in the Netherlands early in June.

Headquarters 2nd Canadian Corps disbanded 25th June, Headquarters 1st Canadian Corps disbanded 17th July and Headquarters First Canadian Army ceased operations 30th July. Headquarters of the divisions disbanded in September, October, November and December.

Personnel proceeded to the Canadian Army Pacific Force, the Canadian Army Occupational Force, departed in priority drafts to Canada or were posted to one of five divisional groups for the return to Canada.

Headquarters First Canadian Army which had ceased operations 30th July 1945, received authorization to disband under General Order 111/46 (Effective 15th February 1946).

Headquarters 3rd Canadian Infantry Division, Canadian Army Occupational Force disbanded 20th June 1946 and Canadian Section, Headquarters British Army of the Rhine (North West Europe) became responsible for the Canadians remaining on the Continent.

* * *

Headquarters First Army Troops —

Headquarters First Army Troops mobilized under General Order 297/44 (Effective 2nd March 1944) and received authorization to disband under General Order 96/46 (Effective 8th January 1946).

* * *

Headquarters of 1st Corps CASF — Serial 1 — Italy & NW Europe

Headquarters of 1st Corps CASF (Including Headquarters Corps Artillery), Serial 1, mobilized under General Order 135/39, 1st September 1939.

A Canadian Corps Headquarters however was not required until the 25th of December 1940 when the Canadian Corps was formed in England with 1st

Canadian Division, Corps Troops, and the recently arrived 2nd Canadian Division under command.

The Canadian troops in England had been serving as a component of 7th Corps, formed 19th July 1940 and disbanded with the forming of the Canadian Corps.

Being the senior Canadian Formation in England the Headquarters found itself responsible for each Canadian Unit as it arrived in England. The Headquarters was given the task of training infantry and reconnaissance personnel in anti-tank weapons, establishing an artillery range, and supervised the tradesmen requirements for all artillery units in the U.K. under instructions from CMHQ.

In November 1941 Headquarters 1st Canadian Corps moved to Haywards Heath, Sussex, and formed part of South Eastern Army, defending the Sussex coast against possible German invasion.

The artillery Order of Battle in the spring of 1942 included: RCA of 1st and 2nd Canadian Infantry Divisions, CCCA — New Haven (four coast artillery regiments), 1st and 5th Medium Regiments RCA, 8th and 11th Canadian Army Field Regiments, 56 Heavy Regiment RA — with under command X and Y Super Heavy Batteries, 1st Canadian Survey Regiment, No. 1 Calibration Troop RCA and 1 Canadian CBO Staff.

CCMA was directly under command of CMHQ and assumed responsibility of 7th Canadian Army Field Regiment, 7th Canadian Anti-Tank Regiment and 2nd Canadian Medium Regiment. 1st Canadian Anti-Aircraft Brigade at Colchester handled all anti-aircraft units.

The need for an enlarged headquarters was evident with the arrival in England of 3rd and 5th Divisions and 1st Army Tank Brigade plus ancillary units during 1941, followed by 4th Division in 1942.

Headquarters First Canadian Army came into being 1st April 1942, to comprise two corps. 1st Canadian Survey Regiment moved under command of First Canadian Army to become Army Troops, and Army Headquarters as senior formation assumed a number of responsibilities being administered to by the Corps. 1st Light Anti-Aircraft Regiment RCA and 7th Light Anti-Aircraft Regiment RCA came under command. Headquarters 1st Canadian Anti-Aircraft Brigade moved down from Colchester but remained under Anti-Aircraft Command in an operational role.

The existing Canadian Corps became 1st Canadian Corps. Headquarters 2nd Canadian Corps came into existence early 1943, authorized under General Order 281/43 (Effective 14th January 1943), and Headquarters 1st Corps Artillery (included in Serial 1), disbanded under General Order 336/43 (Effective 14th January 1943).

Departure to the Mediterranean of 1st Canadian Infantry Division and 1st Canadian Army Tank Brigade for the invasion of Sicily 10th July 1943 lightened the load of 1st Canadian Corps. Before the end of the year however, the Corps too found itself sailing to assume an operational role in Italy.

Headquarters sailed from Greenock, Scotland on board the Edmund B. Alexander, 29th October 1943 and disembarded at Augusta, Sicily on the 9th of November 1943, settling in at Taormina. On the 9th of January 1944 Corps Headquarters moved by transport to Messina and crossed to the Italian mainland by landing craft, then by box car to Altamura, Italy.

On the 28th January 1944, Headquarters 1st Canadian Corps moved north to Rocca San Giovanni in the Ortona Sector on the Adriatic coast and assumed an operational role 31st January-1st February 1944 in relief of 5 British Corps. 1st Canadian Corps was to serve in a defensive role north of Ortona with 1st Canadian Infantry Division and 8th Indian Division under command. 5th Canadian Armoured Division joined the Corps later in the month and 8th Indian Division moved to 13 British Corps. During March and April 1944 1st Canadian Corps moved to the Foggia Plain for a period of rest and training for the forthcoming Liri Valley battle.

The assault on the Gustav Line began 11th May 1944 with 1st Canadian Armoured Brigade and the Canadian Artillery in support. 8th Indian Division of 13 British Corps breached the Gustav Line and 1st Canadian Infantry Division of 1st Canadian Corps which had been in army reserve for Eighth Army moved forward on the 16th in relief of the Indian Division. 1st Canadian Infantry Division clawed its way to the Hitler Line and penetrated the line near Pontecorvo west of Cassino on the 23rd of May following stiff fighting. 5th Canadian Armoured Division entered the breach in the line and continued the 1st Corps advance into the Liri Valley.

On the 4th of June Rome was captured by US forces and 1st Canadian Corps having reached Agnani, its objective in the advance toward Rome, passed into army reserve. Two days later, 6th June 1944, word was received of the Allied invasion of Normandy. During this period in army reserve 1st Canadian Corps assumed a new look as 12th Canadian Infantry Brigade was formed of existing regiments, 4th Reconnaissance Regiment (4th Princess Louis Dragoon Guards) from 1st Division, 1st Light Anti-Aircraft Regiment (Lanark and Renfrew Scottish Regiment) from 1st Corps, The Westminster Regiment (Motor) from 5th Division which also provided 12th Independent Machine Gun Company (The Princess Louise Fusiliers), and 11th Army Field Regiment RCA of Army Troops became 11th Field Regiment RCA to provide the field artillery support for the new brigade in 5th Canadian Armoured Division.

The advance continued beyond Rome toward the Gothic Line and 1st Canadian Corps returned to action in the Adriatic Sector 24th August. For this attack by Eighth Army 1st Canadian Corps was in the centre, the Polish Corps on the coast to the right and 5 British Corps on the left. The CCRA 1st

Canadian Corps had under direct command Corps Troops Artillery, 1st Canadian AGRA, 5th Canadian Armoured Division and 4 British Division Artilleries. 1st Canadian Corps had British, Greek, New Zealand and Polish troops under command at various times.

1st Division in the first phase of the operation was to secure a bridgehead over the Metauro River, then advance ten miles to the Foglia River where the main defences of the Gothic Line began on the far bank. Four assaulting battalions crossed the Metauro before midnight 25th August and upon reaching the Foglia River 3rd Brigade relieved 1st Brigade and 5th Division's 11th Brigade entered the drive in relief of 1st Division's 2nd Brigade to win the distinction of penetrating the Gothic Line.

Following the breakthrough of the Gothic Line units of 1st Canadian Corps crossed the Conca River on the 2nd of September and having taken over the coastal sector to the sea from the Polish Corps the Canadian Divisions prepared to crack the Rimini Line.

From the 5th to 22nd September RCA 1st Canadian Corps utilized the firepower of seven Royal Navy ships operating off Rimini. The Air OP, ground FOO and Arty R, directed the fire of the 4.7 inch and 6 inch naval guns.

1st Canadian Corps assumed the responsibility of capturing the seaward side of the Coriano Ridge which was captured by 5th Division 13th September and Coriano was cleared on the 14th. 4 British Division took over the 5th Canadian Armoured Division front on the Corps left and with 1st Canadian Infantry Division advanced to the Marano River.

1st Canadian Division secured a bridgehead over the Marano River on the 14th and met fierce enemy resistance before capturing San Lorenzo and San Martino on the ridge before the Ausa River and the San Fortunato Ridge beyond, which formed part of the Rimini Line. 4 British Division employed the use of artificial moonlight in its attack on the Rimini Line and in crossing the Ausa River 17th/18th September.

Units of 1st Canadian Infantry Division reached the crest of San Fortunato Ridge at daybreak 20th September and during the morning of the 21st crossed the Marecchia River. The Greek Mountain Brigade advancing to the right under command of 1st Canadian Corps entered Rimini the same morning. The crossing of the Marecchia ended the battle of the ridges, the battle in which 657 Air OP Squadron RAF had provided an invaluable service.

On the 22nd September 2nd New Zealand Division which had relieved 1st Canadian Infantry Division on the right and on the 23rd, 5th Canadian Armoured Division in relief of 4 British Division on its left between the two main highways, moved into their respective bridgeheads across the Marecchia to continue the 1st Canadian Corps drive toward Ravenna and the north.

5th Division's 12th Brigade crossed the Uso River on the 26th of September then 11th Brigade in relief crossed the Salto and advanced to the Fiumicino as the rainy season began, halting the Corps operations at the east bank of the river from San Metauro to the sea. The artillery of the two armoured divisions however remained quite active and were joined by the 1st Division artillery 1st October.

During the pause at the Fiumicino the Canadian Corps front was enlarged to eight miles and now included both main highways. 1st Canadian Infantry Division relieved 56 British Division in the enlarged area with 2nd New Zealand Division on its right and Cumberlandforce under Headquarters 5th Canadian Armoured Brigade covered the right flank as the bulk of 5th Canadian Armoured Division passed into army reserve.

1st Canadian Infantry Division entered 56 Division's bridgehead across the Fiumicino at Savignano and began moving forward on the 11th October. The enemy resisted stubbornly at the Scolo Regussa and at the Pisciatello. Cesena fell on the 19th and the Savio was reached on the 20th by 1st Canadian Infantry Division with 2nd New Zealand Division and Cumberlandforce keeping pace on the right. 1st Div began crossing the Savio the evening of the 20th and Private E.A. Smith of the Seaforths was to earn the Victoria Cross during the action in the bridgehead on the 21st October.

Artillery of the New Zealand Division fired in support of 1st Division's crossing of the Savio River then passed into army reserve and 5th Canadian Armoured Division in relief, with Cumberlandforce under command, returned to action 22nd/23rd October. 5th Division units crossed the Savio on the 24th establishing a bridgehead at Mensa, reached the Bevano on the 25th and advanced to the Conca with Cumberlandforce conforming on the right.

Upon reaching the Conca 1st Canadian Infantry Division and 5th Canadian Armoured Division passed into army reserve with 1st Canadian Corps 28th October. Porterforce was formed at this time and Cumberlandforce phased out. Porterforce became responsible for the Eighth Army right flank. The composition of the force was changed periodically and included a number of Canadian units.

Eighth Army's plan for a concerted effort was launched on a three corps front with 1st Canadian Corps on the right, 5 British Corps centre and the Polish Corps on the left. 1st and 5th Canadian Divisions entered 10th Indian Division's bridgehead across the Montone River and launched their attack 2nd December.

Spitbombers of the Desert Air Force joined in the attack by strafing and bombing enemy positions ahead of the artillery curtain of fire. 3rd Brigade led the 1st Div attack as 12th Brigade of 5th Division cleared the west bank of the

Montone River to San Pancrazio in readiness for bridging operations. 3rd Brigade making slow progress against a determined enemy entered Russi on the 3rd and reached the Lamone on the 4th. The attempted river crossing in the afternoon cost 1st Brigade heavily.

5th Division in addition to clearing the banks of the Montone were to advance to the Lamone, capturing Godo enroute. Elements of the Division were directed toward Ravenna which was captured on the 4th December by 4th Princess Louise Dragoon Guards, and 27th Lancers (British) of Porterforce, also under 5th Div. Italian Partisans, too, made a valuable contribution to the fighting in the 1st Canadian Corps coastal area.

By the 6th of December 5th Division had reached the Lamone on a five mile front. At the Lamone 1st Canadian Corps awaited favourable weather for the river crossing on a two-division front. Four miles beyond the Lamone the Senio River flowed and was the final goal of the Corps operation. However a series of strongly defended water barriers between the two rivers faced the advancing troops, the Fosso Vecchio, the Canale Naviglio and the Fosso Munio, plus the Fosso Vetro for 5th Div.

5th Div moved off on the 10th December crossing the Lamone River near Villanova and Borgo di Villanova. On the 11th counter-attacks on the north end of the bridgehead were beaten off and the advance proceeded favorably until reaching the Naviglio canal on the 12th December and the crossing was delayed until the 14th. The struggle continued over the Fosso Munio.

1st Div crossed the Lamone 10th December at the wrecked Bagnacavallo road bridge at the point of its earlier reverse, then crossed the Naviglio canal the night of 12th/13th December and clung to the bridgehead against fierce attacks. The vicious fighting continued to the banks of the Senio River which was reached by both Canadian Divisions on the 20th December 1944.

On the 30th December the decision was made to go on the defensive for the winter and prepare for the spring offensive, however, there were still some areas in the 1st Canadian Corps sector leading to the Senio River still to be cleared of the enemy before a satisfactory winter defence line could be established.

The Granarolo salient on the Canadian Corps left boundary was attacked on the 3rd January 1945 by 1st Canadian Infantry Division. 56 British Division and 7 Armoured Brigade joined the attack on the 4th and the salient was eliminated on the 5th of January.

An area between Ravenna and the Valli di Comacchio on the Corps right was attacked 2nd January 1945 by 5th Canadian Armoured Division. Conventello defences were first to receive attention, the Canale di Bonifica crossed on the 4th, Sant Alberto cleared on the 5th in one thrust, then in another thrust along the Canale di Bonifica, Mandriole, and Casal Borsetti on the coast were captured by the 6th January. The area between the canal and Valli di Comacchio was cleared as was the coastal belt north from Porto Corsini.

With the enemy cleared from both flanks the units of 1st Canadian Corps settled into the winter line along a 27 mile front and active patrolling was initiated by both the Canadians and the enemy. The relief of brigades and battalions was begun and the Cremona battle group joined 1st Canadian Corps 14th January in relief of 5th Canadian Armoured Division as the division moved into army reserve.

Corps Headquarters received instructions to move into army group reserve 10th February with 1st Canadian Infantry Division becoming responsible for the Corps front. 1st Division remaining in the Senio Line came under command on 5 British Crops 16th February and in a sharp skirmish the night of 24th/25th February repelled an enemy attack. The relief of 1st Canadian Infantry Division by 8th Indian Division began on the 23rd February with the last Brigade being relieved on the 27th February 1945.

Upon receiving notice of its transfer from Italy to NW Europe Headquarters 1st Canadian Corps began the long move from Ravenna to Naples by road 13th February and sailed for Marseilles, France 22nd February, disembarking on the 24th. The Headquarters travelled in convoy through France to Renaix, Belgium, coming under Headquarters First Canadian Army and given responsibility for the left sector of 21 Army Group.

5th Canadian Armoured Division sailed from Leghorn 15th February and upon arrival in NW Europe 12th Canadian Infantry Brigade was disbanded as the division reverted to the official armoured division organization. 1st Armoured Car Regiment (The Royal Canadian Dragoons) returned from 1st Canadian Infantry Division and 1st Light Anti-Aircraft Regiment (Lanark and Renfrew Scottish) RCA once more became the Corp Light Anti-Aircraft Regiment as the components of 12th Brigade returned to their original formations.

1st Canadian Armoured Brigade returned to the fold having served with 13 British Corps during most of the Italian campaign. The armoured brigade departed Italy 8th March from Leghorn.

1st Canadian Infantry Division sailed from Leghorn, Italy, 7th March and came under command 2nd Canadian Corps for its first action in NW Europe 7th April 1945, returning to under command 1st Canadian Corps 13th April.

Headquarters 1st Canadian Corps became operational 15th March 1945 in Holland with 49 (West Riding) Division under command and assumed responsibility for the front from Arnhem west to the sea. 74th Anti-Aircraft Brigade came under command, followed by 5th Canadian Armoured Division and 1st Canadian Infantry Division.

With the capture of Arnhem and the opening of a route to Emmerich as the objective the operations of 1st Canadian Corps were to be coordinated with the 2nd Canadian Corps plan to attack the Ijssel defences from the rear to capture Apeldoorn and the high ground between Apeldoorn and Arnhem.

In readiness 1st Canadian Corps began the task of clearing the enemy from the northern section of the island between the Waal and Neder Rijn. On the 2nd April 49 (West Riding) Division presently holding the southern part of the island with a number of Canadian units under command began clearing the south-east sector, then with 5th Canadian Armoured Division began clearing the remainder of the island which was accomplished 3rd April and the enemy driven back to the north bank of the Neder Rijn.

Deteriorating conditions on the island necessitated attacking Arnhem from the east across the Ijssel in the vicinity of Westervoort. During the attack on the 12th April, 5th Canadian Armoured Division remained on the island and carried out diversionary measures in the Driel area. The capture of Arnhem was completed on the 14th and 49 Div was ordered to open the road from Arnhem to Zutphen then clear the bank of the Neder Rijn to the Grebbe Line, capturing Wageningen and Ede.

5th Canadian Armoured Division was relieved of its role on the island by 1st Canadian Armoured Brigade with two battalions of 1st Belgian Infantry Brigade and a composite Canadian group under command. 5th Div was directed to pass through 49 Div bridgehead and drive north thirty miles to the Ijsselmeer, then pass under command of 2nd Canadian Corps for duty in north-east Holland. 1st Canadian Corps now comprised 1st Canadian Infantry Division and 49 (WR) Division.

On the 11th April 1st Canadian Infantry Division under 2nd Canadian Corps began its attack across the Ijssel River and as it neared Apeldoorn 13th April the division reverted to under the command of 1st Canadian Corps. Apeldoorn was cleared on th 17th and from Apeldoorn 1st Div was directed west in a line parallel to 49 (WR) Division to an area between Barneveld and Voorthuizen where the division relieved 5th Canadian Armoured Division for its role with 2nd Canadian Corps, and continued the advance toward Amersfoort and the Grebbe Line on the Eem River, where the Corps was instructed to hold the line until receiving further orders.

A temporary truce was arranged to permit the delivery of supplies to the starving people of western Holland. The supplies came by air, land and sea and while the truce was in effect the enemy in NW Europe surrendered unconditionally with the 8th of May 1945 being designated "VE" Day.

Headquarters moved to Hilversum, Holland, and controlled the move of all German forces in Holland back to Germany via the Zuider Zee.

The run-down of Canadian units was begun and Headquarters of 1st Corps CASF, received authorization to disband under General Order 388/45 (Effective 17th July 1945).

*   *   *

1st Cdn Infantry Division — Serial 2 — Sicily, Italy & NW Europe

Serial 2, Headquarters of 1st Division, CASF, was named as part of the Canadian Active Service Force under General Order 135/39, 1st September 1939.

The Division was to comprise Headquarters of 1st Division, CASF, Serial 2, 1st Hussars, CASF, Serial 3, Headquarters of 1st Divisional Artillery, RCA, CASF, Serial 4, Headquarters of 1st, 2nd and 3rd Field Brigades RCA, CASF, each with four component batteries, 1st Anti-Tank Regiment RCA, CASF (without batteries).

Divisional Engineers included headquarters, one field park company and three field companies, Divisional Signals contained headquarters and three companies. Divisional RCASC included headquarters, an ammunition company, petrol company and supply column. RCAMC contained three field ambulances and a field hygiene section. No. 1 Provost Company (RCMP), a postal unit and No. 1 Employment Platoon, CASF, was included. A number of Corps Troops, Army Troops and Lines of Communication Troops also mobilized with 1st Division, CASF.

Each infantry brigade included one Permanent Force battalion and a brigade machine gun battalion. 1st Brigade comprised The Royal Canadian Regiment (PF), 48th Highlanders of Canada, The Hastings and Prince Edward Regiment, and The Toronto Scottish Regiment (MG).

2nd Brigade included The Princess Patricia's Canadian Light Infantry (PF), The Seaforth Highlanders of Canada, The Edmonton Regiment, and The Saskatoon Light Infantry (MG).

3rd Brigade was composed of Royal 22e Regiment (PF), The West Nova Scotia Regiment, The Carleton and York Regiment, and the Royal Montreal Regiment (MG).

Headquarters of 1st Division, CASF, departed for overseas on board the Aquitania in the First Flight, 10th December 1939, and arrived at Greenock, Scotland, 17th December 1939. The Division proceeded by troop trains to Aldershot, Hampshire, in the south of England.

The Second Flight departed Canada 22nd December 1939, and arrived in Scotland, 30th December 1939, carrying the balance of the Division. The Third Flight carrying Ancillary Troops and Technical Troops sailed the latter part of January and arrived in Scotland 7th February 1940.

Two battalions of 1st Canadian Infantry Division's 2nd Canadian Infantry Brigade were selected for an attack on Trondhjem Fiord, Norway, April 1940, which in turn was cancelled.

The next excursion planned for the Division was a trip to France by 1st Canadian Infantry Brigade Group in June 1940, as part of the "Second B.E.F.". The vehicle group crossed to Brest, France, 12th June and the main body of 1st Brigade Group landed early on the 14th and proceeded to an assembly area approximately halfway between Brest and Paris.

The disintegrating situation in France brought about the recommendation that no further troops be brought from England, and the withdrawal of those not directly under French Orders. 1st Canadian Brigade Group received orders to return to England via Brest. Vehicles were to be destroyed prior to boarding, however, 1st Field Regiment managed to bring a full complement of guns, less vehicles, back to England.

Brigade Headquarters and The 48th Highlanders of Canada in the leading train boarded ship at St. Malo and disembarked on the 16th at Southampton. Units leaving from Brest departed on the 17th and disembarked at Plymouth and Falmouth.

The two brigade groups which had remained in England with their equipment, along with the artillery units, machine gun battalions and supporting units, prepared to repel the certain attack.

The Canadian Force, with the exception of 1st Brigade, moved from Aldershot 23rd June to the Oxford area to serve in a mobile reserve role directly under GHQ Home Forces.

Brigade reconnaissance squadrons were formed with a self-contained troop in each of the infantry battalions of the infantry brigades. The ancillary artillery units and the machine gun battalions formed a reserve brigade group. The immobilized 1st Brigade remained at Aldershot until the 16th of July.

This organization was soon bolstered by the rebuilt British units and on the 21st of July 1940, 7th Corps, to be commanded by General A.G.L. McNaughton came into being and as components the Canadian units moved south into Surrey. General G.R. Pearkes, V.C. became GOC 1st Canadian Division.

The arrival overseas of 2nd Canadian Division during 1940 made the forming of the Canadian Corps possible. The Canadian Corps came into being on the 25th of December 1940, and 7th Corps disbanded.

Divisional machine gun battalions replaced brigade machine gun battalions and The Saskatoon Light Infantry (MG) remained with 1st Division. The Toronto Scottish Regiment (MG) became 2nd Division machine gun battalion, and The Royal Montreal Regiment (MG) became Canadian Corps machine gun battalion.

Headquarters 2nd Light Anti-Aircraft Regiment RCA, CASF, was authorized under General Order 184/40 and joined 1st Division in England in 1941 as divisional light anti-aircraft regiment. 4th Princess Louise Dragoon Guards of Ottawa incorporated the brigade reconnaissance squadrons and became the divisional reconnaissance battalion.

Detachments from The Edmonton Regiment, The Saskatoon Light Inantry (MG), RCE, signals, medical and a pay detachment landed on the Norwegian island of Spitsbergen 25th August 1941, remaining until the 3rd September during which time the group evacuated the inhabitants and destroyed coal facilities, communications and the harbour, then returned to England.

Headquarters 1st Division, Serial 2, was redesignated Headquarters 1st Infantry Division, Serial 2, under General Order 283/43 (Effective 7th January 1943).

The decision to send Canadian units to the Mediterranean theatre saw 1st Canadian Infantry Division and 1st Canadian Army Tank Brigade sail from Scotland 28th June 1943 and land in the assault on the island of Sicily, 10th July 1943 as a component of 30 British Corps, British Eighth Army. With the fall of Sicily the division crossed the Strait of Messina to the Italian mainland 3rd September 1943 with 13 British Corps, British Eighth Army.

3rd Brigade of 1st Canadian Infantry Division and 5th British Division landed in the assault on the toe of Italy. The British division on the left proceeded up the western coastal road. The Canadians moved inland from Reggio and to the right along the coast road to midway along the Gulf of Taranto coastline, then headed north.

From Reggio the pursuit led through Locri, Cantanzaro, Altamura, Gravina, and on to Foggia where the division turned west toward Campobasso, meeting stiffening resistance enroute. Campobasso was captured 14th October by 1st Brigade. 2nd Brigade closed on Vinchiaturo on the left and by the 21st the enemy had been driven beyond the Biferno River. The Biferno was crossed on the 24th and on the 6th of November the division had completed its allotted task.

During November, 3rd Canadian Infantry Brigade with 13 British Corps executed a diversionary attack on the left toward Castel di Sangro and Sant Angelo.

1st Canadian Infantry Division moved to the Adriatic front on the 1st of December 1943 to continue the attack on the enemy winter line and 1st Brigade entered the bridgehead across the Moro River established by 5 British Corps in the advance toward Ortona.

2nd Canadian Infantry Brigade to the left was given the task of crossing the Moro River and capturing San Leonardo and Villa Regatti. The river was crossed on the 6th of December and heavy fighting stalled the advance which was resumed on the 10th.

In the 3rd Brigade sector Captain Paul Triquet of the Royal 22nd Regiment was awarded the Victoria Cross for heroism in the action at Casa Berardi on the 14th of December 1943.

The Seaforth Highlanders of Canada advancing toward the left section of the city and The Loyal Edmonton Regiment advancing toward the right section of the city began the task of clearing Ortona. Both units reached the outskirts of the city on the 20th of December, however, the vicious struggle continued until the 28th of December before the enemy was driven beyond Ortona.

Operation "Timberwolf" and "Timberwolf II" in October and November 1943 transferred Headquarters 1st Canadian Corps, Corps Troops, 5th Canadian (Armoured) Division, 1st Canadian AGRA plus ancillary units to the Mediterranean theatre of operations.

1st and 3rd Canadian Infantry Brigades advancing to the left of Ortona crossed the Riccio River and the Carleton and York Regiment arrived at Torre Mucchia on the 4th of January 1944, ending the winter offensive.

The battalions of 11th Canadian Infantry Brigade, 5th Canadian Armoured Division relieved 3rd Brigade of 1st Canadian Infantry Division north of Ortona 13th January 1944. The holding role developed into an attack across the Riccio River toward the Arielli River. 11th Brigade was in turn relieved by 2nd Canadian Infantry Brigade.

1st Canadian Corps formally relieved 5 British Corps on the Adriatic front 31st January-1st February 1944 and all Canadian units with the exception of 1st Canadian Armoured Brigade were under command by the 9th of February. 1st Canadian Corps was in turn relieved by 5 British Corps 7th March 1944. 1st Canadian Infantry Division remained in the Ortona salient until the 23rd of April when 10th Indian Division assumed responsibility and 1st Division headquarters was established at Vinchiaturo, once again under 1st Canadian Corps.

The Division with 1st Canadian Corps played an important role in a deception scheme during April and May prior to the attack on the Gustav Line. The divisional artillery fired in support of the Eighth Army attack on the Gustav Line which was launched shortly before midnight 11th May. Shortly after midnight the assaulting units of 13 British Corps crossed the Gari River and were successful in penetrating the line.

The breaching of the Gustav Line by 13 Corps on the 12th of May signalled the entry of 1st Canadian Corps to the battle. 1st Brigade on the left and 3rd Brigade on the right joined in the attack on the 16th with 2nd Brigade in reserve as 1st Canadian Infantry Division advanced toward the next formidable defence line barring the route to Rome along the Liri Valley, the Hitler Line.

Upon reaching the outer defences of the Hitler Line 1st and 3rd Canadian Infantry Brigades began feint attacks to the left of 2nd Brigade's Seaforth Highlanders and Princess Patricia's Light Infantry who were delivering the main attack 23rd May. The 48th Highlanders of 1st Brigade, the Carleton and York's of 3rd Brigade and the Seaforths of 2nd Brigade effected a penetration of the Hitler Line. The attack was directed through the Carleton and York breach in the line which was enlarged by the remainder of 3rd Brigade. 5th Canadian Armoured Division entered the enlarged bridgehead to continue the advance to the Melfa River, and on to Ceprano.

"Adams Force" was formed of 4th Reconnaissance Regiment (4th Princess Louise Dragoon Guards) and The Carleton and York Regiment of 1st Division, two squadrons of 1st Armoured Car Regiment (The Royal Canadian Dragoons) of 1st Corps, and one squadron of 12th Armoured Regiment (The Three Rivers Regiment) of 1st Canadian Armoured Brigade. This composite force advanced along the left flank of the 1st Canadian Corps sector to the Melfa River where a bridgehead was established and the West Nova Scotia Regiment crossed the river to strengthen the bridgehead.

The country between the Pofi and Frosinone approached by 5th Canadian Armoured Division in the main advance proved unsuitable for armour and 1st Canadian Infantry Division assumed the lead from 5th Div 31st May and captured Frosinone, then was directed toward Valmontone. On the 4th of June 1st Canadian Corps reached Agnani its objective in the advance to Rome and passed into army reserve. Fifth United States Army entered Rome on the 4th of June 1944, two days before the allied armies stormed ashore in Normandy.

During the absence of the Canadian corps Eighth Army advanced from Rome to the Arno River at Florence. While in army reserve the future of 1st Canadian Corps came under scrutiny and it was decided to add an extra infantry brigade (the 12th) to 5th Canadian Armoured Division. 1st Canadian Infantry Division's 4th Reconnaissance Regiment (4th Princess Louise Dragoon Guards) moved to the new brigade and 1st Armoured Car Regiment (The Royal Canadian Dragoons) joined 1st Division as a replacement from 1st Corps.

On the 5th of August 1944, 1st Canadian Infantry Division moved into the line south of Florence under 13 British Corps and caught up with 1st Canadian Armoured Brigade which had been continuously in action with Eighth Army.

A change of plan saw the division move to the Adriatic front 10th August to prepare for the 1st Canadian Corps attack on the Gothic Line. 1st Canadian Infantry Division in the 1st Canadian Corps initial assault was to establish bridgeheads and crossings over the Metauro River. Shortly before midnight 25th August 1944 the 48th Highlanders and the Royal Canadian Regiment of 1st Brigade and the Princess Patricia's Canadian Light Infantry and the Loyal Edmonton Regiment of 2nd Brigade crossed the Metauro River.

In the second phase of the operation the two battalions of each brigade were joined by the brigade's third battalion, the Hastings and Prince Edward Regiment of 1st Brigade and the Seaforths of 2nd Brigade and set about clearing the heights between the Metauro and the Foglia River which was accomplished by the 29th of August.

The 3rd Canadian Infantry Brigade of 1st Canadian Infantry Division and 11th Canadian Infantry Brigade of 5th Canadian Armoured Division relieved 1st and 2nd Brigades and were given the task of crossing the Foglia River and establishing a bridgehead through the Gothic Line for their division. The attack was launched on the 30th of August and to the Perth Regiment of 5th Canadian Armoured Division went the honour of being first through the Gothic Line.

On the 1st Division front the Princess Patricia's Canadian Light Infantry of 2nd Brigade relieved the West Nova Scotia Regiment of 3rd Brigade and fought through to the objective, completing phase three of the Eighth Army plan. Units of the division advanced to the Conca River and beyond by the 3rd of September.

With the crossing of the Conca River 1st Canadian Infantry Division set its sights on Rimini and the Marecchia River. The division in its advance along the Adriatic coast however had to contend with crossing the Marano River, the Ausa River, San Martino in Monte l'Abate, leading up to the Rimini Line and San Fortunato Ridge between the Rimini Line and the Marecchia River.

The Princess Patricia's Canadian Light Infantry advanced toward Monticello and crossed the Marecchia River the morning of the 21st of September and proceeded to enlarge the bridgehead. The 48th Highlanders of Canada crossed the river toward the village of Celle later in the day and linked up with the PPCLI in the bridgehead. The capture of Celle completed 1st Division's part of the plan. 5th Canadian Armoured Division and 2nd New Zealand Division in relief were to assume the corps advance into the valley of the Po toward Ravenna and the north.

12th Canadian Infantry Brigade of 5th Canadian Armoured Division began the advance 23rd September and crossed the Uso River, then advanced to the Salto River, having been joined by 11th Canadian Infantry Brigade and 1st Armoured Car Regiment (The Royal Canadian Dragoons) enroute, in the advance to the Fiumicino River.

Cumberland Force came into being 10th October upon the crossing of the Fiumicino River, to operate in the 5th Canadian Armoured Division sector along the coast. The composition of the force varied and two dismounted Canadian Recce Regiments, 1st Armoured Car Regiment (The Royal Canadian Dragoons) and 3rd Armoured Reconnaissance Regiment (Governor General's Horse Guards), with tank support of 9th Armoured Regiment (British Columbia Dragoons), played an important role with the force.

1st Canadian Infantry Division returned to action 11th October to continue the drive from Savignano to Cesena and Martorano at the Savio River. In the bridgehead established by 2nd Canadian Infantry Brigade across the Savio River at Pieve Sestina 22nd October 1944 in recognition of his heroism, Private E.A. "Smokey" Smith of The Seaforth Highlanders of Canada was awarded the Victoria Cross.

By the 25th October 1944, 1st Canadian Infantry Division, 5th Canadian Armoured Division and Cumberland Force were across the Senio River. This marked the end of Cumberland Force and on the 28th of October 1st Canadian Corps passed into Eighth Army reserve. 1st Canadian Infantry Division positions along the Ronco River south of Bagnolo were taken over by 5 Corps and "Porterforce", incorporating a number of Canadian units, including 1st Armoured Car Regiment (The Royal Canadian Dragoons) of 1st Division, was formed to protect 5 Corps right flank in relief of 1st Canadian Corps. 1st Division units moved to Riccione and Cattolica during its period of absence from front-line duty.

1st Canadian Corps returned to Eighth Army's right flank for a concerted two army attack delivered by 1st Canadian Corps, 5 British Corps and the Polish Corps, right to left. The attack was to begin from bridgeheads across the Santerno River. The Lamone and Senio Rivers however had to be crossed before the main attack could be launched.

On the 2nd December 1944, 1st Canadian Infantry Division's 3rd Brigade attacked through the 10th Indian Division bridgehead across the Montone River between Albereto and Casa Bettini and attacked toward Russi with 1st Armoured Car Regiment (RCD) protecting the left flank. 5th Canadian Armoured Division's 12th Brigade attacked to the right of 1st Division, and Ravenna was captured on the 4th of December.

In the 1st Canadian Corps assault the Lamone River was crossed by both

Canadian divisions 10th and 11th December then stiffening enemy resistance, the weather and numerous waterways combined to slow the advance. However, by the 21st December the Canadians had closed to the Senio River which was 1st Canadian Corps goal in the operation. Early in the new year 1st Div cleared a salient on the Corps left flank and 5th Div cleared a salient along the right flank then settled into the 1st Canadian Corps second winter line at the Senio River.

On the 14th January the Italian Cremona battle group relieved 5th Canadian Armoured Division and the division moved into army reserve. Corps Headquarters followed 5th Div into army reserve 10th February and 1st Canadian Infantry Division became responsible for the Corps front until 5 British Corps assumed responsibility on the 16th. 1st Division's 2nd Brigade repelled a sharp enemy attack the night of 24th/25th February, the last action for the division on the Senio front upon its relief by 8th Indian Division which was begun on the 23rd and completed on the 27th February 1945.

The transfer of 1st Canadian Corps to NW Europe saw 1st Canadian Infantry Division proceed to Leghorn in March 1945 to board LSTs for the crossing to Marseilles, France. Twenty months had passed since its assault on the island of Sicily with the famous British Eighth Army, now new adventure beckoned under First Canadian Army in NW Europe.

The division travelled by road in convoy and congregated in Belgium, then on the 3rd of April moved to the Reichswald Forest in Germany to bivouac awaiting its commitment to battle.

1st Canadian Infantry Division came under command of 2nd Canadian Corps and on the 7th of April proceeded to a concentration area east of Zutphen in readiness for its attack across the Ijssel River to capture Apeldoorn.

2nd Brigade's PPCLI and Seaforth Highlanders led the advance across the Ijssel River on the 11th, establishing a bridgehead for 1st Division's advance into western Holland. 1st Brigade directed toward Apeldoorn passed through 2nd Brigade on the 12th followed by 3rd Brigade, then on the 13th, 1st Canadian Infantry Division returned to under command of 1st Canadian Corps and the Corps objective was revised to the clearing of the enemy from western Holland between the Ijssel River and the Grebbe Line.

A linkup with 49 (WR) Division operating from the south was effected at Eerbeck and following the capture of Apeldoorn 1st Div headed for Barneveld where the division relieved 5th Canadian Armoured Division for its role with 2nd Canadian Corps in the northward advance. 1st Canadian Infantry Division continued its westward advance to the Grebbe Line with 49 (West Riding) Division clearing the area between the right bank of the Neder Rijn and 1st Div.

Offensive operations on the 1st Canadian Corps front had practically ceased by the 19th April. 3rd Brigade captured Nijkerk as 1st Division cleared the area east of the Eem River to a point slightly over a mile from Amersfoort where on the 22nd April 1st Canadian Corps received instructions to hold the line until further orders were issued. As events were to prove, this was the final offensive action of 1st Canadian Corps in NW Europe.

A temporary truce was arranged for the delivery of supplies by land, sea and air to the starving people of the western Netherlands and this truce was still in effect when the "Cease Fire" was received 5th May, followed by "VE" Day, 8th of May 1945.

With the cessation of hostilities 1st Canadian Infantry Division supervised the return of German army personnel to Germany and upon completion of this task disbandment proceedings were begun. Personnel began moving to the Nijmegen repatriation centre between the 25th August and 15th September and Headquarters 1st Infantry Division received authorization to disband under General Order 52/46 (Effective 15th September 1945).

*   *   *

Special Artillery Group Headquarters RCA — Serial 807

Special Artillery Group Headquarters RCA, Serial 807, was placed on Active Service under General Order 218/41 (Effective 28th January 1941).

Special Artillery Group Headquarters RCA, Serial 807, was redesignated 1st Anti-Aircraft Brigade Headquarters RCA, Serial 807, under General Order 219/41 (The Effective Date is not listed).

1st Anti-Aircraft Brigade Headquarters RCA, Serial 807, was redesignated Special Artillery Group Headquarters RCA, Serial 807, under General Order 307/41 (Effective 1st October 1941).

Special Artillery Group Headquarters RCA, Serial 807, received authorization to disband under General Order 136/44 (Effective 28th September 1943).

*   *   *

1st Anti-Aircraft Brigade Headquarters RCA — Serial 842 — Army Tps

1st Anti-Aircraft Brigade Headquarters RCA, Serial 842, was placed on active service under General Order 306/41 (Effective 1st October 1941), the same date 1st Anti-Aircraft Brigade RCA, Serial 807 became Special Artillery Group Headquarters.

The Brigade was located at Colchester, Essex, and all Light Anti-Aircraft units

RCA formed in England or upon arrival in England came under 1st Anti-Aircraft Brigade RCA for training prior to joining their Division, Corps, or First Canadian Army, in the field. These units periodically returned to Colchester for refresher courses.

1st Anti-Aircraft Brigade Headquarters moved to the south of England to serve under Army Troops, First Canadian Army and the brigade was to comprise 2nd Heavy Anti-Aircraft Regiment RCA, 7th Light Anti-Aircraft Regiment RCA and 11th Light Anti-Aircraft Regiment RCA.

Anti-Aircraft Brigade Headquarters were normally allotted whenever three or more anti-aircraft regiments came under one commander, who may control up to five regiments, and each Army was to have at least one anti-aircraft brigade under command. The anti-aircraft brigade was occasionally placed in support or under command of a Corps.

1st Anti-Aircraft Brigade Headquarters RCA, Serial 842, however, was deprived of a chance to serve on Continental Europe with First Canadian Army due to the manpower shortage and was authorized to disband along with headquarters and batteries of 7th and 11th Light Anti-Aircraft Regiments RCA, under General Order 357/44 (Effective 1st March 1944).

*   *   *

HQ No. 1 Army Group RCA — Serial 63 — Army Troops

Headquarters 1st Corps Medium Artillery, RCA, CASF, Serial 63, received authorization to mobilize under General Order 135/39, 1st September 1939, however, it was not until 22nd September 1941 that the Formation was organized at Bordon, Hampshire, in England, utilizing accommodation at No. 1 and No. 2 Canadian Artillery Holding Units.

The nucleus of Headquarters Canadian Corps Medium Artillery moved to Cobham, Surrey, on 27th September 1941 and on 13th October 1941, 8th and 11th Canadian Army Field Regiments, 1st and 5th Canadian Medium Regiments, 7th Canadian Anti-Tank Regiment, 1st Canadian Survey Regiment, and No. 1 Canadian Calibration Troop RCA, came under command. On the 14th of October, 7th Canadian Army Field Regiment with several other Units came under direct command and a larger group came under direct command for administration purposes only.

On 19th November 1941 Headquarters CCMA moved to Surrey and took over command of Canadian Corps Area (Surrey) and inherited a large number of incomplete Units left behind by the recently departed 1st Canadian Corps. A number of the Units were Army Troops awaiting the forming of Headquarters First Canadian Army which was authorized 1st of April 1942. Most of these Units were ready to be sent to their proper Formations by the 11th of April 1942.

Headquarters 1st Corps Medium Artillery RCA, Serial 63, was redesignated Headquarters No. 1 Artillery Group RCA, Serial 63, under General Order 447/42 (Effective 7th September 1942).

Headquarters No. 1 Artillery Group RCA, Serial 63, was redesignated Headquarters No. 1 Army Group RCA, Serial 63, under General Order 341/43 (Effective 20th May 1943).

The Headquarters together with 1st, 3rd and 4th Canadian Medium Regiments moved to Lydd Range for training 31st August 1943 and in September moved under 2nd Canadian Corps in support of 1 Polish Division. Units of the AGRA participated in two Exercises without the Headquarters participating.

On 12th October 1943 orders for exercise "Timberwolf" were received and Regiments under command were to be 11th Canadian Army Field Regiment, 1st, 2nd and 5th Canadian Medium Regiments, plus an attached Meteorological Section.

Headquarters 1st Canadian AGRA boarded the SS Argentina at Liverpool, 24th October 1943, along with 2nd Medium Regiment RCA and 11th Army Field Regiment RCA. The ship paused at Gourock, Scotland, then set sail for the Mediterranean. The Headquarters landed by barge at Augusta, Sicily, and proceeded to Aci Trezza, the new Headquarters location.

1st Medium Regiment RCA crossed to Italy for duty in November 1943 and the remainder of the AGRA crossed to the Italian mainland, 4th January 1944. 1st Counter Battery Officers Staff RCA was placed under command 15th January 1944.

The Headquarters settled in at Lanciano, 17th January 1944. On the 18th January a temporary Army Group under Eighth Army was formed consisting of 66 Medium Regiment RA, 70 Medium Regiment RA and two Batteries of 54 Heavy Regiment RA, grouped under Headquarters 1st Canadian AGRA, designated Headquarters Canadian AGRA and became operational 21st January with 66 Medium Regiment RA in action.

On the 4th of February 1944 Headquarters received warning that it would relieve 1 British AGRA, 4th February 1944 with 1st Canadian Medium Regiment, 4 British, 58 British, 70 British Medium, 54 Heavy Regiment RA, and "A" Flight 651 Air OP Squadron under command. The Headquarters moved to Ortona. 2nd Canadian Medium Regiment relieved 4 Medium Regiment RA, 21st February and 5th Canadian Medium Regiment came under command 27th February 1944.

On the 4th March 1944 the Headquarters assumed the commitments of 6 British AGRA, returning to Lanciano, adding 66 and 78 Medium Regiments

RA and losing the two Batteries of 54 Heavy Regiment RA. "A" Flight 657 Air OP Squadron relieved "A" Flight 651 Air OP Squadron, 21st March 1944.

The Headquarters moved to Guardia where Headquarters 1st Canadian AGRA was to come under command 13 British Corps on the 15th April, and in addition to the Canadian Regiments, 51 Medium Regiment RA and 32 Heavy Regiments RA, were to be added. Tactical Headquarters 1st Canadian AGRA left for battle positions NW of Mignano, leaving the Canadian Regiments under command of Headquarters RCA 1st Canadian Corps. The Headquarters came under command of 13 Corps on the 15th of April 1944.

On the 17th May 1944 the Headquarters returned to under command of 1st Canadian Corps and supported 1st Canadian Infantry Division's assault on the Hitler Line, 23rd May 1944.

16th August 1944, 3 Medium Regiment RA and 32 Heavy Regiment RA came under command followed by CBO 1st Canadian Corps on the 17th in readiness for a new operation. 214 Heavy Anti-Aircraft Battery RA was added on the 23rd of August.

The Commander, Corps, Royal Artillery 1st Canadian Corps laid down a policy of dividing the AGRA in two and leap-frogging forward.

By the 6th September 1944 the AGRA consisted of 1st, 2nd and 5th Canadian Medium Regiments, 3, 4 and 26 Medium Regiments RA, 32 and 56 Heavy Regiments RA, with two Batteries of 57 and 97 Heavy Anti-Aircraft Regiments RA and "A" Flight 657 Air OP Squadron in support.

On the 3rd October 1944 the AGRA gained two Polish Regiments, 10 and 11 Medium Regiments, plus an interpreter. On the 29th October 1st Canadian Corps went out of action and 1st Canadian AGRA with it. The non-Canadian Units were posted to other Formations during this period.

On the 25th of November 1944 two Batteries of 61 Heavy Regiment RA came under command and on the 26th, 1st Canadian Counter Battery Officers Staff and 81 Artillery Company RCASC reverted to command of 1st Canadian AGRA as the AGRA moved forward to battle positions at Villa Torre.

Operation "Chuckle" began 2nd December 1944 with 1st, 2nd and 5th Canadian Medium Regiments, 3 Medium Regiment RA, and two Batteries of 61 Heavy Regiment RA, with 213 Heavy Anti-Aircraft Battery RA in support. On the 4th of December the Headquarters moved into the village of Russi and billets on the via Roma. ·

Headquarters 1st Canadian AGRA moved from Russi to Villa Raisa near Godo, on the 1st February 1945. This location turned out to be the last Battle position for the AGRA in Italy as 1 British AGRA assumed responsibility for the sector 18th February 1945.

The main body of the Unit embarked at Naples, Italy, on the Liberty Ship SS Samwye, 8th March 1945 and disembarked at Marseilles, France, 11th March 1945.

Headquarters concentrated in Waregen, Belgium, 17th March and Units now under command include, 1st, 2nd, 5th Canadian Medium Regiments, 1st Canadian CBO Staff, 1st Canadian Survey Regiment, 7th Canadian Anti-Tank Regiment, PLDG, 1st Canadian Light Anti-Aircraft Regiment and all Corps Troops, Army and L of C Units in the Area.

On 30th March 1945, Headquarters was established near Nijmegen, Holland and the AGRA supported 49 (WR) Division in an attack to clear the Island, cross the Neder Rijn and capture Arnhem. On the 8th of April two Special Radar Units RA came under command, the location however caused a number of problems.

Many shoots and small fire plans were passed out by Headquarters supporting 5th Canadian Armoured Division and 49 (WR) Infantry Division in their attacks, and an occasional Air OP shoot was carried out. The AGRA crossed the Neder Rijn to an area near Otterloo on 18th April, then moved to Lunteren, 26th April 1945.

While at Lunteren hostilities ceased and the 8th of May 1945 was designated "VE" Day. The AGRA moved into NW Holland, with Headquarters on the outskirts of Bergen. The AGRA was divided into Powis Force and Dalby Force, each in charge of a concentration area.

Staging camps were set up in each area for the German evacuation where the German troops were disarmed. The Air OP flight was instructed to maintain a continuous watch over the main evacuation routes from Holland to Germany. Guards were also required for ammunition and supply dumps and permanent installations.

Upon completion of this duty the AGRA moved from Bergen to Maarssen and the run-down of the AGRA components was begun.

Headquarters No. 1 Army Group RCA, Serial 63, received authorization to disband under General Order 321/45 (Effective 3rd July 1945).

*   *   *

Headquarters 2nd Canadian Corps — Serial 1701 — NW Europe

Headquarters 2nd Canadian Corps, Serial 1701, received authorization to mobilize under General order 281/43 (Effective 14th January 1943).

Headquarters RCA 2nd Canadian Corps came into being near Cobham, Surrey, in January 1943 and in February training schemes were begun with 5th Canadian Armoured Division under command. Spartan scheme began in March with 2nd Counter Battry Officers Staff, 6th Light Anti-Aircraft Regiment RCA, 6th Heavy Anti-Aircraft Regiment and 99th Anti-Tank Regiment RA, and 5th Canadian Armoured Division under command. Later in the month schemes were held with the artillery of 4th and 5th Canadian Armoured Divisions at Alfriston, Westdown and Sennybridge, which continued into April. An exercise to the north of England with 2nd Canadian AGRA, 2nd CBO, 6th LAA and 1st Canadian Survey Regiment RCA under command, completed the month of April.

Training continued with 4th and 5th Canadian Armoured Divisions, the artillery carrying out firing practice at Alfriston and anti-tank firing at Lydd. In June 6th Light Anti-Aircraft Regiment RCA visited St. Agnes, Cornwall practice camp.

In July 1943, 11th Army Field Regiment RCA fired at Larkhill, 6th LAA Regiment RCA attended Penny Bont, Wales battle school. 19th and 23rd (Self-Propelled) Field Regiments arrived from Canada and came under command.

In October 1943 headquarters moved to the Three Bridges area. 6th Anti-Tank Regiment RCA arrived from Canada and came under command 1st October. 5th Canadian Armoured Division went under command 1st Canadian Corps 14th October and were replaced by RCA 2nd Canadian Infantry Division. 19th Army Field Regiment went under command 3rd Canadian Infantry Division. A scheme was held with all artillery units of 5th Canadian Armoured Division, with under command 5th Medium Regiment RCA and 11th Army Field Regiment RCA, followed by a similar scheme with 4th Canadian Armoured Division.

In November sub-units of 6th LAA Regiment RCA assumed duty on ADGB sites. 660 AOP Squadron RAF came under command, 19th Army Field Regiment returned under command temporarily, 23rd Field Regiment (SP) RCA went under command 4th Canadian Armoured Division and training continued with corps artillery units, 2nd Canadian Infantry Division and 4th Canadian Armoured Division. A number of staff officers attended a Combined Operations training course in Scotland and in December 2nd Canadian Survey Regiment RCA came under command.

Toward the end of April 1944 the headquarters moved to Eastling Wood, Kent, north of Dover, where the headquarters was to spend the months of May and June awaiting the enlarging of the beachhead in Normandy where 3rd Canadian Infantry Division and 2nd Canadian Armoured Brigade of 2nd Canadian Corps had been engaged since landing in the assault on D-Day, 6th June, under 1 British Corps, Second British Army.

On the 29th June the headquarters moved from the Dover area to the marshalling area in NE London and close contact with the V-1 or flying bomb. While at Dover the cross-channel guns had directed shelling at the ports of Dover and Folkestone.

Personnel boarded Liberty ships the evening of the 30th June and late afternoon the following day the convoy set sail. Off-loading into tank landing craft, headquarters landed in Normandy on the 3rd of July 1944. Headquarters proceeded to the assembly area where waterproofing material was removed prior to moving to the village of Camilly, where it immediately deployed. Space nearby was eventually found for Corps Troops and 2nd Canadian AGRA.

2nd Canadian Infantry Division came under command upon arrival and was allotted the Carpiquet area, and 3rd Canadian Infantry Division came under command following the crossing of the Orne River. 2nd Canadian Corps in turn came under command of Second British Army.

Headquarters moved to a location near Lasson with 2nd Canadian AGRA deployed in support of both 2nd and 3rd Canadian Infantry Divisions, as were flights of 660 AOP Squadron RAF, which began to arrive. A towed anti-tank battery from 6th Anti-Tank Regiment RCA was placed under each of the divisions and 2nd Canadian Survey Regiment also deployed under the CCRA's control.

2nd Canadian Corps artillery fired in support of the 3rd Canadian Infantry Division assault crossing of the River Orne and clearing the western sector of Faubourg de Vaucelles. 2nd Canadian Corps was to continue applying pressure in the area. 8 British AGRA came under command to deploy north of Caen and made possible the allotment of an AGRA for each Division. 2nd Canadian Infantry Division was involved in clearing the east bank of the Orne with 53rd Division artillery in support.

The latter part of July the buildup for the breakout from the bridgehead by 2nd Canadian Corps continued. 9 British AGRA replaced 8 AGRA, 7th and Guards Armoured Divisions joined 2nd and 3rd Canadian Infantry Divisions under command of 2nd Canadian Corps. The operation bogged down and the armour was not committed.

4th Canadian Armoured Division relieved 3rd Canadian Infantry Division and 3rd Div reorganized from an assault formation to an infantry division.

Operation Totalize in August was to be a First Canadian Army operation and

2nd Canadian Corps came under command of First Canadian Army completely and operationally for the first time. 51 (Highland) Division with one self-propelled and one towed anti-tank battery of 6th Canadian Anti-Tank Regiment under command moved into the left of the line, and 2nd Canadian Infantry Division on the right, poised for the attack. 1st Polish Armoured Division and 4 British Armoured Brigade came under command, with 3rd Canadian Infantry Division in reserve. 2nd Canadian AGRA and 9 British AGRA augmented by two Heavy Anti-Aircraft Regiments, 3 and 4 AGRAs plus 49 British Division artillery were placed in support of 2nd Canadian Corps.

A creeping barrage was fired as the two leading infantry divisions advanced led by tanks, and the infantry were carried in armoured tracked troop carriers developed from the self-propelled field artillery guns with guns removed, which 3rd Canadian Infantry Division had recently exchanged for towed 25 pounders. Searchlights provided artificial moonlight, Bofors light anti-aircraft batteries fired directional tracer and field artillery fired coloured flares to guide the advance.

4th Canadian Armoured Division moved forward the following afternoon and by nightfall had secured the high ground. Heavy bombers were called in prior to the armour advancing south of Cintheaux and the "fortresses" bombed on the wrong side of the ridge much to the regret of a number of their allies.

Operation Tractable was undertaken to complete the objective of operation Totalize. 2nd Canadian Infantry Division was to capture Falaise from the right, 3rd Canadian Infantry Division in a frontal attack seized the high ground north of Falaise, 4th Canadian Armoured Division passed through to capture Trun, 1st Polish Armoured Divisions in an attack on Chambois from the left was to link up with US troops and close the Falaise Gap. Heavy bomber support was provided to demolish the Quesnay Wood fortifications and both friend and foe were subjected to the same treatment by the Lancasters.

With the closing of the Falaise Gap 2nd Canadian Corps began the chase to the River Seine with 4th Canadian Armoured Division on the right, 3rd Canadian Infantry Division centre and 2nd Canadian Infantry Division on the left, with a medium regiment under command of each division. 9 AGRA reverted to command of Army. 2nd Canadian Infantry Division met stiff opposition in the Foret de la Londe before crossing the Seine at Elbeuf.

2nd Canadian Infantry Division moved on to Dieppe and held a triumphal march through the city, then moved toward Dunkirk to aid in clearing the coast. 2nd Div was diverted from the task of capturing Dunkirk and moved through Antwerp to South Beveland.

3rd Canadian Infantry Division with the support of 2nd and 9 AGRA, each with a heavy anti-aircraft regiment, a heavy regiment, plus four medium regiments under command and 51 (Highland) Division artillery, was directed up the coast to clear Boulogne and Calais which were given top priority. The cooperation of the Dover batteries was enlisted to silence enemy guns at Cap Gris Nez with the aid of the Air OP during the Boulogne operation.

4th Canadian Armoured Division proceeded to Abbeville then moved toward Bruges, Belgium, to begin the battle to clear the south side of the Scheldt Estuary and to contain a large enemy force north of the Leopold Canal. 1st Polish Armoured Division also advanced into Belgium. Headquarters 2nd Canadian Corps made brief stops at Abbeville and Cassel.

A new method of obtaining meteor data was introduced in readiness for the battle of the Scheldt as GL Mk III sets and balloons were used to obtain meteor readings. At the end of September headquarters moved to an area east of Ghent, Belgium and preparations were made for the assault across the Leopold Canal by 3rd Canadian Infantry Division. 2nd Canadian Infantry Division which had been attached temporarily to 1 British Corps, returned to 2nd Canadian Corps.

The AGRAs, 3rd and 4th Canadian Divisions were concentrated in the Maldegem area and portions of 3 and 4 AGRAs were to be made available. Ammunition restirctions were rigidly controlled at this time as the flooding, the condition of the roads, and the distance from the ammunition dumps increased the urgency of opening the port of Antwerp to shipping.

A brigade of 3rd Canadian Infantry Division established a bridgehead across the Leopold Canal and grimly held on as extra artillery was obtained from 21 Army Group. 76 AA Brigade arrived to protect the left flank. 3 Super Heavy Regiment joined 9 AGRA. 59 AGRA, formerly 59 Division artillery, was placed under command 2nd Canadian Infantry Division along with two medium regiments. Two other heavy regiments were placed under the two AGRAs.

Assaults on Walcheren Island and south Beveland were to begin following the clearing of the Breskens pocket by a brigade of 3rd Canadian Infantry Division and this area south of the Scheldt was cleared by 31st October. As soon as the headland was cleared 2nd and 9 AGRA, 2nd Division artillery and two field regiments of 59 AGRA moved into the area to support the South Beveland assault and 2nd Division's advance up the isthmus. 59 AGRA departed and 7th Medium Regiment RCA came under command. The newly formed Rocket Battery manned by 6th Canadian Light Anti-Aircraft Regiment personnel also took part in the barrage, with coast guns included as prime targets. Elements of 4 SS Brigade and 52 (Lowland) Division launched amphibious attacks on South Beveland and Walcheren Island during the clearing of the area leading to the port of Antwerp.

2nd Canadian Corps in relief of 30 British Corps in the Nijmegen area began to move four divisional artilleries, one AGRA, one AA Brigade and Corps Troops. Headquarters relieved Headquarters RA 30 Corps, 8th November.

3rd Canadian Infantry Division artillery relieved RA Guards Armoured Division in support of 82nd US Airborne Division. then 2nd Canadian Infantry Division moved into the salient. 2nd Canadian AGRA relieved 5 AGRA and 2nd Survey Regiment RCA relieved 30 Corps Survey regiment with one flash spotting post in Germany.

A special formation of infantry, machine guns, anti-tank guns, anti-aircraft guns and searchlights was formed for the river defence of the Nijmegen bridge against damage from miniature submarines, swimmers and water-borne devices floated downstream bearing explosives. The enemy also attempted to damage the bridge at Grave with long range guns.

The corps light anti-aircraft regiment was placed under 74 AA Brigade which came under command of 2nd Canadian Corps and was responsible for the AA defence of the area. The division LAA regiments operated in their own gun area. Headquarters RCA 2nd Canadian Corps at Wychen, Holland, was in the path of Antwerp-bound buzz-bombs.

During the month of November 82nd and 101st US Airborne Divisions, 50 (Northumbrian) Division and 51 (Highland) Division (on the island) were attached. 2nd and 3rd Canadian Divisions remained in the Reichswald sector with 4th Canadian Armoured Division guarding the western approaches. The Ardennes offensive in December interrupted 30 Corps attack into the Rhineland.

1st Radar Battery RCA less one troop came under command 2nd Canadian Corps in a counter-mortar role and the counter-mortar sections of 2nd Canadian Survey Regiment received their equipment and both units were fully employed with positive results.

49 (WR) Division moved to the island and 51 (H) Division came under command 30 Corps. 50 (N) Division bagan disbandment proceedings early in December. 2nd Corps armoured car regiment arrived to protect the western approaches and 2nd Canadian Armoured Brigade concentrated as mobile reserve. 3 British Division also came under command during the paratroop threat and a brigade group of 2nd Canadian Infantry Division moved from its position to form a mobile army reserve.

The enemy air force ushered in the new year with a mass air attack. The Ardennes offensive began to fizzle and planning resumed for the attack southeast from the Nijmegen salient through the Reichswald Forest. The initial stages of the First Canadian Army attack was to be the responsibility of 30

Corps and for reasons of secrecy 2nd Canadian Corps artillery was heavily involved in the preparation for the attack. In three days and four nights previous to the attack four divisions, two independent brigades, six divisional artilleries, four AGRAs, 30 Corps Headquarters and numerous other units moved into the area — a triumph in inter-corps cooperation.

The attack was launched 8th February 1945 by 30 Corps with 2nd and 3rd Canadian Infantry Divisions under command. The main thrust was made by 53 (Welsh) Division, 15 (Scottish) Division and 2nd Canadian Infantry Division, with 51 (Highland) Division and 3rd Canadian Infantry Division entering the drive at staggered intervals bringing the total of assaulting divisions to five. 43 (Wessex) Division, Guards Armoured Division, Guards Independent Armoured Brigade, 34 Armoured Brigade, 11 Armoured Division and 4th Canadian Armoured Division provided the reserve strength.

Mid-February 2nd Canadian Corps moved into the line on the left of 30 Corps in the NE corner of the Reichswald Forest and the advance was continued on a two-corps front. 2nd Corps with 2nd, 3rd and 4th Canadian Divisions, 2nd Canadian Armoured Brigade, 11 Armoured Division and elements of 79 Armoured Division under command attacked the Hochwald defences to clear the Hochwald Forest, advance to Xanten and on to Wesel to effect a junction with the Ninth US Army. Artillery support was provided by four divisional artilleries plus 19th Army Field Regiment RCA which had been supporting 53 (Welsh) Division, 2nd Canadian Infantry Division, and now 4th Canadian Armoured Division. 2nd Canadian AGRA, 4th and 5th British AGRAs added their firepower, with other units of 30 Corps on call.

43 (W) Division came under command and was given the task of clearing the area north of the Hochwald between the forest and the Rhine, 4th Canadian Armoured Division was directed to clear the area south of the forest with 11 Armoured Division providing flank protection. 2nd Div was given the responsibility of clearing the north section of the forest and 3rd Division the south section, and the Hochwald Forest was cleared after extremely bitter fighting.

52 (L) Division came under command and advancing on the right flank made contact with the US Army. As the advance of 2nd Canadian Corps and the Ninth US Army began to narrow the front 30 Corps was pinched out and began preparing for its next assignment, the assault crossing of the Rhine. Until the divisions could be withdrawn one by one they were controlled by 2nd Canadian Corps for several days. The Corps returned to normal 12th March with 2nd, 3rd and 4th Canadian Divisions under command.

Ninth US Army remained under 21 Army Group for the Rhine crossing which was to be made by Ninth US Army and Second British Army. 30 Corps reverted to under command of Second British Army for the assault which began 23rd March and 3rd Canadian Infantry Division's Highland Brigade (9th Brigade) accompanied 51 (Highland) Division of Scotland across the Rhine.

Second British Army was to attack on a two-corps front with 2nd Canadian Corps to the left of 30 Corps. Crossing in the Xanten area 30 Corps fanned out and 3rd Canadian Infantry Division turned left to capture Emmerich and the Hoch Elten feature. 107 AA Brigade was placed under command to protect the area during the construction of a bridge at Emmerich. The bridge was to become the Corps lifeline as 2nd Canadian Corps crossed the bridge and began its drive due north into northern Holland and western Germany.

In April events developed too rapidly for Corps control of the guns and one medium regiment was permanently attached to the two armoured divisions and the two infantry divisions in 2nd Canadian Corps. Corps Headquarters moved north of Emmerich 4th April, then back into Holland to Lochem on the south bank of the Twente Canal 5th April, as 3rd Division moved toward Zutphen, 2nd Division was directed due north to the high ground north of the Twente Canal and 4th Division advanced toward Meppen.

Shortage of troops on the ground saw the corps anti-tank regiment in an infantry role and with one squadron of 1st Armoured Car Regiment (The Royal Canadian Dragoons) of 1st Canadian Corps, was responsible for the 15 mile line of the Ijssel from the Rhine to the south of Deventer.

1st Canadian Infantry Division moved into the Reichswald, coming under command 6th April, and under 2nd Canadian Corps the division was to attack across the Ijssel between Zutphen and Deventer to capture Apeldoorn. The remaining medium regiment of 2nd Canadian AGRA and CBO Staff supported the 1st Div attack and upon clearing Deventer 3rd Div artillery became available to 1st Div. 1st Canadian Infantry Division reverted to under command of 1st Canadian Corps 13 April, accompanied by the medium regiment from 2nd AGRA.

4th Division cleared Meppen, 1st Polish Armoured Division returned to 2nd Canadian Corps and passed through 4th Div on the way to Leer, 2nd Div continued its advance in the direction of Groningen as 3rd Division moved into Deventer.

Corps Headquarters moved to Meppen 13th April. 3rd Division moved on to Zwolle and continued to drive into NE Holland. 2nd Div captured Groningen then were whisked away into Germany, through Meppen, and to an area at the mouth of the Weser River opposite Bremerhaven.

4 AGRA came under command 21st April in suport of the Polish Division. 5th Canadian Armoured Division came under command from 1st Canadian Corps 29th April, relieving 3rd Canadian Infantry Division in NE Holland, and 3rd Div returned to Germany to aid in the capture of Leer.

660 AOP Squadron RAF, with the corps throughout departed for the Far East and 664 Air OP Squadron RCAF arrived to serve with 2nd Canadian Corps.

1st Canadian Rocket Battery fired in support of 4 Div south of Bad Zwische-nahn and May was ushered in with 4th Division beyond Bad Zwischenahn, 1st Polish Armoured Division beyond Leer and heading in the direction of Wil-helmshaven. 3rd Div moved toward Aurich, then left to Emdem and 2nd Division entered Oldenburg.

The CBO and extra guns were deployed west of Leer under 4 AGRA for CB fire on Emdem. Activities were mainly on a division level with the front widely spread out. 6th Light Anti-Aircraft Regiment RCA corps LAA regiment, with elements of 107 AA Brigade in support were widely dispersed guarding vital areas. 6th Anti-Tank Regiment RCA had two batteries on infantry duty west of Leer and 1st Canadian Rocket Battery were assisting 4th Division.

On the morning of 5th May 1945 Headquarters RCA 2nd Canadian Corps forwarded the cease fire message to RCA 2nd, 3rd, 4th, 5th Canadian Div-isions, artillery of 1st Polish Armoured Division, 2nd Canadian AGRA, 4 British AGRA, 2nd Canadian CBO Staff, 6th Canadian Anti-Tank Regiment, 6th Canadian LAA Regiment, 2nd Canadian Survey Regiment, 660 AOP Squadron RAF, 664 AOP Squadron RCAF, B Troop, 1st Canadian Radar Battery and 557 Searchlight Battery (Ind) (ML) RA.

Headquarters 2nd Canadian Corps moved to Bad Zwischenahn 6th May where orders were received for clearing the corps area between the Weser and Ems rivers of weapons, ammunition and equipment which was completed by mid-June.

The divisions under command began to depart in turn and 15th June Head-quarters moved back to Holland between Hengelo and Enschede where all corps artillery troops came under command 1st Canadian AGRA.

Headquarters 2nd Canadian Corps which had begun its service in France 3rd July 1944, moved to Belgium 30th September, Holland 8th November, Ger-many 18th February 1945, Holland 4th April, back to Germany 13th April, then returned to Holland 15th June 1945 receiving authorization to disband as Headquarters 2nd Corps, Serial 1701, under General Order 321/45 (Effective 25th June 1945) in NW Europe. Personnel joined the Canadian Army Pacific Force, the Canadian Army Occupational Force, or were posted to divisional groups for the return to Canada.

*   *   *

2nd Canadian Infantry Division — Serial 152 — Dieppe & NW Europe

Headquarters 2nd Division, CASF, Serial 152, mobilized under General Order

135/39, 1st September 1939. 2nd Division was to comprise The Fort Garry Horse, CASF, Headquarters of 2nd Divisional Artillery RCA, CASF, Serial 154, Headquarters of 4th, 5th and 6th Field Brigades RCA, CASF, with their four component batteries and 2nd Anti-Tank Regiment RCA, CASF (less batteries).

Headquarters divisional engineers, one field park company and three field companies, HQ divisional signals and three companies. HQ divisional RCASC, an ammunition company, petrol company, and supply column. RCAMC with three field ambulances and a field hygiene section. No. 2 Provost Company, a postal unit, and No. 2 Employment Platoon, CASF. A number of Corps Troops, Army Troops and L of C Troops also mobilized with 2nd Division, CASF.

Each infantry brigade included a machine gun battalion. Headquarters of 4th Infantry Brigade, CASF, encompassed The Essex Scottish Regiment, CASF, The Royal Hamilton Light Infantry, CASF, The Royal Regiment of Canada, CASF, and The Cameron Highlanders of Ottawa (MG), CASF.

Headquarters of 5th Infantry Brigade, CASF, took under its wing 1st Battalion, The Black Watch (Royal Highland Regiment) of Canada, CASF, Les Fusiliers Mont-Royal, CASF, Le Regiment de Maisonneuve, CASF, and Le Regiment de la Chaudiere (Mitrailleuses), CASF, brigade machine gun battalion.

6th Infantry Brigade included Headquarters of 6th Infantry Brigade, CASF, The South Saskatchewan Regiment, CASF, The Calgary Highlanders, CASF, The Queens Own Cameron Highlanders of Canada, CASF, and The Winnipeg Grenadiers (MG), CASF, brigade machine gun battalion, all mobilized under General Order 135/39, 1st September 1939.

In most cases units remained in the area of their mobilization or moved to more suitable quarters for the winter, then in the spring of 1940, 2nd Division Headquarters was formed and the brigades moved to designated military camps in Ontario, Quebec, and Manitoba.

4th Brigade assembled at Camp Borden, Ontario in May and June 1940, 5th Brigade congregated at Valcartier Camp, P.Q., and 6th Brigade units converged on Camp Shilo, Manitoba, along with The Fort Garry Horse which had mobilized with 2nd Division.

4th Field Regiment RCA and 5th Field Regiment RCA settled in at Camp Petawawa, Ontario. 2nd Anti-Tank Regiment RCA and 6th Field Regiment RCA spent the summer at Camp Shilo, Manitoba, with 6th Brigade.

Normal brigade organization was soon disrupted with the departure of 1st

Battalion Black Watch (RHR) of Canada for duty in Newfoundland mid-June to 11th August 1940. Brigade machine gun battalions were soon discontinued and a divisional machine gun battalion instituted. The CH of O (MG) and the Chaudieres moved to 3rd Division. The Winnipeg Grenadiers (MG) of 6th Brigade, upon becoming surplus to the division proceeded to the Caribbean in May and June 1940, and upon their return to Canada in 1941 crossed to the west coast and sailed for Hong Kong.

"Z" Force for Iceland, to be drawn from 2nd Division, saw The Royal Regiment of Canada of 4th Brigade arrive in Iceland 16th June 1940, to be followed by Les Fusiliers Mont Royal of 5th Brigade, and The Cameron Highlanders of Ottawa (MG) plus signal units and details on the 7th of July 1940.

Divisional Headquarters, The Essex Scottish and The Royal Hamilton Light Infantry of 4th Brigade departed for overseas 23rd July 1940, and upon disembarking at Gourock, Scotland 2nd August 1940, entrained for Aldershot, Hampshire, in the south of England. Headquarters 4th Canadian Infantry Brigade joined its two battalions at Aldershot, 23rd August 1940.

1st Battalion Black Watch (RHR) of Canada returned to Canada from duty in Newfoundland and following embarkation leave proceeded to Halifax to board the Duchess of York with 2nd Anti-Tank Regiment RCA. The convoy which also included the Empress of Australia, the Oronsay, and the Pasteur, with 4th, 5th and 6th Field Regiments RCA, The Calgary Highlanders and Le Regiment de Maisonneuve aboard sailed 27th August 1940. The units disembarked at Gourock, Scotland on the 4th of September 1940 and journeyed south to Aldershot to join the division.

"Z" Force Headquarters, The Royal Regiment of Canada and Fusiliers Mont-Royal departed from Iceland 31st October 1940 on the Empress of Australia and disembarked at Greenock, Scotland, 3rd November 1940, rejoining 2nd Division at Aldershot, England. The Cameron Highlanders of Ottawa (MG), slated to become 3rd Division machine gun battalion, remained in Iceland for the winter.

The Queens Own Cameron Highlanders of Canada and The South Saskatchewan Regiment arrived overseas in December 1940 completing the brigade structure, then with two Canadian Divisions plus ancillary units, the Canadian Corps was formed 25th December 1940, a proud moment in Canadian history.

The Toronto Scottish (MG) joined 2nd Division from 1st Division and during 1941, 3rd Light Anti-Aircraft Regiment RCA arrived overseas to join 2nd Division as division LAA regiment, and 8th Reconnaissance Regiment (14th Canadian Hussars) became div recce regiment. The divisional recce regiments evolved from the brigade reconnaissance squadrons in each infantry brigade.

4th Infantry Brigade now comprised The Royal Regiment of Canada, The Royal Hamilton Light Infantry and The Essex Scottish Regiment.

5th Infantry Brigade units were The Black Watch (RHR) of Canada, Le Regiment de Maisonneuve and The Calgary Highlanders.

6th Infantry Brigade now included Les Fusiliers Mont-Royal, the Queens Own Cameron Highlanders of Canada and The South Saskatchewan Regiment.

On the 19th of August 1942, 4th and 6th Infantry Brigades with representatives from the majority of 2nd Canadian Infantry Division units, launched an attack on the French seaport of Dieppe. The brigades received support from the tanks of The Calgary Regiment, the Commandos, Royal Navy, RCN, RAF, Royal Canadian Air Force and US Rangers. The assaulting force suffered heavily in killed, wounded and prisoners.

Lieutenant-Colonel C.C.I. Merritt of The South Saskatchewan Regiment and Honorary Captain J.W. Foote, Chaplain of The Royal Hamilton Light Infantry (Wentworth Regiment), were awarded the Victoria Cross for heroism at Dieppe, 19th August 1942, and both remained prisoners of war. The shattered units returned to England where the Division absorbed the shock and set about readying itself for the return to the Continent.

Headquarters 2nd Division, Serial 152, was redesignated Headquarters 2nd Infantry Division, Serial 152, under General Order 283/43 (Effective 7th January 1943).

2nd Division returned to France in July 1944, skirting the defended ports, and landed on the beaches of Normandy, joining 3rd Canadian Infantry Division in the beachhead.

2nd Canadian Infantry Division moved into the Carpiquet sector under 2nd Canadian Corps, which in turn came under command of Second British Army, then on the 31st of July 1944 all Canadian units moved under the command of First Canadian Army and participated in the vicious fighting in the breakout from Caen and the closing of the Falaise Gap.

2nd Division units captured Falaise and advanced toward the River Seine where a stiff battle ensued in the Foret de la Londe. The division crossed the Seine and moved on to Dieppe, where on the 3rd of September 1944, following the capture of the city, units of the division paused for a service of remembrance in the cemetery, followed by a divisional parade through the city streets.

2nd Div was then directed along the Channel ports and aided in clearing the coast toward Ostend, however, before Dunkirk was captured the division was whisked away through Antwerp for the attack on South Beveland, to clear the Port of Antwerp to shipping.

Following the clearing of the Scheldt, 2nd Canadian Infantry Division moved to the Nijmegen sector to prepare for the invasion of western Germany by First Canadian Army. The attack was launched 8th February 1945 by 30 British Corps and the initial attack was delivered by five Divisions, including 2nd and 3rd Canadian Infantry Divisions. 2nd Div was to capture the strongpoint of Wyler, and upon the capture of the original objectives the Canadian divisions were to return to under the command of 2nd Canadian Corps.

The Reichswald Forest was cleared and the Siegfried Line breached. 2nd Division reentered the drive and became involved in a stiff battle for the Goch-Calcar Road near Moyland Wood. The enemy resisted stubbornly as the Hochwald Forest area was cleared and the attack closed up to the River Rhine.

The brigades of 2nd Div crossed the Rhine the last week of March and the early days of April. The energies of the division were then directed due north toward Groningen and on to the North Sea, in Holland.

From Groningen in Holland 2nd Division was rushed back into Germany to a point on the mouth of the Weser River opposite Bremen, and on the 3rd of May units of the division entered Oldenburg, Germany. It was here that the war ended for the division in NW Europe upon receiving the "Cease Fire" on the 5th of May and the designation of the 8th of May 1945 as "VE" Day.

2nd Canadian Infantry Division remained in Germany on duty until July, being relieved by 3rd Canadian Infantry Division, Canadian Army Occupational Force, then returned to Holland to await repatriation.

Units of 2nd Canadian Infantry Division returned to Canada and disbandment from September to December 1945. Disbanding under General Order 52/46 during September 1945 were 4th, 5th and 6th Field Regiments RCA, 2nd Anti-Tank Regiment RCA, 3rd Light Anti-Aircraft Regiment RCA, Headquarters 4th, 5th and 6th Infantry Brigades. The Infantry battalions disbanded along with the div recce regiment and the divisional machine gun battalion under General Order 85/46 during November and December 1945.

Headquarters 2nd Infantry Division received authorization to disband under General Order 52/46 (Effective 13th October 1945), and under the same General Order Headquarters of 2nd Divisional Artillery, RCA received authorization to disband (Effective 4th October 1945).

*   *   *

No. 2 Army Group RCA — Serial 1158 — Army Troops — First Cdn Army

Headquarters No. 2 Artillery Group RCA, Serial 1158, mobilized under General Order 446/42 (Effective 7th September 1942).

The Artillery Group was formed in England with 7th Army Field Regiment

RCA, 8th Army Field Regiment RCA and 11th Army Field Regiment RCA under command, followed by 2nd Medium Regiment RCA and 5th Medium Regiment RCA in January 1943.

Headquarters No. 2 Artillery Group RCA, Serial 1158, was redesignated Headquarters No. 2 Army Group RCA, Serial 1158, under General Order 341/43 (Effective 20th May 1943).

Toward the end of September 1943, 2nd and 5th Medium Regiments RCA became components of 1st Canadian AGRA and proceeded to the Mediterranean to support 1st Canadian Corps in action. 3rd and 4th Medium Regiments RCA came under command 2nd Canadian AGRA as replacements.

In October the AGRA began to take its final form with the arrival of 1 Heavy Regiment, Royal Artillery and 191 Regiment, Royal Artillery, and the conversion of 7th Army Field Regiment RCA to 7th Medium Regiment RCA.

In January 1944, 191 Field Regiment RA was replaced by 15 Medium Regiment RA in the AGRA. The regiments now under command were 3rd, 4th and 7th Canadian Medium Regiments, 15 Medium Regiment RA, and 1 Heavy Regiment RA. 82 Artillery Company Royal Canadian Army Service Corps and "C" Flight 661 Air OP Squadron, RAF, also came under command.

The AGRA concentrated on readying itself for the cross-channel invasion, then on the 5th of July 1944 Headquarters 2nd Canadian AGRA, with 3rd, 4th and 7th Canadian Medium Regiments, 15 Medium Regiment RA and 1 Heavy Regiment RA under command joined the action 12th July 1944 at Vieux Cairon, in Normandy, under 2nd Canadian Corps, Second British Army.

2nd Canadian AGRA moved to under the command of First Canadian Army 31st July 1944 in the Caen Sector where the AGRA suffered heavily in the August bombing. With the breakout from Caen effected and the closing of the Falaise Gap the headquarters with 19th Army Field Regiment RCA under command, began to follow the advance, crossing the River Seine, 1st September.

19th Army Field Regiment RCA moved on to 4th Canadian Armoured Division 5th September and 1 Heavy Regiment RA left for 9 British AGRA. On the 6th of September 3rd Canadian, 15, 11 and 107 Medium Regiments RA came under command in a concentration area.

For the attack on Boulogne 11th September headquarters had under command 3rd and 4th Medium Regiments RCA and 15 Medium Regiment RA, and 14th September 53 Heavy Regiment RA and 60 Heavy Anti-Aircraft Regiment RA came under command. Boulogne surrendered on the 22nd September and Calais was the next target.

Calais surrendered on the 30th September and the next objective was the crossing of the Leopold Canal in Belgium, with 3rd, 4th and 7th Canadian Medium Regiments, 15 Medium Regiment RA, 1 and 52 Heavy Regiments RA under command.

63 Super Heavy Regiment RA came under command for the clearing of Walcheren Island as 2nd Canadian AGRA deployed in Holland, then on the 9th of October AGRA Headquarters moved to the Nijmegen area in Holland under 2nd Canadian Corps. 10 Medium Regiment RA arrived to replace 15 Medium Regiment RA in the AGRA, 4th December 1944.

On the 1st of January 1945 AGRA Headquarters less its regiments moved under 1 British Corps with 65 and 68 Medium Regiments RA under command and supported 1st Polish Armoured Division in the battle of Kapelsche Veer, and supported 47 (RM) Commando in a second attack.

On the 18th of January Headquarter 2nd Canadian AGRA resumed command of its own units in the Nijmegen area in preparation for the drive into Germany. The first unit moved forward 11th February and headquarters moved to Cleve, Germany, 19th February 1945.

In March 2nd Canadian AGRA supported the crossing of the Rhine River and returned to Holland to support 1st Canadian Infantry Division's crossing of the Ijssel River 11th april 1945, then returned to Germany where cessation of hostilities came about and the 8th of May 1945 was designated "VE" Day.

The run-down of the AGRA was begun in June, and Headquarters No. 2 Army Group RCA, Serial 1158, received authorization to disband under General Order 321/45 (Effective 11th July 1945).

*   *   *

3rd Canadian Infantry Division — D-Day to VE Day, NW Europe

Headquarters, 3rd Division, CASF, Serial 700, was authorized as a component of the Canadian Active Service Force under General Order 184/40.

3rd Division was to comprise Headquarters, 3rd Division, CASF, Serial 700, Headquarters 3rd Divisional Artillery RCA, CASF, Serial 704, three Field Regiments, 12th, 13th and 14th Field Regiments RCA, CASF, each with two combined field batteries, in the era of hyphenated batteries. 3rd Anti-Tank Regiment RCA, CASF mobilized with a full slate of four anti-tank batteries.

Headquarters 3rd Divisional Engineers, divisional signals, divisional RCASC, dental company, CDC, provost company, postal unit, employment platoon and mobile bath unit, CASF, also mobilized.

The original infantry brigade alignment contained Headquarters 7th Infantry Brigade, CASF, 7th Infantry Anti-Tank Company, CASF, The North Nova Scotia Highlanders, CASF, The Cameron Highlanders of Ottawa (MG), CASF and The Canadian Scottish Regiment, CASF.

Headquarters 8th Infantry Brigade, CASF, 8th Infantry Anti-Tank Company, CASF, The North Shore (New Brunswick) Regiment, CASF, Le Regiment de la Chaudiere, CASF, and The Regina Rifle Regiment, CASF.

Headquarters 9th Infantry Brigade, CASF, contained 9th Infantry Anti-Tank Company, CASF, The Stormont, Dundas and Glengarry Highlanders, CASF, The Queen's Own Rifles of Canada, CASF, and The Highland Light Infantry of Canada, CASF.

The brigade components were not finalized at this time for in addition to The Cameron Highlanders of Ottawa (MG) and Le Regiment de la Chaudiere from 2nd Division, The Royal Winnipeg Rifles arrived from its intended formation, 4th Division.

Headquarters 3rd Division, 7th and 9th Infantry Brigades, 13th and 14th Field Regiments RCA and 3rd Anti-Tank Regiment RCA assembled at Debert, Nova Scotia, Headquarters 8th Infantry Brigade and 12th Field Regiment RCA congregated at Camp Sussex, New Brunswick.

Previous to joining the brigade, The Queen's Own Rifles of Canada boarded the Duchess of Richmond at Montreal and disembarked on the 10th August 1940 at Botwood, Newfoundland, in relief of The Black Watch (RHR) of Canada of 2nd Division. Part of the unit stopped at Botwood and the remainder continued by train to Gander Airport. A detachment was also placed at Lewisporte.

The Regina Rifle Regiment arrived at Camp Debert, Nova Scotia, the end of September 1940 from Dundurn Camp, Saskatchewan, The Canadian Scottish Regiment arrived at Debert from Macaulay Camp, Victoria-Esquimalt, British Columbia, 9th October 1940, The Royal Winnipeg Rifles arrived from Camp Shilo, Manitoba, 28th October, to round out 7th Brigade.

Late in September 1940 the Chaudieres arrived at Camp Sussex, New Brunswick and were joined by The North Shore (New Brunswick) Regiment at Sussex, 5th December. The Queen's Own Rifles were relieved by The Royal Rifles of Canada in Newfoundland and joined 8th Brigade at Sussex, early December 1940, to complete 8th Infantry Brigade.

The Highland Light Infantry of Canada completed its duty at Quebec City and arrived at Debert early March 1941 to form 9th Infantry Brigade along with The North Nova Scotia Highlanders, and The Stormont, Dundas and Glengarry Highlanders.

4th Light anti-Aircraft Regiment RCA encompassed four surplus field batteries to become 3rd Division light anti-aircraft regiment at Camp Sussex, New Brunswick, during 1941, and 7th Reconnaissance Battalion (17th Duke of York's royal Canadian Hussars) joined 3rd Division at Debert to serve as divisional reconnaissance battalion.

Headquarters 3rd Division departed Debert, Nova Scotia by train for Halifax on the 19th of July 1941 to board the Empress of Canada and the convoy sailed for Gourock, Scotland where the units disembarked 29th July 1941. Headquarters and the 3rd Div units proceeded by train to Aldershot, Hampshire, to join the Canadian corps in an anti-invasion role in the south of England. The Cameron Highlanders of Ottawa (MG) joined 3rd Division in England following service in Iceland with "Z" Force, and became divisional machine gun battalion.

Headquarters 3rd Division, Serial 700, was redesignated Headquarters 3rd Infantry Division, Serial 700, under General order 283/43 (Effective 7th January 1943).

1st Canadian Infantry Division proceeded to the Mediterranean for the invasion of Sicily in July 1943. Headquarters 1st Canadian Corps and 5th Canadian Armoured Division followed toward the end of the year to become operational in Italy.

3rd Canadian Infantry Division of 2nd Canadian Corps was selected to land in the assault under 1 British Corps, Second British Army on D-Day, 6th June 1944, in the Allied invasion of Normandy. 3rd Canadian Infantry Division landed between 3rd British Division on its left and 50th (Northumbrian) Division on the right. 1st and 4th US Divisions assaulted farther to the right toward the Cotentin Peninsula. 82nd and 101st US Airborne Divisions and 6th British Airborne Division, with 1st Canadian Parachute Battalion as a component landed beyond the beaches before daylight.

Divisional field artillery, 12th, 13th and 14th Field Regiments RCA plus 19th Army Field Regiment RCA had been issued self-propelled 105mm guns for the assault, and fired the 105mm SPs from the landing craft in support of the assaulting 7th and 8th Canadian Infantry Brigades prior to landing on the beaches of Normandy.

3rd Canadian Infantry division cleared Carpiquet Airfield and a number of villages leading to Caen and aided in the capture of the city which had been bombed by several hundred bombers of the RAF, bombarded by ships of the Royal Navy, and guns of two AGRAs and by Corps and several divisional artilleries.

3rd Canadian Infantry Division moved from 1 British Corps, Second British Army to 2nd Canadian Corps, Second British Army, and during the night of

18th July the division crossed the River Orne. 2nd Canadian Corps, with all Canadian units in Normandy, came under command of First Canadian Army on the 31st of July 1944.

On the 1st of August, with the beachhead secured, the self-propelled 105s were exchanged for towed 25 pounders by the divisional field artillery, conforming to infantry division War Establishment, and later in August 19th Army Field Regiment RCA was issued self-propelled 25 pounders.

3rd Canadian Infantry Division under 2nd Canadian Corps, First Canadian Army, participated in the vicious fighting in the breakout from Caen and the closing of the Falaise Gap.

The pursuit across France began and 3rd Division was given the task of clearing the Channel Port towns of Boulogne and Calais. The attack on Boulogne was launched 17th September and the fortress surrendered 22nd September. The attack on Calais and Cap Gris Nez was begun 25th September and concluded 1st October 1944, silencing the cross-channel guns. While so-employed, operation "Market Garden", the Arnhem Airborne drop had taken place.

From Calais 3rd Canadian Infantry Division remained on the left flank and moved into Belgium where 7th and 8th Brigades were delegated to establish a bridgehead across the Leopold Canal as the need to open the Port of Antwerp to shipping was paramount.

North of Ghent, Belgium, 9th Brigade boarded Buffaloes for a waterborne attack to clear the area between the Leopold Canal and the North Sea, leading to the West Scheldt, which was accomplished by 3rd Div on the 3rd of November 1944, and the division moved to the Nijmegen area as 2nd Canadian Corps took over the Nijmegen Salient from Second British Army 9th November, and from this static position preparations were made for the invasion of Germany.

Headquarters First Canadian Army was given the responsibility of planning and executing the advance across the border into Germany. 30 British Corps, attached to First Canadian Army, led the attack on the 8th of February 1945 with 15 (Scottish) Division, 51 (Highland) Division, 53 (Welsh) Division, 2nd Canadian Infantry Division and 3rd Canadian Infantry Division under command.

In the initial phase 3rd Canadian Infantry Division advanced on the left flank over a water covered area and upon completion of the first phase the two Canadian Divisions reverted to under command of 2nd Canadian Corps and the advance continued on a two-corps front, meeting fierce resistance. Each infantry brigade added to its battle honours, and Sergeant Aubrey Cosens of

The Queen's Own Rifles of Canada was posthumously awarded the Victoria Cross for heroism 26th February 1945.

Upon reaching the banks of the Rhine River, Second British Army became responsible for the river crossing, with 30 British Corps and 2nd Canadian Corps under command. 9th Canadian Infantry Brigade (Highland Brigade) of 3rd Canadian Infantry Division was attached to 51 (Highland) Division and was 2nd Canadian Corps representative for the Rhine crossing. The remainder of 3rd Division crossed into the bridgehead and operating on the left flank of 30 Corps, cleared the city of Emmerich and occupied the wooded promontory of Hoch Elten.

The three Canadian Divisions under 2nd Canadian Corps began a northward drive and on the 1st of April Headquarters First Canadian Army took control of the corps drive. 1st Canadian Corps arrived from Italy and moved into the Arnhem area under First Canadian Army and 1 British Corps returned to Second British Army.

3rd Canadian Infantry Division advancing toward the North Sea with 2nd Canadian Infantry Division on its right, cleared Zutphen, Deventer and Zwolle on the banks of the Ijssel River and Meppel, Steenwijk and Leeuwarden to the right of the Ijsselmeer.

2nd Div reached Groningen then was moved back to Germany to assist in the drive on Oldenburg and 3rd Div having reached the North Sea beyond Leeuwarden moved to the right to clear the area between Groningen and the North Sea.

As 3rd Canadian Infantry Division approached Delfzijl it was relieved by 5th Canadian Armoured Division and returned to Germany in the 1st Polish Armoured Division sector. The Polish Division proceeded in the direction of Varel and 3rd Canadian Infantry Division crossed the Ems and Leda Rivers, captured Leer, then advanced north into the Emdem-Wilhelmshaven Peninsula to reach the Ems-Jade Canal at Aurich. When operations were suspended on the 4th of May elements of the division were advancing on Emdem and upon the designation of the 8th of May "VE" Day the war in NW Europe ended. 3rd Canadian Infantry Division remained on duty in the area until the end of May, then moved to Utrecht, Holland, to await repatriation.

Headquarters 3rd Infantry Division received authorization to disband under General Order 52/46 (Effective 23rd November 1945). Headquarters 3rd Divisional Artillery RCA, Headquarters 7th, 8th and 9th Infantry Brigades also disbanded at that time. Artillery regiments and batteries disbanded during October and November under the same General Order and by the end of 1945 all units of the division had disbanded.

*   *   *

Headquarters 3rd Canadian Infantry Division — CAOF

The forming of a division to serve with the Canadian Army Occupational Force saw a reconstituted 3rd Division mobilized for duty with the force. Headquarters 3rd Canadian Infantry Division, CAOF, was authorized under General Order 319/45 (Effective 1st June 1945).

The divisional recce regiment mobilized as 2nd 7th Reconnaissance Regiment, CAC, and the divisional machine gun battalion mobilized as 3rd Battalion the Cameron Highlanders of Ottawa (Machine Gun), CIC.

The artillery components became 2nd 3rd Anti-Tank Regiment RCA, 2nd 4th Light Anti-Aircraft Regiment RCA, 2nd 12th Field Regiment RCA, 2nd 13th Field Regiment RCA and 2nd 14th Field Regiment RCA. The artillery batteries also added the 2nd prefix.

The War Diary of 2nd 14th Field Regiment RCA confirms that 2nd 81st Field Battery RCA was a component and not 2nd 87th Field Battery RCA as suggested in General Order 319/45.

The Infantry Brigades were redesignated 2nd 7th, 2nd 8th and 2nd 9th Infantry Brigades, CIC. Infantry components, depending on the number of active and reserve battalions, became 3rd or 4th Battalions.

2nd 7th Infantry Brigade, CIC comprised Headquarters 2nd 7th Infantry Brigade, CIC, 2nd 7th Infantry Brigade Ground Defence Platoon (Lorne Scots), CIC, 4th Battalion The Royal Winnipeg Rifles, CIC, 4th Battalion The Regina Rifle Regiment, CIC, 4th Battalion The Canadian Scottish Regiment, CIC.

2nd 8th Infantry Brigade, CIC included Headquarters 2nd 8th Infantry Brigade, CIC, 2nd 8th Infantry Brigade Ground Defence Platoon (Lorne Scots), CIC, 4th Battalion The Queen's Own Rifles of Canada, CIC, 3rd Battalion Le Regiment de la Chaudiere, CIC, 3rd Battalion The North Shore (New Brunswick) Regiment, CIC.

2nd 9th Infantry Brigade, CIC, was composed of Headquarters 2nd 9th Infantry Brigade, CIC, 2nd 9th Infantry Brigade Ground Defence Platoon (Lorne Scots), CIC, 3rd Battalion The Highland Light Infantry of Canada, CIC, 3rd Battalion The Stormont, Dundas and Glengarry Highlanders, CIC, and 3rd Battalion The North Nova Scotia Highlanders, CIC.

The Canadian Scottish moved to 2nd 8th Brigade and the Queen's Own Rifles of Canada joined 2nd 7th Brigade to form a "Rifle Brigade" with The Royal Winnipeg Rifles and The Regina Rifle Regiment.

3rd Canadian Infantry Division, CAOF, concentrated at Amersfoort, Holland, and on the 5th of July began moving to NW Germany in relief of 2nd

Canadian Infantry Division under Headquarters 30 Corps District in the Aurich, Oldenburg area with CAOF Headquarters situated at Bad Zwishenahn.

Units forming an integral part of the division included the RCE, RC Sigs, RCASC, RCAMC, CDC, RCOC, RCEME, CPC, C pro C and the Air OP Squadron.

3rd Canadian Infantry Division, CAOF remained on occupational duty until relieved by 52nd (Lowland) Division on the 15th of May 1946. Units of the Canadian Division were phased out during March, April and May, receiving authorization to disband under General Order 162/46 and General Order 201/46.

Headquarters 3rd Canadian Infantry Division, CAOF, was authorized to disband under General Order 238/46 (Effective 20th June 1946).

* * *

4th Canadian Armoured Division — First Canadian Army — NW Europe

Headquarters, 4th Division, CASF, Serial 900, and Headquarters 4th Divisional Artillery RCA, CASF, Serial 904, mobilized under General Order 184/40 (Effective 24th May 1940).

Mobilized as an infantry division, 15th, 16th and 17th Field Regiments plus 4th Anti-Tank Regiment RCA, comprised the divisional artillery. 10th, 11th and 12th Infantry Brigades were designated the infantry brigade components and mobilized at that time with 4th Division, CASF.

Upon arrival at Nanaimo Camp, British Columbia in October 1940, 10th Infantry Brigade comprised Headquarters 10th Infantry Brigade, CASF, 10th Infantry Anti-Tank Company, CASF, The British Columbia Regiment (Duke of Connaught's Own Rifles), CASF, The South Alberta Regiment, CASF and The 16th/22nd Saskatchewan Horse, CASF.

11th Infantry Brigade components upon arriving at Camp Borden, Ontario, October 1940, included Headquarters 11th Infantry Brigade, CASF, 11th Infantry Anti-Tank Company, CASF, The Lake Superior Regiment, CASF, The Irish Regiment of Canada, CASF and The Grey and Simcoe Foresters.

12th Infantry Brigade in January 1941 included Headquarters 12th Infantry Brigade, CASF, 12th Infantry Anti-Tank Company, CASF, The Governor General's Food Guards, CASF, The Canadian Grenadier Guards, CASF and The Elgin Regiment, CASF.

Division Headquarters was established at Debert, Nova Scotia, and battalions were stationed at Niagara-on-the-Lake and Camp Borden, Ontario, Valcartier,

P.Q., Sussex, New Brunswick, and at Debert, during which time units aided in protecting vulnerable locations and coastal forts.

The request that Canada's next contribution to the overseas force be an armoured division slowed the forming of 4th Division and a number of 4th Division units were diverted to the new formation which mobilized as 1st Canadian Armoured Division, then was redesigned 5th Canadian (Armoured) Division.

4th Anti-Tank Regiment RCA was transferred, the batteries of 15th and 16th Field Regiments moved to other regiments in February 1941, and 18th Field Regiment RCA replaced 17th Field Regiment RCA in 4th Division.

18th (Manitoba) Reconnaissance Battalion, Serial 977, and Headquarters 18th Field Regiment RCA, Serial 982, mobilized under General Order 160/41 (Effective 10th May 1941). 15th and 16th Field Regiments RCA were allotted new batteries.

5th Anti-Tank Regiment RCA, Serial 992, and Headquarters 5th Anti-Tank Regiment RCA, Serial 992A, mobilized under General Order 240/41 (Effective 5th September 1941), to replace the departed 4th Anti-Tank Regiment RCA.

6th Light Anti-Aircraft Regiment RCA, Serial 991, also mobilized under General Order 240/41 (Effective 5th September 1941), to serve as 4th Division light anti-aircraft regiment.

Headquarters 4th Division, Serial 900, was redesignated Headquarters 4th (Armoured) Division, Serial 900, under General Order 132/42 (Effective 26th January 1942). The armoured division was to comprise an armoured car regiment (18th (Manitoba) Armoured Car Regiment), two armoured brigades, the 3rd and 4th, and a support group.

Headquarters 10th Infantry Brigade, Serial 930, was redesignated Headquarters 3rd Armoured Brigade, Serial 930, and Headquarters 12th Infantry Brigade, Serial 950, was redesignated Headquarters 4th Armoured Brigade, Serial 950, under General Order 132/42 (Effective 26th January 1942).

The British Columbia Regiment was redesignated 28th Armoured Regiment (The British Columbia Regiment), CAC, The Elgin Regiment was redesignated 25th Armoured Regiment (The Elgin Regiment), CAC, The South Alberta Regiment was redesignated 29th Armoured Regiment (The South Alberta Regiment), CAC, and The Lake Superior Regiment was redesignated The Lake Superior Regiment (Motor), to serve under Headquarters 3rd Armoured Brigade, 4th Canadian Armoured Division.

The Governor General's Foot Guards became 21st Armoured Regiment (The

Governor General's Foot Guards), CAC, The Canadian Grenadier Guards became 22nd Armoured Regiment (The Canadian Grenadier Guards), CAC, The Sherbrooke Fusiliers Regiment was redesignated 27th Armoured Regiment (The Sherbrooke Fusiliers Regiment), CAC, and The Princess Louise Fusiliers (MG) was redesignated The Princess Louise Fusiliers (Motor), to serve under Headquarters 4th Armoured Brigade, 4th Canadian Armoured Division.

Headquarters 4th Divisional Artillery, RCA, Serial 904, was redesignated Headquarters 4th (Armoured) Divisional Support Group, under General Order 132/42 (Effective 26th January 1942), to comprise 15th Field Regiment RCA, 5th Anti-Tank Regiment RCA, 8th Light Anti-Aircraft Regiment RCA, and The Irish Regiment of Canada.

Headquarters 16th Field Regiment RCA, Serial 906A, was redesignated Headquarters 8th Light Anti-Aircraft Regiment RCA, Serial 1906A, under General Order 132/42 (Effective 26th January 1942), and Headquarters 18th Field Regiment RCA, Serial 982, was redesignated Headquarters 2nd Medium Regiment RCA, Serial 982A, under General Order 104/42 (Effective 26th January 1942). 6th Light Anti-Aircraft Regiment RCA became 2nd Canadian Corps light anti-aircraft regiment at a later date. Headquarters 11th Infantry Brigade became Headquarters 2nd Army Tank Brigade and The Grey and Simcoe Foresters and The 16th/22nd Saskatchewan Horse followed the headquarters to the new army tank brigade.

Headquarters 4th (Armoured) Division with its two Armoured Brigades and Support Group proceeded overseas the latter part of 1942.

One of the armoured brigades in the division was replaced by an infantry brigade shortly after the division arrived overseas. 3rd Armoured Brigade was phased out and 4th Armoured Brigade remained a component retaining two of its regiments, 21st Armoured Regiment (The Governor General's Foot Guards) and 22nd Armoured Regiment (The Canadian Grenadier Guards), and added two units, 28th Armoured Regiment (The British Columbia Regiment) (DCOR) and The Lake Superior Regiment (Motor), from the disbanding 3rd Armoured Brigade. 29th Armoured Regiment (The South Alberta Regiment) became 29th Armoured Reconnaissance Regiment (The South Alberta Regiment), divisional recce regiment.

18th Armoured Car Regiment (12th Manitoba Dragoons) moved under Headquarters 2nd Canadian Corps, 25th Armoured Regiment (The Elgin Regiment) moved to Army Troops as 25th Armoured Delivery Regiment. 27th Armoured Regiment (The Sherbrooke Fusiliers Regiment) moved to 3rd Army Tank Brigade, then 2nd Canadian Armoured Brigade. The Irish Regiment of Canada and The Princess Louise Fusiliers moved to 5th Canadian Armoured Division.

10th Independent Machine Gun Company (The New Brunswick Rangers), The Lincoln and Welland Regiment, The Algonquin Regiment and The Argyll and Sutherland Highlanders of Canada (Princess Louise's), arrived from Canada during 1943 to form 10th Canadian Infantry Brigade in 4th Canadian Armoured Division.

Headquarters 4th (Armoured) Divisional Support Group, Serial 904, was redesignated Headquarters 4th Armoured Divisional Artillery, Serial 904, under General Order 335/43 (Effective 1st January 1943). A fourth anti-tank battery was added to 5th Anti-Tank Regiment RCA, and in August 1943, 23rd Field Regiment (SP) RCA arrived in England to complete the divisional artillery, which now included 15th Field Regiment RCA, 23rd Field Regiment (SP) RCA, 5th Anti-Tank Regiment RCA and 8th Light Anti-Aircraft Regiment RCA.

4th Canadian Armoured Division landed in Normandy on the 26th July 1944 and became operational under 2nd Canadian Corps 29th July on the Caen Front. The division with the bulk of Canadian units in Normandy came under command of First Canadian Army 31st July 1944 and participated in the vicious fighting in the breakout from Caen and the closing of the Falaise Gap.

During the fierce battle at St. Lambert sur Dives 18th to 21st August, 1944, Major David Vivian Currie of 29th Armoured Reconnaissance Regiment (The South Alberta Regiment) was awarded the Victoria Cross for heroism.

2nd Canadian Corps, with 2nd Canadian Infantry Division on the left, 3rd Canadian Infantry Division centre and 4th Canadian Armoured Division on the right, advanced to the River Seine where the enemy resisted stubbornly, enabling a large portion of troops and equipment to escape to form another defence line.

The infantry of 4th Canadian Armoured Division crossed the Seine near Criquebeuf, above Elbeuf, 26th August and Rouen fell to 3rd Canadian Infantry Division of 2nd Canadian Corps 30th August. 4th Div advanced NE from the River Seine to the next water barrier, the River Somme, which was crossed by 4th Division infantry on the 2nd of September, and by the armour on the 3rd, at Pont Remy. 1st Polish Armoured Division crossed on the left and 3rd Canadian Infantry Division next to the sea, as 2nd Canadian Infantry Division returned to Dieppe, and 4th Division paused at Abbeville.

The rapid advance by Second British Army's 30 Corps interrupted the building of a defence line by the enemy at the River Somme and armoured units reached Brussels on the 3rd of September, and Antwerp on the 4th of September. The port of Antwerp, however, was approximately fifty miles from the sea and a determined enemy prepared to deny the use of the port to the Allies by retaining heavily defended areas along the southern and northern approaches.

As Second British Army advanced into Belgium, First Canadian Army moved to the coast to clear the Channel ports, destroy the fortresses and eliminate the flying-bomb launching sites.

1 British Corps, 2nd and 3rd Canadian Infantry Divisions proceeded to clear their allotted fortresses and 4th Canadian Armoured Division resumed its advance from St. Omer on the 6th of September directed at Bruges and Eecloo in Belgium. The division was organized into two battle groups and reached the Ghent Canal on the 8th of September.

The canal which was the beginning of the Scheldt defences was crossed by a battalion of infantry on the 8th and 9th, and on the 10th the recce regiment joined the two battalions and slowly extended the bridgehead. On the 12th of September 4th Brigade of 2nd Division aided in clearing the city of Bruges.

From the Ghent Canal 4th Division advanced to the Canal de Derivation de la Lys and the Leopold Canal which ran side by side. Moerkerke proved too difficult an area for a bridgehead on the 14th of September and a crossing was made NW of Eecloo on the 15th. The two canals divided north of Maldegem to form a wedge-shaped area which was cleared by the division, along with a narrow area leading to the West Scheldt between the Braakman and the Terneuzen Canal. 1st Polish Armoured Division cleared the area to the right of the Terneuzen Canal in conjunction with the 4th Div operation.

2nd Canadian Infantry Division upon being diverted from its duty at Dunkirk began the move to Antwerp 16th September where it undertook the task of clearing the area north of Antwerp leading to South Beveland.

The airborne drop at Arnhem began 17th September, and the resultant penetration to the Nijmegen area was to provide the launching area for the attack into Germany early in the new year. Freeing the port of Antwerp was becoming more important.

Part of 4th Canadian Armoured Division moved north of Antwerp to the Brecht and Brasschaet area 9th October, leaving elements of the Div to patrol the Leopold Canal and contain the enemy in the Breskens Pocket. Upon being relieved by 3rd Canadian Infantry Division in the Breskens Pocket the remainder of 4th Division arrived north of Antwerp 17th October.

The division came under 1 British Corps to aid 2nd Canadian Infantry Division in its attack on South Beveland, then was directed on Esschen, which was captured on the 22nd of October, and Bergen op Zoom, which fell on the 27th.

Beyond Bergen op Zoom 4th Div cleared Steenbergen 4th November and advanced to the Hollandschdiep completing the operation in a naval engagement directed at the harbour of Zijpe on Schoen Island. The battle of the

Scheldt ended 8th November, and supplies began to arrive at the port of Antwerp on the 1st of December 1944.

Upon bringing the Scheldt operation to a successful conclusion Headquarters First Canadian Army and 2nd Canadian Corps assumed control of the Nijmegen bridgehead from 30 British Corps, Second British Army, 9th of November.

4th Canadian Armoured Division, still under command 1 British Corps, First Canadian Army, held the right section of 1 British Corps line on the south bank of the lower Maas River. 52 (Lowland) Division relieved 4th div from 26th November to 5th December, at which time 52 Div departed for Second Army and 4th Division resumed its role in the 's-Hertogenbosch sector of the Maas River under 1 British Corps.

4th Division was relieved by 1st Polish Armoured Division 21st December during the Ardennes offensive and was placed in army reserve occupying positions in the Breda-Tilburg area under 1 British Corps.

Kapelsche Veer, on an island in the Maas River near Geertruidenberg was added to the Battle Honours of 4th Canadian Armoured Division's Lincoln and Welland Regiment and became well known to 1st Polish Armoured division whose troops made the first attack the end of December without success, the 47th Royal Marine Commando unsuccessful attack two weeks later, and 10th Canadian Infantry Brigade's attack 26th January which was terminated the night of 30th/31st January when the enemy was cleared from the island.

The attack into Germany was launched from the Nijmegen salient on the 8th of February 1945 and Headquarters First Canadian Army was entrusted with the planning and execution. 30 British Corps under First Canadian Army was to lead the attack with the two Canadian Infantry Divisions and three British Infantry Divisions involved in the initial drive. 2nd Canadian Corps which was protecting 30 Corps left flank was to enter the drive a week later to continue the advance on a two-corps front.

4th Canadian Armoured Division and 11 British Armoured Division were brought forward as 2nd Canadian Corps was to mount an attack on the 26th February to regain the momentum of the drive. 4th Division concentrated at Cleve, Germany, ready to advance between 2nd and 3rd Canadian Infantry Divisions.

The division formed into five battle groups for the attack on the Hochwald Forest defences 26th February and in a series of attacks by each battle group had cleared the ridge from Calcar to Udem early on the 27th. The attack through the Hochwald Gap ran into difficulty and it was not until 4th March that 2nd Canadian Infantry Division completed the occupation of the Hochwald.

The next objective for the division was the village of Veen which was bitterly defended and was entered by 10th Canadian Infantry Brigade, 9th March. Winnenthal with its monastery was captured on the 10th March ending 4th Canadian Armoured Division's operations west of the Rhine.

2nd Canadian Corps passed under complete operational command of Second British Army 20th March for the Rhine River crossing and 3rd Div moved under 30 Corps. 9th Canadian Infantry Brigade (The Highland Brigade) was selected to accompany 51 (Highland) Division on the Rhine assault. 4th Div artillery fired in support of the Rhine crossing 23rd March. The remainder of 3rd Division along with Headquarters 2nd Canadian Corps had crossed the Rhine by the 28th and 2nd Canadian Corps under Second British Army became responsible for 3rd Canadian Infantry Division and its territory.

2nd Div crossed the Rhine 28th/29th March and entered the line to the right of 3rd Div and 4th Div entered the bridgehead to the right of 2nd Div, 1st April. Headquarters First Canadian Army took control of 2nd Canadian Corps operations across the Rhine 1st/2nd April and was now responsible for the front from the left of Second British Army to the sea. 1st Canadian Corps arrived from Italy and moved into the Arnhem Sector 15th April and replaced 1 British Corps in First Canadian Army.

2nd Canadian Corps with 3rd Division on the left, 2nd Division centre and 4th Division on the right began the northward drive to clear northeast Holland. 2nd Canadian Armoured Brigade joined the advance in support of 2nd and 3rd Canadian Infantry Divisions.

4th Canadian Armoured Division advanced to the Twente Canal where it established a crossing west of Delden, 3rd April, captured the town and moved through Borne. Almelo was cleared on the 4th/5th April and at Almelo 1st Polish Armoured Division returned to 2nd Canadian Corps to operate between 4th and 2nd Canadian Divisions.

4th Canadian Armoured Division was directed into Germany toward Meppen on the Ems River, clearing Neuenhaus, Emlichheim and Coevorden enroute. The division crossed the Ems River at Meppen and proceeded to clear the area east of the river to the Kusten Canal, the infantry brigade in the direction of Leer, on the Leda River, and the armoured brigade captured Sogel, Borger, and Friesoythe on the 14th. 10th Infantry Brigade moved east along the canal and crossed on the 17th at Edewechterdamm, eleven miles SW of Oldenburg and held the bridgehead against fierce counter-attacks.

By the 21st the brigade had extended the bridgehead to the River Aue near Ostercheps, slightly over two miles. Edewecht fell on the 25th and the armoured brigade assumed the lead in the advance toward Bad Zwischenahn, with the aid of rocket firing aircraft. Ekern was captured on the 28th and Bad Zwischenahn fell on the 30th.

2nd Division, in a change of plans, was directed to capture Oldenburg and 4th Division moved north toward Varel and Wilhelmshaven. On the 4th of May 10th Canadian Infantry Brigade neared Mollberg, 4th Canadian Armoured Brigade captured Rastede and had reached the outskirts of Bekhausen, ten miles north of Oldenburg when the "Cease Fire" was received 5th May.

On the 30th April, Hitler committed suicide, the capitulation of the German armies in Italy followed on the 2nd May and now, on the 5th May active operations ceased in NW Europe.

The 8th of May 1945 was designated "VE" Day and the disarming of the Germans and arrangements for their return to Germany was begun.

4th Canadian Armoured Division concentrated near Almelo, Holland late in May and the run-down of the Canadian units was begun. Volunteers proceeded to the Canadian Army Pacific Force joined the Canadian Army Occupational Force, departed on priority drafts, or were posted to divisional units originating in the military district of their enlistment for the return to Canada.

Headquarters 4th Armoured Divisional Artillery, RCA, received authorization to disband under General Order 71/46 (Effective 22nd December 1945) and Headquarters 4th Canadian Armoured Division received authorization to disband under the same General Order (Effective 27th December 1945).

*　　*　　*

5th Canadian (Armoured) Division — Italy and NW Europe

The request that an Armoured Division be dispatched overseas during 1941 saw the suspension of recruiting for 4th (Infantry) Division and energies diverted to the forming of the new Armoured Division which was to comprise two armoured brigades, a support group and an armoured car regiment.

The composition of 1st Canadian Armoured Brigade is listed as Serial 571, Headquarters 1st Canadian Armoured Brigade, 2nd Armoured Regiment (Lord Strathcona's Horse) (Royal Canadians), 6th Armoured Regiment (1st Hussars), and 10th Armoured Regiment (The Fort Garry Horse), authorized under General Order 79/41 (Effective 11th February 1941).

2nd Canadian Armoured Brigade was to comprise Serial 564, Headquarters 2nd Canadian Armoured Brigade, 3rd Armoured Regiment (The Governor General's Horse Guards), 5th Armoured Regiment (8th Princess Louise's (New Brunswick) Hussars), and 9th Armoured Regiment (The British Columbia Dragoons), authorized under General Order 79/41 (Effective 11th February 1941).

Headquarters 1st Canadian Armoured Division, Serial 562, was placed on active service under General order 88/41 (Effective 27th February 1941).

6th Duke of Connaught's Royal Canadian Hussars (Armoured Car) became 5th Canadian (Armoured) Division Headquarters Squadron (6th Duke of Connaught's Royal Canadian Hussars), The Prince Edward Island Light Horse was designated 1st Canadian Armoured Brigade Headquarters Squadron (The Prince Edward Island Light Horse), and 7th/11th Hussars became 2nd Canadian Armoured Brigade Headquarters Squadron (7th/11th Hussars), under General Order 260/41 (Effective 27th February 1941).

A number of 4th Division units were transferred to the new armoured division, along with three motorcycle units previously mobilized, 1st Armoured Car Regiment (The Royal Canadian Dragoons) and the existing 1st Armoured Brigade, slightly altered.

17th Field Regiment RCA and 4th Anti-Tank Regiment RCA also arrived from 4th Division, and they along with 5th Light Anti-Aircraft Regiment RCA formed of field batteries from 15th and 16th Field Regiments, and an infantry battalion, comprised the armoured division support group. Each armoured brigade was allotted a motor battalion of infantry.

The artillery regiments of the division, 17th Field Regiment RCA, 5th Light Anti-Aircraft Regiment RCA and 4th Anti-Tank Regiment RCA concentrated at Camp Petawawa, Ontario, and the armoured and infantry units congregated at Camp Borden, Ontario during the early months of 1941.

Authority was granted to substitute the term "5th Canadian (Armoured) Division" for the term "1st Canadian Armoured Division", under General Order 135/41 (Effective 5th June 1941).

During September, October and November 1941 units of 5th Canadian (Armoured) Division converged on Halifax, Nova Scotia to board ship for the overseas journey and upon arrival in Scotland or Liverpool, England, the division journeyed to Aldershot, Hampshire, in the south of England for duty with the Canadian Corps guarding the coast, interspersed with training for an armoured role.

5th Canadian (Armoured) Division was rocked with reorganization early 1943 as the division trimmed to one armoured brigade, and added more infantry and artillery. Serial 571, Headquarters 1st Canadian Armoured Brigade was redesignated Headquarters 11th Infantry Brigade, under General Order 282/43 (Effective 1st January 1943), and Serial 578, Headquarters 5th Canadian (Armoured) Division Support Group, was redesignated Serial 578, Headquarters 5th Armoured Divisional Artillery, under General Order 335/43 (Effective 1st January 1943).

Serial 564, Headquarters 2nd Canadian Armoured Brigade was redesignated Serial 564, Headquarters 5th Canadian Armoured Brigade C.A.C., under General Order 224/43 (Effective 1st January 1943).

5th Canadian (Armoured) Division Headquarters Squadron (6th Duke of Connaught's Royal Canadian Hussars) disbanded under General Order 225/43 (Effective 1st January 1943), upon being absorbed by Headquarters 5th Canadian (Armoured) Division, and 2nd Canadian Armoured Brigade Headquarters Squadron (7th/11th Hussars) disbanded under General Order 225/43 (Effective 1st January 1943) and was absorbed by Headquarters 5th Canadian Armoured Brigade.

1st Armoured Car Regiment (The Royal Canadian Dragoons) became 1st Canadian Corps Armoured Car Regiment, 1st Canadian Armoured Brigade Headquarters Squadron (The Prince Edward Island Light Horse) was redesignated 2nd Corps Defence Company. 6th Armoured Regiment (1st Hussars) and 10th Armoured Regiment (The Fort Garry Horse) became components of an ad hoc 3rd Army Tank Brigade previous to the forming of 2nd Armoured Brigade (an independent armoured brigade).

3rd Armoured Regiment (The Governor General's Horse Guards), C.A.C. was redesignated 3rd Armoured Reconnaissance Regiment (The Governor General's Horse Guards), C.A.C., under General Order 223/43 (Effective 1st January 1943) and remained with 5th Canadian (Armoured) Division along with the armoured components which included 2nd Armoured Regiment (Lord Strathcona's Horse (Royal Canadians), 5th Armoured Regiment (8th Princess Louise's (New Brunswick) Hussars), 9th Armoured Regiment (The British Columbia Dragoons), and The Westminster Regiment (Motor), under Headquarters 5th Canadian Armoured Brigade, C.A.C.

Grouped under Headquarters 11th Infantry Brigade were The Perth Regiment, The Cape Breton Highlanders, The Irish Regiment of Canada, and 11th Independent Machine Gun Company (The Princess Louise Fusiliers).

Headquarters 5th Armoured Divisional Artillery encompassed 4th Anti-Tank Regiment RCA (now a four-battery regiment), 5th Light Anti-Aircraft Regiment RCA, 17th Field Regiment RCA, and 8th Field Regiment (Self-Propelled) RCA which was added to the order of battle later in the year.

In October and November 1943 units of 5th Canadian Armoured Division departed England for the Mediterranean theatre of operations where a Canadian Corps was to become operational under Headquarters 1st Canadian Corps, with 1st Canadian Infantry Division, 5th Canadian (Armoured) Division, 1st Canadian Armoured Brigade, 1st Canadian AGRA, and attached units, under command.

The fighting squadrons and self-propelled artillery batteries disembarked at Algiers for a three week stay, then proceeded to Naples to rejoin their regiments in Italy in time for Christmas 1943.

Two battalions of the division's 11th Canadian Infantry Brigade with artillery support relieved 3rd Canadian Infantry Brigade of 1st Division north of Ortona, between Ortona and the Riccio River on the 13th of January 1944. The brigade role of holding the front and patrolling was suddenly altered and an attack across the Riccio River toward the Arielli River was ordered to relieve the pressure on the Anzio landing. Both battalions suffered heavily in the vicious fighting.

11th Canadian Infantry Brigade was relieved by 2nd Canadian Infantry Brigade and moved to 13 British Corps sector north-east of Orsogna under 4th Indian Division 21st/22nd January, for an attack on Orsogna. The Westminster Regiment (Motor) and 2nd Armoured Regiment (Lord Strathcona's Horse (Royal Canadians) also entered the line under 4th Indian Division. The attack however was cancelled with two divisions whisked away to duty with Fifth Army.

5th Canadian (Armoured) Division moved to the Orsogna sector on the 31st of January 1944 as 1st Canadian Corps formally relieved 5 British Corps on the Adriatic front, 31st January-1st February 1944 and all Canadian units with the exception of 1st Canadian Armoured Brigade were under command by the 9th of February. The Canadian Corps in turn was relieved by 5 British Corps 7th March 1944.

1st Canadian Corps and 5th Canadian (Armoured) Division surfaced again in the battle to penetrate the Gustav Line which was anchored to Monte Cassino. The assault on the line began 11th May and the guns of the Canadian artillery fired in support of the initial attack.

13 British Corps breached the Gustav Line defences and 1st Canadian Corps passed through with 1st Canadian Infantry Division continuing the advance to the Hitler Line, the next heavily fortified position barring the route to Rome.

1st Canadian Infantry Division of 1st Canadian Corps was given the task of cracking the Hitler Line. The attack was launched 23rd May and the line was breached by The Carleton and York Regiment of 3rd Canadian Infantry Brigade and the Seaforths of 2nd Brigade. The successful penetration of the Hitler Line signalled the breakout from the Anzio beachhead by VI US Corps.

5th Canadian (Armoured) Division entered 1st Canadian Infantry Division's breach in the Hitler Line and in the second phase of the attack 5th Canadian Armoured Brigade of 5th Canadian (Armoured) Division was to advance up the Liri Valley to the Melfa River where 11th Canadian Infantry Brigade was to pass through and proceed to Ceprano.

Brigade Groups were formed to leapfrog to the Melfa River. "Vokes Force" comprising 9th Armoured Regiment (The British Columbia Dragoons), The Irish Regiment of Canada, a self-propelled anti-tank battery, engineers, and medical corps, led the advance to a designated area where a firm base was established for the final leap forward to the Melfa by "Griffin Force" composed of 2nd Armoured Regiment (Lord Strathcona's Horse (Royal Canadians), a company of The Westminster Regiment (Motor), a self-propelled anti-tank battery, engineers and medical corps. The third group of 5th Armoured Regiment (8th Princess Louise's (New Brunswick) Hussars) was held in reserve. 3rd Armoured Reconnaissance Regiment (The Governor General's Horse Guards) was responsible for covering both flanks of the advancing column.

Major J.K. Mahony of The Westminster Regiment (Motor) was awarded the Victoria Cross for heroism 25th May 1944, in the Melfa River bridgehead.

11th Canadian Infantry Brigade crossed the Melfa River, advanced to the Liri River and beyond to capture Ceprano on the 27th May. The British Columbia Dragoons, The Westminster Regiment (Motor) and a self-propelled anti-tank battery took the lead with Pofi and Arnaro as their objective. The villages were captured by 11th Canadian Infantry Brigade and the division formed a firm base for the relieving 1st Canadian Infantry Division 31st May, which completed 5th Canadian (Armoured) Division's phase of the battle. Rome was captured on the 4th of June, the day 1st Canadian Corps was placed in army reserve, and while in reserve news of the invasion of Normandy 6th June was received.

1st Canadian Armoured Brigade however, serving with British formations remained in action during the period of 1st Canadian Corps' reserve role. While in reserve an extra infantry brigade was added to 5th Canadian (Armoured) Division. The new brigade was designated 12th Canadian Infantry Brigade, comprising, from 1st Canadian Corps, 1st Light Anti-Aircraft Regiment RCA, from 1st Canadian Infantry Division, 4th Canadian Reconnaissance Regiment (4th Princess Louise Dragoon Guards), from 5th Canadian (Armoured) Division, The Westminster Regiment (Motor), The Princess Louise Fusiliers formed 12th Independent Machine Gun Company, and from 1st Canadian AGRA, Army Troops, 11th Army Field Regiment RCA was aligned with the brigade to provide field artillery support.

1st Canadian Corps returned to action north of Rome as the Allied units approached the Gothic Line. Shortly before midnight on the 25th of August 1944 two brigades of 1st Canadian Infantry Division led the 1st Canadian Corps attack across the Metauro River. 3rd Canadian Infantry Brigade of 1st Division relieved 1st Canadian Infantry Brigade of 1st Division and 11th Canadian Infantry Brigade of 5th Canadian (Armoured) Division relieved 2nd Canadian Infantry Brigade on the 29th as the attack neared the Foglia River. 5th Division continued the advance to the left of 1st Division and The Perth Regiment of 5th Canadian (Armoured) Division won the distinction of first unit to penetrate the Gothic Line.

4th Princess Louise Dragoon Guards of the recently formed 12th Canadian Infantry Brigade came under 11th Canadian Infantry Brigade 25th August and entered the battle 1st September 1944. The other two battalions of the brigade joined the attack 2nd September at Tomba Di Pesaro and advanced to the Conca River in the breakout from the Gothic Line. On the 14th of September following the capture of Coriano 5th Canadian (Armoured) Division was relieved by 4 British Division in 1st Canadian Corps.

Artificial moonlight provided by searchlights was introduced to the field of battle in Italy 17th/18th September in the advance of 4th British Division to the Rimini Line. The Rimini Line was breached and by the 22nd of September 1944, 1st Canadian Corps had crossed the Marecchia River the full length of its front.

The advance was resumed 22nd September with 5th Canadian (Armoured) Division entering the battle on the 23rd September 1944, crossing the Uso River and several water barriers as the division closed to the Fiumicino.

1st Canadian Corps remained in action until 28th October 1944 and was placed in reserve upon being relieved by "Porterforce". 5th Div units in Porterforce included 3rd Armoured Reconnaissance Regiment (Governor General's Horse Guards), The Westminster Regiment, and 12th Independent Machine Gun Company (The Princess Louise Fusiliers).

5th Canadian (Armoured) Division and 1st Canadian Infantry Division entered 10th Indian Division's bridgehead across the Montone River as 1st Canadian Corps began its battle 2nd December 1944 over numerous rivers and canals to the Senio River, which on the 5th of January 1945 became the Winter Line.

5th Canadian (Armoured) Division moved into Eighth Army reserve 14th January 1945, and 1st Canadian Corps turned over the responsibility of its front on the 10th of February 1945. 1st Canadian Infantry Division remained in the Senio Line under 5 Corps and fought its last battle on the Italian front 25th February 1945. 1st Canadian Armoured Brigade remained with 13 British Corps.

While in its reserve role 5th Canadian (Armoured) Division received word of the transfer of 1st Canadian Corps from Italy to NW Europe to join First Canadian Army. The division sailed from Leghorn, Italy, 15th February 1945 to Marseilles, France, and proceeded to Dixmude, Belgium. 12th Canadian Infantry Brigade was disbanded upon arrival in NW Europe and the units reverted to their former designation and returned to their original formation as 5th Canadian (Armoured) Division trimmed to an armoured division war establishment.

5th Canadian Armoured Division became operational 31st March in the

Arnhem sector where 1st Canadian Corps was delegated the task of capturing Arnhem and opening the route to Emmerich. The attack was to be coordinated with the 2nd Canadian Corps drive to the North Sea.

In the Arnhem sector the enemy still controlled the northern section of the "Island" between the Waal and Neder Rijn rivers when 1st Canadian Corps assumed responsibility for the area 15th March. 49 (WR) Division occupying the southern section of the "Island" was placed under command of 1st Canadian Corps and cleared the eastern end of the "Island" 2nd/3rd April supported by the 11th Armoured Regiment (The Ontario Regiment), 11th Army Field Regiment RCA, 1st Canadian AGRA, 1st Rocket Battery RCA and elements of 79 Armoured Division.

5th Canadian Armoured Division's 11th Infantry Brigade and 3rd Armoured Reconnaissance Regiment (The Governor General's Horse Guards) to the left of 49 Div captured Randwijk, Heteren, and Driel and by the 3rd of April had cleared the remainder of the "Island" to the banks of the Neder Rijn. On the far banks of the Neder Rijn stood the elusive city of Arnhem.

Conditions on the "Island" due to flooding saw a change of plan and instead of crossing the Neder Rijn to capture Arnhem 49th Division crossed the Ijssel River at Westervoort late in the evening of the 12th, and on the 13th had firm control of the bridgehead assisted by The Ontario Regiment tanks.

Westervoort became the main crossing point utilizing "Buffaloes", rafts and a prefabricated Bailey bridge floated into position from five miles along the Pannerdensch Canal. Arnhem was cleared on the 14th and 49 Div advanced in the direction of Utrecht, clearing between the highway and the banks of the Neder Rijn River.

On the 13th and 14th April 5th Canadian Armoured Division crossed the Ijssel River through the bridgehead at Westervoort to begin a quick thrust north to the Ijsselmeer through Otterloo, Barneveld, Voorthuizen and Putten.

In mid-April the corps objective was changed from clearing the enemy from western Holland, to clearing the enemy from western Holland between the Ijssel River and the Grebbe Line, a system of fortifications along the Eem and Grebbe rivers between the Ijsselmeer and the Neder Rijn River.

Upon reaching Otterloo divisional headquarters became involved in a sharp encounter the night 16th/17th April as the enemy endeavoring to withdraw from Apeldoorn to the Grebbe Line attempted to break through the extended line at Otterloo and were repulsed in a concerted effort by headquarters tanks, The Irish Regiment of Canada and 17th field Regiment RCA of 5th Div, and 3rd Medium Regiment RA.

From Otterloo the division continued north reaching the Ijsselmeer at Harderwijk on the 18th, having cleared Barneveld, Nijkerk and Putten enroute. Having completed its assignment 5th Div handed the sector over to 1st Div on the 19th and departed for duty with 2nd Canadian Corps in the north-east in relief of 3rd Canadian Infantry Division.

5th Canadian Armoured Division had completed its relief of 3rd Division by the 24th April and under the command of 2nd Canadian Corps assumed responsibility for the provinces of Friesland, Groningen, Drenthe, and the northern portion of Overijssel to the Netherlands-German border.

The northward drive from the Rhine to the North Sea by 2nd Canadian Infantry Division terminated with the capture of the city of Groningen 16th April. 3rd Canadian Infantry Division upon reaching Leeuwarden and the North Sea, relieved 2nd Div at Groningen as 2nd Div returned to Germany to operate on the right flank of 2nd Canadian Corps. As 3rd Canadian Infantry Division neared Delfzijl its services were required for an amphibious attack on Leer, and 5th Canadian Armoured Division arrived in relief.

11th Canadian Infantry Brigade of 5th Canadian Armoured Division was delegated the task of clearing the Delfzijl pocked and capturing the port. The attack was launched from two sides 25th April as the reduction of the pocket was begun. The infantry brigade had in support The Westminster Regiment (Motor), two armoured regiments, 11th Independent Machine Gun Company, a light anti-aircraft battery, two anti-tank batteries and the divisional artillery. A British AA Brigade and a heavy battery RA supported the latter stages of the operation.

The port was captured 1st May against stiff resistance and the area was cleared the following day. The capture of Delfzijl ended active operations for 5th Canadian Armoured Division in NW Europe upon the receipt of the "Cease Fire" 5th May and the 8th of May 1945 being designated "VE" Day.

5th Canadian Armoured Division remained in the north-eastern Netherlands with headquarters at Groningen and supervised the march of the German forces from the Ijsselmeer causeway to the Netherlands-German border where 2nd Canadian Corps took control.

With cessation of hostilities the run-down of Canadian units was begun. Volunteers proceeded to the Canadian Army Pacific Force, the Canadian Army Occupational Force, departed on priority drafts or were posted to divisional groups from the military districts of their enlistment for the return to Canada.

Headquarters 5th Canadian Armoured Divisional Artillery and Headquarters

5th Canadian Armoured Brigade received authorization to disband under General Order 71/46 (Effective 29th November 1945). Headquarters 11th Infantry Brigade, CIC disbanded under the same General Order (Effective 3rd December 1945). Headquarters 5th Canadian (Armoured) Division disbanded under General Order 71/46 (Effective 12th December 1945).

*   *   *

6th Division, Esquimalt, B.C. — Pacific Command and Kiska

Serial 1030, Headquarters 13th Infantry Brigade, CASF, mobilized under General Order 184/40 (Effective 24th May 1940) as an independent brigade and was employed in the Niagara Peninsula. In May 1941, 13th Brigade arrived at Nanaimo, British Columbia, on Vancouver Island, in relief of 10th Brigade of 4th Division.

Headquarters 14th and 15th Infantry Brigades, Headquarters 19th, 20th and 21st Field Regiments RCA mobilized under General Order 63/42 (Effective 29th July 1941). Brigade groups less artillery were formed in August 1941, then in September 1941, 21st Field Regiment RCA was aligned with 13th Brigade Group, 19th Field Regiment RCA, with 14th Brigade Group and 20th Field Regiment RCA with 15th Brigade Group. 14th Brigade remained in eastern Canada on duty in the Niagara Peninsula and 15th Brigade was stationed at Valcartier, P.Q.

Serial 1800, Headquarters 6th Division, 6th Division Intelligence Section, No. 6 Field Security Section, No. 6 Defence and Employment Platoon, 31st (Alberta) Reconnaissance Battalion CAC, Headquarters 6th Divisional Artillery RCA, Headquarters 9th Light Anti-Aircraft Regiment RCA, with four batteries, Headquarters 6th Anti-Tank Regiment RCA, with four batteries, Headquarters 6th Divisional Engineers, RCE, Headquarters 6th Divisional Signals RCCS, No. 13, 14 and 15 Defence Platoons, a machine gun battalion, RCASC, RCAMC, RCOC, a provost company, and a postal unit, were authorized to mobilize under General Order 147/42 (Effective 18th March 1942). Headquarters 6th Division found accommodation at Esquimalt, British Columbia, on Vancouver Island.

The brigade group organization remained in effect until July 1942 when the division conformed to infantry division organization. The division reconnaissance battalion, the divisional artillery of three field regiments, a light anti-aircraft regiment and an anti-tank regiment were grouped under Headquarters 6th Division. The three infantry brigades, now 13th, 18th and 19th, each contained one defence platoon and three infantry battalions. Each infantry brigade had one designated regiment of field artillery for support, plus anti-tank and light anti-aircraft elements.

21st Field Regiment remained aligned with 13th Brigade and 13th Brigade remained at Nanaimo, 19th Field Regiment accompanied 14th Brigade to 8th Division and 20th Field Regiment remained in eastern Canada with 15th Brigade, now with 7th Division.

24th and 25th Field Regiments RCA accompanied 18th and 19th Infantry Brigades to 6th Division and were grouped with the divisional artillery under division headquarters, along with 21st Field Regiment RCA, 9th Light Anti-Aircraft Regiment RCA, and 6th Anti-Tank Regiment RCA. 18th Infantry Brigade was posted to Port Alberni, on Vancouver Island and 19th Infantry Brigade was stationed at Vernon, in the interior of the province and served as reserve for Pacific Command.

In January 1943, 79th Light Anti-Aircraft Battery RCA of 9th Light Anti-Aircraft Regiment RCA became 79th Anti-Aircraft Battery RCA, remaining in Pacific Command in a coast defence role and 48th Light Anti-Aircraft Battery RCA moved to 8th Division, then in May, Headquarters 9th Light Anti-Aircraft Regiment RCA disbanded. 21st Field Regiment RCA and 6th Anti-Tank Regiment RCA overseas-bound, departed 6th Division. 24th and 25th field Regiments RCA remained.

In June, 13th Infantry Brigade became part of the Kiska "Greenlight" Force and 19th Infantry Brigade moved under command of 8th Division, returning to 6th Division in July. 16th and 20th Infantry Brigades joined 6th Division during July and the division remained a four-brigade division until mid-October 1943 at which time Headquarters 7th Division and Headquarters 8th Canadian Division, Headquarters 16th, 18th, 19th, 20th and 21st Infantry Brigades disbanded. Headquarters 17th Infantry Brigade disbanded 15 November 1943.

13th Brigade at Kiska, 14th Brigade of 8th Division, and 15th Brigade of 7th Division survived the cut and returned as the components of 6th Division. Headquarters 6th Division moved from Esquimalt to Prince George in October 1943 and the division reorganized to comprise three brigade groups of four infantry battalions, one defence platoon, one machine gun company, one three-battery field regiment RCA and one light anti-aircraft battery RCA.

The components of 13th Brigade Group as it landed at Kiska in the Aleutians August 1943 included 24th Field Regiment RCA, 46th Light Anti-Aircraft Battery RCA, The Canadian Fusiliers (City of London Regiment), The Winnipeg Grenadiers, The Rocky Mountain Rangers, Le Regiment de Hull, and "C" Company, The St. John Fusiliers (MG).

Upon landing in Kiska the Canadians found the enemy had vacated the island and the brigade group returned to Canada in January 1944 resuming its home defence role with 6th Division in Pacific Command.

25th Field Regiment RCA and 48th Light Anti-Aircraft Battery RCA joined 14th Brigade Group, 20th Field Regiment RCA along with 15th Brigade Group returned to 6th Division and 25th Light Anti-Aircraft Battery joined 15th Brigade Group. 22nd Heavy Anti-Aircraft Battery (Mobile), RCA joined the division 1st February 1944.

Headquarters 13th Infantry Brigade CASF departed the division in May 1944 and sailed for England where it became Headquarters 13th Canadian Training Brigade, authorized under General Order 78/45 (Effective 1st November 1944). A new Headquarters 16th Infantry Brigade was mobilized to replace 13th Brigade under General Order 405/44 (Effective 20th August 1944) and disbanded under General Order 213/15 (Effective 15th April 1945).

Headquarters 14th Infantry Brigade and Headquarters 15th Infantry Brigade were despatched overseas and were authorized to disband under General Order 114/45 (Effective 10th and 18th January 1945) respectively. Personnel joined the reinforcement pool.

Serial 1800, Headquarters 6th Division, received authorization to disband under General Order 208/45 (Effective 31st January 1945).

Headquarters 13th Canadian Infantry Training Brigade became Headquarters "D" Group Canadian Reinforcement Units under General Order 38/45 (Effective 31st July 1945).

Headquarters "D" Group Canadian Reinforcement Units was redesignated Headquarters "D" Group Canadian Repatriation Units under General Order 399/45 (Effective 30th August 1945).

Headquarters "D" Group Canadian Repatriation Units received authorization to disband under General Order 85/46 (Effective 28th January 1946).

*   *   *

6th Canadian Infantry Division — Canadian Army Pacific Force (CAPF)

Headquarters 6th Canadian Infantry Division mobilized under General Order 241/45 (Effective 1st June 1945) with its components, Headquarters Special Troops 6th Canadian Infantry Division, Headquarters Company 6th Canadian Infantry Division, Medical Detachment RCAMC, 6th Canadian Infantry Division, 6th Canadian Military Police Platoon C Pro C, 6th Canadian Ordnance Light Maintenance Company RCEME, 6th Canadian Quartermaster Company RCASC, 6th Canadian Signal Company RC Sigs. Headquarters 6th Canadian Infantry Division and these components disbanded under General Order 425/45 (Effective 1st November 1945).

Also mobilizing were Headquarters 1st, 2nd and 3rd Canadian Infantry Regiments, each comprising Headquarters Company, Service Company RCASC, a cannon company (The Saskatoon Light Infantry (MG)), an anti-tank company RCA, three infantry battalions and a medical detachment RCAMC.

1st Canadian Infantry Regiment was formed of 1st Canadian Infantry Battalion (The Royal Canadian Regiment), 2nd Canadian Infantry Battalion (The Hastings and Prince Edward Regiment), 3rd Canadian Infantry Battalion (48th Highlanders of Canada).

2nd Canadian Infantry Regiment comprised 1st Canadian Infantry Battalion (Princess Patricia's Canadian Light Infantry), 2nd Canadian Infantry Battalion (The Seaforth Highlanders of Canada), 3rd Canadian Infantry Battalion (The Loyal Edmonton Regiment).

3rd Canadian Infantry Regiment was composed of 1st Canadian Infantry Battalion (Royal 22e Regiment), 2nd Canadian Infantry Battalion (The Carleton and York Regiment) and 3rd Canadian Infantry Battalion (The West Nova Scotia Regiment), completing the infantry components of the division. With the exception of The Royal Canadian Regiment, Princess Patricia's Canadian Light Infantry and Royal 22e Regiment who became components of the Postwar Permanent Force, the above units disbanded under General Order 425/45 (Effective 1st November 1945). The Permanent Force bound 1st Canadian Infantry Battalions of each Canadian Infantry Regiment became 2nd Battalions, authorized under General Order 378/45 (Effective 2nd September 1945) and under General Order 138/46 (Effective 1st March 1946), the 2nd Battalion portion of the title was discontinued.

Headquarters 6th Canadian Division Artillery encompassed Headquarters Battery 6th Canadian Division Artillery, Medical Detachment RCAMC, 6th Canadian Division Artillery, four field artillery battalions RCA and four service batteries RCASC.

1st Canadian Field Artillery Battalion RCA, included Headquarters 1st Canadian Field Artillery Battalion RCA, Headquarters Battery 1st Canadian Field Artillery Battalion RCA, A, B and C Battery 1st Canadian Field Artillery Battalion RCA, Service Battery RCASC, 1st Canadian Field Artillery Battalion. 2nd, 3rd and 4th Canadian Field Artillery Battalions were similarly organized.

Headquarters 6th Canadian Division Artillery and its components, with the exception of 1st Canadian Field Artillery Battalion RCA, Headquarters 1st Canadian Field Artillery Battalion RCA, A, B and C Batteries 1st Canadian Field Artillery Battalion RCA, which became components of the Postwar Permanent Force, disbanded under General Order 425/45 (Effective 1st November 1945), and Headquarters Battery 1st Canadian Field Artillery Battalion RCA which disbanded under General Order 347/45 (Effective 1st September 1945).

6th Canadian Infantry Division Reconnaissance Troop (The Royal Montreal Regiment) CAC, 6th Canadian Engineer Combat Battalion RCE, 6th Canadian Medical Battalion RCAMC, 22nd Canadian Tank Battalion (The Canadian Grenadier Guards) CAC, were included, along with RCOC, Canadian Postal Corps, and a number of specialized units. These units also disbanded under General Order 425/45 (Effective 1st November 1945).

The Canadian Army Pacific Force was to comprise an infantry division, a tank battalion, service and supporting troops. The Canadians, retaining the Canadian uniform, were to be organized along US Army lines, use US equipment and be supplied as a normal US Division.

1st Canadian Infantry Division units were selected as components of the force, 1st Canadian Infantry Division, however, was still operational in NW Europe and the CAPF Division assumed the designation 6th Canadian Infantry Division, CAPF.

The units assembled at a number of camps in Canada with a projected move to Camp Breckenridge, Kentucky. Instructional cadres proceeded to US Army Schools, with the Royal Canadian Artillery cadre posted to the Artillery School at Fort Sill, Oklahoma, and the Royal Canadian Engineers journeying to Fort Belvoir, Virginia.

The division's operational role was slated to begin early in 1946. Plans were to change however with the dropping of atomic bombs at Hiroshima 6th August and at Nagasaki on the 9th of August. The surrender documents were signed 2nd September 1945 ending the conflict and the Canadian Army Pacific Force disbanded, the training cadres only, having departed for the USA. A number of units of the CAPF were diverted to the postwar Active Force.

1st Canadian Field Artillery Battalion became 2nd-1st Field Regiment RCHA. Headquarters 1st Canadian Field Artillery Battalion RCA was redesignated Headquarters 2nd-1st Field Regiment RCHA. A, B and C Batteries 1st Canadian Field Artillery Battalion RCA became A, B and C Batteries 2nd-1st Field Regiment RCHA. The redesignations were authorized under General Order 345/45 (Effective 1st September 1945).

2nd/1st Field Regiment RCHA was redesignated 71st Regiment RCHA, Headquarters 2nd/1st Field Regiment RCHA was redesignated Headquarters 71st Regiment RCHA, "A" Battery and "B" Battery 2nd/1st Field Regiment RCHA were redesignated "A" Battery and "B" Battery RCHA, and "C" Battery 2nd/1st Field Regiment RCHA became "C" Battery (Self-Propelled) RCHA, under General Order 138/46 (Effective 1st March 1946).

71st Regiment Royal Canadian Horse Artillery consisting of Headquarters, "A" Battery, "B" Battery and "C" Battery (Self-Propelled), was permanently embodied in the postwar Permanent Force (Active Force), under General Order 158/46 (Effective 27th June 1946).

Royal Canadian Horse Artillery was redesignated 71st Regiment (Royal Canadian Horse Artillery), under General Order 259/46 (Effective 16th October 1946), amending Canadian Expeditionary Force Routine Order 1716 of January 1919.

*   *   *

7th Division, Debert, Nova Scotia — Atlantic Command

Headquarters 16th, 17th and 18th Infantry Brigades, Headquarters 22nd, 23rd and 24th Field Regiments RCA, Royal Canadian Engineers, Royal Canadian Corps of Signals, Royal Canadian Army Service Corps, Royal Canadian Army Medical Corps, and Royal Canadian Ordnance Corps, mobilized under General Order 147/42 (Effective 18th March 1942).

Brigade Groups were formed comprising brigade headquarters, a field artillery regiment and three infantry battalions. 22nd Field Regiment RCA was aligned with 16th Brigade Group, 23rd Field Regiment RCA with 17th Brigade Group and 24th Field Regiment was aligned with 18th Brigade Group. This organization remained in effect until 7th Division Headquarters was formed in June.

Serial 1400, Headquarters 7th Division, 7th Divisional Intelligence Section, No. 5 Field Security Section, No. 7 Defence and Employment Platoon, 30th Reconnaissance Battalion (The Essex Regiment) CAC, Headquarters 7th Divisional Artillery RCA, 10th Light Anti-Aircraft Regiment RCA, 8th Anti-Tank Regiment RCA, divisional RCE, RCCS, No. 16 Defence Platoon, No. 17 Platoon, No. 18 Platoon, RCASC, RCAMC, RCOC, and Postal Corps, mobilized under General Order 309/42 (Effective 12th May 1942).

Headquarters 7th Division settled in at Debert, Nova Scotia, in Atlantic Command and the Divisional Artillery was grouped under Division Headquarters.

A shuffle of infantry brigades also took place and 15th, 17th and 20th Infantry Brigades were now the 7th Division components. The divisional artillery included 20th, 23rd, 26th Field Regiments RCA, 8th Anti-Tank Regiment RCA and 10th Light Anti-Aircraft Regiment RCA.

24th Reconnaissance Battalion (Voltigeurs de Quebec) replaced 30th Reconnaissance Battalion (The Essex Regiment) CAC in September and 23rd Field Regiment RCA departed the division in October to prepare for an overseas role. The infantry components of the division changed periodically. 24th Reconnaissance Battalion (Voltigeurs de Quebec) departed 7th Division in January 1943 and the division operated without a reconnaissance battalion until disbandment. 8th Anti-Tank Regiment RCA disbanded in May to become 28th Field Regiment RCA in 7th Division.

10th Light Anti-Aircraft Regiment RCA of 7th Division trimmed to three batteries in June 1943, conforming to the new war establishment for an infantry division light anti-aircraft regiment. 8th Light Anti-Aircraft Battery RCA was redesignated 63rd Anti-Aircraft Battery RCA and assumed a coast defence role.

In July 1943, 20th Infantry Brigade moved to 6th Division in Pacific Command, and in August one battery from 10th Light Anti-Aircraft Regiment RCA, 7th Division, provided protection for the Quebec Conference.

Toward the end of 1943 the run-down of units on the home front was begun and 7th and 8th Divisions were phased out. 6th Division survived the cut and reorganized to comprise its original brigades. 15th Infantry Brigade and 20th Field Regiment RCA moved from 7th Division to 6th Division, in Pacific Command.

Serial 1400, Headquarters 7th Division, received authorization to disband under General Order 15/44 (Effective 15th October 1943). Headquarters 16th and 18th Infantry Brigades, 7th Divisional Intelligence Section, No. 7 Defence and Employment Platoon, Headquarters Divisional Artillery and Engineers, RCASC, No. 16 Defence Platoon, No. 18 Platoon, 22nd, 27th and 28th Field Regiments RCA, also disbanded under General Order 15/44 (Effective 15th October 1943).

7th Canadian Divisional Signals RCCS disbanded under General Order 15/44 (Effective 25th October 1943). Headquarters 17th Infantry Brigade, 26th Field Regiment RCA, Headquarters 10th Light Anti-Aircraft Regiment RCA, and No. 17 Platoon, disbanded under General Order 15/44 (Effective 15th November 1943). A number of other 7th Division units disbanded at the same time (Effective 1st December 1943).

*   *   *

8th Canadian Division, Prince George, B.C. — Pacific Command

Headquarters 19th, 20th and 21st Infantry Brigades, 25th, 26th and 27th Field Regiments RCA, RCE, RCCS, nine infantry battalions, RCASC, RCAMC, RCOC, and The Princess of Wales' Own Regiment (MG) mobilized under General Order 309/42 (Effective 12th May 1942).

Serial 1600, Headquarters 8th Canadian Division, Divisional Intelligence Section, Field Security Section, Defence and Employment Platoon, Headquarters 8th Divisional Artillery, Headquarters 8th Divisional Engineers and Commander 8th Divisional RCASC, received authorization to mobilize under General Order 301/42 (Effective 15th June 1942).

The Headquarters began to assemble at Bolton Public School, Ottawa, 25th June 1942, then moved west to Jasper, Alberta, 2nd September, prior to congregating in British Columbia. On the 1st October 1942, 14th and 16th Brigade Groups came under command of 8th Division in a shuffle of brigades in the home defence divisions. The Prince Rupert Defences also came under command of the division 9th October 1942. In November 1942, 19th Field Regiment RCA moved from 8th Division to prepare for an overseas posting and 22nd Field Regiment RCA arrived as a replacement.

Headquarters 8th Division and Headquarters 16th Infantry Brigade were situated at Prince George, Headquarters 14th Infantry Brigade was at Terrace, along with 22nd Field Regiment RCA which had one battery serving in a detached role in the Prince Rupert Defences from 11th November 1942.

The division operated an armoured train along the banks of the Skeena River between Terrace and Prince Rupert. The train carried infantry and artillery with the gunners manning the two searchlights, two 75mm guns and four 40mm Bofors light anti-aircraft guns on board.

The battery at Prince Rupert was joined by the remainder of the regiment 5th June 1943. The regiment with all three batteries returned to Terrace 24th July 1943, then on the 29th and 30th July, 3rd and 80th Batteries of 22nd Field Regiment RCA, with 16th Infantry Brigade moved to 6th Division. The batteries returned to the regiment at Terrace under 8th Division, 2nd October 1943.

18th Brigade Group came under command in the Prince Rupert Defences in September, and the division was to comprise 14th and 18th Brigade Groups until the disbandment of Headquarters 8th Canadian Division, authorized under General Order 15/44 (Effective 15th October 1943).

Headquarters 19th, 20th and 21st Infantry Brigades, No. 8 Field Security Section, No. 8 Defence and Employment Platoon, Headquarters 8th Divisional Artillery, Headquarters 8th Divisional Engineers, Commander 8th Divisional RCASC, No. 19, 20 and 21 Defence Platoon, 22nd, 27th and 28th Field Regiments RCA also disbanded under General Order 15/44, the effective date however varied.

6th Division returned to its original brigade structure, 13th, 14th and 15th Infantry Brigades. 14th Brigade Group, which included 25th Field Regiment RCA, returned to 6th Division from 8th Division and 15th Brigade Group with 20th Field Regiment RCA left 7th Division for 6th Division. 24th Field Regiment RCA which had accompanied 13th Brigade Group to Kiska, in the Aleutians, August 1943 remained with 13th Brigade Group.

8th Canadian Division having made a valuable contribution to the security of the west coast, now turned its responsibilities over to 6th Division.

*　　*　　*

Postwar Permanent Force (Active Force)

Headquarters 23rd Infantry Brigade Group, comprising 1st Armoured Regiment (Royal Canadian Dragoons), 2nd Armoured Regiment (Lord Strathcona's Horse (Royal Canadians)), 71st Regiment Royal Canadian Horse Artillery consisting of Headquarters, "A" Battery, "B" Battery, "C" Battery (Self propelled), 68th Medium Battery RCA, 127th Anti-Tank Battery RCA, 128th Heavy Anti-Aircraft Battery RCA, 129th Light Anti-Aircraft Battery RCA, 23rd Brigade Group signals, RC Sigs, "E" Section Signals (71st Regiment Royal Canadian Horse Artillery), RC Sigs, "X" Troop Signals (1st Armoured Regiment (Royal Canadian Dragoons)), RC Sigs, "Y" Troop Signals (2nd Armoured Regiment (Lord Strathcona's Horse (Royal Canadians)), RC Sigs.

The Royal Canadian Regiment, Princess Patricia's Canadian Light Infantry, Royal 22e Regiment, No. 23 Infantry Brigade Company RCASC, No. 37 Light Field Ambulance RCAMC, No. 23 Composite Brigade Group Workshop RCEME, No. 158 Light Aid Detachment (Type C) RCEME, No. 159 Light Aid Detachment (Type C) RCEME and No. 170 Light Aid Detachment (Type D) RCEME, were named as a permanently embodied Corps of the Postwar Permanent Force (Active Force), under General Order 158/46 (Effective 27th June 1946).

*   *   *

Headquarters Atlantic Command, Serial 2914 — Halifax, N.S.

Headquarters Atlantic command, Serial 2914, was authorized to mobilize under General Order 264/43 (Effective 7th August 1940) with Headquarters at Halifax, Nova Scotia. Atlantic Command incorporated Military Districts No. 6 and 7, a slice of Military District No. 5, and Newfoundland.

Headquarters Atlantic Command received authorization to disband under General Order 305/45 (Effective 31st July 1945).

*   *   *

Armament Maintenance Establishments RCA —

No. 6, 7 & 11 District Establishments RCA mobilized under General Order 53/45 (Effective 1st September 1944) for No. 11 and (Effective 2nd September 1944) for No. 6 and No. 7. No. 6, 7 & 11 District Establishments RCA were redesignated No. 6, 7 & 11 Armament Maintenance Establishments RCA under General Order 216/45 (Effective 1st June 1945), and disbanded under General Order 227/46 (Effective 31st July 1946).

Newfoundland Armament Maintenance Establishment RCA was placed on active service under General Order 256/45 (Effective 10th June 1945), and disbanded under General Order 205/46 (Effective 14th May 1946).

*   *   *

Berlin Brigade —

A Canadian brigade group for inclusion in a proposed Allied garrison for Berlin proceeded to take shape with self-propelled batteries selected. Following a month of preparation the "Berlin Brigade" was disbanded and its components returned to their units. A Canadian battalion less artillery proceeded to Berlin, remaining for the month of July 1945.

*   *   *

"B" Force (Bermuda) —

The Winnipeg Grenadiers provided one company for Bermuda in relief of a British unit. The regiment sailed in two groups, 24th May and 13th June 1940. The company, relieved by a British unit, departed 27th August to rejoin the regiment in Jamaica. The Pictou Highlanders provided a company which arrived in Bermuda, 12th November 1942, in relief of the British company. The companies were relieved periodically and "B" Force remained in Bermuda until after the end of hostilities.

*   *   *

Botwood (Newfoundland) —

Headquarters Botwood Defences (Newfoundland), Serial 873, mobilized under General Order 264/43 (Effective 1st July 1940) and was redesignated Headquarters Defended Port of Botwood under General Order 206/44 (Effective 15th April 1944). Headquarters Defended Port of Botwood disbanded under General Order 213/45 (Effective 31st March 1945).

*   *   *

British Guiana —

No. 34 Company Veterans Guard of Canada mobilized for duty in British Guiana, arrived in Georgetown, June 1942 and returned to Canada in January 1945.

*   *   *

"C" Force (Hong Kong) —

The Winnipeg Grenadiers recently returned from Jamaica, and the Royal Rifles of Canada sailed 27th October 1941 on the Awatea for garrison duty in Hong Kong. The Canadians arrived 16th November 1941 and following 17½ days of fighting surrendered on Christmas day 1941.

*   *   *

Exercise "Eskimo" —

Exercise "Eskimo" was initiated to test equipment under "dry cold" conditions in north-central Saskatchewan by a skeleton brigade group and an Army Co-operation Unit, Royal Canadian Air Force, during January and February 1945. A skeleton 13th Infantry Brigade, lines of communication units, 116th Field Battery of 25th Field Regiment RCA and 46th Light Anti-Aircraft Battery RCA with Bofors 40mm guns tested during the Kiska expedition, accompanied the force 183 miles northward from Prince Albert, Saskatchewan, and returned to the railhead at Prince Albert.

*   *   *

Headquarters Fixed Defences —

Headquarters Fixed Defences East Coast, RCA was placed on active service under General Order 256/45 (Effective 10th June 1945) and Headquarters Fixed Defences West Coast RCA was placed on active service under General Order 351/45 (Effective 15th September 1945).

*   *   *

Headquarters Gaspe Defences, Serial 874 — Gaspe, P.Q.

Headquarters Gaspe Defences, Serial 874, mobilized under General Order 264/43 (Effective 1st July 1940) then was redesignated Headquarters Defended Port of Gaspe under General Order 206/44 (Effective 15th April 1944). 105th Coast Battery RCA manned the three forts until disbandment in August 1945. Headquarters Gaspe Defences had disbanded earlier under General Order 208/45 (Effective 31st October 1944).

*   *   *

Headquarters Goose Bay Defences, Serial 2940 — Labrador

In June 1942 the vanguard of Force "G" which included 15th AA Battery (H) RCA, 30th AA Battery (2L) RCA, 108th Coast Battery RCA and The New Brunswick Rangers, arrived at Goose Bay, Labrador, to protect the new airport. The garrison became a Canadian responsibility under operational control of Atlantic Command, and under Military District No. 6 for administration.

Headquarters Goose Bay Defences, Serial 2940, mobilized under General Order 171/44 (Effective 1st June 1943), was redesignated Headquarters Defended Area Goose Bay, under General Order 206/44 (Effective 15th April 1944) and received authorization to disband under General Order 18/46 (Effective 25th August 1945).

*   *   *

Headquarters Halifax Fortress, Serial 2916 — Halifax, N.S.

Headquarters Halifax Fortress, Serial 2916, mobilized under General Order 264/43 (Effective 1st September 1939). 1st (Halifax) Coast Regiment RCA manned the forts and 21st Anti-Aircraft Regiment RCA provided Ack-Ack protection. The headquarters continued to serve under the same designation until authorized to disband under General Order 85/46 (Effective 29th November 1945).

*　　*　　*

Jamaica, B.W.I.

The Winnipeg Grenadiers had mobilized as a machine gun battalion aligned with 6th Infantry Brigade of 2nd Division in 1939. The division reorganized from brigade machine gun battalions to a divisional machine gun battalion, creating a surplus of machine gun battalions. The Winnipeg Grenadiers became an infantry battalion and sailed for the West Indies in two groups 24th May and 13th June 1940. One company stopped off at Bermuda and the main body of the regiment disembarked in Jamaica, 20th June 1940. The company arrived from Bermuda to join the regiment in Jamaica 27th August 1940.

The Winnipeg Grenadiers were in turn relieved by The Argyll and Sutherland Highlanders of Canada. The main body of the Argyll's arrived 26th September and the rear party of The Winnipeg Grenadiers departed on the 28th of September. Shortly after arriving back in Canada The Winnipeg Grenadiers boarded ship at Vancouver for its next assignment where the name of "Hong Kong" was to be added to its list of battle honours.

The Argyll and Sutherland Highlanders of Canada remained in Jamaica until relieved by The Irish Fusiliers of Canada in May 1943 and the Argyll's disembarked at New Orleans, USA. The Irish Fusiliers of Canada served in Jamaica from May 1943 to August 1944. The Brockville Rifles closed out the Canadian garrison in Jamaica and returned to Canada in the spring of 1946.

*　　*　　*

Kiska, Aleutian Islands —

A combined Canadian-United States "Greenlight" Force was formed to drive the enemy from the island of Kiska in the Aleutian chain. 13th Brigade Group of 6th Canadian Division, Home Defence, supplied the Canadian component and the force was organized along US lines. The force sailed for Adak, also in the Aleutians, for further training and acclimatization.

The Canadian and United States troops landed at Kiska in August 1943 to discover the Japanese had vacated the island. 13th Brigade Group remained on garrison duty until the end of the year and returned to Canada to resume its duty with 6th Division in Pacific Command.

*   *   *

"N" Force (Nassau) in the Bahamas —

No. 33 Company Veterans Guard of Canada, Serial 2264, mobilized under General Order 355/42 Part "A" (Effective 1st May 1942), to aid in the defence of the Bahamas, of which His Royal Highness the Duke of Windsor was Governor.

No. 33 Company arrived in June 1942 and remained until relieved by a company of The Pictou Highlanders in the autumn of 1943. The Pictou's remained until the spring of 1946, then returned to Canada.

*   *   *

Headquarters Pacific Command — moved from Victoria to Vancouver November 1942.

Headquarters Pacific Command, Serial 2915, mobilized under General Order 264/43 (Effective 2nd December 1940). Headquarters Pacific command was redesignated Headquarters Military District No. 11, under General Order 56/46 (Effective 23rd January 1946).

Other areas requiring military protection provided by units in Pacific Command included Patricia Bay, Port Alberni, Bamfield, Ucluelet, Tofino, Comox, Coal Harbour, Port Hardy, Alliford Bay, Sea Island, Boundary Bay, New Westminster, Abbotsford, Bella Bella, Smithers, Fort St. John, in B.C., Fort Nelson and Watson Lake, Y.T., and Annette Island, Alaska.

*   *   *

Headquarters Prince Rupert Defences — Pacific Command

Headquarters Prince Rupert Defences, Serial 2917, mobilized under General Order 264/43 (Effective 1st September 1939) and in October 1942 Prince Rupert Defences came under command of 8th Division, remaining under 8th Division until its disbandment October 1943.

17th (North British Columbia) Coast Regiment's 9th and 102nd Coast Batteries manned the forts at Fairview Point, Casey Point, Frederick Point, Barrett Point and Dundas Point, and 29th AA Regiment provided ack-ack defence with detached units at Alliford Bay, Queen Charlotte Islands, Annette Island, Alaska and Whitehorse, Y.T.

Headquarters Prince Rupert Defences remained operational until receiving authorization to disband under General Order 18/46 (Effective 31st October 1945).

* * *

Headquarters Saint John Defences — (N.B.) — Atlantic Command

Headquarters Saint John Defences, Serial 2908, mobilized under General Order 264/43 (Effective 1st July 1940), at Saint John, New Brunswick. The headquarters was redesignated Headquarters Defended Port of Saint John under General Order 206/44 (Effective 15th April 1944), and disbanded under General Order 305/45 (Effective 31st July 1945).

* * *

Headquarters Shelburne Defences — (N.S.) — Atlantic Command

Headquarters Shelburne Defences, Serial 875, mobilized under General Order 264/43 (Effective 1st September 1939), then was redesignated Headquarters Defended Port of Shelburne under General Order 206/44 (Effective 15th April 1944), and disbanded under General Order 208/45 (Effective 30th September 1944).

* * *

Headquarters St. John's Defences (Newfoundland) — "W" Force

Headquarters St. John's Defences (Newfoundland), Serial 872, mobilized under General Order 264/43 (Effective 1st July 1940), then was redesignated Headquarters Defended Port of St. John's under General Order 206/44 (Effective 15th April 1944), and disbanded under General Order 379/45 (Effective 15th August 1945).

* * *

Headquarters Sydney-Canso Defences — (N.S.) — Atlantic Command

Headquarters Sydney-Canso Defences, Serial 2920, mobilized under General Order 264/43 (Effective 1st September 1939), at Sydney, Nova Scotia, then was redesignated Headquarters Defended Port of Sydney under General Order 206/44 (Effective 15th April 1944), and disbanded under General Order 379/45 (Effective 15th August 1945).

* * *

Headquarters Vancouver Defences — Pacific Command

Headquarters Vancouver Defences, Serial 2919, mobilized under General Order 264/43 (Effective 1st September 1939), at Vancouver, British Columbia. Vancouver defences included the Vancouver area and Yorke Island, in Johnstone Strait, with 15th (Vancouver) Coast Regiment RCA on manning duty at

Stanley Park, Point Atkinson, Narrows North, Point Grey, Steveston and on Yorke Island.

The coast regiment assumed the searchlight manning duties following the disbandment of 3rd Searchlight Battery (CD) RCA in July 1942, and also manned the Bofors 40mm light anti-aircraft guns at the forts. 28th Anti-Aircraft Regiment RCA provided the anti-aircraft protection for the Vancouver area.

Headquarters Vancouver Defences remained under the same designation until authorized to disband under General Order 208/45 (Effective 15th February 1945).

*   *   *

Headquarters Victoria and Esquimalt Fortress — Pacific Command

Headquarters Victoria and Esquimalt Fortress, Serial 2918, mobilized under General Order 264/43 (Effective 1st September 1939) to administer the forts on southern Vancouver Island.

Headquarters Pacific Command which was located in Victoria moved to Vancouver 30th November 1942 and 6th Division Headquarters moved from Esquimalt to Prince George in October 1943 following the disbandment of 8th Division. While in Victoria the headquarters contributed three infantry battalions and the divisional reconnaissance regiment to the local defence. Two field artillery guns served in a semi-detached role at Otter Point and at Jordan River. The Pacific Coast Militia Rangers made a valuable contribution to the local defences beginning in 1942.

Headquarters Victoria and Esquimalt Fortress was redesignated Headquarters Esquimalt Fortress under General Order 517/44 (Effective 8th August 1944) and 5th (B.C.) Coast Regiment RCA continued to man the forts at Christopher Point, Mary Hill, Albert Head, Belmont, Duntze Head, Black Rock, Macaulay Point, Golf Hill and Ogden Point. The coast batteries also manned the coast defence LAA sections and assumed the searchlight manning duties following the phasing out of 17th Searchlight Battery (CD) RCA in 1942. Anti-Aircraft protection was provided to the area by 27th Anti-Aircraft Regiment RCA.

"VJ" Day signalled the end of World War II and Headquarters Esquimalt Fortress received authorization to disband under General Order 18/46 (Effective 31st October 1945).

*   *   *

"W" Force (Newfoundland) — Atlantic Command

Newfoundland was still not a part of Canada when on the 22nd of June 1940

The Black Watch (Royal Highland Regiment) of Canada of 2nd Division arrived to become the first unit from Canada to aid in its defence.

In August 1940 a 3rd Division unit The Queen's Own Rifles of Canada arrived in relief of The Black Watch (RHR) of Canada, soon to proceed overseas. August 1940 also saw the Newfoundland forces placed under Canadian command and Newfoundland was included in Atlantic Command.

As the size of the force grew, "W" Force Brigade Headquarters, Serial 1140, was authorized to mobilize under General Order 61/41 (Effective 31st October 1940) and was to command all Canadian units in the Newfoundland defences, Atlantic Command.

The Victoria Rifles of Canada and The Royal Rifles of Canada arrived in November 1940 as the infantry components of the force was increased to two battalions and The Queen's Own Rifles of Canada returned to Canada and 3rd Division.

The Royal Rifles of Canada returned to Canada in August 1941 and on the 27th October 1941 boarded ship at Vancouver for Hong Kong where the unit and The Winnipeg Grenadiers were destroyed Christmas day 1941 and the survivors were taken prisoner.

The Prince Edward Island Highlanders, The Sherbrooke Fusiliers Regiment, The Lincoln and Welland Regiment, The Algonquin Regiment, Le Regiment de Joliette, The Pictou Highlanders, Le Regiment de St. Hyacinthe, Le Regiment de Montmagny, Le Regiment de Quebec, 1st Airfield Defence Battalion (Le Regiment de Chateauguay), one company of the Veterans Guard, 25th and 26th Anti-Aircraft Regiments RCA, three coast batteries, plus supporting units, served with "W" Force in Newfoundland.

"W" Force Brigade Headquarters, Serial 1140, remained operational until cessation of hostilities and received authorization to disband under General Order 227/46 (Effective 30th July 1946).

*   *   *

Newfoundland Regiments RA —

Two regiments of Newfoundlanders were mobilized for overseas service, the 57th (Newfoundland) Heavy Regiment, Royal Artillery, was formed in April 1940 and 59th (Newfoundland) Heavy Regiment, Royal Artillery, was formed in June 1940.

57th Regiment became 166th (Newfoundland) Field Regiment, Royal Artillery in November 1941, and in January 1943 proceeded to North Africa for action in Tunisia. The regiment also served in Italy where it fired in support of

Canadian, Indian, British, New Zealand, and United States formations.

59th (Newfoundland) Heavy Regiment, Royal Artillery with its 7.2 inch Howitzers and 155mm guns prepared for the invasion of the continent. The regiment landed in Normandy on the 5th of July 1944 under 1 British Corps, then in September moved under command of First Canadian Army and provided heavy artillery support to the components of First Canadian Army in Belgium, Holland and Germany.

*   *   *

"Z" Force (Iceland) —

"Z" Brigade Headquarters, CASF, Serial 1040, mobilized under General Order 243/40 (Effective 28th September 1940) for service in Iceland. The components of the force were drawn from 2nd Division. The force headquarters and The Royal Regiment of Canada arrived in Iceland 16th June 1940. Les Fusiliers Mont-Royal and The Cameron Highlanders of Ottawa (MG) arrived on the 9th of July 1940.

The Cameron Highlanders of Ottawa (MG) remained in Iceland for the winter and the remainder of the force sailed for England 31st October 1940 to join the main body of 2nd Division.

"Z" Brigade Headquarters, Serial 1040, received authorization to disband under General order 375/43 (Effective 1st December 1940).

The Cameron Highlanders of Ottawa (MG) arrived in England, April 1941, to become 3rd Canadian Infantry Division machine gun battalion.

*   *   *

Armoured and Army Tank Brigades —

An interest in armoured units was evident in 1936 when six NPAM units were designated "Tank" Regiments. However, only two tank regiments and "Details" of regiments called out for local protective duty were included in General Order 135/39, 1st September 1939, authorizing the mobilization of the CASF.

The "Canadian Armoured Corps" was named as a corps of the active militia under General order 250/40 (Effective 13th August 1940), and under General Order 251/40, Corps Headquarters, Canadian Armoured Corps, CASF, was placed on active service (Effective 13th August 1940). Serial 571, Headquarters 1st Canadian Armoured Brigade, Canadian Armoured Corps, CASF, was placed on active service under the same general order and on the same date.

The Fort Garry Horse, CASF and The First Canadian Cavalry Regiment

(Mech.), CASF, were allocated to the Canadian Armoured Corps under General Order 253/40 (Effective 13th August 1940), in the Canadian Armoured Corps organization with reference to General Order 250/40.

Also under General Order 253/40 (Effective 13th August 1940) 1st Canadian Armoured Brigade CASF was formed comprising Serial 571, Brigade Headquarters, Serial 153, The Fort Garry Horse, CASF, Serial 229, The Ontario Regiment (Tank), CASF, Serial 108, The Three Rivers Regiment (Tank), CASF, and Serial 3, The First Canadian Cavalry Regiment (Mech.), attached.

All four units had mobilized under General Order 135/39, 1st September 1939, 1st Hussars, CASF, mobilized with 1st Division, then under General Order 81/40 (Effective 1st March 1940), Serial No. 3, 1st Hussars, CASF disbanded and Serial No. 3, 1st Canadian Cavalry Regiment (Mechanized), CASF, was placed on active service. The Fort Garry Horse, CASF, had mobilized with 2nd Division in a similar capacity, The Three Rivers Regiment (Tank), CASF, mobilized under Corps Troops mobilizing with 1st Division, and The Ontario Regiment (Tank), CASF, under Corps Troops mobilizing with 2nd Division.

Five motorcycle regiments mobilized under General Order 184/40 (Effective 24th May 1940). The two Permanent Force cavalry units formed 1st Canadian Motorcycle Regiment, CASF, (RCD/LSH (RC)). These two units were given individual identity, effective 21st September 1940, and were allocated to the Canadian Armoured Corps under General Order 296/40 (Effective 15th November 1940). 3rd Canadian Motorcycle Regiment (17 H) became 17th (Active) Duke of York's Royal Canadian Hussars under General Order 60/41 (Effective 1st February 1941). 2nd, 4th and 5th Canadian Motorcycle Regiments were converted to armoured regiments in General Order 88/41 (Effective 9th February 1941), and were included in the thirteen armoured corps units given a numerical designation under General Order 79/41 (Effective 11th February 1941).

Headquarters 1st Canadian Army Tank Brigade, Canadian Armoured Corps, Serial 583, and The Calgary Regiment (Tank), Serial 582, mobilized under General Order 71/41 (Effective 11th February 1941), then under General Order 79/41, effective the same date, 11th Army Tank Battalion (The Ontario Regiment (Tank)), and 12th Army Tank Battalion (The Three Rivers Regiment (Tank)) joined 14th Army Tank Battalion (The Calgary Regiment (Tank)) and Headquarters, to form 1st Canadian Army Tank Brigade.

A reconstituted 1st Canadian Armoured Brigade comprising Serial 571, Headquarters 1st Canadian Armoured Brigade, 2nd Armoured Regiment (Lord Strathcona's Horse (Royal Canadians), 6th Armoured Regiment (1st Hussars) and 10th Armoured Regiment (The Fort Garry Horse), was authorized under General Order 79/41 (Effective 11th February 1941).

Headquarters 2nd Canadian Armoured Brigade, Serial 564, with under command 3rd Armoured Regiment (The Governor General's Horse Guards), 5th Armoured Regiment (8th Princess Louise's (New Brunswick) Hussars) and 9th Armoured Regiment (The British Columbia Dragoons), also came into being 11th February 1941, authorized under General Order 79/41. The armoured brigades became components of 1st Canadian Armoured Division.

Headquarters 1st Canadian Armoured Division, Serial 562, received authorization to mobilize under General Order 88/41 (Effective 27th February 1941). The designation of 1st Canadian Armoured Division was authorized to become 5th Canadian (Armoured) Division, under General Order 135/41 (Effective 5th June 1941).

Mobilized 27th February 1941 and allocated to the Canadian Armoured Corps, 6th Duke of Connaught's Royal Canadian Hussars (Armoured Car) became 5th Canadian (Armoured) Division Headquarters Squadron (6th Duke of Connaught's Royal Canadian Hussars), 7th/11th Hussars became 2nd Canadian Armoured Brigade Headquarters Squadron (7th/11th Hussars), and The Prince Edward Island Light Horse became 1st Canadian Armoured Brigade Headquarters Squadron (The Prince Edward Island Light Horse). 5th Canadian Armoured Division concentrated at Camp Borden and Petawawa in Ontario, then proceeded overseas toward the end of 1941 to join the Canadian Corps in the south of England.

The New Brunswick Regiment (Tank) was allocated to the Canadian Armoured Corps 24th April 1941 and on the same date became 1st Canadian Army Tank Brigade Headquarters Squadron (The New Brunswick Regiment (Tank)). 1st Canadian Army Tank Brigade departed for overseas during June 1941 and concentrated in the south of England.

Headquarters 4th Division, Serial 900, was redesignated Headquarters 4th (Armoured) Division, Serial 900, under General Order 132/42 (Effective 26th January 1942). No. 4 Defence and employment Platoon was redesignated 4th (Armoured) Division Headquarters Squadron CAC, Headquarters 10th Infantry Brigade became Headquarters 3rd Armoured Brigade, No. 10 Defence Platoon became Headquarters Squadron 3rd Armoured Brigade CAC, Headquarters 12th Infantry Brigade was redesignated Headquarters 4th Armoured Brigade and No. 12 Defence Platoon formed Headquarters Squadron 4th Armoured Brigade CAC.

18th (Manitoba) Reconnaissance Battalion was redesignated 18th (Manitoba) Armoured Car Regiment CAC with the armoured division. 28th Armoured Regiment (The British Columbia Regiment) CAC, 25th Armoured Regiment (The Elgin Regiment) CAC, The Lake Superior Regiment (Motor), 21st Armoured Regiment (The Governor General's Foot Guards) CAC, 29th Armoured Regiment (The South Alberta Regiment) CAC, 27th Armoured

Regiment (The Sherbrooke Fusiliers Regiment) CAC, 22nd Armoured Regiment (The Canadian Grenadier Guards) CAC, and The Princess Louise Fusiliers (Motor), comprised the two armoured brigades in 4th Canadian (Armoured) Division.

Headquarters 11th Infantry Brigade from 4th Division was redesignated Headquarters 2nd Army Tank Brigade and No. 11 Defence Platoon became Headquarters Squadron 2nd Army Tank Brigade CAC. 26th Army Tank Battalion (The Grey and Simcoe Foresters) CAC, 24th Army Tank Battalion (Les Voltigeurs de Quebec) CAC, 23rd Army Tank Battalion (The Halifax Rifles) CAC, became the components of 2nd Army Tank Brigade, under General Order 132/42 (Effective 26th January 1942).

Serial 1053, 16/22 Saskatchewan Horse was redesignated Serial 1053, 20th Reconnaissance Battalion (16/22 Saskatchewan Horse), under General Order 104/42 (Effective 26th January 1942).

Serial 824, 31st (Alberta) Reconnaissance Battalion CAC, mobilized with 6th Division, Home Defence, under General Order 147/42 (Effective 18th March 1942), and Serial 1424, 30th Reconnaissance Battalion (The Essex Regiment) CAC, mobilized with 7th Division, Home Defence, under General Order 309/42 (Effective 12th May 1942).

11th, 12th, 14th, 20th, 23rd and 26th Army Tank Battalions were redesignated Army Tank Regiments CAC, under General Order 302/42 (Effective 15th May 1942).

24th Army Tank Battalion (Les Voltigeurs de Quebec) CAC, was redesignated 24th Reconnaissance Battalion (Les Voltigeurs de Quebec) CAC, and 20th Reconnaissance Battalion (16/22 Saskatchewan Horse) CAC, was redesignated 20th Army Tank Battalion (16/22 Saskatchewan Horse) CAC, under General Order 248/42 (Effective 22nd May 1942).

4th, 7th, 8th, 24th, 30th and 31st Reconnaissance Battalions were redesignated reconnaissance regiments under General Order 455/42 (Effective 8th June 1942).

On the 19th of August 1942, 14th Army Tank Regiment (The Calgary Regiment) (Tank) CAC accompanied 2nd Canadian Infantry Division on the Dieppe Raid to become the first unit of the Canadian Armoured Corps committed to battle. Toward the end of 1942, 4th Canadian Armoured Division arrived overseas and congregated in the south of England. Serial 977, 18th (Manitoba) Armoured Car Regiment CAC, was redesignated Serial 977, 18th Armoured Car Regiment (12th Manitoba Dragoons) CAC, under General Order 66/43 (Effective 16th December 1942).

A new war establishment for an armoured division was introduced in January 1943 at which time an infantry brigade replaced one armoured brigade, an anti-tank battery was added to the three-battery anti-tank regiment, and the addition of a self-propelled regiment of field artillery was authorized. The new organization created a surplus of armoured corps regiments from 4th and 5th Canadian Armoured Divisions.

Serial 564, Headquarters 2nd Canadian Armoured Brigade of 5th Canadian Armoured Division was redesignated Serial 564, Headquarters 5th Canadian Armoured Brigade CAC, under General Order 224/42 (Effective 1st January 1943), and served as 5th Canadian Armoured Division's armoured brigade throughout. 3rd Armoured Regiment (The Governor General's Horse Guards) CAC, was redesignated 3rd Armoured Reconnaissance Regiment (The Governor General's Horse Guards) CAC, under General Order 223/43 (Effective 1st January 1943) and remained with the division, along with 2nd Armoured Regiment (Lord Strathcona's Horse (Royal Canadians)) CAC, 5th Armoured Regiment (8th Princess Louise's (New Brunswick) Hussars) CAC, and 9th Armoured Regiment (The British Columbia Dragoons) CAC, all former motorcycle regiments. The Westminster Regiment (Motor) remained with the brigade to provide the support of a motorized battalion of infantry. 1st Armoured Car Regiment (The Royal Canadian Dragoons) CAC, became 1st Canadian Corps armoured car regiment.

5th Canadian (Armoured) Division Headquarters Squadron (6th Duke of Connaught's Royal Canadian Hussars), 2nd Canadian Armoured Brigade Headquarters Squadron (7th/11th Hussars), 1st Canadian Army Tank Brigade Headquarters Squadron (The New Brunswick Regiment (Tank)), and Headquarters Squadron 2nd Army Tank Brigade CAC, disbanded under General Order 225/43 (Effective 1st January 1943).

29th Armoured Regiment (The South Alberta Regiment) CAC was redesignated 29th Armoured Reconnaissance Regiment (The South Alberta Regiment) CAC and remained with 4th Canadian Armoured Division which also retained 4th Canadian Armoured Brigade. 21st Armoured Regiment (The Governor General's Foot Guards) CAC, 22nd Armoured Regiment (The Canadian Grenadier Guards) CAC, 28th Armoured Regiment (The British Columbia Regiment) CAC, and The Lake Superior Regiment (Motor), comprised 4th Canadian Armoured Brigade CAC.

Headquarters 3rd Armoured Brigade, Serial 930, was redesignated Headquarters 3rd Army Tank Brigade CAC, Serial 930, under General Order 223/43 (Effective 1st January 1943). 4th (Armoured) Division Headquarters Squadron CAC, Headquarters Squadron 4th Armoured Brigade CAC and Headquarters Squadron 3rd Armoured Brigade CAC, were authorized to disband under General Order 225/43 (Effective 1st January 1943).

Serial 1035, 24th Reconnaissance Battalion (Les Voltigeurs de Quebec) CAC was redesignated Serial 1035, 1st Battalion, Les voltigeurs de Quebec, under General Order 106/43 (Effective 16th January 1943).

Serial 44, The Royal Montreal Regiment (MG) was redesignated 32nd Reconnaissance Regiment (The Royal Montreal Regiment) CAC, under General Order 187/43 (Effective 25th January 1943).

Serial 944B, 1st Canadian Tank Delivery Squadron CAC, mobilized under General Order 20/44 (Effective 6th May 1943).

Headquarters 2nd Army Tank Brigade with 20th Army Tank Regiment (16/22 Saskatchewan Horse) CAC, 23rd Army Tank Regiment (The Halifax Rifles) CAC, and 26th Army Tank Regiment (Grey and Simcoe Foresters) CAC arrived overseas in June 1943 where the brigade vied for survival with the ad hoc 3rd Army Tank Brigade formed of two surplus 5th Canadian Armoured Division units and one surplus 4th Canadian Armoured Division unit.

During the last week of June 1st Canadian Army Tank Brigade and 1st Canadian Tank Delivery Squadron CAC, accompanied 1st Canadian Infantry Division to the Mediterranean for the invasion of Sicily, 10th July 1943.

Effective 22nd July 1943, under General Order 88/44, Headquarters 2nd Army Tank Brigade Serial 940, was redesignated Serial 940, Headquarters 2nd Armoured Brigade, and 2nd Armoured Brigade was to comprise 6th Armoured Regiment (1st Hussars), 10th Armoured Regiment (The Fort Garry Horse) and 27th Armoured Regiment (The Sherbrooke Fusiliers Regiment).

In Sicily, Serial 583, Headquarters 1st Canadian Army Tank Brigade, Canadian Armoured Corps was redesignated Serial 583, Headquarters 1st Armoured brigade, and its components 11th, 12th and 14th Army Tank Regiments were redesignated armoured regiments CAC, under General Order 88/44 (Effective 26th August 1943). The brigade crossed the Strait of Messina to the Italian mainland in September.

Serial 944, 25th Armoured Regiment (The Elgin Regiment) CAC was redesignated Serial 944, 25th Canadian Tank Delivery Regiment (The Elgin Regiment) CAC. Headquarters, Serial 944A, along with "C", "D", "E", "F", "G" and "H" Squadrons were authorized under General Order 21/44 (Effective 15th September 1943). "C" Squadron was aligned with 2nd Canadian Armoured Brigade, "D" Squadron with 4th Canadian Armoured Division, "E" Squadron with 2nd Canadian Corps, "F" Squadron with First Canadian Army, "G" Squadron with 5th Canadian Armoured Division and "H" Squadron with 1st Canadian Corps.

CAC, not included in previous designations was added to 6th Armoured Regiment (1st Hussars), 1st Armoured Car Regiment (The Royal Canadian Dragoons), 2nd Armoured Regiment (Lord Strathcona's Horse (Royal Canadians)), 5th Armoured Regiment (8th Princess Louise's (New Brunswick) Hussars), 9th Armoured Regiment (The British Columbia Dragoons), 10th Armoured Regiment (The Fort Garry Horse), and the CAC designation was discontinued following the titles of Headquarters 5th Canadian Armoured Brigade, Headquarters 1st Canadian Army Tank Brigade and Headquarters 3rd Army Tank Brigade, under General Order 476/43 (Effective 15th October 1943).

Serial 944B, 1st Canadian Tank Delivery Squadron CAC, was redesignated Serial 944B, "A" Squadron 25th Cdn Tank Delivery Regiment (The Elgin Regiment) CAC, under General Order 21/44 (Effective 21st October 1943). Serial 944C, "B" Squadron was formed at the same time, under the same general order.

Serial 571A, 1st Canadian Armoured Brigade Headquarters Squadron (The Prince Edward Island Light Horse), was redesignated Serial 571A, 2nd Corps Defence Company (The Prince Edward Island Light Horse) under General Order 486/43 (Effective 1st November 1943).

Headquarters 1st Canadian Corps, Corps Troops, 5th Canadian Armoured Division and 1st Canadian AGRA, plus supporting units, departed for the Mediterranean toward the end of 1943 and 1st Canadian Corps became operational in Italy early in the new year. 1st Canadian Infantry Division joined 1st Canadian Corps upon the Corps becoming operational, 1st Canadian Armoured Brigade for the most part served under 13 British Corps.

25th Cdn Tank Delivery Regiment (The Elgin Regiment) CAC, was redesignated 25th Armoured Delivery Regiment (The Elgin Regiment) CAC, under General Order 298/44 (Effective 15th March 1944). Headquarters, along with C, D, E and F Squadrons were altered accordingly under General Order 298/44 (Effective 15th March 1944). The designation "Tank" was changed to "Armoured" in "A", "B" and "G" Squadrons, under General Order 455/44 (Effective 15th March 1944). Serial 944J, "H" Squadron 25th Cdn Tank Delivery Regiment (The Elgin Regiment) CAC, disbanded under General Order 456/44 (Effective 15th March 1944).

Serial 1424, 30th Reconnaissance Regiment (Essex R) CAC received authorization to disband under General Order 299/44 (Effective 31st March 1944).

32nd Reconnaissance Regiment (Royal Montreal Regiment) CAC became First Army Headquarters Defence Company (Royal Montreal Regiment) under General Order 345/44 (Effective 12th April 1944). No. 9 Defence and Employment Platoon (Royal Montreal Regiment) CIC, was authorized under General Order 462/44 (Effective 24th May 1944).

2nd Canadian Armoured Brigade of the Canadian Armoured Corps and detachments of 3rd Canadian Infantry Division's reconnaissance regiment landed in the assault on the coast of Normandy on D-Day, 6th June 1944. One Squadron of 25th Armoured Delivery Regiment (The Elgin Regiment) CAC landed 8th June to service the armoured brigade. Other squadrons followed in July with 2nd Canadian Corps, 4th Canadian Armoured Division and First Canadian Army.

An extra infantry brigade designated 12th Canadian Infantry Brigade was added to 5th Canadian Armoured Division in Italy and 4th Reconnaissance Regiment (4th Princess Louise Dragoon Guards) CAC, of 1st Canadian Infantry Division was redesignated 4th Princess Louise Dragoon Guards CIC, under General Order 18/45 (Effective 13th July 1944) and served with the new brigade.

The "Kangaroo" armoured personnel carrier was introduced in August 1944 in the drive from Caen to Falaise. The Squadron grew into 1st Canadian Armoured Personnel Carrier Regiment of two Squadrons in October, and served under 79 British Armoured Division.

31st (Alberta) Reconnaissance Regiment CAC, disbanded under General Order 231/45 (Effective 15th February 1945).

1st Canadian Corps departed Italy early in 1945 and joined First Canadian Army in NW Europe. Upon arrival in NW Europe 12th Canadian Infantry Brigade disbanded. 4th Princess Louise Dragoon Guards CIC once more became 4th Reconnaissance Regiment (4th Princess Louise Dragoon Guards) CAC, under General Order 252 (Effective 15th March 1945) and the regiment resumed its duties with 1st Canadian Infantry Division. 1st Armoured Car Regiment (The Royal Canadian Dragoons) CAC, which had replaced the PLDGs in 1st Division, returned to 1st Canadian Corps.

First Canadian Army with 8th Reconnaissance Regiment (14th Canadian Hussars) CAC of 2nd Canadian Infantry Division, 7th Reconnaissance Regiment (17th Duke of York's Royal Canadian Hussars) CAC of 3rd Canadian Infantry Division, 18th Armoured Car Regiment (12th Manitoba Dragoons) CAC of 2nd Canadian Corps, and the armoured units of 4th Canadian Armoured Division under command, advanced along the coastal area in France, where 2nd Div paused for a service or Remembrance at Dieppe, then continued the coastal route into Belgium and Holland.

The advance into Germany was launched 8th February 1945, the River Rhine crossed in March and the three Canadian Divisions, with 2nd Canadian Armoured Brigade in support of the two infantry divisions, advanced toward the North Sea, clearing NE Holland and a section of Germany.

1st Canadian Corps arrived from Italy and became operational in the Arnhem,

Holland Sector, 15th March 1945, under Headquarters First Canadian Army. First Canadian Army now had 1st Canadian Corps and 2nd Canadian Corps under command and was predominantly Canadian. The armoured corps units of 1st Canadian Corps aided in clearing western Holland of the enemy and liberated the starving people. The "Cease Fire" was received 5th May and the 8th May 1945 was designated "VE" Day, ending hostilities.

The run-down of units in NW Europe was begun. Volunteers proceeded to the Canadian Army Pacific Force which was being formed in Canada under the designation 6th Canadian Infantry Division, authorized under General Order 241/45 (Effective 1st June 1945), with 6th Canadian Infantry Division Reconnaissance Troop (The Royal Montreal Regiment) CAC and 22nd Canadian Tank Battalion (The Canadian Grenadier Guards) CAC, representing the Canadian Armoured Corps in the new formation.

Headquarters 3rd Canadian Infantry Division CAOF mobilized under General Order 319/45 (Effective 1st June 1945) and 2nd 7th Reconnaissance Regiment CAC, mobilized as a component.

General Order 321/45 authorized the disbandment of 1st Armoured Personnel Carrier Regiment CAC (Effective 20th June 1945), Headquarters 2nd Corps and Headquarters 2nd Armoured Brigade (Effective 25th June 1945), and Headquarters 1st Armoured Brigade (Effective 1st July 1945).

The Canadian Armoured Corps became the "Royal Canadian Armoured Corps" under General Order 275/45 (Effective 2nd August 1945).

2nd-1st Armoured Car Regiment (The Royal Canadian Dragoons) RC Armd C and 2nd-2nd Armoured Regiment (Lord Strathcona's Horse (Royal Canadians)) RC Armd C were placed on active service under General Order 344/45 (Effective 1st September 1945).

With "VJ" Day heralding the end of World War II, 6th Canadian Infantry Division and its components not required in the Postwar Permanent Force were authorized to disband. 6th Canadian Infantry Division Reconnaissance Troop (The Royal Montreal Regiment) CAC, and 22nd Canadian Tank Battalion (The Canadian Grenadier Guards) CAC, disbanded under General Order 425/45 (Effective 1st November 1945).

2nd 1st Armoured Car Regiment (The Royal Canadian Dragoons) RC Armd C, was redesignated 2nd 1st Armoured Regiment (The Royal Canadian Dragoons) RC Armd C, under General Order 404/45 (Effective 15th November 1945).

2nd Corps armoured car regiment, divisional reconnaissance regiments, armoured reconnaissance regiments, the armoured delivery squadrons, 1st,

2nd, 4th and 5th Armoured Brigades, disbanded from October 1945 to February 1946, under General Orders 52, 71, 85, 111, 139 and 201 of 1946. 2nd 7th Reconnaissance Regiment RCAC, disbanded under General Order 201/46 (Effective 24th May 1946), following service with the Canadian Army Occupational Force in Germany.

1st Armoured Car Regiment (The Royal Canadian Dragoons) (CASF) RCAC and 2nd Armoured Regiment (Lord Strathcona's Horse (Royal Canadians) (CASF) RCAC, received authorization to disband under General Order 139/46 (Effective 1st March 1946). Effective the same date under General Order 138/46, with the disbanment of the CASF units, 2nd/1st Armoured Regiment (Royal Canadian Dragoons) RCAC became 1st Armoured Regiment (Royal Canadian Dragoons) RCAC, and 2nd/2nd Armoured Regiment (Lord Strathcona's Horse (Royal Canadians) RCAC was redesignated 2nd Armoured Regiment (Lord Strathcona's Horse (Royal Canadians) RCAC.

In the organization of the Postwar Permanent Force (Active Force), 1st Armoured Regiment (Royal Canadian Dragoons), and 2nd Armoured Regiment Lord Strathcona's Horse (Royal Canadians) became components of 23rd Infantry Brigade Group, authorized under General Order 158/46 (Effective 27th June 1946).

In a redesignation of Permanent Force units authorized under General Order 259/46 (Effective 16th October 1946), The Royal Canadian Dragoons became 1st Armoured Regiment (Royal Canadian Dragoons) RCAC, and Lord Strathcona's Horse (Royal Canadians) became 2nd Armoured Regiment (Lord Strathcona's Horse (Royal Canadians) RCAC.

*   *   *

Organization of Commands —

In organization of commands authorized under General Order 21/46 (Effective 23rd January 1946), Western Command was to include Military District Number 11, British Columbia, Military District Number 13, Alberta, the Northwest Territories and Yukon.

Prairie Command was to include Manitoba and Western Ontario of Military District Number 10, and Military District Number 12, the province of Saskatchewan.

Central Command included Military Districts Number 1, 2 and 3 in Ontario (less the districts of Thunder Bay, Rainy River and Kenora).

Quebec Command was to include Military Districts Number 4 and 5 in the province of Quebec.

Eastern Command included Nova Scotia, Prince Edward Island, and New Brunswick of Military Districts Number 6 and 7.

The headquarters of each command was placed on active service under General Order 203/46 (Effective 13th August 1946).

*   *   *

REGIMENTS

The component batteries of each regiment are readily identified in the "Regiments" section as the batteries and regiments are brought together in a brief account.

Anti-aircraft and anti-tank were unknown quantities in 1939 and it was not until May 1940 that a light anti-aircraft regiment was formed for 1st Division, followed by the forming of 2nd Division LAA Regiment September 1940, and 3rd Div LAA Regiment in January 1941. Light anti-aircraft regiments were also formed for 4th, 5th, 6th and 7th Divisions.

Two LAA regiments mobilized to serve as Army Troops and one regiment each for 1st Corps and 2nd Corps. 3rd LAA Regiment RCA participated in the Dieppe Raid 19th August 1942 with 2nd Canadian Infantry Division. In England the LAA regiments and 2nd HAA Regiment RCA manned ADGB sites.

The anti-tank regiments for 1st and 2nd Divisions mobilized without batteries 1st September 1939 and were staffed by the batteries of 1st and 2nd Army Field Brigades. The importance of anti-tank soon became evident and anti-tank regiments were allotted to 1st Corps, the five overseas divisions, two for home defence, one of which became 2nd Corps anti-tank regiment overseas and the other became 28th Field Regiment RCA, leaving the home defence divisions without anti-tank support.

Coast Brigades were called out to man the forts 26th August 1939. The Coast Brigades became Coast Regiments in 1942. The composition of the regiments varied and 5th (B.C.) Coast Regiment RCA with 55th, 56th, 60th, 68th and

109th Coast Batteries under command at its peak was probably the largest regiment. Coast batteries manned the forts in British Columbia, Quebec, New Brunswick, Nova Scotia, Labrador and Newfoundland. Anti-aircraft regiments were formed and operated in conjunction with the fortresses.

The Permanent Force RCHA became 1st Field Brigade and was joined by 2nd and 3rd Field Brigades in 1st Division, 4th, 5th and 6th Field Brigades mobilized with 2nd Division, followed by five army field brigades, then 12th, 13th and 14th Field Regiments RCA with 3rd Division. 15th, 16th, 17th and 18th Field Regiments mobilized with 4th Division, and 19th to 28th Field Regiments were allotted to 6th, 7th and 8th Divisions, Home Defence.

1st and 2nd Army Field Brigades became anti-tank regiments, 3rd was redesignated 11th Army Field, 4th changed to 8th Army Field, then 8th field Regiment (SP) RCA with 5th Canadian Armoured Division. 5th Army Field became 21st Army Field Regiment, then 7th Army Field Regiment and finally 7th Medium Regiment RCA. Numbers 9 and 10 were not required.

15th Field Regiment remained with 4th (Armoured) Division, 16th Field became 8th LAA Regiment, 17th Field served with 5th Canadian Armoured Division, 18th Field became 2nd Medium Regiment RCA, 19th, 21st and 23rd Field Regiments departed overseas during 1943. 21st Field Regiment RCA disbanded, 23rd Field Regiment became an SP regiment with 4th Canadian Armoured Division and served in NW Europe. 19th Army Field Regiment RCA landed in Normandy on D-Day, 6th June 1944 in support of 3rd Canadian Infantry Division's 8th Brigade.

Home defence field regiments were aligned with the infantry brigades and shortly after mobilizing the brigades were shuffled between the three home defence divisions. In August 1943, 24th Field Regiment RCA and 46th LAA Battery RCA accompanied 6th Division's 13th Brigade Group in an expedition to Kiska in the Aleutians as part of a Canadian-US Force.

1st, 2nd and 5th Medium Regiments RCA, 1st Canadian AGRA accompanied 1st Canadian Corps to Sicily late 1943. 1st Medium Regiment RCA crossed to Italy in November to fire in support of Fifth US Army, the remainder of the AGRA joined 1st Medium in Italy in January 1944 to support 1st Canadian Corps and served until early 1945, then accompanied the corps to NW Europe to join First Canadian Army. 1st Canadian AGRA joined the action 1st April 1945 in Holland and served until cessation of hostilities.

3rd, 4th and 7th Medium Regiments RCA became operational with 2nd Canadian AGRA in Normandy mid-July 1944 in support of 2nd Canadian Corps and served with First Canadian Army in France, Belgium, Holland and Germany.

1st and 2nd Survey Regiments RCA conclude the "Regiments" section. 1st Survey Regiment mobilized in September 1939 and proceeded overseas in three groups during 1940. Early 1942 the regiment became an army survey regiment of Sound Ranging Battery and four survey batteries, one for each division overseas at that time. The regiment was split in two in October 1943 to form two regiments and the regiments became Corps Troops. 1st Survey Regiment RCA accompanied 1st Canadian Corps to the Mediterranean, 2nd Survey Regiment RCA was formed and served with 2nd Canadian Corps, First Canadian Army, in France, Belgium, Holland and Germany.

* * *

1st Anti-Aircraft Regiment RCA, Vancouver, B.C. — Serial 417

Headquarters 1st Anti-Aircraft Regiment RCA, NPAM, with its component batteries, 9th Anti-Aircraft Battery RCA, 10th Anti-Aircraft Battery RCA and 11th Anti-Aircraft Battery RCA, were localized at Vancouver, British Columbia, MD No. 11, in May 1939.

"Details" of the regiment were placed on active service with the Canadian Active Service Force, 1st September 1939 in Military District No. 11. The "Details" were absorbed into the regiment upon the regiment being placed on active service under General Order 44/41 (Effective 1st January 1941).

The regiment however was being phased out at this time as Headquarters 1st Anti-Aircraft Regiment RCA Serial 417 had received authorization to disband under General Order 314/44 (Effective 11th September 1940).

Serial 418, 9th Anti-Aircraft Battery RCA, Serial 419, 10th Anti-Aircraft Battery RCA and Serial 419A, 11th Anti-Aircraft Battery RCA, disbanded under General Order 183/42 (Effective 13th April 1942).

* * *

1st Light Anti-Aircraft Regiment RCA — Serial 505 — 1st Canadian Corps

35th Battery, Sherbrooke, P.Q. from 2nd Field Regiment RCA, 5th Field Regiment's 89th Battery, Woodstock, New Brunswick and 109th Battery of Trail, British Columbia, from 3rd Field Regiment RCA, were redesignated light anti-aircraft batteries under General Order 57/41 (Effective 1st January 1941), and became the components of 1st Light Anti-Aircraft Regiment RCA.

Headquarters 1st Light Anti-Aircraft Regiment RCA, Serial 505, mobilized under General Order 56/41 (Effective 1st February 1941), incorporating batteries left surplus in a recent reorganization of field regiments. 1st Light Anti-Aircraft Regiment RCA was delegated 1st Canadian Corps Light Anti-Aircraft Regiment.

In England the regiment manned Air Defence of Great Britain sites and manned sites on the south coast of England as protection against tip-and-run-raiders.

The regiment accompanied Headquarters 1st Canadian Corps to the Mediterranean, departing 27th October 1943 from Gourock, Scotland, and disembarked at Augusta, Sicily 8th November 1943.

1st Light Anti-Aircraft Regiment RCA crossed to the Italian mainland 8th January 1944 and continued to serve as 1st Canadian Corps light anti-aircraft unit until July 1944 when the regiment became 89/109 or 1 LAA Infantry Battalion in 5th Canadian Armoured Division and as a component of the newly formed 12th Canadian Infantry Brigade fought its initial engagement 1st/2nd September 1944.

Headquarters 1st Light Anti-Aircraft Regiment RCA and is three batteries became The Lanark and Renfrew Scottish Regiment CIC, under General Order 18/45 (Effective 13th July 1944). This designation remained in effect until the regiment with 1st Canadian Corps moved to NW Europe early March 1945 and 5th Canadian Armoured Division reverted to the official war establishment.

12th Canadian Infantry Brigade disbanded and The Lanark and Renfrew Scottish Regiment, CIC, was redesignated 1st Light Anti-Aircraft Regiment (Lanark and Renfrew Scottish Regiment) RCA, under General Order 295/45 (Effective 15th March 1945). The regiment resumed its Ack-Ack role with 1st Canadian Corps in Holland under First Canadian Army and served until cessation of hostilities, receiving authorization to disband under General Order 321/45 (Effective 29th June 1945).

*   *   *

1st Searchlight Regiment RCA, Vancouver, B.C. — Serial 419B

Headquarters 1st Searchlight Regiment RCA, NPAM, 1st Searchlight Battery RCA and 3rd Searchlight Battery (CD) RCA were authorized in Military District No. 11 and localized at Vancouver, B.C. in May 1939.

"Details" of the regiment were named components of the Canadian Active Service Force, 1st September 1939. The future of the regiment however seemed rather uncertain and 1st Searchlight Battery RCA, Serial 419c, received authorization to disband under General Order 314/44 (Effective 31st August 1940). Headquarters 1st Searchlight Regiment RCA, Serial 419B, received authorization to disband under General Order 314/44 (Effective 10th September 1940). 3rd Searchlight Battery (CD) RCA, Serial 393, received authorization to disband under the same general order, effective 18th July 1942, at which time the coast batteries assumed the searchlight manning duties and absorbed the searchlight battery personnel.

*   *   *

2nd Anti-Aircraft Regiment RCA, CASF — Serial 127

Headquarters 2nd Anti-Aircraft Regiment RCA, CASF, Serial 127, 4th Anti-Aircraft Battery RCA, CASF, Serial 128, from the Permanent Force at Kingston, Ontario, 14th Anti-Aircraft Battery RCA, CASF, Serial 129, 15th Anti-Aircraft Battery RCA, CASF, Serial 130, and 1st (Yorkton) Light Anti-Aircraft Battery RCA, CASF, Serial 131, mobilized prematurely with Army Troops mobilizing with 1st Division in the Canadian Active Service Force, 1st September 1939.

Headquarters and 15th Anti-Aircraft Battery disbanded, 14th Battery joined coast defence, 1st and 4th Batteries moved to 2nd Light Anti-Aircraft Regiment RCA of 1st Division.

Headquarters 2nd Anti-Aircraft Regiment RCA, CASF, Serial 127, is listed as receiving authorization to disband under General Order 438/43 (Effective 1st September 1939), 15th Anti-Aircraft Battery RCA, Serial 130, received authorization to disband under General Order 183/42 (Effective 13th April 1942).

*   *   *

2nd Heavy Anti-Aircraft Regiment (Mobile) RCA — Serial 69 — Army Tps

Headquarters of 2nd Medium Brigade, RCA, CASF, Serial 69, 8th Medium Battery (H) RCA, CASF, Serial 70, Charlottetown, P.E.I., 57th Medium Battery (H) RCA, CASF, Serial 71, Levis, P.Q., 11th Medium Battery (H) RCA, CASF, Serial 72, Winnipeg, Manitoba, and 1st Medium Battery RCA, CASF, Serial 73, Montreal, P.Q., mobilized as components of the Canadian Active Service Force, under General Order 135/39, 1st September 1939, Corps Troops mobilizing with 1st Division.

Headquarters of 2nd Medium Brigade RCA, CASF, Serial 69, was redesignated Headquarters of 2nd Medium Regiment RCA, CASF, Serial 69, and the regiment was to comprise two hyphenated batteries, 8th/11th Medium Battery RCA, CASF and 1st/57th Medium Battery RCA, CASF, authorized under General Order 123/40 (Effective 1st June 1940).

The batteries regained individual identity and Headquarters 2nd Medium Regiment RCA, Serial 69, was redesignated Headquarters 2nd Heavy Anti-Aircraft Regiment (Mobile) RCA, under General Order 149/41 (Effective 24th May 1941). 1st, 8th and 11th Medium Batteries were redesignated Heavy Anti-Aircraft Batteries and 57th Medium Battery RCA became 57th Light Anti-Aircraft Battery RCA, under the same General Order. 57th Battery joined 7th Light Anti-Aircraft Regiment RCA, Army Troops.

2nd Heavy Anti-Aircraft Regiment RCA arrived overseas toward the end of September 1941 and joined 1st Canadian Anti-Aircraft Brigade in the Air Defence of Great Britain and remained with the brigade until the brigade disbanded 1st March 1944.

2nd Heavy Anti-Aircraft Regiment RCA, Army Troops, First Canadian Army, landed in Normandy on the 6th of August 1944 and served with 107th British Anti-Aircraft Brigade which had replaced 1st Canadian Anti-Aircraft Brigade in First Canadian Army.

The regiment served in France, Belgium, Holland and Germany in a ground role and in an ack-ack role, serving until cessation of hostilities. 2nd Heavy Anti-Aircraft Regiment RCA (Mobile) received authorization to disband under General Order 401/45 (Effective 7th September 1945).

*   *   *

2nd Light Anti-Aircraft Regiment RCA — Serial 141 — 1st Cdn Inf Div

Headquarters 2nd Light Anti-Aircraft Regiment RCA, CASF, Serial 141, mobilized under General Order 184/40 (Effective 24th May 1940), 5th Light Anti-Aircraft Battery RCA, CASF, Serial 141A also mobilized under General Order 184/40, and 4th AA Battery became 4th Light Anti-Aircraft Battery RCA, CASF, Serial 128.

1st (Yorkton) Light Anti-Aircraft Battery arrived overseas 5th September 1940 and was redesignated 2nd (Yorkton) Light Anti-Aircraft Battery RCA, under General Order 86/41 (Effective 18th March 1941). The regiment assembled at Colchester, Essex, in March 1941, with 54th Battery arriving from 1st Field Regiment to complete its components.

The regiment manned Air Defence of Great Britain sites and gun positions on the south coast of England. Divisional Light Anti-aircraft Regiments trimmed to three batteries in March 1943 and 4th LAA Battery RCA, the former PF battery moved from 2nd Light Anti-Aircraft Regiment RCA, 1st Canadian Infantry Division, to 11th Light Anti-Aircraft Regiment RCA, Army Troops. 2nd Light Anti-Aircraft Regiment RCA now comprised 2nd (Yorkton) Light Anti-Aircraft Battery RCA, 5th and 54th Light Anti-Aircraft Batteries RCA. On the 25th June 1943 the regiment accompanied 1st Canadian Infantry Division to the Mediterranean for the invasion of Sicily.

2nd Light Anti-Aircraft Regiment RCA, 1st Canadian Infantry Division, landed in Sicily, 10th and 11th July 1943 with 30 Corps, British Eighth Army, then with the fall of Sicily crossed to the Italian mainland 4th September with 13 British Corps.

The regiment joined 1st Canadian Corps early in 1944 and with the division served as a component in Italy until March 1945, then moved with the corps to NW Europe. 2nd Light Anti-Aircraft Regiment RCA joined the action in Holland the first week of April under First Canadian Army and served until cessation of hostilities, receiving authorization to disband under General Order 401/45 (Effective 31st August 1945).

*   *   *

2nd Searchlight Regiment RCA, CASF — Serial 132

Headquarters 2nd Searchlight Regiment RCA, CASF, Serial 132, 4th Searchlight Battery RCA, CASF, Serial 133, and 5th Searchlight battery RCA, CASF, Serial 134, Army Troops mobilizing with 1st Division, were listed as components of the Canadian Active Service Force under General Order 135/39, 1st September 1939.

Headquarters 2nd Searchlight Regiment RCA, CASF, Serial 132 and its batteries had mobilized prematurely and disbanded. The disbandment is listed in General Order 438/43 (Effective 1st September 1939).

* * *

3rd Light Anti-Aircraft Regiment RCA — Serial 142 — 2nd Cdn Inf Div

Headquarters 3rd Light Anti-Aircraft Regiment RCA, CASF, Serial 142, 15th (38th) Light Anti-Aircraft Battery RCA, CASF, Serial 142A, of Winnipeg, Manitoba, 16th Light Anti-Aircraft Battery RCA, CASF, Serial 142B, Vancouver, British Columbia, and 17th Light Anti-Aircraft Battery RCA, CASF, Serial 142C, Calgary, Alberta, mobilized under General Order 243/40 (Effective 28th September 1940), to serve with 2nd Division in the Canadian Active Service Force.

Lieutenant-Colonel B.R. Ker from 5th (B.C.) Coast Brigade RCA in the Victoria-Esquimalt Fortress was given command of 3rd Light Anti-Aircraft Regiment RCA and led the regiment overseas early in 1941. The regiment assembled at Colchester, Essex, and 53rd Battery of Toronto, arrived from 4th Field Regiment RCA to complete the components.

Serial Numbers were altered in December 1941, 38th Battery changed to 142B, 16th Battery to 142C, 17th Battery to 142D, 53rd Battery changed from Serial 157 to 142E, and Headquarters assumed Serial Number 142A. The regiment manned Air Defence of Great Britain sites and manned sites along the south coast of England, interspersed with training.

2nd Canadian Infantry Division, at the peak of its training, was selected to participate in a raid on the coast of France and a total of ten officers and 236 other ranks from 3rd Light Anti-Aircraft Regiment's four batteries, accompanied 4th and 6th Canadian Infantry Brigades of 2nd Canadian Infantry Division to Dieppe, 19th August 1942. 16th LAA Battery casualties included one officer killed, one officer wounded and taken prisoner, eight other ranks killed and five of the nine taken prisoner were wounded. Three wounded returned to England.

The regiment reorganized in March 1943 and 53rd LAA Battery RCA moved to 11th Light Anti-Aircraft Regiment RCA, Army Troops, which in turn was disbanded in March 1944.

The three battery 3rd Light Anti-Aircraft Regiment RCA returned to the Continent, landing in Normandy 7th July 1944 as a component of 2nd Canadian Corps, then with 2nd Canadian Corps came under command of First Canadian Army 31st July 1944.

The regiment participated in the vicious fighting in the breakout from Caen and the closing of the Falaise Gap, then moved on to Dieppe 3rd September 1944 with 2nd Division for a service of remembrance and a divisional parade through the streets of the city.

Returning to action with First Canadian Army 3rd Light Anti-Aircraft Regiment RCA continued the advance through France, Belgium, Holland and Germany, receiving authorization to disband under General Order 52/46 (Effective 24th September 1945).

*   *   *

4th Light Anti-Aircraft Regiment RCA — Serial 449 — 3rd Cdn Inf Div

The three field regiments of 3rd Division each contibuted a battery number, and with 100th Battery RCA from 7th Army Field Regiment RCA, formed 4th Light Anti-Aircraft Regiment RCA, Serial 449.

32nd (Kingston) Light Anti-Aircraft Battery RCA, Serial 452, arrived from 14th Field Regiment RCA, 62nd Light Anti-Aircraft Battery RCA, of Duncan, British Columbia, arrived from 13th Field Regiment RCA and 69th Light Anti-Aircraft Battery RCA, Serial 450, Brantford, was 12th Field Regiment's contribution. 100th Light Anti-Aircraft Battery RCA, Serial 453, of Listowel, Ontario, completed the components of 4th Light Anti-Aircraft Regiment RCA, 3rd Division.

The battery serial numbers were aligned with the regiment's 449, in December 1941, and in March 1943, 62nd Light Anti-Aircraft Battery RCA departed for 11th Light Anti-Aircraft Regiment RCA, Army Troops.

3rd Canadian Infantry Division was selected as an assault division for the invasion of Normandy in 1944 and 4th Light Anti-Aircraft Regiment's 32nd LAA Battery landed with 3rd Canadian Infantry Division on D-Day, 6th June 1944, and was joined by the remainder of the regiment in the beachhead.

The regiment served with 1 British Corps, Second British Army, in the early days of the invasion, then 2nd Canadian Corps, Second British Army, and on 31st July 1944 with 2nd Canadian Corps moved under the command of First Canadian Army for the breakout from Caen and the closing of the Falaise Gap.

3rd Canadian Infantry Division continued the advance with First Canadian Army along the coastal route, clearing the channel ports and overrunning the buzz-bomb launching sites. The regiment served with the division in France, Belgium, Holland and Germany until cessation of hostilities and received authorization to disband under General Order 52/46 (Effective 13th November 1945).

A reconstituted 2nd 4th Light Anti-Aircraft Regiment RCA mobilized under General Order 319/45 (Effective 1st June 1945) and following service with the Canadian Army Occupational Force in Germany received authorization to disband under General Order 162/46 (Effective 4th April 1946).

*   *   *

5th Light Anti-Aircraft Regiment RCA — Serial 454 — 5th Cdn Armd Div

Headquarters 5th Light Anti-Aircraft Regiment RCA, Serial 454, mobilized under General Order 85/41 (Effective 27th February 1941). The original 15th Field Regiment contributed 41st Battery of Simcoe and 47th (Napanee) Battery, 88th Battery, Dartmouth, N.S. came from the original 16th Field Regiment.

41st Battery mobilized as 41st/102nd Field Battery RCA, CASF, with 15th Field Regiment RCA, CASF, 4th Division, CASF, and 47th Battery too, mobilized with 15th Field Regiment RCA, CASF, 4th Division, CASF, as the combined 3rd/47th Field Battery RCA, CASF. 88th Battery mobilized as the combined 87th/88th Field Battery RCA, CASF, with 16th Field Regiment RCA, CASF, 4th Division, CASF, under General Order 184/40 (Effective 24th May 1940).

The batteries were given individual identity as field batteries and redesignated 41st Light Anti-Aircraft Battery RCA, 47th (Napanee) Light Anti-Aircraft Battery RCA, and 88th Light Anti-Aircraft Battery RCA, under General Order 85/41 (Effective 27th February 1941) and became components of 5th Light Anti-Aircraft Regiment RCA, 1st Canadian, redesignated 5th Canadian (Armoured) Division, under General Order 135/41 (Effective 5th June 1941). The battery serial numbers were aligned with Serial 454 of the regiment toward the end of the year.

5th Light Anti-Aircraft Regiment RCA, 5th Canadian Armoured Division arrived overseas toward the end of September 1941 and settled in the Garrison town of Colchester, Essex, under Headquarters 1st Canadian Anti-Aircraft Brigade, then moved to the south of England for duty on Air Defence of Great Britain sites, training with the division and manning sites along the south coast.

The regiment departed for the Mediterranean 27th October 1943 and disembarked at Naples, Italy, 8th November 1943. 1st Canadian Infantry Division and 5th Canadian Armoured Division were to be the main components of 1st Canadian Corps which became operational in Italy early in the new year. A number of the regiment's guns deployed during December protecting gun concentration areas.

5th Light Anti-Aircraft Regiment RCA served in Italy as a component of 1st Canadian Corps until the end of February 1945, then with the corps moved to NW Europe to join First Canadian Army.

The regiment deployed in the Arnhem Sector in Holland, 31st March 1945 and continued in action until cessation of hostilities, receiving authorization to disband under General Order 71/46 (Effective 27th November 1945).

*   *   *

6th Light Anti-Aircraft Regiment RCA — Serial 991 — 2nd Cdn Corps

6th Light Anti-Aircraft Regiment RCA, Serial 991, Headquarters 6th Light Anti-Aircraft Regiment RCA, Serial 991A, 112th Light Anti-Aircraft Battery RCA, Serial 991B, Lethbridge, Alberta, 101st Light Anti-Aircraft Battery RCA, Serial 991C, Moosomin, Saskatchewan, 30th Light Anti-Aircraft Battery RCA, Serial 991D, Toronto, and 1st Light Anti-Aircraft Battery RCA, Serial 991E, Ottawa, mobilized under General Order 240/41 (Effective 5th September 1941) to serve with 4th Division.

4th Division became an armoured division and 16th Field Regiment RCA was redesignated 8th Light Anti-Aircraft Regiment RCA to become Div LAA Regiment. 101st LAA Battery RCA moved to 8th LAA Regiment from 6th Light Anti-Aircraft Regiment and 6th Light Anti-Aircraft Regiment assembled at Petawawa, February 1942.

A composite troop proceeded to Prince Rupert, B.C. in March 1942, the remainder of 112th Battery arrived in June to aid in manning the Prince Rupert defences which included the airfield on Annette Island, Alaska. 30th LAA Battery also moved west in June and manned sites on Vancouver Island in the Victoria-Esquimalt Fortress, and on Yorke Island under Headquarters Vancouver Defences.

The regiment returned to Petawawa in September and departed for overseas 30th October 1942. 6th Light Anti-Aircraft Regiment RCA proceeded to Colchester, Essex, for duty and training under 1st Canadian Anti-Aircraft Brigade, then mid-February 1943 came under command of 2nd Canadian Corps for all purposes. The regiment manned sites on the south coast of England and prepared for the cross-Channel invasion as 2nd Canadian Corps Light Anti-Aircraft Regiment.

6th Light Anti-Aircraft Regiment RCA and 2nd Canadian Corps landed in Normandy early in July 1944. 2nd Canadian Corps served under Second British Army until 31st July 1944 when all Canadian units in Normandy came under command of First Canadian Army. The corps played an important role in the breakout from Caen and the closing of the Falaise Gap.

6th Light Anti-Aircraft Regiment RCA with 2nd Canadian Corps, First Canadian Army, continued the advance along the coastal sector in France, Belgium, Holland and Germany. 112th Battery received instruction on operating rocket launchers and during November 1944 manned the launchers in support of attacks by 52nd (Lowland) Division, and 1st Polish Armoured Division. 30th LAA Battery RCA and two British batteries also manned the launchers of the unit which came to be known as 1st Rocket Battery RCA.

6th Light Anti-Aircraft Regiment RCA remained operational until cessation of hostilities and received authorization to disband under General Order 321/45 (Effective 24th June 1945), in NW Europe.

* * *

7th Light Anti-Aircraft Regiment RCA — Serial 458 — Army Troops

Headquarters 7th Light Anti-Aircraft Regiment (RCA, Serial 458, 67th (Rosetown) Light Anti-Aircraft Battery RCA, Serial 460, Rosetown, Saskatchewan, 42nd Light Anti-Aircraft Battery RCA, Serial 461, of Delhi, Ontario, were joined by 57th Light Anti-Aircraft Battery RCA, Serial 71, of Levis, P.Q. from the original 2nd Medium Regiment to complete the components of the regiment in May 1941.

7th Light Anti-Aircraft Regiment RCA arrived overseas 22nd November 1941 and proceeded to Colchester, Essex, where its association with 1st Canadian Anti-Aircraft Brigade was begun. Both 1st Canadian Anti-Aircraft Brigade and 7th Light Anti-Aircraft Regiment RCA were to become Army Troops, First Canadian Army.

Serial numbers within the regiment were aligned with Serial Number 458, under General Order 54/42 (Effective 22nd December 1941). The regiment proceeded to Northern Ireland in December 1941 and returned to England in May 1942 to assume its intended role of protecting Headquarters First Canadian Army and Army Troops area.

Headquarters 1st Canadian Anti-Aircraft Brigade, 7th Light Anti-Aircraft Regiment RCA and 11th Light Anti-Aircraft Regiment RCA, on the eve of going into battle were authorized to disband under General Order 357/44 (Effective 1st March 1944). The disbanded units were replaced by British units in First Canadian Army to help ease the shortage of manpower.

* * *

8th Light Anti-Aircraft Regiment RCA — Serial 1906 — 4th Cdn Armd Div

4th Division was converted to an armoured division under General Order 132/42 (Effective 26th January 1942). Headquarters 16th Field Regiment RCA was redesignated Headquarters 8th Light Anti-Aircraft Regiment RCA under the same general order and on the same date and became 4th Canadian Armoured Division Light Anti-Aircraft Regiment.

70th Light Anti-Aircraft Battery RCA, Serial 1906B, Brandon, Manitoba, and 102nd Light Anti-Aircraft Battery RCA, Serial 1906C, Dundas, Ontario, were joined by 101st Light Anti-Aircraft Battery RCA, Serial 1906D, Moosomin, Saskatchewan, from 6th LAA Regiment, to comprise 8th Light Anti-Aircraft Regiment RCA, 4th Canadian Armoured Division. Troops from the regiment served in Newfoundland and Arvida, P.Q.

The regiment arrived overseas 18th August 1942 and following training at Colchester under 1st Canadian Anti-aircraft Brigade, moved to the divisional area in the south of England for training and duty on gun sites along the coast.

8th Light Anti-Aircraft Regiment RCA, 4th Canadian Armoured Division crossed the Channel to Normandy between the 25th and 27th of July 1944. The regiment joined 2nd Canadian Corps 29th July on the Caen Front and with 2nd Canadian Corps came under command of First Canadian Army 31st July 1944, participating in the vicious fighting in the breakout from Caen and the closing of the Falaise Gap.

The regiment, division and corps under First Canadian Army continued the advance along the coastal route in France, Belgium, Holland and Germany, then with cessation of hostilities received authorization to disband under General Order 71/46 (Effective 12th December 1945).

*   *   *

9th Light Anti-Aircraft Regiment RCA — Serial 813 — 6th Div & Kiska

9th Light Anti-Aircraft Regiment RCA, Serial 813, Headquarters 9th Light Anti-Aircraft Regiment RCA, Serial 813A, 48th Light Anti-Aircraft Battery RCA, Serial 813B, Watford, 46th Light Anti-Aircraft Battery RCA, Serial 813C, Simcoe, 25th Light Anti-Aircraft Battery RCA, Serial 813D, Ottawa, all of Ontario, and 79th Light Anti-Aircraft Battery RCA, Serial 813E, of Montreal, mobilized with 6th Divisional Artillery, RCA, under General Order 147/42 (Effective 18th March 1942).

The regiment concentrated at Petawawa, then proceeded to Vancouver, British Columbia in October 1942 to provide Anti-Aircraft protection for the three brigade groups of 6th Division in Pacific Command. RHQ moved to Victoria in January 1943, 25th Battery to Port Alberni, 46th Battery to Nanaimo, on Vancouver Island, 48th Battery moved to Terrace on the mainland, as the batteries moved with their allotted brigade groups. 79th Battery remained at Hastings Park, Vancouver.

Headquarters 9th Light Anti-Aircraft Regiment RCA received authorization to disband under General Order 251/43 (Effective 15th May 1943) and the batteries came under control of the Mobile Brigade Groups of 6th Division, then in June the regiment reorganized to comprise three batteries. 79th LAA Battery RCA became 79th AA Battery Type "2L" RCA under General Order 366/43 (Effective 15th June 1943) and joined coast defence, Pacific Command.

46th Battery landed on the island of Kiska in the Aleutian Chain mid-August 1943 as part of the joint Canada-US Force and upon landing discovered the enemy had vacated the island. The battery remained on garrison duty until the end of the year then returned to Vancouver and resumed its home defence role with 6th Division.

One troop of 46th Battery took part in exercise "Eskimo" with a skeleton 13th Brigade Group and the RCAF, January and February 1945, testing equipment under dry cold conditions in Northern Saskatchewan, and while so-engaged 25th and 48th Light Anti-Aircraft Batteries had disbanded (Effective 31st January 1945), 46th Light Anti-Aircraft Battery RCA disbanded under General Order 213/45 (Effective 31st March 1945).

* * *

10th Light Anti-Aircraft Regiment RCA — Serial 1413 — 7th Division

10th Light Anti-Aircraft Regiment RCA, Serial 1413, Headquarters 10th Light Anti-Aircraft Regiment RCA, Serial 1413A, 6th Light Anti-Aircraft Battery RCA, Serial 1413B, 7th Light Anti-Aircraft Battery RCA, Serial 1413C, 8th Light Anti-Aircraft Battery RCA, Serial 1413D, and 9th Light Anti-Aircraft Battery RCA, Serial 1413E, mobilized with Headquarters 7th Divisional Artillery, RCA, Serial 1405, under General Order 309/42 (Effective 12th May 1942), for service in eastern Canada.

Divisional Light Anti-Aircraft Regiments trimmed to three batteries and 8th LAA Battery RCA, Serial 1413D became surplus and joined coast defence with 24th AA Regiment RCA at Arvida, P.Q. upon being redesignated 63rd Anti-Aircraft Battery Type 3L, RCA, under General Order 366/43 (Effective 15th June 1943).

6th LAA Battery RCA provided protection for the First Quebec Conference, 11th to 24th August 1943. The batteries were redesignated 96th, 97th and 99th Light Anti-Aircraft Batteries under General Order 412/43 (Effective 1st September 1943) and remained with 10th Light Anti-Aircraft Regiment RCA under their new designation, its existence however was of rather short duration with the phasing out of 7th Division.

Headquarters 10th Light Anti-Aircraft Regiment RCA received authorization to disband under General Order 15/44 (Effective 15th November 1943). The regiment supplied a cadre base for 1st Light Anti-Aircraft Training Battery RCA at Debert, Nova Scotia.

*   *   *

11th Light Anti-Aircraft Regiment RCA — Serial 1170A — Army Troops

Headquarters 11th Light Anti-Aircraft Regiment RCA, Serial 1170A, mobilized under General Order 242/43 (Effective 6th March 1943) to encompass batteries left surplus to divisional light anti-aircraft regiments in a recent reorganization from four to three batteries. The former Permanent Force 4th LAA Battery RCA, Serial 141C, from 2nd Light Anti-Aircraft Regiment RCA, 1st Canadian Infantry Division, 53rd LAA Battery RCA, Serial 142E, from 3rd Light Anti-Aircraft Regiment RCA, 2nd Canadian Infantry Division, and 62nd LAA Battery RCA, Serial 449C, from 3rd Canadian Infantry Division's 4th Light Anti-Aircraft Regiment RCA, arrived to form the new Army Troops Light Anti-Aircraft Regiment.

11th Light Anti-Aircraft Regiment came under command of 1st Canadian Anti-Aircraft Brigade which had become operational in the south of England and the Army Troops regiments manned their Bofors 40mm LAA guns along the coast, interspersed with training for the new role.

The life of the regiment which showed a lot of promise with its fine array of batteries was of rather short duration for early in the new year the decision was made to replace 1st Anti-Aircraft Brigade Headquarters RCA, and the two Army Troops Artillery regiments with similar British units in First Canadian Army to help ease the manpower shortage.

1st Anti-Aircraft Brigade Headquarters RCA, Serial 842, 7th Light Anti-Aircraft Regiment RCA, Serial 458, HQ 11th Light Anti-Aircraft Regiment RCA, Serial 1170A, 4th, 53rd and 62nd LAA Batteries RCA disbanded under General Order 357/44 (Effective 1st March 1944).

*   *   *

21st Anti-Aircraft Regiment RCA — Serial 527 — Halifax Fortress, N.S.

Headquarters 21st Anti-Aircraft Regiment RCA, Serial 527, mobilized under General Order 256/42 (Effective 1st June 1942). 1st Anti-Aircraft Battery (Type "H") RCA, Serial 344, 4th Anti-Aircraft Battery (Type L) RCA, Serial 890, 18th Anti-Aircraft Battery Type "H", RCA, Serial 723, 19th Anti-Aircraft Battery Type "H", RCA, Serial 724, 49th Anti-Aircraft Battery, Type H, RCA, Serial 788, No. 2 Anti-Aircraft Machine Gun Troop RCA, Serial 429, 1st Anti-Aircraft Searchlight Battery RCA, Serial 878, No. 1 Anti-Aircraft Gun Operation Room (Class B) RCA, 20th Anti-Aircraft Battery Type "H", RCA,

Serial 725, 14th Anti-Aircraft Battery Type "M" and Type "H", RCA, Serial 129, and 146th Anti-Aircraft Battery Type 3L, RCA, Serial 784, served as components of 21st Anti-Aircraft Regiment RCA under Headquarters Halifax Fortress, Atlantic Command, prior to the regiment receiving authorization to disband under General Order 305/45 (Effective 31st July 1945).

*   *   *

22nd AA Regiment RCA — Serial 528 — HQ Defended Port of Saint John

Headquarters 22nd Anti-Aircraft Regiment RCA, Serial 528, mobilized under General Order 256/42 (Effective 1st June 1942) for service under Headquarters Saint John Defences (New Brunswick).

8th Anti-Aircraft Battery Type H, RCA, Serial 376, 25th Anti-Aircraft Battery Type 3L RCA, Serial 738, became 125th AA Battery Type 3L RCA, 52nd Anti-Aircraft Troop Type L RCA, Serial 791 was enlarged to a battery and served in a semi-detached role in the Gaspe Defences, P.Q. 53rd Anti-Aircraft Battery Type H, RCA, Serial 792, also served at Gaspe, these and No. 8 Anti-Aircraft Gun Operations Room (Class B) RCA, Serial 1390, served under command of 22nd Anti-Aircraft Regiment RCA previous to its disbandment under General Order 208/45 (Effective 1st September 1944).

*   *   *

23rd Anti-Aircraft Regiment RCA — Serial 530 — Defended Port of Sydney

Headquarters 23rd Anti-Aircraft Regiment RCA, Serial 530, mobilized under General Order 256/42 (Effective 1st June 1942) to serve in the Sydney-Canso Defences and its later designation Headquarters Defended Port of Sydney.

6th Anti-Aircraft Battery Type H, RCA, Serial 363, 50th Anti-Aircraft Battery Type 2H, RCA, Serial 789, 51st Anti-Aircraft Battery Type 2H, RCA, Serial 790, 24th Anti-Aircraft Troop and Battery Type "L", 4L and 3L, RCA, Serial 737, and No. 7 Anti-Aircraft Gun Operations Room (Class B) RCA, Serial 1389, served as components of 23rd Anti-Aircraft Regiment RCA, Serial 530, during its period on active service, terminating under General Order 208/45 (Effective 31st December 1944).

*   *   *

24th AA Regiment RCA — Serial 533 — Arvida, P.Q. Defences

Headquarters 24th Anti-Aircraft Regiment RCA, Serial 533, mobilized under General Order 256/42 (Effective 1st June 1942) to serve in the Arvida, P.Q. Defences.

17th Anti-Aircraft Battery Type M and Type 2H, RCA, Serial 882, 41st Anti-Aircraft Battery Type 2H, RCA, Serial 779, 12th Anti-Aircraft Battery

Type 4L, 3L and 4L RCA, Serial 883, formerly No. 3 Anti-Aircraft Machine Gun Troop, Type L, RCA, along with 3rd Anti-Aircraft Searchlight Battery RCA, Serial 880, served as components of the regiment.

In July 1943 these units were joined by all active AA units located in Military District No. 5 which were placed under command of 24th Anti-Aircraft Regiment RCA for administration and training supervision.

63rd Anti-Aircraft Battery Type 3L RCA, Serial 1338 (Formerly 8th LAA Battery of 7th Division), at Arvida, 52nd Anti-Aircraft Troop, Type L, RCA, Serial 791, at Gaspe, 60th Anti-Aircraft Battery, Type H, RCA, Serial 1128, which provided AA protection for the First Quebec Conference, 11th to 24th August 1943, and 61st Anti-Aircraft Troop, Type L, RCA, Serial 1129, the latter two at Levis, P.Q., completed the roster.

Headquarters 24th Anti-Aircraft Regiment RCA, Serial 533, received authorization to disband under General Order 208/45 (Effective 15th January 1945).

* * *

25th AA Regiment RCA — Serial 534 — St. John's-Torbay, Newfoundland

Headquarters 25th Anti-Aircraft Regiment RCA, Serial 534, mobilized under General Order 256/42 (Effective 1st June 1942) to encompass the anti-aircraft units serving in the St. John's-Torbay, Newfoundland Defences, Atlantic Command.

14th Anti-Aircraft Battery Type M and Type H, RCA, Serial 129, 27th Anti-Aircraft Battery Type 4L and 2L, RCA, Serial 745, 48th Anti-Aircraft Battery Type 2L, RCA, Serial 787, 54th Anti-Aircraft Battery Type 2H, RCA, Serial 793, 55th Anti-Aircraft Section Type L, and Anti-Aircraft Troop Type LS, RCA, Serial 794, along with 16th Anti-Aircraft (MG) Battery (CD) RCA, Serial 434, completes the list of units under command of 25th Anti-Aircraft Regiment RCA during its period on active service, June 1941 to July 1945.

Headquarters 25th Anti-Aircraft Regiment RCA, Serial 534, received authorization to disband under General Order 305/45 (Effective 31st July 1945).

* * *

26th AA Regiment RCA — Serial 537 — "W" Force, Newfoundland

Headquarters 26th Regiment RCA Regiment RCA, Serial 537, mobilized under General Order 256/42 (Effective 1st June 1942) and commanded anti-aircraft units at Gander Lake, Botwood and Lewisporte in Newfoundland.

2nd Anti-Aircraft Searchlight Battery RCA, Serial 879, No. 4 Anti-Aircraft Gun Operation Room (Class B) RCA, Serial 1344, 5th Anti-Aircraft Battery

Type L, 2L and 4L, RCA, Serial 891, became 105th AA Battery Type 4L, 7th Anti-Aircraft Battery Type M and Type 2H, RCA, Serial 364, 28th Anti-Aircraft Troop and Battery Type L and 2L, RCA, Serial 746, 29th Anti-Aircraft Troop Type L and Type LS, RCA, Serial 747, 56th Anti-Aircraft Battery Type H, RCA, Serial 795, and 57th Anti-Aircraft Battery Type H, RCA, Serial 796, served as components of 26th Anti-Aircraft Regiment RCA during its period of active operations previous to being converted to FS, late 1943.

* * *

26th Anti-Aircraft Regiment RCA — Serial 537 (FS) — "W" Force

The original 26th Anti-Aircraft Regiment RCA was converted to French speaking toward the end of 1943. Headquarters 26th Anti-Aircraft Regiment RCA, No. 4 Anti-Aircraft Gun Operation Room (Class B) RCA and 29th Anti-Aircraft Troop were converted to French speaking and a new slate of batteries arrived, 52nd Anti-Aircraft Battery from Gaspe, 60th and 61st Anti-Aircraft Batteries from Levis, and 17th Anti-Aircraft Battery from Arvida. The new regiment assumed the duties of the previous regiment at Gander, Newfoundland. Headquarters 26th Anti-Aircraft Regiment RCA, Serial 537, disbanded under General Order 379/45 (Effective 15th August 1945).

* * *

27th Anti-Aircraft Regiment RCA — Serial 538 — Victoria-Esquimalt

Headquarters 27th Anti-Aircraft Regiment RCA, Serial 538, mobilized under General Order 256/42 (Effective 1st June 1942) to encompass all anti-aircraft units in the Victoria and Esquimalt Fortress on Vancouver Island, British Columbia.

No. 1 Anti-Aircraft Machine Gun Troop RCA, Serial 428, No. 2 Anti-Aircraft Gun Operation Room (Class B) RCA, Serial 1342, 2nd Anti-Aircraft Battery Type H, RCA, Serial 392, 9th Anti-Aircraft Battery Type H and 2H, RCA, Serial 709, 10th Anti-Aircraft Battery Type 2L and 3L, RCA, Serial 710, 13th Anti-Aircraft Battery Type 2L, 3L and 4L RCA, Serial 712, 22nd Anti-Aircraft Battery Type 2H, RCA, Serial 735, 23rd Anti-Aircraft Battery Type 2H, RCA, Serial 736, 42nd Anti-Aircraft Battery Type 2H, RCA, Serial 780 (became 42nd Composite Anti-Aircraft Battery (Type 1H and 1L) 15th September 1945), and 43rd Anti-Aircraft Battery Type 2H, RCA, Serial 781, served under the command of Headquarters 27th Anti-Aircraft Regiment RCA as its components frequently changed.

Headquarters 27th Anti-Aircraft Regiment RCA, Serial 538, received authorization to disband under General Order 18/46 (Effective 31st October 1945).

* * *

28th Anti-Aircraft Regiment RCA — Serial 539 — HQ Vancouver Defences

Headquarters 28th Anti-Aircraft Regiment RCA, Serial 539, mobilized under General Order 256/42 (Effective 1st June 1942) and served under Headquarters Vancouver Defences in Pacific Command.

No. 6 Anti-Aircraft Gun Operation Room (Class B) RCA, Serial 1372, 11th Anti-Aircraft Battery Type 2L, 3L and 4L, RCA, Serial 711, 21st Anti-Aircraft Battery Type H and 2H, RCA, Serial 729, 31st Anti-Aircraft Battery Type 3L, RCA, Serial 749, 43rd Anti-Aircraft Battery Type 2H, RCA, Serial 781, and 23rd Anti-Aircraft Battery Type 2H, RCA, Serial 736, served with 28th Anti-Aircraft Regiment RCA at some period during the regiment's existence. (See also 47th AA Troop, Serial 785).

Headquarters 28th Anti-Aircraft Regiment RCA, Serial 539, received authorization to disband under General Order 208/45 (Effective 31st December 1945).

* * *

29th AA Regiment RCA — Serial 1346 — HQ Prince Rupert Defences, B.C.

Headquarters 29th Anti-Aircraft Regiment RCA, Serial 1346, mobilized under General Order 208/43 (Effective 29th March 1943) and encompassed the anti-aircraft units serving under Headquarters Prince Rupert Defences, in Pacific Command.

No. 9 Anti-Aircraft Gun Operations Room (Class B) RCA, Serial 1391, 9th Anti-Aircraft Battery Type 2H, RCA, Serial 709, 11th Anti-Aircraft Battery Type 4L, RCA, Serial 711, 22nd Anti-Aircraft Battery (Annette Island, Alaska), Type 2H, RCA, Serial 735, which became "Mobile" with 6th Division, 32nd Anti-Aircraft Battery Type 2L and 3L, RCA, Serial 755, 34th Anti-Aircraft Battery Type 2L, RCA, Serial 758 (Annette Island), 35th Anti-Aircraft Troop Type L, RCA, Serial 759, 36th Anti-Aircraft Troop Type L, RCA, Serial 764, 44th Anti-Aircraft Battery Type H, RCA, Serial 782, and 62nd Anti-Aircraft Troop Type LS, RCA, Serial 1180 (Whitehorse, Y.T.), served under Headquarters 29th Anti-Aircraft Regiment RCA at some period during its existence from March 1943 to 31st July 1945.

Headquarters 29th Anti-Aircraft Regiment RCA, Serial 1346, received authorization to disband under General Order 305/45 (Effective 31st July 1945).

* * *

30th Anti-Aircraft Regiment RCA — Serial 1347 — Port Alberni, B.C.

Headquarters 30th Anti-Aircraft Regiment RCA, Serial 1347, mobilized under General Order 208/43 (Effective 29th March 1943) to encompass the anti-aircraft units in the outlying areas of Vancouver Island, British Columbia, with regimental headquarters at Port Alberni, B.C.

33rd Anti-Aircraft Battery Type 2L and 4L, RCA, Serial 757 (Tofino and Ucluelet), 36th Anti-Aircraft Troop, Type L, RCA, Serial 764 (Comox), 39th Anti-Aircraft Troop, Type L, RCA, Serial 771 (Bella Bella), and 59th Anti-Aircraft Battery Type 2L and 3L, RCA, Serial 797 (Port Hardy and Coal Harbour), served under Headquarters 30th Anti-Aircraft Regiment RCA during its short existence. 25th LAA Battery RCA of 6th Division's 9th Light Anti-Aircraft Regiment RCA was attached to 30th AA Regiment at Port Alberni in June 1943.

Headquarters 30th Anti-Aircraft Regiment RCA, Serial 1347, received authorization to disband under General Order 80/44 (Effective 31st December 1943). 59th AA Battery remained operational until September 1944. 33rd Anti-Aircraft Battery RCA, Serial 757, became 129th Light Anti-Aircraft Battery RCA of the Post-war Permanent Force.

* * *

1st Anti-Tank Regiment RCA — Serial 20 — 1st Cdn Infantry Division

1st Anti-Tank Regiment RCA, Serial 20, less batteries, mobilized with the Canadian Active Service Force under General Order 135/39, 1st September 1939. 1st Army Field Brigade batteries were allotted to 1st Anti-Tank Regiment RCA, CASF and remained components until the regiment disbanded in 1945.

1st Anti-Tank Regiment RCA, Serial 20, comprised Headquarters 1st Anti-Tank Regiment RCA, Serial 20A, 51st Anti-Tank Battery RCA, Serial 20B, Ottawa, 57th Anti-Tank Battery RCA, Serial 20C, Quebec, P.Q., 27th Anti-Tank Battery RCA, Serial 20D, Montreal, and 90th Anti-Tank Battery RCA, Serial 20E, Fredericton, New Brunswick.

1st Anti-Tank Regiment RCA, CASF, arrived overseas 30th December 1939 and in June 1940 elements of the regiment accompanied 1st Brigade Group to France and upon its return to England prepared to repel the imminent invasion.

1st Canadian Infantry Division was selected as an assault division for the invasion of Sicily and the regiment departed for the Mediterranean 28th June 1943. The division landed 10th July with 30 Corps, British Eighth Army, then with the fall of Sicily crossed to the Italian mainland in September with 13 Corps, Eighth Army.

1st Canadian Corps became operational early in the new year and as a component 1st Anti-Tank Regiment RCA with 1st Canadian Infantry Division served in Italy until March 1945, then moved with the corps to NW Europe to join First Canadian Army.

1st Anti-Tank Regiment RCA joined the action in Holland 11th April 1945 and served until cessation of hostilities. The run-down of Canadian units was begun and 1st Anti-Tank Regiment received authorization to disband under General Order 401/45 (Effective 28th August 1945).

*   *   *

2nd Anti-Tank Regiment RCA — Serial 170 — 2nd Cdn Infantry Division

2nd Anti-Tank Regiment RCA, Serial 170, less batteries, mobilized with the Canadian Active Service Force under General Order 135/39, 1st September 1939. 2nd Army Field Brigade batteries were allotted to 2nd Anti-Tank Regiment RCA, CASF and remained components until the regiment disbanded in 1945.

2nd Anti-Tank Regiment RCA, Serial 170, comprised Headquarters 2nd Anti-Tank Regiment RCA, Serial 170A, 18th Anti-Tank Battery RCA, Serial 170B, Regina, 20th Anti-Tank Battery RCA, Serial 170C, Lethbridge, 108th Anti-Tank Battery RCA, Serial 170D, Kimberley, B.C., and 23rd Anti-Tank Battery RCA, Serial 170E, Calgary.

2nd Anti-Tank Regiment RCA, 2nd Canadian Infantry Division's Anti-Tank Regiment, arrived overseas 4th September 1940 and with the arrival of the division the Canadian Corps was formed December 1940.

2nd Canadian Corps was formed in January 1943 and 2nd Div moved to 2nd Corps upon the departure of 1st Canadian Corps to the Mediterranean with a new alignment toward the end of the year.

2nd Anti-Tank Regiment RCA accompanied 2nd Canadian Infantry Division to Normandy in July 1944 and became operational in the Carpiquet area under 2nd Canadian Corps, Second British Army. 2nd Canadian Corps and its components came under command of First Canadian Army 31st July 1944 and participated in the vicious fighting in the breakout from Caen and the closing of the Falaise Gap.

The regiment entered Dieppe 3rd September 1944 and paraded with the division through the streets of the city, then with the division returned to action under First Canadian Army and following the coastal route, served in France, Belgium, Holland and Germany until cessation of hostilities.

2nd Anti-Tank Regiment RCA received authorization to disband under General Order 52/46 (Effective 23rd September 1945).

*   *   *

3rd Anti-Tank Regiment RCA — Serial 708 — 3rd Cdn Infantry Division

3rd Anti-Tank Regiment RCA, CASF, Serial 708, Headquarters 3rd Anti-

Tank Regiment RCA, CASF, Serial 708A, 4th Anti-Tank Battery RCA, CASF, Serial 708B, Peterborough, Ontario, 94th Anti-Tank Battery RCA, CASF, Serial 708C, Quebec, P.Q., 52nd Anti-Tank Battery RCA, CASF, Serial 708D, Weymouth, Nova Scotia, and 105th Anti-Tank Battery RCA, CASF, Serial 708E, St. George, New Brunswick, mobilized with Headquarters 3rd Divisional Artillery RCA, CASF, under General Order 184/40 (Effective 24th May 1940).

The regiment arrived overseas 18th October 1941 and joined the Canadian Corps in the south of England. The corps was becoming more offensive minded and the division began preparing for a cross-Channel invasion.

3rd Anti-Tank Regiment RCA landed in the assault on the coast of Normandy on D-Day, 6th June 1944 attached to 1 British Corps, Second British Army, then moved to 2nd Canadian Corps early July. 2nd Canadian Corps and its components moved under the command of First Canadian Army 31st July 1944 on the Caen Front and the regiment advanced with First Canadian Army along the coastal sector in France, Belgium, Holland and Germany until cessation of hostilities. 3rd Anti-Tank Regiment RCA received authorization to disband under General Order 52/46 (Effective 14th November 1945).

A reconstituted 2nd 3rd Anti-Tank Regiment RCA mobilized under General Order 319/45 (Effective 1st June 1945) and following service with the Canadian Army Occupational Force in Germany received authorization to disband under General Order 201/46 (Effective 14th May 1946).

*　　*　　*

4th Anti-Tank Regiment RCA — Serial 908 — 5th Cdn Armoured Division

4th Anti-Tank Regiment RCA, CASF, Serial 908, Headquarters 4th Anti-Tank Regiment RCA, CASF, Serial 908A, 98th (Bruce) Anti-Tank Battery RCA, CASF, Serial 908B, Port Elgin, 24th Anti-Tank Battery RCA, CASF, Serial 908C, Toronto, 82nd Anti-Tank Battery RCA, CASF, Serial 908D, Gaspe, P.Q., and 104th Anti-Tank Battery RCA, CASF, Serial 908E, Fredericton, N.B., mobilized with Headquarters 4th Divisional Artillery RCA, CASF, under General Order 184/40 (Effective 24th May 1940).

Headquarters 1st Canadian Armoured Division, authorized under General Order 88/41 (Effective 27th February 1941), was changed to 5th Canadian (Armoured) Division under General Order 135/41 (Effective 5th June 1941). 4th Anti-Tank Regiment was transferred to the new formation as a three battery regiment. The regiment retained 98th (Bruce) Anti-Tank Battery RCA, 24th Anti-Tank Battery RCA, and 82nd (Gaspe) Anti-Tank Battery RCA, 104th Anti-Tank Battery RCA became surplus.

The regiment arrived overseas 17th October 1941 and shortly after arrival 24th

Battery was redesignated 49th Anti-Tank Battery RCA, Serial 908C. 16th Anti-Tank Battery RCA, Serial 908F, joined the regiment in England January 1943 as armoured division anti-tank regiments became four-battery regiments.

4th Anti-Tank Regiment RCA departed for the Mediterranean 15th November 1943 with 5th Canadian Armoured Division and 1st Canadian Corps became operational in Italy early in 1944. The SP batteries, 98th and 82nd stopped off at Algiers, the remainder of the regiment disembarked at Naples, Italy 1st December. The SP batteries rejoined the regiment 1st January and served in Italy until the last week of February 1945 when the corps transferred to NW Europe to join First Canadian Army.

The regiment joined the action in Holland the 1st week of April 1945 and served until cessation of hostilities, receiving authorization to disband under General Order 71/46 (Effective 28th November 1945).

*   *   *

5th Anti-Tank Regiment RCA — Serial 1992 — 4th Cdn Armoured Division

5th Anti-Tank Regiment RCA, Serial 992, Headquarters 5th Anti-Tank Regiment RCA, Serial 992A, 96th Anti-Tank Battery RCA, Serial 992B, Edmonton, 65th Anti-Tank Battery RCA, Serial 992C, Grenfell, Sask., mobilized under General Order 240/41 (Effective 5th September 1941) and were joined by 3rd Anti-Tank Battery RCA, Serial 1992D, formerly 3rd (Gananoque) Field Battery RCA, Serial 905C, 18th Field Regiment RCA, to complete the component batteries of 5th Anti-Tank Regiment RCA.

The Serial Number of 5th Anti-Tank Regiment RCA was changed from 992 to 1992, headquarters and the batteries were changed correspondingly, authorized under General Order 438/42 (Effective 12th February 1942).

The regiment arrived overseas 13th June 1942 and on the 1st January 1943 the regiment resumed the four battery organization discarded a year previous. A new battery designated 14th Anti-Tank Battery RCA, Serial 1992E, was formed in England to serve with 5th Anti-Tank Regiment RCA in 4th Canadian Armoured Division.

5th Anti-Tank Regiment RCA, 4th Canadian Armoured Division landed in Normandy 26th/27th July 1944, joining 2nd Canadian Corps in the beachhead, then with 2nd Canadian Corps came under command of First Canadian Army 31st July. The regiment participated in the vicious fighting in the breakout from Caen and the closing of the Falaise Gap. 4th Canadian Armoured Division continued the advance with First Canadian Army along the coastal sector in France, Belgium, Holland and Germany until cessation of hostilities.

5th Anti-Tank Regiment RCA received authorization to disband under General Order 71/46 (Effective 10th December 1945).

* * *

6th Anti-Tank Regiment RCA — Serial 814 — 2nd Canadian Corps

6th Anti-Tank Regiment RCA, Serial 814, Headquarters 6th Anti-Tank Regiment RCA, Serial 814A, 33rd Anti-Tank Battery RCA, Serial 814B, Simcoe, Ontario, 74th Anti-Tank Battery RCA, Serial 814C, Rock Island, P.Q., 56th Anti-Tank Battery RCA, Serial 814D, Lindsay, Ontario, and 103rd Anti-Tank Battery RCA, Serial 814E, Campbellton, New Brunswick, were authorized as components of 6th Divisional Artillery, RCA, in General Order 147/42 (Effective 18th March 1942).

The regiment was selected for overseas service January 1943 and joined 2nd Canadian Corps in England as Corps Troops. 6th Anti-Tank Regiment crossed the Channel to Normandy with Headquarters 2nd Canadian Corps 9th/10th July 1944, then with 2nd Canadian Corps came under command of First Canadian Army 31st July 1944, serving in France, Belgium, Holland and Germany until cessation of hostilities. 6th Anti-Tank Regiment RCA received authorization to disband under General Order 321/45 (Effective 23rd June 1945), in NW Europe.

* * *

7th Anti-Tank Regiment RCA — Serial 506 — 1st Canadian Corps

Headquarters 7th Anti-Tank Regiment RCA, Serial 506, mobilized under General Order 56/41 (Effective 1st February 1941), to encompass 111th (Nelson) Anti-Tank Battery RCA, Serial 167, from 6th Field Regiment RCA, 113th Anti-Tank Battery RCA, Serial 217, Regina, from 8th Army Field Regiment RCA, 15th Anti-Tank Battery RCA, Serial 211, Toronto, from 11th Army Field Regiment RCA, and 104th Anti-Tank Battery RCA, Serial 908E, Fredericton, N.B., a surplus 4th Infantry Division Battery. The regiment was to serve as 1st Canadian Corps A/T unit.

Serial Numbers were realigned with 7th Anti-Tank Regiment RCA, Serial 506, Headquarters 7th Anti-Tank Regiment RCA assumed Serial 506A and the batteries were designated accordingly, under General Order 54/42 (Effective 22nd December 1941).

7th Anti-Tank Regiment RCA accompanied Headquarters 1st Canadian Corps to the Mediterranean in November 1943, stopping at Algiers. The regiment, less 113th Battery arrived at Catania, Sicily, 8th December 1943. 113th Battery caught up with the regiment on the 31st and crossed to the Italian mainland 3rd January 1944. 7th Anti-Tank Regiment RCA served as 1st

Canadian Corps Anti-Tank Regiment in Italy until the end of February 1945 when the regiment accompanied Corps Headquarters to NW Europe to join First Canadian Army.

7th Anti-Tank Regiment became operational 7th April 1945 in the Netherlands and served until cessation of hostilities, receiving authorization to disband under General Order 321/45 (Effective 27th June 1945), in NW Europe.

* * *

8th Anti-Tank Regiment RCA — Serial 1414 — 7th Division, Home Defence

8th Anti-Tank Regiment RCA, Serial 1414, Headquarters 8th Anti-Tank Regiment RCA, Serial 1414A, 10th Anti-Tank Battery RCA, Serial 1414B, 11th Anti-Tank Battery RCA, Serial 1414C, 12th Anti-Tank Battery RCA, Serial 1414D, and 13th Anti-Tank Battery RCA, Serial 1414E, mobilized under General Order 309/42 (Effective 12th May 1942) to serve with 7th Division Home Defence, Eastern Canada.

The departure overseas of 19th, 21st and 23rd Field Regiments sadly depleted the ranks of the Home Defence Divisions and it was decided to disband 8th Anti-Tank Regiment and form a field regiment. 8th Anti-Tank Regiment RCA, Serial 1414, Headquarters and its component batteries disbanded under General Order 292/43 (Effective 15th May 1943). 28th Field Regiment RCA mobilized under General Order 289/43 (Effective 15th May 1943).

* * *

Headquarters 1st (Halifax) Coast Regiment RCA — Serial 339 — Halifax

Headquarters and batteries of the NPAM units were called out for duty at the forts 26th August 1939, then 1st September "Details" were authorized as components of the CASF. The "Details" were absorbed into headquarters and the batteries under General Order 44/41 (Effective 1st January 1941) as Headquarters 1st (Halifax) Coast Brigade RCA, Serial 339, 51st Heavy Battery RCA, Serial 340, 52nd Heavy Battery RCA, Serial 341, 53rd Heavy Battery RCA, Serial 342, 9th Heavy Battery (H) RCA, Serial 343, 1st Anti-Aircraft Battery RCA, Serial 344, 9th Searchlight Battery (CD) RCA, Serial 345, and 10th Searchlight Battery (CD) RCA, Serial 346, were placed on active service in Military District No. 6 and continued to man the forts.

9th Heavy Battery moved to Prince Rupert, British Columbia in March 1942 and 54th Heavy Battery RCA, Serial 893, mobilized under General Order 164/42 (Effective 10th April 1942). Brigades became regiments and heavy batteries became coast batteries under General Order 386/42 (Effective 1st August 1942). Headquarters 1st (Halifax) Coast Regiment RCA served under Headquarters Halifax Fortress, Atlantic Command, until authorized to disband under General Order 18/46 (Effective 15th August 1945).

* * *

Headquarters 3rd (New Brunswick) Coast Regiment RCA — Serial 365

Headquarters 3rd (New Brunswick) Coast Brigade RCA, NPAM, 4th Heavy Battery RCA and 1st Searchlight Battery (CD) RCA, were called out on service in Military District No. 7, 26th August 1939, for duty in the Saint John defences. "Details" of 4th and 15th Heavy Batteries and headquarters became components of the CASF, 1st September 1939. The "Details" were absorbed into the unit as Headquarters 3rd (New Brunswick) Coast Brigade RCA, Serial 365, 4th Heavy Battery RCA, Serial 366, and 15th Heavy Battery RCA, Serial 378, were placed on active service under General Order 44/41 (Effective 1st January 1941).

Headquarters 3rd (New Brunswick) Coast Brigade RCA became Headquarters 3rd (N.B.) Coast Regiment RCA, 15th Heavy Battery RCA became 15th Coast Battery RCA, under General Order 37/43 and 4th Heavy Battery RCA was redesignated 4th Coast Battery RCA under General Order 386/42 (Effective 1st August 1942), for all three. The regiment continued to serve under Headquarters Saint John Defences, and its later designation Headquarters Defended Port of Saint John, until authorized to disband under General Order 55/45 (Effective 1st September 1944).

*   *   *

Headquarters 5th (B.C.) Coast Regiment RCA — Serial 383 — Victoria

Headquarters, 5th (British Columbia) Coast Brigade RCA, NPAM, 55th, 56th, 60th Heavy Batteries RCA, 2nd Anti-Aircraft Battery RCA, and 17th Searchlight Battery (CD) RCA, were called out on service 26th August 1939 to man the forts under Headquarters Victoria and Esquimalt Fortress. "Details" of the brigade became components of the CASF 1st September 1939 and the "Details" were absorbed into headquarters and the batteries as the coast brigade was placed on active service under General Order 44/41 (Effective 1st January 1941). 68th Heavy Battery RCA, mobilized under General Order 155/41 (Effective 11th June 1941).

Headquarters 5th (British Columbia) Coast Brigade RCA, Serial 383, was redesignated Headquarters 5th (B.C.) Coast Regiment RCA, Serial 383, 55th Heavy Battery RCA became 55th Coast Battery RCA, Serial 384, 56th Heavy Battery RCA became 56th Coast Battery RCA, Serial 385, 60th Heavy Battery RCA became 60th Coast Battery RCA, Serial 386, and 68th Heavy Battery RCA became 68th Coast Battery RCA, Serial 382, under General Order 37/43 (Effective 1st May 1942).

The regiment manned forts at Christopher Point, Mary Hill, Albert Head, Belmont, Duntze Head, Black Rock, Macaulay, Golf Hill and Ogden Pier. 109th Coast Battery RCA, Serial 1722, mobilized under General Order 298/43 (Effective 1st June 1943), to aid in manning the forts under Headquarters Victoria and Esquimalt Fortress, and its later designation Headquarters Esquimalt Fortress.

Headquarters 5th (B.C.) Coast Regiment RCA, Serial 383, remained operational until cessation of the war in the Pacific and received authorization to disband under General Order 18/46 (Effective 31st October 1945).

*   *   *

Headquarters 15th (Vancouver) Coast Regiment RCA — Serial 387 — B.C.

Headquarters, 15th (Vancouver) Coast Brigade RCA, NPAM, 31st Heavy Battery RCA, 58th Heavy Battery RCA, and 3rd Searchlight Battery (CD) RCA, were called out on service in Military District No. 11, 26th August 1939, for duty in the Vancouver defences. "Details" of the brigade and batteries became components of the CASF, 1st September 1939. The "Details" were absorbed into headquarters and the batteries under General Order 44/41 (Effective 1st January 1941) as the unit was placed on active service.

Headquarters 15th (Vancouver) Coast Brigade RCA was redesignated 15th (Vancouver) Coast Regiment RCA, 31st Heavy Battery RCA, 58th Heavy Battery RCA and 85th Heavy Battery RCA were redesignated Coast Batteries under General Order 37/43 (Effective 1st June 1942) for Headquarters, 31st and 58th Batteries. 85th Battery's effective date was 1st April 1942.

85th Coast Battery manned the Yorke Island fort. 31st Coast Battery and 58th Coast Batteries manned the guns at Point Atkinson, Narrows North, Stanley Park, Point Grey and Steveston, under Headquarters Vancouver Defences, Pacific Command.

Headquarters 15th (Vancouver) Coast Regiment RCA, Serial 387, and 31st Coast Battery RCA, Serial 388, received authorization to disband under General Order 149/44 (Effective 1st March 1944). 58th and 85th Coast Batteries remained operational as independent coast batteries, 58th on the mainland and 85th Coast Battery RCA at Yorke Island.

58th Coast Battery RCA, Serial 389, received authorization to disband under General Order 208/45 (Effective 1st September 1944), 85th Coast General Order RCA, Serial 390, received authorization to disband under General Order 18/46 (Effective 31st October 1945).

*   *   *

Headquarters 16th Coast Regiment RCA — Serial 335 — Sydney-Canso

Headquarters 16th Coast Brigade RCA, NPAM, 6th Heavy Battery RCA, 36th Heavy Battery RCA, and 86th Heavy Battery RCA, were called out on service in Military District No. 6, 26th August 1939, for duty in the Sydney-Canso defences. "Details" of the coast brigade and batteries became components of the CASF, 1st September 1939. The "Details" were absorbed into headquarters and the batteries under General Order 44/41 (Effective 1st January 1941) as Headquarters 16th Coast Brigade RCA and its batteries were placed on active service.

Headquarters 16th Coast Brigade RCA, was redesignated Headquarters 16th Coast Regiment RCA, and 6th, 36th and 86th Heavy Batteries RCA were redesignated coast batteries, under General Order 399/42 (Effective 1st August 1942). The batteries manned guns at Fort Melford and Beacon on the Canso Strait, and Lingan, Petrie, Edward, Chapel, South Bar, Stubbert and Oxford in the Sydney area. The regiment continued to serve under Headquarters Sydney-Canso Defences and its later designation Headquarters Defended Port of Sydney until authorized to disband under General Order 18/46 (Effective 15th August 1945).

*   *   *

Headquarters 17th (North British Columbia) Coast Regiment RCA — 560

Headquarters 17th (North British Columbia) Coast Regiment RCA, Serial 560, was placed on active service under General Order 309/42 (Effective 1st May 1942) for duty under Headquarters Prince Rupert Defences, Pacific Command.

102nd (North British Columbia) Heavy Battery RCA, Serial 391, was redesignated 102nd Coast Battery RCA, Serial 391, and with 9th Coast Battery RCA, Serial 343, became components of 17th (North British Columbia) Coast Regiment RCA, absorbing 2nd Searchlight Battery (CD) RCA, Serial 394.

17th (North British Columbia) Coast Regiment RCA manned guns at Fairview Point, Frederick Point, Casey Point, Barrett Point and Dundas Point at Prince Rupert, British Columbia, and with Headquarters Prince Rupert Defences served under command of 8th Canadian Division from October 1942 to October 1943.

Headquarters 17th (North British Columbia) Coast Regiment RCA, Serial 560, along with 102nd Coast Battery RCA, Serial 391, 9th Coast Battery RCA, Serial 343, and Headquarters Prince Rupert Defences, Serial 2917, received authorization to disband under General Order 18/46 (Effective 31st October 1945).

*   *   *

1st Field Regiment RCHA — Serial 5 — 1st Canadian Infantry Division

The three Permanent Force field batteries "A" and "B" Batteries, Kingston, and "C" Battery, Winnipeg of the RCHA were named components of the Canadian Active Service Force, and with 54th Field Battery (H) RCA, CASF, Brantford, formed 1st Field Brigade RCA, CASF, under General Order 135/39, 1st September 1939.

The brigade arrived overseas December 1939 where it became a regiment of two combined batteries, "A"/"B" Field Battery RCA, CASF, and "C"/54th Field Battery RCA, CASF, under Headquarters 1st Field Regiment RCA, CASF, authorized under General Order 44/40 (Effective 21st December 1939). The regiment with 1st Brigade Group journeyed to France in June 1940 and due to the deteriorating conditions on the Continent boarded ship with a full complement of guns, less vehicles which due to lack of space aboard ship were destroyed on the beach prior to the ship sailing to England.

Headquarters 1st Field Regiment RCA, Serial 5, was redesignated 1st Field Regiment RCHA, Serial 5, and batteries were given individual identity in a three battery regiment. "A", "B" and "C" Batteries RCHA remained with the regiment and 54th Battery joined 2nd LAA Regiment RCA, 1st Division.

1st Canadian Infantry Division was selected to land in the assault on the island of Sicily in the Mediterranean in July 1943. "A" and "C" Batteries of the RCHA landed 13th July with the reserve 3rd Canadian Infantry Brigade and "B" Battery RCHA in a later sailing arrived 27th August.

The regiment in support of 3 CIB landed in the assault on the Italian mainland with 13 Corps, British Eighth Army, 3rd September 1943. The division came under command of 1st Canadian Corps upon the corps becoming operational early in 1944 and the regiment served with the corps in Italy until 17th March 1945, then moved with the corps to NW Europe.

1st Field Regiment RCHA, 1st Canadian Infantry Division, 1st Canadian Corps, joined the action in Holland 7th April near Joppe, under Headquarters First Canadian Army, and served until cessation of hostilities.

1st Field Regiment RCHA received authorization to disband under General Order 401/45 (Effective 25th August 1945).

* * *

Headquarters of 1st Army Field Brigade RCA, CASF — Serial 74 — 1st A/T

Headquarters of 1st Army Field Brigade RCA, CASF, Serial 74, 51st Field Battery RCA, CASF, Serial 75, 57th Field Battery RCA, CASF, Serial 76, 27th Field Battery (H) RCA, CASF, Serial 77, 90th Field Battery (H) RCA, CASF, Serial 78, were named components of the Canadian Active Service Force, Corps Troops mobilizing with 1st Division, under General Order 135/39, 1st September 1939.

The batteries of 1st Canadian Army Field Brigade RCA, CASF, were aligned with 1st Anti-Tank Regiment RCA, CASF, Serial 20, under General Order 201/39 (Effective 1st October 1939). The field batteries were redesignated anti-tank batteries under General Order 75/40 (Effective 1st December 1939)

and continued the war with 1st Anti-Tank Regiment RCA, 1st Canadian Infantry Division.

* * *

2nd Field Regiment RCA — Serial 10 — 1st Canadian Infantry Division

Headquarters of 2nd Field Brigade RCA, CASF, Serial 10, 10th (St. Catharines) Field Battery RCA, CASF, Serial 11, 7th Field Battery RCA, CASF, Serial 12, Montreal, and 8th Field Battery RCA, CASF, Serial 13, Moncton, mobilized as components of the Canadian Active Service Force with 1st Division, CASF, under General Order 135/39, 1st September 1939. 35th Field Battery (H) RCA, CASF, adopted Serial Number 14, with 2nd Field Brigade RCA, CASF, 1st Division, CASF, under General Order 206/39 (Effective 1st September 1939), in an exchange with 73rd Field Battery (H) RCA, CASF.

Headquarters of 2nd Field Brigade RCA, CASF, Serial 10, arrived overseas 18th December 1939 and was redesignated Headquarters, 2nd Field Regiment RCA, CASF, Serial 10, under General Order 44/40 (Effective 21st December 1939). The regiment was now composed of two batteries, 7th/35th and 8th/10th Field Batteries RCA, CASF, and remained a two hyphenated battery regiment until 1st January 1941 on which date the batteries regained individual identity as 7th, 8th and 10th Field Batteries RCA under General Order 45/41, remaining with the regiment. 35th Battery moved to 1st Light Anti-Aircraft Regiment RCA of 1st Canadian Corps.

2nd Field Regiment RCA, 1st Canadian Infantry Division, landed in the assault on the island of Sicily, 10th July 1943 with 30 Corps, British Eighth Army, then with the fall of Sicily the regiment crossed to the Italian mainland 3rd September 1943 with 13 Corps, British Eighth Army.

1st Canadian Infantry Division served under 13 Corps until 1st Canadian Corps became operational early in 1944 and served in Italy until March 1945 when the corps moved to NW Europe.

2nd Field Regiment RCA became operational in NW Europe under First Canadian Army 8th April 1945 in Holland and served until cessation of hostilities in May 1945, receiving authorization to disband under General Order 401/45 (Effective 25th August 1945).

* * *

Headquarters of 2nd Army Field Brigade RCA, CASF — Serial 79 — 2nd A/T

Headquarters of 2nd Army Field Brigade RCA, CASF, Serial 79, 18th Field Battery RCA, CASF, Serial 80, 20th Field Battery RCA, CASF, Serial 81, 108th Field Battery (H) RCA, CASF, Serial 82, and 23rd Field Battery (H) RCA, CASF, Serial 83, were named components of the Canadian Active

Service Force, as Corps Troops mobilizing with 1st Division, under General Order 135/39, 1st September 1939.

The batteries of 2nd Army Field Brigade RCA, CASF, were aligned with 2nd Anti-Tank Regiment RCA, CASF, Serial 20, under General Order 201/39 (Effective 1st October 1939). The field batteries were redesignated anti-tank batteries under General Order 75/40 (Effective 1st December 1939) and continued the war with 2nd Anti-Tank Regiment RCA, 2nd Canadian Infantry Division.

*   *   *

3rd Field Regiment RCA — Serial 15 — 1st Canadian Infantry Division

Headquarters of 3rd Field Brigade RCA, CASF, Serial 15, 19th Field Battery RCA, CASF, Serial 16, Winnipeg, 77th Field Battery RCA, CASF, Serial 18, Moose Jaw, and 92nd Field Battery (H) RCA, CASF, Serial 19, Edmonton, mobilized under General Order 135/39, 1st September 1939. 109th Field Battery RCA, CASF, of Trail, B.C., adopted Serial Number 17, with Headquarters of 3rd Field Brigade RCA, CASF, in an exchange with 111th Field Battery RCA, CASF, authorized under General Order 220/39 (Effective 1st September 1939).

Headquarters of 3rd Field Brigade RCA, CASF, Serial 15, arrived overseas 18th December 1939 and was redesignated Headquarters, 3rd Field Regiment RCA, CASF, Serial 15, under General Order 44/40 (Effective 21st December 1939). The regiment now comprised two batteries, 19th/77th and 92nd/109th Field Batteries RCA, CASF.

Reorganization to a three battery regiment saw the batteries regain individual identity under General Order 45/41 (Effective 1st January 1941). 19th, 77th and 92nd Field Batteries remained with 3rd Field Regiment RCA and 109th Battery moved to 1st Light Anti-Aircraft Regiment RCA of 1st Canadian Corps.

3rd Field Regiment RCA, 1st Canadian Infantry Division, landed in the assault on the island of Sicily 10th July 1943 with 30 Corps, British Eighth Army, then with the fall of Sicily crossed the Strait of Messina to the Italian mainland 3rd September 1943 with 13 Corps, Eighth Army.

1st Canadian Infantry Division came under command of Headquarters 1st Canadian Corps early in the new year and as a component the regiment served in Italy until March 1945, then moved with the corps to join First Canadian Army in NW Europe.

3rd Field Regiment RCA, 1st Canadian Infantry Division, became operational in Holland 7th April 1945 under Headquarters First Canadian Army and served until cessation of hostilities, receiving authorization to disband under General Order 401/45 (Effective 27th August 1945).

*   *   *

Headquarters of 3rd Army Field Brigade RCA — Serial 209 — 11th A/Fd

Headquarters of 3rd Army Field Brigade RCA, CASF, Serial 209, 40th Field Battery RCA, CASF, Serial 210, Hamilton, 15th Field Battery RCA, CASF, Serial 211, Toronto, 29th Field Battery (H) RCA, CASF, Serial 212, Guelph, and 9th (Toronto) Field Battery (H) RCA, CASF, became components of the Canadian Active Service Force under General Order 135/39, 1st September 1939.

The army field brigade arrived overseas 10th February 1940 and proceeded to the south of England where Headquarters of 3rd Army Field Brigade RCA, CASF, Serial 209, was redesignated Headquarters 11th Army Field Regiment RCA, CASF, Serial 209, and the batteries were paired in a two battery regiment, authorized under General Order 44/40 (Effective 12th February 1940). The regiment comprised 9th/15th Field Battery RCA, CASF, and 29th/40th Field Battery RCA, CASF.

11th Army Field Regiment RCA reorganized to a three battery regiment. Batteries regained individual identity under General Order 45/41 (Effective 1st January 1941), and the regiment retained 9th (Toronto) Field Battery RCA, 29th Field Battery RCA and 40th Field Battery RCA. 15th Battery moved to 7th Anti-Tank Regiment RCA of 1st Canadian Corps. The three surviving batteries continued to serve with the regiment until cessation of hostilities.

*   *   *

4th Field Regiment RCA — Serial 155 — 2nd Canadian Infantry Division

Headquarters of 4th Field Brigade RCA, CASF, Serial 155, 26th Field Battery RCA, CASF, Serial 156, Sarnia, 53rd Field Battery RCA, CASF, Serial 157, Toronto, 14th (Midland) Field Battery RCA, CASF, Serial 158, Cobourg, and 2nd (Ottawa) Field Battery (H) RCA, CASF, Serial 159, mobilized with 2nd division as components of the Canadian Active Service Force under General Order 135/39, 1st September 1939.

2nd Battery combined with 14th Battery to become 2nd/14th Field Battery RCA, CASF, 26th Battery combined with 53rd Battery to become 26th/53rd Field Battery RCA, CASF, and 4th Field Brigade became 4th Field Regiment RCA, CASF, under General Order 123/40 (Effective 1st June 1940).

The regiment arrived overseas 4th September 1940 and reorganized to comprise three batteries, authorized under General Order 45/41 (Effective 1st January 1941). 26th (Lambton) Field Battery RCA, 14th (Midland) Field

Battery RCA, and 2nd (Ottawa) Field Battery RCA regained individual identity and remained with 4th Field Regiment RCA. 53rd Battery joined 3rd Light Anti-Aircraft Regiment RCA of 2nd Division.

Three officers and twenty ORs participated in the raid on Dieppe, 19th August 1942 where three ORs were killed and the remainder taken prisoner. 2nd Canadian Infantry Division returned to the Continent in July 1944. 4th Field Regiment RCA landed in Normandy 7th July and following the breakout from Caen returned to Dieppe 3rd September 1944 for a service of remembrance in the cemetery, and a divisional parade through the streets of the city.

4th Field Regiment RCA, 2nd Canadian Infantry Division, 2nd Canadian Corps, served as a component of First Canadian Army in France, Belgium, Holland and Germany, then with cessation of hostilities received authorization to disband under General Order 52/46 (Effective 19th September 1945).

* * *

Headquarters of 4th Army Field Brigade RCA — Serial 214 — (8th Fd Regt)

Headquarters of 4th Army Field Brigade, RCA, CASF, Serial 214, 61st Field Battery RCA, CASF, Serial 215, 107th Field Battery RCA, CASF, Serial 216, 113th Field Battery (H) RCA, CASF, Serial 217, and 71st Field Battery (H) RCA, CASF, Serial 218, were authorized as components of the Canadian Active Service Force, Corps Troops mobilizing with 2nd Division, under General Order 135/39, 1st September 1939.

Headquarters of 4th Army Field Brigade RCA, CASF, Serial 214, was redesignated Headquarters 8th Army Field Regiment RCA, CASF, Serial 214, under General Order 44/40 (Effective 12th February 1940) and continued to serve under this designation until being redesignated 8th Field Regiment (Self-Propelled) RCA, under General Order 134/44 (Effective 18th October 1943) as the regiment joined 5th Canadian Armoured Division. The regiment served in Italy and NW Europe as an SP regiment with 5th Canadian Armoured Division.

* * *

5th Field Regiment RCA — Serial 160 — 2nd Canadian Infantry Division

Headquarters of 5th Field Brigade RCA, CASF, Serial 160, 5th (Westmount) Field Battery RCA, CASF, Serial 161, 28th (Newcastle) Field Battery RCA, CASF, Serial 162, and 89th (Woodstock) Field Battery RCA, CASF, Serial 163, were authorized as components of the CASF under General Order 135/39, 1st September 1939. 73rd Field Battery (H) RCA, CASF, adopted Serial Number 164, under Headquarters of 5th Field Brigade RCA, CASF, in an exchange with 35th Field Battery (H) RCA, CASF, authorized under General Order 206/39 (Effective 1st September 1939).

The field brigade became a field regiment of two hyphenated batteries and the regiment comprised 5th/73rd Field Battery RCA, CASF, and 28th/89th Field Battery RCA, CASF, authorized under General Order 123/40 (Effective 1st June 1940).

The regiment arrived overseas 4th September 1940 and under General Order 45/41 (Effective 1st January 1941), became a three battery regiment, retaining 5th (Westmount) Field Battery RCA, Serial 160B, 28th (Newcastle) Field Battery RCA, Serial 160C, and 73rd Field Battery RCA, Serial 160D, Magog, P.Q. 89th Battery RCA, Woodstock, N.B., moved to 1st Light Anti-Aircraft Regiment RCA, 1st Canadian Corps.

Captain W. McCutcheon, the sole member of the regiment on the Dieppe raid 19th August 1942 was killed on the beach. 2nd Canadian Infantry Division returned to the Continent with 5th Field Regiment RCA landing in Normandy 7th July 1944 and following the capture of Dieppe the division paused for a service of remembrance followed by a divisional parade through the city.

2nd Canadian Infantry Division returned to action under Headquarters First Canadian Army and 5th Field Regiment RCA served in France, Belgium, Holland and Germany, then with cessation of hostilities the regiment received authorization to disband under General Order 52/46 (Effective 21st September 1945).

*   *   *

Headquarters of 5th Army Field Brigade RCA — Serial 238 — (7th Med.)

Headquarters of 5th Army Field Brigade RCA, CASF, Serial 238, 100th Field Battery RCA, CASF, Serial 239, 12th Field Battery RCA, CASF, Serial 240, 97th Field Battery (H) RCA, CASF, Serial 241, and 45th Field Battery (H) RCA, CASF, Serial 242, were authorized as components of the Canadian Active Service Force, Corps Troops mobilizing with 2nd Division, under General Order 135/39, 1st September 1939.

Headquarters of 5th Army Field Brigade RCA, CASF, Serial 238, was redesignated Headquarters of 21st Army Field Regiment RCA, CASF, Serial 238, under General Order 123/40 (Effective 1st June 1940). The batteries combined at this time to become 12th/45th and 97th/100th Field Batteries RCA, CASF. The regiment was redesignated 7th Army Field Regiment RCA, CASF, under General Order 195/40 (Effective 15th August 1940), the batteries remained combined until the regiment reorganized to a three battery regiment authorized under General Order 74/41 (Effective 1st January 1941). 12th, 45th and 97th Batteries regained individual identity and remained with 7th Army Field Regiment RCA, 100th Battery moved to 4th Light Anti-Aircraft Regiment RCA, 3rd Division.

7th Army Field Regiment RCA, Serial 238, was redesignated 7th Medium Regiment RCA, Serial 238, retaining 12th and 45th Batteries upon their conversion to medium batteries, authorized under General Order 21/44 (Effective 21st November 1943). 97th Battery disbanded under General Order 22/44 (Effective 21st November 1943), the medium regiment requiring two batteries only.

*   *   *

6th Field Regiment RCA — Serial 165 — 2nd Canadian Infantry Division

Headquarters of 6th Field Brigade RCA, CASF, Serial 165, 13th (Winnipeg) Field Battery RCA, CASF, Serial 166, 91st Field Battery RCA, CASF, Serial 168, Calgary, and 21st Field Battery (H) RCA, CASF, Serial 169, of Saskatoon, mobilized with 2nd Division, CASF, Under General Order 135/39, 1st September 1939. 111th Field Battery RCA, CASF, of Nelson, British Columbia, adopted Serial Number 167, with Headquarters of 6th Field Brigade RCA, CASF, in an exchange with 109th Field Battery RCA, CASF, of Trail, B.C., authorized under General Order 220/39 (Effective 1st September 1939).

The brigade became a two battery field regiment and the batteries were paired to become 13th/21st and 91st/111th Field Batteries, RCA, CASF, under General Order 123/40 (Effective 1st June 1940).

6th Field Regiment arrived overseas in September 1940 and reorganized to a three battery regiment under General Order 45/41 (Effective 1st January 1941), retaining 13th (Winnipeg) Field Battery RCA, 21st Field Battery RCA and 91st Field Battery RCA. 111th (Nelson) Field Battery RCA joined 7th Anti-Tank Regiment RCA of 1st Canadian Corps.

Captain B. Carswell, the sole member of the regiment on the Dieppe raid was wounded and later awarded the Military Cross. 2nd Div returned to the Continent in July 1944, with 6th Field Regiment RCA landing in Normandy 8th July and returned to Dieppe 3rd September 1944 for a memorial service and a divisional parade through the city.

2nd Canadian Infantry Division returned to action under 2nd Canadian Corps, First Canadian Army and the regiment served in France, Belgium, Holland and Germany, then with cessation of hostilities 6th Field Regiment RCA received authorization to disband under General Order 52/46 (Effective 23rd September 1945).

*   *   *

7th Army Field Regiment RCA & 7th Medium Regt — Serial 238 — Army Tps.

Headquarters of 5th Army Field Brigade RCA, CASF, Serial 238, 100th Field Battery RCA, CASF, Listowel, 12th Field Battery RCA, CASF, London, 97th

Field Battery (H) RCA, CASF, Walkerton, and 45th Field Battery (H) RCA, CASF, Lindsay, all from Ontario, mobilized under General Order 135/39, 1st September 1939, Army Troops mobilizing with 2nd Division.

Headquarters of 5th Army Field Brigade RCA, CASF, Serial 238, became 21st Army Field Regiment RCA, CASF, with 12th/45th and 97th/100th Field Batteries RCA, CASF, as components, under General Order 123/40 (Effective 1st June 1940), then under General Order 195/40 (Effective 15th August 1940), 21st Army Field Regiment RCA, CASF and its hyphenated batteries became 7th Army Field Regiment RCA, CASF. Batteries were given individual identity under General Order 74/41 (Effective 1st January 1941) and the regiment retained 12th, 45th and 97th Field Batteries RCA, 100th Battery joined 4th Light Anti-Aircraft Regiment RCA to serve with 3rd Division.

7th Army Field Regiment RCA arrived overseas 21st November 1941 to join 1st Corps Medium Artillery, which evolved into 1st Canadian AGRA, then with the forming of 2nd Canadian AGRA 7th Army Field Regiment RCA became a component.

7th Army Field Regiment RCA, Serial 238, was redesignated 7th Medium Regiment RCA, Serial 238, under General Order 21/44 (Effective 21st November 1943), and remained with 2nd Canadian AGRA, Army Troops. The medium regiment required two batteries only and 97th Field Battery RCA disbanded.

7th Medium Regiment RCA, 2nd Canadian AGRA, Army Troops, landed in Normandy 11th July 1944 to support 2nd Canadian Corps, then with 2nd Canadian Corps moved under the command of First Canadian Army, 31st July 1944 and served in France, Belgium, Holland and Germany until cessation of hostilities in NW Europe.

7th Medium Regiment RCA received authorization to disband under General Order 52/46 (Effective 25th September 1945).

* * *

8th Field Regiment (Self-Propelled) RCA — Serial 214 — 5th Cdn Armd Div

Headquarters of 4th Army Field Brigade RCA, CASF, Serial 214, 61st Field Battery RCA, CASF, Serial 215, Edmonton, 107th Field Battery RCA, CASF, Serial 216, Cranbrook, B.C., 113th Field Battery (H) RCA, Serial 217, Regina, Sask. and 71st Field Battery (H) RCA, Serial 218, Brandon, Man., became components of the Canadian Active Service Force, Corps Troops mobilizing with 2nd Division, under General Order 135/39, 1st September 1939.

Headquarters of 4th Army Field Brigade RCA and the batteries arrived overseas 8th February 1940 and was redesignated Headquarters 8th Army

Field Regiment RCA, CASF, under General Order 44/40 (Effective 12th February 1940). The regiment was to comprise 61st/107th Field Battery RCA, CASF, and 71st/113th Field Battery RCA, CASF, then under General Order 45/41 (Effective 1st January 1941), batteries were given individual identity as the regiment reorganized to three batteries. 113th Battery moved to 7th Anti-Tank Regiment RCA, 1st Canadian Corps.

8th Army Field Regiment RCA shed its role as an army field regiment and joined 5th Canadian Armoured Division upon being redesignated 8th Field Regiment (Self-Propelled) RCA, Serial 214, under General Order 134/44 (Effective 18th October 1943), and joined 5th Canadian Armoured Division in Italy, 22nd December 1943.

8th Field Regiment (Self-Propelled) RCA joined the action early in the new year and served with 5th Canadian Armoured Division, 1st Canadian Corps until February 1945, then moved with the corps to NW Europe to join First Canadian Army.

The regiment deployed in the Arnhem, Holland, Sector 6th April and served until cessation of hostilities, receiving authorization to disband under General Order 71/46 (Effective 27th November 1945).

*   *   *

11th Army Field Regiment RCA — Serial 209 — Army Troops & 5th Div

Headquarters of 3rd Army Field Brigade RCA, CASF, Serial 209, 40th Field Battery RCA, CASF, Serial 210, Hamilton, 15th Field Battery RCA, CASF, Serial 211, Toronto, 29th Field Battery (H) RCA, CASF, Serial 212, Guelph, and 9th (Toronto) Field Battery (H) RCA, Serial 213, all from Ontario, became components of the Canadian Active Service Force, Corps Troops mobilizing with 2nd Division, under General Order 135/39, 1st September 1939.

The brigade arrived overseas 10th February 1940, and under General Order 44/40 (Effective 12th February 1940), Headquarters of 3rd Army Field Brigade RCA, CASF, Serial 209, was redesignated Headquarters 11th Army Field Regiment RCA, CASF, Serial 209. Batteries were paired and the regiment comprised 9th/15th Field Battery RCA, CASF, and 29th/40th Field Battery RCA, CASF.

The regiment reorganized to a three battery regiment, retaining 9th (Toronto) Field Battery RCA, 29th Field Battery RCA and 40th Field Battery RCA, upon the batteries regaining individual identity under General Order 45/41 (Effective 1st January 1941). 15th Battery moved to 7th Anti-Tank Regiment RCA, 1st Canadian Corps.

11th Army Field Regiment RCA accompanied 1st Canadian AGRA to Sicily, where the regiment disembarked 8th November 1943 and crossed the Strait of Messina to the Italian mainland 7th January 1944. 11th Army field Regiment fired its first rounds 18th February, then in July the regiment changed from Army Troops to divisional troops, becoming 11th Field Regiment RCA with 5th Canadian Armoured Division's new infantry brigade and served with the armoured division until its departure from Italy toward the end of February 1945.

Upon arrival in NW Europe the regiment exchanged the 5th Division maroon patch for the Army Troops Artillery diamond and resumed its role as Army Troops artillery. 11th Army Field Regiment RCA joined First Canadian Army and from positions in Germany fired in support of the Rhine crossing by 2nd and 3rd Canadian Division regiments 31st March, then returned to the Arnhem Sector in Holland and served until cessation of hostilities, receiving authorization to disband under General Order 401/45 (Effective 4th September 1945).

* * *

12th Field Regiment RCA — Serial 705 — 3rd Canadian Infantry Division

12th Field Regiment RCA, CASF, Serial 705, Headquarters 12th Field Regiment RCA, CASF, Serial 705A, 16th/43rd Field Battery RCA, CASF, Serial 705B, and 11th/69th Field Battery RCA, CASF, Serial 705C, with Headquarters, 3rd Divisional Artillery RCA, CASF, were named components of the Canadian Active Service Force under General Order 184/40 (Effective 24th May 1940).

Batteries were given individual identity and the regiment retained 11th, 16th and 43rd Field Batteries as the regiment reorganized to comprise three batteries, authorized under General Order 45/41 (Effective 1st January 1941). 69th Battery joined 4th Light Anti-Aircraft Regiment RCA, 3rd Division light anti-aircraft regiment.

12th Field Regiment RCA, 3rd Canadian Infantry Division proceeded overseas during July 1941 and joined the Canadian Corps in the south of England. 3rd Div was selected as a participant in the Normandy assault and 12th Field Regiment RCA fired its 105mm self-propelled guns from the landing craft in support of 3rd Canadian Infantry Division's 7th Brigade prior to landing on the Normandy beaches on D-Day, 6th June 1944.

During the early days of the invasion the division served with 1 British Corps, Second Army, moving under 2nd Canadian Corps mid-July, then with 2nd Canadian Corps moved under command of First Canadian Army 31st July 1944. The 104mm SPs were exchanged for towed 25 pounders 1st August, with the beachhead secured. 3rd Canadian Infantry Division advanced with First Canadian Army along the coast and the many amphibious operations earned the division the title "Water Rats".

12th Field Regiment RCA served in France, Belgium, Holland and Germany until cessation of hostilities and received authorization to disband under General Order 52/46 (Effective 31st October 1945).

A 2nd 12th Field Regiment RCA mobilized for the reconstituted 3rd Canadian Infantry Division, CAOF, under General Order 319/45 (Effective 1st June 1945) and following occupational duty in Germany received authorization to disband under General Order 201/46 (Effective 18th May 1946).

*   *   *

13th Field Regiment RCA — Serial 706 - 3rd Canadian Infantry Division

13th Field Regiment RCA, CASF, Serial 706, Headquarters 13th Field Regiment, RCA, CASF, Serial 706A, 44th/62nd Field Battery RCA, CASF, Serial 706B and 22nd/78th Field Battery RCA, CASF, Serial 706C, mobilized with Headquarters 3rd Divisional Artillery RCA, CASF, authorized as components of the Canadian Active Service Force under General Order 184/40 (Effective 24th May 1940).

The regiment retained 22nd, 44th and 78th Batteries in a three battery regiment as the batteries were given individual identity under General Order 45/41 (Effective 1st January 1941). 62nd Battery moved to 4th Light Anti-Aircraft Regiment RCA, 3rd Division LAA Regiment.

13th Field Regiment RCA, 3rd Canadian Infantry Division, arrived overseas during November 1941 and as thoughts turned from defense to offense the division was selected as a participant in the invasion of Normandy in 1944. 13th Field Regiment RCA in support of 7th Canadian Infantry Brigade, fired its 105mm self-propelled guns from the assault craft prior to landing on D-Day, 6th June 1944.

3rd Canadian Infantry Division served under 1 British Corps, Second British Army until the beachhead was enlarged and 2nd Canadian Corps became operational early in July. On the 31st July the regiment with 2nd Canadian Corps came under command of First Canadian Army, and following the coastal route, served in France, Belgium, Holland and Germany, then with cessation of hostilities received authorization to disband under General Order 52/46 (Effective 14th November 1945).

A reconstituted 2nd 13th Field Regiment RCA was formed under General Order 319/45 (Effective 1st June 1945) and disbanded under General Order 201/46 (Effective 13th April 1946), following service with the Canadian Army Occupational Force in Germany.

*   *   *

14th Field Regiment RCA — Serial 707 — 3rd Canadian Infantry Division

14th Field Regiment RCA, CASF, Serial 707, Headquarters 14th Field Regiment RCA, CASF, Serial 707A, 32nd/34th Field Battery RCA, CASF, Serial 707B and 66th/81st Field Battery RCA, CASF, Serial 707C, with Headquarters 3rd Divisional Artillery RCA, CASF, were authorized as components of the Canadian Active Service Force under General Order 184/40 (Effective 24th May 1940).

14th Field Regiment RCA, 3rd Canadian Infantry Division arrived overseas 29th July 1941 and joined the Canadian Corps in the south of England. 3rd Canadian Infantry Division was chosen an assault division for the Normandy invasion in 1944 and 14th Field Regiment RCA fired its 105mm self-propelled guns from the assault craft in support of 8th Canadian Infantry Brigade of 3rd Canadian Infantry Division prior to landing on the Normandy beach on D-Day, 6th June 1944.

3rd Canadian Infantry Division served under 1 British Corps, Second British Army until 2nd Canadian Corps became operational early in July, then 14th Field Regiment RCA, with 3rd Canadian Infantry Division and 2nd Canadian Corps, came under command of First Canadian Army 31st of July 1944 and played a leading role in the breakout from Caen and the closing of the Falaise Gap.

The division continued the advance under First Canadian Army along the coastal sector in France, Belgium, Holland and Germany, then with the cessation of hostilities 14th Field Regiment RCA received authorization to disband under General Order 52/46 (Effective 2nd November 1945).

A reconstituted regiment, 2nd 14th Field Regiment RCA was formed under General Order 319/45 (Effective 1st June 1945), and following service with the Canadian Army Occupational Force in Germany was authorized to disband under General Order 162/46 (Effective 28th March 1946).

*   *   *

15th Field Regiment RCA — Serial 1905 — 4th Cdn Armoured Division

Headquarters, 4th Division, CASF, Serial 900, Headquarters, 4th Divisional Artillery RCA, CASF, Serial 904, 15th Field Regiment RCA, CASF, Serial 905, Headquarters 15th Field Regiment RCA, CASF, Serial 905A, 41st/102nd Field Battery RCA, CASF, Serial 905B, 3rd/47th Field Battery RCA, CASF, Serial 905C, mobilized as components of the Canadian Active Service Force, under General Order 184/40 (Effective 24th May 1940).

3rd Battery regained individual identity as 3rd (Gananoque) Field Battery RCA, under General Order 85/41 (Effective 27th February 1941), and in May 1941 joined 18th Field Regiment RCA in 4th Division, then became 3rd Anti-Tank Battery RCA with 5th Anti-Tank Regiment RCA, 4th Division.

41st and 47th Batteries joined 5th Light Anti-Aircraft Regiment RCA, and 102nd Battery became 102nd (Wentworth) Field Battery with 16th Field Regiment RCA, which in turn was redesignated 8th LAA Regiment RCA.

15th Field Regiment RCA received a new slate of batteries, 17th Field Battery RCA, Winnipeg, mobilized under General Order 85/41 (Effective 1st January 1941), 95th Field Battery RCA, Calgary, and 110th Field Battery RCA, Broadview, Sask., mobilized under General Order 160/41 (Effective 10th May 1941) to complete the three battery regiment.

4th Division was converted to an armoured division under General Order 132/42 (Effective 26th January 1942) and 15th Field Regiment RCA remained the sole field regiment in the armoured division. Serial Numbers were revised under General Order 438/42 (Effective 12th February 1942). 15th Field Regiment RCA assumed Serial 1905, Headquarters 15th Field Regiment RCA, Serial 1905A, 95th Field Battery RCA, Serial 1905B, 110th Field Battery RCA, Serial 1905C, and 17th Field Battery RCA, Serial 1905D.

15th Field Regiment RCA arrived overseas in August 1942 and remained a towed regiment, equipped with towed 25 pounders, and welcomed 23rd Field Regiment (Self-Propelled) RCA to the divisional artillery in 1943.

15th Field Regiment RCA, 4th Canadian Armoured Division crossed the Channel to Normandy 26th July 1944 to join 2nd and 3rd Divisions in the beachhead under 2nd Canadian Corps, then with 2nd Canadian Corps moved under the command of First Canadian Army 31st July 1944 on the Caen Front.

Following the breakout from Caen and the closing of the Falaise Gap the regiment advanced with First Canadian Army along the coastal sector and served in France, Belgium, Holland and Germany, then with cessation of hostilities received authorization to disband under General Order 71/46 (Effective 12th December 1945).

*   *   *

16th Field Regiment RCA — Serial 906 — 4th Division, CASF

16th Field Regiment RCA, CASF, Serial 906, Headquarters 16th Field Regiment RCA, CASF, Serial 906A, 24th/75th Field Battery RCA, CASF, Serial 906B, and 87th/88th Field Battery RCA, CASF, Serial 906C, mobilized with Headquarters 4th Division, CASF, as components of the Canadian Active Service Force under General Order 184/40 (Effective 24th May 1940).

Under General Order 240/41 (Effective 5th September 1941), 24th and 75th Batteries regained individual identity as 24th (Shefford) Field Battery RCA, and 75th Field Battery RCA, then under the same General Order the batteries were redesignated 24th Anti-Tank Battery RCA and 75th Anti-Tank Battery

RCA. Serial Numbers suggest both batteries were slated for 5th Anti-Tank Regiment RCA, a four battery regiment in 4th Division. 4th Division became an armoured division requiring a three battery anti-tank regiment and 20th Field Regiment RCA was in need of two batteries, 24th and 75th Batteries became field batteries once more and moved to 20th Field Regiment RCA. 87th Battery moved to 18th Field Regiment RCA, then to 3rd Medium Regiment RCA. 88th Battery joined 5th Light Anti-Aircraft Regiment RCA and served with 5th Canadian Armoured Division.

With its original slate of batteries employed elsewhere 16th Field Regiment RCA was allotted three new batteries in May 1941. 70th Field Battery RCA arrived from Brandon, Manitoba, 102nd (Wentworth) Field Battery RCA of Dundas, Ontario, and 18th Field Battery RCA, Port Arthur, Ontario, became the new components.

Reorganization struck again. Headquarters 4th Division, Serial 900, was redesignated Headquarters 4th (Armoured) Division, Serial 900. Headquarters 16th Field Regiment RCA, Serial 906A, was redesignated Headquarters 8th Light Anti-Aircraft Regiment RCA, Serial 1906A, under General Order 132/42 (Effective 26th January 1942), and the regiment continued to serve with the division under its new designation.

*   *   *

17th Field Regiment RCA — Serial 907 — 5th Canadian Armoured Division

17th Field Regiment RCA, CASF, Serial 907, Headquarters 17th Field Regiment RCA, CASF, Serial 907A, 60th/76th Field Battery RCA, CASF, Serial 907B, and 37th Field Battery RCA, CASF, Serial 907C, mobilized under General Order 184/40 (Effective 24th May 1940), with Headquarters 4th Division, CASF.

The composition of the regiment was rather unique for in the era of combined battery field regiments 17th Field Regiment mobilized with one hyphenated battery and one individual battery. The combined battery became two batteries as the batteries were given individual identity under General Order 85/41 (Effective 1st January 1941) and the regiment became a three battery regiment comprising 37th Field Battery RCA, Portage La Prairie, Manitoba, 60th Field Battery RCA, Aneroid, Saskatchewan and 76th Field Battery RCA, Indian Head, Saskatchewan.

17th Field Regiment RCA was withdrawn from 4th Division and joined the Support Group of 1st Canadian Armoured Division, authorized under General Order 88/41 (Effective 27th February 1941) and redesignated 5th Canadian (Armoured) Division under General Order 135/41 (Effective 5th June 1941). 17th Field Regiment RCA was the sole field artillery unit in the armoured division.

17th Field Regiment RCA, 5th Canadian Armoured Division arrived overseas in November 1941 and joined the Canadian Corps in the south of England. 5th Canadian Armoured Division was selected to join 1st Canadian Infantry Division and 1st Canadian Armoured Brigade under Headquarters 1st Canadian Corps in an operational role in Italy. 17th Field Regiment RCA sailed 26th October 1943 and disembarked at Naples, Italy, 8th November, to inherit equipment 7th Armoured Division (The Desert Rats) had initiated in desert warfare.

The regiment fired its first rounds 14th January 1944 and equipped with towed 25 pounders served as a towed regiment throughout. 8th Field Regiment (Self-Propelled) RCA joined the division in Italy to serve as divisional self-propelled regiment.

Transfer of 1st Canadian Corps to NW Europe saw 17th Field Regiment RCA depart from Leghorn, Italy the last week of February 1945 and join the action in the Arnhem Sector in Holland, 29th March 1945 under First Canadian Army. The regiment served until cessation of hostilities and received authorization to disband under General Order 71/46 (Effective 29th November 1945).

*   *   *

HQ 18th Field Regiment RCA — Serial 982 — 4th Division

Headquarters 18th Field Regiment RCA, Serial 982, and 25th Field Battery RCA, Serial 983, Toronto, mobilized under General Order 160/41 (Effective 10th May 1941). 3rd (Gananoque) Field Battery from the original 15th Field Regiment and 87th Field Battery, Dartmouth, N.S., from the original 16th Field Regiment RCA, arrived to complete the new Regiment which had mobilized to replace the departed 17th Field Regiment RCA in 4th Division.

4th Division was converted to an armoured division under General Order 132/42 (Effective 26th January 1942) requiring one regiment of field artillery only. 18th Field Regiment became surplus and Headquarters 18th Field Regiment RCA, Serial 982, was redesignated Headquarters 2nd Medium Regiment RCA, Serial 982A, under General Order 104/42 (Effective 26th January 1942). 25th Battery accompanied the headquarters to the new regiment and was joined by 18th Battery from 16th Field Regiment RCA to complete 2nd Medium Regiment RCA. 3rd (Gananoque) Battery joined 5th Anti-Tank Regiment RCA, and 87th Battery became a component of 3rd Medium Regiment RCA.

*   *   *

19th Army Field Regiment RCA - Serial 810 - Army Troops

Headquarters 19th Field Regiment RCA, Serial 810A, 55th Field Battery RCA, Serial 810B, London, 63rd Field Battery RCA, Serial 810C, Guelph, and 99th Field Battery RCA, Serial 810D, Wingham, mobilized with 6th Division, Home Defence, under General Order 63/42 (Effective 29th July 1941). Serial

Number 810 was authorized for 19th Field Regiment RCA, under General Order 438/42 (Effective 12th February 1942).

Aligned with 14th Brigade Group the regiment served at Prince Rupert, British Columbia and manned the armoured train running along the Skeena River between Prince Rupert and Terrace. While at the west coast 19th Field Regiment RCA received notice of an overseas posting and Headquarters 19th Field Regiment RCA was redesignated Headquarters 19th Self-Propelled Regiment RCHA, under General Order 328/43 (Effective 15th May 1943).

The regiment arrived overseas in July 1943, and under General Order 396/43 (Effective 15th August 1943) 19th Self-Propelled Regiment RCHA, was redesignated 19th Regiment (Self-Propelled) RCA. 19th Regiment (Self-Propelled) RCA, Serial 810, was redesignated 19th Field Regiment (Self-Propelled) RCA, under General Order 452/43 (Effective 1st September 1943).

19th Field Regiment (Self-Propelled) RCA was attached temporarily to 5th Canadian Armoured Division in a self-propelled role, then was redesignated 19th Army Field Regiment RCA, Serial 810, under General Order 134/44 (Effective 18th October 1943), and was attached to 3rd Canadian Infantry Division to prepare for the Normandy assault.

A fourth regiment of field artillery was required to provide the support of two regiments of field artillery to each of the two assaulting infantry brigades of 3rd Canadian Infantry Division, and as an army field regiment the regiment's firepower was added to that of 12th, 13th and 14th Field Regiments RCA of 3rd Division.

19th Army Field Regiment RCA fired its 105mm self-propelled guns from the landing craft in support of 3rd Canadian Infantry Division's 8th Brigade prior to landing on the beaches of Normandy on D-Day, 6th June 1944. The remainder of 2nd Canadian Corps arrived during July and on the 31st July 1944 the Canadian units in Normandy came under command of First Canadian Army for the breakout from Caen and the closing of the Falaise Gap.

The regiment exchanged the 105mm SPs for 25 pounder SPs in August with the beachhead secured and with First Canadian Army 19th Army Field Regiment RCA advanced along the coastal sector in France, Belgium, Holland and Germany, firing in support of the multi-national components of First Canadian Army until cessation of hostilities.

19th Army Field Regiment RCA received authorization to disband under General Order 52/46 (Effective 16th November 1945).

*   *   *

20th Field Regiment RCA — Serial 811 — 6th and 7th Divisions

Headquarters 20th Field Regiment RCA, Serial 811A, 58th Field Battery RCA, Serial 811B, Quebec, P.Q., 72nd Field Battery RCA, Serial 811C, Coaticook, P.Q., and 50th Field Battery RCA, Serial 811D, Montreal, mobilized under General Order 63/42 (Effective 29th July 1941) with 6th Division, Home Defence. The regiment aligned with 15th Brigade Group 6th Division was transferred to 7th Division for service in eastern Canada.

50th and 58th Batteries were redesignated medium batteries 26th January 1942 and joined 4th Medium Regiment RCA. 24th and 75th Field Batteries arrived as replacements. The batteries had mobilized as the combined 24th/75th Field Battery in the original 16th Field Regiment RCA, CASF, 4th Division, and became surplus upon regaining individual identity. 20th Field Regiment RCA was allotted Serial Number 811, under General Order 438/42 (Effective 12th February 1942).

7th and 8th Divisions disbanded October 1943 and 6th Division returned to its original brigade alignment. 20th Field Regiment RCA with 15th Brigade returned to 6th Division and served at Prince George and Nanaimo, British Columbia, Wainwright, Alberta, returning to Prince George, then moved to Valcartier, P.Q. 1st December 1944, where 20th Field Regiment RCA received authorization to disband under General Order 208/45 (Effective 31st December 1944).

*   *   *

21st Field Regiment RCA — Serial 812 — 6th Division & reinforcements

Headquarters 21st Field Regiment RCA, Serial 812A, 59th Field Battery RCA, Serial 812B, Brandon, 64th (Yorkton) Field Battery RCA, Serial 812C, and 39th Field Battery RCA, Serial 812D, Lethbridge, mobilized with 6th Division, Home Defence, under General Order 63/42 (Effective 29th July 1941). 21st Field Regiment RCA was allotted Serial Number 812, under General Order 438/42 (Effective 12th February 1942).

21st Field Regiment RCA aligned with 13th Brigade Group arrived at the west coast in December 1941, then on the 13th March 1942, 21st Field Regiment RCA moved from Westminster Camp on the mainland to Nanaimo tent camp on Vancouver Island, from which location detached unit gun positions were manned at Otter Point and Jordan River.

21st Field Regiment RCA moved from Nanaimo to Port Alberni 1st March 1943, then on the 17th of April proceeded to Willows Camp, Victoria. Eastward bound, 21st Rield Regiment RCA crossed from Victoria to the mainland 22nd May and arrived at Petawawa, Ontario, 26th May 1943.

The eastward journey was resumed 12th August as the regiment left Petawawa For Debert, Nova Scotia, then on to Halifax 26th August to board the Queen

Mary on which Winston Churchill had travelled to attend the First Quebec Conference. The ship sailed 27th August and the regiment disembarked at Gourock, Scotland, 1st September 1943.

21st Field Regiment RCA proceeded to the south of England, where the die had been cast for the 1st Canadian Corps operation in italy and the 2nd Canadian Corps operation in NW Europe. 21st Field Regiment RCA was not included, and left without an active role. The regiment received authorization to disband under General Order 149/44 (Effective 11th October 1943). Personnel joined the reinforcement pool.

* * *

Headquarters of 21st Army Field Regiment RCA, CASF — Serial 238 — 7 Med

Headquarters of 5th Army Field Brigade RCA, CASF, Serial 238, 100th Field Battery RCA, CASF, Serial 239, Listowel, Ontario, 12th Field Battery RCA, CASF, Serial 240, London, Ontario, 97th Field Battery (H) RCA, CASF, Serial 241, Walkerton, Ontario, and 45th Field Battery (H) RCA, CASF, Serial 242, Lindsay, Ontario, were authorized as components of the Canadian Active Service Force, Corps Troops mobilizing with 2nd Division, under General Order 135/39, 1st September 1939.

Headquarters of 5th Army Field Brigade RCA, CASF, Serial 238, was redesignated Headquarters of 21st Army Field Regiment RCA, CASF, Serial 238, under General Order 123/40 (Effective 1st June 1940), and the batteries were paired at this time to become 12th/45th and 97th/100th Field Batteries RCA, CASF.

The 21st Army Field Regiment RCA, CASF, was redesignated 7th Army Field Regiment RCA, CASF, under General Order 195/40 (Effective 15th August 1940). The batteries remained combined until the regiment reorganized to comprise three batteries in January 1941. 12th, 45th and 97th Batteries survived, 100th Battery joined 4th LAA Regiment RCA, 3rd Division.

7th Army Field Regiment RCA, Serial 238, was redesignated 7th Medium Regiment RCA, Serial 238, under General Order 21/44 (Effective 21st November 1943). 12th and 45th Batteries remained components of the two battery medium regiment and served in France, Belgium, Holland and Germany until cessation of hostilities.

* * *

22nd Field Regiment RCA — Serial 1410 — 7th and 8th Divisions

22nd Field Regiment RCA, Serial 1410, Headquarters 22nd Field Regiment RCA, Serial 1410A, 3rd Field Battery RCA, Serial 1410B, MD No. 4, 6th Field Battery RCA, Serial 1410C, MD No. 4, and 80th Field Battery RCA, Serial

1410D, Quebec-Levis, mobilized under General Order 147/42 (Effective 18th March 1942), aligned with 16th Brigade Group, 7th Division, Home Defence.

In June 1942, 16th Brigade was transferred to 8th Division in Pacific Command and the regiment followed 16th Infantry Brigade to the west coast. 22nd Field Regiment RCA served at Terrace and Prince Rupert in British Columbia with 8th Canadian Division until the division and 22nd Field Regiment RCA received authorization to disband under General Order 15/44 (Effective 15th October 1943).

*   *   *

23rd Field Regiment (Self-Propelled) RCA — Serial 1411 — 4 Cdn Armd Div

23rd Field Regiment RCA, Serial 1411, Headquarters 23rd Field Regiment RCA, Serial 1411A, 31st Field Battery RCA, Serial 1411B, Toronto, 36th Field Battery RCA, Serial 1411C, Cobourg, and 83rd Field Battery RCA, Serial 1411D, Niagara District, Ontario, mobilized under General Order 147/42 (Effective 18th March 1942), aligned with 17th Brigade Group, 7th Division, Home Defence, Eastern Canada.

The regiment was withdrawn from 7th Division in October 1942 to prepare for an overseas posting to 4th Canadian Armoured Division as a self-propelled regiment.

23rd Field Regiment RCA, Serial 1411, was redesignated 23rd Self-Propelled Regiment RCHA, under General Order 243/43, Headquarters 23rd Field Regiment RCA, Serial 1411A, was redesignated Headquarters 23rd Self-Propelled Regiment RCHA, 31st Field Battery RCA became 31st Self-Propelled Battery RCHA, 36th and 83rd Batteries were similarly redesignated under General Order 328/43 (Effective 15th May 1943).

The regiment arrived overseas the latter part of July 1943 and its designation changed to 23rd Regiment (Self-Propelled) RCA. The batteries were altered accordingly under General Order 396/43 (Effective 15th August 1943), then a final designation to 23rd Field Regiment (Self-Propelled) RCA, under General Order 452/43 (Effective 1st September 1943).

23rd Field Regiment (Self-Propelled) RCA, 4th Canadian Armoured Division landed in Normandy 26th July 1944 and moved into the line south of Caen 29th July under 2nd Canadian Corps, then with 2nd Canadian Corps moved under command of First Canadian Army 31st July 1944.

The regiment participated in the vicious fighting in the breakout from Caen and in closing the Falaise Gap, then advanced with First Canadian Army along the coastal sector in France, Belgium, Holland and Germany.

23rd Field Regiment (Self-Propelled) RCA served until cessation of hostilities and received authorization to disband under General Order 71/46 (Effective 18th December 1945).

*   *   *

24th Field Regiment RCA — Serial 1412 — 7th Div, 6th Div and Kiska

24th Field Regiment RCA, Serial 1412, Headquarters 24th Field Regiment RCA, Serial 1412A, 49th Field Battery RCA, Serial 1412B, Kenora, Ontario, 84th Field Battery RCA, Serial 1412C, Moosomin, Saskatchewan, and 85th Field Battery RCA, Serial 1412D, Calgary, Alberta, mobilized under General Order 147/42 (Effective 18th March 1942), aligned with 18th Brigade Group, 7th Division, Home Defence.

24th Field Regiment RCA and 18th Infantry Brigade moved to 6th Division 15th July 1942. In June 1943 the regiment was selected to accompany 13th Brigade Group of 6th Division in a joint Canadian-US attack on the Island of Kiska in the Aleutian Chain. 13th Brigade landed 15th/16th August 1943 to discover the enemy had vacated the island. The regiment remained on garrison duty until the end of the year then returned to Canada, and a reorganized 6th Division.

During the absence of 24th Field Regiment 7th and 8th Divisions had been phased out and 6th Division returned to its original brigade alignment. 13th Brigade Group, intact, resumed its home defence role with 6th Division until May 1944 when the infantry components were posted overseas.

24th Field Regiment remained with 6th Division and following postings to Vernon, B.C., Wainwright and Suffield, Alberta, the regiment returned to Vernon where authorization was received to disband under General Order 213/45 (Effective 31st March 1945).

*   *   *

25th Field Regiment RCA — Serial 1610 — 6th Division — Pacific Command

25th Field Regiment RCA, Serial 1610, Headquarters 25th Field Regiment RCA, Serial 1610A, 114th Field Battery RCA, Serial 1610B, MD No. 13, 115th Field Battery RCA, Serial 1610C, MD No. 10, 116th Field Battery RCA, Serial 1610D, MD No. 12, mobilized under General Order 309/42 (Effective 12th May 1942), aligned with 19th Infantry Brigade.

In a shuffle of infantry brigades within the home defence divisions in July 1942, 19th Infantry Brigade became a component of 6th Division with Brigade Headquarters situated at Vernon, British Columbia, and the brigade was held in Pacific Command reserve.

Following the disbandment of 7th and 8th Divisions October 1943, 6th Division reverted to its original brigade structure. 15th Brigade returned from 7th Division, 14th Brigade returned from 8th Division and 13th Brigade returned from Kiska. 25th Field Regiment RCA joined 14th Infantry Brigade Group and continued its home defence role until authorized to disband under General Order 213/45 (Effective 31st March 1945).

*   *   *

26th Field Regiment RCA — Serial 1611 — 7th Division

26th Field Regiment RCA, Serial 1611, Headquarters 26th Field Regiment RCA, Serial 1611A, 117th Field Battery RCA, Serial 1611B, Toronto, 118th Field Battery RCA, Serial 1611C, Toronto, and 119th Field Battery RCA, Serial 1611D, Toronto, mobilized under General Order 309/42 (Effective 12th May 1942) aligned with 20th Infantry Brigade and in a shuffle of brigades within the home defence divisions in July 1942, 20th Infantry Brigade joined 7th Division.

26th Field Regiment RCA continued to serve in eastern Canada under 7th Division until receiving authorization to disband under General Order 15/44 (Effective 15th November 1943).

*   *   *

27th Field Regiment RCA — Serial 1612 — 8th Division

27th Field Regiment RCA, Serial 1612, Headquarters 27th Field Regiment RCA, Serial 1612A, 120th Field Battery RCA, Serial 1612B, Montreal, 121st Field Battery RCA, Serial 1612C, Montreal, and 122nd Field Battery RCA, Serial 1612D, Montreal, mobilized under General Order 309/42 (Effective 12th May 1942).

27th Field Regiment RCA mobilized with a brigade group of 8th Division as mobile reserve for eastern Canada and served in eastern Canada in a home defence role until authorized to disband (with the exception of 122nd Field Battery RCA), under General Order 15/44 (Effective 15th October 1943).

122nd Battery RCA did not disband but was redesignated 127th Anti-Tank Battery RCA under General Order 138/46 (Effective 1st March 1946) and was permanently embodied in the Postwar Permanent Force under General Order 158/46 (Effective 27th June 1946).

*   *   *

28th Field Regiment RCA — Serial 1814 — 7th Division

28th Field Regiment RCA War Diary excerpt "8th Anti-Tank Regiment RCA was converted to Field Artillery and redesignated 28th Field Regiment RCA".

28th Field Regiment RCA, Serial 1814, Headquarters 28th Field Regiment RCA, Serial 1814A, 123rd Field Battery RCA, Serial 1814B, 124th Field Battery RCA, Serial 1814C, and 125th Field Battery RCA, Serial 1814D, mobilized under General Order 289/43 (Effective 15th May 1943), and served with 7th Division, Home Defence, in eastern Canada.

The run-down of home defence units was begun toward the end of 1943 and 28th Field Regiment RCA, Serial 1814, received authorization to disband along with Headquarters 7th Division, under General Order 15/44 (Effective 15th October 1943).

*   *   *

1st Medium Regiment RCA — Serial 64 — 1st Canadian AGRA — Army Troops

Headquarters of 1st Medium Brigade RCA, CASF, Serial 64, 7th Medium Battery (H) RCA, CASF, Serial 65, Montreal, 2nd Medium Battery (H) RCA, CASF, Serial 66, Charlottetown, 23rd Medium Battery (H) RCA, CASF, Serial 67, Toronto, and from the Permanent Force, 3rd Medium Battery RCA, CASF, Serial 68, mobilized under Headquarters 1st Corps Medium Artillery, RCA, CASF, Corps Troops mobilizing with 1st Division, authorized under General Order 135/39, 1st September 1939.

1st Medium Brigade RCA, CASF arrived overseas 8th February 1940 in the third flight and moved to the south of England where 1st Medium Brigade RCA, CASF became 1st Medium Regiment RCA, CASF, comprising two batteries. The existing batteries were paired to become 2nd/7th Medium Battery RCA, CASF, and 3rd/23rd Medium Battery RCA, CASF, under General Order 44/40 (Effective 12th February 1940).

The era of hyphenated batteries ended and the batteries were given individual identity under General Order 45/41 (Effective 1st January 1941). Medium regiments now comprised two individual batteries and 1st Medium Regiment RCA retained 2nd and 3rd Medium Batteries RCA. 7th and 23rd Batteries moved to 5th Medium Regiment RCA.

1st Medium Regiment remained in England until departing for the Mediterranean theatre of operations with 1st Canadian AGRA in October 1943. The regiment disembarked in Sicily 8th November and on the 19th of November 1943 crossed to the Italian mainland to fire in support of Fifth American Army, then returned to 1st Canadian AGRA and served in italy until early 1945 supporting units of 1st Canadian Corps.

1st Medium Regiment RCA sailed to Marseilles, France 11th March as 1st Canadian Corps moved to NW Europe to join First Canadian Army. The regiment became operational in Holland 1st April 1945 and served until cessation of hostilities, receiving authorization to disband under General Order 401/45 (Effective 1st September 1945).

*   *   *

2nd Medium Regiment RCA — Serial 982 — 1st Cdn AGRA — Army Troops

Headquarters 18th Field Regiment RCA, Serial 982, was redesignated Headquarters 2nd Medium Regiment RCA, Serial 982A, under General Order 104/42 (Effective 26th January 1942). 2nd Medium Regiment RCA was allotted Serial Number 982, under General Order 438/42 (Effective 9th January 1942).

25th Battery of Toronto accompanied Headquarters 18th Field Regiment RCA to the new 2nd Medium Regiment and 18th Battery of Port Arthur, Ontario arrived from 16th Field Regiment RCA to complete the components.

Previously, Headquarters 2nd Medium Regiment RCA, CASF, Serial 69, had been redesignated Headquarters 2nd Heavy Anti-Aircraft Regiment (Mobile) RCA, Serial 69, under General Order 149/41 (Effective 24th May 1941).

2nd Medium Regiment RCA, Serial 982 arrived overseas 29th March 1942 and departed for the Mediterranean 24th October 1943. The regiment disembarked in Sicily 8th November 1943 and crossed to the Italian mainland 5th January 1944. As a component of 1st Canadian AGRA, 2nd Medium Regiment RCA added its firepower to the divisional artilleries of 1st Canadian Infantry Division and 5th Canadian Armoured Division of 1st Canadian Corps, British Eighth Army.

The transfer of 1st Canadian Corps to NW Europe saw 2nd Medium Regiment RCA depart Italy 11th March 1945 and become operational in Holland 30th March 1945, under First Canadian Army. The regiment served until the cessation of hostilities and 2nd Medium Regiment RCA, less 25th Medium Battery, received authorization to disband under General Order 52/46 (Effective 3rd October 1945).

25th Medium Battery RCA was redesignated 68th Medium Battery RCA, under General Order 138/46 (Effective 1st March 1946), and under General Order 158/46 (Effective 27th June 1946), 68th Medium Battery RCA became part of the Postwar Permanent Force.

*   *   *

3rd Medium Regiment RCA — Serial 1050 — 2nd Cdn AGRA — Army Troops

Headquarters 3rd Medium Regiment RCA, Serial 1050A, and 5th Medium Battery RCA, Serial 1050C, of Vancouver, British Columbia, mobilized under General Order 103/42 (Effective 26th January 1942). 87th Medium Battery

RCA, Serial 1050B, of Dartmouth, Nova Scotia, arrived to complete the components of 3rd Medium Regiment RCA.

87th Battery had mobilized as the combined 87th/88th Field Battery in the original composition of 16th Field Regiment RCA, CASF, 4th Division, CASF, in May 1940, and upon regaining individual identity was posted to 18th Field Regiment RCA, which in turn disbanded and 87th Battery joined 3rd Medium Regiment RCA.

3rd Medium Regiment RCA was allotted Serial Number 1050, under General Order 438/42 (Effective 30th January 1942). The regiment arrived overseas mid-June 1942 and came under command of Headquarters Medium Artillery, 1st Canadian Corps, in the south of England, moving to 2nd Canadian AGRA late 1943.

3rd Medium Regiment RCA, 2nd Canadian AGRA, Army Troops, landed in Normandy 9th July 1944 to support 2nd Canadian Corps in the beachhead. The Canadian units in Normandy moved under command of First Canadian Army 31st July 1944 and the regiment advanced with First Canadian Army along the coastal sector, serving in France, Belgium, Holland and Germany.

With the cessation of hostilities in May 1945, the run-down of Canadian units was begun and 3rd Medium Regiment RCA received authorization to disband under General Order 52/46 (Effective 16th November 1945).

* * *

4th Medium Regiment RCA — Serial 1051 — 2nd Cdn AGRA — Army Troops

50th Battery of Montreal and 58th Battery of Quebec, P.Q. had mobilized with 20th Field Regiment RCA for service with 6th Division, home Defence in July 1941 and early in the new year an opportunity for overseas service saw 50th Field Battery RCA, Serial 811D and 58th Field Battery RCA, Serial 811B redesignated 50th Medium Battery RCA, Serial 1051C and 58th Medium Battery RCA, Serial 1051B, under General Order 104/42 (Effective 26th January 1942).

4th Medium Regiment RCA was allotted Serial Number 1051, under General Order 438/42 (Effective 2nd February 1942), and Headquarters 4th Medium Regiment RCA, Serial 1051A, was authorized to mobilize under General Order 103/42 (Effective 1st March 1942).

4th Medium Regiment RCA arrived overseas in August 1942 and came under command of Headquarters Canadian Corps Medium Artillery, which in time became Headquarters 1st Canadian AGRA. The AGRA reorganized prior to its departure to the Mediterranean and the regiment became a component of 2nd Canadian AGRA and readied itself for the invasion of the Continent.

4th Medium Regiment RCA landed in Normandy 9th July 1944 with 2nd Canadian AGRA and fired its first rounds 13th July 1944 in support of 2nd Canadian Corps, Second British Army.

The Canadian units in Normandy came under command of First Canadian Army 31st July 1944 and following the breakout from Caen the regiment advanced with First Canadian Army along the coastal sector in France, Belgium, Holland and Germany, then with cessation of hostilities 4th Medium Regiment RCA received authorization to disband under General Order 52/46 (Effective 26th September 1945).

*   *   *

5th Medium Regiment RCA — Serial 507 — 1st Canadian AGRA

Medium regiments reorganized from hyphenated batteries to individual batteries and 2nd/7th Medium Battery RCA and 3rd/23rd Medium Battery RCA became 2nd, 3rd, 7th and 23rd Medium Batteries RCA, authorized under General Order 45/41 (Effective 1st January 1941). 1st Medium Regiment retained 2nd and 3rd Medium Batteries RCA in a two battery regiment and 7th Medium Battery RCA of Montreal, with 23rd Medium Battery RCA of Toronto became the components of 5th Medium Regiment RCA.

Headquarters 5th Medium Regiment RCA, Serial 507, was authorized under General Order 56/41 (Effective 1st February 1941) and in an alignment of Serial Numbers within the regiment under General Order 54/42 (Effective 22nd December 1941), 5th Medium Regiment RCA, was allotted Serial 507, Headquarters 5th Medium Regiment RCA assumed Serial 507A, 7th Medium Battery RCA changed to Serial 507B, and 23rd Medium Battery adopted Serial Number 507C.

5th Medium Regiment RCA with 1st Canadian AGRA departed from Scotland for the Mediterranean 25th October 1943 and disembarked in Sicily 8th November 1943, then on the 7th January 1944 the regiment crossed to the Italian mainland to lend support to 1st Canadian Corps in its forthcoming operations.

The regiment joined the action in the Lanciano campaign at the end of February 1944 and served in Italy until mid-March 1945, then moved with 1st Canadian Corps to NW Europe.

5th Medium Regiment RCA joined the action under First Canadian Army in NW Europe 1st April 1945 in the Arnhem, Holland sector and served until cessation of hostilities, receiving authorization to disband under General Order 321/45 (Effective 30th June 1945).

*   *   *

7th Medium Regiment RCA — Serial 238 — 2nd Cdn AGRA — Army Troops

The regiment mobilized as Headquarters of 5th Army Field Brigace RCA, CASF, 1st September 1939, with 100th Battery of Listowel, 12th Battery, London, 97th Battery, Walkerton, and 45th Battery, Lindsay, Ontario, as components.

Headquarters of 5th Army Field Brigade RCA, CASF, Serial 238, was redesignated Headquarters 21st Army Field Regiment RCA, CASF, Serial 238, and the batteries combined to become 12th/45th and 97th/100th Field Batteries RCA, CASF, in a two battery regiment, authorized under General Order 123/40 (Effective 1st June 1940).

The 21st Army Field Regiment RCA, CASF, was redesignated 7th Army Field Regiment RCA, CASF, under General Order 195/40 (Effective 15th August 1940). The batteries remained combined until given individual identity under General Order 74/41 (Effective 1st January 1941), at which time 7th Army Field Regiment RCA became a three battery regiment retaining 12th, 45th and 97th Field Batteries. 100th Battery moved to 4th Light Anti-Aircraft Regiment RCA, authorized under the same general order.

7th Army Field Regiment RCA, Serial 238, was converted and redesignated 7th Medium Regiment RCA, Serial 238, under General Order 21/44 (Effective 21st November 1943). 12th Field Battery RCA, Serial 238B, was redesignated 12th Medium Battery RCA, Serial 238B, and 45th Field Battery RCA, Serial 238D, was redesignated 45th Medium Battery RCA, Serial 238D. Medium regiments required two batteries only and 97th Field Battery RCA, Serial 238C, disbanded under General Order 22/44 (Effective 21st November 1943).

7th Medium Regiment RCA with 2nd Canadian AGRA, landed in Normandy 11th July 1944 and joined the action under 2nd Canadian Corps, then on the 31st July 1944 the Canadian units in Normandy came under command of First Canadian Army and participated in the breakout from Caen and the closing of the Falaise Gap.

7th Medium Regiment RCA continued the advance with First Canadian Army along the coastal sector and fired in support of its multi-national components in France, Belgium, Holland and Germany, then with cessation of hostilities received authorization to disband under General Order 52/46 (Effective 25th September 1945).

*   *   *

1st Survey Regiment RCA — Serial 84 — 1st Canadian Corps

1st (P) Survey Battery RCA, Serial 84E and 2nd (Q) Survey Battery RCA, Serial 84F.

1st Survey Regiment RCA, Serial 84, mobilized under General Order 135/39, 1st September 1939. The regiment departed for overseas in three groups in January, August, and December 1940.

In May 1941 the regiment did the original survey of the Poling Calibration Base and in the Dover area did fall of shot calibration of railroad guns defending the coast of England.

The regiment experimented with a composite battery and carried out technical shoots with 1st and 2nd Divisions, did airburst renging with 3rd Division and tested the 222 Fuze with an army field regiment. During the latter part of 1941 1st Survey Regiment RCA moved to Worthing and manned the calibration base at Poling.

In February 1942 the regiment became an Army Survey Regiment of four divisional survey batteries and Sound Ranging Battery. The survey battery was composed of battery headquarters, survey troop, observation troop and ranging section. Flash Spotting Battery was phased out.

Mid-September 1943 the order was received to congregate and the regiment was split in two to form two regiments. 1st Survey Regiment RCA became Corps Troops, 1st Canadian Corps, and 2nd Survey Regiment RCA was formed to serve with 2nd Canadian Corps.

"A" Survey Battery RCA, Serial 84E was redesignated 1st Survey Battery RCA, Serial 84E, and "B" Survey Battery RCA, Serial 84F, was redesignated 2nd Survey Battery RCA, Serial 84F, under General Order 486/43 (Effective 18th October 1943). The batteries continued as composite batteries, composed of a flash spotting troop, sound ranging troop, and survey troop. Grouped under RHQ was a meteorological section, a survey troop, LAD and RAP. Sound Ranging Battery Headquarters moved to 2nd Survey Regiment RCA as Regimental Headquarters.

1st Survey Regiment RCA sailed for Algiers, North Africa where the regiment disembarked 25th November 1943 remaining at Blida until 8th December, then resumed its journey and disembarked at Catania, Sicily mid-December.

The regiment crossed to the Italian mainland 4th January 1944 to assume an operational role in relief of 5 British Survey Regiment at San Vito. 5 British Survey Regiment in turn relieved 1st Canadian Survey Regiment and 1st (P) Battery remained attached to 5 British Survey Regiment for three months replacing one of its batteries operating in the Anzio bridgehead.

The assault on the Gustav Line 11th May 1944 heralded the beginning of the spring offensive. On the Eighth Army front, 1st Canadian Corps entered the drive through the breach in the line on the 16th and 1st Canadian Infantry

Division penetrated the Hitler Line on the 23rd. 5th Canadian Armoured Division entered the gap in the line and assumed the lead in the advance along the Liri Valley toward Rome.

Rome fell to US forces 4th June 1944 and the fighting north of Rome reached the Gothic Line which was cracked by 5th Canadian Armoured division 31st August/1st September. 1st Canadian Corps advanced to the Senio River which became the Winter Line. 5th Canadian Armoured Division was relieved mid-January 1945, Corps Headquarters passed into army reserve 10th February, the relief of 1st Canadian Infantry Division was completed 27th February 1945 and the transfer of the corps to NW Europe was begun.

1st Survey Regiment RCA arrived at Marseilles, France from Naples, Italy 28th February 1945 and proceeded to corps concentration area in Belgium. 2nd (Q) Battery became operational on the "Island" in front of Nijmegen in Holland in support of 49 (WR) Division, 21st March 1945. 1st (P) Battery concentrated near Oss, Holland, 27th March in support of 1st Canadian Infantry Division and 5th Canadian Armoured Division.

1st Survey Regiment RCA, Serial 84, served until cessation of hostilities and received authorization to disband under General Order 321/45 (Effective 28th June 1945), in NW Europe.

*   *   *

2nd Survey Regiment RCA — Serial 1790 — 2nd Canadian Corps

2nd Survey Regiment RCA, Serial 1790, Headquarters 2nd Survey Regiment RCA, Serial 1790A, 5th Survey Battery RCA, Serial 1790B and 6th Survey Battery RCA, Serial 1790C, mobilized under General Order 485/43 (Effective 18th October 1943).

1st Survey Regiment RCA as an Army Survey Regiment of Sound Ranging Battery and four survey batteries, one for each division overseas, was providing services for the whole of First Canadian Army. First Canadian Army was split in two with 1st Canadian Corps about to move to the Mediterranean. Survey became a Corps responsibility, 1st Survey Regiment RCA became Corps Troops 1st Canadian Corps and 2nd Survey Regiment RCA was formed to serve with 2nd Canadian Corps.

A and B Survey Batteries were retained by 1st Survey Regiment and C and D Survey Batteries became part of 2nd Survey Regiment RCA. Battery Headquarters Sound Ranging Battery became Regimental Headquarters 2nd Survey Regiment. Both regiments comprised two composite survey batteries with a flash spotting troop, sound ranging troop and survey troop. The designation of the troops of the composite batteries were identical in both regiments. A meteorological section, a survey troop, LAD and RAP were grouped under regimental headquarters.

General Order 488/43 (Effective 18th October 1943) authorized the disbandment of C Survey Battery RCA, Serial 84G and D Survey Battery RCA, Serial 84H, severing connections with the previous organization and 2nd Survey Regiment components were aligned under Serial 1790.

X Survey Troop of 2nd Survey Regiment RCA landed in Normandy 6th July 1944, the remainder of the regiment arrived on the 9th of July. The regiment deployed in the Carpiquet area on the 11th and 12th, suffering its first casualties. Airburst ranging and calibration was done for a number of regiments in the bridgehead.

2nd Survey Regiment RCA suffered a number of casualties during the USAAF bombing 8th August and in the RAF bombing 14th August. With the breakout from Caen effected the regiment raced across France to Boulogne and Calais, then into Belgium and Holland for the battle of the Scheldt, to clear the Port of Antwerp to Allied shipping.

The regiment moved to the Nijmegen, Holland sector in November following the battle of the Scheldt and the drive into Germany was launched 8th February 1945 by First Canadian Army, 30 British Corps leading with 2nd and 3rd Canadian Divisions under command for the initial attack. The Canadians returned to 2nd Canadian Corps for the second phase and the advance continued on a two corps front. The Siegfried Line was breached, the Reichswald and Hochwald Forests cleared, the Rhine crossed and the three Canadian Divisions on a parallel course advanced northward through NE Holland and a section of Germany to the North Sea. The regiment provided survey for 2nd, 3rd and 4th Canadian Divisions, 2nd Canadian AGRA and 11 British Armoured Division prior to "VE" Day.

Headquarters 2nd Survey Regiment RCA, 5th and 6th Survey Batteries RCA received authorization to disband under General Order 238/46 (Effective 22nd June 1945), in NW Europe.

*   *   *

ILLUSTRATIONS AND FLASHES

Copy

H.Q. Cdn Corps
9 Sep 41

The Senior Officer,
Canadian Military Headquarters.

1. The Officer i/c Records has requested two complete sets of shoulder titles, distinguishing patches and copies of any plates showing the approved designs for those patches and for helmet flashes. It is suggested that these might best be provided from Cdn Ordnance Depot from existing stocks and as they become available:—

(a) **Formation H.Qs.**
Cdn. Corps — plain red diamond.
1 Cdn Div — plain red rectangle.
2 Cdn Div — plain blue rectange.
3 Cdn Div — plain french grey rectangle.
1 Cdn Army Tank Bde.
Inf Bdes — green, red and blue bars.

(b) **2 Cdn Div Inf etc Bns.**
Circles, semi-circles and triangles in green, red and blue as worn above div patch. Also distinguishing patches of div recce bn and div M.G. Bn; and shoulder titles of Tor Scot R.

(c) **Shoulder Titles of Inf etc Bns of 1 and 3 Cdn Divs.**

R.C.R.	R.Wpg.Rif.
Hast. & P.E.R.	1.C.Scot.R.
48 Hghrs	Regina Rif.
P.P.C.L.I.	N.Shore.R.
Seaforth of C.	R.de Chaud.
Edmn.R.	Q.O.R. of C.
R.22e.R.	S.D. & G. Highrs.
Carlt & York R.	Nth N.S. Highrs.
West N.S.R.	H.L.I. of C.
Sask. L.I.(M.G.)	C.H. of O. (M.G.)
4 Recce Bn.	7 Recce Bn.

(d)   Miscellaneous
R.M.R. — (Corps M.G. Bn) — shoulder title.
Lorne Scots — shoulder title.
Army Tank Bde units — "ram" and "tank" badges.

(e)   Corps and Services — two samples of each div and Corps Tps patch
with abbreviated designations of corps or service superimposed
viz:—
R.C.E.
R.C.C.S.
R.C.A.S.C.
R.C.A.M.C.
R.C.O.C.
R.C.A.P.C. (Corps Tps patch/and shoulder title only)
Cdn Postal Corps.
Cdn Dental Corps.
Cdn Chaplain Service

(f)   R.C.A. — Embroidered titles for wear at the base of the shoulder
strap; two samples of each:—
R.C.H.A.
A Fd Regt
an A.Tk Regt
a Lt. A.A. Regt
a Med Regt
1 Cdn Svy Regt
Corps Tps Arty distinguishing patch.

2. This H.Q. is providing for Officer i/c Records, copies of the plates showing
the approved designs for the distinguishing patches of the corps and services
in the three divisions.

3. It would be appreciated if you would inform Officer i/c Records whether
you can provide the samples indicated in para above.

— signed —

(N.E. Rodger) Major,
Cdn. Liaison, Cdn. Corps.

An excerpt from correspondence dated 12 Sep 41 notes:—

"The plates forwarded with my letter of 9 Sep 41 are the only ones
which have been made. Shoulder titles for infantry units, etc, have
been supplied from actual samples submitted from the units concerned. In some cases the unit itself purchased the titles and in

other cases they were or are being provided by Ordnance. It was for this reason that C.M.H.Q. was asked to provide samples through Cdn Ordnance Depot."

Signed by the above.

Author's note — "1st and 3rd LAA Regiments with titles red on royal blue for the initial issue were no doubt purchased by the regiments. The author still has in his possession his original issue of 3 LAA RCA red on royal blue. Later issues were red on a darker blue, Ordnance issue, common to all regiments."

5th Canadian Armoured Division arrived overseas the latter part of 1941 and 4th Canadian Armoured Division arrived during 1942, adding 5th Division maroon and 4th Division dark green flashes to those of the Canadian Corps in England.

The rebuilding of 2nd Canadian Infantry Division following the disastrous Dieppe Raid of August 1942 saw the division discontinue the wearing of geometrical patches and the battalions began wearing shoulder titles, conforming to other Canadian Divisions.

On the home front diamonds of Atlantic Command grey and Pacific Command green were authorized as were flashes for 6th, 7th and 8th Divisions.

Excerpts from a letter dated 22nd September 1942 from the Master-General of the Ordnance to G.O.C.-in-C, Headquarters Atlantic Command, Halifax, N.S. — "It is proposed to combine colours now in use by two of the Divisions overseas into a single patch of two colours for one of the Divisions in Canada where this is possible. Enclosed is a sample patch of French Gray and Dark Green (3rd and 4th Divisions) which it is proposed to supply for the 7th Canadian Division. For information, the 6th and 8th Divisions are being similarly treated."

A letter dated 24th October, 1942, notes — "A distinguishing patch as follows, has been approved for 7th Canadian Division.

"A French gray and dark green patch divided diagonally from upper right to lower left, French gray uppermost."

The overall dimensions of the patch are 3 inches horizontally, by 2 inches vertically." This letter was to the G.O.C., 7th Canadian Division, Debert, N.S., from the Master-General of the Ordnance.

Distinguishing Patch 6th Division. A red and blue patch divided diagonally from upper right to lower left, red uppermost, with overall dimensions of 3" horizontally by 2" vertically, will be worn by all ranks of 6th Division. Issued in pairs and worn with the wide edge of the red triangle to the front, authorized 5 Nov 1942. (See Routine Order 1567 d/Dec 42.)

Description and authorization of badges on the colour pages including Badge, embroidered, Canadian Infantry Corps, the General Service (G.S.) Badge, and the Mars (Trained Soldier's Badge) are included in this section, also a description of the Patch, Distinguishing, Winter Warfare, Distinguishing Patch, Canadian Army Pacific Force, and an excerpt from the War Diary of 84 Field Battery RCA, CA (A), showing the battery's mobilization at Moosomin, Saskatchewan, March 1942 and its move to Camp Shilo, Manitoba in June 1942 to join 24th Field Regiment, RCA CA (A).

3rd Div was still in NW Europe when 3rd Canadian Infantry Division CAOF was formed and to differentiate the occupation force division wore a half-inch strip of french grey below the french grey 3rd Div patch.

An interesting combination resulted when a half-inch strip in the brigade colour was worn above the div patch by the staff of brigade headquarters. Green denoted 7th Brigade, red, 8th Brigade and royal blue, 9th Brigade.

In correspondence with D Hist, Ottawa, during the 1960s to clarify a number of issues I received the following information — *"With regard to the formation patches, they are as described by you including the 1st Corps RCA patch"*, and, *"There were no Armoured Brigade Groups. We have no knowledge of a black horizontal diamond patch with red zig-zag. Artillery 2 Corps wore a blue diamond with a red zig-zag."*

Unofficial flashes also made an appearance, one of which was issued to the members of 4th AA Searchlight Battery at Victoria, B.C., and is included with the shoulder flashes. Projected expansion in some cases spurred the manufacture of patches and RCA titles which were not required due to organizational changes.

6th Armoured Regiment (1st Hussars), 10th Armoured Regiment (The Fort Garry Horse) and 27th Armoured Regiment (The Sherbrooke Fusiliers Regiment), the components of the ad hoc 3rd Army Tank Brigade, remained designated armoured regiments during their service with the army tank brigade and if 3rd Army Tank Brigade flashes, a French grey diamond with centre bar of black, exist with 6th, 10th or 27th CTR imprinted they no doubt fit the unofficial category.

HQ 21 Army Group

First Canadian Army

HQ and Army Troops

Army Troops Artillery

1st and 2nd Canadian AGRA

1st Corps

HQ and 1st Corps Units

1st Corps Artillery

2nd Corps

HQ and 2nd Corps Units

2nd Corps Artillery

30 Corps

1 British Corps

49(WR) Division

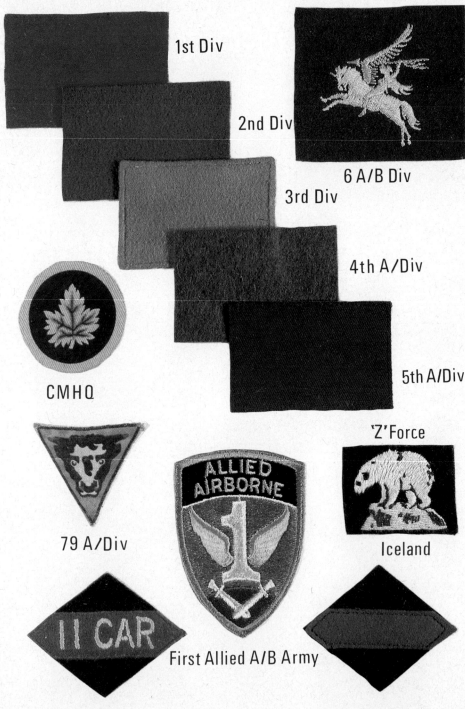

1st Div

2nd Div

6 A/B Div

3rd Div

4th A/Div

5th A/Div

CMHQ

79 A/Div

First Allied A/B Army

'Z' Force

Iceland

1st Cdn A/Bde w imprint

2nd Cdn A/Bde

Pacific Command

Headquarters

6th Division

8th Division

Mars Badge

Kiska Flash
Aleutians

6th Div CAPF

First Special Service Force

6th Div CAPF
miniature

Hong Kong
Battle Flash

Atlantic Command

Headquarters

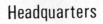

7th Division

GS Badge

`W´ Force
Newfoundland

Exercise `Eskimo´

Winter Warfare

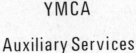

Cdn Inf Corps

Salvation Army

YMCA

Legion

Auxiliary Services

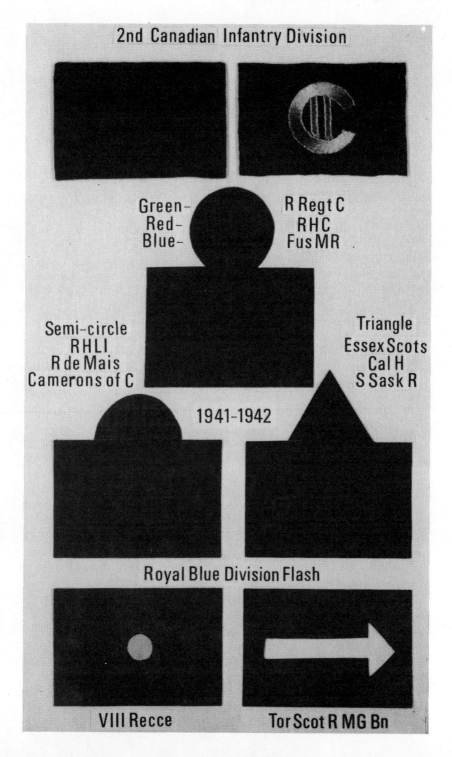

2nd Canadian Infantry Division

Green–   R Regt C
Red–   RHC
Blue–   Fus MR

Semi-circle   Triangle
RHLI   Essex Scots
R de Mais   Cal H
Camerons of C   S Sask R

1941–1942

Royal Blue Division Flash

VIII Recce   Tor Scot R MG Bn

UNOFFICIAL UNIT FLASH

Worn by Col. Ransome's 4th Anti-Aircraft Searchlight Battery while serving at Victoria, British Columbia. The accompanying photo shows members of the unit wearing the flashes on the upper sleeve. The BQMS proudly displays the flashes on both lower sleeves.

The Battery manned two 18 inch searchlights atop the Bay Street Armoury, and later, on the ground in the vehicle compound, from October 1941 to May 1943. Then as a group the Battery departed for Long Beach on the west coast of the Island, to form 23rd AA Battery of 27 AA Regiment RCA. Information and flash courtesy Mr. George A. Warren, Victoria, B.C.

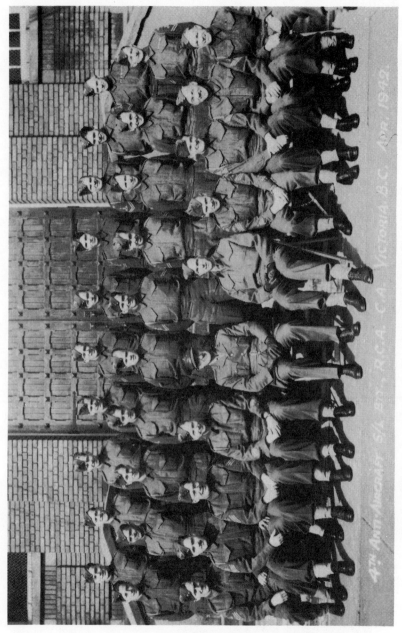

From the G.A. Warren Collection courtesy Mr. George A. Warren, 5th (B.C.) Regiment Museum Society, Victoria, B.C.

Photo of CWAC uniform showing the location of the "Mars" badge, the Pacific Command flash and two service chevrons, courtesy of Phylis Bowman, Prince Rupert, British Columbia, author of "We Skirted the War", a story of the Canadian Women's Army Corps.

WAR DIARY

OR

~~INTELLIGENCE SUMMARY~~

(Erase heading not required)

84 Field Battery RCA CA (A)

Original, duplicate and triplicate to be forwarded to O. i/c 2nd Echelon for disposal.

M41   X.39 (1798)
H.Q. 1772-45-18

tained in F.S. Regt. Vol. 1.
Title pages will be prepared.

Place	Date	Hour	Summary of Events and Information	Remarks, references to Appendices and initials
Moosomin, Sask.	12 Apr.42.		84 Field Battery RCA CA (A) formed as a Field Battery of the 7th.Div.,(H.Q.S.20-1-6,F.D.2 M.R.1 dated 24 Mar.1942)with Serial142)with Serial1412 C.W.E.10 officers and 194 O.Rs.Temporary mobilization point at Moosomin Sask.	App.1
			Capt.W.J.Brown,M.M.arrived Moosomin to take temporary command of Bty,RQMS J.W.Walton WO 11, 22 Fd.Bde,RCA temporarily detailed to assist in recruiting.	
	13		offices taken up in Moosomin Armouries.Hot water for showers connected up.	
	14		One recruit sent to Regina for Medical Board.	
	15		Capt.W.J.Brown proceeded to Indian Head area to visit Civilian Recruiting Committees.	
	16		Capt.W.J.Brown returned to Moosomin via Windthorst and #16 Hway.	
	17		Capt.Brown inspected potential campsite on Pipestone R.5½ miles South Moosomin.Site good good swimming area,well for drinking water untested.Alternative site just north of Moosomin requiring water to be piped ½ mile.	
	18		BQMS Walton in charge of office.Capt.Brown on interviews Fairlight Maryfield Wawota.	
	19		Capt.J.O.Probe arrived from Regina to take temporary Cmd.Bty.on assignment of Capt.Brown to Reserve Brigade HQ.	
			-Continued-	
Camp Shilo, Manitoba.	June 19th/42		All Battery personnel are Struck of Strength, 84th Field Battery, R.C.A. CA (A), to the 24th Field Regiment, R.C.A. CA (A) on change of station from Moosomin, Saskatchewan to Camp Shilo, Manitoba.	

(C.A. Smith) Major.,
Officer Commanding.,
84th Field, Battery., R.C.A. CA (A).,,

CAROs

4851—DRESS—GENERAL SERVICE BADGE —4851

1. A badge known as the "General Service Badge" is authorized to be worn, except in the United Kingdom or other theatre of war, by all other ranks who have undertaken to serve "in any Active Formation or Unit of the Active Army" for the duration of the present war and who have been appointed to or enlisted in the Active Army under such conditions.

2. The badge consists of the initials "G.S." in red embroidery on a black circular patch, one inch in diameter. The badge will be worn on the left forearm of the battle dress blouse, jacket khaki drill and jacket serge drab open collar, 5½ inches above the bottom of the sleeve or immediately above any badge of rank worn on the forearm.

3. The General Service Badge will be removed by personnel who have qualified for the award of the Canadian Volunteer Service Medal and who have, by authority, taken the ribbon of the Medal into wear.

4. The General Service Badge will be removed by personnel proceeding overseas for service in the United Kingdom or such other theatre of war as may be laid down by the Adjutant General from time to time, the day after embarkation, except that personnel of the Canadian Hospital Ship and personnel of the permanent Ships Conducting Staffs, remaining on Canadian strength, will not remove the badge except as otherwise directed in para. 3 above.

5053—BADGE, EMBROIDERED, CANADIAN INFANTRY CORPS— —5053
INTRODUCTION

1. Authorization has been given to the adoption of a Badge, embroidered, Canadian Infantry Corps, described as follows:—
    White, three red maple leaves conjoined on one stem with the words "INFANTRY CORPS" in white on a red base.
    The badge is in the form of an inverted shield 3¼ inches in height and 2⅛ inches in width.

2. The badge will be worn by all general service personnel, both officers and other ranks, of the Canadian Infantry Corps who are not allocated to or affiliated with a specific Infantry Unit for which distinctive badges are authorized.

3. In addition, general service personnel of Home War Establishments who are members of the Canadian Infantry Corps may wear the Canadian Infantry Corps badge in which case unit badges will not be worn.

4. Badges, embroidered, Canadian Infantry Corps will not be worn by N.R.M.A. soldiers of the Canadian Infantry Corps.

5. The badge will be worn:—
    (a) *by officers*—on both sleeves of the blouse, battle dress, and the greatcoat but not on the service dress jacket or khaki drill jacket, and,
    (b) *by other ranks*—on both sleeves of the blouse, battle dress; jacket, serge, drab, open collar; jacket khaki, drill, and the greatcoat.
with the uppermost point ½ inch below the shoulder seam. In cases where a Command patch is worn, such patch may be lowered sufficiently to allow correct positioning of the badge.

6. Personnel wearing the Badge, embroidered Canadian Infantry Corps, will not wear the worsted "CANADA" badge.

7. Supplies of the badge will be demanded and issued on the same basis as Badges embroidered, unit title, prs.

8. Distribution of quantities estimated to meet initial requirements, is being made to commands and districts.

9. The badge will not be taken into wear prior to 10th November, 1944.

(H.Q. 54-27-144-2)

5782—BADGE, EMBROIDERED, COLOURED, CANADIAN INFANTRY CORPS —5782

1. The pattern of badge, embroidered, coloured, Canadian Infantry Corps, described in RO 5053 will be modified as follows:—
    The white portion of the shield bearing three red maple leaves will be cut off and discarded. The red portion bearing the words "Infantry Corps" will henceforth be the approved pattern and will be worn ½ inch below the shoulder seams.

2. Para 1 of RO 5053 is accordingly amended as follows:—
    Delete lines 3 to 6 inclusive and *insert*, "The words "INFANTRY CORPS" in white on a red bar."

3. It will be the responsibility of Officers Commanding units to take such steps as are necessary to ensure that badges in possession of personnel, and those which are issued until stocks of this pattern are exhausted, are modified as outlined in para 1 above.

4. Stocks of the superseded pattern in Ordnance Depots will not be modified by the RCOC but will continue to be issued to units, in their present state, until exhausted.

5. The "CANADA" badge will again be taken into wear by personnel wearing the modified "Infantry Corps" badge. Para 6 of RO 5053 is, in consequence, hereby cancelled.

6. This order will be read in conjunction with RO 5053.

(Effective 30th May 1945)

(HQ 54-27-60-21)

5833—DISTINGUISHING PATCH—CANADIAN ARMY PACIFIC FORCE   —5833

1. A patch as described hereunder and designated "Patch, Distinguishing, CAPF", has been approved for wear by all ranks of the Canadian Army Pacific Force,—

> A hexagon, three inches in diameter; six equal segments of red, blue, French grey, green, maroon and black, clockwise respectively.

Each segment is representative of an overseas Canadian Division except the black segment, which represents the independent Armoured Brigades overseas.

  (a) This patch will be taken into wear following the posting of a volunteer to a Unit of Pacific Force. Unposted reinforcements will also wear this patch but only after departure from Canada.

  (b) Patch will be worn on both sleeves, with the uppermost point 3 inches below the shoulder seams; the division between the black and red segments being at 12 o'clock.

2. (a) A miniature of the patch, 1½ inches in diameter, will be worn by all ranks
    (i) Who have completed MFM 2J (Supplementary Declaration of Service Pacific Theatre) and
    (ii) Who on 14 Jun 45 had not reached their 45th birthday, and
    (iii) Whose PULHEMS Profile is not lower than 3333321 or such other PULHEMS Profile as may later be decided acceptable for CAPF.

  (b) Personnel who, subsequent to being accepted for the Canadian Army Pacific Force, are reduced in PULHEMS below the required minimum standard due to hospitalization or medical board, may continue to wear the miniature patch only, as in para 3 (b) below. This will not apply to personnel who proceed overseas with the force; such personnel then become entitled to continued wear of the large patch.

3. (a) The miniature will be taken into wear only after an entry indicating entitlement has been published in Part I Orders of the unit concerned.

  (b) Where an overseas distinguishing formation patch, other than the large CAPF patch is worn, the miniature will be superimposed. Otherwise, it will be worn as in para 1 (b) of this order.

(HQC 9131-17 FD 2)

6405—DISTINGUISHING PATCH—WINTER WARFARE   —6405

1. A patch as described hereunder and designated "Patch, Distinguishing, Winter Warfare" has been approved for wear of all ranks taking part in Exercise Musk-Ox.

A circle, 2½ inches in diameter, with white foreground and mountains and light blue water and sky and embroidered thereon a Naval Craft, an Igloo and an Aircraft in black.

2. This patch will be worn only for the duration of the exercise for which it is authorized.

(HQC 9012-544)

**6430—WAR DRESS REGULATIONS FOR THE OFFICERS AND OTHER   —6430
RANKS OF THE CANADIAN ARMY (1943) AMENDMENTS
(No. 22)**

War Dress Regulations for the Officers and Other Ranks of the Canadian Army (1943) are hereby amended as follows:—

Section XII

Page 56. (B) Mars Badge (Trained Soldier's Badge)
Cancel paras 1 to 8 and *substitute* new paras as follows:—

1. A trained soldier's badge is authorized for private soldiers of the Canadian Army (Active), and Volunteers of the CWAC. The badge will be in the form of the Zodiac Sign for Mars, 1½ inches long in red embroidery on a khaki background.

2. The badge will be worn on the right forearm of the battle dress blouse, jacket khaki drill, jacket barathea CWAC, and jacket summer CWAC, with the point of the badge up at an angle of 45 degrees to the front. The badge will be worn 4½ inches from the bottom of the sleeve or, where other authorized insignia are worn, immediately above such insignia.

3. To be eligible to wear the trained soldier's badge, the soldier must be in receipt of second increase of pay (i.e.) $1.50 per diem, or, in the case of the CWAC, $1.20 per diem.

4. Permission to wear the trained soldier's badge will be authorized in Part II Daily Order.

5. NCOs who have been reduced or have reverted to the ranks will be eligible for the award of the badge, provided they fulfil the conditions of para. 3 above.

6. The Mars badge (trained soldier's badge) will be taken down by personnel proceeding overseas for service in the United Kingdom, or such other theatre of war as may be laid down by the Adjutant-General from time to time, the day after embarkation, except that personnel of the Canadian Hospital Ship and personnel of the permanent Ships Conducting Staffs, remaining on Canadian strength, will not remove these badges.

7. Each soldier or Volunteer of the CWAC who may be entitled to wear the trained soldier's badge, as detailed above, will receive a free issue as follows:—

  (a) Initial issue one badge for each battle dress blouse, jacket khaki drill, jacket barathea CWAC, and jacket summer CWAC, issued under authorized scales of issue.

  (b) Badges will be replaced at Public expense when worn out. Units will indent on Ordnance for their requirements of badges and on issue to personnel they will be accounted for as an expendable store in accordance with para. 100 "Unit Accounting Instructions for Ordnance Stores."

(HQ 54-27-60-3 FD 79)

The following is compiled from a list of unit shoulder flashes at D Hist, Ottawa, and includes shoulder titles as well as flashes.

First Canadian Army Troops

The Elgin Regiment — The Royal Montreal Regiment — Artillery Flash — 1 Med RCA — 2 Med RCA — 2 HAA — 3 Med RCA — 4 Med RCA — 5 Med RCA — 7 RCA — 7 LAA RCA — 7 Med RCA — 8 RCA — 11 RCA — 11 LAA RCA — 19 RCA — Army Medical Flash — Army RCE Flash — Army RCCS Flash — Army RCASC Flash — Army CDC Flash — Army RCOC Flash — Army CPC Flash, and the Army Flash without printing.

1st Canadian Corps Troops

Royal Canadian Dragoons — Lorne Scots Canada — 1 Svy RCA — 1 LAA RCA — 7 A/T RCA — Corps RCA Flash — Corps RCE Flash — Corps RCCS Flash — Corps RCASC Flash — Corps CDC Flash — Corps RCOC Flash and Corps CPC Flash.

2nd Canadian Corps

XII Manitoba Dragoons Canada — Prince Edward Island Light Horse Canada — 2 Svy RCA — 6 A/T RCA — 6 LAA RCA — Plain Corps Flash — Corps Artillery Flash — Corps RCE Flash and Corps RCCS Flash.

1st Canadian Infantry Division

The Royal Canadian Regiment — Hastings and Prince Edward Regiment Canada — 48th Highlanders of Canada — P.P.C.L.I. — Seaforth Canada — 49th The Loyal Edmonton Regiment Canada — Royal 22e Regiment — Carleton and York Regiment Canada — West Nova Scotia Regiment Canada — 4th Princess Louise Dragoon Guards Canada — Sask. L.I. M.G. Canada — Royal Canadian Mounted Police (1st Provost Company) — RCHA — 2 RCA — 3 RCA — 1 A/T RCA — 2 LAA RCA — Div RCE Flash — Div RCCS Flash — Div RCASC Flash — Div Medicals Flash — Div CDC — Div RCOC and Div CPC.

2nd Canadian Infantry Division

The Royal Regiment of Canada — Royal Hamilton Light Infantry Canada — Essex Scottish Canada — The Black Watch R.H.R. of Canada — Regiment de Maisonneuve Canada — Calgary Highlanders Canada — Toronto Scottish — Fusiliers Mont-Royal Canada — Queens Own Cameron Highrs Canada — South Saskatchewan Regiment Canada — VIII Cdn Recce Regt 14 CH — 2 A/T RCA — 3 LAA — 4 RCA — 5 RCA — 6 RCA — Div M.G. Flash — Div Medicals Flash — Div RCE Flash — Div RCCS Flash — Div RCASC Flash — Div CDC Flash — Div RCOC Flash — Div CPC Flash and the Div Recce bull's-eye circles.

3rd Canadian Infantry Division

Royal Winnipeg Rifles Canada — Regina Rifle Regiment Canada — Canadian Scottish — Queen's Own Rifles — Le Regiment de la Chaudiere — North Shore Regiment New Brunswick — Highland Light Infantry Canada — Glengarrians Canada — North Nova Scotia Highlanders — Cameron Highlanders of Ottawa M.G. — 17th Duke of York's Royal Canadian Hussars — 3 A/T RCA — 4 LAA RCA — 12 RCA — 13 RCA — 14 RCA — Div Medicals Flash — Div RCE Flash — Div RCCS Flash — Div RCASC — Div CDC Flash — Div RCOC Flash and Div CPC Flash.

4th Canadian Armoured Division

Governor General's Foot Guards — Canadian Grenadier Guards — British Columbia Regiment Canada — South Alberta Regiment Canada — The Lake Superior Regiment — N.B. Rangers — Lincoln & Welland Regt. — The Algonquin Regiment — Argyll & Sutherland Highlanders Canada — 5 A/T RCA — 8 LAA — 15 RCA — 23 RCA — Div Flash — Div RCE Flash — Div RCCS Flash — Div RCASC Flash — Div CDC Flash — Div RCOC Flash — Div RCAPC Flash and Div CPC Flash.

5th Canadian Armoured Division

Lord Strathcona's Horse Royal Canadians — 8th New Brunswick Hussars Canada — British Columbia Dragoons Canada — The Perth Regiment Canada — The Cape Breton Highlanders Canada — The Irish Regiment of Canada — The Governor General's Horse Guards Canada — Princess Louise Fusiliers — The Westminster Regiment Canada — Lanark and Renfrew Scottish Canada — 7/XI Hussars Canada — 6 Royal Hussars Canada — 4 A/T RCA — 5 LAA RCA — 8 RCA — 11 RCA — 17 RCA — 5 CAD Flash — Div RCE Flash — Div RCCS Flash — Div RCASC Flash — Div RCAMC Flash — Div RCOC Flash — Div CPC Flash and Div CMSC Flash. Printing on 5th Div Flash also included FGH — 1H — 6H — 7-11H — LSH — BCD — CBH — GGHG — Perth R. — Westmr. R. and 8 NBH.

1st Canadian Armoured Brigade

The "Canada" is printed above the name of the regiment on the shoulder titles of the three regiments — The Ontario Regiment — Three Rivers Regiment and The Calgary Regiment. Brigade Flashes include 11 CTR — 12 CTR — 14 CTR — Brigade Medicals Flash — Brigade RCCS Flash — Brigade RCASC Flash and Brigade RCOC Flash.

2nd Canadian Armoured Brigade

2nd Canadian Armoured Brigade Flash — First Hussars Canada — Fort Garry Horse Canada and Sherbrooke Fusilier Regiment Canada shoulder titles.

Miscellaneous Titles and Flashes

RCEME — Canadian Chaplain Service — CWAC — Civilian Concert Party — Canadian Film and Photo Unit — 13th Brigade units — Canadian Fusiliers (city of London Regt.) — Le Regt. de Hull Canada — Rocky Mountain Rangers and Winnipeg Grenadiers. The Veterans Guard of Canada title, the dark green Forestry Corps triangle and the Royal Winnipeg Rifles right and left black on green triangular shaped patches are included in the list.

The following list includes a number of flashes for Canadian Reinforcement Units circa 1942, at which time Canadian Holding Units were redesignated Canadian Reinforcement Units.

A plain gold circle 2½ inches in diameter denoted CRU.

All circles were gold and headquarters of the various groups wore designs superimposed on the gold circles identified at D Hist, Ottawa, as:

A green 1¼ inch capital letter on the gold circle identified HQ A, B, C, D or E Groups.

Headquarters 1 Div IRU, HQ 2 Div IRU and HQ 3 Div IRU wore a 1¼ inch circle in red, blue and French grey respectively on the gold circle.

Headquarters 1 Canadian Armoured Corps Reinforcement Unit wore a tank on the gold circle.

Headquarters 1 RCA Reinforcement Unit wore a 1¼ inch square divided in two, red uppermost and blue below, on the gold circle.

HQ 1 Engineer RU wore a 1¼ inch square with equally proportioned strips of red, blue, red, a narrow blue strip, then equal strips of red, blue, red, on the gold circle.

Headquarters 1 Signal RU was identified by a 1¼ inch square divided equally white above blue, on the gold circle.

HQ 1 CMG RU wore a green arrow on the gold circle.

Headquarters CRU RCAMC were issued the gold circle with a central maroon strip ¾ of an inch high and 1¼ inches wide.

HQ CDC RU wore CDC in green ½ inch high on the gold circle.

HQ 1 Ordnance RU was identified by two ³⁄₁₆th of an inch red stripes above centre on a 1¼ inch blue square on the gold circle.

*   *   *

ABBREVIATIONS

A/B	Airborne
ADGB	Air Defence of Great Britain
AOP	Air Observation Post
ASSU	Air Support Signal Unit
Ammo, amn	ammunition
AA, Ack Ack	Anti-Aircraft
AAGOR, AAOR	Anti-Aircraft Gun Operation(s) Room
AA S/L	Anti-Aircraft Searchlight
A/T, A/Tk	Anti-Tank
Armd	Armoured
A/Bde	Armoured Brigade
A/Div	Armoured Division
AGRA	Army Group Royal Artillery
Arty	Artillery
Bn	Battalion
Bty	Battery
BHQ	Battery Headquarters
Bde	Brigade
Brig	Brigadier
Brit	British
BAOR	British Army of the Rhine
B.C.	British Columbia
BCD	British Columbia Dragoons
BCR	British Columbia Regiment
BEF	British Expeditionary Force
Buffaloes	Landing Vehicles Tracked
Cal H	The Calgary Highlanders
Camerons of C	The Queen's Own Cameron Highlanders of Canada
Cdn	Canadian
CASF	Canadian Active Service Force
CAC	Canadian Armoured Corps
CA	Canadian Army
CAOF	Canadian Army Occupation(al) Force
CAPF	Canadian Army Pacific Force
CAG	Canadian Army Group
CARU	Canadian Artillery Reinforcement Unit
CATC	Canadian Artillery Training Centre

CA (A)	Canadian Army Active
CBRG	Canadian Base Reinforcement Group
CD	Canadian Forces Decoration
CGA	Canadian Garrison Artillery
CIC	Canadian Infantry Corps
CMHQ	Canadian Military Headquarters
CPSS	Canadian Pacific Steamship
CRLE	Canadian Radio Location Establishment
CWAC	Canadian Women's Army Corps
(CD)	Coast Defence
Comd	Commander
CCRA	Commander, Corps Royal Artillery
CBO	Counter Battery Officers Staff
CMO	Counter Mortar Officers Staff
Det	Detachment
D Hist	Directorate of History, Ottawa
D.S.O.	Distinguished Service Order
Div	Division
DUKW (Duck)	2½ ton amphibian truck
Ed Fus	Edmonton Fusiliers
E.D.	Canadian Efficiency Decoration
Esq	Esquimalt
E & N	Esquimalt and Nanaimo Railway
Essex Scots	The Essex Scottish Regiment
Fd	Field
FOO	Forward Observation Officer
FS	French Speaking
Fus MR	Les Fusiliers Mont-Royal
Gen	General
G.O.C.	General Officer Commanding
Gp	Group
HQ	Headquarters
(H)	Howitzer, or Heavy for Ack Ack
HAA	Heavy Anti-Aircraft
HD	Home Defence
Inf	Infantry
IsG	Instructors in Gunnery
Kangaroo	Armoured Personnel Carrier
KORC	The King's Own Rifles of Canada

LCA	Landing Craft Assault
LCI	Landing Craft Infantry
LCT	Landing Craft Tank
LST	Landing Ship Tank
Lieut, Lt	Lieutenant
Lieut.-Col.	Lieutenant Colonel
(L)	LAA components of AA Regiments
(LS)	Six LAA guns
L of C	Lines of Communication
MG	Machine Gun
Maj	Major
Med, (M)	Medium
M.B.E.	Member of the Order of the British Empire
M.C.	Military Cross
MD	Military District
mm	millimetre
MT	Motor Transport
NDHQ	National Defence Headquarters
N.B.	New Brunswick
Nfld	Newfoundland
NCO	Non-commissioned officer
NPAM	Non-Permanent Active Militia
N.S.	Nova Scotia
No.	Number
Off.	Officer
O.B.E.	Officer of the Order of the British Empire
Ont.	Ontario
ORs	Other ranks
P & O	Pacific and Orient
Pat Bay	Patricia Bay, B.C.
PF	Permanent Force
P.E.C.	Photo Electric Cell
Pt.	Point
Pr	pounder
P.P.C.L.I.	Princess Patricia's Canadian Light Infantry
Pte	Private
P.Q.	Province of Quebec
"QE"	Queen Elizabeth, transport
Ram	Canadian tank, SP, personnel carrier and gun tower
R & Q	Rations and quarters

Recce	Reconnaissance
Regt	Regiment
R de Mais	Le Regiment de Maisonneuve
RHQ	Regimental Headquarters
RAF	Royal Air Force
RA	Royal Artillery
RCAF	Royal Canadian Air Force
RCAMC	Royal Canadian Army Medical Corps
RCA	Royal Canadian Artillery
RCCS	Royal Canadian Corps of Signals
RCHA	Royal Canadian Horse Artillery
RHLI	The Royal Hamilton Light Infantry
RHC	The Black Watch (Royal Highland Regiment) of Canada
R Regt C	The Royal Regiment of Canada
SP	Self-Propelled
Sgt	Sergeant
Sqn	Squadron
S Sask Regt	South Saskatchewan Regiment
SAS	Special Air Service
SOS	Struck off Strength
Svy	Survey
TOS	Taken on Strength
TLC	Tank Landing Craft (Dieppe)
Tor Scots	The Toronto Scottish Regiment (MG)
trg	training
Tp	Troop
US	United States
Van	Vancouver
V.C.	Victoria Cross
V & E	Victoria and Esquimalt
"VE"	Victory Europe
"VJ"	Victory Japan
W.D.	War Diary
(WR)	West Riding
YMCA	Young Men's Christian Association
Y.T.	Yukon Territory
Zuider Zee	Ijsselmeer

*   *   *

BIBLIOGRAPHY

General Orders 1939 to 1946.

The Canadian Army 1939-1945 — An Official Historical Summary by Colonel C.P. Stacey, King's Printer, Ottawa, 1948.

Official History of The Canadian Army in the Second World War — Volume I Six Years of War The Army In Canada, Britain and the Pacific by Colonel C.P. Stacey, Queen's Printer, Ottawa, 1955.

Official History of the Canadian Army in the Second World War Volume II The Canadians in Italy 1943-1945, by Lt. Col. G.W.L. Nicholson, Queen's Printer, Ottawa, 1957.

Official History of the Canadian Army in the Second World War Volume III The Victory Campaign The Operations in North-West Europe 1944-1945, by Colonel C.P. Stacey, The Queen's Printer and Controller of Stationery, Ottawa, 1960.

The Gunners of Canada The History of the Royal Regiment of Canadian Artillery Volume II 1919-1967, by Colonel G.W.L. Nicholson, McClelland and Stewart Limited, Toronto/Montreal.

History Headquarters Royal Canadian Artillery 1 Canadian Corps Covering World War II (Unpublished).

HQ RCA 2 Cdn Corps War History (Unpublished).

Unit History HQ 1 Cdn Army Group RA (Unpublished).

History of the Headquarters 2 Canadian Army Group Royal Artillery, Holland, July 1945 (Unpublished).

Meteor Memoirs, 1 Cdn Army Met Group, Apeldoorn, Netherlands, 31 July 1945 (Unpublished).

History of 1 Cdn Calibration Troop RCA from Sept 41 to June 45 World War II (Unpublished).

Notes on History of 1 Canadian CBO Staff RCA (Unpublished).

The History of 2 Cdn CBO Staff, RCA, 21 October 1942 - 26 June 1945 (Unpublished).

History of 1 Cdn CMO Staff from 15 Feb 44 to 21 June 45, World War II (Unpublished).

History of 2nd Cdn Counter Mortar Officers Staff R.C.A. From 14 June 1944 to 22 June 1945, World War II, Lt. R.J. Hauser Unit Historian (Unpublished).

21st AA Regiment RCA, Halifax, 22nd AA Regiment RCA, Saint John, N.B., 23rd AA Regiment RCA, Sydney, N.S., 24th AA Regiment RCA, Arvida, P.Q., 25th AA Regiment RCA, St. John's-Torbay, Newfoundland, and 26th AA Regiment RCA, Gander, Newfoundland, are listed in Operational Units — Artillery — Cdn Army, North American Zone, 24 April 1943, D Hist, Ottawa, and in Atlantic Command — AA Radars — Time in Operating Condition Jan 1944 - July 1945. (5th (B.C.) Regiment RCA Museum and Archives, Victoria). Regimental Files, D Hist, Ottawa also provided information on each regiment.

The Site Fighting Book, V.H. 2 Colwood, B.C., 11 Nov 42 to 19 Feb 45 contains a list of 27th AA Regiment batteries on manning duty. Operational Units — Artillery — Cdn Army, North American Zone, 24 April 1943, D Hist, Ottawa, and Pacific Command — AA Radars, Time in Operating Condition Jan 1944 - July 1945 include 27th AA Regiment RCA, Victoria-Esquimalt, 28th AA Regiment RCA, Vancouver, B.C., and 29th AA Regiment RCA, Prince Rupert, B.C. 29th AA Regiment is also included in the Order of Battle 8th Cdn Div, Prince Rupert Defences, Public Archives Canada, Ottawa.

Information on 30th AA Regiment RCA, Port Alberni, B.C. was garnered from Organizational Orders 8 July 1943 and 31 Dec 1943, D Hist, Ottawa.

A History of 2 Cdn HAA Regt 1939-1945 by Major J.E. Wilson, Major D.N. Byers, Capt F.E.E. Darling, Lieut W.F. Northcott and BQMS J.S. Phelps, Soesterberg, Holland, August, 1945.

History of 1 Cdn LAA Regiment RCA (Lanark & Renfrew Scottish Regiment) From 10 Mar 41 to 29 Jun 45, World War II (Unpublished). D Hist, Ottawa.

2 Cdn LAA Regt Regimental History (Unpublished). D. Hist.

The History of Third Canadian Light Anti-Aircraft Regiment From August 1940 to 7 May 1945, World War II. Kellaway Printing Ltd., Calgary, Alberta.

History of 4th Canadian Light Anti-Aircraft Regiment From 18 February 1941 to 8 May 1945, World War II (Unpublished).

The Story of 69th Light Anti-Aircraft Battery R.C.A. by B.S.M. Rimmer, T.G., Gnr. Boyle, H.C., Sgt. Geale, H., Capt. D.M. Dunlap and Capt. H.L. Waterous. T.H. Best Printing Co. Limited, Toronto, 1947. (69th Battery was a component of 4th LAA Regiment RCA.)

5th Canadian Light Anti-Aircraft Regiment Regimental History World War II (1 March 1941 - 8 May 1945) Capt A. Noblston. Printed by De Waal, Groningen, Holland, 1945.

Regimental History 6 LAA Regt. (Unpublished), D Hist, Ottawa. (See also The Royal Regiment of Artillery, Ottawa, 1855-1952, a history, by Lt. Col. H.M. Jackson, page 292 to page 335.

Notes From War Diary 7 Cdn LAA Regt (Unpublished), D Hist, Ottawa.

The History of the 8th Canadian Light Anti-Aircraft Regiment, R.C.A. by Captain W.S. Russell, Amersfoort, Holland, December 1945.

9th LAA Regiment RCA is included in 6th Cdn Div Components, Public Archives Canada, Ottawa, also an account of the regiment is included in The Royal Regiment of Artillery, Ottawa, 1855-1952, a history, by Lt. Col. H.M. Jackson, Industrial School for the Deaf, Montreal, 1952.

10th LAA — Notes from the files of 10th LAA Regiment, D Hist, Ottawa.

11th LAA — Notes from War Diary of 11 Cdn LAA Regt, D Hist, Ottawa. 4th LAA Battery information may be found in 2nd AA Regiment text, and 2nd LAA War Diary and Regimental History. 53rd LAA Battery's history is contained in the Regimental History and War Diaries of 4th Field Regiment and 3rd LAA Regiment. 62nd LAA Battery served with 13th Field Regiment, 4th LAA Regiment and 11th LAA Regiment, each regiment contains a segment of the battery's history.

Unit History 16 Canadian Anti/Aircraft Operational Room. Royal Canadian Artillery. Royal Canadian Corps of Signals. (Unpublished), RCA Museum and Archives, CFB Shilo.

History 1 Anti-Tank Regiment R.C.A. 5 Sep 39 to 31 July 45 World War II (Unpublished).

History of 2nd Canadian A/T Regiment Royal Canadian Artillery Sept 1939 to Sept 1945 (Unpublished).

History of the 3rd Anti-Tank Regiment RCA October 1st 1940 - May 8th 1945 (Unpublished).

History of the 4 Canadian Anti-Tank Regiment Royal Canadian Artillery 1940-1945 (Unpublished).

The History of the 5th Canadian Anti-Tank Regiment 10 Sept. 1941 - 10 June 1945, Captain J.P. Claxton, Editor, assisted by Major J.M. Savage and Regimental Sergeant-Major W. Cunningham, printed by J.H. Scheen, Lochem, Holland, under the supervision of Gnr. A.J. Morrison of 23rd Field Regiment (SP) RCA.

6th Cdn Anti-Tank Regiment Royal Canadian Artillery Regimental History (Unpublished).

A History of The 7th Anti-Tank Regiment Royal Canadian Artillery (Unpublished).

Included in the Summary of Coast Defences Table I — East Coast 15 Jan 43 are the names of the forts at Halifax, Sydney, and Shelburne in Nova Scotia, Saint John Area, Saint John, New Brunswick, Arvida, Gaspe, and Quebec, P.Q., Bell Island, St. John's-Torbay, Botwood, and Lewisporte, Newfoundland, and at Goose Bay in Labrador.

Summary of Coast Defences Table II — West Coast 15 Jan 43 includes the forts at Victoria-Esquimalt and other areas on Vancouver Island, the Vancouver Area including Yorke Island, the Prince Rupert Defences, Bella Bella, and at Alliford Bay, Queen Charlotte Islands.

Operational Units — Artillery — Cdn Army North American Zone 24 April 1943 lists the regiments and batteries manning the forts on both East and West Coasts.

Coast Artillery Installations — Pacific Coast of Canada, D. Mumford, Fort Rodd Hill National Historic Park, 1976. Unpublished.

Through the kindness of 5th (B.C.) Regiment Museum and Archives, Part II Orders for HQ 5th (B.C.) Coast Brigade RCA, 26 Aug/39 - 15 Sept/42, 2nd AA Battery RCA, 26 Aug/39 - 17 July/42 and 17th Searchlight Battery RCA, 26 Aug/39 - 31 Oct/41, were made available, as were Fort Record Books for Albert Head, Belmont, Black Rock, Christopher Point, Duntze Head, Golf Hill and Ogden Point.

History of 1st Field Regiment R.C.H.A., World War II (Unpublished).

Regimental History 2nd Canadian Field Regiment RCA (Unpublished).

History of The 3rd Canadian Field Regiment Royal Canadian Artillery September 1939 to July 1945 World War II (Unpublished).

The History of the 4th Field Regiment by Captain G.G. Blackburn (Unpublished).

5 Cdn Fd Regt, RCA (Unpublished).

The Six Years of 6 Canadian Field Regiment Royal Canadian Artillery September 1939 - September 1945, Bilthoven, Holland, September, 1945.

7th Army Field Regiment, 5th Army Field and 21st Army Field information is included in the History of 7th Canadian Medium Regiment R.C.A. From 1st September 1939 to 8th June 1945 World War 2 — Capt A.M. Lockwood.

History of 8 Canadian Field Regiment (Self-Propelled) Royal Canadian Artillery From 1 September 1939 to 31 May 1945 — World War II (Unpublished).

History of the 11 Canadian Army Field Regiment RCA From 1 September 1939 to 5 May 1945 Compiled by Captain A.G. Campbell, printed by Kemink & Zoon N.V., Utrecht, 1945.

Into Action With The 12th Field, 1940-45 by Captain T.J. Bell MC, Sgt J. Daimer and Lt. T.E. Jarvis.

The History of 13 Canadian Field Regiment Royal Canadian Artillery 1940-1945 by Lieut W.W. Barrett.

The History of 14 Field Regiment 1940-1945 by Lieut G.E.M. Ruffee and L/Bdr J.B. Dickie, Amsterdam, Sept 1945.

Fifteen Canadian Field Regiment Royal Canadian Artillery 1941-1945 by Captain Robert A. Spencer, Elsevier. Printed in Holland by Meijer's Boeken Handelsdrukkerij at Wormerveer.

A sketch of 16 Cdn Fd Regt RCA is included in The History of the 8th Canadian Light Anti-Aircraft Regt. R.C.A. by Capt. W.S. Russell (pages 15 to 18), Amersfoort, Holland, December 1945.

History of 17th Field Regiment Royal Canadian Artillery 5th Canadian Armoured Division 1946. J. Niemeijer's Publishing Company, Groningen (Holland).

A short account of 18th Field Regiment and 25th Field Battery is recorded in Appendix 3, pages 102 to 104, 2nd Canadian Medium Regiment R.C.A. Regimental History 18th January 1942 - 30th June 1945 by Major John G. Osler, Nederlandsche Diepdruk Inrichting N.V. Deventer (Holland).

19 Canadian Army Field Regiment RCA Regimental History September 1941 - July 1945. Printed by Nederlandsche Diepdruk Inrichting N.V., Deventer.

20th Field Regiment RCA is listed with 6th Canadian Division Components 10th Sept/41 to 15th July 1942 and in the Order of Battle of 7th Canadian Division from mid 1942 until October 1943, then with 6th Division from 16th October 1943 to 31st December 1944. A short account of the regiment is included in The History of the 4 Canadian Medium Regiment R.C.A. and 2nd Medium Regiment History contains a sketch of 24th/75th Field Battery RCA.

21st Field Regiment RCA, Serial 812, is included in 6th Canadian Division Components (Public Archives Canada, Ottawa).

22nd Field Regiment RCA is included in the Order of Battle of 7th and 8th Canadian Divisions (Public Archives Canada, Ottawa).

The History of 23rd Field Regiment (SP) RCA (Unpublished). The regiment is also included in the Order of Battle 7th Cdn Div, 6th Apr/42 to 10th Oct/42 (Public Archives Canada, Ottawa).

24th Field Regiment RCA, Serial 1412, is listed in the Order of Battle of 7th Canadian Division 6 Apr/42 to 15 July/42, and with 6th Canadian Division 15th July 1942 until 6th Div disbanded 31st January 1945. The regiment disbanded 31st March 1945. The unit War Diary confirms the location of 84th Battery.

25th Field Regiment RCA, Serial 1610, is included in the Order of Battle of 6th Canadian Division.

26th Field Regiment RCA, Serial 1611, is included in the Order of Battle of 7th Canadian Division.

27th Field Regiment's story is told in Six Years of War, pages 172 to 176, Col. C.P. Stacey, Queen's Printer Ottawa, 1955.

The 28th Field Regiment RCA, Serial 1814 information was gleaned from the regiment's War Diary, RCA Museum and Archives, CFB Shilo, Shilo, Manitoba.

The History of the First Med. Regt. 1940-1945, prepared by Lieut. R.Y. Walmsley and Lieut. B.J.P. Whalley, Spin's Publishing Comp. Amsterdam.

2nd Canadian Medium Regiment R.C.A. Regimental History 18th January 1942 - 30th June 1945 by Major John G. Osler, Nederlandsche Diepdruk Inrichting N.V. Deventer (Holland).

3rd Canadian Medium Regiment R.C.A. Regimental History, 21 Aug 45 (Unpublished).

The History of the 4 Canadian Medium Regiment R.C.A., Lt.-Col. J.H.R. Gagnon, Lieut. P.L. Cote, Lieut. J.R. Gouin, Lieut. P.M. Pelletier, Holland, 1945 (Unpublished).

The History of 5 Medium Regiment RCA by Lt Robt. J. Giles, Holland, 30 June 1945 (Unpublished).

History of the 7th Canadian Medium Regiment R.C.A. From 1st September, 1939 to 8th June, 1945 World War 2, by Captain A.M. Lockwood, Major W.H. Gillespie and Major W.G. Ferguson.

History of 1 Canadian Radar Battery R.C.A. from September 1944 to May 1945 (Unpublished).

History of 1 Canadian School of Artillery (Overseas) 21 Nov 1942 to 21 Jun 1945 (Unpublished).

The Story of 1 Canadian Survey Regiment RCA 1939-1945 Captain T.M. Gavin RCA Editor-in-Chief, Holland 29 June 1945.

History of 2 Canadian Survey Regiment RCA From Oct 43 To Jun 45 (Unpublished).

The 1st Centaur Battery R.C.A. (Unpublished).

History of 3rd Counter Mortar Officers Staff Type "A" RCA From 19 July 1944 To 9 May 1945 (Unpublished).

Regimental History of 1st Rocket Battery R.C.A. June 44 to June 45 (Unpublished).

Canadian Army No. 1 Armoured Train, 1942-44 by C.J. Dillon (Unpublished). See also "We Helped Win The War" in Muskeg, Rocks and Rain By Phylis Bowman Prince Rupert 1973.

The Calgary Regiment 14 CAR pamphlet printed by Printingworks De Jong & Co Hilversum, Holland, 1945. Thanks to Mr. Ivan Smith, Victoria, B.C.

A History of the First Hussars Regiment 1856-1945, compiled by Lieutenant Foster Stark, Hunter Printing London Limited, London, Canada, 1951.

Vanguard The Fort Garry Horse in The Second World War printed in Doetinchem (Holland) 1945.

The Sherbrooke Regiment (12th Armoured Regiment) by Lt.-Col. H.M. Jackson, M.B.E., E.D., 1958.

The Regiments and Corps of The Canadian Army. Prepared by the Army Historical Section. Volume 1 of the Canadian Army List. Published by Authority of the Minister of National Defence. Roger Duhamel, F.R.S.C. Queen's Printer and Controller of Stationery, Ottawa, Canada, 1964.

Associate Readings:

The Argyll and Sutherland Highlanders of Canada (Princess Louise's) 1928-1953 Compiled by officers of the Regiment. Edited by Lieut-Colonel H.M. Jackson, M.B.E., E.D. 1953.

The Story of The British Columbia Regiment 1939-1945 by D.E. Harker. (1950).

The History of The Calgary Highlanders 1921-54 by Major Roy Farran, D.S.O., M.C. Printed by Bryant Press Limited. (1954).

The History of the 1st Battalion Cameron Highlanders of Ottawa (MG) 1939-1946 by Lieutenant Colonel Richard M. Ross, O.B.E. Runge Press Limited, Ottawa, Canada.

History of the Canadian Grenadier Guards 1760-1964 by Colonel A. Fortescue Duguid, D.S.O., O.B.E., C.D., B.Sc., Royal Canadian Artillery. Gazette Printing Company (Limited) Montreal, 1965.

An Historical Account of the 7th Canadian Reconnaissance Regiment (17th Duke of York's Royal Canadian Hussars) in The World War 1939-1945 by Capt. Walter G. Pavey, Montreal.

1 Bn. The Essex Scottish Regiment (Allied with the Essex Regiment) 1939-1945. A Brief Narrative. R.W. Meanwell, Captain, Adjutant, September, 1945.

A History of the First Hussars Regiment 1856-1980. Committee of E. Frank Hull, W. Robert Newman and Sam W. Pawley. Foreword by A. Brandon Conron, February, 1981.

The Regimental History of the Governor General's Foot Guards. Ottawa, Canada, 1948. Printed by Mortimer Limited, Ottawa, 1948.

1st Battalion The Highland Light Infantry of Canada 1940-1945, researched by Capt. R. Glanville. Published by Highland Light Infantry of Canada Association, Galt, Ontario, 1951.

In The Face of Danger. The History of The Lake Superior Regiment by Lieut. Colonel George F.G. Stanley, introduction by Colonel R.A. Keane and maps by Major C.C.J. Bond. Published by The Lake Superior Scottish Regiment, Port Arthur, Ontario, 1960.

Service The Story of the Canadian Legion 1925-1960 by Clifford H. Bowering. Published by Dominion Command, Canadian Legion, Legion House, Ottawa. Published November 1960. Printed by Canadian Printing and Lithographing Company, Ltd., Montreal.

History of the Lincoln and Welland Regiment by Major R.L. Rogers 1954. 2nd Printing October 1979. Litho'd in Canada by Lincoln Graphics.

Regimental History of the 18th Armoured Car Regiment (XII Manitoba Dragoons), France, Belgium, Holland, Germany 8 July 1944 - 8 May 1945, by Capt. C.E. Henry. Printed by Nederlandsche Diepdruk Inrichting N.V. Deventer. Compliments of Mr. R. Neale, 26th Field Regiment Museum, Brandon, Manitoba.

Official History of The Canadian Medical Services 1939-1945. Edited By W.R. Feasby, B.A., M.D., Lieutenant Colonel, R.C.A.M.C., Supplementary Reserve. Published by Authority of the Minister of National Defence. Edmond Cloutier, C.M.G., A.O., D.S.P., Ottawa, 1956, Queen's Printer and Controller of Stationery.

No Retreating Footsteps the story of the North Novas by Will R. Bird. The 2nd printing of The Story of the North Nova Scotia Highlanders by Lancelot Press Limited, Hantsport, Nova Scotia, 1983, was produced in paperback.

History of The Ontario Regiment 1866-1951. Written by Captain Lex Schragg from information derived from the Official War Diary, Regimental Records and Historical Sketches written by Col. Frank Chappell, Major J.E. Slinger and Capt. Arch. Whitelaw. General Printers Limited.

The Princess Louise Dragoon Guards. A History by Lt.-Col. H.M. Jackson, M.B.E., E.D., Foreword by Maj.-Gen. E.L.M. Burns, D.S.O., O.B.E., M.C., C.D., 1951.

1st Battalion The Regina Rifle Regiment 1939-1946. Edited by Captain Eric Luxton. Part I by C.S.T. Tubb, Part II by J.G. Baird, Part III by E.C. Luxton and Part IV by G.E. Rouatt. Commercial Printers, Regina, Saskatchewan.

Sabretache The Memorial Journal of the VIII Recce Association, March 1966. Lt.-Col. C.D. Williams, CD, QC, Editor.

A Resume of the Story of 1st Battalion The Saskatoon Light Infantry (MG),

1939-1945, Canadian Army, Overseas. Compiled by Lt.-Col. D.E. Walker, D.S.O., E.D. General Printing and Bookbinding, Saskatoon, Saskatchewan. Compliments of Mr. A.J. Peacock, Victoria, B.C.

A Short History of the 29 Cdn Armd Recce Regt (South Alberta Regiment) by Major G.L. Macdougall. Spin's Publishing Co., Amsterdam.

"The March of the Prairie Men" being a story of The South Saskatchewan Regiment by Lt.-Col. G.B. Buchanan, M.B.E. 1957. Litho'd by Midwest Litho Ltd., Saskatoon.

Red Shield in Action. A record of Canadian Salvation Army War Services in the Second Great War by Scott Young. Printed in Canada by F.F. Clarke & Company, Toronto. (1949).

History of The Royal Canadian Corps of Signals 1903-1961. Written by Officers of the Corps and edited by John S. Moir, M.A., Ph.D. Published by authority of the Corps Committee Royal Canadian Corps of Signals Ottawa, 1962.

A short history of The Toronto Scottish Regiment by Major D.R. McKillican, CD, Dip, Th., B.A., B.D., M.Th. Regimental Padre 1972. Courtesy Mr. M. Hobbs, Toronto.

Seventy-fifth anniversary Royal Winnipeg Rifles 1883-1958.

The Canadian Y.M.C.A. in World War II by Alan M. Hurst. National War Services Committee of The National Council of Young Men's Christian Association of Canada. Goodfellow Printing Co. Ltd.

INDEX

A

Abbreviations: 483-486

Adak: 217, 238, 393

Abbeville: 370

Adriatic: 287, 288, 329, 338, 340, 377

ADGB: 6, 12, 17, 19, 26, 34, 39, 42, 44, 57, 61, 65, 68, 80, 90, 92, 96, 107, 413, 415, 417

Alaska: 48, 54, 59, 107

Alberta: 203, 388

Albert Head: 86, 162, 167

Aldershot, Hants: 17, 135, 335, 357, 363

Aleutians: 60, 73, 172, 217, 234, 238, 383, 471

Alfriston: 280, 284, 348

Algiers: 121, 122, 126, 129, 137, 141, 143, 147, 222, 228, 246, 294, 303, 376

Alliford Bay: 60, 63, 66

Almanzora: 130

Ambleside: 47

Amersfoort: 278, 325, 334, 343, 366

Amherst: 109, 175, 313

Andes: 118, 131, 139, 144

Andover, Hants: 273, 296, 297, 304

Aneroid, Sask: 220

Annette Island: 7, 47, 54, 59, 107

Anti-Aircraft Artillery: 1-111

Anti-Tank Artillery: 113-150

Antigonish: 173

AMTB: 136, 168, 170, 177

Antwerp: 281, 301, 320, 350, 351, 358, 364, 370

Anzio: 294, 303, 377

Aorangi: 126, 129, 136, 141, 261, 263

Apeldoorn: 123, 278, 290, 295, 305, 324, 334, 342, 380

Aquitania: 121, 192, 207, 213, 255, 258, 262

Ardennes: 133, 312, 322, 352

Argentina: 193, 207, 214, 263, 345

Arielli: 141, 338, 377

Armament Maintenance Establishment: 390, 391

Armoured and Army Tank Brigades: 398-407, 468, 470

Arnhem: 68, 75, 97, 122, 149, 212, 221, 222, 228, 231, 290, 324, 333, 347, 371, 380

Arromanches: 281

Arvida: 4, 13-15, 27, 35, 43-45, 67, 89

Atlantic Command: (See HQ Section).

Augusta: 62, 98, 105, 183, 193, 207, 214, 255, 261, 263, 275, 329, 345

Authie: 189, 206

Aurich: 367

Avonmouth: 129, 149

B

Bad Zwischenahn: 367

Bahamas: 394

Barrett Point: 174

Batory: 41

Bay Street Armoury: 16, 49, 170

Bazan Bay: 28, 48

Beachy Head: 92, 116, 284

Belgium: All Canadian units fighting under Headquarters First Canadian Army in France also served in Belgium. Units of 1st Canadian Corps travelled in convoy from Marseilles, France, to a concentration area in Belgium prior to joining First Canadian Army in NW Europe in 1945.

Belmont Battery: 36, 59, 109, 162, 170, 177

Berlin Brigade: 97, 145, 224, 246, 391

"B" Force (Bermuda): 391

Bexhill on Sea: 80

Bibliography: 487-496

Biggen Hill: 80

Borden, Ont: 223, 243, 367

Bordon, Hants: 227, 276, 283, 298, 344

Botwood: 53, 84, 88, 176, 362, 391

Boulogne: 133, 210, 300, 310, 351, 360, 364

Boundary Bay: 31, 36

Bramshott: 305

S

T

U

V

W

X

Y

Z

Unit Index

A

8th and 8th/10th Bty: 191, 192, 437

9th (Toronto) and 9th/15th Bty: 192-194, 439

10th (St. Catharines) and 8th/10th Bty: 194, 195, 437

11th (Hamilton) and 11th/69th Bty: 195, 196, 445, 446

13th (Winnipeg) and 13th/21st Bty: 196, 197, 442

14th (Midland) and 2nd/14th Bty: 197, 198, 439, 440

16th and 16th/43rd Bty: 198, 199, 445, 446

17th: 199, 200, 447, 448

19th and 19th/77th Bty: 200, 201, 438

21st and 13th/21st Bty: 201, 202, 442

22nd and 22nd/78th Bty: 203, 446

24th (Shefford) and 24th/75th Bty: 204, 451, 452

26th (Lambton) and 26th/53rd Bty: 204, 205, 439, 440

28th (Newcastle) and 28th/89th Bty: 206, 207, 440, 441

29th and 29th/40th Bty: 207, 208, 439

31st: 208, 209, 454, 455

34th and 32nd/34th Bty: 209, 210, 446, 447

36th: 210, 211, 454, 455

37th: 211, 212, 449, 450

39th: 212, 213, 452, 453

40th and 29th/40th Bty: 213, 215, 439

43rd and 16th/43rd Bty: 215, 216, 445, 446

44th and 44th/62nd Bty: 216, 217, 446

49th: 217, 218, 455

55th: 218, 219, 450, 451

59th: 219, 220, 452, 453

60th and 60th/76th Bty: 220, 221, 449, 450

61st and 61st/107th Bty: 221, 223, 443, 444

63rd: 223, 224, 450, 451

64th (Yorkton): 224, 225, 452, 453

66th and 66th/81st Bty: 225, 226, 446, 447

71st and 71st/113th Bty: 226-228, 443, 444

72nd: 228, 229, 451, 452

73rd and 5th/73rd Bty: 229, 230, 440, 441

75th and 24th/75th Bty: 230, 231, 451, 452

76th and 60th/76th Bty: 231, 232, 449, 450

77th and 19th/77th Bty: 232, 233, 438, 439

78th and 22nd/78th Bty: 233, 234, 446

80th: 234, 235, 453, 454

81st and 66th/81st Bty: 235, 236, 446, 447

83rd: 236, 237, 454, 455

84th: 237, 238, 455, 477

85th: 238, 239, 455

91st and 91st/111th Bty: 239, 240, 442

92nd and 92nd/109th Bty: 240, 241, 438, 439

93rd: 241

95th: 241, 242, 448

97th and 97th/100th Bty: 242, 243, 453

99th: 243, 244, 450, 451

107th and 61st/107th Bty: 245, 246, 443, 444

110th: 246, 247, 447, 448

114th: 247, 455, 456

115th: 247, 248, 455, 456

116th: 248, 249, 392, 455, 456

117th: 249, 456

118th: 249, 456

119th: 249, 250, 456

120th: 250, 456

121st: 250, 456

122nd: 149, 150, 250, 251, 456

123rd: 251, 456, 457

124th: 251, 252, 456, 457

125th: 252, 456, 457

Field Regiments:

1st and 1st Fd Bde: 435, 436, 480

2nd and 2nd Fd Bde: 437, 480

3rd and 3rd Fd Bde: 438, 439, 480

4th and 4th Fd Bde: 439, 440, 480

5th and 5th Fd Bde: 440, 441, 480

6th and 6th Fd Bde: 442, 480

7th Army Fd: 441, 442, 461, 480

8th (SP) and 8th Army Fd: 443, 444, 480, 481

11th and 11th Army Fd: 439, 444, 445, 480, 481

12th: 445, 446, 481

11th Armoured Regiment (The Ontario Regiment): 380, 399, 403, 481
12th Armoured Regiment (The Three Rivers Regiment): 339, 399, 401, 403, 481
14th Armoured Regiment (The Calgary Regiment): 80, 358, 399, 401, 403, 481
15th (Reserve) Armoured Regiment (6th Duke of Connaught's Royal Canadian Hussars) and 5th Canadian (Armoured) Division HQ Squadron (6th Duke of Connaught's Royal Canadian Hussars): 400, 402, 481
16th (Reserve) Armoured Regiment (7th/11th Hussars) and 2nd Canadian Armoured Brigade HQ Squadron (7th/11th Hussars): 400, 402, 481
17th (Reserve) Armoured Regiment (Prince Edward Island Light Horse) and 1st Canadian Armoured Brigade HQ Squadron (The Prince Edward Island Light Horse), then 2nd Corps Defence Company (The Prince Edward Island Light Horse): 400, 404
18th Armoured Car Regiment (12th Manitoba Dragoons): 326, 368, 369, 400, 401, 405, 480
19th (Reserve) Army Tank Regiment (The New Brunswick Regiment (Tank)), the Active Battalion served as 1st Cdn Army Tank Brigade HQ Squadron (The New Brunswick Regiment (Tank)): 400, 402
20th Army Tank Regiment (16/22 Saskatchewan Horse): 367, 369, 401, 403
21st Armoured Regiment (The Governor General's Foot Guards): 367-369, 400, 402, 481
22nd Armoured Regiment (The Canadian Grenadier Guards): 367, 369, 401, 402, 406, 481
23rd Army Tank Regiment (The Halifax Rifles): 401, 403
24th Reconnaissance Battalion (Les Voltigeurs de Quebec): 401, 403
25th Armoured Delivery Regiment (The Elgin Regiment): 367-369, 400, 403-405, 480

26th Army Tank Regiment (Grey and Simcoe Foresters): 367, 369, 401, 403
27th Armoured Regiment (The Sherbrooke Fusiliers Regiment): 326, 369, 397, 401, 403, 468, 481
28th Armoured Regiment (The British Columbia Regiment): 367-369, 400, 402, 481
29th Armoured Reconnaissance Regiment (The South Alberta Regiment): 367-370, 400, 402, 481
30th Reconnaissance Regiment (Essex Regiment): 401, 404
31st (Alberta) Reconnaissance Regiment: 401, 405
32nd Reconnaissance Regiment (The Royal Montreal Regiment): 403, 404, 406
1st Canadian Armoured Personnel Carrier Regiment: 324, 405

*   *   *

Infantry and Machine Gun Units:

The Algonquin Regiment: 119, 370, 397
The Argyll and Sutherland Highlanders of Canada (Princess Louise's): 370, 393, 481
The Black Watch (Royal Highland Regiment) of Canada: 356-358, 362, 397, 473, 480
The Brockville Rifles: 393
The Calgary Highlanders: 356-358, 473, 480
The Cameron Highlanders of Ottawa (MG): 356, 357, 362, 366, 465, 481
The Canadian Fusiliers (City of London Regiment): 383, 482
The Canadian Scottish: 362, 366, 465, 481
The Cape Breton Highlanders: 376, 481
The Carleton and York Regiment: 335, 338, 339, 385, 465, 480
The Dufferin and Haldimand Rifles of Canada: 119
The Edmonton Regiment and The Loyal Edmonton Regiment: 335, 337, 338, 385, 465, 480

*   *   *

Allied Units:

Armies:
  First Allied A/B: 470
  Second British: 349, 365, 370, 418, 460
  Fifth US: 339
  Eighth British: 286, 288, 329, 331, 337, 339, 341, 342, 414, 458
  Ninth US: 323, 353
Army Group:
  21 Army Group: 219, 297, 323, 333, 353, 469
Brigades:
  4th British Armoured Bde: 350
  7th British Armoured Bde: 332
  34th British Armoured Bde: 353
  1st Czechoslovak Independent Armoured Brigade Group: 321
  Greek Mountain Brigade: 330
  Guards Independent Armoured Brigade: 353
  4th Special Service Brigade: 321
Corps:
  1 British: 277, 292, 320, 321, 324, 349, 361, 469
  5 British: 286, 288, 289, 329, 331, 338, 341, 342
  7 Corps: 328, 336
  10 British: 289
  13 British: 329, 333, 337, 340, 346, 377, 414, 437
  30 British: 322, 323, 337, 352, 367, 427, 469
  Polish: 287, 329, 331, 341
  XVI US: 323
Divisions:
  3rd British: 352, 363
  4th British: 288, 330

5th British: 337
6th British Airborne: 323, 363, 470
7th British Armoured: 349, 450
11th British Armoured: 311, 353, 464
15th (Scottish): 322
43rd (Wessex): 322, 353
49th (West Riding): 311, 322, 324, 325, 334, 350, 469
50th (Northumbrian): 322, 352, 363
51st (Highland): 311, 322, 350
52nd (Lowland): 311, 312, 321, 353, 367
53rd (Welsh): 322, 353
56th British: 331, 332
59th (Staffordshire): 351
79th British Armoured: 324
Guards Armoured: 323, 349
4th Indian: 377
8th Indian: 342
10th Indian: 331, 338, 341
2nd New Zealand: 330, 331, 340
1st Polish Armoured: 293, 297, 311, 322, 324, 350, 351, 361
6th South African: 287, 288
1st US: 363
4th US: 363
82nd US Airborne: 322, 363
101st US Airborne: 311, 322, 363
104th US: 322
Belgian SAS: 326
Cremona Battle Group: 342
No. 10 (Inter-Allied Commando): 326
First Special Service Force (Canadian-US): 471

*   *   *